CHAPTERS FROM THE AGRARIAN HISTORY OF ENGLAND AND WALES 1500–1750

EDITED BY

JOAN THIRSK

Sometime Reader in Economic History
University of Oxford

VOLUME 1

Economic Change: Prices, Wages, Profits and Rents
1500–1750

With a new Introduction by PETER J. BOWDEN
Senior Economist, Tariff Board, Federal Government of Canada

EDITED BY

PETER J. BOWDEN

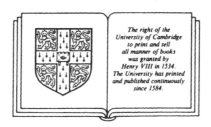

The right of the
University of Cambridge
to print and sell
all manner of books
was granted by
Henry VIII in 1534.
The University has printed
and published continuously
since 1584.

CAMBRIDGE UNIVERSITY PRESS

CAMBRIDGE

NEW YORK   PORT CHESTER   MELBOURNE   SYDNEY

Published by the Press Syndicate of the University of Cambridge
The Pitt Building, Trumpington Street, Cambridge CB2 1RP
40 West 20th Street, New York, NY 10011, USA
10 Stamford Road, Oakleigh, Melbourne 3166, Australia

First published 1990

Printed in Great Britain by the
University Press, Cambridge

British Library cataloguing in publication data
Chapters from the agrarian history of
England and Wales, 1500–1750.
1. England. Agricultural industries,
ca. 1350–1870
1. Thirsk, Joan II. The agrarian
history of England and Wales
338.1'0942

Library of Congress cataloguing in publication data
Chapters from the agrarian history of England and Wales. 1500–1750
edited by Joan Thirsk.
p. cm.
Rev. ed. of: Vols. 4 and 5 of the Agrarian history of England and
Wales. 1967–
Bibliography.
Includes index.
Contents: v. 1. Economic change/edited by Peter J. Bowden – v.
2. Rural society/edited by Christopher Clay – v. 3. Agricultural
change/edited by Joan Thirsk – v. 4 Agricultural markets and
trade. 1500–1750/edited by John Chartres – v. 5. The buildings of
the countryside. 1500–1750/edited by M. W. Barley.
ISBN 0 521 36884 7 (v. 1)
1. Agricultural – Economic aspects – England – History.
2. Agricultural – Economic aspects – Wales – History. 3. England – Rural
conditions. 4. Wales – Rural conditions. 1. Thirsk, Joan.
II. Agrarian history of England and Wales.
HD1930.E5C47 1989
338.1'0942 – dc19 88-38786, CIP
ISBN 0 521 36884 7

CONTENTS

TEXT-FIGURES

TABLES

EDITOR'S PREFACE

Since a survey of English agriculture is a large part of the economic history of England in the sixteenth to eighteenth centuries, it has seemed desirable to make the volumes of *The Agrarian History of England and Wales* available in a cheaper format to a wider readership. With this purpose in mind, each of the general chapters published in volume IV of *The Agrarian History*, and spanning the years 1500–1640, has been combined with its partner in volume V, 1640–1750, to give a survey covering two hundred and fifty years.[1] Here then is a view of a long chain of development. And while the individual authors fix a piercing gaze upon single themes in the sequence, the amalgamation of their studies reveals a larger pattern unfolding. Particularly striking are the differences in the economic circumstances ruling between the two periods, from 1500 to 1650 on the one hand, and from 1650 to 1750 on the other. Whereas rising food prices boosted the production of mainstream crops in the first period, stable or falling prices encouraged diversification, and the commercial production of a more varied range of plants and animals in the second. These differing circumstances also obliged landowners and all other classes living off the land to devise different strategies for survival. Changes in consequence did not follow one linear path. Human ingenuity turned in two different directions in the two periods, and, in fact, some of the subsidiary, not to say frivolous, activities in the first period (such as the production of luxury fruit and vegetables for the rich) proved to be among the most rewarding of the strategies for survival in the second.

The authors of all chapters in these two volumes have been given the chance to bring their surveys up-to-date by drawing attention to new work published since they first wrote. As volume IV was published in 1967, this means that they have more to say about their earlier writing than the later (published in 1985–6). These introductions should guide the reader to the most recent research. But it is also hoped that the juxtaposition of chapters from both volumes will offer a new perspective on the period as a whole, and so promote further discussion and

[1] The only chapters omitted from this paperback series, which appeared in the hardback version, are those describing regional farming systems, namely chapters I and II in volume IV, and all the chapters in part I of volume V.

understanding of the significance of the two phases within it. For while some of the solutions to problems in the second half of the period plainly sprang from developments in the first half, we must also bear in mind that within this whole web of human activity lay certain notable successes with new crops, new farming systems, and new ways of getting a living, which launched another phase of boisterous agricultural, and industrial, expansion in the later eighteenth century. To see agricultural development in a long view across two-and-a-half centuries is a particularly salutary experience for us who live in another changing agricultural world.

ABBREVIATIONS

Agric. Hist.	*Agricultural History*
AHEW	*Agrarian History of England and Wales*, Cambridge 1967–
AHR	*Agricultural History Review*
Amer. Hist. Rev.	*American Historical Review*
AO	Archives Office
APC	*Acts of the Privy Council*, London, 1890–
Arch. Aeliana	*Archaeologia Aeliana*
Arch. Camb.	*Archaeologia Cambrensis*
Arch. Cant.	*Archaeologia Cantiana*
Arch. J.	*Archaeological Journal*
B. Acad.	British Academy
BE	N. Pevsner, *The Buildings of England*, London, 1951–74
BL	British Library
BM	British Museum
Borthwick IHR	Borthwick Institute of Historical Research
BPP	British Parliamentary Papers
Bull. BCS	*Bulletin of the Board of Celtic Studies*
Bull. IHR	*Bulletin of the Institute of Historical Research*
Bull. JRL	*Bulletin of the John Rylands Library*
CCC	M.A.E. Green, *Calendar of the Proceedings of the Committee for Compounding. etc., 1643–1660*, 5 vols. London, 1889–92
C,Ch.	Proceedings in the Court of Chancery
CJ	Commons Journals
CP 40	Court of Common Pleas, Plea Rolls, PRO
CPR	Calendar of Patent Rolls
CRO	Cumbria Record Office, Carlisle
CSPD	*Calendar of State Papers Domestic*
CW2	*Cumb. and Westmor. Antiq. and Arch. Soc.*, 2nd series
E	Exchequer Records, PRO
E 134	Exchequer, Depositions
E 159	Exchequer, King's Remembrancer,

	Memoranda Rolls
E 164	Exchequer, King's Remembrancer, Miscellaneous Books
E 178	Exchequer, Special Commissions
E 315	Exchequer, Augmentations Office, Miscellaneous Books
E 318	Exchequer, Augmentations Office, Particulars for Grants
E 321	Exchequer, Augmentations Office, Proceedings
EcHR	*Economic History Review*
EFC	M. W. Barley, *The English Farmhouse and Cottage*, London, 1961
EHR	*English Historical Review*
EPNS	English Place-Name Society
EVH	Eric Mercer, *English Vernacular Houses: A Study of Traditional Farmhouses and Cottages*, RCHM (England), London, 1975
GLCRO	Greater London Council Record Office
GMR	Guildford Muniment Room
Hist. Mon. C.	Historical Monuments Commission
HMC	Historical Manuscripts Commission
J.	Journal
JCH	*Journal of Comparative History*
JFHS	*Journal of the Friends' Historical Society*
JMH	*Journal of Modern History*
KRO	Cumbria Record Office, Kendal
LAO	Lincolnshire Archives Office
LJ	Lords Journals
LJRO	Lichfield Joint Record Office
LP	*Letters and Papers of Henry VIII*
LPL	Lambeth Palace Library
LR	Exchequer Office of the Auditors of Land Revenue, PRO
LUS	Land Utilization Survey
Mont. Coll.	Montgomeryshire Collections
NLW	National Library of Wales
NQ	*Notes and Queries*
PP	Parliamentary Papers
PP	*Past and Present*
PRO	Public Record Office, Chancery Lane and Kew, London
PS	*Population Studies*
RASE	Royal Agricultural Society of England

RCAM	Royal Commission on Ancient Monuments
RCHM	Royal Commission on Historical Monuments
Req., Req. 2	Proceedings in the Court of Requests
RHS	Royal Historical Society
RO	Record Office
Roy. Inst. Cornwall	*Royal Institution of Cornwall*
SC	Special Collections, PRO
SP	State Papers
T & C	*Seventeenth-Century Economic Documents*, ed. J. Thirsk and J. P. Cooper, Oxford, 1972
TED	*Tudor Economic Documents*, ed. R. H. Tawney and Eileen Power, 3 vols., London, 1924
UCNWL	University College of North Wales Library, Bangor
VCH (name of county in italics)	*Victoria County History*
Yorks. Bull.	*Yorkshire Bulletin of Economic and Social Research*

INTRODUCTION

From the standpoint of economic development the period 1500–1750 as a whole is difficult to characterize in simple terms, comprising as it does two clearly distinguishable epochs, with the middle years of the seventeenth century constituting a watershed. In the first part of the period, encompassing the Tudor and early Stuart eras, population pressure upon land and other productive resources greatly intensified, resulting in higher prices generally and a lowering in the standards of living of the growing numbers of landless poor. Subsequently, reflecting the combined effects of a more productive use of resources and a sharp reduction in the rate of population growth (the underlying causes of which are, as yet, imperfectly understood),[1] the long-term rise in the general level of prices was halted and some gains in family comforts – of unknown, but possibly considerable, proportions – were achieved.

On the subject of wages and employment as viewed from the standpoint of the wage earner, it seems very likely that with the spread of rural industry on the one hand, and the slowing down in the rate of population growth on the other, unemployment and under-employment, particularly among female country-dwellers, tended to decline after 1660. There are no means of knowing this for certain; nor – given that earnings are almost invariably recorded as payments to individual (often unnamed) workers – does there appear to be much prospect of developing some authentic measures of changes in family living standards over time, even if we knew much more than we do about the spending patterns of the poorer sections of the population.[2]

[1] The subject is one which has attracted a considerable literature in recent years. For a cross-section of views, see the collection of essays in *J. of Interdisciplinary Hist.*, xv, 4 (Spring, 1985).

[2] For a selection of studies and data bearing on these issues, see *infra*, pp. 190–4; Joan Thirsk, 'Industries in the Countryside' in *Essays in the Economic and Social History of Tudor and Stuart England*, ed. F. J. Fisher, Cambridge, 1961, pp. 70–88; Elizabeth Waterman Gilboy, 'Labour at Thornborough: An Eighteenth Century Estate', EcHR, iii, 1931–2, pp. 388–98; Sir Frederick M. Eden, *The State of the Poor*, iii, 1797, pp. 754–7, 794–9; E. Lipson, *The Economic History of England*, ii, London, 1947 edn, pp. 392–3, 501; Jerome Blum, 'The Condition of the European Peasantry on the Eve of the Emancipation', *JMH*, xlvi, 1974, pp. 408–19; E. H. Phelps Brown and Sheila V. Hopkins, 'Builder's Wage-rates, Prices and Population: Some Further Evidence', *Economica*, ns, xxvi, 1959, p. 59; A. Kussmaul, *Servants in Husbandry in Early Modern England*, Cambridge, 1981; K. D. M. Snell, *Annals of the Labouring Poor. Social Change and Agrarian England, 1660–1900*, Cambridge, 1985; Donald Woodward, 'Wage Rates and Living Standards in Pre-Industrial England', *Past and Present*, 91, 1981, pp. 28–45.

The extent to which the economy during these years experienced subsistence crises of a Malthusian kind has recently been the subject of some debate. Thus, in acknowledging the occurrence of severe food shortages in 1555–7, 1586–8, 1596–8, 1622–3 and 1647–9, Palliser states that the chronology of famines during this period "shows that they were generally diminishing both in intensity and in geographical range, rather than worsening as population increased".[3] This is essentially a backward extension of the position put forward earlier by Appleby, who claimed that the last severe famine to affect most parts of the country was in 1596–8, and that "after 1649 England was free of subsistence crises".[4] Noting the conjunction of high grain prices and sharply higher mortality in various dispersed parishes during the years 1661–2, 1678–9 and 1693–4, Outhwaite has recently been led to conclude that Appleby's argument "may not be chronologically correct".[5] Further, in reference to the views of Palliser, he cites, with approval, the finding of Schofield, with particular reference to the period 1548–1640, that "there was ... a time when mortality in England fluctuated with the harvest".[6] In Outhwaite's view, "the mortality response might have been even more considerable, if the population had not experienced that other 'Malthusian check', ignored by Palliser, a rise in female age at marriage".[7]

In the context of the present study, we have allowed that, over the period 1650–1750 as a whole, subsistence crises were indeed tending to become less severe and more narrowly localized than in the past, although critical shortages did occur from time to time. In this connection, the attainment of greater stability with respect to the supply of food is suggested by our data pertaining to the prices of grains,[8] which not only exhibit less volatility than in earlier years, but also indicate a narrowing of regional price differentials.

Obviously, since, to a very large extent, the English economy at this time generated its own basic food requirements, any diminution in the country's susceptibility to subsistence crises must have been effected

---

[3] D. M. Palliser, 'Tawney's Century: Brave New World or Malthusian Trap?', EcHR, 2nd ser., xxxv, 1982, pp. 344–5.

[4] Andrew B. Appleby, 'Grain Prices and Subsistence Crises in England and France, 1590–1740', J. of Econ. Hist., xxxix, 1979, p. 867.

[5] R. B. Outhwaite, 'Dearth and Government Intervention in English Grain Markets, 1590–1700', EcHR, 2nd ser., xxxiv, 1981, pp. 401–2.

[6] R. S. Schofield, 'The Impact of Scarcity and Plenty on Population Change in England, 1541–1871', J. of Interdisciplinary Hist., xiv, 1983, p. 286.

[7] R. B. Outhwaite, 'Progress and Backwardness in English Agriculture, 1500–1650', EcHR, 2nd ser., xxxix, 1986, p. 17.

[8] These price data will be found in the Statistical Appendices, infra, pp. 117–23, 320–3, 350–1.

through changes in the relationship between the size of the consuming population and the volume of food produced. However, to seek an explanation for such changes solely, or even mainly, in terms of the two variables indicated may be to ignore the effects of other highly significant influences. The processes of agricultural production and distribution did not take place in a vacuum, neither did they remain unchanged. Surprisingly, since we live in a world of constantly changing weather conditions, the importance of which for food production is universally recognized, economic historians and demographers have been slow to integrate climatic influences as an independent variable in the Malthusian equation.[9] The position taken here is that, throughout the period under review, cyclical changes in weather conditions, by influencing the volume of agricultural output, served to disturb the balance between population and food, thus alternately providing a catalyst and then a depressant to economic well-being.

If climatic changes, being cyclical in nature, were inimical to a steadily improving situation, this was not the case with certain other underlying factors, the combined effects of which were to make the consequences of phases of bad weather progressively less calamitous with the passage of time. Thus, improvements in the food distribution system, involving better-organized dealer networks and storage facilities and more effective arrangements for the transportation of goods, served to bring areas of food production and need closer together, thereby reducing the threat of widespread famine. At the same time, the heavy dependence of the mass of the population upon the traditional grain staples was somewhat reduced as a result of a marked increase in the domestic production of fruits and vegetables and the limited importation of non-indigenous foodstuffs such as rice and citrus products.

The extent to which the provision of these additional supplies of food gave rise to a net increase in agricultural output is impossible to determine with any degree of accuracy. However, insofar as imports were obtained mainly in exchange for industrial exports, while market gardening represented the most intensive use of land for agricultural purposes, it may be asserted with a fair degree of confidence that the opportunity cost in terms of alternative agricultural production foregone would have been comparatively small.

On the broader issue of aggregate agricultural output, there are no

[9] However, see Ronald Lee, 'Short-Term Variation: Vital Rates, Prices and Weather' in E. A. Wrigley and R. S. Schofield, *The Population History of England, 1541–1871: A Reconstruction*, London, 1981, pp. 386–98.

reliable data to guide us, although it is clear that English agriculture must have developed considerably during the period under review: in 1750 it essentially supported a population of perhaps six million, compared with less than half that number in 1500. As already implied,[10] during much of the earlier part of the period, ending in the middle years of the seventeenth century, agricultural output lagged well behind the growth of population and, in consequence, *per capita* levels of production and consumption fell significantly. With respect to the later years, starting at about the time of the Restoration, the most widely accepted estimates until comparatively recently have been those of Deane and Cole, which, in broad terms, suggested that real agricultural output grew slowly and unevenly until about 1740 and accelerated thereafter.[11] More recently, studies by Crafts and Jackson have undermined these estimates, placing the period of most rapid growth before, rather than after, 1740.[12] Our own conclusions are in line with these more recent studies.

There remains the question of how far any increases in agricultural output were the result of improvements in productivity and how far they were attributable to other considerations, most notably an extension in the area of farmland. Some specifics with respect to crop yields will be noted subsequently.[13] For the present, it may be stated that the weight of evidence, such as it is, appears to suggest that in the century and a half before 1650 increases in the output of arable crops[14] were due more to an expansion in the acreage under cultivation than to higher yields per acre. After 1650, farmland was less noticeably in short supply, and increased arable output seems to have been achieved primarily as a result of farming and estate improvements undertaken in the context of a generally more favourable climatic environment. It should be noted that, while the above view of development before 1650 commands the support of a number of leading scholars,[15] it runs

---

[10] *Supra*, p. 1.

[11] Phyllis Deane and W. A. Cole, *British Economic Growth, 1688–1959: Trends and Structure*, Cambridge, 1962, ch. II.

[12] N. F. R. Crafts, 'English Economic Growth in the Eighteenth Century: A Re-Examination of Deane and Cole's Estimates', EcHR, 2nd ser., XXIX, 1976, pp. 226–35; R. V. Jackson, 'Growth and Deceleration in English Agriculture, 1660–1790', EcHR, 2nd ser., XXXVIII, 1985, pp. 333–51.

[13] *Infra*, pp. 71–2, 197–8, 280, 288, 374–5.

[14] The position with respect to livestock is less certain (see *infra*, pp. 22–5).

[15] Joan Thirsk, 'The Farming Regions of England' in Thirsk (ed.), *The Agrarian History of England and Wales, IV, 1500–1640*, Cambridge, 1967, p. 199; D. B. Grigg, *Population Growth and Agrarian Change*, Cambridge, 1980, p. 91; C. G. A Clay, *Economic Expansion and Social Change: England, 1500–1700*, 2 vols., Cambridge, 1984, I, pp. 66, 72, 109; A. R. Bridbury, 'Sixteenth-Century Farming', EcHR, 2nd ser., XXVII, 1974, pp. 538–56; Outhwaite, 'Progress and Backwardness', pp. 7–11.

counter to the position of certain other authorities, such as Kerridge and Hoskins, who have argued for a substantial increase in crop yields during the earlier period.[16] Indeed, in Kerridge's view, "yields per acre in the seventeenth century compare not unfavourably with modern English ones, the average of which has only increased as it has in more recent times through the abandonment of poorer lands".[17] However, while we are hesitant to subscribe to the generality of this observation, we are, in fact, persuaded that high yields were at times obtained in the seventeenth century on land where growing conditions, in terms of soil, management and climate were especially favourable.

The change in economic circumstances which occurred during the two and a half centuries encompassed by this study was paralleled by a change in the emphasis of government economic policy. Whereas, before the middle decades of the seventeenth century, measures to maintain the level of agricultural (notably, grain) production and to contain the rise in food prices were high on the list of governmental priorities, after the Restoration there was a growing preoccupation with overseas trade and export markets. Since, with the exception of wool in early Tudor times, agricultural products in their raw state were consumed almost entirely at home throughout the period under review,[18] measures to promote exports were concerned primarily with the establishment and maintenance of conditions conducive to the efficient production and effective marketing of industrial products.

In this schema, agriculture, while constituting the largest single sector of the economy, played an essentially supportive role, providing a source of cheap raw materials for industrial processing and – by means of increased output – making possible the deployment of capital and labour into manufacturing activity and other forms of business enterprise.

Reflecting these various tendencies, there were significant changes in the terms of trade between agricultural goods and industrial products and in the relative prices of different agricultural commodities. These changing price relationships are brought out in Table 1, which brings together on a common statistical base certain of the price indices previously compiled separately with reference to the periods 1500–

---

[16] E. Kerridge, *The Agricultural Revolution*, London, 1967, pp. 328–31; W. G. Hoskins, 'Harvest Fluctuations and English Economic History', AHR, XVI, pp. 25–8.

[17] Kerridge, *op. cit.*, p. 330.

[18] For exports of grain in the latter part of the period, see *infra*, pp. 379–80.

Table 1. *Commodity price indices: selected decades (1450–99 = 100)*[a]

| | | | (a) Field crops | | | | | |
	Wheat	Rye	Barley	Oats	Peas	Beans	Hay	Straw
1540–9	171	–	197	191	177	170	140	118
1590–9	499	651	600	638	475	464	385	401
1640–9	717	860	796	843	622	620	768	612
1690–9	683	678	753	762	548	596	969	759
1740–9	472	485	674	682	443	496	1039	968

| | | | (b) Livestock and animal produce | | | | | |
| | | | | | Sheep | | Dairy | |
	Oxen	Cows	Calves	Wethers	(unspec.)	Lambs	Produce	Wool
1540–9	195	171	155	207	221	203	139	153
1590–9	428	517	449	460	492	458	313	315
1640–9	600	823	733	740	587	684	439	396
1690–9	594	878	964	778	624	711	359	259
1740–9	566	925	781	816	624	752	325	195

| | (c) All agricultural commodities and industrial products | | |
	Agricultural commodities	Industrial products	Agricultural × 100 industrial
1540–9	169	127	133
1590–9	451	238	189
1640–9	644	306	210
1690–9	669	331	202
1740–9	619	293	212

Note: [a] Based on data contained in the Statistical Appendices. The figures for 1640–1749 have been recast with reference to the base period indicated.

1640 and 1640–1750 respectively.[19] The figures in this table further illustrate how, in the determination of long-term statistical trends, conclusions can be greatly influenced by the choice of terminal points.

Thus, the rise in the price of grains, which is generally recognized by historians as the most notable aspect of the Tudor 'price revolution', assumes a somewhat different complexion when viewed from the

[19] See Statistical Appendices, *infra*, pp. 158–64, and 342–8. It was possible to make the aforementioned consolidation due to the fact that the price indices for the earlier period were carried forward to 1649, thereby providing a ten-year overlap with the series for the later period. Thus, for the decade 1640–9, wheat has a price index number of 717, using 1450–99 as the base period, and 126, using 1640–1749 as base. Hence, by applying a multiplication factor of 717 ÷ 126 (or 5.69), it is possible to re-cast the price indices for wheat in the years 1640–1749 so that they have reference to the same base period as the earlier price series. For example, 120, the index number for 1690–9, becomes 684 (i.e. 120 × 5.69) and 83, the index number for 1740–9, becomes 472 (i.e. 83 × 5.69).

standpoint of the economically less agitated years of the mid-eighteenth century. Likewise, adoption of the latter standpoint serves to enhance awareness of the underlying strength of demand for livestock and fodder crops throughout the period under review. In this regard, the imbalance between supply and demand appears to have been particularly great in the case of hay, which underwent a more than tenfold increase in price during the period 1500–1750 as a whole. While it is possible that this imbalance could have resulted, in part, from the conversion of grassland to other uses, the growing feed requirements of a bigger and/or better fed livestock population would appear to provide a more comprehensive and more likely explanation.

The rise in the price of hay and of other traditional fodder crops, such as straw and oats, makes it clear why supplies of clover, rye grass, sainfoin and turnips were such a boon to the cattle grazier and sheepmaster in the post-Restoration period, but it also underlines the fact that, in spite of the diffusion of these new crops, and in spite of innovations, such as the floating of water meadows to increase the yield per acre of common hay, problems with respect to the supply of feed had been by no means resolved by the mid-eighteenth century.

As is discussed in more detail in the main body of the text,[20] increases in the weight and size of livestock would appear to provide at least a partial explanation as to why stock prices rose more than grain prices over the period 1500–1750 as a whole. One would also expect the same factor – through the production of more meat, milk, hide and wool per beast – to have a moderating effect on the rise in the price of animal produce, and this expectation would appear to be borne out by the data in Table 1.[21] Increases in the longer-term yields of farm produce – whether of animal origin or grain – could, of course, help to compensate the farmer when prices tended to fall, as in the decades after the Restoration.

Unfortunately, with respect to the period under review, there are few quantitative data to guide us in regard to the yields of farm produce. Indeed, while the data upon which our price series have been

---

[20] Infra, pp. 22–5, 198–201.

[21] An indication of the possible dimensions involved is provided by the sheep-farming accounts of the Temple family. In the 1540s and 1550s sheep grazed by Peter Temple in the vicinity of Burton Dassett, War., had an average fleece weight of 2–2.5 lb. The price received by Temple for the wool of his flock ranged between 12s. 8d. per tod (of 28 lb) in 1544 and 25s. 4d. per tod in 1550 (when cloth exports were booming). Almost two centuries later, in 1740, the average weight of the fleeces produced by sheep belonging to Richard Temple Grenville of Wootton, Bucks., was 7.8 lb, the wool being sold for 12s. 3d. per tod. See N. W. Alcock, ed., *Warwickshire Grazier and London Skinner, 1532–1555. The Account Book of Peter Temple and Thomas Heritage*, British Academy, Records of Social and Economic History, NS, IV, Oxford, 1981, pp. 99–101; Bucks. RO, D/MH/33/1; Reading Univ. Lib., Farm Rec. Coll. BUC 11/1/5.

based are far from perfect, being of a piecemeal nature for some commodities and almost completely lacking for others, there is a much greater paucity of information respecting physical measures of all kinds. So far as the studies reproduced in the following pages are concerned, the lack of a solid foundation of physical facts becomes very evident when attempts are made to establish a rigorous framework for analysing the economic circumstances of the individual farm entity. Of necessity, such attempts have to rely mainly upon shreds of evidence from whatever source and upon a considerable element of guesswork.

This weakness in the data base applies to measures of both input and output. With respect to the latter, extant farm accounts contain surprisingly few entries indicating the yields per acre of arable crops or hay, and are even less informative concerning the yields of animal produce such as milk or wool. On the input side, we remain largely in the dark in regard to such critical variables as the sowing rates of seed per acre and the stock-carrying capacity of land.[22] Likewise, with respect to labour inputs, many account books record a variety of wage payments, but none of those examined contains any useful data on total hours worked per week or total days worked per year.

Among the dangers associated with reliance upon a weak data base is the tendency to accept unrepresentative situations as typical simply because they are the only ones evidenced in extant documentation. In view of the dearth of information on the subject, one might easily assume, for example, that grain crop yields in the early decades of the seventeenth century were generally of the order of those obtained by Robert Loder of Harwell, Berks., during the years 1612–20.[23] This period, however, included several years in which bumper harvests were obtained as a result of exceptionally favourable weather conditions. Moreover, there would have been differences in yields per acre in any given year as between Loder's farm and farms in other parts of the country, depending upon such factors as soil type, terrain and the amounts of sunshine and rainfall. By the same token, rates of return on expenditure in agriculture must have varied enormously from time to time and from one farming enterprise to another; accordingly, the likelihood that some farmers occasionally achieved "incredible" profits needs to be recognized.[24]

[22] These topics are discussed in more detail *infra*, pp. 72–4, 84–7, 274–5, 280–1, 292–305. See also Ian Blanchard, 'Population Change, Enclosure, and the Early Tudor Economy', EcHR, 2nd ser., XXIII, 1970, pp. 443–5.

[23] See *infra*, pp. 39, 71.

[24] For example, by Holderness, who expresses reservations regarding the rates of return achieved on certain of our 'hypothetical' farms in the period 1600–20. See B. A. Holderness, *Pre-industrial England: economy and society, 1500–1750*, London, 1976, p. 201; *infra*, pp. 70–93.

The problems inherent in the determination of national crop yields have recently been resurrected in studies by Turner and Overton,[25] who have reviewed and revamped the bases for the most commonly accepted estimates of wheat yields in the latter part of our period. Unfortunately, but perhaps not surprisingly, the resultant findings have been neither definitive nor unambiguous. Rather, the effect has been to widen the range of previous estimates at both ends of the scale – to between 8 and 20 bushels per acre with respect to the period 1650–1700, and to between 14 and 27 bushels per acre with reference to the 1760s. At the local level, using data derived from probate inventories, Overton has produced estimates of the average yields of the major grains in the counties of Norfolk and Suffolk over the period 1585–1735.[26] Given that care is taken to compensate for the intrusion of extraneous factors, this kind of exercise has a possibly wider application, and could prove particularly useful in the determination of trends in crop yields.

Of course, economic variables such as crop yields varied not only from year to year and locality to locality but also, it may be suspected, in relation to the size of the individual farm enterprise. However, while it may be safely assumed that the majority of agricultural producers during the period under review were smallholders and subsistence cultivators selling little in the open market, 'first hand' information respecting the business of farming is derived mainly from the farm accounts and estate records of substantial yeomen, country gentlemen and the aristocracy. Clearly, considerable caution is necessary in relating the evidence contained in such documentation to the circumstances of the farming community in general.

Size – and the possession of capital – conferred upon the big producer a degree of flexibility denied to the small operator.[27] Even so, at all levels of enterprise, farming was – and remains – an activity circumscribed and controlled by external and impersonal influences to an extent unknown in virtually all other areas of economic endeavour.

In the first place, save in highly exceptional circumstances – as in the case of a very large producer and an isolated local market – farmers could do little to influence the price of produce. Individual farmers might higgle over a few pence, or even a shilling or two in the case of a

[25] M. Turner, 'Agricultural Productivity in England in the Eighteenth Century: Evidence from Crop Yields', EcHR, 2nd ser., xxxv, 1982, pp. 489–510; 'Agricultural Productivity in Eighteenth-Century England: Further Strains of Speculation', EcHR, 2nd ser., xxxvii, 1984, pp. 252–7; M. Overton, 'Agricultural Productivity in Eighteenth-Century England: Some Further Speculations', ibid., pp. 244–51.

[26] M. Overton, 'Estimating Crop Yields from Probate Inventories: An Example from East Anglia, 1585–1735', J. Econ. Hist., xxix, 1979, pp. 363–78.

[27] See infra, pp. 91–3, 305–6.

large transaction, but essentially they were at the mercy of market forces.

Secondly, a range of factors, entirely or largely outside the farmer's control, effectively limited his options with respect to production possibilities. Reference has already been made to the weather; this not only exerted a major impact on the size of the harvest, but also (at least before the advent of temperature-controlled production under glass) effectively ruled out as economically – if not technically – unfeasible various farm activities in different regions. Also of critical concern in this regard were the nature of the soil and the topography of the farmland. The composition of the soil could, of course, be changed by dressings of various sorts, but considerable capital was required and there were limits to what could be done. With respect to the terrain, some levelling of uneven land might be undertaken, but fundamental changes to the basic configuration of the countryside were obviously out of the question.

Marketing considerations imposed a further set of constraints upon production for commercial disposition. Costs of transportation overland were especially high by present-day standards, and farmers operating at a distance from navigable water were unlikely to engage in the commercial production of crops such as hay or oats which were bulky and/or of low value in relation to weight. Likewise, market-oriented producers of liquid milk and most types of horticultural produce needed to be located within close proximity of their customers in the urban centres, both on account of the perishable nature of their wares and in order to facilitate frequent deliveries.

Most of the aforementioned restrictions still remained at the end of the period under review, although their impact and frequency had in some instances been considerably reduced. At the level of the individual farm, impediments arising out of the particular circumstances of the individual enterprise tended to become less widespread or less intractable with the passage of time. In the first place, the percentage of enclosed farmland was increasing throughout the period, and in the study of agrarian history it has long been axiomatic that a much more flexible system of farming was possible when land was enclosed than when it was cultivated in strips in the open fields. The imposition of market value rents – with or without enclosure – was another feature of the period. Concomitant with these expressions of a growing commercialism in agriculture, the number of subsistence operators (whose ranks were also thinned with every harvest failure) became an ever-declining force. Though no figures are available, it would seem safe to assume that over the period 1500–1750 as a whole there was an increase in the average size of farm and in the credit-worthiness of the average farmer.

The operational flexibility conferred by these changes in individual circumstances was buttressed on the production front after the Restoration by the possibilities provided by the new crops and new rotations.

At the same time, external constraints – especially in the related spheres of distribution and marketing – were tending to become less confining. Thus, by the middle years of the eighteenth century, the heavy burden of transportation costs had been eased somewhat in certain instances as a result of new highway construction, improvements in the system of inland water navigation, and a greater use of coastal shipping.[28] As a corollary of these developments and of the accompanying growth in the volume of trade, the network for the distribution of agricultural (and non-agricultural) products became better organized, with the emergence of specialized classes of dealers, jobbers, factors, carriers and drivers, whose intervention in the business of buying, selling and transporting goods attracted the hostile attention of entrenched manufacturing and trading interests.[29] As part of this process of development and change, the sixteenth century witnessed a significant increase in the number of open markets and fairs. Subsequently, these institutions tended to decline in numbers and importance, as new trading possibilities opened up and were exploited elsewhere.[30]

Finally, the developments which have been outlined in these introductory pages, and which are described in greater detail in the main body of the text, had an important unifying influence on the national economy, for with them the degree of economic interdependence between different parts of the country increased. Thereby, the more remote regions – notably, the pastoral areas of the North and West – were brought into the mainstream of economic development, from which further advance over the next one hundred and fifty years was to be rapid.

Within this framework, agriculture was, and remains, an activity of great diversity, practised in a wide range of physical environments by operators falling into numerous farm types and size categories. As should become clear in the following pages, there was not one agricultural interest, but many, frequently with differing views and with differing responses to economic conditions. Thus, speaking pri-

[28] See *infra*, pp. 31–5, 207–9; J. A Chartres, 'The Marketing of Agricultural Produce', in *The Agrarian History of England and Wales, V, 1640–1750*, ed. Joan Thirsk, Cambridge, 1985, pp. 465–8 (reprinted in vol. 4 of this series, pp. 216–19).

[29] R. B. Westerfield, *Middlemen in English Business*, New Haven, 1915, *passim*; N. S. B. Gras, *The Evolution of the English Corn Market*, Cambridge, Mass., 1926, *passim*; P. J. Bowden, *The Wool Trade in Tudor and Stuart England*, London, 1962, *passim*; Chartres, *op. cit.*, pp. 469–502.

[30] Alan Everitt, 'The Marketing of Agricultural Produce' in *The Agrarian History of England and Wales, IV*, pp. 475–6 (reprinted in vol. 4 of this series, pp. 24–5); Chartres, *op. cit.*, pp. 409–21.

marily with reference to European experience, Professor Abel has reinforced our conclusion that "the sheep farmer's chance of profit rose or fell in inverse proportion to the price of corn";[31] while recent work by Beckett has underlined the unevenness of the impact of the 'depression' in the second quarter of the eighteenth century on farmers and landowners in different parts of the country.[32] On another plane, there were significant differences in the responses of large arable producers and small subsistence cultivators to changes in the economic environment. Whereas the latter were primarily concerned to obtain a sufficiency of output, the former were more largely interested in market prices. Since the size of the harvest and the level of prices tended to move in contrary directions, contentment among arable farmers was never universal. However, even as fundamental a proposition as this may escape recognition when, as is the case, extant documentation is highly selective in its representation of the fortunes and experiences of the different social and economic classes. Thus, while the generally acknowledged decline of the smallholder during the period under review has been variously ascribed to the effects of the enclosure movement, loopholes in the system of land tenure and legal niceties, it may be suspected that a more pervasive influence in many instances was the debilitating effects of disastrous harvests. At the level above the subsistence cultivator, on farms where a moderate proportion of output was for commercial disposition, a prolonged period of low prices could also cause bankruptcy and the vacation of holdings.

PETER J. BOWDEN

[31] Wilhelm Abel, *Agricultural Fluctuations in Europe from the Thirteenth to the Twentieth Centuries*, London, 1980 edn, translated by Olive Ordish, p. 114.

[32] J. V. Beckett, 'Regional Variation and the Agricultural Depression, 1730–50', EcHR, 2nd ser., xxxv, pp. 35–51; 'Yorkshire and the Agricultural Depression, 1730–1750', *Yorks. Arch. J.*, 54, 1982, pp. 119–23.

1

AGRICULTURAL PRICES,
FARM PROFITS, AND RENTS, 1500–1640[1]

A. THE LONG-TERM MOVEMENT OF
AGRICULTURAL PRICES

1. *Introduction*

Though much obscurity still exists about the origins, extent, and even
the nature of agrarian changes in the Tudor and early Stuart periods,
certain broad generalizations may be made. Under the stimulus of
growing population, rising agricultural prices, and mounting land
values, the demand for land became more intense and its use more
efficient. The area under cultivation was extended. Large estates were
built up at the expense of small-holdings, and subsistence farming lost
ground to commercialized agriculture. Changes in the balance of land
distribution were accompanied by an increase in the number of agricultural wage-earners and a decline in their standard of living. There
was a growing inequality of income among the different classes of
rural society.

These features, indicative of growing population pressure and land
hunger, are familiar to all students of thirteenth-century agrarian
history. During the greater part of the fourteenth and fifteenth centuries, however, conditions were far otherwise. Severe and recurrent
outbreaks of plague, of which the Black Death of 1348–9 is the most
notable instance, resulted in extremely high mortality and a marked
reduction of population. Beginning in the early decades of the fourteenth century and continuing until the third quarter of the fifteenth,
agriculture, together with other sectors of the economy, experienced
a prolonged recession; agricultural prices and rents fell, and the area of
cultivated land contracted. The task of land reclamation, actively
pursued in the thirteenth century, petered out, and on marginal lands

[1] I wish to thank the University of Sheffield for financial assistance from the
Knoop Research Fund, which helped make possible the examination of a wide range
of source material for this study. I am grateful to many colleagues and friends for
constructive criticism and advice, but especially should like to mention Dr Joan Thirsk,
Mr R. Wilkinson, Prof. M. W. Beresford, Prof. A. J. Brown, Mr J. L. J. Machin, and
Mr A. J. Odber. Any errors remain my own. The diagrams were kindly prepared by
Miss M. Lawson, and the manuscript typed by Mrs M. L. Smith and Mrs B. Jobling.
—P.J.B.

colonized during the earlier period of expanding demand and high prices, whole settlements were abandoned. Tenants were hard to find in the fifteenth century, and farms were at a discount. Unfavourable land, whether it was infertile or burdened with a heavy rent or an irksome customary service, reverted to nature. On large estates it became increasingly common for the lords to retire wholly or in part from direct farming and to lease their demesnes to tenants on easy terms. On peasants' customary holdings rents were reduced, and labour services, once rigorously exacted, were now commuted. This was "an age of recession, arrested economic development, and declining national income."[1] But if there were losses in the national product, there were gains in social distribution. The latter change resulted partly from the increase in the average size of peasant holdings and their multiplication at the expense of commercialized agriculture. The ease with which a tenancy could be obtained resulted in a general 'upgrading' of the village community, and this, together with the decline in the population as a whole, greatly reduced the size of the wage-labour force. While agricultural prices declined, money wages increased. Between 1300 and 1480, on the estates of the bishop of Winchester, the purchasing power of wages in terms of wheat more than doubled.[2] It is not surprising that Thorold Rogers should refer to the fifteenth century as "the golden age of the English labourer."[3] Not until the nineteenth century was the wage-earner's standard of living again so high.

2. The long-term trend of prices

The question of the antecedent conditions, out of which the agrarian changes of the Tudor period arose, is obviously an important one for our study; just how important becomes apparent when the pressure exerted by the market is considered. The century and a half before 1650 was marked by a long, large rise in the general level of prices. This rise was greater for agricultural commodities than for other products. If the period 1450–99 is taken as base (= 100),[4] the average price of agricultural goods had increased to 644 by the decade 1640-9. This compares with price indices of 524 for timber and 306 for industrial

---

[1] M. M. Postan, 'The Fifteenth Century', EcHR, IX, 1939, p. 161.
[2] Ibid., pp. 161–7; M. M. Postan, 'Some Economic Evidence of Declining Population in the later Middle Ages', EcHR, 2nd Ser., II, 1950, pp. 221–46; 'The Chronology of Labour Services', RHS, 4th Ser., XX, 1937, pp. 169–93; J. Saltmarsh, 'Plague and Economic Decline in England', Camb. Hist. J., VII, 1941, pp. 23–41.
[3] J. E. T. Rogers, Six Centuries of Work and Wages, London, 1886, p. 326.
[4] All subsequent price indices mentioned in the text refer to this base, unless otherwise specified.

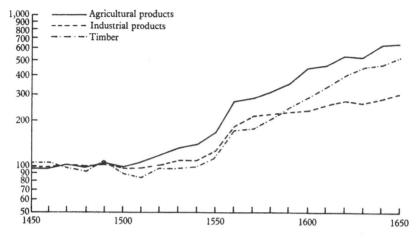

Fig. 1. Prices of agricultural products, industrial products and timber.
1450–99 = 100.

products.[1] The position is graphically represented in Fig. 1. The secular movement of prices was similar throughout Europe.[2]

There had been periods of rising prices in earlier ages, but the inflation of the sixteenth and early seventeenth centuries was of hitherto unprecedented proportions. Until recent decades, explanations of this

[1] Statistical Appendix, Table XIII.
[2] See Statistical Appendix, Tables VII and XIV; G. Wiebe, *Zur Geschichte der Preisrevolution des XVI. und XVII. Jahrhunderts*, Leipzig, 1895; M. J. Elsas, *Umriss einer Geschichte der Preise und Löhne in Deutschland vom ausgehenden Mittelalter bis zum Beginn des Neunzehnten Jahrhunderts*, I, II, Leiden, 1936–49; A. F. Pribram, *Materialien zur Geschichte der Preise und Löhne in Österreich*, I, Vienna, 1938; F. Simiand, *Recherches Anciennes et Nouvelles sur le Mouvement Général des Prix du 16e au 19e Siècle*, Paris, 1932; E. J. Hamilton, *Money, Prices, and Wages in Valencia, Aragon, and Navarre, 1351–1500*, Harvard, 1936; *American Treasure and the Price Revolution in Spain, 1501–1650*, Harvard, 1934; G. Parenti, *Prime ricerche sulla rivoluzione dei prezzi in Firenze*, Florence, 1939; J. Pelc, *Ceny w Krakowie w latach, 1369–1600, Badania z dziejow spolecznych i gospodarczych*, Lwow, 1935; C Verlinden *et al.*, 'Mouvements des prix et des salaires en Belgique au xvi⁰ siècle', *Annales E.S.C.*, 1955, pp. 173–98; C. M. Cipolla, 'La prétendue "révolution des prix," Réflexions sur l'expérience italienne', *Annales E.S.C.*, 1955, pp. 513–16; H. G. Koenigsberger, 'Property and the Price Revolution (Hainault, 1474–1573)', EcHR, 2nd Ser., IX, 1956, pp. 1–15; D. I. Hammarström, 'The Price Revolution of the Sixteenth Century: Some Swedish Evidence', *Scand. Econ. Hist. Rev.*, v, 1957, pp. 118–58; E. H. Phelps Brown and S. V. Hopkins, 'Wage-rates and Prices: Evidence for Population Pressure in the Sixteenth Century', *Economica*, NS XXIV, 1957, pp. 289–306; 'Builders' Wage-rates, Prices, and Population: Some Further Evidence', *Economica*, NS XXVI, 1959, pp. 18–38.

sustained fall in the value of money emphasized the effect of monetary influences, and in particular laid stress on the debasements of the coinage and the influx of precious metals into Europe from Spanish America. These monetary factors may have been partly responsible for the inflationary process, but by themselves they do not appear to provide a complete explanation.

The upward movement of prices was far greater than can be allowed for by reductions in the fineness and weight of the coinage, as Wiebe showed when he translated all his money-of-account values into silver prices.[1] Moreover, on close examination, the relationship between currency debasement and rising prices appears less positive than is sometimes suggested.[2] The general level of agricultural prices showed no tendency to rise in the years immediately following 1465, when the quantity of silver in English coins of a given nominal value was cut by 20 per cent. Prices moved upward in the decade following 1526, when the metal weight of coins was reduced by 8 per cent, but the increase was not steep and by then a rising trend had already set in. During the period of the great debasements between 1542 and 1551, the metal content of coins was progressively reduced, eventually by 75 per cent for silver and by 25 per cent for gold.[3] But the rise in prices at this time was not uninterrupted—the price of wheat, for instance, was lower in 1547 than it had been for more than twenty years—and not until the end of the 1540's did the general price level move sharply upwards. Even then, continental prices followed a broadly similar curve, and this suggests other, probably real, economic factors at work.[4] The re-coinage of 1560–25 had no noticeable effect on the level of prices, and the upward trend continued until the middle years of the seventeenth century.

How far the price inflation was a direct consequence of the influx of silver and gold into Europe from Spanish America is an open question. The upward movement of prices began in the early years of the sixteenth century, before the import of bullion into Spain had assumed very substantial proportions.[6] In several continental countries the price rise commenced even earlier, in the closing decades of the fifteenth century.

[1] Wiebe, op. cit., pp. 354–62, 374–7.
[2] See, for example, Y. S. Brenner, 'The Inflation of Prices in Early Sixteenth-century England', EcHR, 2nd Ser., XIV, 1961, pp. 227–8.
[3] Sir John Craig, The Mint. A History of the London Mint from A.D. 287 to 1948, Cambridge, 1953, pp. 94, 109, 111.
[4] See Statistical Appendix, pp. 116ff. below.
[5] For details, see Craig, op. cit.; A. E. Feaveryear, The Pound Sterling. A History of English Money, Oxford, 1933, pp. 71–8.
[6] E. H. Hamilton, 'American Treasure and Andalusian Prices, 1503–1660', J. Econ. & Bus. Hist., I, 1928–9, p. 6.

There may, of course, have been some relationship between these earlier price movements and the fact that silver production in Central Europe entered upon a phase of secular expansion in the second half of the fifteenth century, to reach a peak in the decade 1526–35.[1] But even at its peak, Europe's output of coinage metal was only small compared with American production later in the century; and the theoretical substitution of European for American silver still leaves certain apparent contradictions unresolved.

In England, output of silver was insignificant, while the activities of privateers and bullion smugglers in bringing treasure into the realm have probably been exaggerated. This being so, the major part of any additions to the country's monetary stocks must have come by way of a favourable external balance of trade. Statistics of overseas commerce during this period are incomplete, but a favourable balance may have been achieved in the first half of the sixteenth century, when England's export trade underwent a marked expansion.[2] In the second half of the century, however, when the price rise was at its height, the export trade ceased to grow, and England's overall external balance was probably either slightly adverse or in rough equilibrium.[3] Moreover, the level of export-goods prices rose less than that of domestic products. Finally, it is only during the second quarter of the seventeenth century that there is any definite evidence of large quantities of silver from Spain actually reaching England. Most of the silver was, however, re-exported, and, in any case, by this time the inflationary movement of prices was coming to an end.[4]

A factor which undoubtedly exercised a powerful stimulating influence on prices in the sixteenth and early seventeenth centuries was population growth. Precise population statistics for this period are not available, and such estimates as there are contain a very large element of guesswork. According to Sir John Clapham, the population of England and Wales increased, after the setbacks of the earlier period, to perhaps 2,500,000 or 3,000,000 in the year 1500, and to 5,800,000 in 1700.[5]

[1] J. U. Nef, 'Silver production in Central Europe', *J. Pol. Econ.*, XLIX, 1941, pp. 584–6; 'Mining and Metallurgy in Medieval Civilisation', *The Cambridge Economic History of Europe*, ed. M. Postan and E. E. Rich, II, Cambridge, 1952, pp. 469–70.

[2] F. J. Fisher, 'Commercial Trends and Policy in Sixteenth-century England', EcHR, X, 1939–40, pp. 95–7.

[3] L. Stone, 'Elizabethan Overseas Trade', EcHR, 2nd Ser., II, 1949, pp. 36, 54.

[4] Y. S. Brenner, 'The Inflation of Prices in England, 1551–1650', EcHR, 2nd Ser., XV, 1962, pp. 277–8.

[5] Sir John Clapham, *A Concise Economic History of Britain from the Earliest Times to 1750*, Cambridge, 1949, pp. 77–8, 186. For other estimates of population in this period see J. C. Russell, *British Medieval Population*, Albuquerque, 1948, *passim*; D. V. Glass, 'Gregory King's Estimates of the Population of England and Wales, 1695', *Population Studies*, III, 1950, p. 338.

On the basis of these estimates, a growth of population of 75–100 per cent between the mid-fifteenth and mid-seventeenth century seems likely. Although the actual extent of demographic change is unknown, the evidence of mounting land hunger, increasing poverty, and diverging relative price movements, in sum, leaves no doubt that the rise in population must have been substantial. The subject of land hunger will be discussed later. For evidence of declining living standards we must look first at changes in the wage-earner's position.

Wage-earning is not a pursuit that is normally engaged in for its own sake, and in a peasant economy it is followed only by men with little or no land of their own. At the beginning of the Tudor period, many—perhaps the majority—of agricultural wage-earners were sons or brothers waiting to take over the family holding. At this time, lifelong agricultural wage-earners, who had no such prospect ahead of them, were probably outnumbered by the land-holders. But as the sixteenth century progressed the position changed, with an increasing proportion of the population becoming dependent upon wages or poor relief for the major part of their livelihood. In 1641 the opinion was expressed that "the fourth part of the inhabitants of most of the parishes of England are miserable poor people, and (harvest time excepted) without any subsistence," while towards the end of the seventeenth century it was estimated that labourers, cottagers, and paupers constituted as much as 47 per cent of the total population.[1]

This growth in the size of the labour force need not have resulted in a decline in the wage-earner's standard of living had there been a compensating increase in the amount of employment available; but there was not. Employment in agriculture, which was much the most important economic activity, may well have fallen, despite an increase in the area under cultivation. Enclosures, especially for pasture farming, engrossing, evictions of small cultivators, and the creation of large estates, meant fewer agricultural holdings and probably less work for labourers. Manufacturing industry could not have employed more than one fifth of the working population, even in 1650, and its expansion was quite inadequate to absorb the surplus labour made available by population growth and agrarian change. Government measures served to aggravate the situation. The free movement of labour, which would have facilitated economic expansion and the absorption of unemployed workers, was impeded by Poor Law enactments and the Statute of Artificers (1563)[2] as well as by the restrictions of the gild system. One

[1] Clapham, op. cit., pp. 212–13; Considerations Touching Trade, with the Advance of the King's Revenue, 1641, p. 15; Gregory King, Natural and Political Observations, 1696, reprinted in G. Chalmers, An Estimate of the Comparative Strength of Great Britain, 1820, pp. 424–5.   [2] Statutes of the Realm, 5 Eliz. I, c. 4.

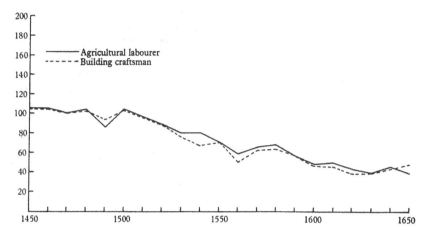

Fig. 2. Purchasing power of wage rates. 1450–99 = 100.

clause of the afore-mentioned Statute sought to preserve the wage-earner's standard of life by putting the power of assessing wage-rates into the hands of the employer class! However, in practice, the machinery of assessment seems to have exercised little long-term influence over actual wage levels, one way or the other; the wage-earner's position had been deteriorating before this measure was passed, and it was to become even worse in the future. There was some improvement in the worker's position in the decade or so following the 1563 Act; but this was not a purely English phenomenon, and was associated with the return of better harvests after the famine years of the 1550's and the probable temporary slowing down of population growth.[1]

Some idea of the extent of the fall in the wage-earner's standard of living is provided by Fig. 2, which indicates changes in the purchasing power of the daily wage-rates of agricultural labourers and building craftsmen in southern England in the period under review. In both cases money wages increased: from 4d. to 1s. 0d. a day for agricultural labourers, and from 6d. to 1s. 5d. for building craftsmen.[2] These increases, though substantial, did not offset the much greater advance in the general level of prices. In real terms, therefore, these workers became much poorer. Beginning in the early years of the sixteenth

[1] Real wages in, for example, Antwerp and Valencia temporarily improved after 1560. See C. Verlinden et al., *Annales E.S.C.*, 1955, pp. 191–8; E. H. Phelps Brown and S. V. Hopkins, 'Builders' Wage-rates, Prices and Population: Some Further Evidence', *Economica*, NS XXVI, 1959, pp. 35–6.

[2] See Tables XV and XVI; E. H. Phelps Brown and S. V. Hopkins, 'Seven Centuries of Building Wages', *Economica*, NS XXII, 1955, p. 205.

century the purchasing power of the daily wage-rate declined, though not continuously. There was a sharp fall in the middle years of the century, when prices rapidly increased, and this was followed by a partial recovery. The improvement in the worker's position, however, was not maintained. At the lowest point, in the second decade of the seventeenth century, the purchasing power of the agricultural labourer's daily wage-rate was only 44 per cent of its level in the second half of the fifteenth century, and the building craftsman's wage-rate was only 39 per cent of the comparable level. Possibly workers in other industries fared somewhat better, for agriculture and the building trades are occupations where rates of pay tend by tradition to be relatively inelastic.[1] The number of wage-earners in other industries, however, was probably only a small proportion of the total working population.

It should be further borne in mind that, for several reasons, Fig. 2 represents only an approximation of changes in the standard of living of agricultural labourers and building craftsmen. In the first place, because of the lack of statistical data, any 'cost of living' index for this period must be based largely on the prices of primary products, such as grain. The prices of the processed products and the manufactured goods actually bought by wage-earners would have risen less than those of the relevant primary commodities, since they would have been influenced to a greater extent by comparatively rigid labour costs.[2] Furthermore, changes in daily wage-rates do not provide an exact measure of changes in the wage-earner's income over a period of time; the number of days in which employment is found must also be taken into account. It has been argued that the Reformation resulted in an increase of one fifth in the number of working days in the year.[3] Such may have been the case; but, against this, it seems probable that employment became more irregular as the general level of unemployment among the working population increased. Again, the daily wage may not have been the wage-earner's only source of livelihood. Many agricultural labourers (if not building craftsmen) possessed an acre or two of land and enjoyed traditional rights to graze livestock on the common, while in some parts of the country the pursuit of a by-occupation in the home was encouraged by the predominantly rural form of industrial organization. For numbers of wage-earners these supplementary sources of income may well have spelt the difference between existence and starvation.

[1] T. S. Ashton, *An Economic History of England: the Eighteenth Century*, London, 1955, pp. 224–6.
[2] The possibility of reductions in manufacturing costs due to improvements in production methods will be discussed later, see pp. 28–9.
[3] E. H. Phelps Brown and S. V. Hopkins, 'Wage-rates and Prices: Evidence for Population Pressure in the Sixteenth Century', *Economica*, NS XXIV, 1957, p. 293.

The significance of all these various factors, however, cannot be accurately determined. On balance, it seems probable that the deterioration in the average wage-earner's position was not as drastic as Fig. 12 suggests. Nevertheless, the decline in living standards must still have been very considerable.

3. The long-term movement of relative prices

If, as seems probable, a growing surplus of labour arising from population pressure was mainly responsible for increasing poverty among the labouring classes, we should expect to find confirmatory evidence of this in the relative long-term price movements of different commodities.

In the first place, we should expect a rise in the relative price of foodstuffs, reflecting increased pressure on the country's limited natural resources, especially land. Since most other European countries were experiencing similar demographic changes, and since imports were, in any case, restricted by relatively high costs of transport, the major part of any increase in food supplies must have come from home production. There were three principal ways in which domestic farm output could have been increased: by extensions to the agricultural area; by the application of improved technical methods; and by changes involving the better utilization of land, i.e. by specialization upon those products which gave the highest physical returns. Apart from enclosures, improved methods of agricultural production were little in evidence before the mid-sixteenth century, while, with the notable exception of wool production, limitations of transport and marketing organization still imposed severe restrictions on the use of land. This being so, the extra food required by a growing population must have been obtained mainly by bringing more land into cultivation. In the late fifteenth century good agricultural land was probably still lying idle in many parts of the country, and its cultivation need not have led to any significant increase in the price of food. But as the demand for agricultural produce continued to rise, less fertile soils and more remote areas would be taken in hand, necessitating heavier outlays and transport over greater distances. Marginal costs of production, particularly for arable crops, would increase.

If the supply of agricultural products was inelastic, so also was the demand. There was no substitute for bread in the diet of the mass of the people. With falling real wages and increasing unemployment, it can be assumed that a relatively larger proportion of consumer demand was directed towards the necessities of life, such as bread. Moreover, in an effort to keep down their expenditure on food, there would be a tendency for consumers to buy less of the more expensive foods and more of the cheaper ones—for example, to buy less wheaten bread, and more rye and barley bread. If we compare the movement of grain prices between the mid-fifteenth and mid-seventeenth centuries we do, in fact, find that whereas the price of wheat increased sevenfold, that of the cheaper grains increased eightfold.[1] Other arable crops—hay, straw, peas, and beans—went up less in price. The demand for these other crops would have been influenced as much by the needs of the animal as of the human population, and the actual increase in price to between six and seven times the 1450-9 level was approximately the same as for livestock.

This line of argument can be developed further. One measure of a country's standard of living is the amount of dairy produce, eggs, and meat consumed per head of the population. At the stage above bare subsistence, expenditure on these products tends to rise proportionately more than income. But in Tudor and Stuart England many families were living at the very margin of subsistence, and though milk, butter, cheese, eggs, and meat may not have been classed as luxuries, they probably did not figure very prominently in the landless labourer's diet, and may well have become less important as his real income declined. When, in addition to this consideration, we allow for a more responsive supply than in the case of arable crops, it is not surprising that edible animal products should have risen less than fivefold in price between the mid-fifteenth and mid-seventeenth centuries. To the very poor man clothing is much less vital than food, and the comparatively small rise in the price of cloth in the latter part of our period suggests that this was an item on which substantial economies in expenditure were made. The price of wool reflected the demand for cloth, and although wool prices rose more than cloth prices during the two hundred years under consideration, the increase over the period was only fourfold. There was a somewhat greater rise in the price of hides and skins, possibly because a higher proportion of leather goods than of cloth was sold to the middle and upper classes.

Another feature which calls for comment is the considerable divergence between the movement of livestock prices, on the one hand, and animal produce prices, on the other, as illustrated in Table 2.

It will be noted that the animal products listed above do not include meat; and it might conceivably be argued that if meat were also brought into the reckoning, the disparity between stock and produce prices would largely disappear. However, the weight of evidence is against this supposition. In the first place, pigs and rabbits, which—to a greater extent than other farm animals—would be purchased mainly

[1] For these and subsequent prices mentioned, see Statistical Appendix, pp. 116ff.

for their flesh, rose much less in price than other livestock, the comparable indices being 575 (pigs) and 463 (rabbits). Secondly, beef and mutton prices little more than doubled between the mid-sixteenth and mid-seventeenth centuries, the increase being of the same order of magnitude as for other edible animal products. At Cambridge, for example, the price of beef increased from an average of 1s. 5¼d. per stone in the decade 1550–9 to 3s. 3½d. in 1640–9.[1]

Table 2. *Prices of livestock and animal products in 1640–49*
as percentages of prices in 1450–99

Cows and heifers	823	Dairy products	439
Cattle	713	Hides	577
Poultry	698	Eggs	500
Sheep	681	Wool	396

One possible explanation of the divergence between the prices of livestock and animal products is that improvements in management and feed were resulting in larger and healthier stock, with corresponding increases in the yield of meat, wool, and other produce. The increased supplies would thus tend to exercise a restraining effect on the rise in the prices of these commodities. How far this actually happened is unknown. There is certainly evidence that, compared with nearby common-field areas, enclosed lands in the Midlands produced larger sheep with heavier fleeces, and it is not unreasonable to suppose that, under similar circumstances, the size and yield of other livestock may also have improved. Unfortunately, information about the weights of livestock before the nineteenth century is extremely sparse, and there are insufficient data to enable any clear trend to be established. Such evidence as there is, however, suggests that Gregory King's estimates made at the end of the seventeenth century—which put the average weight of a bullock at 370 lb. and of a sheep at 28 lb.—were too low. Oxen purchased for the household of the bishop of Winchester in 1567–8 averaged 484 lb. in weight, while the figure for wether sheep was 44 lb. The average weight of runts (i.e. undersized bullocks) killed for domestic consumption on the Kentish estate of Sir Roger Twysden in 1641–2 was 370 lb. (allowing 8 lb. to the stone, in accordance with

[1] For meat prices see J. E. T. Rogers, *A History of Agriculture and Prices in England*, III, Oxford, 1882, pp. 119–202, 692–6; *ibid.*, VI, Oxford, 1887, pp. 241–306, 671; W. Beveridge *et al.*, *Prices and Wages in England from the Twelfth to the Nineteenth Century*, I, London, 1939, pp. 83, 144–5, 236.

common contemporary practice) or 647 lb. (allowing 14 lb. to the stone). It is not clear from Twysden's accounts whether these figures include the weight of hides (average, 12·1 lb.), tallow (11·7 lb.), and suet (8·7 lb.).[1] However, in view of what has already been said concerning changes in the pattern of consumer expenditure in times of falling real wages, the main feature of Table 2 that calls for explanation is probably not so much the comparatively small increase in the price of animal products, as the much greater increase in the price of stock. On the demand side, one factor which must have exercised some influence on the prices of cattle, horses, and sheep, was the area of arable cultivation. Not only were oxen and horses (price index number, 675) used for draught purposes, but, before the age of artificial fertilizers, animal manure was essential if the fertility of the arable land was to be maintained. The common-field system of agriculture and, at a more refined level, the growing practice of ley farming demonstrated this interdependence of livestock and tillage. It may, therefore, be assumed that the extension of arable cultivation, unless undertaken at the expense of pasture farming, was accompanied by an increase in the demand for stock. This was one reason why in many common-field villages it became increasingly necessary to stint rights of common as the sixteenth century progressed: the extension of the arable area often meant less waste on which to support more livestock.

Moreover, the overcrowding of the common land was associated with another feature of the period, which also probably exercised a stimulating effect on livestock prices. Attention has already been drawn to the growth in the number of cottagers and labourers with little or no land of their own, but with the traditional right to graze livestock on the common. The land available to such peasants, together with their lack of capital resources, imposed very strict limits on the nature of their farming activities, if, indeed, they were able to farm at all. The urgent need to obtain regular returns in the form of produce directed the attention of many cottagers to the keeping of one or two cows and a few hens, whose milk, cheese, butter, and eggs could be consumed at home, or perhaps sold at the local market. Other stock were also sometimes kept but in general were of subsidiary importance. The disappearance from the agrarian scene of the poor man and his cow was later to be lamented by a generation of economic historians. The very marked rise in the price of dairy animals noted in Table 2 suggests that these partnerships of man and beast were still very much

---

[1] P. J. Bowden, *The Wool Trade in Tudor and Stuart England*, London, 1962, pp. 26–7; Phyllis Deane and W. A. Cole, *British Economic Growth, 1688–1959*, Cambridge, 1962, pp. 69–70; Surrey RO, Loseley MS 927, 4; BM Add. MS 34162, f. 5. See also BM Add. MS 37419, f. 11ᵛ; Bury and W. Suff. RO, Tem. 1, 7, f. 6.

in evidence in the sixteenth and early seventeenth centuries, and indeed were probably becoming increasingly numerous.

So far, our analysis of relative price movements has been concerned with the period 1450–1650 as a whole. The analysis may now be taken further by breaking down the period into four parts, as in Table 3.

Table 3. *Percentage change in price*

	Agricultural commodities	Timber	Industrial products	Agricultural wage-rates
1450/9—1490/9	+3	−14	−2	—
1490/9—1540/9	+71	+26	+31	+17
1540/9—1590/9	+167	+151	+87	+86
1590/9—1640/9	+43	+81	+29	+39

From the above figures it can be seen that the level of agricultural prices tended to rise throughout the period, with the most rapid rate of advance occurring in the second half of the sixteenth century.

The rise was by no means even or uninterrupted. In the 1490's agricultural prices fell on average 7 per cent compared with the level reached in the previous decade; in the 1550's they jumped 60 per cent. A comparable increase of 26 per cent in the 1590's was followed by a slowing down in the inflationary process. The high point was reached in the fifth decade of the seventeenth century, but by then the prices of some agricultural products (e.g. barley, wool, fells, eggs, and poultry) had already ceased to rise. In the second half of the seventeenth century the general trend of agricultural prices was downward.

If we are looking for a real, as opposed to a monetary, explanation of this slowing down in the upward movement of prices in the early Stuart period, there seems good reason to believe that the forces both of demand and of supply were working in this direction. On the demand side, the probability is that the rate of population growth was greatly slowed down after 1620. In a society where many went hungry, even in prosperous times, and where medical knowledge was practically non-existent, famine or plague could double the mortality rate almost overnight. Neither was ever far away, but both scourges visited the 1620's and 1630's with particular severity. Whether the population actually decreased at this time is not known; in some parts of Europe apparently it did.[1] When we recall the rise in real wages after 1620 and

[1] See, for example, E. J. Hamilton, 'The Decline of Spain', EcHR, VIII, 1938, p. 171; M. J. Elsas, 'Price Data from Munich, 1500–1700', *Econ. Hist.*, III, 1935, p. 77.

the comparatively small increase in the price of grain in the first half of the seventeenth century (33 per cent, as against 43 per cent for all agricultural commodities), a similar occurrence in England does not seem wholly improbable.

On the supply side, various factors were making for an increased output of agricultural commodities and a reduction in prices. Improved farming techniques, described in detail elsewhere in this volume, such as the enclosure of common-field land, the use of lime and marl, the floating of water meadows, and the practice of 'convertible husbandry', all tended to increase the yield from arable and pasture. It would be wrong to infer that these improved methods of agriculture (apart from enclosure) had more than a limited application in the early Stuart period, but certainly they were becoming more widely adopted. Other factors were also working in the same direction. Though some contemporaries were inclined to believe that the concentration of agricultural holdings in fewer hands resulted in the engrossing of produce and rising agricultural prices, the probability is that the trend in favour of the larger farming unit made for more efficient production and lower costs.[1] The market for many commodities in the early Stuart period was still largely local; but the rise of classes of professional middlemen and carriers, together with developments in coastwise transportation, were gradually facilitating the growth of regional economic specialization, with resulting increased farming efficiency. The overall effect of all these influences cannot be precisely measured. One modern authority estimates that the average British wheat yield per acre may have risen from $8\frac{1}{4}$ to 11 bushels in the period 1450–1650; but this is very much guesswork. Also not entirely reliable is the statement made in 1610 that "one sheepe beareth as muche woolle as twoe or three did" formerly.[2] However, the evidence points the same way, and there seems some justification for supposing that towards the end of our period, if not before, improved farming techniques were having some effect in raising yields, at least on the lands of the more progressive farmers.

The increase in the country's agricultural output in the two centuries before 1650, however, probably owed less to improvements in productivity than to extensions in the cultivated area. The breaking in of new land was a piecemeal process, and at first was achieved mainly by intakes from the forest and waste. Later, as the area of easily accessible land diminished, attention was increasingly turned in marshy regions to reclamation by means of drainage. The sixteenth century

[1] TED III, pp. 52, 319; Bowden, op. cit., pp. 2–3.
[2] M. K. Bennett, 'British Wheat Yield Per Acre for Seven Centuries', Econ. Hist., III, 1935, pp. 23–6; BM Lansdowne MS 152, f. 229.

saw, for instance, the embankment of the Greenwich, Plumstead, and Wapping marshes, and the stock these newly-created grazings supported helped to supply the needs of the growing London market. In the middle decades of the seventeenth century some thousands of acres of fertile land were drained in the Fenlands in the biggest and most expensive reclamation scheme yet attempted. The resulting addition to the country's output of agricultural produce must have been considerable, and came at a time when other factors were also tending to check the rise in agricultural prices.[1]

The process of land reclamation, which continued throughout the Tudor and early Stuart periods, exercised an important influence on the price of timber. This is understandable, when it is recalled that to bring land under the plough often involved the clearance of woodland areas. The revival of economic activity in the second half of the fifteenth century is suggested, not only by the slight rise in the general level of agricultural prices, but also by the significant fall in the price of timber (see Table 3). It is evident that, at this phase of agricultural expansion, the clearing of woodland was outstripping the demand for wood. In the sixteenth century timber prices, though increasing, still tended to lag behind agricultural prices, but the position was changing. As remoter areas were cleared for cultivation, timber had to be moved greater distances at high and steeply rising costs of transport. Moreover, the growth of population and industry meant a greater demand for wood as fuel or raw material. More timber was needed, for example, for ordinary domestic use, house-building, ship-building, and the manufacture of iron. By the early decades of the seventeenth century, therefore, as a result of all these various influences, wood prices were rising more rapidly than agricultural prices, thus giving emphasis to contemporary complaints about a growing shortage of timber.

If the gap between agricultural prices and timber prices was narrowing during the early Stuart period, it was not until the middle years of the seventeenth century that industrial prices also began to catch up. During the preceding century and a half the purchasing power of industrial goods over agricultural products had progressively declined. By 1630–9 it needed 226 units of industrial goods to buy the same volume of agricultural commodities that 100 industrial units would have bought in the late fifteenth century.[2]

This lag of industrial prices behind other prices is probably to be explained largely in terms of changes in the pattern of consumer expenditure over the period. As real wages fell, so the proportion of

[1] H. C. Darby, *The Draining of the Fens*, Cambridge, 1940, *passim;* N. Harvey, 'Farm and Estate under Elizabeth the First', *Agriculture*, LX, 1953, pp. 108–11.
[2] Statistical Appendix, Table XIII.

income spent on industrial goods declined, while the proportion spent on foodstuffs and other essential items increased. Since agricultural prices kept ahead of most other prices, the class with the largest proportionate increase in income must have been those agricultural producers who farmed primarily for the market. The growing purchasing power of this section of the community would have helped to stimulate the demand for industrial goods, but only to a limited extent. In the first place, farmers with large marketable surpluses were very much a minority group. The great majority of agricultural producers were subsistence farmers with little to spare for the market; indeed, in times of harvest failure many small cultivators were turned into buyers of grain. Secondly, as a group, the large and middling farmers who engaged in commercialized agriculture seem also to have possessed a comparatively high propensity to save. Many yeomen and gentlemen, as well as the occasional lord, practised thrift, not only to accumulate capital for the future enlargement of their estates, but also simply in order to hoard. It is unlikely, therefore, that the growth in the income of these agricultural producers was accompanied by a corresponding increase in the demand for industrial products.

On the supply side, the probability is that industrial costs of production rose less than agricultural costs. Professor J. U. Nef has claimed that technological changes in the period 1540–1640 amounted to a minor 'industrial revolution'. How far industrial costs of production were lowered in real terms is a matter for debate, but the extent of the application of new industrial techniques has probably been exaggerated by Nef. Certainly, the main manufacturing activity—the production of cloth—was scarcely affected by cost-reducing innovations. Moreover, agricultural and industrial prices were diverging before 1540, i.e. before the technological advances described by Nef could have exercised any effect on costs. Even after 1540 it is doubtful whether technical progress in most spheres of industry greatly exceeded that in agriculture. The growing shortage of fuel, which Nef singles out as supplying the mainspring of industrial advance in the period 1540–1640, did not, in fact, become a major problem, to judge by timber prices, before the early decades of the seventeenth century. To say all this, however, is not to deny that, even with static techniques, there were probably factors on the supply side which tended towards a relative cheapening of industrial products. The greater elasticity of supply of industrial goods, as compared with agricultural commodities, meant that the output of the former could be increased more quickly and at smaller marginal cost. Industrial prices were probably influenced to a greater extent than agricultural prices by comparatively sticky labour costs. Evidence concerning industrial wage movements in the Tudor and

Fig. 3. Agricultural prices and wage-rates in southern England. 1450–99 = 100.

early Stuart periods is scanty, but available data suggest that the wages of industrial workers followed a broadly similar trend to the wages of agricultural labourers and building craftsmen. If this was so, then the alleged widening profit-margin, between industrial prices and labour costs, which Professor Earl Hamilton saw as the main causative factor in the development of early capitalism, disappears. As can be seen from Table 3 (p. 25), industrial prices and (agricultural) wage-rates moved very closely together during the late sixteenth century, and in the first half of the seventeenth century—when population may have temporarily stopped growing and the rate of technological advance may have increased—wages began to move ahead of prices. In so far as there was a 'profit inflation' in the Tudor and early Stuart periods, clearly, as Fig. 3 indicates, it must have been in agriculture and not in industry.[1]

4. Regional prices

So far, our discussion has been in terms of the secular movement of prices in the national economy as a whole. The market, however, was very imperfect, and while the long-term trend of agricultural prices was

[1] J. U. Nef, *The Rise of the British Coal Industry*, London, 1932; 'The Progress of Technology and the Growth of Large-Scale Industry in Great Britain, 1540–1640', EcHR, v, 1934, pp. 3–24; 'A Comparison of Industrial Growth in France and England, 1540–1640', EcHR, vII, 1937, pp. 155–85; E. J. Hamilton, *American Treasure and the Price Revolution in Spain*; D. C. Coleman, 'Industrial Growth and Industrial Revolutions', *Economica*, NS, xxIII, 1956, p. 14; D. Felix, 'Profit Inflation and Industrial Growth', *Quart. J. Econ.*, Lxx, 1956, pp. 441–6.

similar in all regions, there were significant differences in relative regional price-levels. Thorold Rogers, in discussing this subject (with reference to a later historical period), argued that regional price differences were the outcome of an unequal distribution of money throughout the country, the Thames valley area having a disproportionately large share of the nation's monetary resources, and therefore the highest prices. This, however, can be no more than a partial, and probably minor, explanation, for it fails to account for the divergence in relative regional price movements of different commodities. These can only be explained in terms of real economic differences.[1]

Production and distribution costs varied, not only from region to region, but from district to district within each region; and the demand for agricultural produce was by no means evenly distributed. On the supply side, labour was an important element in the costs of commercial agriculture, especially for the arable farmer.[2] Assuming that there were no significant differences in the productivity of labour as between regions, a comparison of agricultural wage-rates in different parts of the country may be expected to provide an indication of relative regional labour costs. Wage data for this period are, unfortunately, piecemeal, but there is sufficient evidence to suggest that London, the south-eastern and south-western parts of the country, were high wage-cost areas, that northern and central England were low wage-cost, and that the southern and eastern regions occupied an intermediate position. It is perhaps not without significance that the high wage-cost areas were also high-price areas for arable produce. The relatively high level of wages in the vicinity of London may be attributed to a growing demand for labour engendered by general economic expansion, while in south-western England the developing textile industry was effectively competing with agriculture for workers. To account for the low level of wages in the northern region it should be recalled that this, like parts of the west Midlands, was primarily a pastoral region, and that pasture farming requires less labour than arable production. Elsewhere in central England, where common-field farming was the rule, population growth unsupported by compensating industrial development was creating an unemployment problem of formidable proportions, and one would expect this to be reflected in a relatively low level of agricultural wages.

The costs of agricultural production, however, are affected more by climate and by the nature and fertility of land than by the price of labour. Where soil is rich and well-drained wheat is comparatively cheap to produce; on thin sandy soils rye is a better economic proposi-

---

[1] Rogers, *Agriculture and Prices*, v, p. 241.
[2] See further on this, pp. 81–3, *infra*.

tion. Barley does well on light, calcareous ground; while oats, being a hardy crop, will grow almost anywhere. Tudor and Stuart farmers were well aware of these differences. They were also aware that wet soils are better suited to pasture than arable, and that on coarse grassland cattle are preferable to sheep. Where market conditions were favourable this knowledge was reflected in the regional farming pattern. Thus, on the drier, lighter soils of eastern and southern England, barley and sheep predominated; further inland, the claylands grew much wheat, as well as wool; the wet uplands of northern and western England, on the other hand, specialized more on cattle breeding and forage crops. Types of farming, however, varied, not merely from region to region, but from locality to locality. Thus, in the early seventeenth century a sheep-corn husbandry was practised on the chalklands of Sussex, while on the heavier land of the Weald arable farming was subordinate to cattle grazing. Such examples could be multiplied.[1]

Had there been in Tudor and Stuart England a cheap and efficient means of transport, there seems little doubt that the pattern of farming everywhere would have conformed closely to the potentialities of the soil, given the relative level of prices. In some areas, as we have seen, it did, but in others, high costs of transport imposed severe limitations on the nature of agricultural production. Most roads were extremely difficult to negotiate with goods, and many were impassable in winter. The transport of heavy products, therefore, even over comparatively short distances, was normally by water, whenever possible. When, in 1631, the J.P.'s for Essex stated that the inhabitants of the hundred of Dengie "by reason of foulness of ways, have not vented their corn at any country markets, but have always sent it to the City of London by sea and there sold it," they were describing a situation which would have surprised nobody.[2]

The availability of water communications, inadequate though they may seem by present-day standards, was an immense advantage to the farmer in the disposal of his produce, and in spite of the ever-present dangers of famine, permitted a degree of economic specialization in some parts of the country which was impossible in areas less well-endowed with transport possibilities. While central England had perforce to produce its own grain, it was thought unnecessary in 1620 for the coal-mining and lead-mining districts of Nottinghamshire and Derbyshire to be self-supporting in this respect, since the port of Hull

[1] J. C. K. Cornwall, *The Agrarian History of Sussex, 1560–1640*, University of London M.A. thesis, 1953, p. 146. See further on this subject, *AHEW, IV*, chapter 1.
[2] SP 16, 182, 67.

and the river Trent had always been found capable of meeting any deficiency in local corn production. London, which is estimated to have increased threefold or fourfold in size during the course of the sixteenth century, and which by the year 1600 probably contained something like 300,000 people, was a monument to the efficacy of water transport; so too, on a smaller scale, were Bristol and the other major provincial ports. Indeed, there were few important urban areas in predominantly pastoral districts which were not within comparatively easy reach of river transport or coastal shipping.[1]

The significance of water-carriage can be more readily understood when the relative costs of the different methods of transportation are examined. In the late fifteenth and early sixteenth centuries, when the average price of barley was approximately 3s. per quarter, and the normal cost of transporting grain by land carriage was 1d. per ton mile (at 5 quarters to the ton), a journey of 180 miles by road would have meant a doubling of the price of this commodity. At 2d. per ton mile, a rate occasionally charged, a journey of 90 miles would have achieved the same effect. By comparison, the conveyance of a load of barley from Wroxham to Yarmouth by the river Bure, at a slightly earlier period, was undertaken at a freight charge of ¼d. per ton mile—i.e. at between one-quarter and one-eighth of the above-specified rates for land carriage. Wheat, being more than twice the price of barley, was cheaper to transport in relation to its value, and so could be carried longer distances. As a cash crop it had obvious advantages over barley in those parts of the Midlands poorly served by inland waterways. On the other hand, soil and climatic considerations apart, it is hardly surprising that East Anglia, with its excellent water communications, should have been a leading centre for the production of barley. Similarly, the comparatively cheap and perishable nature of dairy produce was reflected in the siting of the principal dairy farming districts along the eastern seaboard and near major groupings of population. In relation to the value of the product, timber was the most expensive agricultural commodity to transport, and since a formidable number of horses, oxen, carriages, and men were normally involved in the passage of any significant quantity overland, water carriage was essential if the destination were more than a few miles away. In an estimate made in the early seventeenth century of the cost of conveying a large consignment of sawn timber from Conisbrough Parks, in the West Riding, to London, we find 5s. per ton allowed for carriage overland to Doncaster, only five miles distant, as against 6s. per ton for the very much

[1] SP 14, 112, 12 (i); SP 14, 112, 91; SP 14, 113, 17: SP 14, 113, 22; SP 14, 142, 14 (vii, viii); SP 16, 175, 35 (i); G. N. Clark, *The Wealth of England, from 1496 to 1760,* Oxford, 1947, pp. 5, 43, 93.

longer journey, in miles, by sea from Hull to London.[1] Accessibility by water, in fact, gave the capital a comparative advantage over many other parts of the country in respect of the price of timber.

Of all agricultural products, wool was the cheapest to transport, by virtue of its high value in relation to weight, and, as in the case of livestock (which were generally driven on the hoof to fattening pastures or to market), wool destined for home use was normally conveyed overland. The wool dealer and his packhorse were a familiar part of the rural and industrial scenes. The corn badger paid much more dearly for transporting his produce in this way. In relation to value, and at the level of prices ruling in the late fifteenth century, wheat was twenty to thirty times more expensive to transport by land carriage than the equivalent weight of good-quality wool, and barley fifty to seventy times more expensive. It should therefore occasion no surprise to recall that the trade in fine wool was the first to be developed on an extensive scale; nor is it difficult to explain the attraction of wool growing (and, to some extent, cattle feeding) for large numbers of capitalistic farmers in the Midlands cut off by transport deficiencies from profitable extra-regional markets in grain.

Efforts to improve the country's transport system were concentrated primarily on the ports, harbours, and inland waterways, whose effective working was especially vital to the economical carriage of corn. A series of statutes was passed, especially in the reign of Henry VIII, with the object of facilitating the removal of obstructions from rivers and clearing them of silt. The first pound-locks in England were built on the canal at Exeter in about 1564; Dover pier was financed, and Trinity House chartered. Such improvements became essential with the growth of London and other urban areas, and particular attention was paid to the removal of obstacles from the Thames, where pound-locks were also constructed. In 1541, as in the fourteenth century, Henley appears to have been the furthest point to which the Thames was ordinarily navigable. But in the early seventeenth century it became possible for barges to navigate as far as Oxford and even beyond.[2]

Such developments as these were bound to have an effect on regional price levels. The growing influence of London demand on the Thames valley area is suggested by Table 4, which indicates the prices of wheat in selected markets in the various regions.[3]

---

[1] Rogers, *Agriculture and Prices*, IV, pp. 694–710; V, pp. 755–77; Worcester RO, 705, 24, 355 (89).

[2] Clark, *op. cit.*, pp. 45, 95–6; Rogers, *op. cit.*, V, pp. 757–60; T. S. Willan, *River Navigation in England, 1600–1750*, Manchester, 1936, *passim*.

[3] For the sources of these and other prices mentioned in the text, see the 'Note on Sources and Methods' in the Statistical Appendix, pp. 167–72.

Table 4. *Decennial average prices of wheat (s. per quarter)*

Market	1450–9	1640–9	Prices in 1640–9 as percentages of prices in 1450–9
London	6·88	49·91	725
Exeter	6·44	44·95	698
Winchester	5·24	38·75	740
Cambridge	4·70	36·76	783
Oxford	4·63	42·53	919
Canterbury	6·79	—	—
Durham	5·85	—	—
Windsor	—	47·04	—
Nottingham	—	46·59	—
Shrewsbury	—	43·84	—

The figures shown in the table make it quite clear that the market for wheat was very local in the mid-fifteenth century, and there seems no doubt that prices were greatly influenced by the availability of supplies grown in the immediately surrounding districts. At this time, much of the fertile Thames valley region was apparently little affected by metropolitan demand, since prices in the London area were very nearly 50 per cent higher than in Oxford, a town less than sixty miles distant. It seems probable that any deficiency in the balance of production and consumption in the vicinity of the capital was met mainly from the south-eastern sector of the country rather than from further inland. This view is supported, not only by the relatively high price of grain in Canterbury in the fifteenth century, but also by the heavy dependence of London on wheat imports from Kent later in the period. Among the other towns indicated in Table 4, relative price-levels were much as one would expect. In Exeter and Durham, both situated in regions relying mainly on spring-sown cereals and pastoral activities, wheat was dear; in Cambridge and Winchester it was cheap.

Two hundred years later the pattern of regional price differences was in many respects the same as in the mid-fifteenth century, but some significant changes had taken place in the intervening period. The most remarkable of these was a narrowing of regional price-differentials, this being a development which one would expect to occur as the market became wider and better organized. Prices in different regions often diverged widely in years of scarcity, but the general tendency was for them to converge more closely together. The latter was particularly the case with prices in London and the Thames valley area; by 1640–9, a margin of only 17 per cent separated Oxford prices from those in the capital. At Windsor the difference was 6 per cent. However, since the districts through which the upper reaches of the Thames flowed had developed greater pastoral interests in the early Tudor period it would probably be unwise to attribute a ninefold increase in the price of wheat since 1450–9 solely to the growing influence of the London food market. In eastern and southern England (as illustrated by the data relating to Cambridge and Winchester), the growth of London had apparently exercised a much less stimulating effect on prices, and it was in these two regions, and no longer in the Thames valley area, that the cheapest wheat was to be obtained in the mid-seventeenth century.

The scattered nature of the data makes it impossible to attempt a regional analysis of the prices of other grains in the same detail as for wheat; nevertheless, the general picture which emerges is clear enough. Owing to the limitations of the transport system, the prices of inferior cereals varied much more widely from locality to locality than the prices of wheat, since the markets for these cheaper grains were more narrowly restricted. The broad pattern of regional prices, however, was much the same for rye and barley as for wheat, with each grain tending to become more expensive as one moved north, west, and south-east from the low-cost producing areas of eastern and southern England. Barley was a speciality in the eastern districts, being much in demand by the maltsters and brewers of East Anglia and London, though the capital appears to have relied more upon Kentish sources for the supply of this commodity. The production of barley was the principal aim of the sheep-corn husbandry of Norfolk, and it was a major crop in all the main farming regions of Lincolnshire. In the early 1620's the average price of barley in Oxford, at 17s. 7d. per quarter, was 11 per cent higher than in Lincoln. By way of comparison, barley sold at Theydon Garnon, in Essex, was 29 per cent dearer. At Laughton, in the pastoral Weald of Sussex, where oats competed strongly with barley for spring-sown land, barley prices in the 1630's were about on a level with those in Oxford.[1]

The chief strength of the pastoral areas lay in their fodder crops, and both barley and rye prices were often higher in the northern and south-western parts of the country than in the London region. The production of oats was strongly favoured in northern districts, where soils were generally poor and where oatcake and porridge provided the major sustenance of the human population. Thus, the average price of

[1] F. J. Fisher, 'The Development of the London Food Market, 1540–1640', EcHR, v, 1935, pp. 47–51; Joan Thirsk, *English Peasant Farming: the Agrarian History of Lincolnshire From Tudor to Recent Times*, London, 1957, p. 103; BM Add. MS 33147.

oats at Worksop in the 1590's, at 9s. 3d. per quarter, was approximately 13 per cent less than that in Cambridge. In western England a greater emphasis was placed on the production of peas and beans than of oats, and this was reflected in a corresponding price advantage in respect of these commodities. The eastern and south-eastern districts, on the other hand, with their fens and marshes, had generally less need to grow crops for fodder purposes, since hay was in many places plentiful and cheap, though extremely costly to transport any distance. Thus we find that, throughout the Tudor and early Stuart periods, the price of hay at Cambridge was constantly some 40 per cent lower than that at Eton. In general, it was in the central and southern parts of England that hay, oats, and pulses commanded the highest prices. This fact should occasion little surprise, for it fits in well with our knowledge of the growing pressure on common grazing land in these areas and underlines their concentration upon the major bread and drink cereals.

Differences in the cost of feed, not unexpectedly, exercised a strong influence on the price of livestock and animal produce. Pigs, for example, were generally cheapest in woodland and dairy-farming districts, where they could be fed on acorns, beechmast, and the waste-products of dairying, and dearest in unwooded areas devoted largely to tillage. Again, all kinds of poultry, and especially geese, were exceedingly cheap in the north of England, where extensive commons often existed, while they were dearest in London, the south-east, and south. In these latter regions the prices of dairy produce, cattle, horses, and sheep were also generally higher than those elsewhere; but in the absence of comparative data relating to the quality of produce and the size, age, and condition of stock, any attempt at detailed regional price analysis would be unwise.

Local differences in the price of stock arose partly from differences in the value of their produce, and this was especially so in the case of sheep and wool. The quality of wool and weight of fleece varied enormously in different parts of the country, depending largely upon the nature of pasturage and climate. In the south and east Midlands, where the quality of wool was generally good and the fleece weight often considerable, sheep fetched high prices and wool growing was a major occupation of many capitalist farmers. In northern and south-western England, on the other hand, sheep were comparatively inexpensive, since they produced a fleece of coarse quality and inconsiderable weight. This fact doubtless helps to explain the greater emphasis on cattle rearing and dairy farming in these areas, once the market had become sufficiently well organized.[1]

[1] Bowden, *op. cit.*, pp. 25–37.

B. FLUCTUATIONS AND TRENDS IN THE AGRARIAN ECONOMY

1. *Introduction*

The upward movement of agricultural prices which has been described in the earlier part of this study did not proceed without interruption and prices varied widely from season to season, year to year, and decade to decade. These fluctuations had to be endured as one of the penalties of a backward economic system and of the narrowly confined physical world in which Europeans lived. Agricultural prices always tend to fluctuate more markedly than other prices because in the short run the supply of agricultural produce is mainly dependent upon variable weather conditions. But in respect of the weather, as well as in various other respects, modern economic systems are provided with a number of built-in stabilizing influences which have the effect of offsetting the worst consequences of scarcity and glut. The wide dispersal of primary producing countries over the globe ensures that climate and crop yields will be favourable in some parts of the world, if not in others, while the operation of an efficient marketing mechanism permits the storage and cheap distribution of stocks, for domestic and foreign consumption, as and when required.

These conditions, which tend towards the stabilization of prices, were largely absent in England and the rest of western Europe in the sixteenth and seventeenth centuries. The agricultural potentialities of the New World had yet to be developed, so there was little hope of outside relief in times of harvest failure. Meanwhile, extreme climatic conditions in the Old World tended to affect all countries in greater or lesser degree.[1] This is clearly brought out in Fig. 4, which compares wheat prices in England between the mid-fifteenth and mid-seventeenth centuries with the average of wheat prices in Germany, France, and the Netherlands during the same period. Bearing in mind the comparatively wide geographical area covered by the latter countries, the coincidence, both as regards short-term fluctuations and long-term trends, is striking. The broad similarity of climatic conditions throughout western Europe, together with limitations of the transportation system, largely explain why, even in famine years, the amount of grain imported into England was only a negligible proportion of domestic output and why exports were never very large. The year ending December 1638 was one of extreme food shortage. During this period London, which accounted for the bulk of the country's external

[1] See further on this, G. Utterström, 'Climatic Fluctuations and Population Problems in Early Modern History', *Scand. Econ. Hist. Rev.*, III, 1955, pp. 3–47.

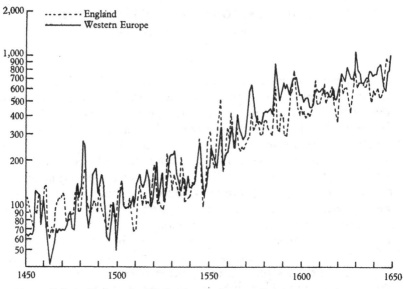

Fig. 4. Price of wheat in England and western Europe. 1450–99 = 100.

trade, imported from abroad a record quantity of 160,545 quarters of different types of grain.[1] If we allow an average crop yield of two quarters per acre, this quantity of produce could have been grown on 125 sq. miles, or about 1 per cent of the nation's arable area. Doubtless, the greater climatic differences of the Baltic countries, as compared with those of western Europe, partly explain why Danzig should have been looked upon as a principal source of supply in times of need.

Adequate storage facilities, which would have helped to mitigate the worst effects of harvest failure, were largely lacking. The corn trade was mainly in the hands of small dealers—an indication of the limited extent of the market. These lacked the necessary capital for the provision of warehousing, and in the face of government intervention when food was scarce must have been hard put to it at times to carry on their business. Larger merchants who dealt in grain did so mainly on an occasional and speculative basis, and were said to lack "the pollices to kepe Corne and wheate for the space of vj or vij yeres good if nede require."[2]

Among the growers of corn, small producers had little to spare for market, and many were forced by necessity to sell their surplus as soon

---

[1] PRO E 190, 41, 145. Information kindly supplied by Mrs A. M. Millard.

[2] Fisher, EcHR, v, 1935, p. 59; TED III, pp. 329–30; Gervase Markham, *Markham's Farewell to Husbandry*, London, 1638, pp. 110 *sqq.*; John Worlidge, *Systema Agriculturae*, 1675, pp. 52, 53.

as crops had been harvested, irrespective of the current market price. The larger farmers were generally in a better position, when prices were low, to wait for a favourable market. That some adopted this course is shown by the practice of Robert Loder, who in 1619, a year of bumper harvest, stored part of his wheat crop in a rick, selling it three years later at twice the original value. Self-interest thus helped to stabilize prices, but only to a limited extent. Not all large corn-growers followed Loder's example, and some, especially in inland areas, made a constant practice of selling their grain in small quantities every week or few days to local buyers. This could suggest an inability to store large quantities of grain for any appreciable length of time; but on the other hand, these small sales may have been forced on growers by the limited nature of the accessible market, or have been preferred because a higher unit price was obtainable than on larger transactions. Local and conciliar regulation also aimed at keeping markets regularly supplied in times of scarcity. Government proposals made in 1619 for the provision of public granaries received no support from J.P.'s in several corn-growing counties, on the ground of the expense involved in providing the necessary buildings. One suspects that this was not the real reason, but that the J.P.'s were looking to their own profit, as Loder had done. Subsequently, the public storage of grain figured prominently in the government's programme to combat the effects of a series of disastrous harvests.[1]

Storage facilities for the other main marketable commodity—wool— were better organized than for grain, since the wool trade was well developed and had long attracted men with substantial amounts of capital. Many large growers also stored wool when prices were low, in order to await a seller's market; but the small sheep farmers, like the arable husbandmen, were often in urgent need of cash and seldom lost much time in the disposal of their produce.[2]

2. Seasonal fluctuations

Even in a highly developed economy, some seasonal movement in the prices of agricultural commodities can be expected, since the supply of some types of produce varies considerably with the seasons, while other

[1] G. E. Fussell (ed.), *Robert Loder's Farm Accounts, 1610–1620*, Camden Soc., 3rd Ser., LIII, 1936, pp. 158–9, 161, 174, 177; BM Add. MS 34682; BM Add. MS 37419; Beds. RO, D.D.T.W. i, i; Herts. RO, 6604 and 6718; Kent AO, U 269, A 418, 5, ff. 11–16; SP 14, 112, 91; SP 14, 113, 26; SP 14, 113, 90; SP 14, 128, 65; SP 14, 144, 24; SP 14, 144, 32; SP 16, 117, 61; SP 16, 185, 6; SP 16, 186, 16; SP 16, 186, 62.

[2] Bowden, *op. cit.*, pp. 77–80, 86–7, 91–2; A. Simpson, *The Wealth of the Gentry, 1540–1660: East Anglian Studies*, Cambridge, 1961, pp. 188–93.

crops, such as corn, hay, and wool, are gathered only once a year. Adequate statistical material for an analysis of seasonal movements in the price of grain in the Tudor period is unfortunately lacking, but when the relevant data relating to the early Stuart period are analysed, an unfamiliar picture meets the eye. Normally, we should expect grain prices to be lowest in the months immediately following the harvest, since at this time supplies would be at their most plentiful. Subsequently, as stocks dwindled, we should expect prices to rise, reaching a peak in the late summer months before the next harvest, though the actual extent of the price rise would obviously be influenced in some degree by forecasts, which could be made with reasonable accuracy as early as April, about forthcoming crop yields. This seasonal pattern had clearly established itself by the late eighteenth century and may also have been normal in the earlier part of the period covered by our study. It does not, however, appear to have been the experience in the early Stuart period, as Table 5, relating to the price of wheat in Exeter, suggests.[1]

Table 5. *Price of wheat in Exeter (1626–40)*

(Average quarterly price as percentage of average annual price)

Oct.–Dec.	Jan.–March	April–June	July–Sept.
98·9	100·1	102·7	98·7

The most striking feature of this table is the fall in the price of wheat in the late summer months, when the presumption is that growing scarcity should have forced prices to rise. The only feasible explanation of this must be that growing scarcity was more than offset by declining demand. Either people ate less bread of any kind at this time of the year or they turned from the consumption of wheaten bread to the consumption of bread made from inferior cereals. Price data for other grains, had they been available, would have enabled the probability of these two hypotheses to have been tested. Irrespective of which is the more likely explanation, however, the evidence presented above points to a society where many experienced extreme poverty, living desperately from one meagre harvest to the next. Wheat prices fell in the late summer months because, by then, any capital accumulated from the sale of produce the previous year had largely disappeared, and starvation stared many starkly in the face. This viewpoint is supported

---

[1] T. S. Ashton, *Economic Fluctuations in England, 1700–1800*, Oxford, 1959, p. 11. Exeter wheat prices have been obtained from the Beveridge collection of price material at the Library of the London School of Economics.

by the fact that the steepest fall in prices in the late summer months occurred at the end of years of severe harvest failure, as was the case in 1630 and 1637, when August wheat prices in Exeter were only 77 per cent and 81 per cent respectively of those obtaining the previous June. The whole weight of evidence, in fact, of this and other sections of this study indicates that the third, fourth, and fifth decades of the seventeenth century witnessed extreme hardship in England, and were probably among the most terrible years through which the country has ever passed. It is probably no coincidence that the first real beginnings in the colonization of America date from this period.

If seasonal fluctuations in the level of consumer income and capital played an important part in determining the price of grain, the same was probably less true of livestock, since large farmers, whose receipts were usually spread throughout the year, figured more prominently as purchasers. However, many small men must have found it necessary to sell stock before the arrival of harvest time in order to raise capital for food and other necessary expenses, and this would obviously have tended to exert a depressing influence on prices. Figures relating to sales of livestock at Shrewsbury, as given in Table 6, appear to lend support to this supposition.[1]

Table 6. *Average prices of livestock at Shrewsbury, 1600–12 (s. each)*

	May	June	August	September
Horses	63·13	45·71	48·71	49·69
Mares	53·05	52·66	46·33	46·36
Oxen	74·50	74·75	70·51	64·76
Cows	49·14	45·46	44·78	44·20
Heifers	39·56	46·09	40·53	35·85

Probably the most decisive factor in the seasonal movement of stock prices, however, was the availability of feed. In the spring and early summer months the growth of natural pasture encouraged the purchase of stock, which could be fed cheaply on grass, but with the approach of autumn and winter it became increasingly necessary to rely upon hay and other fodder crops, which were not only expensive but sometimes almost impossible to obtain. Hay might double in price between one crop and the next, though a rise of about one-third was more usual. Unwanted stock, which could not be supported, were therefore usually sold off before winter set in. The difficulties which were

[1] Figures from the Beveridge collection of price material.

encountered even by large farmers in respect of feed are clearly brought out by two mid-sixteenth-century entries in the account books of the depopulated manor of Misterton, in Leicestershire, belonging to the Poulteney family, but at this time under the wardship of Sir William Paget. The first entry, relating to the sale of 66 lambs in July and August 1553, reads: "Recept for culling lambes not fatt this yere for wante grasse to the ewes and yet sold for haueing their dames depryving them," £3 11s. 8d.; and the second entry, in a list of cattle sales the following year: "Item, of Wallener the bocher for an other Runte despayring in the cold weder and sold partelye for lakke of haye," £1 7s. 8d.[1] Such sales as these naturally tended to affect the price of animal products. Cheap livestock in the autumn meant cheap meat. By the early spring the number of animals being sent to market had dwindled, and meat, especially beef, was at its dearest. Cows could be made to yield milk in winter, but only at a disproportionate cost and in comparatively small quantities. Dairy produce was therefore usually much dearer, sometimes by as much as 50 per cent, in winter and early spring than in summer. Thus at Wormleighton, in Warwickshire, in 1621-2, the price of butter in April was 5¼d. per lb.; in June it was 3¾d. Since a considerable part of the value of the sheep consisted of its fleece, the curve of sheep prices normally reached a peak just before shearing time—usually between the beginning and middle of June—and thereafter fell to a low point towards the end of the year. The price of wethers in May was commonly twice that in November. The movement of sheep-skin prices followed a broadly similar curve, since the value of the pelt depended primarily on the amount of wool covering the animal when it was slaughtered or otherwise died. Thus, an entry made in 1583 in the farming accounts of the Clopton family of Kentwell, in Suffolk, notes a price of 2s. 6d. for the fells of sheep killed between Shrovetide and shearing time, as against 7d. for those killed between clipping time and Michaelmas. Wool, itself, tended to increase in price with the coming of autumn and was generally at its most expensive in the late spring. Detailed information about the seasonal movement of wool prices is, unfortunately, not available, but this must have been considerable since many wealthy growers held back their clips from the market until late in the wool-growing year.[2]

[1] Beveridge, op. cit., pp. 21-2; W. G. Hoskins, Essays in Leicestershire History, Liverpool, 1950, pp. 88-9; William Salt Library, D 1734, 22, f. 4; D 1734, 38, f. 6.
[2] Rogers, Agriculture and Prices, IV, p. 308; V, pp. 337, 358-60; Bowden, op. cit., pp. 3-4, 13, 14, 87; Beveridge, op. cit., pp. 238-9; BM Harl. MS 127, f. 36; Val Cheke, The Story of Cheese-Making in Britain, London, 1959, p. 84.

3. Annual fluctuations

The prime cause of annual fluctuations in agricultural prices was the weather. In the short run, this largely determined the supply of agricultural produce. Moreover, changes arising from supply conditions affected the level and distribution of agricultural income, and in a predominantly agrarian economy this was bound to influence significantly the demand, not only for agricultural commodities, but for things in general.

The weather, however did not affect all branches of farming equally, since different crops and kinds of livestock react differently to climatic conditions. Moreover, as the climate must have varied somewhat from one locality to another, and as sowing and reaping times also differed, an unfavourable spell of weather would have affected some districts more adversely than others. However, the possibilities of bumper harvests in some areas coinciding with crop failures elsewhere were extremely remote.

In England drought is normally advantageous to the wheat harvest and, unless prolonged, is seldom a cause of failure among the other cereal crops. This, as Professor Ashton has pointed out, is due to the predominance of heavy, moisture-retaining clayland over lighter, sandy soils. The majority of serious crop failures in Tudor and early Stuart times do not appear to have been the result of excessive drought, but one of the most disastrous harvests to be experienced—that of 1637—was apparently due to this cause. The main danger to cereal farming was heavy and prolonged rainfall in summer, accompanied by an almost total absence of sunshine. Under such conditions crops failed to ripen, yields were poor, and prices rose to famine heights. An excessively cold winter and frosty spring were also harmful to the wheat harvest. The weather in winter scarcely affected barley, oats, and pulses, which were spring-sown cereals, but a cold spring could add to the difficulties of sowing, since the ground would be hard, while a late frost might do damage to the crops.[1]

The climatic conditions which ensured a bumper cereal harvest were, in general, less suitable for a plentiful crop of hay. This explains why grain prices and hay prices in Tudor and early Stuart England frequently diverged, with the noticeable exception of the decade which marked the Civil Wars. Since the growth of grass depended primarily on moisture and warmth, a plentiful supply of hay required a mild, wet spring followed by a spell of dry, sunny weather in the early summer months. Late frosts, low rainfall, or prolonged drought were generally

[1] Ashton, *Economic Fluctuations*, p. 15; Yorks. Arch. Soc. Lib., MS 311; SP 14, 123, 62; SP 14, 187, 20; SP 14, 187, 90; SP 16, 90, 35; SP 16, 167, 28; SP 16, 168, 126.

harmful, tending to reduce the supply of good-quality hay and leading to a rise in price.

While farmers in the sixteenth and seventeenth centuries were by no means entirely dependent upon hay for the winter keep of their livestock, since peas, beans, tares, straw, oats, and, occasionally, other grains were used for fodder purposes, hay played a much more vital rôle in the animal husbandry of these earlier centuries than it does today. In the period with which we are concerned, the large-scale use of roots, artificial grasses, oilcake, and the other aids of the modern breeder or grazier were still in the future. A failure of the hay crop meant that the ability of many farmers to carry their stock through the winter months was seriously impaired, and large numbers of animals were slaughtered or sold. This tended to create a short-run buyers' market in respect of livestock, meat, hides, and tallow, followed inevitably by a shortage of these commodities, as well as of dairy produce and young stock. This sequence of events was outlined by the Lord Mayor of London to the Privy Council in a letter dated 26 May 1630, wherein the causes of "the excessive prices of victuals" were set out. The Privy Council was informed that in 1629 "spring fell out so unseasonable that grass grew very short...so much smaller store of hay, straw, and stover for feeding cattle...the last winter...causing a great slaughter in the end of last summer and the winter following and discouraged the Butchers from making their provision of fat cattle and the country people here about London from storing themselves with Cowes as formerly they have done...Of late years have been brought to Cheapside market upon a Saturday 1700 or 1800 veals and this spring not above 200 or 300..." In 1629-30, in fact, the prices of both calves and dairy produce were higher than in any previous year. The state of the hay crop was of special concern to the cattle-farming industry, for other kinds of livestock were probably less dependent than cattle upon hay. Horses were fed mainly on oats, while the practice of feeding pulses to sheep appears to have become increasingly common throughout the period. Pigs and poultry grubbed around for much of their keep, and the acorns favoured by the former were at their most plentiful following the kind of hot summer weather so detrimental to hay.[1]

Apart from influencing the price of livestock and animal produce through the supply of feed, the climate had an important direct bearing on the mortality of stock. Extreme cold in winter, whereby animals may perish from lack of food or shelter, has always been a major hazard in the English livestock industry, and in the sixteenth and

---

[1] Rogers, *Agriculture and Prices*, IV, pp. 295–6; V, p. 305; Ashton, *Economic Fluctuations*, pp. 15–16; W. Salt Lib., D 1734, 22, ff. 4, 22, 24ᵛ; D 1734, 38, f. 6; SP 14, 113, 89; SP 16, 167, 28.

seventeenth centuries it was a problem which caused farmers much concern. High mortality among stock, however, was probably due less to the effects of cold than to outbreaks of animal diseases, such as the liver fluke in sheep and lung worm in cattle. Though runs of very dry summers were conducive to the spread of disease, the main danger was excessive rain, from which sheep, in particular, were liable to suffer. In such periods one would expect the initial tendency to be for livestock prices to fall, since the reaction of owners of infected animals would be to sell them as quickly as possible, while buyers would be wary. Subsequently shortages of stock and animal produce would tend to develop and prices to rise. The "great rottes and murryns, bothe of sheepe and bullockes" referred to by Hales in his *Defence* of 1549 suggests that this year experienced abnormal climatic conditions: an impression which gains support from a consideration of the relevant price data relating to stock and corn. Similarly "sore winters" and "immoderate rains" were partly responsible for "great decay and dearth of cattle and sheep" in the early and late 1620's. The loss of stock at such times was often considerable. In 1627–8 disease eliminated one third of the flock of twelve or thirteen hundred sheep kept by Sir Ralph Delaval at Seaton Delaval in Northumberland; while in the stormy weather of 1570 Sir Henry Lee of Quarrendon, in Buckinghamshire, was alleged—probably with great exaggeration—to have lost three thousand sheep besides other horned cattle.[1]

Apart from its effect on the *supply* of agricultural commodities, the climate also indirectly influenced *demand* since, in a peasant economy, purchasing power was largely determined by the size of the harvest. A crop failure, however, did not affect all classes equally, and it was followed by a shift in the distribution of income from other people to large arable farmers, whose propensity to consume was low. Since the demand for bread was inelastic (i.e. only a little less was consumed when the price increased substantially), large grain-growers who produced for the market could expect to enjoy increased receipts in times of general harvest failure. But for most agriculturalists, as well as for the industrial sections of society, a bad harvest meant high bread prices, with less to spend on other things, and a general decline in the standard of living. For the many small subsistence farmers, who normally sold a little surplus produce in the market in order to raise money for rent and other necessary expenses, a crop failure was disastrous. These now found themselves buying grain at famine prices, using up any small

---

[1] Bowden, *op. cit.*, pp. 15–16; W. Salt Lib., D 1734, 22, f. 4ᵛ; E. Lamond (ed.), *A Discourse of the Common Weal of this Realm of England*, Cambridge, 1929, pp. 149–50; SP 14, 131, 29; SP 16, 90, 35; SP 16, 167, 28; *Dictionary of National Biography*, ed. S. Lee, xxxii, London, 1892, p. 356.

reserves of capital and falling into arrears with their rent. Preparations for the coming year's harvest might also be threatened by inability to purchase seed-corn and other essential supplies. For the large and growing class of agricultural labourers a bad harvest meant not only a higher price of subsistence, but less opportunities for work and reductions in already pitifully small incomes. A crop flattened by heavy rain may not have required less labour than usual to reap it, but fewer workers would have been needed to move, stack, thresh, and winnow the grain. Moreover, these reductions in demand for labour may have been preceded by many months of unfavourable weather conditions in which opportunities for work in the fields were restricted. With meagre earnings and dear food, survival for agricultural wage-earners and other depressed sections of society could only have been accomplished by a lowering in the standard of diet and a reduction of expenditure on the minor luxuries, and even bare essentials, of working-class life. One would thus expect to find a contraction in demand for such goods as clothing and footwear, with consequent unemployment in these industries. The consumption of ale, beer, dairy produce, and meat would also be affected, though, in the case of meat, it appears that beef and, to a lesser extent, mutton were supplied mainly to a middle and upper-class market, while bacon and pork were more commonly eaten by the poor. These contractions in demand would in turn be transmitted back to the primary producers, and, above all, to the growers of wool. However, if the hay crop had been good, and if the farming enterprise were of a mixed character, as was often the case, any fall in receipts from the sale of livestock and animal produce might be carried without too great difficulty.[1]

The arguments outlined above can be developed further by reference to our price data. The movement of grain prices in the period under review is illustrated by Fig. 5. This graph has several interesting features, one of which is the wide fluctuation in prices from year to year, this being a consequence of the inelasticity in demand and supply conditions which distinguishes arable agriculture from most other economic activities. The short-term movements in the price of each of the main cereals—wheat, barley, oats, and rye—were broadly similar, since each grain was, in some degree, a substitute for the others, while any extremes of climate in spring or summer affected the yield of all. The degree of price fluctuation, however, varied from one grain to another, being greatest in respect of the inferior cereals. This tendency seems to have become more pronounced in the latter part of our period, when the standard of life of the mass of the people was at its lowest level.

[1] Ashton, *Economic Fluctuations*, pp. 42–4; W. Salt Lib., D 1734, 22, f. 24^v; D 1734, 38, f. 28^v.

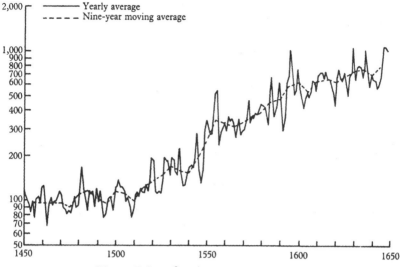

Fig. 5. Price of grains. 1450–99 = 100.

Thus, while wheat harvested in 1637 was only 16 per cent dearer than in the previous year, the prices of rye, barley, and oats were increased by 59 per cent, 50 per cent, and 22 per cent respectively. The climatic conditions of 1636–7 were probably less unfavourable to wheat than to the other cereals. In 1595–6 barley seems to have been the crop least adversely affected by the weather, since the price of barley, like the price of wheat, increased by only approximately one third. By comparison, oats doubled in price, while rye advanced by more than 50 per cent. At Worksop seed rye was more expensive than wheat. During the same period peas and beans, which, because of their comparative cheapness, were consumed in the form of bread by many people in years of famine, increased in price by 78 per cent and 68 per cent respectively. Barley was primarily a drink cereal, although it was also a principal breadcorn of the poor, and in times of great scarcity was used mainly for this purpose. In this connection it is instructive to note that the price of hops fell sharply in years of harvest failure. This suggests a contraction in the output of the brewing industry, due mainly, one supposes, to the income-effect of dearer bread on consumers, and the inability of brewers and maltsters to obtain supplies of scarce grain, rather than to the efforts of the government to curb the activities of the alehouses and their suppliers.[1]

[1] SP 14, 112, 91; SP 14, 132, 52; SP 14, 142, 14 (ii); SP 16, 177, 43; SP 16, 182, 40; SP 16, 186, 62; SP 16, 186, 98; G. E. Fussell, *The English Rural Labourer. His Home, Furniture, Clothing and Food from Tudor to Victorian Times*, London, 1949, pp. 31–3. For hop prices, see Beveridge, *op. cit.*, pp. 143–5 and 193–4.

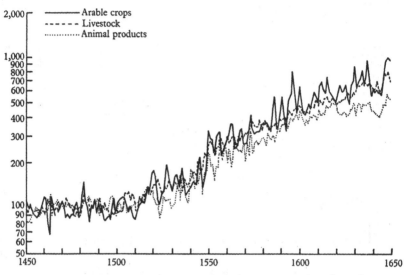

Fig. 6. Annual movements in the price of main agricultural products.
1450–99 = 100

The relationship between the price of arable crops (including hay)
and other agricultural commodities is illustrated in Fig. 6. It should be
borne in mind that our price data, especially those relating to livestock
and animal produce, have certain basic weaknesses (discussed in the
Statistical Appendix) which make it unwise to push year-to-year
comparisons very far. Nevertheless, the evidence presented in Fig. 6
does appear to lend support to the thesis outlined earlier, especially in
respect of the latter part of the period, for which data are more plentiful.

Compared with the wide fluctuations which characterized the short-
term movement in arable crop prices, those for livestock and animal
produce were much less volatile. Both tended to fall after a crop
failure and to rise after a good harvest, but this tendency was much
stronger in the case of produce than of stock. Probably part of the
explanation of the smaller degree of sensitivity of livestock prices to
harvest conditions is the fact that the poorer classes who suffered most
severely in times of scarcity were, in general, more important as
consumers of produce than as buyers of stock, though many cottagers
kept one or two hens, pigs, or a cow. Beef production and sheep
husbandry, on the other hand, were mainly the business of substantial
and well-to-do farmers for whom a contraction in demand for animal
products might mean smaller profits but not an immediate contraction
in the scale of enterprise. Moreover, owing to the heavy dependence of

arable farming on animal manure, livestock were often not easily dispensed with, and large cereal growers who made windfall gains from the failure of crops might decide to invest some of their profits in adding to their flocks and herds. The demand for livestock, as we have seen, was also greatly influenced by the state of the hay crop, and this was more likely to be good than bad when the harvest was poor.

Among livestock farmers the adverse effects of a harvest failure were felt with particular severity by the wool growers, since clothing was the principal consumer good on which income might be saved in times of food scarcity. The production of cloth was the main industrial activity in many parts of the country, and its export, together with that of raw wool in the earlier part of our period, accounted for between 75 and 90 per cent of England's total export trade. Any large contraction in demand was therefore likely to create unemployment for many hundreds of industrial workers and adversely affect the balance of payments position. A comparison of statistics relating to cloth exports, wool prices, and English and continental grain prices leaves little doubt that good harvests, at home and abroad, were fundamental to the industry's prosperity, leading to a buoyant demand for wool. Such harvests occurred towards the end of the 1540's, and gave a final great boost to a broadcloth industry already producing at its longer-term equilibrium level; they occurred again at the very beginning of the seventeenth century to inject some life into a trade by then almost stagnant. On the other hand, bad harvests in years such as the early 1550's, mid- 1580's, late 1590's, and early 1620's had the effect of contracting home and export demand for cloth, resulting in a substantial fall in the price of wool.[1]

In much the same manner, though not to the same extent, the prices of dairy produce and meat (e.g. rabbits) tended to rise after a good harvest and fall after a bad one. On the other hand, egg prices usually increased after a crop failure, this suggesting either that necessity had forced cottagers and other small poultry keepers to part with their birds, thus creating a shortage of eggs, or that there was a rising demand for eggs because these were found to be a cheap substitute for dear bread. Since the general tendency was for the prices of capons, hens, geese, and ducks to decline after a bad harvest, the supply of poultry was apparently more plentiful at such times, in relation to demand, than was the supply of eggs. Pigs generally seem to have maintained their price in years of crop failure, this suggesting, perhaps, that there was a switch on the part of some consumers from beef and mutton to the inferior meat, though there are insufficient data for testing the accuracy of this hypothesis.

[1] Bowden, *op. cit.*, pp. xv–xviii.

The general economic effect of changes in the size of the harvest can be further illustrated with specific reference to the years around 1550 and 1620, when comparative prosperity was changed within a short span of time to deep depression. The 1540's have long been thought of as a period of rising prices, for which the debasements of the coinage have been held mainly responsible. The point has generally been missed that, although wheat prices at the very end of the decade were more than double those in 1540, and other prices also much enhanced, the crops harvested in 1546, 1547, and 1548 were exceptionally bountiful and grain prices in those years were very low. This fact did not escape the attention of contemporaries, who were at a loss to explain the apparent paradox of "dearth of victuals" in the midst of abundance. The main blame was laid at the door of land-hungry sheep masters and beef farmers, though covetous engrossers and rack-renting landlords were also roundly condemned.[1]

It is possible that part of the price rise was due to the usurpation of common land for grazing sheep and oxen, since the presumption is that this would tend to result in a shortage of other stock; the high incidence of animal diseases, alleged by contemporaries in the late 1540's, could also have temporarily reduced the supply of livestock and victuals. We must also admit the possibility that the depreciations of the coinage helped to stimulate the price rise in its final stages. But when all this has been said, it still seems reasonable to suppose that the purchasing power engendered by the abundant harvests of 1546–8 not only acted as a stimulus to the economy during these years but also helped to carry it along on a crest of buoyant demand for a period afterwards. Moderately good harvests on the continent in 1549 and 1550, together with the need of foreign armies for clothing, served to sustain the demand for English cloth, and the economy remained active, in spite of a jump in the price of home-produced grain. By 1550, however, the prices of some commodities had already begun to fall, and cloth exports in this year were no higher than in the mid-1540's, in spite of the devaluation of sterling. In the following year a combination of exchange appreciation and poor crop yields led to a marked contraction of trade and a general collapse of prices.

Cloth exports from London, which had amounted to almost 132,800 pieces in 1550, fell to less than 112,800 pieces in 1551 and 85,000 in 1552. Wool prices, which had more than doubled between 1546 and 1550, fell sharply. At Misterton, in Leicestershire, wool sold for 12s. 6d. per stone in 1550–1 fetched only 6s. 8d. per stone a year later; while an entry made in the manorial accounts in 1552 recorded that "shepe

[1] Lamond, *op. cit.*, pp. lvix–lxv, 15, 17, 38, 48, 52–3, 104, 122, 149–51, 162–3, 167, 185–7; TED III, pp. 37–8, 40, 51–4, 57, 59, 61, 316, 319–21, 337–8.

fells kept from Februare bycase the price then was small" were sold in July for "lesse price." The wheat harvests of 1552 and 1553 appear to have been somewhat better than those in the two preceding years, but the prices of spring-sown cereals remained high, this suggesting not only less favourable yields as compared with wheat, but also a change in the pattern of consumer expenditure in favour of the inferior grains. The depression continued, and at Misterton receipts from the sale of wool averaged only £93 per annum in the three years 1552–4, as compared with £171 in 1550–1. The depth of the slump was reached in 1553, with livestock and animal produce prices well below the levels of 1550. Thereafter, recovery was uncertain and irregular.[1]

The depression of the early 1620's had much in common with that just described. As with the slump of the mid-sixteenth century, several excellent harvests were followed by a number of crop failures. This combination, of a run of exceptionally good harvests followed by a series of crop failures, by impoverishing first one section of the community and then other sections, appears to have provided the optimum conditions for the onset of trade depression. The harvests of 1618 and 1619 were very good, while that of 1620 was even better. A "marvellous yield," noted Loder in his account books in 1620, scarcely able to believe in crops which gave a return of 14·55 quarters of wheat and 8·43 quarters of barley for each quarter of seed sown—figures which represented increases of 36 per cent and 27 per cent respectively over the average yields obtained in the years 1612–17. To Loder, and other substantial arable farmers, the price, as against the yield, of grain gave less cause for rejoicing. For wheat sold in 1620 Loder received only 17s. 7¼d. per quarter, compared with an average price of 32s. 0½d. in the period 1612–17; for barley he received 14s. 4d. per quarter, as against an average price of about 22s. 5d. in the earlier years. While the low price of wheat was enabling many poor people to enjoy wheaten bread for possibly the first time in their lives, the J.P.'s of Norfolk were reporting to the Privy Council in November 1619, "that divers farmers, whose farms consisted upon tilth and corn, are utterly disabled and enforced to leave the same and the owners to leese their farms." From Lincolnshire, in March 1620, the J.P.'s argued that it was "better to endure with patience the present inconvenience" than to adopt the Privy Council's proposal for public granaries. The complaints of abundance continued, Sir Symonds Dewes noting in his diary in 1621 that as a result of the excessive cheapness of wheat the price of some

[1] L. Stone, 'State Control in Sixteenth-Century England', EcHR, XVII, 1947, pp. 106, 119; F. J. Fisher, 'Commercial Trends and Policy in Sixteenth-Century England', EcHR, X, 1940, pp. 96, 103–4; W. Salt Lib., D 1734, 4 and 5 Edward VI (not numbered); D 1734, 24, ff. 3, 4ᵛ; D 1734, 22, fo. 4ᵛ; D 1734, 38, fo. 5ᵛ.

lands had been reduced from twenty years' purchase to sixteen or seventeen.[1]

Meanwhile, a number of factors had combined to undermine the prosperity of the livestock industry. The hay crops of 1619 and 1620 were disappointing, while the difficulties experienced by mixed farmers with substantial arable interests also encouraged the disposal of stock on easy terms. Abroad, English cloth exporters were meeting with increased foreign competition and trade protection. Bad harvests in 1621 and 1622 underlined the cloth industry's weak position, which was reflected in a rising level of unemployment at home and a steep fall in the price of wool. In 1622—a year which saw a trebling of rye prices in parts of Germany—cloth exports from London amounted to 75,600 pieces: a decline of some 26,700 pieces on the 1618 figure. During the same period the price of Lincolnshire wool sold by Sir George Heneage of Hainton fell from 14s. to 10s. per stone.[2]

Reports received by the government from the northern counties between 1621 and 1623 spoke of great distress among livestock farmers occasioned by recent crop failures and by the "abatement of the wonted prices of cattle, sheep, and wool." Many small tenants, it was stated, had been unable to pay their rents, and had left "their farms untimely to their landlords"—a position reminiscent of that reported from the bishopric of Durham after the disastrous harvest failure of 1597. From Cambridgeshire, in May 1622, the J.P.'s informed the government that many small husbandmen had been forced to sell crops not yet harvested in order to provide for themselves in the meantime. The following year witnessed no perceptible improvement, and the terrible hardship which many endured was vividly described by Sir William Pelham of Brocklesby, Lincs., in a letter to his brother-in-law, Sir Edward Conway, in 1623. He wrote: "There are many thousands in these parts who have sold all they have even to their bed-straw, and cannot get work to earn any money. Dog's flesh is a dainty dish, and found upon search in many houses, also such horse flesh as hath lain long in a deke for hounds, and the other day one stole a sheep, who for mere hunger tore a leg out, and yet the great time of scarcity not yet come." During the course of the next thirty years suffering and extreme hunger were to become all too familiar.[3]

[1] *Robert Loder's Farm Accounts*, passim; T. Tooke, *A History of Prices and of the State of the Currency from 1793 to 1837*, London, I, 1838, pp. 23–4; SP 14, 111, 11; SP 14, 113, 26.

[2] Bowden, *op. cit.*, pp. 187–90; M. J. Elsas, 'Price Data from Münich, 1500–1700', *Econ. Hist.*, III, 1935, p. 65; F. J. Fisher, 'London's Export Trade in the Early Seventeenth Century', EcHR, 2nd Ser., III, 1950, p. 153; Lincs. AO, HEN. 3/2.

[3] CSPD 1621–23, p. 305; SP 14, 113, 21; SP 14, 130, 107; SP 14, 130, 9; SP 14, 131, 9; SP 14, 131, 25; SP 14, 131, 29; SP 14, 140, 10; SP 14, 144, 24 (xii); Joan Thirsk, 'Industries in the Countryside', *Essays in the Economic and Social History of*

Recurrent outbreaks of plague added to the distress caused by famine and trade depression. As Creighton noted many years ago, it is possible to search through the annals of Tudor and early Stuart times, and find scarcely a year when pestilence was not reported from one or another part of the country. The striking coincidence of serious plague outbreaks with harvest failures, however, leaves no doubt that these two events were closely related. Whether this was because the rat hosts of the fleas (*Xenopsylla cheopis*) which carried the plague migrated to towns and granaries in search of food in times of crop failure and were imported with shipments of foreign grain, or whether it was because these fleas multiplied most rapidly in climatic conditions conducive to bad harvests, need not concern us here. Whatever the explanation, the mortality rate in plague years was often extremely high. In London, where many of the severest outbreaks occurred, a record number of 41,313 people were registered in the mortality bills as having died of the plague in 1625. Total recorded mortality in London for this year amounted to 63,001 persons, so if we allow for a population of some 400,000, the death rate in the capital in 1625 approximated to 150 per 1,000 inhabitants. In 1563, another year of severe plague epidemic, the death-rate in London was possibly 100 per 1,000. Outbreaks of this order not only adversely affected the economy by sweeping away large numbers of consumers and producers, but also led directly to stoppages of trade. Few buyers visited markets and risked infection when the plague was rampant, as at least one seller of oxen found after a fruitless visit to Smithfield market in the 1590's. The plague of 1625 stopped all organized trade in the city of London for a season, and subsequent outbreaks of the pestilence in some of the provincial towns, such as Plymouth, also brought commerce to a halt. From Essex, in September 1625, the Deputy Lieutenants informed the Privy Council: "Scarce any man has half an ordinary crop of corn, clothiers have no vent of their wares, graziers and marketmen have no sale on account of the infection in London, hopmasters cannot sell at Stourbridge fair or London, Michaelmas rents and an assessment of the subsidy are becoming due, and extraordinary taxes for the relief of the sick poor." It is not surprising that, at such times, attempts at arbitrary taxation should have met with opposition.[1]

Tudor and Stuart England, ed. F. J. Fisher, Cambridge, 1961, pp. 82–3; J. W. F. Hill, *Tudor and Stuart Lincoln*, Cambridge, 1956, p. 142.

[1] C. Creighton, *A History of Epidemics in Britain from* A.D. *664 to the Extinction of Plague*, Cambridge, 1891, pp. 202, 229 *sqq.*, 304, 470, 507–12; L. F. Hirst, *The Conquest of Plague. A Study of the Evolution of Epidemiology*, Oxford, 1953, pp. 213, 260 *sqq.*, 303 *sqq.*; E. Hobsbawm, 'The General Crisis of the European Economy in the Seventeenth Century', *Past and Present*, v, 1954, p. 35; PRO E 133, 1224, 37–8 Eliz. I; SP 16, 29, 46; SP 16, 6, 77.

4. Cycles and trends

Though agricultural prices, and especially grain prices, were subject to violent fluctuations from one year to another, some regularity in the longer-term movement of prices can be discerned (see Figs. 4–6). More than forty years ago Lord Beveridge commented on the periodicity which he had discovered in the movement of European wheat prices in the early modern period, stating that "this would establish climatic variations as one cause, not as the whole or perhaps even the main cause, of cyclical fluctuations of industry." Our own investigations lend support to this view. Whatever we may think of Jevons's sunspot theory, it does appear that good harvests and bad harvests tended to cluster together, and that at fairly regular intervals—e.g. 1551, 1562, 1573, 1586, 1597, 1608—exceptionally bad harvests occurred as a result of a deterioration in weather conditions. To some extent also, one bad harvest helped to generate others, hunger resulting in the consumption of corn intended for the next year's seed. Conversely, with good harvests.[1]

Moreover, apart from recurrent trade cyclical fluctuations, it is possible to denote alternate periods of ten or more years when the predominant tendency was for the price of grain to rise in relation to other agricultural prices or for other agricultural prices to rise in relation to the price of grain. These different phases or cycles are set out in Tables 7 and 8 and provide a key to the main trends in the agrarian economy during our period. The outstanding feature of those years when grain prices surged upwards, was relative economic stagnation or decline; whereas in the alternate periods when corn was cheap, the economy was buoyant and growth comparatively rapid.

Doubtless, part of the explanation of these different phases can be traced to deliberate shifts in the balance of agricultural production in favour of one or another branch of farming activity. When grain prices were relatively low consumers would have surplus purchasing power to spend on other things and these would tend to rise in price, while producers would be encouraged to move out of corn into the

[1] W. H. Beveridge, 'British Exports and the Barometer', *Econ. J.*, XXX, 1920, pp. 13–25, 209–13; 'Weather and Harvest Cycles', *Econ. J.*, XXXI, 1921, pp. 429–52; W. S. Jevons, *The Solar Period and the Price of Corn*, 1875; *The Periodicity of Commercial Crises and its Physical Explanation*, 1878; *Commercial Crises and Sun-spots*, 1879 —all reprinted in *Investigations in Currency and Finance*, 2nd edn., London, 1909. See also H. S. Jevons, *The Causes of Unemployment, The Sun's Heat and Trade Activity*, London, 1910; 'Trade Fluctuations and Solar Activity', *Contemporary Review*, August, 1909; H. L. Moore, *Economic Cycles: their Law and Cause*, New York, 1914; *Generating Economic Cycles*, New York, 1923; W. G. Hoskins, 'Harvest Fluctuations and English Economic History, 1480–1619', AHR, XII, 1964, pp. 31–3.

Table 7. Percentage change in average annual price and volume

Percentage change in average annual price — Harvest years

Commodity	1450-61/ 1462-86	1462-86/ 1487-1503	1487-1503/ 1504-18	1504-18/ 1519-36	1519-36/ 1537-48	1537-48/ 1549-73	1549-73/ 1574-84	1574-84/ 1585-1600	1585-1600/ 1601-20	1601-20/ 1621-49
Grain	-2	+6	+2	+49	+2	+104	+15	+49	+3	+26
Wool	+29	-11	+12	+9	+19	+45	+21	+14	+25	+9
Wethers	+27	-2	+23	+17	+27	+73	+23	+8	+21	+30
Lambs	+15	-8	+17	+41	+22	+55	+28	+20	+9	+17

Percentage change in average annual volume — Calendar years

	1450-62/ 1462-82	1510-19/ 1520-37	1520-37/ 1538-47	1536-47/ 1550-73	1550-73/ 1574-85	1574-85/ 1586-1600	1586-1600/ 1601-20	1601-20/ 1622-40
Total exports of wool and cloth[a]	+15	—	—	-8	+6	—	—	—
Exports of short-cloths from London[b]	—	-7	+20	—	—	+0.4[c]	+7[d]	-15[e]

a Based on figures given in M. Postan, 'The Trade of Medieval Europe', *The Cambridge Economic History of Europe*, ed. M. Postan and E. E. Rich, Cambridge, 1952, II, p. 193; L. Stone, 'State Control in Sixteenth-Century England', EcHR, XVII, 1947, p. 119.

b Based on figures given in F. J. Fisher, 'Commercial Trends and Policy in Sixteenth-century England', EcHR, x, 1940, p. 96; 'London's Export Trade in the Early Seventeenth Century', EcHR, 2nd Ser, III, 1950, p. 153. These figures exclude exports of raw wool and worsted fabrics and exports of woollen cloth from the provincial ports. In the period 1549-73 exports of raw wool almost completely dwindled away, while exports of worsted cloth were also of relatively small importance. Subsequently, especially after the beginning of the seventeenth century, there was a marked expansion in the export of worsted fabrics. Throughout the period the overwhelming bulk of cloth exports were shipped from London.

c Statistics of cloth exports in the famine years of 1595-7 are not available. Had they been included, the figure in the table would probably indicate a substantial decline.

d Owing to the probable decline in the preceding period (*vide* c above) and to the fact that statistics of shipments by alien merchants are not available for every year, this figure almost certainly underestimates the growth in cloth exports.

e This figure probably underestimates the decline in cloth shipments (*vide* d above).

production of these other, more profitable, commodities. Eventually this movement would lead to a shortage of grain and a rise in its relative price, as a result of which producers would again find it profitable to devote more attention to cereals. This argument, of course, assumes that farmers possessed the necessary flexibility to switch from one crop to another in response to relative price movements. Most large farmers had room for manœuvre, within limits. But there must also have been many producers who were greatly restricted in their activities by limitations of marketing, capital, or soil.

The main explanation of these price cycles, however, seems to lie less with the decisions of planned farming enterprise than with the impersonal intervention of the weather, which affected not only crops, but also, indirectly, population. Periods of predominantly good weather and predominantly bad weather appear to have alternated with considerable regularity. Moreover, one finds that records of contemporary complaints about severe weather conditions relate primarily to phases when grain prices were relatively high and when outbreaks of disease (with the notable exception of the London plague of 1603) were most severe. The main explanation would seem to be that in a good weather cycle the low price of subsistence and the reduced incidence of disease encouraged population to grow comparatively rapidly. In the ensuing phase of worsened climatic conditions population was found to have outgrown the means of subsistence. The Malthusian checks of famine and pestilence thus served to restrict further growth for a period, and in some cases, as with the 'Sweating Sickness' of 1551 (from which 50,000 people were estimated to have died in England), the dreadful famine of 1556, and the virulent plague of 1563, probably exacted such a toll that population took some years to recover.[1] The pressure on grain supplies would eventually be eased as a result of improved weather conditions, aided by a possible reduction of population, and a switch to grain on the part of some producers affected by a relative fall in the prices of other commodities.

Since the income-elasticity of demand for clothing was high, the sheep-farming industry was particularly sensitive to changes in harvest conditions, and its fortunes fluctuated inversely with the level of grain prices at home and abroad. A long run of good harvests meant a rising demand for clothing and the need for more wool. Under such conditions cloth exports increased, wool prices rose, and the sheep-farming industry expanded. It seems quite clear from Table 7 that the urge towards increased wool production was very strongly felt in the years 1462–86, when the average annual price of wool was almost one third

[1] Barbara Winchester, *Tudor Family Portrait*, London, 1955, p. 272; Creighton, *op. cit.*, pp. 304, 470, 477; Hoskins, AHR, XII, 1964, p. 36.

higher than in the previous period. On the evidence of prices alone it seems possible to pinpoint these years as marking the most destructive phase in the sheep enclosure-movement. But other evidence is not lacking. The author of the *Discourse of the Common Weal*, an acute Midland observer, stated that the great decay of husbandry was before the reign of King Henry VII (i.e. before 1485), while the impressive array of case-histories, investigated by Professor M. W. Beresford in his work on depopulated villages, lends irrefutable support to this view.[1]

The evidence of relatively high grain prices and relatively low wool prices during the next sixteen years or so, suggests that this spectacular phase in the development of the sheep-farming industry was succeeded by a period of contracting demand. In the early years of the sixteenth century, however, demand revived and wool growers enjoyed a further period of rising prosperity. In the years 1450–62, before the boom in sheep farming had commenced, annual exports of raw wool and cloth (allowing 4⅓ cloths to one sack of wool) had averaged 15,690 sacks of wool or its equivalent. By the decade 1511–20 this figure had risen to 30,440 sacks. Following two exceptionally good harvests on the continent, a peak export was reached in 1519–20 of 35,890 sacks: a level that was not to be attained again until the boom years of the 1540's. The rise in the price of wool which accompanied this growth in export demand (and also, it may be assumed, home demand) encouraged the resumption and expansion of demesne agriculture by monastic and lay landowners alike. The flocks of Norwich Cathedral Priory, which had averaged some 2,700 sheep in the 1470's, increased to a peak of more than 8,600 sheep in 1517 (a year of exceptionally high wool prices and the appointment of the first royal commission on depopulation) and thereafter declined. In 1520–1 Sir William Fermour of East Barsham, Norfolk, possessed some 17,000 sheep, distributed among twenty-five flocks; but, by this time, the boom was already receding, and a sharp contraction followed. While grain prices continued on an upward trend, wool prices in the years 1520–35 were, on average, 4 per cent lower than those in 1511–20. During the same period the volume of wool and cloth exports fell by 13 per cent to an annual average of 26,560 sacks, the growth of cloth exports being more than offset by a decline in the shipment of wool.[2]

By 1537 another cycle of good harvests had set in, providing the

[1] Lamond, *op. cit.*, p. lxiii; M. W. Beresford, *The Lost Villages of England*, London, 1954, pp. 142, 148; 'The Lost Villages of Medieval England', *Geog. J.*, cxvii, 1951, pp. 145–6.
[2] K. J. Allison, *The Wool Supply and the Worsted Cloth Industry in Norfolk in the Sixteenth and Seventeenth Centuries*, University of Leeds Ph.D. thesis, 1955, p. xli; Simpson, *op. cit.*, pp. 182–3.

necessary purchasing power and incentive for a resurgence of sheep-farming activities. Both date and motive are clearly stated by the Husbandman in the *Discourse:* "manie of vs saw, xij yere ago [i.e. 1537], that oure proffittes was but small by the plowes; and therfore divers of my neighboures that had, in times past, some two, some thre, some fowre plowes of their owne, have laid downe some of them (parte, and som of theym) all theire teames, and turned ether part or all theire arable grounde into pasture, and therby haue wexed verie Rich men." The year 1548 marked the last of a series of exceptional harvests and the appointment of the second royal commission on depopulation. Even before the crash of 1550–1 some producers had ceased to expand their sheep-farming activities, and with the sharp decline of cloth exports and wool prices in the early 1550's the business of raising sheep lost much of its former attraction.[1]

Exports of cloth and raw wool in the third quarter of the sixteenth century were at a distinctly lower level than in the boom years of the late 1540's. Assuming that there was a proportionate contraction in the home market for cloth, the total demand for English wool in the third quarter of the century was only between two thirds and three quarters of demand in the years immediately preceding 1550. Supply had now to adjust itself to a lower level of demand, and it was not until the late 1570's that wool prices showed any definite tendency to rise. Many large landowners who had been drawn into wool production during the earlier period of rising demand now decided to reduce the size of their flocks or to give up sheep farming altogether. In Northamptonshire the Fitzwilliams were leasing out whole manors in 1549, and by 1576, at the latest, even the home farm at Milton had ceased to support sheep. Subsequently a comparatively small number were kept on the family's newly acquired estate at Dogsthorpe, a hamlet of Peterborough. Similarly the Brudenells of Deene, Northants., began to abandon wool production after 1551, at first on their Leicestershire pastures and then elsewhere. In East Anglia Sir Nicholas Bacon, the rising lawyer, had six flocks totalling about four thousand sheep in 1556. By 1561 the foldcourses on which these sheep ran had all been leased, and the same practice was followed with subsequent acquisitions of land. Indications of a substantial fall in the size of the total sheep population during the third quarter of the sixteenth century are suggested, not only by the aforementioned facts, but also by a consideration of certain other price movements. We find, for example, that sheepskins, which are a by-product of wool production, doubled in price between 1550–9

[1] Lamond, *op. cit.*, p. 56; W. Salt Lib., D 1734, 2–4 Edward VI (not numbered); D 1734, 56; K. J. Allison, 'Flock Management in the Sixteenth and Seventeenth Centuries', EcHR, 2nd Ser., XI, 1958, p. 100.

and 1560–9, and continued to rise at a less rapid rate thereafter. If this suggests a reduced supply of pelts as compared with the earlier period, the tendency of pea and bean prices to fall in the decades before 1580 suggests a reduced demand for feed.[1]

The price of grain, which had almost doubled between 1540–9 and 1550–9, fell slightly in the subsequent decade, owing partly, it would seem, to fewer years of severe harvest failure, and partly to an expansion in the area devoted to corn production. The increase in the acreage under grain was achieved in several ways. More land was taken in from the unproductive waste; many acres of pasture were probably converted to tillage; more intensive rotations may have been used, giving more years of grain crops and fewer fallows; and arable land was reallocated with less emphasis on fodder crops such as peas and beans. We should also expect the relatively greater rise in the prices of inferior cereals to encourage grain growers to give more attention to these crops and less to wheat. Some of these tendencies were clearly at work in Leicestershire during this period. Comparing the distribution of arable land in the county in 1558 with that in the early years of the sixteenth century, Dr Hoskins found a substantial decline in the proportion of land devoted to pulses and wheat, and a marked increase in that given over to rye and oats.[2]

By the early 1570's the demand and supply of grain were tending towards equilibrium, and with the return of better harvests the economy again entered upon a phase of comparatively rapid growth. A partial recovery was made in cloth exports, but probably more important in providing an impetus to the revival of sheep farming in the Midlands and East Anglia was the growth in the production of the new draperies, these being worsted fabrics made wholly or in part from long-staple wool. The growing raw material requirements of this new manufacture was clearly the main reason why the Clopton family of Kentwell, in Suffolk, extended their sheep-farming interests in the 1570's and early 1580's, making periodic purchases of long-wool Northamptonshire and Norfolk sheep. References to dairy cattle and beef animals also figure prominently in this family's account books during much of the period, but such references cease after 1582. Another landowner to be attracted by the profits from wool at this time was Sir Thomas Tresham of Rushton, Northants., who turned sheep farmer in the 1570's and by January 1581 had a total flock of 3,600 head.[3]

This boom in the economy, however, was of comparatively short

[1] Finch, op. cit., pp. 114, 117, 122, 147; Northants. RO, F. (M) Misc. vol. 52.
[2] Hoskins, op. cit., p. 169.
[3] Bowden, op. cit., pp. 64–5, 130; BM Harl. MS 127, ff. 17–33; Finch, op. cit., pp. 73–5.

duration. A series of severe crop failures and plague epidemics in the last fifteen years of the sixteenth century depressed trade and cast an air of gloom over the country. Cloth exports stagnated, and while some sheep farmers maintained their flocks, others, like John Isham of Lamport, Northants., cut back their production of wool.[1]

Economic revival came at the turn of the century with the beginning of an exceptional cycle of good harvests, which continued until 1620. In England the long-term rise in the price of grain was halted, while in western Europe wheat prices in the period 1601–20 were, on average, 14 per cent lower than in the years 1585–1600. This stimulus generated a rate of economic growth which was probably as great, if not greater, than in any other comparable period of our study. As in the case of other periods of buoyant demand, growth was greatest in the wool-textile industry. There was a marked expansion in the output and export of woollen cloth, and a much more spectacular development in the production of worsted fabrics. Since the new draperies were well suited to the Spanish and Mediterranean markets, the ending of the Anglo-Spanish war in 1604 provided the worsted industry with an additional stimulus to growth. By 1620 the volume of worsted exports was possibly treble that at the beginning of the seventeenth century.[2]

This expansion of the wool-textile industry brought with it a rising demand for wool, and sheep farmers were not slow in responding. Contemporary complaints made in the early years of the seventeenth century about the conversion of arable land to pasture give emphasis to this point. Some large landowners who had abandoned direct farming for the market in former years of trade depression were now lured back by the expectation of high profits from the sale of wool. The Fitz-williams of Northamptonshire, for example, resumed their pastures in or before 1605, and their sheep-farming activities were no longer confined to Milton or Dogsthorpe but embraced surrounding manors which the family owned. Other landowners extended the scale of existing sheep-farming enterprises, adding to their flocks and utilizing additional pastures whenever possible. Among these was Sir Thomas Temple of Stowe, who had more than 6,600 sheep (excluding lambs) grazing on lands in Buckinghamshire, Warwickshire, and Leicester-shire in 1605. Temple's receipts from the sale of wool in this year exceeded £1,260, as compared with receipts which were never in excess of £800 in the 1590's.[3]

The events leading up to the economic collapse of the early 1620's have already been described. Coming after a period of unusual abun-

---

[1] Finch, *op. cit.*, pp. 19, 74; Simpson, *op. cit.*, p. 190; Northants. RO, F. (M) Misc. vol. 52.   [2] Fisher, EcHR, 2nd Ser., III, 1950, pp. 153, 155.
[3] Finch, *op. cit.*, pp. 115, 117, 128; Henry E. Huntington Library, ST. 48.

dance and prosperity, the contrast in conditions was striking. Bad harvests, plague outbreaks, poverty, and unemployment were among the dominant characteristics of this and the two subsequent decades. The woollen-cloth industry was as depressed in the 1640's as it had been twenty years earlier. Efforts to export cloth to western Europe, also struggling in the throes of economic malaise, were made even more difficult by a deterioration in the quality of English wool, which had been very gradually changing its character since the days of the early Tudors. An increasing proportion of longer and coarser wool was being produced. This wool was eminently suitable for use by the worsted industry, whose exports (mainly to southern Europe and the East) continued on an upward trend throughout the period, thus providing the most encouraging feature in an otherwise very gloomy picture. The demands of the worsted manufacturers for more raw material, however, failed to make the business of wool production as profitable as it had been in the early decades of the century—even in the Midlands, where the bulk of the country's long-staple wool was produced. The English wool-grower's position, already undermined by the chronic depression in the domestic cloth industry, was further aggravated by increased imports of the raw material from Ireland and Spain. The price of wool remained low; and many landowners let their sheep pastures or turned their attention to other forms of farming enterprise. In 1622, a year which saw the lowest wool prices for more than three decades, the Ishams of Lamport were leasing out grazing land, while still apparently retaining a direct interest in sheep. In 1623 and 1624 Sir Thomas Temple of Stowe disposed of his flocks and established a system of leaseholds on his pastures. A few years later the Fitzwilliams of Milton followed his example. In 1628 Sir George Heneage of Hainton, in Lincolnshire, sold the bulk of his sheep for £400 and let out some of his best grazing land. In November 1630 Lionel Cranfield, first earl of Middlesex, had more than 6,780 sheep and lambs, besides cattle, grazing on his recently acquired estates in the west Midlands. Within four years his flocks had been reduced by more than half and some of his pastures let out on lease. Even the Spencers of Althorp, the outstanding flock masters of the age, lost their appetite for sheep farming in the conditions of the second quarter of the seventeenth century. By 1639 the family flocks in Warwickshire and Northamptonshire had been reduced to about one third their former size of 10,000 sheep plus lambs, and in the next few years direct farming was abandoned altogether.[1]

[1] Bowden, op. cit., pp. 6–7, 25–7, 43–5, 214–17; Finch, op. cit., pp. 31, 46, 48, 130, 166; E. F. Gay, 'The Temples of Stowe and their Debts', Huntington Lib. Quart., II, 1938–9, p. 430; Lincs. AO, HEN. 3/2; Kent AO, U 269, A 421; U 269, A 423.

How far the pastures let out by landowners like Spencer in periods of reduced profitability continued to support sheep, and how far they were used for cattle grazing or tillage, cannot be determined. Doubtless much depended on the nature of the land, the accessibility of markets, and the covenants of leases. What does seem to emerge fairly clearly from our study, however, is that for many large Midland landowners, decisions about commercial agriculture and the scale of demesne farming hinged primarily upon the demand for wool. This appears to have been almost as true of the early seventeenth century as it does of the late fifteenth, in spite of a long-term tendency for sheep prices to rise in comparison with wool prices, this suggesting a growing appreciation of the sheep as a supplier of meat, dung, and pelt, as against wool.

It may be safely assumed that sheep's dung increased in value in periods of rising grain prices, and in areas where the lightness of the arable land necessitated heavy applications of manure, as in the sheep-corn regions of Norfolk and Wiltshire, sheep numbers might be maintained, and even increased, in spite of a contraction in the demand for wool. Thus, Sir Richard Southwell of Wood Rising, in Norfolk, possessed an average of approximately 16,850 sheep in 1561–2, as compared with 14,170 in 1544–5.[1]

It seems reasonable to suppose that the *per capita* consumption of mutton and lamb, like that of clothing, tended to decline in periods when poor harvests predominated. Since, however, mutton did not figure prominently in the diet of the lower classes, the income-effect of high bread prices was presumably smaller than in the case of cloth, and overall demand more inelastic. This being so, wool growers whose pastures were eminently suitable for the grazing of sheep, or who for other reasons decided to stay in the industry, had an incentive to concentrate more of their attention upon the production of meat—possibly lamb, but, more especially, prime mutton. The latter entailed an increase in the proportion of wether sheep in the flock, and one would expect this to be reflected in a tendency for the price of wethers to rise more than the prices of other types of sheep and that of wool. A greater emphasis on mutton production appears to have been the main reason why the number of wethers kept by Sir George Heneage, in Lincolnshire, increased, while the proportion of ewes among his sheep declined from 53 per cent in 1618–20 to 23 per cent in 1633–5.[2]

Whether sheep farmers were willing, or even able, to devote their attention to the production of mutton depended, among other things, on the scale of their enterprise and their accessibility to consumers, especially in the larger urban centres. In the Tudor and early Stuart

[1] Allison, *thesis*, pp. xlv–l.
[2] Fussell, *The English Rural Labourer*, pp. 26–9; Lincs. AO, HEN. 3/2.

periods the market for meat was probably never uppermost in the minds of the smallest farmers. The fattening and sale of stock required time, capital, and a knowledge of marketing techniques, and in all these small men were deficient. But even among large producers there is little evidence to support the view sometimes put forward that the mutton market was the primary reason for sheep-farming activities in early Tudor times. The complete absence of price data for beef before the mid-sixteenth century and for mutton before the early seventeenth, together with the fact that many large households and institutions purchased livestock for the kitchen, and not carcasses—a practice which Eton College, for example, continued until the seventeenth century— suggests that the market for meat was very poorly organized before Elizabeth's reign. In the 1540's and 1550's large Norfolk sheep farmers, like Sir Roger Townshend of East Rainham, Coke of Holkham, and Sir Henry Bedingfeld of Oxborough, were selling prime sheep, presumably for use as mutton, but many of their sales were of poor quality stock. At this time, and possibly for more than a century afterwards, the market for meat was supplied with many old, weak, and inferior animals, which were sold either because of a shortage of feed or to make way for stock of higher quality. In the years 1548–51 between one half and two thirds of the sheep pastured at Misterton, in Leicestershire, were ewes. Wethers, as well as oxen, were fattened, but the majority of these were eventually despatched, along with other provisions, to the Paget household at Drayton, in Middlesex. Receipts from the sale of sheep between 1550 and 1554 at no time approached receipts from the sale of wool, and many of the animals which were marketed were noted in the estate account books as being "refuse," "barren," "sick," or "giddy." In only one of these years (1553–4) was the sale made of a substantial number of fat wethers. A basically similar situation was to be found in many other parts of the country at an even later period. On estates in, for example, Lancashire and York-shire (in the 1570's), Buckinghamshire, and Warwickshire (in the 1600's), Lincolnshire, Worcestershire, and Gloucestershire (in the 1630's), a number of substantial and great flock masters, at least, were relying much more upon wool than upon mutton for their income. Similarly, although west country store beasts were coming into Kent as early as the 1530's, indications from later in the century suggest that, with the exception of prime beef produced for the household, many large arable farmers fattened their cattle only at the end of a useful working life.[1]

[1] Simpson, *op. cit.*, p. 192; Rogers, *Agriculture and Prices*, v, pp. 406–7; Allison, EcHR, 2nd Ser., XI, 1958, pp. 108–9; Bowden, *op. cit.*, pp. 4, 8–10; W. Salt Lib., D 1734/22, 24, 38, 56, 2–4 Edward VI (not numbered), 4–5 Edward VI (not numbered);

It is not until the latter half of the sixteenth century that evidence begins to accumulate of the growth of a market-orientated livestock fattening industry of any significance. The main impulse to this development came from the growth of the London food market, and it was in districts adjoining the capital—above all, in the Wealden and marshy coastal regions of the south-east—that specialization on fattening was most pronounced. Already, by the late 1550's, Sir William Petre of Ingatestone, Essex, was placing the emphasis of his demesne farming activities on stock-fattening, mainly of cattle but also other livestock, and was selling considerable numbers of animals to butchers from London and elsewhere. Before the end of the century metropolitan demand was making itself felt much further afield, encouraging an enterprising handful of market-conscious farmers to give more attention to the production of meat. In the summer of 1565, for example, sales made by the Northamptonshire Spencers included 706 fat wethers sold to the butchers of London. In the year ending October 1577 a total of 3,071 lambs and 2,765 sheep (including 1,800 wethers) were sold, partly to local butchers, but mainly, it would seem, to London men. The lambs were almost certainly home-bred, but it is clear from the family estate accounts that some of the sheep were purchased during the year in order to be fattened for the butcher. At a slightly later date Sir Thomas Tresham of Rushton was also selling substantial numbers of sheep: some at Northampton, others in London. In 1581 a Buckinghamshire dealer owed him £400 for fat sheep which had subsequently been resold at Smithfield. At the end of the sixteenth century Sir John Dormer of Rousham, who had extensive pastures in Oxfordshire and Buckinghamshire, was buying large numbers of sheep and cattle for grazing and ultimate despatch to markets in London and its vicinity. In the year 1600 he received at least £797 from the sale of sheep and £1,690 from the sale of cattle. Further expansion of the business brought in gross receipts of almost £8,750 from the sale of cattle, sheep, hides, and fells in the seven-month period 25 March—30 October 1616. Many hundreds of wethers were purchased by Dormer in Wiltshire and elsewhere, while oxen and bullocks were bought mainly at Coventry, Tamworth, Burton, and other places in the west and north Midlands. The pastoral regions of northern and western England were thus caught up in the growth of metropolitan demand, since it was in these districts that many of the livestock destined to satisfy the

Finch, op. cit., p. 18; W. F. Rea, 'The Rental and Accounts of Sir Richard Shireburn, 1571–77', Lancs. & Ches. Hist. Soc., CX, 1959, p. 50; Henry E. Huntington Library, ST. 48; E. F. Gay, op. cit., pp. 421–2; Kent AO, U 269, A 423; Lincs. AO, H 97, 22/1, 2; R. Trow-Smith, A History of British Livestock Husbandry to 1700, London, 1957, pp. 188–9.

appetites of Londoners were bred. The early seventeenth-century account-books of the Toke family, who occupied lands in the Kentish Weald and Romney Marsh, are full of references to "northern" and "country" steers and other beasts. In the years 1618 and 1619 Nicholas Toke estimated that, on average, sheep accounted for 58 per cent of the family's farming assets. A further 20 per cent was attributed to other livestock (mainly oxen and steers "a fattinge") and 11 per cent to wool. Hay, arable crops, and other produce accounted for the remaining 11 per cent. In subsequent valuations made by Toke in the years 1624-30 sheep accounted for an average of only 16 per cent of the gross value of stock and produce, while other livestock were credited with 34 per cent. There was a sharp increase in the relative importance of arable crops and other commodities, these now constituting approximately half the total assets of the enterprise. Considerable quantities of wheat and barley were being grown in the 1620's, but the main expansion was in the output of fodder crops, notably oats, beans, peas, and tares. The fattening of livestock remained a major part of the undertaking, but in the latter part of the decade Toke developed an interest in dairy farming, producing quantities of butter and cheese for sale, while pig-keeping and hop production also claimed more of his attention. These various changes in the farming pattern were doubtless partly due to the fact that at some time between 1619 and 1624 Toke gave up valuable marshland grazings at Cheynecourte, though whether voluntarily or not is uncertain. But it also seems reasonable to suppose that, in part, these changes represented adjustments in response to the pull of market forces, and, in particular, to the reduced profitability of sheep.[1]

Cattle grazing and dairying were not, of course, carried on only as a poor second choice to sheep farming. In some pastoral regions physical conditions were much more suitable for cattle than for sheep; and given accessibility to markets, farmers in such regions were probably little influenced by the ebb and flow in the demand for wool and mutton. In other, more marginal, areas the balance between different pastoral activities was doubtless largely determined, at least as far as market-conscious farmers were concerned, by the relative movements in the prices of the main animal products. We should, however, expect there to be a tendency for these prices to move together, since any large swings in consumer demand would be likely to affect all

[1] W. R. Emerson, *The Economic Development of the Estates of the Petre Family in Essex in the Sixteenth and Seventeenth Centuries*, University of Oxford D.Phil. thesis, 1951, pp. 330-1; Finch, *op. cit.*, pp. 42, 75; Lord Dormer's Papers, 1600-30 (in the possession of T. Cottrell-Dormer, Esq., of Rousham Hall, Oxfordshire); W. Salt Lib., D 1734, 110, 111, 123; Eleanor C. Lodge (ed.), *The Account Book of a Kentish Estate, 1616-1704*, Oxford, 1927, *passim;* BM Add. MSS 34162; 34163; 34166.

animal products in greater or lesser degree. A comparison of Table 7 and Table 8 lends support to this view. The inverse price relationship with grain, already noted in the case of wool, will be seen to apply also to dairy produce and beef. But since the income-elasticity of demand for wool was greater than for the other products, its price increased relatively more in periods when good harvests predominated and less in periods when crops were poor.

On turning more specifically to Table 8, a comparison of oxen and hide prices, on the one hand, with those of kine, calves, and dairy produce, on the other, lends weight to contemporary assertions that the early Tudor enclosure movement was partly motivated by a desire to keep more bullocks and oxen, as well as more sheep. Though the first great spate of depopulating enclosures in the period 1462–86 was apparently directed solely at the production of wool, the resurgence of pasture farming in the years 1504–18 and 1537–48 appears from the evidence of prices, as well as from the statements of contemporaries, to have embraced beef and draught animals as well as sheep. In both of these latter periods the price of oxen substantially increased, while the price of hides (a by-product of cattle farming) changed comparatively little. The relatively greater rise in the price of hides than of oxen in the years 1519–36, when harvests were poor, suggests that sheep farming may not have been the only pastoral industry to contract at this time. Similarly, in the depressed conditions of the second quarter of the seventeenth century, a decline in the numbers of oxen and bullocks can be noted in the account-books of more than one substantial grazier. At the same time, a growth in the import of Irish cattle added to the English stock-breeder's difficulties. The Petres of Ingatestone, who had let out some of their cattle-fattening pastures in 1551, abandoned demesne farming completely for a period after 1638, and they were not the only large graziers to do so. How far the production of hides was a mere by-product of cattle farming, incidental to the business of providing meat for the table or stamina for the plough, is a moot question. The manufacture of leather goods—footwear, gloves, belts, saddles, bellows, and the like—was a major industrial activity, second only to that of cloth; and although the industry was most highly localized in the London area, where it was based upon abundant supplies of hides resulting from the traffic in meat, there were also important centres in cattle rearing and grazing districts, such as south Yorkshire, the east and west Midlands, the Weald, and the Forest of Dean. Accounts relating to the provisioning of the army in 1513 attribute one third of the value of oxen purchased to their hides and tallow. On the other hand, the average price received for ox-hides sold by Eton College in the years 1566–1600 was one eighth of that

Table 8. Percentage change in average annual price

Commodity	Harvest years									
	1450–61/ 1462–86	1462–86/ 1487–1503	1487–1503/ 1504–18	1504–18/ 1519–36	1519–36/ 1537–48	1537–48/ 1549–73	1549–73/ 1574–84	1574–84/ 1585–1600	1585–1600/ 1601–20	1601–20/ 1621–49
Dairy produce	+11	+2	−10	+10	+23	+75	+9	+28	+14	+11
Beef	—	—	—	—	—	—	+7	+26	+22	+17
Hides	−8	+33	+12	+35	+3	+47	+22	+18	+14	+20
Calves	+19	−21	+57	+1	+12	+76	+41	+12	+19	+27
Dairy cattle	+24	−22	−2	+64	+13	+80	+42	+25	+17	+22
Oxen	−8	−8	+28	+25	+22	+59	+21	+20	+16	+16

paid for live oxen purchased for slaughter. It seems unlikely that the value of tallow could account completely for the difference between this and the 1513 figure, and the most likely explanation is that, by the end of the sixteenth century, beef-producing animals were being valued relatively more for their meat and relatively less for their hides than they had been at the beginning of the Tudor period, in spite of an expansion in the long-term demand for leather goods in the intervening years. Table 8 suggests that it was in the closing decades of the sixteenth century that this growing emphasis on meat made itself most strongly felt. From then onwards, the prices of oxen, beef, and hides did not widely diverge as they had done hitherto, but moved much more closely together. This development is significant. It suggests an improvement in the organization of the market, which doubtless owed much to the increasing activity of middlemen, common carriers and drovers, and to the establishment of direct contact with producers by some of the big retailers from the larger towns, especially London.[1]

The operation of similar tendencies is discernible in the movement of the prices of kine, calves, and dairy produce. Table 8 suggests that, whatever the reason for keeping cows in the early Tudor period, it had no strong connection with the market for milk, butter, and cheese. The relationship between the prices of dairy cattle and calves, on the other hand, was much closer, even if, at times, it was a negative relationship. The large rise in the price of calves in the period 1504–18 seems to have been clearly due to a decline in the number of dairy cattle in the face of increased competition for pasture from sheep and bullocks. In the subsequent years, 1519–36, the demand for kine greatly increased, and so presumably did the supply, since there was a sharp fall in the relative price of calves. The greatly increased demand for dairy cattle during these years is interesting. We must reject the hypothesis that this was mainly due to large farmers switching from other, temporarily less profitable, forms of livestock husbandry to the commercial production of milk, butter, and cheese. Not only were the necessary price incentives to do this lacking, but prevailing market conditions were generally unfavourable for the wholesale disposal of produce of this type. Some large farmers may indeed have kept more kine and reared calves, in place of sheep and oxen; but if so, it was

[1] H. B. Cotterill (ed.), *The Utopia of Sir Thomas More*, 1937, p. 30; Lamond, *op. cit.*, pp. xlii, lxiii–lxv, 52–3, 149; Kent AO, U 269, A 421/1, 3, 4, 5; BM Add. MS 33147; Thirsk, *English Peasant Farming*, pp. 151, 192; *House of Commons Journals*, I, pp. 527, 615, 625; CSPD 1621–23, pp. 393, 498; E. Lipson, *The Economic History of England*, III, London, 1947, pp. 198–200; Emerson, *thesis*, pp. 328–9; L. A. Clarkson, 'The Organisation of the English Leather Industry in the late Sixteenth and Seventeenth Centuries', EcHR, 2nd Ser., XIII, 1960, p. 245; LP I, 1118; F. J. Fisher, EcHR, V, 1935, pp. 46–64.

undoubtedly the market for stock, and not dairy produce, which attracted them. There were also large institutions, such as Syon Abbey in Middlesex, Tavistock Abbey in Devon, and Sibton Abbey in Suffolk, which possessed considerable numbers of cows, but these were kept mainly, if not entirely, for the provisioning of the household. It was, however, among small farmers and cottagers that the main market for dairy cattle existed. It therefore seems probable that the fundamental reasons for the marked rise in the price of dairy cattle in the years 1519–36 were an increase in dairying activity in districts where small peasants predominated and a substantial growth in the number of poor farmers and near-landless cottagers, who produced milk, butter, and cheese from grazing on the common.[1]

It was not, it may be suggested, until towards the end of the sixteenth century that dairy farming ceased to be an almost exclusive province of the poorer sections of rural society, and began to be organized on wider commercial lines. With the improved marketing outlets which we have already noted in connection with the meat trade, substantial farmers in districts physically best suited to dairy farming but hitherto tied to the production of beef, mutton, or wool, now found it possible to turn their attention to the output of butter and cheese. In this, they may also have been influenced by the fact that dairy production brings in quicker returns than meat fattening: a not unimportant consideration in such uncertain years as the 1590's or 1630's. Nevertheless, the small man continued as a major support of the industry throughout the period.

C. EXPENDITURE AND INCOME

1. *Introduction*

The profitability of any farming enterprise depended not only upon the prices received for produce and stock, but also upon the costs of production and distribution incurred by the farmer. Our information about costs is, unfortunately, piecemeal, and for it we are dependent upon two main types of record: manorial accounts compiled by officials in the employ of large landowners; and the personally written farm accounts of substantial yeomen and gentry who played a direct part in commercial agriculture. Both types of record have drawbacks which seriously impair their usefulness for any assessment of profitability. Normally no clear distinction is drawn in contemporary accounts between capital and income; no allowance is made for the depreciation of capital assets; farming and non-farming expenditures are occasionally lumped together; little or no attempt is made to

[1] H. P. R. Finberg, *Tavistock Abbey*, Cambridge, 1951, pp. 135–44.

allocate overheads to different parts of the enterprise—indeed, overheads and other items of expenditure are often completely disregarded; while the value of home-consumed produce is also frequently omitted. Moreover, as Mr Batho points out elsewhere in this volume, manorial accounts were essentially statements of the receipts and expenses of the accountants (the bailiffs, sheep-reeves, and receivers) and not of the estate. They were primarily concerned with the liability of the collectors of revenue and not with the determination of profit. Bad debts were not written off, but were carried forward year after year, merely for the record.[1]

A much greater concern with the question of profit is revealed by the surviving account-books of early seventeenth-century yeomen and gentlemen farmers such as Nicholas Toke and Sir Roger Twysden of Kent, Robert Loder of Berkshire, John Hatcher of Lincolnshire, and Henry Best of the East Riding. These men, and others like them, took a direct interest in the running of their estates, noting down particulars of transactions, prices, costs, yields, and other matters relating to the business of farming. The accounts which they left to posterity tell us much; but unfortunately, these records suffer in varying degrees from the defects already mentioned, and are insufficiently detailed or comprehensive for profits to be accurately assessed. This did not prevent some farmers from making the attempt; but the science of accountancy was in its early stages, and the figures which were arrived at should be viewed with great caution. They are probably of more significance as indications of the businesslike approach of the compilers than as accurate statements of their affairs. Our knowledge of small farm units is even less complete, since the great mass of peasants were illiterate, and no accounts for small-holdings (were any compiled) appear to have survived. In spite of these various difficulties, however, it is still possible to comment usefully on the cost-structure of farming in the Tudor and early Stuart periods and to give some consideration to the question of profitability.[2]

2. Arable farming

Most farming enterprises in the sixteenth and seventeenth centuries were of a mixed character. Cereal growers needed livestock to maintain the fertility of their soil, while transport difficulties compelled many

[1] D. Oschinsky, 'Medieval Treatises on Estate Accounting', EcHR, xvii, 1947, pp. 52–7; Simpson, *op. cit.*, pp. 3–9; Kent AO, U 269, A 421; U 269, A 423; BM Add. MS 33147.

[2] Lodge, *op. cit*; BM Add. MSS 34162; 34163; 34166; *Robert Loder's Farm Accounts;* Lincs. AO, H 97, 22/2, 3; C. B. Robinson (ed.), *Rural Economy in Yorkshire in 1641, being the Farming and Account Books of Henry Best of Elmeswell in the East Riding of the County of York,* Surtees Soc., xxxiii, Durham, 1857.

pasture farmers to grow their own food and forage crops, apart from hay. For the purposes of this section of our study, however, we will endeavour to treat each of the main branches of agriculture separately.

Once we turn to a consideration of arable production it becomes apparent that the principal factor determining the farmer's livelihood was his crop yield. This in turn depended upon the efficiency of the farmer, the fertility of his land, and the influence of the climate, though not necessarily in that order. Crop yields varied greatly, not only from one farm to another but from one year to the next. On the demesne lands of the manor of Grantchester, which supplied King's College, Cambridge, with produce in the mid-fifteenth century, the yield of wheat in the years 1455–66 varied between 9·0 and 17·7 bushels per acre, averaging 13·6 bushels over the whole period. On newly enclosed lands at East Peckham in the Weald of Kent the yield in several years between 1639 and 1651 ranged from 11.7 to 14·6 bushels. A questionnaire survey conducted by the Royal Society in 1664–5 revealed even wider differences. On the lighter soils of Devon and Cornwall, for example, the average yield of wheat was stated to range between 10 and 25 bushels per acre according to the character of the season, while on marl land, which was better suited to the cultivation of oats than of other cereals, an average wheat yield of between 5 and 12 bushels was cited as normal. Variations in the size of the crop appear just as marked when measured in terms of the productivity of seed. At Grantchester, in the years already mentioned, the yield of wheat per bushel of seed sown varied between 2·56 and 5·22 bushels. On Robert Loder's farm at Harwell, Berks., in 1612–20, wheat yields ranged between five times and fifteen times, with an average return over the whole period of 10·2 bushels per bushel sown. Some years later, Sir Roger Twysden, who had estates at Great Chart and Romney Marsh, in Kent, was less fortunate. His notes on yields, covering the period 1639–56, suggest that in only one year (1654) did he obtain a return of seed which approximated to the average achieved by Loder in the second decade of the century: in most years his wheat crop showed only a threefold to sixfold increase on seed.[1]

Sufficient has been said for it to be apparent that the yield of wheat was extremely variable, and the same was also true of other grains. This great variability in yield, both from area to area and from year to

[1] J. Saltmarsh, 'A College Home-Farm in the Fifteenth Century', *Econ. Hist.* III, 1936, pp. 156, 165–8; Lord Beveridge, 'The Yield and Price of Corn in the Middle Ages', *Econ. Hist.*, I, 1927, p. 162; R. Lennard 'English Agriculture under Charles II: The Evidence of the Royal Society's "Enquiries"', *EcHR*, IV, 1932, pp. 39–41; *Robert Loder's Farm Accounts*, p. xvii; BM Add. MS 34162.

year, cautions us against placing any great reliance on fragmentary documentary evidence in appraising the average level and trend of crop yields in the country as a whole. M. K. Bennett, who was faced with this problem of unsatisfactory source-material, discarded the use of farm accounts altogether in estimating the yield of wheat in our period, basing his conclusions instead upon an analysis of Gregory King's statistical estimates of national income and output, published in 1695. As a result of his calculations, Bennett concluded that the average British wheat yield per acre increased by about 30 per cent between 1450 and 1650, rising from 8½ bushels to 11 bushels. A consideration of individual farm accounts and other relevant data tends to confirm an increase of the order suggested by Bennett, though his estimates of actual wheat yields, both in 1450 and 1650, may be slightly on the low side.[1]

In order to illustrate the importance of high crop yields to the arable farmer, and the nature of the expenditure incurred by him, we may construct a schedule of costs and output for a hypothetical farm of, say, 30 acres, which we will assume was in existence in the early years of the seventeenth century (see Table 9). For the purposes of our example, we will further assume that the farmer was of average efficiency, that the land which he occupied was moderately fertile, and that weather conditions during the harvest year in question were fair. Under such circumstances a crop yield of 12 bushels per acre for wheat and 16 bushels per acre for barley would have been reasonable. At the level of prices ruling in the early seventeenth century, we may estimate the total market value of the year's crop at £42 10s. od.

On the side of expenditure, we may note first of all that a holding of 30 acres was generally too small to require hired workers. No entry is therefore made for labour costs, our farmer and his family working the land without outside assistance. It will be apparent from Table 9 that a major item of expenditure for the cereal grower was the cost of seed. Even if, as was often the case, the farmer used seed saved from his previous crop, this was a cost to him, and must be entered on the debit side of his account. In respect of the amount of seed used, contemporary practice varied considerably, depending upon the farmer's resources and prejudices and the type of soil. Examples have been found of wheat seed being sown at the rate of 2 bushels to the acre, while occasionally, as at Heighton St Clair in Sussex in 1562, as much as 4 bushels per acre were used. Our figure of 2½ bushels probably represents the most common practice. Similarly with barley—a crop which, like oats, was normally sown more thickly than wheat—sowing rates varied between about 3½ and 8 bushels to the acre. The latter

[1] Bennett, op. cit., pp. 12–29.

Table 9. *Expenditure and output of hypothetical arable farm of 30 acres, c. 1600–20*

	Total cost £ s. d.	Cost per acre s.
Seed:		
25 bushels wheat @ 3s. 9d.	4 13 9 }	6·46
40 bushels barley @ 2s. 6d.	5 0 0 }	
Rent: 30 acres @ 4s. 0d.	6 0 0	4·00
Manure	1 2 6	0·75
Feed for oxen	2 12 0	1·73
Interest and capital depreciation:		
On stock	2 18 2	1·94
On equipment	19 4	0·64
Miscellaneous (e.g. veterinary, marketing)	10 0 0	0·33
Totals	23 15 9	15·86

	Total output £ s. d.	Output per acre s.
10 acres fallow	—	—
10 acres wheat: 120 bushels @ 3s. 9d.	22 10 0	15·00
10 acres barley: 160 bushels @ 2s. 6d.	20 0 0	13·33
Totals	42 10 0	28·33
Tithes	4 5 0	2·83
	38 5 0	25·50
Net Profit	14 9 3	9·64

figure was exceptional; and the rate we have adopted for our farmer, of 4 bushels per acre, was probably close to the norm.[1]

A second major item of expenditure incurred by the arable farmer—assuming payment of the full current market value—was rent. The subject of rent will be discussed in detail later on, but for our present purpose we will assume that land is paid for at the rate of 4s. per acre, this being approximately the commercial rent which moderately good common-field land commanded in the early years of the seventeenth century. We will further assume that the rent paid by our farmer includes interest on the landlord's investment in buildings and improvements, and that the repair and maintenance of fixed capital on the holding is the landlord's responsibility.

In our example, it will be noted that the combined expenditure on rent and seed accounts for approximately two thirds of the farmer's outgoings. This proportion is extremely high by modern standards, and reflects the very uneconomical use of seed and land in earlier times. Other expenditures, which nowadays figure much more prominently in arable-farming costs, were less heavy. The cost of manure to the small cultivator in early Stuart times is difficult to estimate since we know practically nothing about the quantity used or its price. Information relating to later in the seventeenth century suggests that, over a period of years, some farmers with enclosed arable land spread an annual average of about three loads of manure on every acre, apart from other dressings. At this rate, 90 loads of dung would be required for 30 acres. An early seventeenth-century pamphleteer cites a price for manure of 6d. per load, and on this basis the annual cost of dunging 30 acres of enclosed land would amount to £2 5s. 0d. Our farmer, however, occupies common-field land, which would be used during part of the year for grazing the livestock of the village. We will therefore assume that he obtains half of his manure free of charge, and purchases the remainder at a cost of £1 2s. 6d. No allowance is made for other dressings, such as lime and marl, since it seems unlikely that small cultivators in early Stuart times could afford to apply them in worthwhile quantities.[2]

Many peasants who occupied arable land also possessed sheep, from

---

[1] See sources listed in footnotes to pp. 71, 72 supra; Warws. RO, B 13, 998; Worcs. RO, 705, 24, 857; PRO E133, 1625, Eliz. I; Fitzherbert, *The Boke of Husbondrie*, ed. W. W. Skeat, 1882, pp. 23, 40; J. Blagrave, *The Epitomie of the Art of Husbandry*, London, 1669, pp. 22–7; E. Kerridge, 'The Notebook of a Wiltshire Farmer in the Early Seventeenth Century', *Wilts. Arch. &,Nat. Hist. Mag.*, LIV, 1951–2, pp. 417–19; Cornwall, *thesis*, pp. 116–17, 119.

[2] Lennard, EcHR, IV, 1932, pp. 32–4; Edward Maxey, *A New Instruction of Plowing and Setting the Corne, Handled in Manner of a Dialogue betweene a Ploughman and a Scholler*, London, 1601.

which an income was derived by means of the sale of wool, mutton, and pelts. In order to save unnecessary complication, the only livestock which we assume our farmer to possess are four oxen for draught purposes. This appears to have been the minimum number necessary for the plough team. Many farmers, of course, used horses for draught; but where physical conditions were suitable, small men often preferred to employ oxen, since they were less costly to feed in winter, were cheaper to equip, and depreciated less in value. In calculating the cost of feed for our four oxen, it has been assumed that free pasturage on common land, supplemented by straw threshed from the farmer's crop, sufficed to maintain his stock during the spring and summer months, while our estimate of the cost of keep during the remainder of the year has been based on data relating to the amounts paid for agistment—i.e. a practice whereby a man took in some one else's stock to feed in return for a money payment or a share in the progeny of the stock. The amounts charged for this service varied, depending upon the type of animal, the current price of hay, and whether the object was to fatten or merely to keep alive. For oxen, agistment charges in the early seventeenth century appear to have generally ranged between about 4d. and 9d. a week per beast, though occasionally as much as 2s. was charged. Our figure of £2 12s. 0d. for the cost of feed is based on a weekly expenditure of 6d. per beast for 26 weeks. In order to calculate the depreciation on stock, we have assumed that oxen were purchased at £3 10s. 0d. each, and after five years of toil were re-sold at £2 apiece. Thus, we put the total original outlay at £14 and loss of value over the five-year period at £6. By discounting capital at the statutory rate of 10 per cent, we therefore arrive at a figure of £2 18s. 2d. for interest and depreciation on stock. If we add this amount to the expenditure on feed, we find that the farmer's four oxen were costing him £5 10s. 2d. a year: a substantial sum for a husbandman's very limited resources. This cost was evidently too much for many small peasant cultivators, who of necessity had to share a plough team, for we find inventories that list "halfe the teame" among the dead man's possessions.[1]

The sum which we have entered in Table 9 for interest and depreciation on equipment will appear exceedingly small to the eyes of a present-day arable farmer, for whom the operation, repair, and replacement of machinery is a major item of expenditure. The agricultural appliances of Tudor and Stuart times, however, were few, simple, and

---

[1] Markham, *op. cit.*, pp. 146–7; J. Blagrave, *op. cit.*, pp. 9–10; Gloucs. RO, D 621, M 18; Lancs. RO, Derby MS 1553, 51; Kent AO, U 269, A 418/3, 5; BM Add. MS 34166, f. 43ᵛ; Kerridge, *op. cit.*, p. 427; Trow-Smith, *op. cit.*, pp. 239–40; Hoskins, *op. cit.*, p. 149.

cheap. In sixteenth-century Leicestershire Dr Hoskins found that the average farmer above the poorest possessed a plough, one or two carts, and two or three harrows, apart from such implements as spades, scythes, and rakes. Wagons and rollers were uncommon, even in the early seventeenth century. The farm gear of small cultivators was made mainly from wood, since equipment which used iron was very much more expensive. Many husbandmen probably fashioned some of their implements themselves, using timber to which they may have been entitled under the terms of their tenancy. In any case, the cost of construction by country carpenters and smiths was not high. The most expensive part of the arable farmer's equipment was the cart or wain, and the cost of this depended very largely upon whether the wheels were iron-shod or bare. In 1610, for example, King's College paid 15s. for a pair of new wheels, and 42s. 2d. for the tire of them. It seems very unlikely that small farmers would be able or willing to incur the latter expense. Other agricultural appliances were much cheaper. It was possible to buy a new plough for 1s. 8d. in Staffordshire in 1582, and for 3s. in Norfolk in 1621.[1] Altogether, it seems doubtful whether the small arable farmer's equipment in the early seventeenth century was worth more than about £3, and this is the figure which we have adopted for our calculations. We have further assumed that appliances were replaced every five years and have discounted capital at the same rate of interest as before. On the basis of these assumptions we find that only 4 per cent of our farmer's total expenditure was attributable to the cost of equipment. Clearly, this fact had considerable significance for the pattern of farming in our period; and the small capital outlay needed to equip the typical arable farm must have played an important part in deciding the majority of peasant cultivators to concentrate upon tillage or mixed farming rather than upon livestock husbandry, where total capital requirements were much greater.

Apart from the main items of cost already analysed, our hypothetical arable farmer was likely to be faced with some small expenses of an occasional nature. If his oxen fell sick he might find it necessary to purchase medicaments or have the cattle blooded. He might also incur some small marketing charges when purchasing supplies or disposing of produce. We have allocated an arbitrary sum of 10s. per year to cover these incidental outgoings. Since we have assumed our farmer to be paying a full market-value rent, we have made no estimate for the

[1] Hoskins, op. cit., pp. 149–50, 154; R. E. Prothero (Lord Ernle), English Farming Past and Present, London, 1912, pp. 91–2; C. M. L. Bouch and G. P. Jones, A Short Economic and Social History of the Lake Counties, 1500–1830, Manchester, 1961, p. 104; Rogers, Agriculture and Prices, v, p. 676; W. Salt Lib., D 1734, 118; Norwich Pub. Lib., Townshend Coll. 88, MS 1505, f. 15; BM Add. MS 33147, f. 17ᵛ.

payment of local rates and taxes. This was a burden which landlords sometimes passed on to tenants occupying under-rented holdings.[1]

In Table 9 the total value of the farmer's crop is estimated at £42 10s. 0d. After deduction of tithes, assuming that these were paid at the full rate, the profit remaining after all farming expenses have been met is £14 9s. 3d. Not unexpectedly, this sum compares favourably with the income of the agricultural wage-earner in the early years of the seventeenth century. At the prevailing ordinary wage-rate of 8d. per day, and excluding the payment of higher rates for special tasks, the maximum annual earnings of an agricultural labourer in southern England at this time could not have exceeded £10 8s. 0d. This figure makes no allowance for public holidays or unemployment, and if these factors are taken into account, it is doubtful whether the wage-earnings of even the fullest employed agricultural labourers were more than about £9 per annum. Ignoring possible subsidiary sources of livelihood open to both cottagers and peasant cultivators, this means that, in a normal year, the income of an arable farmer with a holding of 30 acres may have been some 60–70 per cent higher than that of a better-off agricultural wage-earner. This suggests that, in times of moderate plenty, a net farming profit of £14–£15 per annum made possible a tolerable, though by no means easy, existence. If we accept eighteenth-century estimates, the average size of a working-class family was six (mother, father, and four children), while the consumption of breadcorn per head totalled six bushels a year. Expenditure on farinaceous products seems to have amounted to about 50 per cent of total essential personal expenditure. On the basis of these figures, the family of a farmer with a small-holding of 30 acres in the early decades of the seventeenth century could have subsisted in years of moderate harvest on an annual income of about £11 5s. if wheaten and barley bread were consumed in equal proportions, and on somewhat less if only inferior bread were eaten. In such years, our small arable farmer would therefore have a margin of about £3–£5 to spend on raising the standard of life of his family above the bare minimum. This margin was small and could easily disappear in times of crop failure: a point which is illustrated by Table 10.[2]

Referring to this table, it will be seen that, even though we assume a substantial increase in the market value of the farmer's produce when his crop was poor (because of the inelasticity of demand for grain), the value of corn remaining for sale after all other commitments have

[1] Oxford RO, Garsington Estate Accounts, 1625–98, temp. no. 41, f. i; see also *infra*, pp. 100–1.

[2] Lipson, *op. cit.*, III, pp. 392–3, 501; Phelps Brown and Hopkins, *Economica*, NS XXVI, 1959, p. 29.

Table 10. *Effect of change in crop yield on income of small farmer*

Moderate crop

	£	s.	d.		£	s.	d.
Value of output:							
120 bushels wheat @ 3s. 9d.				22	10	0
160 bushels barley @ 2s. 6d.				20	0	0
Tithes	4	5	0			
Home consumption of grain:						
18 bushels wheat @ 3s. 9d.	3	7	6			
18 bushels barley @ 2s. 6d.	2	5	0			
Required for next year's crop:						
25 bushels wheat seed @ 3s. 9d.	4	13	9			
40 bushels barley seed @ 2s. 6d.	5	0	0			
Other farm expenses	14	2	0			
	33	13	3	42	10	0
Remaining				8	16	9

Poor crop

	£	s.	d.		£	s.	d.
Value of output:							
70 bushels wheat @ 7s. 6d.				26	5	0
100 bushels barley @ 5s. 0d.				25	0	0
Tithes	5	2	6			
Home consumption of grain:						
18 bushels wheat @ 7s. 6d.	6	15	0			
18 bushels barley @ 5s. 0d.	4	10	0			
Required for next year's crop:						
25 bushels wheat seed @ 7s. 6d.	9	7	6			
40 bushels barley seed @ 5s. 0d.	10	0	0			
Other farm expenses	14	2	0			
	49	17	0	51	5	0
Remaining				1	8	0

been met is insufficient to cover the full cost of the succeeding year's farm expenses and also provide an adequate income for the absolute minimum of personal expenditure (say, £5) on non-farinaceous products. In the event, unless capital had been put aside in other years, both the home and the farm were likely to suffer, and the payment of rent, in particular—since this was the least essential expense from the farmer's point of view—to fall into arrears. Several such bad harvests in succession could hardly fail to bring complete ruin to many small cultivators. This prospect diminished as farms became larger, until a point was reached, at probably somewhere between about 50 and 100 acres, when a general crop failure meant an increase in net income for the producer. With very large arable farms the gain would be considerable. The main reason for these differences in fortune was that the larger farmer, even if he were no more efficient than the small producer, had a proportionately greater marketable surplus. A smaller proportion of his output would be retained for domestic consumption, since the farmer with 300 acres could not easily consume ten times as much bread as the cultivator with 30 acres. Moreover, the assumption about equal efficiency is questionable, and although the large grower may have sown seed in the same quantities per acre as the subsistence farmer, there seems good reason to think that his yield per bushel of seed was in some cases much higher.

There is little information to guide us on the respective profit-margins per unit of output of the large and small arable enterprise. It appears likely, however, that the big farmer obtained a higher yield at a greater cost per unit of land. There was probably little difference between the large and small farm in the cost of seed per acre, since there is no evidence to invalidate our suggestion that sowing rates were roughly similar. On the other hand, the acreage rent (or value) of land occupied by the large producer was likely to be greater than for a small-holding, since it would more probably be enclosed or otherwise improved by the farmer or his landlord. In some cases, part, at least, of this enhanced value could be attributed to a comparatively large expenditure on manures and other dressings, though there is little evidence of such expenditure before the last quarter of the sixteenth century. In 1600 James Bankes of Winstanley, in Lancashire, advised his son to marl the lands which he would eventually inherit, informing him that "the charg of the marlying of an acare wyll stand you in fyfe markes [i.e. £3 6s. 8d.] so that therby you shall incres your Rentes in good sort." At Chute, in Wiltshire, during the reign of James I, Francis Golding, yeoman, claimed to have spent £100 about "the scyleinge, manuringe, marlinge and betteringe" the land of Escott farm, improving the annual value by £30. In Sussex, in the

1630's, Sir Thomas Pelham laid out considerable sums on denshiring and liming land. In 1634 he spent over £21 on such work: more than the value of many a farmer's stock. It was cheaper to apply raw chalk than lime, but even this was generally too expensive for the husbandman, since to be effective it required 20 or 30 tons to the acre. Some years ago Sir William Ashley suggested that the expense of marling land encouraged small cultivators to grow rye instead of wheat, but there is no real evidence in support of this view. In sixteenth-century Leicestershire Dr Hoskins found that, as a general rule, it was the large farmers, rather than the small, who grew some rye; and it seems reasonable to suppose that peasant cultivators, with a limited acreage and no labour costs but their own, would prefer whenever possible to grow the more highly valued wheat. In some districts, of course, this was out of the question owing to the unsuitability of physical conditions; but where the nature of the soil was such that wheat was an uncertain proposition, a compromise solution which was sometimes adopted was the sowing of a blend of wheat and rye, termed maslin.[1]

If the large farmer generally spent more on soil dressings and rent per acre than the husbandman, the reverse probably applied to outlays on stock and equipment. In regard to these costs the small farmer suffered from the economic problem of 'indivisibility'—i.e. he still required a full plough-team and an adequate range of appliances with which to cultivate his land, no matter how limited its acreage. Unless his team and implements were hired out to his neighbours or otherwise shared, they would often be under-utilized and would be relatively expensive in terms of output or land. Up to a certain point the size of farm could be increased with little or no additional expenditure on these items. In the chalk districts of Wiltshire, for example, Dr Kerridge found that a ploughteam of three or four horses was normally used to work an arable area of up to 60 acres. On his farm in Suffolk in 1630-1 Paul Dewes, Esq., had seven horses and geldings "with their furniture for plough and carte" (valued in all at £30), to cultivate a total arable area which probably amounted to between about 100 and 150 acres, since his autumn-sown land, alone, consisted of seven acres of wheat and 31 acres of rye (valued, in this period of scarcity, at £3 10s. and £2 per acre respectively, after deduction of rent).[2]

[1] Joyce Bankes (ed.), *The Memoranda Book of James Bankes, 1586–1617*, Inverness, 1935, p. 8; E. W. J. Kerridge, *The Agrarian Development of Wiltshire, 1540–1640*, University of London Ph.D. thesis, 1951, pp. 133, 181–2; Cornwall, *thesis*, pp. 117, 178, 212–13; BM Add. MS 33147; Ashley, *The Bread of Our Forefathers*, Oxford, 1928, pp. 137–42; Hoskins, *op. cit.*, p. 163; J. Blagrave, *op. cit.*, p. 24.
[2] Kerridge, *thesis*, pp. 165, 443–4, 551; BM Harl. MS 7657.

With fewer draught animals in relation to acreage than the small cultivator, the large arable farmer was also likely to have a proportionately lower feed bill, in spite of the fact that his horses and oxen were probably better fed; and though he may have invested in higher-quality stock and equipment than the husbandman, this was by no means a dis-economy, since the life of these assets would presumably be longer than in the case of the average small farm.

A major item in the costs of the large arable enterprise, which scarcely affected the typical unit of peasant agriculture, was the cost of hiring labour. The relative importance of labour costs varied with the size and efficiency of the undertaking, the level of wages, and the type of crops cultivated. In general, it appears that a single-plough farm could be managed by the occupier and his family with little need of wage-labour; but a two-plough farm of between, say, 60 and 120 acres, would probably provide fairly regular employment for one, two, or three labourers, plus additional workers at harvest time. On very large arable farms as many as twenty workers, including a bailiff and various specialists, might be employed. Some of these would be boarded farm servants, hired perhaps on a yearly basis at one of the local hiring fairs, and receiving a large part of their wages in kind—e.g. grain, pasturage for stock, and, occasionally, their employer's discarded clothes and boots! Other workers, many of whom had small plots of their own to cultivate, were engaged irregularly on a day or piece-rate basis. Wages were graded according to the character of the work; but in some instances relatively high rates, especially at harvest time, reflected the seasonal demand for labour, rather than any peculiar differences in skill.[1]

When we come to consider more closely the labour costs incurred by the large arable farmer, we are again faced with problems posed by the inadequate and unsystematic nature of contemporary accounts, and it once more becomes necessary to visualize the position as it might apply to a hypothetical producer. In order to facilitate comparison with our earlier example relating to the 30-acre farm, we will assume, first of all, that the acreage of land, the total of non-wage expenditure, the yield of crops, and the value of produce are as previously set out in Table 9. Given these assumptions, and basing our estimates of wage-expenditure on piecemeal data gleaned from various estate accounts, we conclude that the annual labour costs involved in the cultivation of an arable area of 30 acres in the early years of the seventeenth century were not markedly dissimilar to those indicated in Table 11.

[1] Kerridge, *thesis*, pp. 441–5, 561; W. Hasbach, *A History of the English Agricultural Labourer*, London, 1908, pp. 67, 83–4, 86; Cornwall, *thesis*, p. 390; Robinson, *op. cit.*, *passim*; Saltmarsh, *Econ. Hist.*, III, 1936, pp. 160–1.

Table 11. *Estimated annual labour costs on 30 acres of arable land, 1600–20*

	£	s.	d.
Ploughing 30 acres twice @ 2s. per acre	6	0	0
Harrowing and sowing 20 acres at 2s. per acre	2	0	0
Weeding 20 acres @ 4d. per acre		6	8
Reaping and binding 10 acres of wheat @ 3s. per acre	1	10	0
Mowing and raking 10 acres of barley @ 1s. 7d. per acre		15	10
Threshing 120 bushels of wheat @ 1s. 6d. per quarter	1	2	6
Threshing 160 bushels of barley @ 1s. 0d. per quarter	1	0	0
Miscellaneous (dunging, carting, etc.)		10	0
Total labour costs	13	5	0
Other costs	23	15	9
Total costs	37	0	9
Value of crop after deduction of tithes	38	5	0
Net profit	1	4	3

It will be noted that the most important single item of expenditure related to ploughing. Normally land (including fallow) was ploughed at least twice a year; and where soils were heavy, three and even four ploughings might be given. The cost of weeding was negligible, since many farmers appear to have attached little importance to the practice, and it was usually undertaken by female workers at about half the ordinary daily wage for men. At harvest time, when piece-rate incentives were often used, some workers were able to double their normal daily earnings, but the cost, in wages, of gathering the harvest was not especially high, amounting, in our example, to only 17 per cent of total labour costs. Wheat was a more expensive crop to gather than barley and it was also dearer to thresh. The cost per acre of harvesting oats was about the same as for barley, but owing to the higher yield normally obtainable, the cost per unit of output was often well below that for other grains. Threshing costs (at 8d. per quarter in the early seventeenth century) were also less. Thus, on the lands of Sir Charles Morison at Cassiobury in Hertfordshire, in 1609, the yield of oats—the major crop in terms of output—amounted to 29·4 bushels per acre, as against 16·6 bushels for barley and 12·8 bushels for wheat. The average cost of harvesting and threshing oats amounted to 1·09s. per quarter, as compared with 1·76s. for barley and 3·37s. for wheat. The task of threshing a large grain crop was a formidable one, and on a big estate might employ several workers well into the following year.[1]

It will be evident from Table 11 that wages constituted a major element in the cost-structure of the large arable farm: in our example they account for 36 per cent of total costs, and exceed expenditure on either seed or rent. It will also be evident that the income remaining to the farmer after all outgoings had been met would be quite inadequate to permit a reasonable standard of living, unless the enterprise were very large indeed. In other words, in the conditions of the early seventeenth century, the large farmer who paid a full market-value rent on moderately good arable land, could not make a livelihood from yields of 12 bushels per acre of wheat and 16 bushels per acre of barley. Either he had to grow other, more profitable, crops, if this were possible, or he had to increase productivity. The difference which higher productivity could make to the farmer's position may be illustrated if we assume that his crop yields per acre averaged 16 bushels of wheat and 20 bushels of barley. At the level of prices previously stipulated—viz., 30s. per quarter for wheat and 20s. for barley—the value of produce grown on 30 acres of land (10 being fallow) would amount to £55. If this were achieved with no addition to total costs, net profit would amount to £12 9s. 3d.: almost as much as the income of our small peasant cultivator employing no hired labour. The assumption about total costs remaining unchanged is, of course, unrealistic, since any significant rise in productivity would probably have been impossible without some additional outlay. This, however, need not have been large in relation to the returns achieved; and it seems probable that the big arable farmer in circumstances such as those described would have a good margin on which to operate, except in years when the price of grain was very low.

3. Pasture farming

The business of pasture farming in the Tudor and early Stuart periods is relatively better documented than that of tillage, partly because rearing and grazing were more likely to attract the attention of large landowners, and it is mainly in relation to the conduct of large estates that accounts have survived. In their existing form, however, contemporary accounts

[1] Norwich Pub. Lib., Townshend Coll. 88, MS 1505, ff. 1–5; Maxey, *op. cit.*, *passim;* Lennard, EcHR, IV, 1932, pp. 31–2; Essex RO, D, DP, A 18; A 22; F. Hull, *Agriculture and Rural Society in Essex, 1560–1640*, University of London, Ph.D. thesis, 1950, pp. 88, 498–500, 536–51; Lodge, *op. cit., passim;* W. Salt Lib., D 1734, 22 and 38; BM Add. MSS 28242; 33147; 34166; Kent AO, U 269, A 417; A 418; *Robert Loder's Farm Accounts, passim;* Herts. RO, 6604; 6718.

of sheep and cattle-farming enterprises give a very misleading impression of profitability, since certain costs are generally taken for granted or otherwise omitted, including the most vital costs of all—those of pasture and feed. To obtain an insight into the income and cost-structure of the pastoral undertaking, therefore, it again becomes necessary to construct a model based as closely as our information permits on the conditions of the period. In Table 12 we have set down the possible expenditures and receipts of a sheep farm consisting of 400 acres of good pasture and 100 acres of rich meadowland in the early years of the seventeenth century. A problem arises in connection with the form which our enterprise is to take, since sheep were kept for a number of reasons and for varying lengths of time. For example, many farmers concerned themselves primarily with the production of wool, breeding their own stock and selling animals which were mainly old, inferior, or diseased. On the other hand, farmers with good fattening pastures might do little or no breeding, buying in stock in order to sell again at a higher price later on. At Dogsthorpe, near Peterborough, where Fitzwilliam had a mixed pastoral enterprise, beasts were generally kept for only a short time before resale. Most of the sheep were bought between Lady Day and May Day and were sold before the following Michaelmas, having been clipped in the intervening period. The principal purchases were of couples of ewes and lambs bought in the spring and sold separately in the autumn.[1] In enterprises where the production of mutton was a major aim of sheep-farming activity, mainly wethers would probably be kept, perhaps for a few months, possibly for a year or longer, depending upon the age and condition of the stock and the movement of market prices.

The farm which is envisaged in Table 12 combines most of the elements mentioned above. Wethers are purchased in the spring at 12s. each, and after clipping and fattening are sold the following spring for 16s. 6d. Ewes cost 10s. each, and after three years of bearing lambs and providing wool are completely replaced, being sold at 8s. 6d. apiece. All lambs are marketed at an average price of 6s. without being sheared. Rams, which like other stud animals did not normally command very high prices at this time, are purchased at 15s. and sold three years later at 12s. 6d. All these prices are based upon the transactions of Toke's sheep-farming enterprise in the late 1610's. In order to save unnecessary complication, it is assumed that all farm output (apart from hay) is sold, and that interest charges on credit purchases and sales cancel out. A more difficult problem concerns the number of stock which our sheep farm of 500 acres could maintain. At the present day, stocking rates vary between about one ewe to every five acres on the mountains to

[1] Finch, *op. cit.*, p. 122; Northants. RO, F. (M) Misc. vol. 52.

Table 12. *Expenditure and output of hypothetical sheep farm of 500 acres, 1600–20*

	Expenditure £ s. d.	Cost per acre s.		Output £ s. d.	Income per acre s.
Rent:					
400 acres pasture @ 12s.	240 0 0 }	13·20	Wool: ewes and rams, 4133¼ lb. @ 1s.	206 13 6 }	17·27
100 acres meadow @ 18s.	90 0 0 }		wethers, 4500 lb @ 1s.	225 0 0 }	
Feed:					
For sheep	130 0 0 }	5·41	Lambs: 1029 @ 6s.	308 14 0	12·35
For oxen	5 4 0 }		Gross profit of 4s. 6d. each on sale	215 6 6	8·61
Interest and capital depreciation:			of 957 wethers		
On equipment	9 13 3 }	0·39			
On oxen	5 16 4 }				
On ewes and rams	96 7 4 }	7·26			
On wethers	79 7 0 }				
Materials: tar, pitch, ruddle, grease	5 7 3	0·21			
Marketing expenses: driving charges, tolls, grass	20 10 11	0·82			
Labour:					
Shepherds' wages	48 0 0				
Shearing time	7 10 0				
Haymaking @ 4s. per acre	20 0 0	3·42			
Miscellaneous	10 0 0				
Totals	767 16 1	30·71	Totals	955 14 0	38·23
			Tithes	74 0 9	2·96
				881 13 3	35·27
			Net profit	113 17 2	4·55

twelve sheep to the acre on the best fattening pastures on Romney Marsh. We have assumed that the grassland in our example is of high quality and that it is supplemented by a generous allowance of meadow-land and purchased winter feed. Under such circumstances a stocking rate of five to six sheep per acre of pasture may not be unrealistic, and gains some support from other evidence. We have therefore assumed that our sheep farm supports 1,000 wethers, 1,143 ewes, and 38 rams, the original outlay on sheep amounting to £1,200. The ratio of rams to ewes is 1:30, which accords with the advice given by Henry Best and the practice followed by some large sheep farmers during our period.[1]

The income of our farmer is assumed to be derived from the sale of wool, lambs, and fattened wethers. Any significant fall in the price of one of these commodities (especially wool) could substantially affect the level of profits and might even lead to a net loss. In order to calculate the value of wool sales it is necessary to make assumptions about fleece weights and wool prices. We have estimated the average weight of a wether's fleece at 4½ lb. and of other fleeces at 3½ lb. Such weights were not uncommon on good-quality enclosed pasture at this time, and in some Midland districts fleeces weighing 6–7 lb. were obtained. The price of wool is assumed to be 28s. per tod (i.e. 1s. per lb.), which was the price received by Sir Thomas Temple of Stowe for several wool clips marketed in the early years of the seventeenth century. In Table 12 the total value of wool sold by our farmer is given as £431 13s. 6d., this accounting for 45 per cent of the gross value of output.[2]

The income derived from the sale of lambs depended not only on their price but on the ewes' fertility. Nowadays, lambing rates in Britain seldom fall below 1·0 and sometimes rise to 2·0 lambs per ewe per annum. In Tudor and Stuart England lambing rates varied a great deal from flock to flock and from year to year, but seldom, if ever, reached an average of 1·0. On a large well-managed sheep farm, such as that owned by the Bacon family at Culford in west Suffolk at the beginning of the seventeenth century, a lambing rate of approximately 0·9 was normally achieved, and this is the figure which we have adopted in our calculations. Our 1,143 ewes are therefore assumed to produce an average of 1,029 lambs per year.[3]

The fact that only 957 wethers are recorded in Table 12 as being sold, out of the original total of 1,000 calls for explanation. This

[1] Lodge, *op. cit., passim;* R. Dexter and D. Barber, *Farming for Profits,* London, 1961, p. 44; PRO E 133, 657 East. 28 Eliz. I; Robinson, *op. cit.,* pp. 2, 4; Bowden, *op. cit.,* p. 21.
[2] Bowden, *op. cit.,* pp. 30–3; Henry E. Huntington Library, ST. 48.
[3] Bowden, *op. cit.,* p. 22; Simpson, *op. cit.,* pp. 185, 190–1.

adjustment has been made in order to allow for casualties among the
farmer's flock. The casualty rate among sheep could be very high in
years when rot was prevalent; and even in comparatively favourable
years common-field farmers may have suffered quite severe losses. In
normal years, however, and on large enclosed farms, losses seem to have
averaged between about 1 per cent and 3½ per cent each year. In our
example we have assumed a casualty rate of 2 per cent, which gives us a
figure of forty-three sheep lost by virtue of accident or disease. In
practice, of course, not all casualties would have been of wether sheep,
but it makes our example less involved if we make this assumption and
if we also assume that all losses occurred after shearing time. Dead
sheep, however, did not represent a complete loss to their owner,
since their fells and carcases were of some value and could be sold. We
have assumed that for every dead wether our farmer received 3s.,
thereby losing 9s. on sheep which originally cost 12s. This loss has been
taken into account by including a sum of £19 7s. od. on the expenditure side under the heading of interest and capital depreciation on
wethers. The total of this charge is given as £79 7s. od., the remaining
£60 representing one year's interest at 10 per cent on the original
price of £600 paid for 1,000 wethers.[1]

Turning more specifically to the expenses incurred by the large
sheep farmer, it will be at once apparent from Table 12 that the major
part of expenditure was associated with the provision of pasture and
other feed for stock. If we include haymaking costs, our farmer's
outlay on rent and fodder crops (whether purchased or grown at home)
accounts for almost exactly two thirds of total expenditure. Other costs,
apart from interest forgone and capital depreciation on sheep, were
very much less important. At the same time, the view, which owes
much to Sir Thomas More, that a sheep farm could be run by a shepherd
and his dog, oversimplifies the position, since draught animals, equipment, and additional labour were also required, if not continuously, at
least from time to time. Oxen and carts, together with their owners,
were sometimes hired at the busy haymaking season, but the possession
of transport facilities was also likely to be essential on other occasions.
We have therefore assumed that our farmer owned eight oxen, which
made him self-supporting in this respect. Our figures for interest and
capital depreciation on oxen, and the cost of their feed, are based on similar assumptions to those made in connection with Table 9. The value
of the sheep-farmer's appliances and other equipment is difficult to assess.

[1] *Supra*, p. 45; W. Salt Lib., D 1734/22, 24, 38, 56, 2–4 Edward VI (not numbered),
4–5 Edward VI (not numbered); Kent AO, U 269, A 418, 1; U 269, A 419, 1;
U 269, A 421, 1–5; U 269, A 423; Northants. RO, F. (M) Misc. vol. 52; BM Harl.
MS 127; BM Add. MS 39836; Bowden, *op. cit.*, pp. 15–17.

A large flockmaster would almost certainly possess a number of carts or wains, as well as the usual range of small agricultural implements. Additionally, he would need to invest in specialized equipment, such as hurdles and pens. We have assumed that the total cost of all these assets is £30, and that they are written off over five years. Their annual charge on the enterprise would thus be comparatively insignificant. The same may be said of purchased materials—tar, pitch, ruddle, and grease—used for marking and veterinary purposes. Our figure for the cost of such materials is based on the accounts of William Wickham's farm at Garsington, Oxon., for the period 1625–30, which enable us to calculate expenditure on materials as 1·26 per cent of receipts from the sale of wool.[1]

A somewhat more substantial charge on the sheep-farming enterprise was the expense involved in the marketing of stock. Toll payments and other costs were incurred, both at markets and fairs and on the roads to and from them. Drivers and other helpers had to be hired, and both they and their charges required overnight accommodation and food if on the roads for more than one day. In practice, the total expense involved in despatching or collecting sheep normally varied between about one half and two per cent of the value of the animals concerned, depending primarily upon the distance between the points of departure and destination. The figure in our table assumes an average marketing charge of one per cent on purchases and sales.[2]

A more constant and important element in the costs of sheep farming was that of labour. In common-field villages common shepherds were employed to tend sheep and guard them against thieves and wool pluckers. In large specialized undertakings shepherds were quite often the only permanent employees, though in very big enterprises a sheep-reeve was also usually appointed to exercise general supervision. The number of shepherds employed by large sheep farmers varied with the size of flocks and the nature and geographical distribution of pastures. Obviously it would not have been economically sensible to employ a shepherd to look after a few sheep, while there were limits to the size of the flock which one man could effectively manage alone. On well-stocked and compact pastures a good shepherd could probably handle up to 600 sheep quite competently, requiring assistance only on special occasions; but if the sheep farm were scattered and the terrain difficult, a larger permanent labour force would be required. In the case of the

[1] Kent AO, U 269, A 417; U 269, A 418, 5; Lincs. AO, H 97, 22, 2; Allison, thesis, pp. xxix–lxii; Simpson, op. cit., p. 186; Oxford RO, Garsington Estate Accounts 1625–98, temp. no. 41.

[2] Kent AO, U 269, A 417; U 269, A 418, 2; Lincs. AO, H 97, 22, 1; Lord Dormer's Papers, 1600–30; W. Salt Lib., D 1734, 22 etc.

sheep farm in our example, we will assume that four full-time shep-herds are employed, each receiving money wages and allowances to the value of £12 per annum.[1]

Apart from shepherds' wages, the substantial sheep farmer also incurred other labour charges. Additional workers were required for a variety of purposes during the year, but above all they were needed to gather in the hay crop and to assist at shearing time. On large under-takings the former task was often spread over several weeks and involved considerable expenditure. In 1631 it cost the earl of Middlesex £102 3s. 1d. in wages and other hiring charges to have the hay growing on his West Midland estates mown, transported, and stacked. Without it, the 6,000 or so sheep and other stock which he possessed at this time would have spent a very hungry winter. The expense of gathering the hay crop depended not only upon the local level of wage-rates, but also upon the yield of grass and the distance over which it had to be trans-ported. In 1629 it cost Sir Roger Twysden £2 7s. 0d. before hay, growing on 9 acres of land in Romney Marsh, was home and literally dry. Bearing in mind the probable abundance of the crop, this outlay by Twysden, which averages out at 5s. 2¾d. per acre, may not have been unduly high. However, we have based our estimate of hay-making charges on an average expenditure of 4s. per acre, which allows for the rather lower level of wages at the beginning of the cen-tury and is more in line with evidence from other sources. Even so, it will be noted that the labour costs of our farmer in connection with his hay crop were almost half the annual wages he paid to his shepherds.[2]

Less substantial than either of these charges were the costs incurred at shearing time. In this connection, the main expenditures on labour related to the washing and clipping of sheep and the winding of wool. Other payments were made to helpers who performed such tasks as rounding up sheep and gathering locks. The principal expense was that of shearing. In arriving at the figure given in Table 12, we have assumed that clippers were paid at the same rates as those employed by Sir Richard Townshend in 1626—viz., 3s. for every 100 ewes and rams sheared, and 3s. 4d. for every 100 wethers. This gives us a total of £3 8s. 9d. for shearing, while a further £1 14s. 5d. has been allowed for the driving and washing of sheep. The usual rate of payment for winding wool in the early Stuart period was 4d. per score of fleeces, which puts the cost of this operation at £1 16s. 4d. The remaining sum in our example is made up of 6d. for the gathering of locks and 10s.

[1] Bowden, op. cit., pp. 18–19; Allison, EcHR, 2nd Ser., XI, 1958, p. 110; Lodge, op. cit., pp. xxxvi–xxxvii.
[2] Kent AO, U 269, A 423; BM Add. MSS 34166, f. 42; 33147, ff. 7–7ᵛ; Norwich Pub. Lib., Townshend Coll. 88, MS 1505, f. 3.

to cover the cost of any food and drink which may have been provided by the farmer.[1]

The sum of £10 allowed in Table 12 for miscellaneous labour charges is quite arbitrary, but may not be too wide of the mark. On the large pasture farm there were a variety of tasks which required additional or specialized labour at different times of the year. Among the sheep-farming accounts of the period one finds references to payments for gelding lambs, greasing hoggs, and assisting at lambing time. At Misterton, in the severe winter of 1550–1, helpers were engaged to look for sheep in the snow, watch for foxes, and trap dogs which had been worrying stock. Some sheep farmers paid to have water-furrows ploughed in their pastures and manure spread in their meadows. Hedges and ditches needed to be kept in good repair, since animals could otherwise escape. The extent to which tenants assumed the burden of such repairs depended upon the terms of their tenancy. On most large pasture farms a vigorous battle was waged against moles and mole hills "for encreyce of grasse and meadow grounde to make the graysse fyner grayne." Many accounts record periodic payments for dead moles; and on the earl of Middlesex's estates in the 1630's a "mole taker" was a permanent member of the labour force.[2]

Turning to the overall position on our sheep farm, we find that total expenditure amounts to £767 16s. 1d., while the value of output after deduction of tithes is £881 13s. 3d. The net profit of the enterprise is thus £113 17s. 2d., which averages 4·55s. per acre, or 1·04s. per sheep. These figures are not, of course, absolutely reliable, since in order to arrive at them a certain amount of guesswork has been necessary, but they are much more realistic than the figures of alleged profitability put forward by Professor A. Simpson in connection with certain sheep-farming enterprises in Norfolk during our period. The "profits" of Professor Simpson's study are not, in fact, profits at all, but some form of gross return which contains within itself the rental value of land and interest on capital invested; no allowance is made in respect of depreciation and the maintenance of stock, nor for the value of feed. In fact, all the major elements of the sheep-farmer's expenditure are taken for granted. It follows that Professor Simpson's estimates of changes in the profitability of sheep farming in Norfolk during Tudor and early Stuart times are not very meaningful.[3]

[1] Bowden, op. cit., pp. 22–4; Allison, thesis, pp. 223–4; Kent AO, U 269, A 417; A 418, 5, ff. 50–1; Lincs. AO, H 97, 22, 1 and 2; Lodge, op. cit., p. xxxvi; BM Add. MS 39836.

[2] Allison, EcHR, 2nd Ser., XI, 1958, p. 110; W. Salt Lib., D 1734, 24; Essex RO, D, DP, A 18, A 22; Hull, thesis, pp. 87, 536–7; BM Add. MSS 33147; 34166; Lincs. AO, H 97, 22, 1 and 2; Kent AO, U 269, A 418, 5, f. 29ᵛ.

[3] Simpson, op. cit., pp. 186–96.

Our own figures clearly show why the specialist sheep farmer was unlikely to be a man with less than 50 acres of pasture at his disposal. Compared to tillage, the amount of labour required for sheep farming was small: in Table 12, wages constitute only 11 per cent of total expenditure, compared with our previous estimate of 36 per cent for a large arable undertaking. A small sheep venture was therefore unlikely to keep a peasant farmer fully occupied. More important was the fact that considerable outlay on stock, rent, and feed was required before an adequate income could be secured. In Table 9 we estimated the annual net profit of our small arable cultivator at £14 9s. 3d. or 9·64s. per acre of land. The comparable figure for our large sheep farmer is 4·55s. per acre. If, in the latter case, wage costs are completely excluded, on the assumption that the occupier provides all the labour himself, we obtain a net profit of 7·98s. per acre, or 1·83s. per sheep. On the basis of these figures, we may calculate that it would require 158 sheep (costing between £80 and £90) and 36 acres of good enclosed pasture to make the same net profit of £14 9s. 3d. achieved by our peasant cultivator with 30 acres of common-field land and a much smaller capital outlay. Clearly, requirements of this sort put specialization upon sheep farming out of reach of many small producers, and while most peasants with more than a few acres owned some sheep, it was probably only in districts where pasture land was unusually cheap or common grazing exceptionally abundant that the comparatively small specialized sheep enterprise was able to make any significant impression. Moreover, we need look no further for an explanation of why the small farmer in pastoral areas, as well as in mixed farming districts, strained every effort to increase his acreage under the plough. On the other hand, since the business of sheep farming could be carried on with a minimum of technical organization, it was well suited to the large landowner who desired to participate in commercialized agriculture but did not wish to become too directly involved with matters of detail.

Much of what has been said about sheep farming applies also to cattle grazing. Indeed, sheep and cattle were often combined in the same undertaking, if for no other reason than because of the broadly similar pattern of routine and the complementary feeding habits of the two kinds of stock. As with sheep farming, the main costs of beef production were those of pasture, feed, and interest on capital invested in livestock. Comparatively little was tied up in fixed assets. Marketing expenses may have been somewhat higher, on average, than for sheep, since longer journeys to market were often involved, but labour charges and casualties were probably less. The economics of buying, feeding, and selling cattle during our period are obscure, for few detailed cattle-farming records have survived. An entry in Toke's account book, dated 8 April 1620, notes the sale to a Londoner of seventeen northern oxen for £148 which had cost £83 at St Bartholomew's Fair the previous year, "soe for feedinge £65." This gives a gross return of nearly £4 a head. The net figures would have been very much less by the time all costs had been taken into account. The winter stall-feeding of an ox in order to bring it to prime condition was likely to have required a total ration of at least 40 cwt of hay spread over a period of twenty weeks. At the local level of hay prices in 1619–20, this item alone would have cost Toke between £1 10s. and £3 per beast. According to Lisle, who wrote at the beginning of the eighteenth century, steers would not beef until they were four or five years old, although a heifer would make "very pretty beef" at three. Other considerations apart, this fact alone is sufficient to explain why cattle grazing exercised little attraction for small farmers, who needed a more rapid turnover on capital in order to survive. Small men often engaged in cattle-breeding, but partly, if not mainly, as a complement to dairying, where quick returns could be obtained. Doubtless, the majority of husbandmen and cottagers followed the advice of a contemporary pamphleteer, and disposed of their calves before winter because of the high cost of feed.[1]

Of all the major branches of livestock husbandry, dairy farming was the one best calculated to suit the particular needs of the small producer. Dairying required much more labour than either sheep farming or beef production, not only because cows demanded regular milking, but also because the inadequacies of the transportation system meant that much milk had to be converted into butter and cheese before it could be sold. The sale of dairy produce brought the farmer a regular income, at least during part of the year, while the necessary utensils— the milking pails, sieves, butter churns, cheese tubs, and presses—cost little. Even in a large buttery the value of equipment in the latter part of our period was unlikely to exceed a few pounds. These considerations, though of major importance to the small farmer who possessed little besides his ability to work, carried less weight with the large producer. Moreover, dairy farming necessitated a routine and labour force which did not dovetail neatly into the organization of the specialist sheep venture or cattle-fattening enterprise, and this doubtless helps to explain why, in some instances, even substantial graziers and flockmasters, such as Hatcher of Careby, in Lincolnshire, produced insufficient quantities of butter and cheese to meet ordinary domestic requirements. This was not, of course, always the case. Sir William

[1] Thirsk, op. cit., pp. 175–6; Lord Dormer's Papers, 1600–30; Lodge, op. cit., p. 489; Lisle, Observations in Husbandry, 1757, II, pp. 5–6, 9; J. Blagrave, op. cit., pp. 85–9.

Fitzwilliam kept milch kine, as well as most other types of stock, at Dogsthorpe. Between Michaelmas 1585 and 1594 the values of milk, butter, and cheese produced there averaged £12 7s. 7d. per year, all of which was apparently consumed at home. In Berkshire Robert Loder also kept dairy cattle to supply produce for the needs of the household, rather than for sale. In 1618 his twelve milkers yielded a daily average of one gallon per cow during the 129 days between weaning and drying off. This suggests a whole lactation yield of the order of 200–220 gallons, achieved on downland pasture of not very high quality. At this time milk was priced at about 2½d. per gallon, and Loder believed his kine to be among his most profitable livestock assets, calculating the profit per cow at £1 16s. 8d. Experience of other contemporary accounts, however, leads us to question the reliability of this figure.

Information about the remaining branches of livestock husbandry is, if anything, less precise. It seems clear, however, that the breeding and rearing of horses required more capital than other kinds of stock farming, not only because of the larger initial outlay but also because of the comparatively high cost of feed and slow rate of capital turnover. Obviously these considerations would preclude the small man from concentrating attention upon the raising of horses. Better suited to the limited resources of the small producer was the keeping of pigs and poultry. The organization of pig production on a commercial basis, however, seems to have been limited largely to forest and dairy farming districts where feed was especially cheap. Elsewhere most pig-keepers appear to have aimed primarily at catering for domestic consumption or utilizing the waste of the farmstead. There is even less evidence of specialization upon poultry farming, except in East Anglia, though regular sales of eggs and occasional sales of birds probably enabled many small cultivators to eke out a bare existence. On most large farms pigs and poultry appear to have been of little significance, partly, it may be suspected, because of the attention which these stock required. To some extent this gap might be filled, in the case of landowners, by the receipt of produce rents in the form of hens, eggs, and the like. Even so, the household accounts of many large landed families indicate the expenditure of substantial sums on the purchase of 'white meats'. It is difficult to escape the conclusion that pig-keeping and poultry farming, like dairying, were mainly the concern of the small producer.[1]

[1] G. E. Fussell and Constance Goodman, 'The Eighteenth-century Traffic in Milk Products', Econ. Hist., III, 1937, p. 380; Val Cheke, op. cit., pp. 87, 90; G. D. Ramsay (ed.), John Isham, Mercer and Merchant Adventurer: Two Account Books of a London Merchant in the Reign of Elizabeth I, Northants. Rec. Soc., XXI, 1962, pp. 161, 162; Thirsk, op. cit., pp. 175–6; Northants. RO, F (M) Misc. vol. 52; Robert Loder's Farm Accounts, pp. 153–6; Trow-Smith, op. cit., pp. 185–6, 237–8, 250–5.

4. The landlord

The gross income of the landlord, who had no other source of livelihood but receipts from tenants, depended upon the size of his rent-roll.
Out of this sum he had to finance the expenses of estate management
and—where these burdens were not passed on to tenants—the costs
of the repair and renewal of fixed capital and other charges on land.
The economic changes of Tudor and early Stuart times affected the
landlord, both in his capacity as a *rentier* and as a consumer. Various
factors served to increase the demand for land, and with it the landlord's potential income. In an age of mansion-building, when the
possession of a landed estate was the principal indication of social
status, the non-pecuniary advantages of farming were becoming more
highly regarded. Moreover, during the sixteenth and early seventeenth
centuries rural population was growing faster than opportunities for
industrial employment, and this was bound to lead to strong competition for farms and an upward pressure on rents. More important than
either of these two considerations, however, was the rise in the general
profitability of farming during our period. On the demand side, the
growth of population was reflected in the rising trend of farm produce
prices, which benefited agriculturalists as against other sections of the
community. On the side of supply, the real costs of agricultural
production were tending to decrease, owing to greater productivity
and a fall in factor costs (measured in terms of the value of output).
In respect of costs, we have already noted that agricultural wages
lagged behind commodity prices during much of the period under
review, while in the early decades of the seventeenth century capital
seems to have become available on easier terms. The net effect of
these various changes was to widen the margin between agricultural
prices and non-rent costs (including adequate remuneration to the
farmer of average efficiency). This margin, or surplus, was potentially
available to the landlord as rent, though in practice all or part of it
might be retained by the tenant. It was not, however, necessary for the
landlord to take the entire surplus, or even all that part of it attributable
to the rise in agricultural prices, in order to maintain his standard of
life, since a substantial proportion of his expenditure would presumably
have been on non-agricultural commodities and services, whose prices
increased less markedly than those of farm produce.[1]

The extent to which Tudor and early Stuart landlords were in
practice able to benefit from the general rise in land values depended

---

[1] For a discussion of factors affecting the rent of land, see R. Turvey, *The Economics
of Real Property: an analysis of property values and patterns of use*, 1957, pp. 55–66;
G. Hallett, *The Economics of Agricultural Land Tenure*, London, 1960, *passim*.

largely upon the terms of tenancy by which their lands were let; and here custom played no small part. Nowadays many farms are occupied by tenants under leases terminable by either landlord or tenant at twelve months' notice. Such leases permit rents to be frequently adjusted, if necessary, in line with changes in the market value of land. The tenures inherited by Tudor landlords from an earlier period of land surfeit, in which all the bargaining power had rested with tenants, were, in general, much less flexible. Demesne lands were sometimes leased on a short-term basis, and thus provided the best opportunity for rent revision. But tradition conferred a high degree of security of tenure in the case of many customary holdings, especially the copyholds of inheritance. Leasehold and other forms of tenure were often for lives or for long periods of time. Changes of tenancy might thus be at infrequent intervals, and even then to raise rent on much copyhold land was difficult, if not impossible.

Even under such circumstances as these, however, it did not necessarily follow that the landlord was bound to suffer a decline in real income. The assumption made earlier, that rent was the landlord's only source of revenue, does not, in fact, represent the true position. Landlords' receipts in the sixteenth and seventeenth centuries came from a variety of sources. Most landlords probably engaged in direct farming to cater for the needs of the household, if not for the market. The interest in commercial agriculture varied, as we have seen, according to the pull of economic forces; and the early sheep-enclosure movement clearly showed that, given sufficient incentive, not only demesne land might be farmed, but a covetous eye also cast upon common land and tenants' holdings. The great majority, if not all, of the farmers whose activities have been singled out for special mention in the earlier pages of this study were landlords as well as cultivators, deriving their income from rents as well as from the sale of produce. In the first few years of the seventeenth century the total revenue from the estates of Sir Thomas Temple of Stowe amounted to some £2,500–£2,600 per annum. Of this amount, revenue from rents, including not only rents from land and borough tenements, but also from tithes, mills, and manorial dues, did not account for more than about £500 or £600 a year. The remaining £2,000 came from Temple's own farming enterprise. On the West Midland estates of the first earl of Middlesex in the two years ending 1 November 1631 rents accounted for only 13 per cent of total gross receipts, the bulk of income being derived from sales of wool, livestock, and corn. With the decline of Cranfield's direct farming interests the relative importance of revenue from rents increased, and in the sixteen-month period ending 27 February 1637 some 51 per cent of gross income was obtained from this source. Almost half a century earlier, in the 1590's, the rent-roll of Sir Thomas Tresham of Rushton, Northants., amounted to approximately £1,000 per annum. More than half of Tresham's gross income in this decade, however, came from the sale of farm produce, especially wool and sheep, but most other kinds of livestock were also sold, as well as corn, hops, cheeses, hides, timber, and lime. A substantial income was obtained from the sale of rabbits, this being a business which many large landowners found profitable. At Misterton, in the mid-sixteenth century, the cony warren was a highly-valued asset, its commercial exploitation providing permanent employment for a warrener and a net knitter who made and repaired the nets used for snares. Other workers were engaged on an occasional basis. In the year ending Michaelmas 1551 total expenditure in connection with the warren on wages and materials (including meat and milk for the ferrets) amounted to about £10, while proceeds from the sale of rabbits came to £74 4s. 4d. Total demesne receipts in the same year amounted to £587 10s. 5d., of which wool accounted for £170, while rents from tenanted holdings totalled £206 18s. 8½d. The demesne figure is of gross receipts from sales at Misterton, and makes no allowance for the value of produce consumed by the Paget household at Drayton in Middlesex, nor of receipts arising from the sale of kitchen by-products, notably hides, fells, and tallow. Most substantial landowners, whether they farmed for the market or not, probably obtained some income from the sale of such products, and in large households the receipts were sometimes considerable. Thus, in the year ending Michaelmas 1616, Lord Dormer sold 884 fells for £62 12s., while debts outstanding on wool sold the previous year brought in £773. On the earl of Northampton's estates at Compton, Warws., hides and fells sold in the eight-month period ending 26 March 1631 fetched £70 15s. 1½d., while the sale of tallow realized £55 2s. 9d. The diet of wealthy seventeenth-century landowners may have been deficient in vitamins, but certainly not in proteins! For the landlord who retained in his own possession more grazing land than his livestock required, agistment charges frequently provided a useful supplementary source of income. Alternatively, grass or hay could be sold locally; and since hay was very costly to transport, its sale was also sometimes favoured by the stock-grazing landowner whose properties were widely dispersed. In the late 1590's Thomas Grantham, Esq., who possessed a large scattered estate in Lincolnshire, was selling more than 170 acres of grass each year, despite the fact that he himself owned some 1500–2700 sheep and perhaps 100–200 head of cattle. In 1598 hay and grass sold by Grantham's bailiff at St Katherine's (now part of Lincoln city) brought in £94 16s., while barley—the main arable crop—fetched £119 16s. 2d. The hay was sold unmown at 10s. per acre: a practice which relieved the land-owner of the costs and responsibilities of hay making and marketing.[1]

Apart from rent income and the proceeds of direct farming, how-ever, by far the most important source of receipts for the majority of landlords was timber. In many contemporary estate accounts, especially those relating to the early seventeenth century, references frequently occur to sales of fallen wood or standing timber; and though tenants were occasionally required to plant so many trees of specified kinds, there is little evidence of afforestation by the majority of landowners. It thus appears that in early Stuart times, at any rate, many landlords were living partly on their capital, though how far this was forced upon them by a rigidity in other sources of income in a period of inflation, and how far it was motivated by a desire to benefit from the rising demand for timber, cannot be precisely determined. The largest sales of wood and woodland were, of course, made by the Crown, but comprehensive accounts are few and data are both confused and widely dispersed. The last comprehensive general account to be found for the sixteenth century relates to 1546, when sales of timber brought in gross receipts of about £2,000. By the years 1606–9 this figure had risen to an average of £8,645 per annum, of which something like a quarter to a half may have been swallowed up by costs of administra-tion. In spite of a threefold to fourfold increase in the market price of timber in the intervening period, the receipts for 1606–9 probably represented only a small proportion of the true commercial value of sales; and there seems little doubt that the Crown was making greater inroads into its reserves of woodland in the early seventeenth century than it had done sixty years previously. However, these reserves still remained very large, an estimate made in 1612 putting the value of all royal woods at £403,000. During the years that followed, depletion continued at a more rapid rate, but commercial exploitation was severely restricted by limitations of the transportation system. While, therefore, Crown receipts from wood sales showed a marked increase in districts such as the Forest of Dean, which were relatively densely populated or in close proximity to industrial consumers, royal woods situated in remote and isolated localities were largely unaffected by the rising demand for fuel. The same factor of transport possibilities doubtless played an important part in determining the exploitation of woodland resources by other landowners. Much also depended, of course, upon the extent of such resources, since some regions had been

[1] Gay, *op. cit.*, pp. 421–2; Kent AO, U 269, A 423; Finch, *op. cit.*, pp. 74–5; W. Salt Lib., D 1734, 24; Lord Dormer's Papers, 1600–30; BM Add. MS 33417; Bowden, *op. cit.*, pp. 12–13; Warws. RO, CR 556, 5, f. 22; Gloucs. RO, D 621, M 18; Lincs. AO, And. 1; Thirsk, *op. cit.*, pp. 90–1.

largely cleared of trees by Tudor times or had never possessed a great abundance of forest. In the arable districts of East Anglia, for example, wood sales by landlords in the sixteenth and early seventeenth centuries appear to have seldom made more than a minor contribution to revenue. Southern and central England, on the other hand, were still well-wooded in many districts at the beginning of Elizabeth's reign, and most extant records of substantial wood sales by private landowners relate to these regions of relatively dense settlement. The Cromwell family of Ramsey, Hunts., was selling several hundred pounds-worth of timber annually towards the end of the sixteenth century. Near by, at Leighton Buzzard in Bedfordshire, sales of spires, bark, underwood, and faggots between 1611 and 1614 brought Sir Thomas Leigh gross receipts averaging £130 4s. 3d. per annum. At Finchampstead, Berks., Sir Richard Harrison raised a total of £1,760 17s. 3d. by similar sales in the twenty-five years ending September 1637. On the Oxfordshire and Buckinghamshire estates of Sir Henry Lee, one of the king's wards, receipts for wood sold in the year September 1640–1 amounted to £601 11s. 6d., while sales over the whole 11-year period 1639–50 realized almost £3,000. To the west, in Warwickshire, a single wood, 'Coldoak Coppice', yielded the earl of Northampton £538 14s. 6d. in 1630–1. Further north, on Brudenell's Northamptonshire estate, sales of underwood, oaks, and bark between 1606 and 1635 brought in average gross receipts of £222 13s. 4d. per annum, out of a total estate revenue which varied between about £2,500 and £4,600. In the same county Brudenell's contemporary, Sir William Fitzwilliam, drew more heavily upon his timber supplies. Accounts for the five years 1603–8 show that Fitzwilliam's gross annual receipts from wood sales ranged between £572 0s. 3d. and £691 15s. 10d., while the total yearly revenue from his estate amounted to about £2,500. There seems little doubt that Fitzwilliam, like many other landowners of the period, was utilizing his woodland in order to live beyond his income, but there is no evidence of long-term indebtedness on his part. For the landlord in financial difficulties, depletion of timber reserves was an obvious means of attaining temporary solvency. The earl of Northumberland, for example, sold wood worth almost £2,000 from his Petworth estate in Sussex between 1585 and 1595 in order to satisfy his creditors, and this was not the end of his depredations. From the standpoint of the landowner, particularly if he lacked capital as well as foresight, one of the main attractions which the commercial exploitation of woodland possessed over direct farming, was the smaller outlay incurred in relation to receipts. Expenditure varied, depending not only upon the acreage and location of woodland, but also upon whether sales were made of standing timber or felled wood. In either case, coppices had to be fenced, guarded, and tended; woodwards' wages had to be paid and hedges maintained. But these costs were comparatively small. Thomas Grantham, who possessed at least four separate woods, paid out £14 16s. in woodwards' wages in 1594–5, while hedging and allied charges totalled £8 12s. 1d. Grantham's annual gross receipts from timber sales in the period 1594–8 averaged £130 11s. 3d., which exceeded the value of either barley or hay sales, and accounted for about 10 per cent of total gross revenue. Many landowners sold wood in small quantities to local inhabitants, and in this way disposed of old or fallen timber. Large wood dealers and industrial consumers, however, relied less on casual sales than on purchasing or leasing areas of woodland, paying the landowner a specified annual 'rent' per acre and assuming full responsibility for felling and carriage. Many minute parcels of coppice were also sold in this way, local men buying an interest in perhaps a quarter or half acre of woodland. The 'rents' charged in these transactions varied enormously—the value of the timber, the location of the wood, and the business instincts of the landowner, all playing a part. The average 'rent' received by the Crown for coppices leased in eleven counties in the years 1604–12 worked out at 2s. 3d. an acre. At the other end of the scale, Sir George Heneage of Hainton, in Lincolnshire, was receiving as much as £10 per acre for certain parcels of coppice in the 1630's. The woods in question must have been exceptionally well-stocked, even allowing for the enhanced value of woodland since the beginning of the seventeenth century.[1]

Clearly, as the preceding discussion indicates, to consider the landlord's economic position solely from the standpoint of farm rents may be to ignore other, more important, sources of income. The standard of living of many substantial landowners, however, depended primarily upon their rent receipts, and the ability to adjust these in an age of rising prices afforded a major protection against inflation. One way in which rent revenues could be increased, of course, was by charging more for existing holdings; and much has been written concerning the conflict between landlord and tenant over the "unearned increment" (i.e. the economic rent) of land resulting from its rise in value. The point is obviously a very valid one; but probably no less important to some landowners was the additional revenue derived from the creation

[1] Hull, *thesis*, p. 324; G. Hammersley, 'The Crown Woods and their Exploitation in the Sixteenth and Seventeenth Centuries', *Bull. IHR*, xxx, 1957, pp. 137–59; Simpson, *op. cit.*, *passim;* BM Add. MSS 33458; 33459; Beds. RO, DD. KK. 739; BM Add. MS 34302; Oxford RO, DIL. XVIII, M 121; Warws. RO, CR 556, 5, f. 36; Finch, *op. cit.*, pp. 129, 163; Cornwall, *thesis*, pp. 127–33; Lincs. AO, And. 1; HEN. 3, 2; Kent AO, U 269, A 421, 3; Norwich Pub. Lib., MS 20449; PRO E 133, 465, East. 20 Eliz. I.

of new holdings and farm extensions by intakes from the adjoining forest or waste. Not only were such intakes normally let for market-value rents, but, with growing land hunger, the cultivated area on many manors was greatly increased.[1] On some estates, especially in districts of rapidly expanding population, the income acquired by additions to the acreage of productive land must have largely, if not completely, offset any rise in the landlord's cost of living.

Moreover, an improvement in net rent receipts did not necessarily have to take the form of increased money payments by tenants. The landlord's disposable income depended upon costs of estate administration and maintenance as well as upon rents. If the former charges could be reduced, net estate revenue would rise. In some cases, economies in administration were effected by the sale of outlying properties and the concentration of lands into more compact and easily manageable units. In other instances, part of the burden of estate administration was placed upon tenants in lieu of higher rent charges. This development was not in itself novel, since under the system of feudal agriculture much of the work of manorial administration, as well as the cultivation of the lord's demesne, had been undertaken by customary tenants; indeed, in spite of the widespread commutation of labour services which preceded the Tudor age, vestiges of villein tenure still survived in the occasional boonworks and other obligations exacted on some manors as late as the mid-seventeenth century. These services, however, formed part of a long-established, though greatly weakened tradition, and affected customary tenants rather than other occupiers. The main departure, as far as the period covered by our study is concerned, was the imposition of new services on leaseholders. A feature of the leases granted by Sir William Petre after 1550 was the obligation on lessees to occupy manorial offices, such as those of bailiff, collector, and reeve. Annual surveys of the Petre lands were compiled from terriers drawn up by tenants and completed by an outside surveyor.[2]

While costs of administration might thus be reduced, expenditure on estate maintenance suggested greater possibilities of economy, especially in connection with small under-rented holdings whose upkeep was the landlord's responsibility. Contemporary complaints concerning the

[1] W. G. Hoskins, 'The Reclamation of the Waste in Devon', EcHR, XIII, 1943, pp. 85–9; E. Kerridge, 'The Movement of Rent, 1540–1640', EcHR, 2nd Ser., VI, 1953, pp. 24–31; E. Hopkins, *The Bridgewater Estates in North Shropshire in the First Half of the Seventeenth Century*, University of London M.A. thesis, 1956, pp. 53–63.

[2] Finch, op. cit., p. 44; Kerridge, EcHR, 2nd Ser., VI, 1953, pp. 17–18; Hull, thesis, pp. 340–2; M. Campbell, *The English Yeoman Under Elizabeth and the Early Stuarts*, New Haven, 1942, pp. 142–3; Salop. RO, 123, I, p. 35; Lancs. RO, DDF, 75, f. 11; Emerson, thesis, pp. 134–5, 285.

"decay" and engrossing of farms reflect the widespread nature of this problem and indicate two of the principal solutions which recommended themselves to landowners. In the one case, the landlord allowed the farmstead to "decay," that is, he neglected his obligations on the ground that the rent received scarcely covered the value of the timber used for maintenance. In the other case, small-holdings were thrown together to create large farms, thereby effecting a saving in the cost of repairs. Nor were these the only possibilities. On many holdings responsibility for the upkeep of buildings, generally assumed by the landlord at the beginning of the Tudor period, was increasingly placed on the tenant; so also was the maintenance of hedges, fences, and ditches. For these purposes timber was normally supplied by the landlord, either as a specific allowance or, more generally, in the common terminology of housebote, hedgebote, firebote, ploughbote, and cartbote. Occasionally an upper limit was placed on the cost of repairs for which the tenant was liable, but this was not usual. Moreover, the tenant's responsibility in regard to repairs was sometimes extended beyond the holding which he occupied. He might, for example, be required as a condition of his tenancy to repair and maintain the lord's swinehouse, or any mills, weirs, or fisheries on the manor. In localities where there was a danger of flooding, as in parts of south-east England or Lincolnshire, the repair of sea-walls and dikes, or the payment of "scots" in lieu, was often delegated, in whole or in part, to the occupier. In addition, various other public charges, such as maintenance of bridges and highways and the relief of the poor, were sometimes placed on the tenant, so also was responsibility for the payment of any fee-farm or quit-rent issuing out of the property, together with taxation charges, fifteenths being specifically referred to in certain leases.[1]

Even the cost of estate improvement was sometimes borne by the tenant, although this was not the usual practice. One does, however, find instances, as at Kilpeck in Herefordshire in the 1530's, where long-term leaseholders were required to clear land and bear the costs of its enclosure. Just over a century later, at Ayston in Rutland, tenants had to meet all or most of the costs of enclosure on land belonging to Brudenell of Deene. On Petre's Essex estate in the late sixteenth century several leaseholders were required to put in certain specified buildings

[1] J. Thirsk, *Tudor Enclosures* (Historical Association Pamphlet, General Series: G. 41), 1959, pp. 10–13; Hasbach, *op. cit.*, p. 384; Rogers, *Agriculture and Prices*, IV, p. 62; Hull, *thesis*, pp. 319–22; Emerson, *thesis*, pp. 133–4; Northants. RO, Westmorland-Apethorpe Coll. 4, XVI, 5; Herts. RO, X. C. 7. A, f. 31; Lancs. RO, DDCL, 1660–1685; BM Add. MSS 34163, ff. 21–21ᵛ, 46ᵛ; 34166, f. 25; PRO E 133, 481, Trin. 20 Eliz. I; PRO E 133, 1223, Mich. 37–8 Eliz. I; Lumley MS 2305 (in possession of the earl of Scarbrough).

or other capital improvements on their holdings within a stipulated time of having entered them. At Wrexham, and possibly a number of other places, local custom ruled that landlords should compensate outgoing tenants for the costs of any improvements effected, but legislation provided the occupier with no general protection of this nature. Thus the progressive tenant who improved the value of his holding was as likely to be rack-rented as compensated. The existence of such conditions inevitably tended to act as a brake on agricultural progress, and, particularly towards the end of his tenancy, the occupier must have been tempted to over-crop or under-manure his holding. The husbandry clauses which are to be found in some leases endeavoured to prevent this situation by, for example, stipulating the proportion of arable to pasture or fallow, and by specifying the application of quantities of manure and other dressings.[1]

If a reduction in the burden of estate expenditure enabled some landowners to ride out the worst effects of inflation, additional protection against the fall in the value of money might be obtained by levying rents in kind. Sometimes such provision rents were sold on the open market; but not uncommonly they were used, along with demesne yields and receipts from tithes, if any, to furnish the landlord's household and to provide feed for his stock. Produce rents were not new; indeed, cottagers had long rendered part-payment for their small properties in capons, hens, eggs, and the like, and in the sixteenth and early seventeenth centuries many continued to do so. It was, however, in connection with a different class of tenant and a wider range of agricultural produce that rents in kind began to assume greater significance in the Tudor period. From the early sixteenth century onwards an increasingly common feature of leasehold tenure on many estates was the obligation laid on tenants to pay all or part of their rents in corn or other produce. In the case of stock-and-land leases, whereby the landlord supplied capital apart from land and buildings, such arrangements were normal. Many leases of this type were similar to that renewed by Bacon at Ingham in Suffolk in 1562, which provided for a rent of £93 and 133 combs of barley and rye with an option to pay 5s. a comb. But apart from tenancies of this nature, the payment of rent wholly or partly in the form of produce was frequently stipulated in leases of demesne lands, as, for example, at Wilton in Wiltshire, where leaseholders were required to pay large rents in wheat, barley,

---

[1] Nat. Lib. Wales, Pye of the Mynd Coll. Nos. 65, 73; Kent Church Court Coll., No. 320; Finch, *op. cit.*, p. 161; Emerson, *thesis*, pp. 252–4; PRO E 133, 223, 16–17 Eliz. I; W. Blith, *The English Improver Improved or the Survey of Husbandry Surveyed*, London, 1652, preface; G. Plattes, *A Discovery of Infinite Treasure Hidden Since the World's Beginning*, London, 1639, p. 16; Salop. RO, 320, 5, p. 13.

malt, oats, poultry, and rabbits. Moreover, institutional landowners, as well as private landlords, were affected by this development. In 1576 an Act of Parliament (18 Eliz. I, c. 6) empowered the colleges of Oxford and Cambridge and the schools of Eton and Winchester to take one third of their leasehold rents in corn or its maximum current market value. Even before this act was passed, however, produce rent, at fictitious prices, had for some time been customary at King's College, Cambridge, and had figured in occasional collegiate leases granted elsewhere. In the years immediately preceding the Dissolution many monastic houses were deriving a considerable revenue from rents in kind, chiefly from leased-out portions of the demesne. At St Augustine's, Canterbury, in 1535, almost one fifth of total gross income (£309 out of £1,684) took the form of produce rents, but this proportion was exceptional. On ecclesiastical lands in the seventeenth century rents in kind were, if anything, more important than in early Tudor times, and generally constituted a major element in annual rent receipts. Together with tithes—where these were not leased out or otherwise commuted for fixed money payments—such rents must have provided the clergy with a comforting wind-break against inflation. On the other hand, provision rents, tithes, and other payments in kind were an encumbrance to the Crown, and those arising on former monastic properties were quickly farmed out, exchanged, or commuted.[1] One such payment was heriot: a charge most commonly levied at the death of a tenant, but sometimes additionally demanded on the surrender or alienation of land. Despite its feudal origin, this payment, which normally took the form of the tenant's best beast or chattel (or a money sum in lieu), was a widespread feature of copyhold tenure throughout our period, and it was not in the least unusual for it to be charged against leasehold or freehold land. Heriot was claimed on many of the estates belonging to private landowners, the Church, and the Crown. In the latter case, it featured in two fifths of the leases for lives granted in the final decade of Elizabeth's reign—but as a fixed money payment, and not as a levy in kind.[2]

In spite of provision rents and similar charges, however, it was principally to larger money payments that the majority of landlords looked for an improvement in their rent-rolls. The extent to which such payments could be exacted from tenants depended primarily

[1] Herts. RO, 6604; 6718; Simpson, op. cit., pp. 81–2; Kerridge, EcHR, 2nd Ser., VI, 1958, p. 18; Finch, op. cit., p. 122; Emerson, thesis, pp. 136–49, 154; Bury and W. Suff. RO, E 3, 15. 51, 2, 2; D. Knowles, The Religious Orders in England: The Tudor Age, Cambridge, 1959, p. 251; Hereford Dean and Chapter Lib., 3 A; 3 E; 5096; Norwich Dean and Chapter Lib., Parliamentary Survey of Lands (1649).

[2] Campbell, op. cit., pp. 116–17, 126–7; Hull, thesis, pp. 343–5; Cornwall, thesis, pp. 270, 284; CSPD 1591–1603, passim.

upon the type of land tenure, and this could vary greatly, not only from estate to estate, but also from one property to another. In the case of freehold land, frequently held "by fealty only" or in return for small token payments, rents were fixed and could not be increased. Even at the beginning of the Tudor period such rents had often added little to the landlord's income, and with the fall in the value of money they became less and less significant. Thus, by the middle of the seventeenth century many freeholders had ceased to make any payments whatever, and freehold had almost achieved its modern meaning.[1]

On customary land, tenures at will provided the landlord with the best opportunity to adjust rents in line with rising land values, and it is sometimes claimed that the sixteenth and early seventeenth centuries witnessed the spread of tenancies of this type. Examples of this process can certainly be found; but, on balance, the evidence appears rather more suggestive of a development away from tenures at will in favour of longer-term leaseholds for years or lives. From the landlord's point of view there were disadvantages as well as advantages in the tenancy at will, and flexibility in the matter of rent adjustment was not everything. The tenant who occupied a holding for an uncertain term and was liable to be dispossessed at short notice had little incentive to improve his land, and was not chargeable at law with reparations. Moreover, since the period of tenure was indefinite, the payment of an entry fine, i.e. a premium, on admittance was not practicable. At a time when estate improvement was often financed to a large extent out of fines and receipts from the sale of timber, this could be a big drawback to the progressive but penurious landlord, as well as to the debtor or spendthrift. Thus, on the Ellesmere estate of the financially embarrassed earl of Bridgewater, in north Shropshire, in the years 1637–40, annual lettings at rack-rents were regarded as a poor second choice to long-term leases, and were considered only in the case of tenants who were unable or unwilling to pay the comparatively heavy entry fines demanded for the latter.[2]

Conditions governing the exaction of such fines were of decisive influence in determining the movement of rent on copyhold land, where the occupier paid a premium on admittance and a low annual reserved rent. As a general, though by no means universal, rule, the copyholder of inheritance paid a fixed fine, which normally amounted to the equivalent of one or two years' annual rent, depending on the custom of the manor. With holdings of this type there was little

[1] Campbell, *op. cit.*, pp. 114–15; R. H. Tawney, *The Agrarian Problem in the Sixteenth Century*, 1912, p. 30.

[2] Finch, *op. cit.*, pp. 150, 159, 161; Aaron Rathbone, *The Surveyor in Foure Bookes*, London, 1616, p. 180; Hopkins, *thesis*, pp. 68–72, 155–60.

prospect of rent increase unless the landlord could successfully prove that at some date variable fines had been imposed, or unless he could persuade tenants to exchange copies for leases. Since, by the end of the sixteenth century, rising prices had given the copyholder of inheritance an almost freehold interest in his land, there was no advantage to him in the latter course. Indeed, as in more recent times of inflation, rent restriction helped to pave the way to outright purchase, and we find many instances of copyholders of inheritance enfranchising their holdings on highly favourable terms. In general, the copyholders for lives—who in Tudor times possibly outnumbered those of inheritance by about two to one—were less fortunate. In the first place, their copies were normally granted for not more than three lives, at the end of which the natural heir had no guarantee of succession to a property, but only the right of first refusal. Moreover, the entry fine in this class of tenure was usually arbitrary, and could in practice, as well as in theory, vary from a penny to scores of pounds, according to the size and value of the holding and the amount of the reserved rent. Thus, on the manor of Rivers Hall in Boxted, Essex, copyhold fines in 1620 amounted to £136 2s. 9d., compared with copyhold annual rents of £11 6s. 2d. Where the prospective copyholder lacked capital resources, a high entry fine could preclude occupation of a holding, and the landlord was free, if he wished, to put in a more substantial tenant, or to throw several such properties together in order to create a large leasehold farm. The extent to which this happened is unknown. There is no doubt that on many manors the acreage under lease was growing at the expense of copyhold, but the change of tenure did not necessarily imply a change of tenant. In most parts of England at the end of the sixteenth century copyholders still outnumbered leaseholders, though the latter may well have occupied a larger area of land. Moreover, even arbitrary fines were sometimes regulated by custom, as on certain Norfolk and Suffolk manors in early Stuart times, where premiums on entry varied from a few pence above to a few pence below the sum of 2s. per acre.[1]

It is generally assumed that the entry fine formed an increasingly important element in the rent paid by the leaseholder in the sixteenth and early seventeenth centuries, and on many estates this was undoubtedly so. Information on this score for early Tudor times, however, is piecemeal, but such evidence as there is suggests that, in the matter of

---

[1] Kerridge, EcHR, 2nd Ser., VI, 1953, pp. 18–19; Campbell, *op. cit.*, pp. 134–5, 144–5; Cornwall, *thesis*, pp. 264 ff., 297, 331; Tawney, *op. cit., passim;* Hull, *thesis*, pp. 333, 347, 350–1; Finch, *op. cit.*, pp. 73, 117, 149–50; J. Spratt, *Agrarian Conditions in Norfolk and Suffolk, 1600–1650,* University of London M.A. thesis, 1935, pp. 115–17.

fines, the leaseholder's position at the beginning of the sixteenth century differed little from that of the copyholder, i.e. he paid a premium on the grant or renewal of lease, and this sum was generally equivalent to one or two years' reserved rent. By the Elizabethan period, when our data become more plentiful, this was no longer necessarily the case, and one finds numerous instances of the landlord's interest being asserted by heavy entrance fines combined with low annual rents. Thus, to give but one example of such a "beneficial" lease: in 1571 James Brodribbe (who also possessed 22 acres of freehold land) secured the renewal of a lease for twenty-one years of eight acres of enclosed pasture on the manor of Pill, five miles north-west of Bristol, in return for a fine of £10 and an annual rent of 10s. If we wish to calculate the true rent cost of this holding, we must make allowance, as contemporaries did, for the interest forgone by the tenant on his advance premium payment—i.e. we must discount the amount of the fine at the current rate of interest over the whole of the period of tenure. At 10 per cent compound interest (the maximum statutory rate), Brodribbe's £10 fine would have cost him, on average, £3 10s. 6d. per annum. Added to the reserved annual rent, this gives a total yearly charge of £4 0s. 6d. for the whole holding, or 10s. 1d. per acre. How far the easing of credit facilities in early Stuart times affected this type of tenure is uncertain, but by the mid-seventeenth century there was a growing tendency for the entry fine to be dispensed with altogether, and for the landlord's claim on the lessee to be limited to the annual rent; in other words, leasehold and copyhold were parting company, and the former was assuming its modern shape. Thus, on some leaseholds in Northamptonshire in the early seventeenth century, beneficial leases were superseded by lettings at commercial rents. In Sussex and Yorkshire during the same period premiums were not usually demanded for leasehold land except where an improvident gentleman or nobleman wanted to raise large sums quickly. One such was Josias Lambert of Carlton, father of the parliamentary general, who granted leases for 3,000 and 6,000 years at negligible annual rents and for fines which were almost equivalent to the freehold value of the lands concerned.[1]

The terms of the leases granted by Lambert were, of course, highly exceptional; but there were probably many estates in the early decades

[1] Somerset RO, X, WLM, O, 822, f. 10ᵛ; T. Clay, Briefe, Easie and Necessary Tables, of Interest and Rents Forborne, London, 1624; Anon., Tables of Leases and Interest ..., London, 1628; Kerridge, EcHR, 2nd Ser., VI, 1953, pp. 19–24; Finch, op. cit., p. 49; Cornwall, thesis, pp. 290–2; J. T. Cliffe, The Yorkshire Gentry on the Eve of the Civil War, University of London Ph.D. thesis, 1960, pp. 111, 143–4.

of the sixteenth century where leases for forty years and upwards predominated over those for shorter periods. Thus, a survey made in 1590 of the former monastic property of Brilley, Hereford, reveals that the majority of tenants were still holding under indentures for ninety-nine years granted between 1491 and 1535. The rents received at the time of the survey were far below the commercial letting value of the land, and a memorandum noted that, in future, leases were to be limited to a maximum term of three years. In Devon the lease for three lives, coupled with a definite term of ninety-nine years, remained the predominant form of tenure until the late eighteenth century. Elsewhere in the west of England, and in parts of the north, long leases were also common. In general, however, the tendency was towards shorter terms; and by the end of Elizabeth's reign the lease for twenty-one years had been widely adopted in many places with the lease for three lives next in frequency. How far the prevalence of these terms was the result of the various enabling and restraining statutes is difficult to determine. But the Act of Leases (32 Hen. VIII, c. 28) disallowed reversions of more than twenty-one years or three lives, while legislation passed in Elizabeth's reign (13 Eliz. I, c. 10; 14 Eliz. I, c. 14; 18 Eliz. I, c. 11) limited ecclesiastical and collegiate leases to similar terms. Thus we find, for example, that church leases of land in the Durham Palatinate in the period 1610–31 employed these two terms in roughly equal proportions. Among Crown leases granted in the years 1591–1601 approximately two fifths were for twenty-one years and one quarter for three lives. The same predilection for a term of twenty-one years is to be noted in the records of many private landowners, with a tendency on some estates in favour of even shorter periods in the early seventeenth century.[1]

It will be apparent, however, that, whatever the term of tenure, the lessee benefited from any rise in the value of land between the grant of a lease and its renewal. But on each renewal it was possible for the landlord to adjust rent so that, temporarily at least, it reflected the enhanced value of the land. Such rent adjustments might be very large: indeed, in the conditions of the sixteenth and early seventeenth centuries the *proportionate* increase in rent could be much greater than the rise in the value of land, or in the price of agricultural produce which mainly contributed to it, without reducing farm profits to an unremunerative

[1] Hereford City Lib., L. C. Deeds 6581; W. G. Hoskins and H. P. R. Finberg, *Devonshire Studies*, London, 1952, pp. 84, 337; Campbell, *op. cit.*, pp. 82–4; Hull, *thesis*, pp. 317–8; Cornwall, *thesis*, pp. 31–3; Finch, *op. cit., passim;* R. T. Gent., *Tenants' Law, or The Laws Concerning Landlords, Tenants and Farmers*, London, 1666, pp. 58–61; Prior's Kitchen, Durham, 220,194; 220,240; CSPD 1591–1601, *passim;* HMC, Seventh Report, p. 530a.

level. In order to appreciate the full significance of this argument, we should recall that rent is essentially a residual payment, and in a perfectly competitive market for agricultural land represents the difference between farm costs (including tenant's 'fair' remuneration) and the value of farm output. A simple example will make the position clear.

Table 13. *Effect of change in the value of land on rent and tenant's remuneration*

	Before rise in value of land	After rise in value of land	
		Money rent unchanged	Tenant's real income unchanged
	£	£	£
Landlord's rent	10	10	225
Other farm costs	60	240	240
Value of produce	100	600	600
Tenant's remuneration	30	350	135
		Index number of real income	
Landlord	100	22	500
Tenant	100	259	100

In Table 13 we assume the existence of a large arable holding worked by hired wage labour. No claim is made for the accuracy of figures contained in the table, but the changes which are shown are broadly representative of those which occurred between the beginning and end of the sixteenth century—viz., a sixfold increase in the value of farm output, due mainly to higher prices and partly to improved productivity; a fourfold increase in farm costs, particular allowance being made for the lag of agricultural wages behind prices; and a rise of 450 per cent in the cost of living. On the basis of these assumptions, it can be seen that if rent remains unchanged in spite of a rise in the value of land, the tenant's net income in our example is increased almost twelvefold in money terms, and more than two and a half times in real terms. At the same time, the purchasing power of the landlord's gross income from the holding declines to between one quarter and one fifth of its former level. In the second instance, where it is assumed that the entire economic surplus arising from the holding is taken by the landlord and the tenant's real income remains unchanged, it appears that the landlord's real income increases fivefold, while his money income rises by 2,250 per cent. The *proportionate* increase in rent is thus almost four times greater than the stipulated rise in the value of farm output.

In the context of the sixteenth and early seventeenth centuries the contrast in the two situations illustrated by Table 13 has more than theoretical significance. On the majority of estates at this time long leases and customary tenures restricted the rent of some holdings far below the level of that obtainable on new commercial lettings. The predominant tendency, therefore, was for the range of rents, as between different holdings, to widen. On Petre's Essex lands in 1566 the range of leasehold rents was about 10:1, from the highest to the lowest rented properties on the estate; by 1590 this range had been increased to 24:1, from the Dairy House farm at East Thorndon, renting at 12s. per acre, to Westlands farm in Mountnessing, which was still at the old rent of about 6d. per acre set under the terms of a 1528 monastic lease. This situation was not in any way exceptional, and many similar examples could be cited. In general, it was the large leasehold farm operated on commercial principles by the capitalist farmer which provided the best opportunity for high rent; and the landlord whose estate consisted partly of such properties coming up for periodic revision of rents had little to fear from inflation, even though receipts from other holdings might remain inflexible. The rent of small farm units was often restricted by custom; but even where this was not the case, the economic surplus which the landlord could tap was generally smaller, in relation to size, than with large farm undertakings; for not only was productivity on the small-holding usually lower than on the large, but the subsistence cultivator in some instances supplemented his income by wage earning, and so was more likely to suffer than benefit from the relative fall in agricultural wage costs. Thus, apart from economies in expenditure on estate mainten-ance, there were positive advantages to the landlord in replacing small farmsteads by large holdings. However, security of tenure and artificially low rents doubtless enabled many small tenants to continue in possession who would otherwise have been squeezed out in favour of more efficient producers. Moreover, since the demand for land was rising, tenants who occupied under-rented holdings were well placed to sub-let all or part of their property at enhanced rents; and in many districts there appears to have been a tendency for the number of share-croppers and other undertenants to increase. The rents which figure in manorial surveys and leases, therefore, were not always the rents paid by the ultimate cultivators of the soil.[1]

[1] Emerson, *thesis*, pp. 128, 250, 286; Hull, *thesis*, pp. 354, 369; Kerridge, *thesis*, pp. 385–402; Cornwall, *thesis*, pp. 69, 298–301; Hopkins, *thesis*, p. 61.

When we turn to a detailed analysis of rent data, it becomes apparent that the general movement of rent in Tudor and early Stuart times cannot be measured with any degree of statistical exactness. Most of the relevant material which has come down to us is insufficiently detailed and too unreliable to justify statistical manipulation. But even if this were not the case, the range of rents was so wide that averages calculated from an unrepresentative sample of estates would not be very meaningful. Dr Kerridge has shown how, given a series of comprehensive manorial surveys, it is possible to calculate, for individual estates, the movement of rent on new lettings.[1] But if this enables us to determine the trend of rents, it tells us little about their general level, even on individual estates, since new lettings in any one year would seldom account for more than a small proportion of the total area of tenant-occupied land. Thus, one would expect the curve of total rent receipts to have followed a different course to that of rents on new takings, at first rising more slowly and then more rapidly as old leases fell in and customary rent restrictions were eased in some instances.

The date at which rents generally commenced to rise cannot be fixed with any certainty, and much must obviously have depended upon the type and geographical location of land. It may be suspected that in some pastoral districts rents showed a tendency to increase in the late fifteenth century, but, in general, there is no evidence of a sharp upward movement in arable rents before the 1520's. Thereafter, complaints about the exaction of high entry fines, or *gressums*, abound, and the rack-renting activities of "covetous" landlords become a subject of severe censure by moralists and churchmen. This, however, cannot be taken as evidence of a universal rise in rents; and on the majority of estates the disparity between rent receipts and rent potential widened as old tenancies proceeded to the completion of their terms. For many landowners, a wholesale revision of rents was delayed until the 1570's and 1580's; but from then onward, with land values continuing to rise, rent-rolls on estate after estate doubled, trebled, and quadrupled in a matter of decades. Thus, on manors belonging to the Seymour family in Wiltshire, while rents per acre for new takings approximately doubled, total rent receipts increased from £475 12s. 5½d. in 1575–6 to £1,429 11s. 0d. in 1639–40, and to £3,203 19s. 4d. in 1649–50. On Petre's Essex estate, properties producing annual rents of £1,400 in 1572 were renting for £2,450 in 1595, and for at least £4,200 in 1640. Between 1572 and 1640 the rents on many large leasehold farms on the estate were increased between five and tenfold. In little more than thirty years (1619–51) the rents on twelve Yorkshire

[1] Kerridge, EcHR, 2nd Ser., VI, 1953, pp. 16–34.

manors in the possession of the Saviles of Thornhill were increased by more than 400 per cent, the result of a major change in leasing policy. On the estates of other landed families in Yorkshire, Northampton-shire, East Anglia, and elsewhere, a doubling or trebling of rent receipts in the half century or so preceding the Civil War was by no means exceptional.[1]

Thus, in the late sixteenth and early seventeenth centuries there is evidence of a marked increase in rents on the estates of many private landowners. The same, however, cannot be said of Crown lands, which—thanks to the pressures of inflation and political uncertainty—were regarded less as long-term income-yielding investments than as a means of raising capital and rewarding allegiance. In Wiltshire rents per acre for new takings on lands of the duchies of Lancaster and Corn-wall increased about threefold in the course of the sixteenth century. By comparison, similar rents on the Seymour manors increased almost ninefold. Administration of the Crown estates appears to have been generally inefficient and corrupt. Surveys made in 1608 show that tenants on royal manors in Somerset, Devon, Dorset, and Wiltshire paid rents of £506 for land worth £7,500 per annum; in Cumberland, Westmorland, and the West Riding rents amounting to £2,206 were paid for properties valued at £9,294. These surveys were undertaken as part of a policy, instituted by Salisbury, of raising Crown rents to an economic level. But the policy, at first pushed with vigour, was later allowed to lapse, and the surveys were never completed. In consequence, although some quite sharp rent increases occurred under James I, many traditional rents were allowed to persist unaltered until after the Civil War. On ecclesiastical estates—where not only land but also manorial rights were sometimes farmed out—rents were generally at a less remunerative level than on private properties, though the disparity was not so marked as with Crown lands. On the estates of both the Crown and the Church, lessees—who included many substantial landowners in their own right—were often able to make high profits from direct farming or by sub-letting to undertenants. In 1633 the earl of Pembroke paid the bishop of Salisbury just over £118 rent for manors that he sublet for an upper rent of nearly £206. In 1616 the estate of Sir Timothy Hulton of Marske, whose father had been

[1] *Ibid.;* TED III, pp. 20–1, 39–43, 48–9, 57, 59, 61–3, 71–2, 337–8; Lamond, *op. cit.,* pp. 17–20, 38–9, 40–1, 104, 186–7; A. E. Bland, P. A. Brown, and R. H. Tawney, *English Economic History: Select Documents,* London, 1914, p. 249; LP XII, pt. I, pp. 71, 72, 136, 226, 274, 415; LP XVIII, pt. I, pp. 444–5; LP XX, pt. II, pp. 342–3; Emerson, *thesis,* pp. 232, 236; Cliffe, *thesis,* pp. 112–14; G. R. Batho, 'The Finances of an Elizabethan Nobleman: Henry Percy, Ninth Earl of Northumberland', EcHR, 2nd Ser., IX, 1957, pp. 439, 442; Simpson, *op. cit.,* pp. 196–216; Finch, *op. cit.,* pp. 129, 163.

archbishop of York, was valued at £1,449 per annum, of which no less than £573 was derived from church leases. Also in Yorkshire, at about the same time, the Alfords of Meaux held the Crown property of Meaux Abbey on a lease worth some £320 per annum more than the yearly rent.[1]

It is clear that in Tudor and early Stuart times tenurial relationships played a significant part in the determination of rent; and differences in the system of land tenure and in the disposition of the landlord could lead to wide variations in the rents charged for holdings of essentially similar land. In a perfect market these considerations would cease to exercise any effect, and the determination of rent would depend upon the location of land and the size of the economic surplus arising from it. Whilst the influence of these latter factors is not always easily discernible among the complexities and inconsistencies of Tudor and Stuart land tenure, they nevertheless played a significant part in the determination of rent during our period.

Rents, generally, were highest in the London region and in other districts, such as the south-west, where major groupings of population provided the farmer with an easily accessible market for his produce. In Essex, for example, land on manors furthest away from London was valued at the lowest rates. In most areas the shortage and high cost of transporting hay led to a high premium being placed on meadowland, which frequently commanded two or three times the rent of common-field arable and was usually more expensive than pasture. In marshland districts, however, hay was exceptionally plentiful, and pasture normally fetched the highest rents. Thus, at Trusthorpe and Sutton in Lincolnshire in the early seventeenth century, pasture was worth 9s.–10s. per acre, compared with 7s. for meadow and 5s. for arable. In such areas rent often depended partly upon the state of the drainage works and the expenses needed to keep them efficient. In general, meadowland was highly rented because its economic surplus was large. Unlike arable, which normally lay fallow for one year in three, meadow was cropped annually and was cultivated at low factor cost, apart from rent. The same considerations, applied with rather less force, resulted in higher rents being generally charged for pasture than for arable. The fertility of the soil, whether due to its inherent qualities or man-made improvements, had an important bearing on rent, though high yields and high rents do not inevitably go together. Thus, enclosed arable normally rented at higher rates than common-field land, while good grassland was much dearer than rough grazing. For example, in

---

[1] Kerridge, EcHR, 2nd Ser., VI, 1953, pp. 29–34; F. C. Dietz, *English Public Finance, 1558–1641*, New York, 1932, pp. 297–8; Norwich Dean and Chapter Lib., Parliamentary Survey of Lands (1649); Cliffe, *thesis*, pp. 104–5.

Northamptonshire in the mid-seventeenth century high-quality pasture rented for up to 26s. 8d. per acre, while in the north of England rough grazing could be had for a few pence.[1]

Over the Tudor and early Stuart periods as a whole, one of the most significant features in the long-term movement of rent was the narrowing of the differential between rates charged for poorer and better qualities of land. As a corollary of this, the rent of arable increased to a greater extent than that of pasture or meadow. Thus, between 1556 and 1648 the rents of certain lands in Warwick increased by 1031 per cent, while the rents of better lands in the same place increased by 833 per cent. On one Derbyshire estate between 1543 and 1584 a more than fourfold increase in the rent of meadowland was accompanied by an even greater rise in arable rents. In parts of Norfolk and Suffolk the rent of arable land increased from 4s. per acre in the first decade of the seventeenth century to 10s. the acre in 1640–50; pasture rose from 5s. 11d. to 12s. in the same period, and meadow from 10s. in 1600–10 to 11s. 8d. in 1630–40.[2] The proportionately large increase in arable rents is not unexpected, since the long-term rise in the price of cereals exceeded that for other farm products, while arable production afforded the greatest scope for raising yields and lowering costs in terms of output.

Over shorter periods, also, one might expect to find disparities in the movement of rent on different categories of land, in accordance with changes in the relative profitability of arable and livestock husbandry. In our analysis, made earlier, of trends in the agrarian economy, we indicated alternate phases in which grain prices were either rising or falling in relation to the prices of pastoral products, and it seems reasonable to suppose that the movement of rents on arable and grassland also tended to alternate in sympathy with prices. In the case of lands subject to inflexible tenures any such relationship is difficult to discern, though it appears to emerge fairly clearly on new lettings at commercial rents. Thus, while rents on new (predominantly) arable takings in Wiltshire doubled in the 1530's, when harvests were generally poor, pasture rents changed little. In the succeeding decade rents on new arable takings remained almost static while, according to literary evidence, grassland rents sharply increased. We should note, however, that while land is by no means homogeneous, a considerable degree of substitution between different categories exists, and in

<hr>

[1] TED III, p. 341; Hull, *thesis*, p. 373; Thirsk, *English Peasant Farming*, pp. 60–2; Spratt, *thesis*, pp. 215–7; Finch, *op. cit.*, pp. 48, 157; R. Lennard, *Rural Northamptonshire Under the Commonwealth*, Oxford Studies in Social and Legal History, v, 1916, p. 53; Prior's Kitchen, Durham, M. 80.

[2] Campbell, *op. cit.*, pp. 84–5; VCH *Derbys.*, II, p. 176; Spratt, *thesis*, p. 216; Hull, *thesis*, p. 376; Blith, *op. cit.*, p. 82.

periods of major economic upheaval all land values tend to react sympathetically. Thus, the severe structural adjustments of the 1550's and '60's and 1620's and '30's, which left most large arable farmers better off than before, led to a general slowing down, and even temporary reversal, in the upward movement of arable rents, as well as those on pasture.[1] Clearly, the main explanation for this situation is to be found in a temporary surplus of untenanted land—at ruling levels of rent—attributable to the reduced profitability of pasture farming, and the throwing up of small-holdings by peasant cultivators following adverse harvest conditions.

D. CONCLUSION

The inflation of Tudor and early Stuart times is generally believed to have confronted English landowners with serious problems: problems which derived from the inelasticity of tenures, and which, so it is argued, could only be overcome by the adoption of rational techniques of estate management, or—according to another school of thought— by an injection of income from the proceeds of office or business. Under the influence of these conceptions, historians have envisaged major shifts in the balance of economic, social, and political power in the century preceding the Civil War.[2] If such theories carry great scholarship behind them, they also seem in the light of present evidence to be built on very uncertain foundations. In the first place, our own study suggests that the basic premise of landlord embarrassment has been seriously overstated. Rent was not the landlord's only source of estate revenue, and proceeds from direct farming—not to mention timber sales and other receipts—were sometimes of much greater importance. Moreover, in spite of rigidities due to the prevailing system of land tenure, there were probably few estates where rental revenues remained inflexible for any length of time. In most districts, pressure of population created a constant need for additions to the cultivated area, while on demesne lands, if not on customary holdings, tenancies could be periodically renewed at greatly enhanced rents in money or in

---

[1] See sources listed in note 1, p. 111 *supra*; Kerridge, EcHR, 2nd Ser., VI, 1953, pp. 24–31; Hull, *thesis*, pp. 371, 380; Spratt, *thesis*, p. 216; Cliffe, *thesis*, p. 112; Finch, *op. cit.*, pp. 130, 157.

[2] R. H. Tawney, 'The Rise of the Gentry, 1558–1640', EcHR, XI, 1941, pp. 1–38; 'The Rise of the Gentry; A Postscript', EcHR, 2nd Ser., VII, 1954, pp. 91–7; L. Stone, 'The Anatomy of the Elizabethan Aristocracy', EcHR, XVIII, 1948, pp. 1–53; 'The Elizabethan Aristocracy: A Restatement', EcHR, 2nd Ser., IV, 1952, pp. 302–21; H. R. Trevor-Roper, 'The Elizabethan Aristocracy: An Anatomy Anatomised', EcHR, 2nd Ser., III, 1951, pp. 279–98; *The Gentry, 1540–1640*, EcHR, Supplement No. 1, 1953; J. P. Cooper, 'The Counting of Manors', EcHR, 2nd Ser., VIII, 1956, pp. 377–89; Finch, *op. cit.*, pp. xi–xix; Simpson, *op. cit.*, pp. 179–80, 210–16.

kind. On many properties, as we have seen, much of the burden of estate expenditure was placed upon the tenant; and in some instances large, highly-rented leasehold farms were created out of small holdings. Whatever doubts may linger about the landowner's position in the years before 1580, few can remain in connection with the succeeding period up to 1620, which saw a massive redistribution of income in favour of the landed class: a redistribution which, in the final analysis, was as much at the expense of the agricultural wage-earner and consumer as of the tenant farmer. Even after 1620 the rent-rolls of many landlords continued to increase, though on some estates rents on new commercial lettings, particularly of pasture land, remained stationary or declined. Not all landowners, of course, stayed prosperous, even under the highly favourable conditions of the late sixteenth and early seventeenth centuries; but not every landed family which declined did so because of poor estate management or because agricultural income failed to rise. Where these factors were operative, however, it may be suspected that the social class of the landowner—whether gentry or aristocracy—was of seldom more than marginal significance. In general, given the level of personal expenditure, the prosperity of the landowner in Tudor and early Stuart times must have depended much less upon his social origins than upon the nature of the land which constituted his estate and its sensitivity to economic change.

2

STATISTICAL APPENDIX

A. PRICE OF AGRICULTURAL COMMODITIES: ANNUAL AVERAGES

1450–99 = 100

Table I. *Price of arable crops*

INDEX NUMBER

Harvest year	Grains					Other arable crops					Average—all arable crops
	Wheat	Barley	Oats	Rye	Average—all grains	Hay	Straw	Peas	Beans	Average—all other arable crops	
1450	116	116	100	142	119	95	116	86	148	111	115
1451	112	100	94	121	107	108	112	73	98	98	102
1452	99	97	97	110	101	120	111	84	90	101	101
1453	87	116	106	68	94	105	100	109	97	103	99
1454	73	92	91	74	83	121	115	88	—	108	93
1455	94	102	102	—	99	—	—	55	—	55	88
1456	89	77	91	46	76	116	89	86	90	95	86
1457	116	99	94	103	103	87	118	81	90	94	99
1458	105	105	95	118	106	92	67	74	—	78	94
1459	93	100	100	84	94	146	116	104	104	118	106
1460	132	124	105	128	122	102	—	125	—	114	119
1461	138	115	120	—	124	108	102	108	—	106	115
1462	74	81	86	114	89	64	—	88	97	83	86
1463	60	70	79	59	67	59	69	53	92	68	68
1464	74	106	127	74	95	131	195	146	107	145	120
1465	83	130	106	96	104	95	122	106	110	108	106
1466	92	102	94	80	92	96	81	92	89	90	91
1467	106	97	88	109	98	129	86	94	104	103	101
1468	114	88	88	100	98	104	102	77	82	91	94
1469	114	80	103	121	105	110	105	113	97	106	105
1470	121	95	98	141	114	93	106	120	—	106	111
1471	112	112	109	99	108	84	102	111	—	99	104
1472	79	99	98	74	88	107	72	78	—	86	87

Table I (cont.)

Harvest year	Grains					Other arable crops					Average—all arable crops
	Wheat	Barley	Oats	Rye	Average—all grains	Hay	Straw	Peas	Beans	Average—all other arable crops	
1473	79	93	113	62	87	85	102	107	104	100	93
1474	82	72	90	74	80	88	102	92	—	94	86
1475	89	71	90	95	86	107	102	86	97	98	92
1476	89	72	93	74	82	97	102	126	71	99	91
1477	122	78	89	—	96	123	102	—	—	113	103
1478	130	90	97	101	105	152	—	109	97	119	111
1479	92	95	79	84	88	85	76	110	97	92	90
1480	94	95	79	98	92	76	—	—	119	98	94
1481	132	163	130	117	136	95	80	149	136	115	125
1482	177	184	116	196	168	98	65	220	—	128	151
1483	132	141	90	—	121	74	105	—	—	90	108
1484	98	105	102	96	100	74	110	120	97	100	100
1485	86	82	89	82	85	72	65	99	—	79	82
1486	96	109	103	160	117	75	87	104	—	89	105
1487	108	95	105	133	110	79	81	88	—	83	98
1488	106	113	144	102	116	104	105	103	148	115	116
1489	91	95	90	84	90	113	87	82	102	96	93
1490	127	86	98	168	120	85	86	119	—	97	110
1491	100	116	98	74	97	105	92	95	85	94	96
1492	89	117	143	102	113	85	81	—	—	83	103
1493	81	88	90	97	89	85	81	78	69	78	84
1494	70	77	87	71	76	99	105	73	77	89	82
1495	70	59	93	102	81	106	125	126	106	116	98
1496	103	79	101	124	102	108	106	82	85	95	99
1497	102	113	104	99	105	128	106	55	74	91	98
1498	99	114	134	74	105	135	151	121	124	133	119

1499	72	100	97	74	86	96	95	103	115	102	94
1500	126	113	104	136	120	91	96	—	100	96	109
1501	128	113	119	135	124	95	94	119	101	102	113
1502	147	109	111	184	138	96	89	—	75	87	116
1503	130	117	105	141	123	115	118	121	98	113	118
1504	98	152	127	110	122	110	121	102	—	111	117
1505	99	116	104	149	117	57	94	115	82	87	102
1506	98	95	95	102	98	78	88	106	91	91	94
1507	113	88	104	121	107	93	96	112	102	101	104
1508	85	102	105	83	94	84	118	89	83	94	94
1509	69	77	94	67	77	115	85	86	97	96	86
1510	81	82	97	88	87	100	83	72	69	81	84
1511	111	99	103	112	106	112	91	95	83	95	101
1512	144	93	108	109	114	99	111	90	89	97	105
1513	121	104	101	100	107	123	104	117	—	115	110
1514	102	127	121	132	121	90	102	96	—	96	110
1515	127	112	115	96	113	102	103	105	107	104	108
1516	105	106	124	108	111	113	125	137	145	130	120
1517	109	132	178	97	129	117	152	151	176	149	139
1518	97	114	121	120	113	121	157	159	128	141	127
1519	140	154	127	156	144	160	138	188	279	191	168
1520	191	175	170	235	193	97	181	251	132	165	179
1521	166	176	153	236	183	88	126	162	132	127	155
1522	104	124	121	—	116	94	93	140	136	116	116
1523	109	77	135	118	110	96	99	97	—	97	105
1524	99	121	142	101	116	126	114	132	113	121	119
1525	95	116	129	101	116	115	80	157	156	127	119
1526	110	168	146	—	141	102	135	177	195	152	148
1527	227	121	207	236	198	125	174	239	231	192	195
1528	175	146	138	269	182	89	81	—	158	109	151
1529	165	—	134	269	189	106	87	152	118	116	147
1530	130	160	129	172	148	85	124	115	127	113	130
1531	162	232	152	236	196	117	122	—	107	115	161
1532	150	162	173	267	188	97	173	173	146	147	168

Table I (cont.)

Harvest year	Grains					Other arable crops					Average—all arable crops
	Wheat	Barley	Oats	Rye	Average—all grains	Hay	Straw	Peas	Beans	Average—all other arable crops	
1533	133	127	156	202	155	120	127	160	153	140	147
1534	116	106	145	225	148	113	99	150	122	121	135
1535	213	199	184	303	225	133	118	164	169	146	185
1536	156	124	182	154	154	121	124	149	133	132	143
1537	108	151	139	93	123	81	146	—	119	115	120
1538	113	136	144	102	124	95	144	112	163	129	126
1539	116	184	144	149	148	103	122	112	133	118	133
1540	122	201	140	—	154	111	111	—	143	122	138
1541	146	166	147	—	153	145	108	165	175	148	150
1542	139	239	147	—	175	126	105	—	140	124	149
1543	185	—	143	—	164	120	105	—	154	126	141
1544	192	—	192	—	192	138	119	—	178	145	164
1545	288	319	251	—	286	115	116	199	—	143	215
1546	139	142	200	—	160	131	119	—	166	139	150
1547	99	118	172	—	130	133	121	168	150	143	137
1548	138	—	186	—	162	197	133	—	—	165	164
1549	265	—	330	—	298	181	147	—	256	195	236
1550	294	—	411	—	353	259	212	—	469	313	329
1551	329	—	297	—	313	—	252	—	—	252	293
1552	204	302	337	—	281	277	255	—	332	288	285
1553	179	377	282	—	279	171	250	—	147	190	234
1554	267	—	413	—	340	328	304	—	171	268	297
1555	383	805	374	—	521	327	143	389	461	330	412
1556	528	582	564	—	558	164	184	454	469	318	421
1557	194	237	275	—	235	198	200	226	—	208	222
1558	179	402	270	—	284	160	168	—	256	195	239

1559	291	—	336	—	314	259	260	—	231	250	275
1560	339	340	331	—	337	278	225	224	—	242	290
1561	271	260	356	—	296	319	283	—	338	313	305
1562	426	331	358	—	372	185	472	—	394	350	361
1563	275	436	317	—	343	370	345	316	410	360	353
1564	244	283	247	—	258	257	253	211	211	233	244
1565	394	298	313	—	335	294	259	232	287	268	260
1566	247	252	302	—	267	303	267	244	242	264	265
1567	235	455	313	281	321	360	273	332	372	334	328
1568	252	393	378	395	355	383	307	265	—	318	339
1569	243	—	310	—	277	260	241	241	279	255	262
1570	265	296	291	345	299	267	248	239	220	244	271
1571	288	252	272	406	305	266	255	198	221	235	270
1572	301	343	298	531	368	349	283	269	248	287	328
1573	427	427	417	639	478	285	271	388	495	360	419
1574	328	323	285	399	334	342	234	346	396	330	332
1575	348	467	319	—	378	322	263	235	214	259	310
1576	411	—	306	—	359	302	280	294	326	301	320
1577	369	428	375	—	391	268	263	265	302	275	324
1578	309	345	407	426	372	353	261	269	222	276	324
1579	310	—	461	470	414	280	324	321	—	308	361
1580	379	537	405	456	444	321	296	304	310	308	376
1581	381	—	439	483	434	298	302	300	325	306	361
1582	333	429	396	531	422	340	300	323	316	320	371
1583	316	394	406	365	370	379	293	277	350	325	348
1584	299	409	374	213	324	274	286	364	307	308	316
1585	427	547	472	777	556	244	281	449	481	364	460
1586	626	697	709	703	684	299	285	500	594	420	552
1587	331	361	403	—	365	300	242	370	325	309	333
1588	320	399	502	—	407	276	206	435	312	307	350
1589	437	568	465	652	531	315	254	328	351	312	421
1590	394	720	757	—	624	444	405	592	541	496	550
1591	304	451	573	—	443	306	349	—	383	346	394
1592	295	287	392	210	296	391	365	298	317	343	319

Table I (*cont.*)

Harvest year	Grains					Other arable crops					Average—all arable crops
	Wheat	Barley	Oats	Rye	Average—all grains	Hay	Straw	Peas	Beans	Average—all other arable crops	
1593	388	379	417	216	350	434	423	322	371	388	369
1594	578	520	765	—	621	343	504	506	412	441	518
1595	607	740	574	801	681	489	414	443	487	458	569
1596	811	971	1148	1227	1039	352	436	788	816	598	819
1597	746	779	718	869	778	337	400	585	615	484	631
1598	462	545	535	531	518	323	310	376	356	341	430
1599	407	617	498	706	557	428	403	366	347	386	472
1600	485	816	962	808	768	556	449	548	537	523	645
1601	416	583	526	693	555	504	360	387	525	444	499
1602	432	617	419	450	480	431	323	381	337	368	424
1603	391	338	502	450	420	492	388	357	372	402	411
1604	434	487	581	—	501	510	338	369	450	417	453
1605	401	639	589	—	543	521	529	369	444	466	499
1606	447	506	523	—	492	488	409	385	346	407	443
1607	571	571	519	—	554	658	438	428	479	501	523
1608	715	527	721	—	654	581	448	493	601	531	584
1609	493	759	648	—	633	477	493	530	441	485	549
1610	495	534	633	—	554	561	422	432	440	464	502
1611	545	698	853	—	699	541	663	577	619	600	642
1612	606	792	810	—	736	504	742	593	831	668	697
1613	667	788	721	—	725	466	431	565	—	487	606
1614	504	752	695	—	650	568	504	436	540	512	571
1615	574	749	924	—	749	950	660	592	769	743	745
1616	590	664	717	—	657	529	532	698	469	557	600
1617	647	624	616	747	659	561	519	465	419	491	575
1618	517	565	603	659	586	509	547	412	389	464	525

1619	450	493	661	—	535	589	545	492	461	522	527
1620	366	391	539	—	432	667	548	427	461	526	486
1621	598	670	730	—	666	466	580	513	512	518	581
1622	763	886	596	845	773	634	532	499	528	548	660
1623	573	648	599	845	666	564	502	424	538	507	587
1624	625	614	607	690	634	672	520	524	552	567	601
1625	637	745	768	764	729	535	494	621	751	600	664
1626	521	577	517	798	603	579	494	325	472	468	535
1627	427	443	532	615	504	481	507	388	478	464	484
1628	525	690	667	889	693	—	551	515	717	594	651
1629	609	825	741	717	723	659	674	688	632	663	693
1630	881	1277	1034	—	1064	610	603	873	—	695	880
1631	630	689	639	—	653	489	517	430	820	564	602
1632	684	795	663	1031	793	651	531	459	769	602	698
1633	686	812	754	1024	819	549	575	574	—	566	711
1634	668	862	745	902	794	1454	574	563	—	864	824
1635	645	792	900	331	667	643	612	582	—	612	644
1636	645	817	824	720	752	631	668	741	819	715	733
1637	750	1225	1004	1146	1031	905	687	842	1189	906	969
1638	575	899	764	808	762	549	529	556	—	545	669
1639	507	602	597	—	569	725	488	393	—	535	552
1640	615	728	781	—	708	568	567	536	—	557	633
1641	574	657	717	—	649	684	542	435	513	544	589
1642	616	637	666	—	640	811	547	576	487	605	620
1643	542	582	571	—	565	710	638	412	—	587	576
1644	546	574	680	—	600	539	640	515	614	577	587
1645	590	634	764	—	663	573	512	502	413	500	570
1646	804	736	1000	—	847	571	650	582	922	681	752
1647	997	1191	1085	—	1091	864	596	822	—	761	926
1648	943	1135	1140	—	1073	1250	668	839	—	919	996
1649	942	1097	1030	—	1023	1106	756	998	774	909	958

Table II. *Price of cattle and sheep*

INDEX NUMBER

Harvest year	Cattle				Sheep			
	Oxen	Cows and heifers	Calves	Average—all cattle	Wethers	Type unspecified	Lambs	Average—all sheep
1450	105	—	99	102	106	—	75	91
1451	124	—	70	97	67	—	—	67
1452	112	79	106	99	80	—	—	80
1453	107	69	77	84	68	—	120	94
1454	100	90	73	88	74	79	87	80
1455	111	94	—	103	83	—	101	92
1456	122	87	106	105	81	108	91	93
1457	101	82	111	98	71	56	87	71
1458	115	95	106	105	91	99	85	92
1459	106	93	108	102	88	—	77	83
1460	103	118	61	94	96	—	82	89
1461	108	—	102	105	101	—	—	101
1462	63	98	98	86	84	—	81	83
1463	112	88	101	100	110	—	110	110
1464	92	115	93	100	109	—	135	122
1465	104	113	105	107	98	105	116	106
1466	115	109	95	106	90	113	101	101
1467	105	136	136	126	67	130	109	102
1468	73	113	117	101	—	91	115	103
1469	82	102	113	99	—	103	127	115
1470	127	107	122	119	—	—	104	104
1471	92	113	132	112	—	—	—	—
1472	104	—	125	115	—	104	121	113

Year								
1473	115	109	95	106	133	97	132	121
1474	124	—	—	124	91	—	—	91
1475	109	114	—	112	105	—	—	105
1476	97	115	88	100	80	87	108	92
1477	92	—	—	92	84	—	40	62
1478	109	110	101	107	93	91	118	101
1479	97	81	—	89	—	—	57	57
1480	85	—	—	85	63	—	53	58
1481	107	95	111	104	120	—	93	107
1482	85	103	92	93	210	108	134	151
1483	115	129	133	126	147	128	80	118
1484	—	156	124	140	126	—	80	103
1485	—	115	—	115	98	—	80	89
1486	113	—	—	113	113	—	168	141
1487	80	97	100	92	103	—	138	121
1488	98	90	99	96	99	—	131	115
1489	90	—	74	82	116	—	98	107
1490	72	82	111	88	112	—	201	157
1491	113	—	—	113	114	—	—	114
1492	88	80	59	76	101	—	90	96
1493	—	97	—	97	—	—	101	101
1494	75	67	111	93	116	—	—	116
1495	128	80	55	83	113	—	72	93
1496	76	80	63	73	112	—	64	88
1497	91	80	96	89	92	—	120	106
1498	74	101	135	103	101	—	50	76
1499	87	—	—	87	92	—	70	81
1500	99	89	66	85	109	75	—	92
1501	100	104	68	91	104	—	63	84
1502	93	82	100	92	114	103	47	88
1503	120	—	77	99	63	97	84	81
1504	107	96	—	102	98	—	65	82
1505	108	110	—	109	100	—	76	88
1506	—	88	116	102	92	101	128	107

Table II (*cont.*)

Harvest year	Cattle				Sheep			
	Oxen	Cows and heifers	Calves	Average—all cattle	Wethers	Type unspecified	Lambs	Average—all sheep
1507	121	64	115	100	116	103	105	108
1508	141	—	—	141	130	99	105	111
1509	137	75	102	105	113	107	105	108
1510	103	75	91	90	121	108	105	111
1511	102	79	125	102	138	—	105	122
1512	—	71	139	105	138	—	161	150
1513	—	87	—	87	131	—	85	108
1514	—	107	—	107	165	—	122	144
1515	97	87	170	118	146	—	105	126
1516	94	—	197	146	155	—	136	146
1517	138	—	156	147	142	106	136	128
1518	162	92	150	135	126	—	122	124
1519	159	162	148	156	141	123	105	123
1520	158	—	—	158	152	213	156	174
1521	156	126	97	126	144	—	—	144
1522	163	—	—	163	143	—	—	143
1523	154	—	—	154	130	—	—	130
1524	140	95	112	116	139	103	132	125
1525	108	—	123	116	121	—	—	121
1526	126	—	—	126	151	106	150	136
1527	140	—	161	151	131	—	—	131
1528	153	—	168	161	137	—	—	137
1529	149	—	173	161	151	117	—	134
1530	153	149	109	137	178	159	169	169
1531	181	161	164	169	180	196	175	184
1532	164	142	—	153	139	—	159	149
1533	103	147	108	119	144	138	172	151

Year								
1534	151	—	—	151	179	—	—	179
1535	149	—	128	139	157	107	181	148
1536	169	148	153	157	172	144	164	160
1537	168	142	—	155	174	159	—	167
1538	151	155	—	153	180	102	—	141
1539	152	127	135	140	112	177	109	133
1540	154	168	142	152	167	213	—	190
1541	172	174	174	163	168	168	158	165
1542	170	123	—	156	179	222	—	201
1543	171	—	144	171	150	239	—	195
1544	175	—	158	160	183	167	245	198
1545	192	—	—	175	214	184	191	196
1546	173	112	148	143	226	293	201	240
1547	244	221	178	204	298	233	201	244
1548	249	219	163	215	224	266	226	239
1549	249	183	202	198	258	223	202	228
1550	282	293	194	259	361	266	318	315
1551	319	280	279	264	320	291	227	279
1552	243	210	220	244	292	198	175	222
1553	247	202	177	223	272	196	213	227
1554	247	—	260	212	260	182	169	204
1555	325	188	302	258	320	204	250	258
1556	335	381	240	339	—	271	314	293
1557	313	—	268	277	381	228	246	285
1558	277	301	243	282	281	216	269	255
1559	343	329	266	305	316	267	—	292
1560	298	207	280	257	349	275	285	303
1561	321	328	278	310	342	292	292	309
1562	285	323	—	295	367	331	350	349
1563	256	306	327	281	407	315	—	361
1564	290	284	—	300	343	256	350	316
1565	272	294	346	283	263	265	254	261
1566	255	274	292	292	316	321	321	319
1567	250	314	—	285	287	265	303	285

Table II (cont.)

Harvest year	Cattle				Sheep			
	Oxen	Cows and heifers	Calves	Average—all cattle	Wethers	Type unspecified	Lambs	Average—all sheep
1568	279	254	345	293	259	307	374	313
1569	285	337	301	308	318	293	287	299
1570	257	—	320	289	381	292	419	364
1571	328	360	313	334	414	296	—	355
1572	290	406	319	338	359	307	449	372
1573	338	469	286	364	396	342	421	386
1574	379	502	324	402	447	366	—	407
1575	392	416	386	398	390	367	—	379
1576	311	—	367	339	410	366	—	388
1577	314	—	444	379	372	368	439	393
1578	395	—	402	399	356	368	—	362
1579	305	—	370	338	433	360	—	397
1580	312	—	405	359	464	389	—	427
1581	339	—	388	364	501	391	316	446
1582	329	303	378	337	337	385	366	346
1583	353	439	381	391	374	397	391	379
1584	383	376	351	370	357	381	363	376
1585	434	496	382	437	292	379	363	345
1586	381	477	381	413	396	375	392	388
1587	397	576	314	429	388	413	402	401
1588	358	426	361	382	338	387	464	396
1589	339	462	426	409	399	434	411	415
1590	361	414	421	399	512	466	535	504
1591	394	405	401	400	619	444	495	519
1592	384	505	449	446	605	476	517	533
1593	392	471	441	435	453	467	447	456
1594	444	548	475	489	350	502	420	424

Year								
1595	452	522	476	483	352	512	423	429
1596	502	562	442	502	445	524	449	473
1597	473	680	468	540	343	510	420	424
1598	488	593	450	510	—	503	437	470
1599	393	469	462	441	—	511	437	474
1600	470	—	468	469	589	525	616	577
1601	456	408	478	447	—	482	445	464
1602	423	556	455	478	—	476	—	476
1603	446	559	448	484	—	503	—	503
1604	432	—	464	448	—	503	—	503
1605	477	512	467	485	—	504	446	475
1606	423	627	519	523	—	480	596	538
1607	440	634	501	525	—	477	418	448
1608	475	629	506	537	—	505	456	481
1609	460	—	533	497	—	523	447	485
1610	506	575	519	533	—	491	426	459
1611	495	537	551	528	—	518	410	464
1612	489	500	518	502	—	539	515	527
1613	475	667	535	559	—	548	514	531
1614	509	795	510	605	—	540	497	489
1615	502	621	512	545	431	535	552	544
1616	528	—	531	530	454	537	532	508
1617	551	698	493	581	613	525	568	569
1618	569	658	535	587	608	563	569	580
1619	532	568	564	555	667	570	484	574
1620	457	584	—	521	380	489	487	452
1621	468	—	506	487	—	531	498	515
1622	454	501	534	496	594	532	512	546
1623	456	597	488	514	—	551	423	487
1624	547	399	537	494	—	580	533	557
1625	567	679	556	601	510	582	541	544
1626	576	657	580	604	687	591	567	615
1627	521	683	575	593	685	577	580	614
1628	532	597	—	565	686	568	590	615

Table II (cont.)

Harvest year	Cattle				Sheep			
	Oxen	Cows and heifers	Calves	Average—all cattle	Wethers	Type unspecified	Lambs	Average—all sheep
1629	499	616	618	578	813	574	486	624
1630	512	630	627	590	786	584	514	628
1631	511	646	626	594	635	572	631	613
1632	546	727	591	621	580	580	444	535
1633	569	798	653	673	600	553	532	562
1634	519	734	—	627	652	553	526	577
1635	630	755	—	693	641	582	548	590
1636	557	712	743	671	692	565	563	607
1637	586	765	—	676	604	560	553	572
1638	555	999	535	696	664	559	588	604
1639	568	676	—	622	647	557	526	577
1640	562	650	564	592	581	592	550	574
1641	567	—	505	536	—	542	769	656
1642	473	1046	882	800	653	542	713	636
1643	451	581	743	592	569	542	577	563
1644	498	636	772	635	595	686	582	621
1645	619	744	831	731	831	655	805	764
1646	682	1057	817	852	796	605	—	701
1647	703	970	—	837	807	—	—	807
1648	761	902	861	841	934	558	790	761
1649	687	823	624	711	892	561	—	727

Table III. *Price of poultry and rabbits*

INDEX NUMBER

Harvest year	Capons and hens	Geese and ducks	Average— all poultry	Rabbits	Average— poultry and rabbits
1450	102	99	101	—	101
1451	103	100	102	99	101
1452	103	99	101	—	101
1453	102	99	101	—	101
1454	103	99	101	—	101
1455	100	99	100	—	100
1456	101	99	100	—	100
1457	100	99	100	—	100
1458	101	99	100	122	107
1459	102	99	101	—	101
1460	102	99	101	—	101
1461	102	121	112	—	112
1462	108	102	105	—	105
1463	103	99	101	—	101
1464	102	103	103	—	103
1465	101	97	99	107	102
1466	100	99	100	—	100
1467	99	92	96	84	92
1468	101	99	100	—	100
1469	102	99	101	—	101
1470	101	—	101	—	101
1471	101	—	101	—	101
1472	101	—	101	—	101
1473	101	99	100	—	100
1474	101	125	113	—	113
1475	101	99	100	—	100
1476	103	99	101	—	101
1477	101	—	101	—	101
1478	102	117	110	107	109
1479	101	99	100	115	105
1480	101	96	99	—	99
1481	101	102	102	107	103
1482	104	99	102	—	102
1483	—	—	—	—	—
1484	101	99	100	—	100
1485	84	99	92	92	92
1486	104	—	104	—	104
1487	97	—	97	92	95
1488	104	—	104	99	102
1489	—	—	—	—	—
1490	—	—	—	99	99

Table III (*cont.*)

Harvest year	Capons and hens	Geese and ducks	Average— all poultry	Rabbits	Average— poultry and rabbits
1491	—	—	—	—	—
1492	97	99	98	—	98
1493	101	—	101	—	101
1494	—	—	—	—	—
1495	101	—	101	92	97
1496	92	75	84	115	94
1497	92	72	82	—	82
1498	89	117	103	92	99
1499	91	—	91	84	88
1500	107	123	115	99	110
1501	101	99	100	53	84
1502	101	99	100	84	95
1503	148	132	140	—	140
1504	225	—	225	—	225
1505	161	—	161	—	161
1506	106	180	143	—	143
1507	—	104	104	107	106
1508	—	—	—	—	—
1509	139	105	122	130	125
1510	103	79	91	—	91
1511	77	66	72	—	72
1512	101	86	94	—	94
1513	101	72	87	—	87
1514	101	87	94	—	94
1515	—	87	87	—	87
1516	101	86	94	—	94
1517	101	83	92	—	92
1518	—	111	111	69	90
1519	101	108	105	115	108
1520	101	—	101	—	101
1521	109	—	109	—	109
1522	109	—	109	—	109
1523	—	—	—	—	—
1524	—	—	—	—	—
1525	—	—	—	—	—
1526	—	—	—	—	—
1527	—	—	—	—	—
1528	—	—	—	—	—
1529	131	—	131	—	131
1530	101	—	101	122	112
1531	107	—	107	—	107
1532	153	—	153	—	153
1533	147	128	138	—	138

Table III (cont.)

Harvest year	Capons and hens	Geese and ducks	Average— all poultry	Rabbits	Average— poultry and rabbits
1534	—	—	—	—	—
1535	—	84	84	122	103
1536	—	—	—	—	—
1537	—	—	—	—	—
1538	—	—	—	—	—
1539	—	180	180	—	180
1540	208	180	194	198	195
1541	231	179	205	153	188
1542	169	165	167	137	157
1543	161	—	161	145	153
1544	295	291	293	145	244
1545	243	186	215	160	196
1546	253	171	212	153	192
1547	258	168	213	221	216
1548	276	221	249	221	239
1549	293	291	292	206	263
1550	262	—	262	237	250
1551	235	—	235	—	235
1552	—	—	—	—	—
1553	—	249	249	168	209
1554	483	—	483	168	326
1555	347	—	347	229	288
1556	—	216	216	168	192
1557	425	282	354	191	299
1558	272	—	272	168	220
1559	379	—	379	214	297
1560	388	249	319	183	273
1561	332	249	291	221	267
1562	352	300	326	198	283
1563	—	—	—	252	252
1564	326	276	301	221	274
1565	289	279	284	221	263
1566	315	—	315	214	265
1567	—	—	—	221	221
1568	292	294	293	214	267
1569	—	—	—	244	244
1570	—	—	—	214	214
1571	336	278	307	260	291
1572	470	351	411	252	358
1573	393	345	369	252	330
1574	386	374	380	412	391
1575	393	—	393	260	327
1576	383	318	351	260	320

Table III (cont.)

Harvest year	Capons and hens	Geese and ducks	Average— all poultry	Rabbits	Average— poultry and rabbits
1577	341	314	328	275	310
1578	339	315	327	275	310
1579	406	351	379	275	344
1580	356	300	328	275	310
1581	—	—	—	305	305
1582	275	272	274	282	276
1583	283	281	282	305	290
1584	282	304	293	290	292
1585	302	321	312	298	307
1586	355	263	309	366	328
1587	436	315	372	290	347
1588	343	258	301	267	289
1589	339	273	306	336	316
1590	388	255	322	305	316
1591	404	296	350	237	312
1592	305	329	317	298	311
1593	339	486	413	275	367
1594	493	293	393	336	374
1595	406	470	438	366	414
1596	379	384	382	313	359
1597	—	420	420	328	374
1598	—	419	419	336	378
1599	384	697	541	344	475
1600	426	498	462	344	423
1601	534	404	469	359	432
1602	548	405	477	336	430
1603	417	385	401	389	397
1604	514	351	433	344	403
1605	312	261	287	—	287
1606	—	327	327	366	347
1607	439	374	407	389	401
1608	581	429	505	397	469
1609	671 ·	619	645	260	517
1610	—	426	426	427	427
1611	—	502	502	496	499
1612	—	464	464	504	484
1613	— .	583	583	420	502
1614	567	547	557	435	516
1615	443	449	446	435	442
1616	661	449	555	458	523
1617	464	441	453	389	431
1618	475	547	511	443	488
1619	408	492	450	450	450

Table III (*cont.*)

Harvest year	Capons and hens	Geese and ducks	Average— all poultry	Rabbits	Average— poultry and rabbits
1620	443	519	481	389	450
1621	409	534	472	420	454
1622	502	444	473	443	463
1623	782	489	636	450	574
1624	737	429	583	435	534
1625	611	498	555	397	502
1626	705	—	705	374	540
1627	695	—	695	443	569
1628	802	381	592	344	509
1629	718	—	718	389	554
1630	—	—	—	321	321
1631	852	—	852	427	640
1632	701	—	701	—	701
1633	785	—	785	—	785
1634	805	—	805	—	805
1635	762	—	762	—	762
1636	782	—	782	519	651
1637	—	—	—	—	—
1638	768	874	821	427	690
1639	782	—	782	—	782
1640	579	599	589	466	548
1641	662	646	654	389	566
1642	609	851	730	504	655
1643	702	806	754	458	655
1644	745	637	691	443	608
1645	601	941	771	466	669
1646	—	—	—	—	—
1647	—	—	—	—	—
1648	—	—	—	—	—
1649	—	—	—	519	519

Table IV. *Price of livestock*

INDEX NUMBER

Harvest year	Sheep	Cattle	Horses	Pigs	Poultry and rabbits	Average—all livestock
1450	91	102	101	91	101	97
1451	67	97	98	100	101	93
1452	80	99	148	96	101	105
1453	94	84	113	98	101	98
1454	80	88	86	95	101	90
1455	92	103	97	95	100	97
1456	93	105	109	77	100	97
1457	71	98	81	93	100	89
1458	92	105	97	88	107	98
1459	83	102	113	105	101	101
1460	89	94	78	96	101	92
1461	101	105	64	115	112	99
1462	83	86	196	103	105	115
1463	110	100	—	100	101	103
1464	122	100	—	89	103	104
1465	106	107	58	105	102	96
1466	101	106	73	105	100	97
1467	102	126	135	102	92	111
1468	103	101	77	110	100	98
1469	115	99	—	107	101	106
1470	104	119	70	113	101	101
1471	—	112	94	102	101	102
1472	113	115	143	109	101	116
1473	121	106	86	114	100	105
1474	91	124	86	86	113	100
1475	105	112	102	84	100	101
1476	92	100	59	90	101	88
1477	62	92	—	98	101	88
1478	101	107	69	96	109	96
1479	57	89	69	109	105	86
1480	58	85	96	112	99	90
1481	107	104	111	123	103	110
1482	151	93	157	115	102	124
1483	118	126	72	—	—	105
1484	103	140	149	100	100	118
1485	89	115	84	80	92	92
1486	141	113	73	106	104	107
1487	121	92	77	106	95	98
1488	115	96	133	100	102	109
1489	107	82	104	93	—	97
1490	157	88	123	117	99	117
1491	114	113	115	110	—	113

Table IV (cont.)

Harvest year	Sheep	Cattle	Horses	Pigs	Poultry and rabbits	Average—all livestock
1492	96	76	84	112	98	93
1493	101	97	128	—	101	107
1494	116	93	—	86	—	98
1495	93	83	112	117	97	100
1496	88	73	72	82	94	82
1497	106	89	86	109	82	94
1498	76	103	102	61	99	88
1499	81	87	115	118	88	98
1500	92	85	83	92	110	92
1501	84	91	107	114	84	96
1502	88	92	99	99	95	95
1503	81	99	78	80	140	96
1504	82	102	89	125	225	125
1505	88	109	109	149	161	123
1506	107	102	139	142	143	127
1507	108	100	127	118	106	112
1508	111	141	148	99	—	125
1509	108	105	162	96	125	119
1510	111	90	94	91	91	95
1511	122	102	70	122	72	98
1512	150	105	117	128	94	119
1513	108	87	101	153	87	107
1514	144	107	100	158	94	121
1515	126	118	138	121	87	118
1516	146	146	144	110	94	128
1517	128	147	110	163	92	128
1518	124	135	101	144	90	119
1519	123	156	111	161	108	132
1520	174	158	151	127	101	142
1521	144	126	138	178	109	139
1522	143	163	153	197	109	153
1523	130	154	150	118	—	138
1524	125	116	103	121	—	116
1525	121	116	133	142	—	128
1526	136	126	142	146	—	138
1527	131	151	110	138	—	133
1528	137	161	—	157	—	152
1529	134	161	153	114	131	139
1530	169	137	105	126	112	130
1531	184	169	157	117	107	147
1532	149	153	121	140	153	143
1533	151	119	97	134	138	128
1534	179	151	197	127	—	164
1535	148	139	118	133	103	128

Table IV (cont.)

Harvest year	Sheep	Cattle	Horses	Pigs	Poultry and rabbits	Average— all livestock
1536	160	157	—	144	—	154
1537	167	155	174	103	—	150
1538	141	153	148	94	—	134
1539	133	140	154	126	180	147
1540	190	152	88	130	195	151
1541	165	163	196	139	188	170
1542	201	156	180	141	157	167
1543	195	171	154	144	153	163
1544	198	160	—	—	244	201
1545	196	175	169	146	196	176
1546	240	143	167	138	192	176
1547	244	204	196	164	216	205
1548	239	215	293	164	239	230
1549	228	198	209	169	263	213
1550	315	259	280	184	250	258
1551	279	264	307	292	235	275
1552	222	244	206	352	—	256
1553	227	223	193	219	209	214
1554	204	212	258	243	326	249
1555	258	258	225	228	288	251
1556	293	339	216	447	192	297
1557	285	277	293	220	299	275
1558	255	282	271	256	220	257
1559	292	305	241	140	297	255
1560	303	257	259	382	273	295
1561	309	310	243	171	267	260
1562	349	295	283	216	283	285
1563	361	281	277	—	252	293
1564	316	300	279	170	274	268
1565	261	283	237	197	263	248
1566	319	292	220	394	265	298
1567	285	285	273	309	221	275
1568	313	293	287	317	267	295
1569	299	308	306	—	244	289
1570	364	289	299	373	214	308
1571	355	334	276	244	291	300
1572	372	338	329	231	358	326
1573	386	364	304	307	330	338
1574	407	402	343	292	391	367
1575	379	398	329	296	327	346
1576	388	339	412	238	320	339
1577	393	379	334	285	310	340
1578	362	399	382	428	310	376
1579	397	338	253	279	344	322

Table IV (*cont.*)

Harvest year	Sheep	Cattle	Horses	Pigs	Poultry and rabbits	Average—all livestock
1580	427	359	346	302	310	349
1581	446	364	392	—	305	377
1582	346	337	539	235	276	347
1583	379	391	331	242	290	327
1584	376	370	342	275	292	331
1585	345	437	380	261	307	346
1586	388	413	350	258	328	347
1587	401	429	371	284	347	366
1588	396	382	441	269	289	355
1589	415	409	450	292	316	376
1590	504	399	398	267	316	377
1591	519	400	415	266	312	382
1592	533	446	399	263	311	390
1593	456	435	389	264	367	382
1594	424	489	461	—	374	437
1595	429	483	481	289	414	419
1596	473	502	401	298	359	407
1597	424	540	490	390	374	444
1598	470	510	548	381	378	457
1599	474	441	454	368	475	442
1600	577	469	486	415	423	474
1601	464	447	468	361	432	434
1602	476	478	395	363	430	428
1603	503	484	396	349	397	426
1604	503	448	411	347	403	422
1605	475	485	409	407	287	413
1606	538	523	478	441	347	465
1607	448	525	524	361	401	452
1608	481	537	485	390	469	472
1609	485	497	605	498	517	520
1610	459	533	473	431	427	465
1611	464	528	615	430	499	507
1612	527	502	520	397	484	486
1613	531	559	539	448	502	516
1614	489	605	561	439	516	522
1615	544	545	593	534	442	532
1616	508	530	435	487	523	497
1617	569	581	460	494	431	507
1618	580	587	548	449	488	530
1619	574	555	455	486	450	504
1620	452	521	526	426	450	475
1621	515	487	544	468	454	494
1622	546	496	539	436	463	496
1623	487	514	578	387	574	508

Table IV (cont.)

Harvest year	Sheep	Cattle	Horses	Pigs	Poultry and rabbits	Average—all livestock
1624	557	494	577	384	534	509
1625	544	601	665	368	502	536
1626	615	604	618	531	540	582
1627	614	593	523	445	569	549
1628	615	565	558	389	509	527
1629	624	578	587	499	554	568
1630	628	590	702	511	321	550
1631	613	594	623	596	640	613
1632	535	621	714	567	701	628
1633	562	673	566	572	785	632
1634	577	627	638	598	805	649
1635	590	693	676	661	762	676
1636	607	671	711	582	651	644
1637	572	676	656	602	—	627
1638	604	696	668	605	690	653
1639	577	622	569	600	782	630
1640	574	592	682	589	548	597
1641	656	536	669	587	566	603
1642	636	800	691	581	655	673
1643	563	592	507	611	655	586
1644	621	635	442	598	608	581
1645	764	731	648	510	669	664
1646	701	852	771	—	—	775
1647	807	837	703	591	—	735
1648	761	841	724	—	—	775
1649	727	711	918	534	519	682

Table V. Price of animal products
INDEX NUMBER

Harvest year	Dairy products and eggs						Wool, fells, and hides				Average—all animal products
	Milk and cream	Butter	Cheese	Average—all dairy products	Eggs	Average—all dairy products and eggs	Wool	Sheepskins and wool fells	Cattle hides	Average—wool, fells, and hides	
1450	59	—	—	59	101	80	91	83	74	83	82
1451	—	—	—	—	101	101	70	54	58	61	81
1452	59	106	—	83	101	89	71	77	94	81	85
1453	—	106	—	106	101	104	71	63	106	80	92
1454	59	106	—	83	101	89	80	94	100	91	90
1455	—	106	—	106	101	104	80	60	151	97	101
1456	—	—	—	—	101	101	95	89	105	96	99
1457	—	—	—	—	—	—	85	80	103	89	89
1458	—	—	—	—	—	—	89	76	114	93	93
1459	—	106	—	106	—	106	91	71	104	89	98
1460	—	—	—	—	101	101	84	67	106	86	94
1461	—	—	—	—	—	—	99	—	—	99	99
1462	—	—	91	91	—	91	102	—	—	102	97
1463	—	—	91	91	101	96	152	—	—	152	124
1464	—	—	91	91	101	96	118	—	43	81	89
1465	—	—	—	—	101	—	115	—	111	113	107
1466	—	—	91	91	101	96	118	148	94	120	108
1467	—	—	—	—	101	101	116	161	99	125	113
1468	—	—	—	—	101	101	100	122	114	112	107
1469	—	—	—	—	101	101	89	130	118	112	107
1470	—	—	—	—	101	101	97	—	—	97	99
1471	—	—	—	—	101	101	104	—	—	104	103
1472	—	—	—	—	101	101	109	95	104	103	102

Table V (*cont.*)

Harvest year	Dairy products and eggs						Wool, fells, and hides				Average—all animal products
	Milk and cream	Butter	Cheese	Average—all dairy products	Eggs	Average—all dairy products and eggs	Wool	Sheepskins and wool fells	Cattle hides	Average—wool, fells, and hides	
1473	—	—	—	—	101	101	109	129	—	119	110
1474	—	—	—	—	101	101	99	108	—	104	103
1475	—	—	—	—	101	101	97	116	99	104	103
1476	—	—	—	—	101	101	99	82	—	91	96
1477	—	—	—	—	101	101	92	103	—	98	100
1478	—	—	105	105	101	103	99	103	65	89	96
1479	—	—	—	—	101	101	84	118	—	101	101
1480	—	—	—	—	101	101	88	—	—	88	95
1481	—	108	—	108	101	105	107	—	103	105	105
1482	—	98	111	105	101	103	122	—	—	122	113
1483	—	98	111	105	—	105	128	—	73	101	103
1484	—	98	111	105	—	105	132	—	—	132	119
1485	—	98	111	105	—	105	117	—	—	117	111
1486	—	98	111	105	—	105	116	90	—	103	104
1487	—	94	93	103	89	98	104	—	—	104	101
1488	—	98	111	96	—	96	101	140	87	109	103
1489	118	100	111	110	—	110	112	159	93	121	116
1490	—	95	83	89	—	89	88	—	—	88	89
1491	—	98	111	105	—	105	100	—	—	100	103
1492	—	—	—	—	96	96	83	—	132	108	102
1493	—	—	—	—	96	96	97	—	—	97	97
1494	—	85	—	85	—	85	101	—	114	108	97
1495	—	103	—	103	96	100	101	—	—	101	101
1496	167	104	—	136	—	136	99	90	—	95	116
1497	138	94	—	116	—	116	101	—	138	120	118

Year	C1	C2	C3	C4	C5	C6	C7	C8	C9	C10	C11
1498	97	95	—	—	95	99	96	102	—	102	—
1499	87	93	—	95	91	81	—	81	64	98	—
1500	104	115	179	75	92	92	92	—	—	—	—
1501	107	107	134	96	90	106	96	109	93	131	102
1502	98	104	123	101	87	92	93	91	91	—	—
1503	100	104	117	97	97	96	96	—	—	—	—
1504	109	111	139	95	98	106	—	106	—	106	—
1505	92	102	128	95	83	82	96	75	—	88	62
1506	101	104	116	115	81	97	96	97	—	88	106
1507	97	107	121	110	91	86	96	82	—	91	72
1508	104	113	121	116	101	94	—	94	—	94	—
1509	104	114	139	97	107	94	98	90	—	90	—
1510	107	116	119	120	109	97	98	95	—	95	—
1511	108	111	116	114	103	104	119	88	—	88	—
1512	112	109	—	—	109	115	142	88	—	88	—
1513	113	118	—	129	107	107	126	88	—	88	—
1514	108	119	169	—	119	97	117	87	—	88	—
1515	128	152	192	—	135	103	117	88	86	108	—
1516	134	154	—	142	129	113	117	108	—	88	—
1517	122	141	171	—	141	103	117	88	—	88	—
1518	123	142	171	—	113	104	117	98	—	88	—
1519	127	149	—	—	126	104	117	99	102	88	107
1520	112	117	—	—	117	107	—	107	125	88	107
1521	103	106	—	108	103	99	—	99	107	88	107
1522	104	122	—	—	122	86	—	86	62	89	102
1523	85	94	162	—	94	75	—	75	—	75	107
1524	97	96	162	—	96	97	—	97	97	88	—
1525	119	141	—	—	119	96	—	96	86	106	105
1526	111	144	—	—	126	77	—	77	—	94	—
1527	111	110	—	—	110	112	—	112	122	95	59
1528	112	121	—	—	121	102	—	102	105	98	118
1529	97	102	—	—	102	92	—	92	81	102	—
1530	102	106	—	125	87	97	—	97	99	94	—
1531	108	116	—	—	116	99	—	99	97	101	—

Table V (cont.)

Harvest year	Dairy products and eggs						Wool, fells, and hides				Average—all animal products
	Milk and cream	Butter	Cheese	Average—all dairy products	Eggs	Average—all dairy products and eggs	Wool	Sheepskins and wool fells	Cattle hides	Average—wool, fells, and hides	
1532	166	91	—	129	136	131	131	—	—	131	131
1533	145	91	—	118	136	124	146	—	215	181	153
1534	—	88	—	88	—	88	136	—	—	136	112
1535	—	88	115	102	193	132	121	—	227	174	153
1536	—	133	126	130	193	151	150	—	—	150	151
1537	145	88	—	117	—	117	117	—	—	117	117
1538	—	101	—	101	—	101	108	—	—	108	105
1539	—	—	—	—	—	—	112	—	163	138	138
1540	—	—	—	—	—	—	190	—	166	178	178
1541	—	—	—	—	—	—	155	—	180	168	168
1542	—	—	—	—	—	—	—	103	160	132	132
1543	—	—	—	—	—	—	150	122	208	160	160
1544	—	—	—	—	—	—	141	—	—	141	141
1545	—	—	—	—	—	—	180	—	—	180	180
1546	—	133	136	135	—	135	126	86	—	106	121
1547	—	118	—	118	224	171	120	125	225	157	164
1548	—	151	143	147	—	147	—	144	246	195	171
1549	—	151	162	157	—	157	168	165	254	196	177
1550	—	—	—	—	—	—	281	181	234	232	232
1551	—	—	—	—	—	—	268	121	169	186	186
1552	—	—	—	—	—	—	192	105	280	192	192
1553	—	—	—	—	—	—	124	131	197	151	151
1554	—	—	—	—	—	—	166	—	207	187	187
1555	—	212	—	212	288	250	160	77	—	119	185
1556	—	—	—	—	—	—	262	—	354	308	308

Year											
1557	206	188	—	103	272	224	—	224	224	—	—
1558	224	238	410	160	143	209	188	220	228	211	—
1559	254	299	410	—	187	209	—	209	174	208	246
1560	196	153	—	—	153	239	286	216	—	276	155
1561	248	220	—	—	220	276	—	276	—	276	—
1562	184	150	—	—	150	217	—	217	205	228	—
1563	220	193	—	213	172	246	—	246	242	249	—
1564	294	220	246	254	160	367	728	247	179	303	259
1565	243	219	—	—	219	266	337	242	201	276	248
1566	236	282	253	310	—	189	—	189	189	—	—
1567	237	277	267	290	273	197	—	197	197	—	—
1568	231	253	265	262	231	208	—	208	208	—	—
1569	268	233	262	205	233	302	561	215	177	313	155
1570	199	200	248	167	184	197	—	197	197	—	—
1571	263	266	325	238	234	259	365	224	188	276	207
1572	217	261	372	214	197	172	—	172	172	—	—
1573	314	302	336	350	219	326	550	251	254	293	207
1574	223	261	295	—	226	184	—	184	184	—	—
1575	264	296	388	272	229	231	—	231	232	253	207
1576	274	286	304	303	251	262	—	262	230	294	—
1577	260	296	319	315	254	223	—	223	192	270	207
1578	272	295	319	303	262	248	—	248	207	289	—
1579	284	327	319	383	280	241	—	241	211	253	259
1580	287	327	319	405	257	247	—	247	208	276	257
1581	252	290	346	—	234	213	—	213	213	—	—
1582	310	331	390	339	265	289	365	264	215	293	284
1583	288	304	390	289	234	271	366	239	193	240	284
1584	283	310	408	312	211	255	—	255	217	264	284
1585	298	314	417	312	214	282	—	282	—	286	278
1586	277	255	390	195	179	298	568	298	265	330	—
1587	310	268	361	256	187	351	539	278	224	326	284
1588	332	313	404	318	217	350	371	255	197	313	—
1589	317	333	415	—	250	300	516	277	230	316	284
1590	350	351	390	—	311	349	—	294	260	323	298

145

Table V (*cont.*)

Harvest year	Dairy products and eggs						Wool, fells, and hides				Average—all animal products
	Milk and cream	Butter	Cheese	Average—all dairy products	Eggs	Average—all dairy products and eggs	Wool	Sheepskins and wool fells	Cattle hides	Average—wool, fells, and hides	
1591	310	300	—	305	433	348	322	—	397	360	354
1592	310	299	—	305	580	396	334	348	390	357	377
1593	325	304	158	262	334	280	344	377	392	371	326
1594	—	355	224	290	389	323	346	392	375	371	347
1595	284	349	—	317	593	409	325	—	431	378	394
1596	313	344	315	324	500	368	324	418	429	390	379
1597	284	358	331	324	588	390	279	502	420	400	395
1598	—	357	—	357	562	460	289	442	408	380	420
1599	—	353	—	353	371	362	276	476	425	392	377
1600	292	390	—	341	638	440	296	476	461	411	426
1601	—	465	331	398	—	398	318	468	341	376	387
1602	283	307	241	277	488	330	370	391	362	374	352
1603	227	308	364	300	352	313	412	508	373	431	372
1604	—	326	232	279	—	279	371	537	408	439	359
1605	—	406	199	303	518	374	362	458	432	417	396
1606	—	373	265	319	454	364	356	486	430	424	394
1607	310	394	265	323	475	361	364	529	458	450	406
1608	310	413	298	340	536	389	334	433	460	409	399
1609	407	391	245	348	—	348	297	508	425	410	379
1610	—	386	331	359	726	481	271	454	459	395	438
1611	384	405	331	373	536	414	300	431	481	404	409
1612	341	391	298	343	585	404	286	465	507	419	412
1613	341	418	—	380	481	413	310	—	503	407	410
1614	341	400	430	390	593	441	344	665	489	499	470
1615	341	396	—	369	682	473	371	—	495	433	453

Year											
1616	341	389	275	335	536	385	420	662	510	531	458
1617	341	416	397	385	542	424	400	717	540	552	488
1618	341	372	397	370	476	397	428	680	533	547	472
1619	341	412	397	383	519	417	403	659	521	528	473
1620	341	382	364	362	460	387	338	524	537	466	427
1621	341	390	331	354	463	381	316	469	504	430	406
1622	—	344	298	321	642	428	267	389	493	383	406
1623	341	369	—	355	562	424	316	439	486	414	419
1624	341	379	—	360	476	399	326	478	520	441	420
1625	—	349	331	340	—	340	378	464	511	451	396
1626	—	384	305	345	—	345	377	485	553	472	409
1627	341	389	298	343	497	381	417	529	549	498	440
1628	—	343	362	353	429	378	407	534	588	510	444
1629	341	475	397	404	494	427	—	506	597	552	490
1630	—	309	331	320	—	320	393	508	553	485	403
1631	341	393	—	367	628	454	405	542	516	488	471
1632	—	—	—	—	—	—	405	—	561	483	483
1633	—	406	319	363	—	363	401	500	554	485	424
1634	341	432	405	393	579	439	425	544	547	505	472
1635	341	433	371	382	588	433	428	512	585	508	471
1636	341	430	552	441	515	460	424	466	578	489	475
1637	—	508	401	455	—	455	419	518	585	507	481
1638	348	448	340	394	—	394	403	474	552	476	435
1639	341	426	—	387	519	431	371	357	582	437	434
1640	341	422	—	382	466	410	348	324	621	431	421
1641	341	420	331	364	458	388	337	338	587	421	405
1642	341	418	323	361	493	394	—	254	557	406	400
1643	341	433	342	372	528	411	340	327	457	375	393
1644	341	438	363	381	427	392	—	443	486	465	429
1645	341	426	310	359	481	390	—	558	554	556	473
1646	—	485	—	485	—	485	427	359	578	455	470
1647	—	548	644	596	—	596	497	370	640	502	549
1648	—	574	563	569	—	569	427	372	620	473	521
1649	284	625	644	518	—	518	—	372	665	519	519

Table VI. *Price of all agricultural products and timber*
INDEX NUMBER

Harvest year	Grains	Other arable crops	Livestock	Animal products	Average—all agricultural products	Timber
1450	119	111	97	82	102	83
1451	107	98	93	81	95	100
1452	101	101	105	85	98	115
1453	94	103	98	92	97	124
1454	83	108	90	90	93	107
1455	99	55	97	101	91	124
1456	76	95	97	99	92	82
1457	103	94	89	89	94	—
1458	106	78	98	93	94	93
1459	94	118	101	98	103	124
1460	122	114	92	94	106	124
1461	124	106	99	99	107	100
1462	89	83	115	97	96	—
1463	67	68	103	124	91	—
1464	95	145	104	89	108	88
1465	104	108	96	107	104	97
1466	92	90	97	108	97	94
1467	98	103	111	113	106	89
1468	98	91	98	107	99	92
1469	105	106	106	107	106	100
1470	114	106	101	99	105	87
1471	108	99	102	103	103	—
1472	88	86	116	102	98	—
1473	87	100	105	110	101	—
1474	80	94	100	103	94	—
1475	86	98	101	103	97	—
1476	82	99	88	96	91	94
1477	96	113	88	100	99	—
1478	105	119	96	96	104	96
1479	88	92	86	101	92	96
1480	92	98	90	95	94	96
1481	136	115	110	105	117	104
1482	168	128	124	113	133	136
1483	121	90	105	103	105	125
1484	100	100	118	119	109	104
1485	85	79	92	111	92	—
1486	117	89	107	104	104	—
1487	110	83	98	101	98	—
1488	116	115	109	103	111	98
1489	90	96	97	116	100	99
1490	120	97	117	89	106	—

Table VI (*cont.*)

Harvest year	Grains	Other arable crops	Livestock	Animal products	Average—all agricultural products	Timber
1491	97	94	113	103	102	100
1492	113	83	93	102	98	88
1493	89	78	107	97	93	83
1494	76	89	98	97	90	99
1495	81	116	100	101	100	—
1496	102	95	82	116	99	83
1497	105	91	94	118	102	83
1498	105	133	88	97	106	93
1499	86	102	98	87	93	98
1500	120	96	92	104	103	—
1501	124	102	96	107	107	89
1502	138	87	95	98	105	—
1503	123	113	96	100	108	84
1504	122	111	125	109	117	—
1505	117	87	123	92	105	92
1506	98	91	127	101	104	82
1507	107	101	112	97	104	85
1508	94	94	125	104	104	85
1509	77	96	119	104	99	79
1510	87	81	95	107	93	81
1511	106	95	98	108	102	—
1512	114	97	119	112	111	—
1513	107	115	107	113	111	—
1514	121	96	121	108	112	—
1515	113	104	118	128	116	105
1516	111	130	128	134	126	—
1517	129	149	128	122	132	—
1518	113	141	119	123	124	100
1519	144	191	132	127	149	104
1520	193	165	142	112	153	99
1521	183	127	139	103	138	99
1522	116	116	153	104	122	101
1523	110	97	138	85	108	94
1524	116	121	116	97	113	98
1525	110	127	128	119	121	83
1526	141	152	138	111	136	99
1527	198	192	133	111	159	108
1528	182	109	152	112	139	102
1529	189	116	139	97	135	97
1530	148	113	130	102	123	134
1531	196	115	147	108	142	84
1532	188	147	143	131	151	101
1533	155	140	128	153	144	84

Table VI (cont.)

Harvest year	Grains	Other arable crops	Livestock	Animal products	Average—all agricultural products	Timber
1534	148	121	164	112	136	100
1535	225	146	128	153	163	99
1536	154	132	154	151	148	102
1537	123	115	150	117	126	99
1538	124	129	134	105	123	106
1539	148	118	147	138	138	87
1540	154	122	151	178	151	105
1541	153	148	170	168	160	102
1542	175	124	167	132	150	108
1543	164	126	163	160	153	106
1544	192	145	201	141	170	122
1545	286	143	176	180	196	126
1546	160	139	176	121	149	86
1547	130	143	205	164	161	118
1548	162	165	230	171	182	127
1549	298	195	213	177	221	145
1550	353	313	258	232	289	151
1551	313	252	275	186	257	153
1552	281	288	256	192	254	173
1553	279	190	214	151	209	160
1554	340	268	249	187	261	184
1555	521	330	251	185	322	181
1556	558	318	297	308	370	156
1557	235	208	275	206	231	174
1558	284	195	257	224	240	220
1559	314	250	255	254	268	193
1560	337	242	295	196	268	199
1561	296	313	260	248	279	136
1562	372	350	285	184	298	144
1563	343	360	293	220	304	181
1564	258	233	268	294	263	176
1565	335	268	248	243	274	196
1566	267	264	298	236	266	190
1567	321	334	275	237	292	166
1568	355	318	295	231	300	194
1569	277	255	289	268	272	195
1570	299	244	308	199	263	194
1571	305	235	300	263	276	206
1572	368	287	326	217	300	195
1573	478	360	338	314	373	182
1574	334	330	367	223	314	217
1575	378	259	346	264	312	186
1576	359	301	339	274	318	238

Table VI (*cont.*)

Harvest year	Grains	Other arable crops	Livestock	Animal products	Average—all agricultural products	Timber
1577	391	275	340	260	317	226
1578	372	276	376	272	324	190
1579	414	308	322	284	332	228
1580	444	308	349	287	347	265
1581	434	306	377	252	342	206
1582	422	320	347	310	350	240
1583	370	325	327	288	328	230
1584	324	308	331	283	312	257
1585	556	364	346	298	391	254
1586	684	420	347	277	432	253
1587	365	309	366	310	338	273
1588	407	307	355	332	350	239
1589	531	312	376	317	384	251
1590	624	496	377	350	462	255
1591	443	346	382	354	381	285
1592	296	343	390	377	352	261
1593	350	388	382	326	362	287
1594	621	441	437	347	462	281
1595	681	458	419	394	488	299
1596	1039	598	407	379	606	314
1597	778	484	444	395	525	300
1598	518	341	457	420	434	312
1599	557	386	442	377	441	299
1600	768	523	474	426	548	280
1601	555	444	434	387	455	323
1602	480	368	428	352	407	324
1603	420	402	426	372	405	299
1604	501	417	422	359	425	362
1605	543	466	413	396	455	317
1606	492	407	465	394	440	345
1607	554	501	452	406	478	347
1608	654	531	472	399	514	370
1609	633	485	520	379	504	382
1610	554	464	465	438	480	381
1611	699	600	507	409	554	404
1612	736	668	486	412	576	304
1613	725	487	516	410	535	397
1614	650	512	522	470	539	403
1615	749	743	532	453	619	356
1616	657	557	497	458	542	378
1617	659	491	507	488	536	425
1618	586	464	530	472	513	467
1619	535	522	504	473	509	454

Table VI (cont.)

Harvest year	Grains	Other arable crops	Livestock	Animal products	Average—all agricultural products	Timber
1620	432	526	475	427	465	447
1621	666	518	494	406	521	413
1622	773	548	496	406	556	493
1623	666	507	508	419	525	392
1624	634	567	509	420	533	404
1625	729	600	536	396	565	460
1626	603	468	582	409	516	433
1627	504	464	549	440	489	483
1628	693	594	527	444	565	582
1629	723	663	568	490	611	395
1630	1064	695	550	403	678	445
1631	653	564	613	471	575	428
1632	793	602	628	483	627	503
1633	819	566	632	424	610	449
1634	794	864	649	472	695	429
1635	667	612	676	471	607	429
1636	752	715	644	475	647	538
1637	1031	906	627	481	761	485
1638	762	545	653	435	599	534
1639	569	535	630	434	542	510
1640	708	557	597	421	571	580
1641	649	544	603	405	550	545
1642	640	605	673	400	580	549
1643	565	587	586	393	533	582
1644	600	577	581	429	547	468
1645	663	500	664	473	575	420
1646	847	681	775	470	693	501
1647	1091	761	735	549	784	548
1648	1073	919	775	521	822	504
1649	1023	909	682	519	783	549

Table VII. *Price of wheat in England and western Europe*

INDEX NUMBER

Harvest year	England	Western Europe
1450	116	66
1451	112	64
1452	99	68
1453	87	65
1454	73	70
1455	94	130
1456	89	123
1457	116	121
1458	105	76
1459	93	111
1460	132	90
1461	138	69
1462	74	52
1463	60	42
1464	74	48
1465	83	67
1466	92	72
1467	106	67
1468	114	72
1469	114	70
1470	121	71
1471	112	69
1472	79	76
1473	79	88
1474	82	94
1475	89	71
1476	89	70
1477	122	134
1478	130	144
1479	92	115
1480	94	136
1481	132	273
1482	177	254
1483	132	85
1484	98	72
1485	86	97
1486	96	161
1487	108	170
1488	106	181
1489	91	122
1490	127	137
1491	100	163

Table VII (*cont.*)

Harvest year	England	Western Europe
1492	89	140
1493	81	81
1494	70	64
1495	70	59
1496	103	78
1497	102	109
1498	99	92
1499	72	51
1500	126	85
1501	128	126
1502	147	139
1503	130	102
1504	98	97
1505	99	100
1506	98	101
1507	113	103
1508	85	117
1509	69	100
1510	81	142
1511	111	153
1512	144	166
1513	121	144
1514	102	134
1515	127	152
1516	105	178
1517	109	149
1518	97	99
1519	140	113
1520	191	159
1521	166	196
1522	104	109
1523	109	136
1524	99	168
1525	95	109
1526	110	128
1527	227	175
1528	175	218
1529	165	222
1530	130	221
1531	162	236
1532	150	161
1533	133	146

Table VII (cont.)

Harvest year	England	Western Europe
1534	116	128
1535	213	157
1536	156	153
1537	108	120
1538	113	160
1539	116	133
1540	122	133
1541	146	142
1542	139	148
1543	185	195
1544	192	234
1545	288	270
1546	139	153
1547	99	118
1548	138	137
1549	265	181
1550	294	184
1551	329	247
1552	204	228
1553	179	207
1554	267	181
1555	383	250
1556	528	333
1557	194	186
1558	179	201
1559	291	230
1560	339	229
1561	271	290
1562	426	352
1563	275	243
1564	244	256
1565	394	418
1566	247	335
1567	235	317
1568	252	281
1569	243	291
1570	265	378
1571	288	489
1572	301	582
1573	427	658
1574	328	510
1575	348	410

Table VII (cont.)

Harvest year	England	Western Europe
1576	411	360
1577	369	370
1578	309	355
1579	310	428
1580	379	437
1581	381	431
1582	333	437
1583	316	451
1584	299	411
1585	427	598
1586	626	904
1587	331	588
1588	320	507
1589	437	596
1590	394	675
1591	304	612
1592	295	652
1593	388	561
1594	578	626
1595	607	711
1596	811	720
1597	746	728
1598	462	602
1599	407	549
1600	485	565
1601	416	497
1602	432	528
1603	391	539
1604	434	457
1605	401	453
1606	447	478
1607	571	582
1608	715	616
1609	493	582
1610	495	590
1611	545	619
1612	606	567
1613	667	566
1614	504	584
1615	574	528
1616	590	559
1617	647	616

Table VII (*cont.*)

Harvest year	England	Western Europe
1618	517	515
1619	450	519
1620	366	585
1621	598	657
1622	763	767
1623	573	726
1624	625	686
1625	637	843
1626	521	779
1627	427	713
1628	525	711
1629	609	794
1630	881	1096
1631	630	810
1632	684	764
1633	686	670
1634	668	669
1635	645	715
1636	645	725
1637	750	802
1638	575	784
1639	507	740
1640	615	760
1641	574	761
1642	616	858
1643	542	891
1644	546	761
1645	590	622
1646	804	597
1647	997	783
1648	943	808
1649	942	1022

B. PRICE OF AGRICULTURAL COMMODITIES:
DECENNIAL AVERAGES
1450–99 = 100

Table VIII. *Price of arable crops*
INDEX NUMBER

Decade	Grains					Other arable crops					Average—all arable crops
	Wheat	Barley	Oats	Rye	Average—all grains	Hay	Straw	Peas	Beans	Average—all other arable crops	
1450–9	98	100	97	96	98	110	105	84	102	96	98
1460–9	99	99	100	98	99	100	108	100	97	101	101
1470–9	100	88	96	89	93	102	96	104	94	101	97
1480–9	112	118	105	118	114	86	87	121	121	99	107
1490–9	91	95	104	99	97	103	103	95	92	98	98
1500–9	109	108	107	123	112	93	100	106	92	98	105
1510–9	114	112	119	112	115	114	117	121	134	120	117
1520–9	144	136	148	195	154	104	117	167	152	132	143
1530–9	140	158	155	190	161	106	130	142	137	128	145
1540–9	171	197	191	—	187	140	118	177	170	145	164
1550–9	285	450	356	—	348	238	223	356	317	261	301
1560–9	293	338	322	338	316	301	293	258	317	294	301
1570–9	336	360	343	459	370	303	268	282	294	288	326
1580–9	385	482	457	523	454	305	274	365	367	328	389
1590–9	499	600	638	651	590	385	401	475	464	428	507
1600–9	479	583	599	600	560	522	418	425	453	454	503
1610–9	560	665	723	703	655	578	557	526	548	551	599
1620–9	564	648	630	770	642	584	540	492	564	546	594
1630–9	667	876	792	852	790	721	578	601	899	660	728
1640–9	717	796	843	—	786	768	612	622	620	664	721

Table IX. *Price of cattle and sheep*

INDEX NUMBER

Decade	Cattle				Sheep			
	Oxen	Cows and heifers	Calves	Average—all cattle	Wethers	Type unspecified	Lambs	Average—all sheep
1450–9	110	86	95	98	81	86	90	84
1460–9	96	110	102	102	95	108	108	103
1470–9	107	107	110	108	98	95	97	94
1480–9	97	112	105	105	120	118	106	111
1490–9	89	84	90	90	106	—	96	103
1500–9	114	89	92	103	104	98	86	95
1510–9	122	95	147	119	140	112	118	128
1520–9	144	110	139	143	140	135	146	138
1530–9	154	146	133	147	162	148	161	158
1540–9	195	171	155	174	207	221	203	210
1550–9	293	273	239	266	312	232	242	263
1560–9	279	292	304	290	325	292	313	312
1570–9	331	431	353	358	396	343	432	380
1580–9	362	444	377	389	385	393	388	392
1590–9	428	517	449	465	460	492	458	471
1600–9	450	561	484	489	589	498	489	495
1610–9	516	624	527	553	555	537	507	525
1620–9	508	590	549	545	622	557	522	557
1630–9	555	744	629	646	650	566	542	587
1640–9	600	823	733	713	740	587	684	681

Table X. *Price of poultry and rabbits*

INDEX NUMBER

Decade	Capons and hens	Geese and ducks	Average— all poultry	Rabbits	Average— poultry and rabbits
1450–9	102	99	101	111	101
1460–9	102	101	102	95	102
1470–9	101	106	103	111	103
1480–9	99	99	100	98	100
1490–9	95	91	94	96	95
1500–9	136	120	134	95	132
1510–9	98	86	93	92	91
1520–9	113	—	113	—	113
1530–9	127	131	127	122	132
1540–9	239	206	220	174	204
1550–9	343	249	311	193	257
1560–9	328	275	304	219	261
1570–9	383	331	361	273	320
1580–9	330	288	309	302	306
1590–9	387	405	400	314	368
1600–9	493	405	441	353	411
1610–9	503	490	495	446	476
1620–9	640	471	591	408	515
1630–9	780	874	786	424	682
1640–9	650	747	698	463	603

Table XI. *Price of livestock*
INDEX NUMBER

Decade	Sheep	Cattle	Horses	Pigs	Poultry and rabbits	Average— all livestock
1450–9	84	98	104	94	101	97
1460–9	103	102	98	103	102	102
1470–9	94	108	87	100	103	98
1480–9	111	105	106	104	100	105
1490–9	103	90	104	101	95	99
1500–9	95	103	114	111	132	111
1510–9	128	119	108	135	91	117
1520–9	138	143	137	144	113	138
1530–9	158	147	141	124	132	143
1540–9	210	174	184	148	204	185
1550–9	263	266	249	258	257	259
1560–9	312	290	266	270	261	281
1570–9	380	358	326	297	320	336
1580–9	392	389	394	269	306	352
1590–9	471	465	444	310	368	414
1600–9	495	489	466	393	411	451
1610–9	525	553	520	460	476	507
1620–9	557	545	572	433	515	524
1630–9	587	646	652	589	682	630
1640–9	681	713	675	575	603	667

Table XII. *Price of animal products*
INDEX NUMBER

Decade	Dairy products and eggs						Wool, fells, and hides				Average—all animal products
	Milk and cream	Butter	Cheese	Average—all dairy products	Eggs	Average—all dairy products and eggs	Wool	Sheepskins and wool fells	Cattle hides	Average—wool, fells, and hides	
1450–9	59	106	—	91	101	97	82	75	101	86	91
1460–9	—	—	91	91	101	98	109	126	98	110	105
1470–9	—	—	105	105	101	101	99	107	89	101	101
1480–9	118	99	109	105	98	103	113	130	89	110	107
1490–9	152	97	86	102	96	100	96	93	128	101	101
1500–9	86	99	92	93	96	95	93	100	132	108	102
1510–9	107	91	94	93	119	105	119	126	156	131	118
1520–9	100	92	98	94	—	94	111	108	162	115	105
1530–9	152	97	109	109	165	116	122	125	202	136	127
1540–9	—	138	147	139	224	153	153	124	206	161	159
1550–9	246	210	208	216	238	223	206	126	283	210	213
1560–9	204	274	200	225	478	251	205	256	258	220	236
1570–9	217	275	207	223	458	234	234	283	323	279	257
1580–9	279	294	218	261	442	286	225	303	384	305	295
1590–9	303	334	257	313	487	369	315	422	406	375	372
1600–9	305	377	271	323	494	360	348	479	415	414	387
1610–9	346	398	357	369	568	425	353	592	504	472	448
1620–9	341	380	336	354	503	389	354	482	534	462	426
1630–9	342	421	389	389	566	417	407	491	561	486	455
1640–9	333	479	440	439	500	455	396	372	577	460	458

Table XIII. *Price of all agricultural products, timber, and industrial products*

INDEX NUMBER

Decade	Grains	Other arable crops	Livestock	Animal products	Average—all agricultural products	Timber	Industrial products	Agricultural / Industrial × 100
1450–9	98	96	97	91	96	106	99	97
1460–9	99	101	102	105	102	98	103	99
1470–9	93	101	98	101	98	93	100	98
1480–9	114	99	105	107	106	109	103	103
1490–9	97	98	99	101	99	91	97	102
1500–9	112	98	111	102	106	85	98	108
1510–9	115	120	117	118	118	97	102	116
1520–9	154	132	138	105	132	98	110	120
1530–9	161	128	143	127	139	100	110	126
1540–9	187	145	185	159	169	115	127	133
1550–9	348	261	259	213	270	174	186	145
1560–9	316	294	281	236	282	178	218	129
1570–9	370	288	336	257	313	206	223	140
1580–9	454	328	352	295	357	247	230	155
1590–9	590	428	414	372	451	289	238	189
1600–9	560	454	451	387	463	335	256	181
1610–9	655	551	507	448	540	397	274	197
1620–9	642	546	524	426	535	450	264	203
1630–9	790	660	630	455	634	475	281	226
1640–9	786	664	667	458	644	524	306	210

Table XIV. *Price of wheat in England and western Europe*
INDEX NUMBER

Decade	England	Western Europe
1450–9	98	89
1460–9	99	65
1470–9	100	93
1480–9	112	155
1490–9	91	97
1500–9	109	107
1510–9	114	143
1520–9	144	162
1530–9	140	161
1540–9	171	171
1550–9	285	225
1560–9	293	301
1570–9	336	407
1580–9	385	536
1590–9	499	644
1600–9	479	483
1610–9	560	566
1620–9	564	726
1630–9	667	778
1640–9	717	786

Table XV. *Agricultural day wage-rates*[a] *in southern England*

Decade	Oxford	Cambridge	Eton College	Average	Index number
	d.	d.	d.	d.	
1450–9	4	4	—	4·00	101
1460–9	4	4	—	4·00	101
1470–9	4	4	4	4·00	101
1480–9	4	—	3½	3·75	95
1490–9	4	—	4	4·00	101
1500–9	4	4	4	4·00	101
1510–9	4	4	4	4·00	101
1520–9	4	4	4½	4·17	106
1530–9	4	4	5	4·33	110
1540–9	4	5	5	4·66	118
1550–9	6	6	7	6·33	160
1560–9	8	5	8	7·00	177
1570–9	8	7½	9	8·17	207
1580–9	8	8	8	8·00	203
1590–9	8	10	8	8·66	219
1600–9	8	10	8	8·66	219
1610–9	8	10	9	9·00	228
1620–9	10	10	10	10·00	253
1630–9	10	12	12	11·33	287
1640–9	12	12	12	12·00	304

[a] These are median wage-rates for ordinary day-to-day agricultural operations performed by male workers—e.g. hedging, ditching, spreading dung. Seasonal tasks, such as mowing and haymaking, normally paid at higher rates, are not included. Also excluded are rates supplemented by payments in kind.

Table XVI. *Wage-rates in southern England and their purchasing power*

INDEX NUMBER

	Agricultural labourer			Building craftsman
Decade	Money wage-rate[a]	'Cost of living'[b]	·Purchasing power of wage-rate	Purchasing power of wage-rate[c]
1450–9	101	96	105	104
1460–9	101	101	100	100
1470–9	101	97	104	103
1480–9	95	111	86	93
1490–9	101	97	104	103
1500–9	101	104	97	96
1510–9	101	114	89	88
1520–9	106	133	80	76
1530–9	110	138	80	68
1540–9	118	167	71	70
1550–9	160	271	59	51
1560–9	177	269	66	62
1570–9	207	298	69	64
1580–9	203	354	57	57
1590–9	219	443	49	47
1600–9	219	439	50	46
1610–9	228	514	44	39
1620–9	253	511	50	39
1630–9	287	609	47	—
1640–9	304	609	50	49

[a] Data taken from Table XV.
[b] Based on the preceding price tables, using the following weights: Arable crops, excluding hay and straw (5), animal products (2), livestock (1), timber (1), industrial products (1).
[c] Re-calculated from figures given by E. H. Phelps Brown and Sheila V. Hopkins in 'Seven Centuries of the Prices of Consumables, compared with Builders' Wage-rates', *Economica*, NS, XXIII, 1956, p. 312.

C. NOTE ON STATISTICAL SOURCES AND METHODS

The principal sources of data used in the compilation of our price indices have been J. E. T. Rogers, *A History of Agriculture and Prices in England*, vols. III and VI; W. Beveridge *et al.*, *Prices and Wages in England from the Twelfth to the Nineteenth Century*, vol. I; and unpublished statistics forming part of the Beveridge Collection of Price Material at the London School of Economics. These sources contain many different series of price quotations of varying degrees of usefulness. The series which have been utilized in this study, together with the relevant agricultural commodities, are listed below.

In order to save space, the following abbreviations for commodities are used:

B = Barley	G = Geese or ducks	Pe = Peas
Be = Beans	H = Hens	R = Rye
Bu = Butter	Ha = Hay	Ra = Rabbits
C = Capons	Hi = Hides	S = Straw
Ca = Calves	Ho = Horses	T = Timber
Ch = Cheese	L = Lambs	V = Various: six or
Co = Cows or heifers	O = Oats	more commodities
E = Eggs	Ox = Oxen	W = Wool
F = Fells or skins	P = Pigs	We = Wethers
		Wh = Wheat

Rogers, *History of Agriculture and Prices*

Alciston (C, Co, G)
Alton Barnes (C)
Apuldram (V)
Balneth (E)
Bardney (Bu, Ca, Ch, Co)
Barking (H)
Battle (Co, G)
Beeding (H, T)
Biggin (O, Pe)
¹Cambridge Colleges (V)
Canterbury (P, T, Wh)
Castor (B, P)
Chatham (Hi)
Colchester (C)
Coleshill (V)
D'Ewes Accounts (Ch, Co, H, O)
Downham (V)
Durham Cells:
  Finchale ⎫
  Jarrow   ⎬ (V)
  Wearmouth ⎭
Durham Obedientiary (V)
Ellsworth (C)
Elmswell (B, O, R)
¹Eton College (V)
Fountains Abbey (V)
Gawthorp (V)
Guyton (C, E, H)
Hardwick (Be, R)
Harling (V)
Harting (Hi, We)
Hawkesbury (E)
Heightredbury (H)
Heyford (O, Wh)

Hickling (V)
Hinton (B, R)
Honden (C)
Hornchurch (C, H, O, Wh)
Houghton (E)
Howard Accounts (Ca, Hi, L)
Hunstanton (R, W)
Ipswich (R)
Kirkby Stephen (C)
Kirtling (V)
Laughton (V)
Le Strange Accounts (R, W)
Lewes (B, Hi, Ox)
Loders (G, H, R, Wh)
London (Ha, O, R, T)
Lullington (B, Ox, P, Wh)
Mendham (V)
Metingham College (F, Hi, We)
Newton Longville (C)
Norwich (V)
Ormsby (V)
Osney (Co, F, Hi, L)
Otterton (Be, G)
¹Oxford Colleges (V)
Oxford City (V)
Portsmouth (Hi)
Radcliffe (G, P)
Rochester (Hi)
Rotherham (R)
Royden (Ca)
Ruislip (Be)
St Osyth (Ca, F, Hi, Ho)
Selborne (C, P)
Sion and Isleworth (V)

¹ Sources of data for wage tables.

Skidmore Upton (C)
Spitling (B, C)
Stamford (S)
Stoke (Co, G, Ha, Hi, O)
Sutton-at-Hone (F, Hi, Ox, We)
Takley (C, Co, H, O)
Theydon Garnon (V)
Wardrobe (V)
Winchester College (V)
Worksop (V)

Wormleighton (V)
Writtle (C, G, P)
Wye (V)
Wykenholt (E)
Wymondham (V)
Wythingham (C, E, H)
Yartcombe (C)
Yeovil (B, Be, O, R)
Yotes Court (Be)

Beveridge, London School of Economics

Cambridge Colleges (V)
Dover Assize (Wh)
Durham Cells (V)
Durham Obedientiary (V)
Ely (Wh)
[1]Eton College (V)
[2]Exeter Assize (Wh)
Hungerford (V)
Lambeth Palace (Be)
Laughton (V)
[3]Loder's Accounts (V)
London Assize (Wh)
London City Cos. (Wh)
Norwich Assize (Wh)
Norwich Obedientiary (V)
Nottingham (Wh)
Oxford Colleges (V)

Penshurst and Robertsbridge (V)
[1]Sandwich (Bu, Ch, F, Ha)
Shrewsbury (Co, Ho, Ox, We, Wh)
Tattershall (V)
Taunton (Wh)
[1]Victualling Contracts (Bu, Ch, Hi, T, Wh)
Western Europe:
France ⎫
Germany ⎬ (Wh)
Low Countries ⎭
[1]Westminster School and Abbey (T, Wh)
[1]Winchester College (V)
Winchester Manor (R, Wh)
York (Wh)

Other sources of price material which have been drawn upon are as follows:

K. J. Allison, *thesis*, Appendix Five: Norfolk Sheep and Wool Prices.

P. J. Bowden, 'Movements in Wool Prices, 1490–1610', *Yorks. Bull. Econ. and Soc. Research*, IV, 1952, pp. 109–24.

Durham Parish Books: Churchwardens' Accounts of Pittington and Other Parishes in the Diocese of Durham from A.D. 1580 to 1700, Surtees Soc., LXXXIV, Durham, 1888, *passim*: Wool Prices.

Finch, *op. cit.*, p. 19: John Isham's Wool Sales.

Hill, *op. cit.*, Appendix III: Corn Prices returned by Leet Juries, 1513–1712, Lincoln.

Lodge, *op. cit.*, *passim*: Toke's Purchases and Sales of Livestock.

Henry E. Huntington Library, California, U.S.A., ST. 48: Sir Thomas Temple's Account Book on Wool Sales, 1592–1626.

Kent AO, A 423, Cranfield Family Estate Accounts: Sheep, Wool, and Fell Prices.

[1] Published, in whole or in part, in Beveridge, *Prices and Wages in England*.

[2] Published in W. H. Beveridge, 'A Statistical Crime of the Seventeenth Century', *J. Econ. and Bus. Hist.*, 1929.

[3] See *Robert Loder's Farm Accounts, 1610–1620*, ed. G. E. Fussell, Camden Soc., 3rd Ser., LIII, 1936.

Lincoln, AO, H. 97/22, John Hatcher's Estate Accounts: Livestock and Animal Product Prices.
Lincoln AO, HEN. 3/2, Account Book of Sir George Heneage: Wool and Wether Prices.
Lumley MS 2305, Estate Accounts of Sir Nicholas Saunderson: Wool Prices.
Northants. RO, F(M) Misc. Vol. 52, Fitzwilliam's Dogsthorpe 'Cattle Book': Livestock Transactions.
Oxford AO, DIL III/6/2, Lee Family Wool Sales.
William Salt Library, D 1734, Misterton Manorial Accounts: Livestock and Animal Product Prices.

The main problem confronting the sixteenth- and seventeenth-century price historian is the lack of adequate statistical data. For many commodities long series of observations from the same source are not available, and wheat is the only product for which several series exist covering all or most of the period treated in our study. It is therefore necessary to rely to a considerable extent upon scattered observations covering comparatively short terms of years and derived from a variety of sources. For a number of reasons data from such sources are unlikely to be strictly comparable; for example, there are likely to be differences in local demand and supply conditions; there may be variations in local standards of weights and measures, about which we know little; while there may be differences in the quality of the product or in the conditions of sale. Obviously, there is a risk of serious distortion if scattered observations are simply lumped together indiscriminately. This has been avoided by treating sources separately; and where information has been available, separate price series have been distinguished for each source according to the type of transaction and the narrowest possible definition of product. For example, purchases have been differentiated from sales, and livestock have been distinguished by age as well as by kind. On the other hand, owing to the inadequacy of the data, no attempt has been made to adjust for seasonal price movements. Suspect prices have been discarded.

The statistical procedure used in the compilation of price indices can probably best be illustrated with reference to a specific product, say wheat. The first step was to select a series of wheat prices against which other series of wheat prices could be measured. The Exeter series extended throughout the whole period and so was well suited for this purpose. The next stage was to adjust prices from the remaining thirty-four series to the price of wheat in Exeter. The total price of each series in the years for which quotations were obtained was compared with the total of Exeter wheat prices in the same years, and the ratio between the two totals established. Each individual price quotation was then multiplied by the ratio of the total Exeter price to the total price of the wheat series to which it was related. For example, the total price of wheat in Cambridge was found to be 0·822 times that of wheat in Exeter in the same years. Each Cambridge wheat price was therefore multiplied by a factor of 1·217, or $\dfrac{1}{0\cdot822}$. After each wheat series had been treated in this way, simple arithmetical averages were obtained of each year's adjusted prices. Finally, these averages were expressed in the form of an index, with the average price ruling in the period 1450–99 as base. Essentially the same procedure was followed with all other commodities. Where, as was sometimes the case, it was not possible to establish a direct relationship between a series and the series selected as the standard, an indirect relationship was established through some third overlapping series the ratio of whose total price to the total price of the basic series was known. Yearly averages and indices were calculated as for wheat. Throughout, calculations have been based on harvest years (beginning Michaelmas) and not on calendar years, since, as we have seen, the size of the harvest exercised a major influence on agricultural prices. Thus, harvest year 1620, for example, relates to the period 29 September 1620 to 28 September 1621.

The standard series and base price for each commodity are listed below:

Commodity	Standard Series	Base price (average 1450–99)
Wheat	Exeter	6·32s. per qtr.
Barley	Cambridge	2·82s. per qtr.
Oats	Cambridge	1·92s. per qtr.
Rye	Loders	3·97s. per qtr.
Hay	Cambridge	3·17s. per load
Straw	Cambridge	1·63s. per load
Peas	Cambridge	3·72s. per qtr.
Beans	Oxford	3·90s. per qtr.
Oxen	Cambridge	13·77s. each
Cows (and heifers)	Shrewsbury	8·50s. each
Calves	Cambridge	2·21s. each
Wethers	Wardrobe	1·72s. each
Unspecified sheep	Cambridge	1·84s. each
Lambs	Eton College	1·32s. each
Capons (and hens)	Cambridge	0·30s. each
Geese (and ducks)	Oxford	0·33s. each
Rabbits	Winchester	0·13s. each
Horses	Oxford	33·93s. each
Pigs	Cambridge	8·46s. each (boars)
Cream (and milk)	Cambridge	3·52s. per doz. gall.
Butter	Cambridge	1·30s. per doz. lb.
Cheese	Sandwich	0·76s. per doz. lb. (Suffolk cheese)
Eggs	Cambridge	0·67s. per 120
Wool	Durham	2·30s. per stone
Sheepskins and wool fells	Sandwich (1st qtr)	0·47s. each
Cattle hides	Eton College	2·82s. each
Timber	Cambridge	7·99s. per 100 faggots

In calculating average price indices for each group of commodities (e.g. grains, cattle), no attempt has been made to weight products according to their relative importance, since the necessary information is lacking. In years where all products in a group are not represented, simple arithmetical averages have been taken in respect of those commodities for which data exist. Similarly the indices for 'all agricultural commodities' are simple un-weighted averages of indices of major groups of products.

The unorthodox method of treatment which has been adopted can be criticized on theoretical grounds, but the nature of the material is such that the use of refined techniques is obviously out of the question. Theoretically, there is the possibility that the long-term trend of prices for individual commodities will be misrepresented if the trend of the standard series is markedly different from that of other series, especially if the total number of observations is small. This possibility has been kept in mind as far as practicable in the selection of basic series, and while there may be some distortion from this cause, in most cases it is not likely to be of more than slight significance. As for the shorter term movement of prices, it will be evident that the measurement of year-to-year variations is, in general, less reliable than that for rather longer periods, though the unreliability is more likely to be a matter of degree than of direction. It will be recognized, of course, that the concept of an average price level is an abstraction, and that in the conditions of Tudor and early Stuart times prices might vary widely from one local market to another.

3

SELECT BIBLIOGRAPHY, 1500–1640

Alcock, L., and Foster, I. Ll. (eds.). *Culture and Environment*. London, 1963.

Allan, D. G. C. *Agrarian Discontent under the Early Stuarts and during the last Decade of Elizabeth*. University of London M.Sc. (Econ.) thesis, 1950.

—— 'The Rising in the West, 1628–31', EcHR, 2nd Ser., v, 1952.

Allen, J. Romilly. 'Old Farmhouses with Round Chimneys near St David's', *Arch. Camb.*, ii, 1902.

Allison, K. J. 'Flock Management in the Sixteenth and Seventeenth Centuries', EcHR, 2nd Ser., xi, 1958.

—— 'The Sheep-Corn Husbandry of Norfolk in the Sixteenth and Seventeenth Centuries', AHR, v, 1957.

—— *The Wool Supply and the Worsted Cloth Industry in Norfolk in the Sixteenth and Seventeenth Centuries*, University of Leeds Ph.D. thesis, 1955.

Ambler, L. *Old Halls and Manor Houses of Yorkshire*. London, 1913.

Ascoli, Georges. *La Grande-Bretagne devant L'Opinion Française au XVIIe Siècle*. Travaux et Mémoires de l'Université de Lille, NS, Fascicule 13, 1, Paris, 1930.

Ashley, Sir William J. *The Bread of our Forefathers*. Oxford, 1928.

Ashton, T. S. *An Economic History of England: the Eighteenth Century*. London, 1955.

—— *Economic Fluctuations in England, 1700–1800*. Oxford, 1959.

Aylmer, G. E. *The King's Servants*. London, 1961.

—— 'The Last Years of Purveyance, 1610–1660', EcHR, 2nd Ser., x, i, 1957.

Bacon, Nathaniel. *Annalls of Ipswiche*. Ipswich, 1884.

Bailey, J., and Culley, G. *General View of the Agriculture of the County of Northumberland*. London, 1813.

Bankes, Joyce (ed.). *The Memoranda Book of James Bankes, 1586–1617*. Inverness, 1935.

Barley, M. W. *The English Farmhouse and Cottage*. London, 1961.

Barnes, D. G. *A History of the English Corn Laws from 1660 to 1846*. London, 1930.

Barnes, T. G. *Somerset Assize Orders, 1629–1640*. Som. Rec. Soc., lxv, 1959.

Bates, E. H. *The Particular Description of the County of Somerset, 1633*. Somerset Rec. Soc., xv, 1900.

Batho, G. R. 'The Finances of an Elizabethan Nobleman: Henry Percy, Ninth Earl of Northumberland', EcHR, 2nd Ser., ix, 1957.

—— *The Household Papers of Henry Percy, ninth Earl of Northumberland*. Camden Soc., xciii, 1962.

Beale, John. *Herefordshire Orchards, a Pattern for all England*. London, 1657.

Bean, J. M. W. *The Estates of the Percy Family, 1416–1537*. London, 1958.

Bell, H. E. *An Introduction to the History and Records of the Court of Wards and Liveries*. Cambridge, 1953.

Bennett, M. K. 'British Wheat Yield Per Acre for Seven Centuries', *Economic History*, iii, 1935.

Beresford, M. W. 'Glebe Terriers and Open-Field Buckinghamshire', *Records of Bucks.*, xvi, 1953–4.

—— 'Habitation versus Improvement. The Debate on Enclosure by Agreement', *Essays in the Economic and Social History of Tudor and Stuart England*, ed. F. J. Fisher. Cambridge, 1961.

—— 'A Journey to Elizabethan Market Places', chapter vi in *History on the Ground*. London, 1957.

Beresford, M. W. *The Lost Villages of England*. London, 1954.
—— 'The Lost Villages of Medieval England', *Geog. J.*, cxvii, 1951.
—— 'The Lost Villages of Yorkshire', *Yorks. Arch. J.*, xxxviii, 1952.
Best, Henry. *Rural Economy in Yorkshire in 1641, being the Farming and Account Books of Henry Best of Elmeswell in the East Riding*, ed. C. B. Robinson. Surtees Soc., xxxiii, 1857.
Beveridge, Lord. 'British Exports and the Barometer', *Economic J.*, xxx, 1920.
—— 'The Yield and Price of Corn in the Middle Ages', *Economic History*, ii, 1927.
—— 'Wages in the Winchester Manors', EcHR, vii, 1936–7.
—— 'Weather and Harvest Cycles', *Economic J.*, xxxi, 1921.
Beveridge, Lord, and others. *Prices and Wages in England from the Twelfth to the Nineteenth Century*. London, 1939.
Bickley, W. B. *Abstract of the Bailiffs' Accounts of Monastic and other Estates in the County of Warwick*. Dugdale Soc., ii, 1923.
Bindoff, S. T. *Ket's Rebellion, 1549*. Hist. Assoc. Pamphlet, General Series 12, 1949.
—— *Tudor England*. London, 1950.
Birch, Walter de Gray. *A Descriptive Catalogue of Penrice and Margam Manuscripts*, Series i–iv. London, 1893–5.
Blagrave, J. *The Epitomie of the Art of Husbandry*. London, 1669.
Blake, W. T. 'Hooker's Synopsis Chorographical of Devonshire', *Devon Assoc.*, xlvii, 1915.
Bland, A. E., Brown, P. A., and Tawney, R. H. *English Economic History. Select Documents*. London, 1914.
Blith, Walter. *The English Improver Improved*. London, 1652.
Blome, Richard. *Britannia*. London, 1673.
Bouch, C. M. L., and Jones, G. P. *The Lake Counties, 1500–1830*. Manchester, 1961.
Bourne, George. *The Bettesworth Book. Talks with a Surrey Peasant*. London, 1920.
—— *Memoirs of a Surrey Labourer: a record of the last years of Frederick Bettesworth*. London, 1911.
Bowden, P. J. 'The Home Market in Wool, 1500–1700', *Yorks. Bull. of Econ. and Soc. Research*, viii, ii, 1956.
—— *The internal Wool Trade in England during the Sixteenth and Seventeenth Centuries*. University of Leeds Ph.D. thesis, 1952.
—— 'Movements in Wool Prices, 1490–1610', *Yorks. Bull. of Econ. and Soc. Research*, iv, 1952.
—— *The Wool Trade in Tudor and Stuart England*. London, 1962.
Brace, H. W. *History of Seed Crushing in Great Britain*. London, 1960.
Bradley, Harriet. *The Enclosures in England—an Economic Reconstruction*. New York, 1918.
Brenner, Y. S. 'The Inflation of Prices in Early Sixteenth Century England', EcHR, 2nd Ser., xiv, 1961.
—— 'The Inflation of Prices in England, 1551–1650', EcHR, 2nd Ser., xv, 1962.
Brett-James, N. G. *The Growth of Stuart London*. London, 1935.
Brown, E. H. Phelps, and Hopkins, Sheila V. 'Seven Centuries of Building Wages', *Economica*, NS, xxii, 1955.
—— 'Wage-rates and Prices: Evidence for Population Pressure in the Sixteenth Century', *Economica*, NS, xxiv, 1957.
—— 'Builders' Wage-rates, Prices and Population: Some Further Evidence', *Economica*, NS, xxvi, 1959.
Browning, Andrew (ed.). *English Historical Documents, 1660–1714*. London, 1953.
Brunskill, R. W. 'An Appreciation of Monmouthshire Houses', *Mont. Coll.*, liii, ii, 1954.

Brydson, A. P. *Some Records of two Lakeland Townships—Blawith and Nibthwaite—chiefly from original documents*. Ulverston, 1908.

Burton, William. *The Description of Leicestershire*. London, 1622.

Caley, J., and Hunter, J. (eds.). *Valor Ecclesiasticus temp. Hen. VIII*. . . . (6 vols.). London, 1810–34.

Camden, W. *Britannia*, trans. R. Gough. 3 vols., London, 1789.

Campbell, Mildred. *The English Yeoman Under Elizabeth and the Early Stuarts*. New Haven, 1942.

Carew, Richard. *The Survey of Cornwall*. London, 1602.

Carpenter, H. J. 'Furse of Morhead', *Devon Assoc.*, XXVI, 1894.

Cave, T., and Wilson, R. A. (eds.). *The Parliamentary Survey of the Lands and Possessions of the Dean and Chapter of Worcester*. Worcs. Hist. Soc., 1924.

Chalklin, C. W. 'The Compton Census of 1676: the dioceses of Canterbury and Rochester', *A Seventeenth Century Miscellany*. Kent Arch. Soc., Records Publication Committee, XVII, 1960.

—— 'The Rural Economy of a Kentish Wealden Parish, 1650–1750', AHR, X, 1962.

—— *Seventeenth Century Kent*. London, 1965.

Charles, B. G. 'The Second Book of George Owen's Description of Pembrokeshire', *Nat. Lib. Wales J.*, V, 1947–8.

Charman, D. 'Wealth and Trade in Leicester in the early Sixteenth Century', *Leics. Arch. Soc.*, XXV, 1949.

Cheke, Val. *The Story of Cheese-making in Britain*. London, 1959.

Chippindall, C. L. W. H. (ed.). *A Sixteenth-century Survey and Year's Account of the Estates of Hornby Castle, Lancashire*. Chetham Soc., NS, CII, 1939.

Cipolla, C. M. 'La prétendue "révolution des prix." Réflexions sur l'expérience italienne', *Annales E.S.C.*, 10e année, 4, 1955.

Clapham, Sir J. *A Concise Economic History of Britain from the Earliest Times to 1750*. Cambridge, 1949.

Clark, G. N. *The Wealth of England from 1496 to 1760*. Oxford, 1947.

Clarkson, L. A. 'The Organization of the English Leather Industry in the Late Sixteenth and Seventeenth Centuries', EcHR, 2nd Ser., XIII, 1960.

Clay, J. M. *Yorkshire Monasteries: Suppression Papers*. Yorks. Arch. Soc. Rec. Ser., XLVIII, 1912.

Clay, T. *Briefe, Easie and Necessary Tables of Interest and Rents Forborne*. London, 1624.

Cliffe, J. T. *The Yorkshire Gentry on the Eve of the Civil War*. University of London Ph.D. thesis, 1960.

Coleman, D. C. 'Industrial Growth and Industrial Revolutions', *Economica*, NS, XXIII, 1956.

—— 'Labour in the English Economy of the Seventeenth Century', EcHR, 2nd Ser., VIII, 1955–6.

Collier, C. V. 'Burton Agnes Courts, Miscellanea II', Yorks. Arch. Soc., Rec. Ser., LXXIV, 1929.

Collis, I. P. 'Leases for Term of Years, determinable with Lives', *J. Soc. Archivists*, I, 1957.

Considerations Touching Trade, with the Advance of the King's Revenue. . ., 1641.

Cooper, J. P. 'The Counting of Manors', EcHR, 2nd Ser., VIII, 1956.

—— 'The fortune of Thomas Wentworth, Earl of Strafford', EcHR, 2nd Ser., XI, 1958.

Cordingley, R. A. 'British Historical Roof Types and their Members', *Ancient Monuments Soc.*, NS, IX, 1961.

—— 'Stokesay Castle, Shropshire: The Chronology of its Buildings', *The Art Bulletin* (U.S.), XLV (2), 1963.

Cornwall, J. C. K. *The Agrarian History of Sussex, 1560–1640*. University of London M.A. thesis, 1953.

Cornwall, J. C. K. 'English Country Towns in the Fifteen Twenties', EcHR, 2nd Ser., xv, i, 1962.

—— 'Farming in Sussex, 1560–1640', Sussex Arch. Coll., xcii, 1954.

Cox, J. C. (ed.). The Records of the Borough of Northampton, II. Northampton, 1898.

Craig, Sir J. The Mint. A History of the London Mint from A.D. 287 to 1948. Cambridge, 1953.

Cramer, J. A. (ed.). The Second Book of the Travels of Nicander Nucius of Corcyra. Camden Soc., xvii, 1841.

Creighton, C. A History of Epidemics in Britain from A.D. 664 to the Extinction of Plague. Cambridge, 1891.

Crook, Barbara. 'Newnham Priory: Rental of Manor at Biddenham, 1505–6', Beds. Hist. Rec. Soc., xxv, 1947.

Cross, M. Claire, 'An Exchange of Lands with the Crown, 1587–8', Bull. IHR, xxxiv, 1961.

Cunningham, W. The Growth of English Industry and Commerce in Modern Times, II. Cambridge, 1919.

Daniel-Tyssen, J. R. 'The Parliamentary Surveys of the County of Sussex', Sussex Arch. Coll., xxiii, 1871.

Darby, H. C. The Draining of the Fens. Cambridge, 1940.

—— (ed.). Historical Geography of England before A.D. 1800. Cambridge, 1936.

Darby, H. C., and Saltmarsh, J. 'The Infield-Outfield System on a Norfolk Manor', Economic History, iii, 1935.

Davies, D. J. The Economic History of South Wales prior to 1800. Cardiff, 1933.

Davies, Elwyn. (ed.). Celtic Studies in Wales. Cardiff, 1963.

Deane, Phyllis, and Cole, W. A. British Economic Growth. 1688–1959. Cambridge, 1962.

Defoe, Daniel. A Tour through England and Wales. Everyman edn., London, 1959.

Dendy, F. W. 'The Ancient Farms of Northumberland', Archaeologia Aeliana, 2nd Ser., xvi, 1894.

Denney, A. H. The Sibton Abbey Estates: Select Documents, 1325–1509. Suffolk Rec. Soc., ii, 1960.

Dexter, R., and Barber, D. Farming for Profits. London, 1961.

Dickens, A. G. 'Estate and Household Management in Bedfordshire, c. 1540', Beds. Hist. Rec. Soc., xxxvi, 1956.

—— The Register or Chronicle of Butley Priory, Suffolk, 1510–35. Winchester, 1951.

Dietz, F. C. English Government Finance, 1485–1558. University of Illinois, Studies in the Social Sciences, ix, 3. Urbana, 1920.

—— English Public Finance, 1558–1641. New York, 1932.

Dodd, A. H. Studies in Stuart Wales. Cardiff, 1952.

Edwards, Ifan Ab Owen (ed.). A Catalogue of Star Chamber Proceedings relating to Wales. Cardiff, 1929.

Eland, G. (ed.). Thomas Wotton's Letter-Book, 1574–1586. London, 1960.

Ellis, Sir Henry (ed.). Speculi Britanniae Pars: an Historical and Chorographical Description of the County of Essex by John Norden, 1594. Camden Soc., ix, 1840.

Elsas, M. J. 'Price Data from Münich, 1500–1700', Economic History, iii, 1935.

—— Umriss einer Geschichte der Preise und Löhne in Deutschland vom ausgehenden Mittelalter bis zum Beginn des Neunzehnten Jahrhunderts, i, ii. Leiden, 1936–49.

Elton, G. R. The Tudor Constitution. Cambridge, 1960.

—— The Tudor Revolution in Government. Cambridge, 1953.

Emerson, W. R. The Economic Development of the Estates of the Petre Family in Essex in the Sixteenth and Seventeenth Centuries. University of Oxford D.Phil. thesis, 1951.

Emery, F. V. 'West Glamorgan farming circa 1580–1620', Nat. Lib. Wales J., ix, x, 1955–6, 1957–8.

Emmison, F. G. *Tudor Secretary: Sir William Petre at Court and Home.* London, 1961.
Ernle, Lord. *English Farming Past and Present.* New (sixth) edn., London, 1961.
Evans, A. 'Battle Abbey at the Dissolution', *Huntington Lib. Qtrly.*, IV, 1941–2.
Evans, Elwyn. 'Two Machynlleth Toll-Books', *Nat. Lib. Wales J.*, VI, 1949–50.
Evans, G. Ewart. *The Horse in the Furrow.* London, 1960.
Everitt, Alan. *The Community of Kent and the Great Rebellion, 1640–60,* Leicester, 1966.
—— *The County Committee of Kent in the Civil War.* Leicester, Dept. of English Local History, Occasional Papers, 9, 1957.
—— *Kent and its Gentry, 1640–1660: a political Study.* University of London Ph.D. thesis, 1957.
—— *Suffolk and the Great Rebellion.* Suffolk Rec. Soc., III, 1961.
Farrer, W. *Chartulary of Cockersand Abbey,* III, iii. Chetham Soc., NS, LXIV, 1909.
Feaveryear, A. E. *The Pound Sterling. A History of English Money.* Oxford, 1933.
Felix, D. 'Profit Inflation and Industrial Growth', *Qtrly. J. of Economics,* LXX, 1956.
Fiennes, Celia. *The Journeys of Celia Fiennes.* ed. C. Morris. London, 1947.
Finberg, H. P. R. 'An Early Reference to the Welsh Cattle Trade', AHR, II, 1954.
—— *Gloucestershire Studies.* Leicester, 1957.
—— 'The Gostwicks of Willington', *Beds. Hist. Rec. Soc.,* XXXVI, 1956.
—— *Tavistock Abbey.* Cambridge, 1951.
Finch, Mary. *The Wealth of Five Northamptonshire Families, 1540–1640.* Northants. Rec. Soc., XIX, 1956.
Fisher, F. J. 'Commercial Trends and Policy in Sixteenth Century England', EcHR, X, 1939–40.
—— 'The Development of the London Food Market, 1540–1640', EcHR, V, 1935.
—— 'London's Export Trade in the Early Seventeenth Century', EcHR, 2nd Ser., III, 1950.
Fisher, H. A. L. *The History of England, 1485–1547.* London, 1906.
Fishwick, H. (ed.). *The Survey of the Manor of Rochdale.* Chetham Soc., NS, LXXI, 1913.
Folkingham, W. *Feudigraphia.* London, 1610.
Fowler, J. T. *The Coucher Book of Selby Abbey, II.* Yorks. Arch. Soc., Rec. Ser., XIII, 1893.
Fowler, R. C. 'Inventories of Essex Monasteries in 1536', *Essex Arch. Soc.,* NS, X, 1909.
Fox, Sir Cyril. *A Country House of the Elizabethan Period in Wales: Six Wells, Llantwit Major, Glamorganshire.* Cardiff, 1941.
—— 'The Round-chimneyed Farm-houses of Northern Pembrokeshire', *Aspects of Archaeology in Britain and Beyond, Essays presented to O. G. S. Crawford,* ed. W. F. Grimes. London, 1951.
—— 'Three Rounded Gable Houses in Carmarthenshire', *Arch. Camb.,* 1951.
Fox, Sir C., and Raglan, Lord. *Monmouthshire Houses: A Study of Building Techniques and Smaller House-Plans in the Fifteenth to Seventeenth Centuries.* 3 vols. Cardiff, 1951–4.
Fussell, G. E. 'Adventures with Clover', *Agriculture,* LXII, 7, 1955.
—— 'Cornish Farming, A.D. 1500–1910', *Amateur Historian,* IV, 8. 1960.
—— *The English Rural Labourer.* London, 1949.
—— 'Four Centuries of Cheshire Farming Systems, 1500–1900', *Hist. Soc. Lancs. & Cheshire,* CVI, 1954.
—— 'Four Centuries of Farming Systems in Derbyshire, 1500–1900', *Derbyshire Arch. & Nat. Hist. Soc.,* LXXI, 1951.
—— 'Four Centuries of Farming Systems in Dorset, 1500–1900', *Dorset Nat. Hist. & Arch. Soc.,* LXXIII, 1952.
—— 'Four Centuries of Farming Systems in Hampshire, 1500–1900', *Hants. Field Club & Arch. Soc.,* XVII, iii, 1949.

Fussell, G. E. 'Four Centuries of Farming Systems in Shropshire, 1500–1900', *Salop Arch. Soc.*, LIV, i, 1951–2.

—— 'Four Centuries of Nottinghamshire Farming', *Notts. Countryside*, XVII, 2, 1956.

—— 'History of Cole (*Brassica* Sp.)', *Nature*, 4471 (9 July), CLXXVI, 1955.

—— *Robert Loder's Farm Accounts, 1610–1620*. Camden Soc., 3rd Ser., LIII, 1936.

Fussell, G. E., and Goodman, Constance. 'The Eighteenth-century Traffic in Milk Products', *Economic History*, III, 1937.

Gardiner, Dorothy (ed.). *The Oxinden Letters, 1607–1642*. London, 1933.

Gardiner, S. R. (ed.). *The Constitutional Documents of the Puritan Revolution, 1625–1660*. 1906 edn., Oxford.

Gay, E. F. 'Inclosures in England in the Sixteenth Century', *Qtrly. J. of Economics*, XVII, 1903.

—— 'Inquisitions of Depopulation in 1517 and the Domesday of Inclosures', RHS, NS, XIV, 1900.

—— 'The Midland Revolt and the Inquisitions of Depopulation of 1607', RHS, XVIII, 1904.

—— 'The Rise of an English Country Family: Peter and John Temple, to 1603', *Huntington Lib. Qtrly.*, I, 1938.

—— 'The Temples of Stowe and Their Debts: Sir Thomas Temple and Sir Peter Temple, 1603–1653', *Huntington Lib. Qtrly.*, II, 1938–9.

Gerard, J. *The Herball or Generall Historie of Plantes*. London, 1597.

Glass, D. V. 'Gregory King's Estimates of the Population of England and Wales, 1695', *Population Studies*, III, 1950.

Gough, R. (ed.). *Description des Royaulmes d'Angleterre et d'Escosse composé par Etienne Perlin, Paris 1558*. London, 1775.

Gould, J. D. 'Mr Beresford and the Lost Villages: a Comment', AHR, III, 1955.

—— 'The Inquisition of Depopulation of 1607 in Lincolnshire', EHR, LXVII, 1952.

Grafton, Richard. *A little Treatise conteyning many proper Tables and Rules, very necessary for the use of all men*. 1602 edn., London.

Gras, N. S. B. *The Evolution of the English Corn Market...*, Cambridge, Mass., 1926.

Gray, H. L. *English Field Systems*. Harvard Historical Studies, XXII, 1915.

Green, Mrs J. R. *Town Life in the Fifteenth Century*. London, 1894.

Habakkuk, H. J. 'The Long-term Rate of Interest and the Price of Land in the Seventeenth Century', EcHR, 2nd Ser., V, 1952.

—— 'The Market for Monastic Property, 1539–1603', EcHR, 2nd Ser., X, 3, 1958.

Haldane, A. R. B. *The Drove Roads of Scotland*. London, 1952.

Hallam, H. E. 'Some Thirteenth-century Censuses', EcHR, 2nd Ser., X, 3, 1958.

Hallett, G. *The Economics of Agricultural Land Tenure*. London, 1960.

Hamilton, E. J. 'American Treasure and Andalusian Prices, 1503–1660', *J. Econ. & Bus. Hist.*, I, 1928–9.

—— *American Treasure and the Price Revolution in Spain, 1501–1650*. Harvard, 1934.

—— *Money, Prices, and Wages in Valencia, Aragon, and Navarre, 1351–1500*. Harvard, 1936.

—— 'The Decline of Spain', EcHR, VIII, 1938.

Hammarström, D. I. 'The Price Revolution of the Sixteenth Century: Some Swedish Evidence', *Scand. Econ. Hist. Rev.*, V, 1957.

Hammersley, G. 'The Crown Woods and their Exploitation in the Sixteenth and Seventeenth Centuries', *Bull. IHR*, XXX, 1957.

Harland, John (ed.). *The House and Farm Accounts of the Shuttleworths of Gawthorpe Hall...*, Parts I and II. Chetham Soc., XXXV, XLI, 1856.

Harris, A. 'The Agriculture of the East Riding of Yorkshire before the Parliamentary Enclosures', *Yorks. Arch. J.*, CLVII, 1959.

Harrison, William. *Harrison's Description of England in Shakspere's Youth*, ed. F. J. Furnivall, New Shakspere Soc., 6th Ser. I and VIII. London 1877 and 1881.

Hartlib, Samuel. *Samuel Hartlib his Legacie*. London, 1652.

Harvey, N. 'Farm and Estate under Elizabeth the First', *Agriculture*, LX, 1953.

Hasbach, W.. *A History of the English Agricultural Labourer*. London, 1908.

Hasted, Edward. *History of Kent*. Canterbury, 1797–1801.

Havinden, M. 'Agricultural Progress in Open-field Oxfordshire', AHR, IX, 1961.

Hembry, P. M. *The Bishops of Bath and Wells, 1535–1647: a social and economic study*. London University Ph.D. thesis, 1956.

Hemp, W. J., and Gresham, Colin. 'Park, Llanfrothen and the Unit System', *Arch. Camb.*, XCVII, 1942.

Henman, W. N. 'Newnham Priory: a Bedford Rental, 1506–7', *Beds. Hist. Rec. Soc.*, XXV, 1947.

Hervey, Lord Francis (ed.). *Suffolk in the Seventeenth Century. The Breviary of Suffolk by Robert Reyce, 1618*. London, 1902.

Hexter, J. H. *Reappraisals in History*. London, 1961.

Heylyn, Peter. *A Help to English History*. 1709 edn., London.

Hill, C. *Economic Problems of the Church, from Archbishop Whitgift to the Long Parliament*. Oxford, 1956.

Hill, J. W. F. *Tudor and Stuart Lincoln*. Cambridge, 1956.

Hilton, R. H. *The Social Structure of Rural Warwickshire*. Dugdale Soc. Occasional Paper, 9, 1950.

—— 'Winchcombe Abbey and the Manor of Sherborne', *Gloucestershire Studies*, ed. H. P. R. Finberg. Leicester, 1957.

Hirst, L. F. *The Conquest of Plague*. Oxford, 1953.

Hobsbawm, E. 'The General Crisis of the European Economy in the Seventeenth Century', *Past and Present*, V, VI, 1954.

Holdsworth, W. S. *An Historical Introduction to the Land Law*. Oxford, 1927.

Hopkins, E. *The Bridgewater Estates in North Shropshire in the First Half of the Seventeenth Century*. University of London M.A. thesis, 1956.

Hoskins, W. G. *Devon*. London, 1954.

—— 'English Provincial Towns in the early Sixteenth Century', RHS, 5th Ser., VI, 1956.

—— *Essays in Leicestershire History*. Liverpool, 1950.

—— 'Harvest Fluctuations and English Economic History, 1480–1619', AHR, XII, 1964.

—— *Industry, Trade, and People in Exeter, 1688–1800*. Manchester, 1935.

—— *The Midland Peasant*. London, 1957.

—— 'The Reclamation of the Waste in Devon', EcHR, XIII, 1943.

—— *Two Thousand Years in Exeter*. Exeter, 1960.

Hoskins, W. G., and Finberg, H. P. R. *Devonshire Studies*. London, 1952.

Howells, B. E. 'Pembrokeshire Farming *circa* 1580–1620', *Nat. Lib. Wales J.*, IX, 1955–6.

Hudson, W. H. *A Shepherd's Life*. Everyman edn., London, 1949.

Hughes, H. 'Notes on the Architecture of some old houses in the neighbourhood of Llansilin, Denbighshire', *Arch. Camb.*, XV (5th Ser.), 1898.

Hughes, H., and North, H. L. *The Old Cottages of Snowdonia*. Bangor, 1908.

Hulbert, N. F. 'A Survey of the Somerset Fairs', *Som. Arch. and Nat. Hist. Soc.*, LXXXII, 1937.

Hull, F. *Agriculture and Rural Society in Essex, 1560–1640*. University of London Ph.D. thesis, 1950.

Hurstfield, J. 'Corruption and Reform under Edward VI and Mary: the Example of Wardship', EHR, LXVIII, 1953.
—— 'The Greenwich Tenures of the Reign of Edward VI', *Law Qtrly. Rev.* LXV, 1949.
—— 'Lord Burghley as Master of the Court of Wards', RHS, 4th Ser., XXXI, 1949.
—— 'The Profits of Fiscal Feudalism', EcHR, 2nd Ser., VIII, 1955.
—— *The Queen's Wards: Wardship and marriage under Elizabeth I.* London, 1958.
Jackson, J. N. 'Some Observations upon the Herefordshire Environment of the Seventeenth and Eighteenth Centuries', *Woolhope Nat. Field Club*, XXXVI, i, 1958.
James, M. E. *Estate Accounts of the Earls of Northumberland, 1562–1637.* Surtees Soc., CLXIII, 1955.
Jefferies, Richard. *Field and Hedgerow. Being the Last Essays of Richard Jefferies.* London, 1904.
—— *The Toilers of the Field.* London and New York, 1892.
Jevons, W. S. *Investigations in Currency and Finance.* 2nd edn., London, 1909.
Jevons, H. S. *The Causes of Unemployment, the Sun's Heat, and Trade Activity.* London, 1910.
—— 'Trade Fluctuations and Solar Activity', *Contemporary Rev.*, August, 1909.
Johnson, A. H. *The Disappearance of the Small Landowner.* New edn., London, 1963.
Jones, Emyr G. (ed.). *Exchequer Proceedings (Equity) concerning Wales, Henry VIII–Elizabeth.* Cardiff, 1939.
Jones, E. L. 'Eighteenth-century Changes in Hampshire Chalkland Farming', AHR, VIII, 1960.
Jones, Francis. 'An Approach to Welsh Genealogy', *Trans. Cymmrodorion Soc.*, 1948.
Jones, S. R., and Smith, J. T. 'The Houses of Breconshire, Part I', *Brycheiniog*, 1963.
Jones, T. I. Jeffreys (ed.). *Exchequer Proceedings concerning Wales in Tempore James I.* Cardiff, 1955.
Kennedy, J. *The Dissolution of the Monasteries in Hampshire and the Isle of Wight.* London University M.A. thesis, 1953.
Kenyon, G. H. 'Petworth Town and Trades, 1610–1760: Part I', *Sussex Arch. Coll.*, XCVI, 1958.
Kerridge, E. 'Agriculture, c. 1500–c. 1793', VCH *Wilts.*, IV, 1959.
—— *The Agrarian Development of Wiltshire, 1540–1640.* University of London Ph.D. thesis, 1951.
—— 'The Floating of the Wiltshire Watermeadows', *Wilts. Arch. & Nat. Hist. Mag.*, LV, 1953.
—— 'The Movement of Rent 1540–1640', EcHR, 2nd Ser., VI, 1953.
—— 'The Notebook of a Wiltshire Farmer in the early seventeenth century', *Wilts. Arch. & Nat. Hist. Mag.*, LIV, 1952.
—— 'A Reconsideration of some Former Husbandry Practices', AHR, III, 1955.
—— 'The Returns of the Inquisitions of Depopulation', EHR, LXX, 1955.
—— 'The Revolts in Wiltshire against Charles I', *Wilts. Arch. & Nat. Hist. Mag.*, LVII, 1958–9.
—— 'Ridge and Furrow and Agrarian History', EcHR, 2nd Ser., IV, 1951.
—— 'The Sheepfold in Wiltshire and the Floating of the Watermeadows', EcHR, 2nd Ser., VI, 1954.
—— 'Social and Economic History of Leicester', VCH *Leics.*, IV, 1958.
—— *Surveys of the Manors of Philip, First Earl of Pembroke, 1631–2.* Wilts. Arch. and Nat. Hist. Soc., Records Branch, IX, 1953.
King, G. *Natural and Political Observations and Conclusions upon the State and Condition of England.* 1696.
Klotz, E. L., and Davies, G. 'The Wealth of Royalist Peers and Baronets during the Puritan Revolution', EHR, LVIII, 1943.

Knocker, H. W. 'Sevenoaks: the Manor, Church and Market', *Arch. Cant.*, XXXVII, 1926.

Knowles, D. *The Religious Orders in England*, III. Cambridge, 1959.

Knox, Ronald. *Enthusiasm: a Chapter in the History of Religion*. Oxford, 1950.

Koenigsberger, H. G. 'Property and the Price Revolution (Hainault, 1474–1573)', EcHR, 2nd Ser., IX, 1956.

Lambarde, William. *A Perambulation of Kent*. 1826 edn., Chatham.

Lamond, E. (ed.). *A Discourse of the Common Weal of this Realm of England*. Cambridge, 1954.

Laslett, T. P. R. 'The Gentry of Kent in 1640', *Camb. Hist. J.*, IX, 1948.

Leadam, I. S. *The Domesday of Inclosures, 1517–18*. 2 vols. RHS, 1897.

Le Hardy, W. *County of Buckingham: Calendar to the Sessions Records, I, 1678–1694*. Aylesbury, 1933.

Leland, J. *Itinerary in England*, ed. L. Toulmin Smith. 5 vols. London, 1906–8.

Lennard, R. 'The Alleged Exhaustion of the Soil in Medieval England', *Econ. J.*, CXXXV, 1922.

—— 'English Agriculture under Charles II: The Evidence of the Royal Society's "Enquiries"', EcHR, IV, 1932.

—— *Rural Northamptonshire under the Commonwealth*. Oxford Studies in Social and Legal History, V, 1916.

Leonard, E. M. 'The Inclosure of Common Fields in the Seventeenth Century', RHS, NS, XIX, 1905.

—— 'The Relief of the Poor by the State Regulation of Wages', EHR, XIII, 1898.

Lewis, E. A. (ed.). *An Inventory of the Early Chancery Proceedings concerning Wales*. Cardiff, 1937.

—— 'The Toll-Books of some North Pembrokeshire Fairs (1599–1603)', *Bull.* BCS, VII, 1934.

Lewis, E. A., and Davies, J. Conway (eds.). *Records of the Court of Augmentations relating to Wales and Monmouthshire*. Cardiff, 1954.

Lipson, E. *The Economic History of England*, III. London, 1947.

Lisle, E. *Observations in Husbandry*, II. London, 1757.

Lister, J. 'Some Local Star Chamber Cases', *Halifax Antiq. Soc.*, 1927.

—— *Yorkshire Star Chamber Proceedings*, IV. Yorks. Arch. Soc., Rec. Ser., LXX, 1927.

Lloyd, Nathaniel. *A History of the English House from primitive times to the Victorian Period*. London, 1931.

Lodge, E. C. *The Account Book of a Kentish Estate, 1616–1704*. Records of the Social and Economic History of England and Wales, VI. London, 1927.

Low, David. *On the Domesticated Animals of the British Islands*. London, 1845.

Lyte, Henry. *A Niewe Herbal or Historie of Plantes...translated out of French by H.L.* London, 1578.

McGrath, P. V. *The Marketing of Food, Fodder, and Livestock in the London Area in the Seventeenth Century*. University of London M.A. thesis, 1948.

Malfatti, C. V. *Two Italian Accounts of Tudor England*. Barcelona, 1953.

Markham, Gervase. *Cheape and Good Husbandry*. 1623.

—— *Markham's Farewell to Husbandry*. London, 1625.

Marshall, William. *The Rural Economy of Norfolk*. London, 1787.

—— *The Rural Economy of the Southern Counties*. 2 vols., London, 1798.

Mascall, L. *The Government of Cattell....* London, 1620.

Matthews, C. M. 'Annals of the Poor: taken from the Records of a Hertfordshire Village', *History Today*, V, 1955.

Maxey, E. *A New Instruction of Plowing and Setting of Corne, Handled in Manner of a Dialogue betweene a Ploughman and a Scholler*. London, 1601.

Meekings, C. A. F. *Dorset Hearth Tax Assessments, 1662–1664.* Dorset Nat. Hist. and Arch. Soc., Occasional Publications, Dorchester, 1951.

Mercer, E. 'The Houses of the Gentry', *Past and Present*, v, 1954.

Miller, H. 'The Early Tudor Peerage' (thesis summary), *Bull. IHR*, XXIV, 1951.

—— 'Subsidy Assessments of the Peerage in the Sixteenth Century', *Bull. IHR*, XXVIII, 1955.

Minchinton, W. 'Bristol—Metropolis of the West in the Eighteenth Century', RHS, 5th Ser., IV, 1954.

Moore, H. L. *Economic Cycles: their Law and Cause.* New York, 1914.

—— *Generating Economic Cycles.* New York, 1923.

More, Sir Thomas. *The Utopia of Sir Thomas More*, ed. J. H. Lupton. Oxford, 1895.

Mortimer, J. *The Whole Art of Husbandry.* London, 1707.

Morton, J. *The Natural History of Northamptonshire.* London, 1712.

Mousley, J. E. 'The Fortunes of Some Gentry Families of Elizabethan Sussex', EcHR, 2nd Ser., XI, 1959.

Munby, L. *Hertfordshire Population Statistics, 1563–1801.* Hitchin, 1964.

Nalson, John. *An impartial Collection of the great Affairs of State.* I. London, 1682.

Nef, J. U. 'A Comparison of Industrial Growth in France and England, 1540–1640', EcHR, VII, 1937.

—— 'Mining and Metallurgy in Medieval Civilisation', *The Cambridge Economic History of Europe*, ed. M. Postan and E. E. Rich, II. Cambridge, 1952.

—— 'Silver Production in Central Europe', *J. Polit. Econ.*, XLIX, 1941.

—— *The Rise of the British Coal Industry.* London, 1932.

—— 'The Progress of Technology and the Growth of Large-scale Industry in Great Britain, 1540–1640', EcHR, v, 1934.

Norden, John. *Speculum Britanniae. An Historical and Chorographical Description of Middlesex and Hartfordshire.* London, 1723.

—— *The Surveyors Dialogue.* London, 1607.

Notestein, W., Relf, F. H., and Simpson, H. (eds.). *Commons Debates, 1621.* 8 vols. New Haven, 1935.

Oschinsky, D. 'Medieval Treatises on Estate Accounting', EcHR, XVII, 1947.

Owen, George. *Description of Pembrokeshire*, 2 vols. ed. H. Owen. London, 1892.

—— *The Taylors Cussion*, ed. E. M. Pritchard. London, 1906.

Owen, G. Dyfnallt. *Elizabethan Wales. The Social Scene.* Cardiff, 1962.

Owen, L. 'The Population of Wales in the Sixteenth and Seventeenth Centuries', *Hon. Soc. Cymmrodorion*, 1959.

Page, F. M. *Wellingborough Manorial Accounts, A.D. 1258–1323.* Northants. Rec. Soc., VIII, 1936.

Palmer, A. N. *History of Ancient Tenures of Land in the Marches of North Wales.* Wrexham, 1883. Second edition in collaboration with Edward Owen, 1910.

Parenti, G. *Prime ricerche sulla rivoluzione dei prezzi in Firenze.* Florence, 1939.

Parker, L. A. 'The Agrarian Revolution at Cotesbach, 1501–1612', *Studies in Leicestershire Agrarian History, Leics. Arch. Soc.*, XXIV, 1948.

—— 'The Depopulation Returns for Leicestershire in 1607', *Leics. Arch. Soc.*, XXIII, 1947.

—— *Enclosure in Leicestershire, 1485–1607.* University of London Ph.D. thesis, 1948.

Parliament. House of Commons. *Journals*, I, II, 1547–1642.

Pearce, Brian. 'The Elizabethan Food Policy and the Armed Forces', EcHR, XII, 1942.

Peate, I. C. *The Welsh House, A Study in Folk Culture.* Liverpool, 1944.

Pelc, J. *Ceny w Krakowie w latach 1369–1600, Badania z dziejow spolecznych i gospodarczych.* Lwow, 1935.

Pierce, T. Jones (ed.). 'An Anglesey Crown Rental of the Sixteenth Century', *Bull. BCS*, x, 1940.

Pierce, T. Jones (ed.). *A Calendar of Clenennau Letters and Papers*. Aberystwyth, 1947.
—— 'The Law of Wales—the last Phase', *Trans. Cymmrodorion Soc.*, 1963.
—— 'Notes on the History of Rural Caernarvonshire in the Reign of Elizabeth', *Trans. Caernarvons. Hist. Soc.*, 1940.
—— 'Pastoral and Agricultural Settlements in Early Wales', *Geografiska Annaler*, XLIII, 1961.
Platt, Sir Hugh. *The Jewell House of Art and Nature....* London, 1594.
Plattes, G. *A Discovery of Infinite Treasure Hidden Since the World's Beginning*. London, 1639.
Plot, R. *The Natural History of Oxfordshire....* Oxford, 1677.
Plymley, Joseph. *General View of the Agriculture of Shropshire*. London, 1803.
Pollard, A. F., and Blatcher, M. 'Hayward Townshend's Journals', *Bull. IHR*, XII, 1934–5.
Postan, M. M. 'Some Economic Evidence of Declining Population in the later Middle Ages', *EcHR*, 2nd Ser., II, 1950.
—— 'The Chronology of Labour Services', *RHS*, 4th Ser., XX, 1937.
—— 'The Fifteenth Century', *EcHR*, IX, 1939.
Pribram, A. F. *Materialien zur Geschichte der Preise und Löhne in Österreich*. Vienna, 1938.
Pringle, A. *General View of the Agriculture of the County of Westmorland*. London, 1813.
Public Record Office, London. *Acts of the Privy Council, New Series, 1542–1630*.
Pugh, R. B. *Antrobus Deeds before 1625*. Wilts. Arch. & Nat. Hist. Soc., Records Branch, III, 1947.
—— *The Crown Estate, An Historical Essay*. London, 1960.
Pugh, T. B. (ed.). *The Marcher Lordships of South Wales, 1415–1536*. Cardiff, 1963.
Purvis, J. S. 'A Note on Sixteenth-century Farming in Yorkshire', *Yorks. Arch. J.*, XXXVI, 1944.
—— *A Selection of Monastic Records and Dissolution Papers*. Yorks. Arch. Soc. Rec. Ser., LXXX, 1931.
Ramsay, G. D. (ed.). *John Isham, Mercer and Merchant Adventurer: Two Account Books of a London Merchant in the Reign of Elizabeth I*. Northants. Rec. Soc., XXI, 1962.
Rathbone, A. *The Surveyor in Foure Bookes*. London, 1616.
Rea, W. F. 'The Rental and Accounts of Sir Richard Shireburn, 1571–77', *Hist. Soc., Lancs. & Cheshire*, CX, 1959.
Rees, W. *A Survey of the Duchy of Lancaster Lordships in Wales, 1609–13*. Cardiff, 1953.
Reid, Rachel R. *The King's Council in the North*. London, 1921.
Rew, R. H. *An Agricultural Faggot. A Collection of Papers on Agricultural Subjects*. Westminster, 1913.
Richards, Thomas. *A History of the Puritan Movement in Wales, 1639–53*. London, 1920.
Richardson, H. *Medieval Fairs and Markets of York*. St Anthony's Hall Publications, 20. York, 1961.
Richardson, W. C. *History of the Court of Augmentations, 1536–1554*. Baton Rouge, 1961.
—— *Tudor Chamber Administration, 1485–1547*. Baton Rouge, 1952.
Robinson, Thomas. *The Common Law of Kent; or, the Customs of Gavelkind. With an Appendix concerning Borough English*. London, 1822.
Rodgers, H. B. 'Land Use in Tudor Lancashire: the Evidence of the Final Concords, 1450–1558', *Trans. Inst. British Geographers*, XXI, 1955.
—— 'The Market Area of Preston in the Sixteenth and Seventeenth Centuries', *Geographical Studies*, III, i, 1956.
Rogers, J. E. T. *A History of Agriculture and Prices in England*. Oxford, 1866–1900.
—— *Six Centuries of Work and Wages*. London, 1894.

Rogers, P. G. *Battle in Bossenden Wood*. London, 1961.

Rowse, A. L. *The England of Elizabeth*. London, 1950.

—— *Tudor Cornwall, Portrait of a Society*. London, 1941.

Royal Commission on Ancient Monuments in Wales and Monmouthshire. *Anglesey Inventory*. London, 1937.

—— *Caernarvonshire Inventory*, 3 vols. London, 1956–64.

Royal Commission on Historical Monuments. *Monuments threatened or destroyed: a Select List*. London, 1963.

Royal Commission on Land in Wales and Monmouthshire. *Report*. London, 1896.

Royce, D. (ed.). *Landboc sive Registrum Monasterii...de Winchelcumba...*, II. Exoniae, 1903.

Russell, J. C. *British Medieval Population*. Albuquerque, 1948.

Rye, W. B. *England as seen by Foreigners*. London, 1865.

Sabin, A. *Some Manorial Accounts of Saint Augustine's Abbey, Bristol*. Bristol Rec. Soc., XXII, 1960.

Salter, E. Gurney. *Tudor England through Venetian Eyes*. London, 1930.

Salter, H. E. *Cartulary of Oseney Abbey*, VI. Oxford Hist. Soc., CI, 1936.

Saltmarsh, J. 'A College Home-farm in the Fifteenth Century', *Economic History*, III, 1936.

—— 'Plague and Economic Decline in England', *Camb. Hist. J.*, VII, 1941.

Savine, A. 'Bondmen under the Tudors', RHS, NS, XVII, 1903.

—— *English Monasteries on the eve of the Dissolution*. Oxford Studies in Social and Legal History, ed. P. Vinogradoff, I, 1909.

Sayce, R. U. 'The Old Summer Pastures, Pt II', *Mont. Coll.*, LV, i, 1958.

Schenk, W. *The Concern for Social Justice in the Puritan Revolution*. London, 1948.

Scott, W. D. Robson. *German Travellers in England, 1400–1800*. Oxford, 1953.

Simiand, F. *Recherches anciennes et nouvelles sur le mouvement général des prix du XVIᵉ au XIXᵉ siècle*. Paris, 1932.

Simpson, A. *The Wealth of the Gentry, 1540–1660: East Anglian Studies*. Cambridge, 1961.

Skeat, Rev. W. W. (ed.). *The Book of Husbandry by Master Fitzherbert*. English Dialect Soc., 1882.

Skeel, Caroline. 'The Cattle Trade between Wales and England...', RHS, 4th Ser., IX, 1926.

Slack, W. J. *The Lordship of Oswestry, 1393–1607*. Shrewsbury, 1951.

Smith, J. T. 'The Long-house in Monmouthshire: a Reappraisal', *Culture and Environment*, ed. Alcock & Foster, 1963.

—— 'Medieval Roofs: A Classification', *Arch. J.*, CXV, 1958.

Smith, P. 'The Long-house and the Laithe-house', *Culture and Environment*, ed. Alcock & Foster, 1963.

—— 'Plas Teg', *J. Flints. Hist. Soc.*, XVIII, 1960.

Smith, P., and Gardner, E. M. 'Two Farmhouses in Llanbedr', *J. Merioneth Hist. and Rec. Soc.*, III, iii, 1959.

Smith, P., and Owen, C. E. V. 'Traditional and Renaissance Elements in some late Stuart and early Georgian Half-timbered Houses in Arwystli', *Mont. Coll.*, LV, 1958.

Smith, R. A. L. *Canterbury Cathedral Priory, A Study in Monastic Administration*. Cambridge, 1943.

Smith, W. J. (ed.). *Calendar of Salusbury Correspondence, 1553–1700*. Cardiff, 1954.

Somerville, R. *History of the Duchy of Lancaster*, I, 1265–1603. London, 1953.

Speed, Adolphus. *Adam out of Eden...*, London, 1659.

Speed, Adolphus. *The Husbandman, Farmer, and Grazier's...Instructor...or Country-man's Guide*. London, [1705 or later].

Spratt, J. *Agrarian Conditions in Norfolk and Suffolk, 1600–1650*. Univ. of London M.A. thesis, 1935.

Steer, F. W. (ed.). *Farm and Cottage Inventories of Mid-Essex, 1635–1749*. Chelmsford, 1950.

Stone, L. 'The Anatomy of the Elizabethan Aristocracy', EcHR, XVIII, 1948.

—— 'The Elizabethan Aristocracy—a Restatement', EcHR, 2nd Ser., IV, 1952.

—— 'Elizabethan Overseas Trade', EcHR, 2nd Ser., II, 1949.

—— 'The Fruits of Office: The Case of Robert Cecil, first Earl of Salisbury, 1596–1612', *Essays in the Economic and Social History of Tudor and Stuart England*, ed. F. J. Fisher, Cambridge, 1961.

—— 'The Nobility in Business, 1540–1640', *The Entrepreneur*, Harvard University, 1957.

—— 'State Control in Sixteenth-century England', EcHR, XVII, 1947.

Straker, E. 'Ashdown Forest and its Inclosures', *Sussex Arch. Coll.*, LXXXI, 1940.

Straton, C. R. *Survey of the lands of William, first earl of Pembroke*. Roxburghe Club, 2 vols., 1909.

Summerson, Sir J. N. *Architecture in Britain 1530 to 1830*. London, 1953.

Supple, B. E. *Commercial Crisis and Change in England, 1600–1642*. Cambridge, 1959.

Sylvester, D. 'The Open Fields of Cheshire', *Hist. Soc. Lancs. & Cheshire*, CVIII, 1956.

Sylvester, D., and Nulty, G. *The Historical Atlas of Cheshire*. Chester, 1958.

T., R. Gent. *The Tenants' Law, or the Laws Concerning Landlords, Tenants and Farmers*. London, 1666.

Tables of Leases and Interest..., London, 1628.

Tawney, R. H. *The Agrarian Problem in the Sixteenth Century*. London, 1912.

—— *Business and Politics under James I: Lionel Cranfield as Merchant and Minister*. Cambridge, 1958.

—— 'The Rise of the Gentry, 1558–1640', EcHR, XI, 1941.

—— 'The Rise of the Gentry: A Postscript', EcHR, 2nd Ser., VII, 1954.

Tawney, A. J. and R. H. 'An Occupational Census of the Seventeenth Century', EcHR, V, 1934–5.

Tawney, R. H., and Power, Eileen (eds.). *Tudor Economic Documents*, 3 vols. London, 1924.

Taylor, H. *Old Halls of Lancashire and Cheshire*. Manchester, 1884.

Thirsk, Joan. *English Peasant Farming*. London, 1957.

—— 'Industries in the Countryside', *Essays in the Economic and Social History of Tudor and Stuart England*, ed. F. J. Fisher. Cambridge, 1961.

—— 'The Isle of Axholme before Vermuyden', AHR, I, 1953.

—— *Tudor Enclosures*. Hist. Assoc. Pamphlet, General Ser., 41, 1959.

Thomas, D. R. *The History of the Diocese of Saint Asaph*. 3 vols. Oswestry, 1908.

Thomas, Lawrence. *The Reformation in the Old Diocese of Llandaff*. Cardiff, 1930.

Thompson, Flora. *Lark Rise to Candleford*. 1957 edn., London.

Thorpe, S. M. *The Monastic Lands in Leicestershire on and after the Dissolution*. University of Oxford B.Litt. thesis, 1961.

Topographer and Genealogist, I. London, 1846.

Torr, Cecil. *Small Talk at Wreyland*. 1926 edn., Cambridge.

Trevor-Roper, H. R. 'The Elizabethan Aristocracy: an anatomy anatomized', EcHR, 2nd Ser., III, 1951.

—— *The Gentry, 1540–1640*. EcHR Supplement, I, 1953.

Trow-Smith, R. *A History of British Livestock Husbandry to 1700*. London, 1957.

Tupling, G. H. 'An Alphabetical List of the Markets and Fairs of Lancashire recorded before the Year 1701', *Lancs. and Ches. Antiq. Soc.*, LI, 1936.

—— *The Economic History of Rossendale.* Chetham Soc., NS, LXXXVI, 1927.

—— 'Lancashire Markets in the Sixteenth and Seventeenth Centuries', *Lancs. and Ches. Antiq. Soc.*, LVIII, 1947.

—— 'The Origin of Markets and Fairs in Medieval Lancashire', *Lancs. and Ches. Antiq. Soc.*, XLIX, 1933.

Tyack, N. C. P. *Migration from East Anglia to New England before 1660.* University of London Ph.D. thesis, 1951.

Upton, A. F. *Sir Arthur Ingram, c. 1565–1642.* London, 1961.

Utterström, G. 'Climatic Fluctuations and Population Problems in Early Modern History', *Scand. Econ. Hist. Rev.*, III, 1955.

Verlinden, C. and Others. 'Mouvements des prix et des salaires en Belgique au XVIe siècle', *Annales E.S.C.*, 1955.

Wales. A Bibliography of the History of Wales. Cardiff, 1962. *See also* Supplement I, *Bull.* BCS, 1963.

Walford, Cornelius. *Fairs, Past and Present: a chapter in the History of Commerce.* London, 1883.

Walker, F. *Historical Geography of South-West Lancashire before the Industrial Revolution.* Chetham Soc., NS, CIII, 1939.

Wallen, W. C. 'Tilty Abbey', *Essex Arch. Soc.*, NS, IX, 1904–5.

Watkin, Dom Aelred. 'Glastonbury 1538–9 as shown by its account rolls', *Downside Review*, LXVII, 1949.

Wedgwood, C. V. *The Great Rebellion: II, The King's War, 1641–1647.* London, 1958.

West, T. *The Antiquities of Furness.* Ulverston, 1805.

Westcote, Thomas. *A View of Devonshire in MDCXXX.* Exeter, 1845.

Westerfield, R. B. *Middlemen in English Business, particularly between 1660 and 1760.* Transactions Connecticut Academy of Arts and Sciences, XIX, Connecticut, 1915.

White, Gilbert. *The Natural History of Selborne.* Everyman edn., London, 1945.

Wiebe, G. *Zur Geschichte der Preisrevolution des XVI und XVII Jahrhunderts.* Leipzig, 1895.

Willan, T. S. *The English Coasting Trade, 1600–1750.* Manchester Economic History Series, XII. Manchester, 1938.

—— *River Navigation in England, 1600–1750.* London, 1936.

Willan, T. S., and Crossley, E. W. (eds.). *Three Seventeenth-Century Yorkshire Surveys.* Yorks. Arch. Soc. Rec. Ser., CIV, 1941.

Williams, Clare. *Thomas Platter's Travels in England, 1599.* London, 1937.

Williams, Glanmor. *The Welsh Church from Conquest to Reformation.* Cardiff, 1962.

Williams, N. J. *The Maritime Trade of East Anglian Ports, 1550–1590.* University of Oxford D.Phil. thesis, 1952.

—— 'Sessions of the Clerk of the Market of the Household in Middlesex', *London and Middlesex Arch. Soc.*, XIX, ii, 1957.

—— *Tradesmen in Early-Stuart Wiltshire.* Wilts. Arch. and Nat. Hist. Soc., Records Branch, XV, 1960.

Williams, W. Ogwen. *Calendar of the Caernarvonshire Quarter Sessions Records.* Cardiff, 1956.

Wilson, Rev. J. M. (ed.). *Accounts of the Priory of Worcester for the year 13–14 Hen. VIII, A.D. 1521–2.* Worcs. Hist. Soc., 1907.

Winchester, Barbara. *Tudor Family Portrait.* London, 1955.

Wolffe, B. P. 'The Management of English Royal Estates under the Yorkist Kings', EHR, LXXI, 1956.

Wood, E. B. (ed.). *Rowland Vaughan, His Booke.* London, 1897.

Wood-Jones, R. B. *Traditional Domestic Architecture in the Banbury Region.* Manchester, 1963.

Woodward, G. W. O. *The Benedictines and Cistercians in Yorkshire in the sixteenth century.* Trin. Coll., Dublin, Ph.D. thesis, 1955.

Woodworth, Allegra. 'Purveyance for the Royal Household in the Reign of Queen Elizabeth', *American Philosophical Soc.*, NS, xxxv, 1946.

Worlidge, John. *Systema Agriculturae; the Mystery of Husbandry discovered:* ... *2nd edn. with additions by the author.* London, 1675.

Wright, T. *Three Chapters of Letters relating to the Suppression of the Monasteries.* Camden Soc., 1843.

Wynn, Sir John. *History of the Gwydir Family.* Cardiff, 1927.

Wynn of Gwydir. *Calendar of Wynn of Gwydir Papers, 1515–1690.* Aberystwyth, 1926.

Youings, J. A. *Devon Monastic Lands: Calendar of Particulars for Grants, 1536–58.* Devon and Cornwall Rec. Soc., NS, I, 1955.

—— 'The Terms of the Disposal of the Devon Monastic Lands, 1536–58', EHR, LXIX, 1954.

Young, F. Brett. *Portrait of a Village.* London, 1937.

4

AGRICULTURAL PRICES, WAGES, FARM PROFITS, AND RENTS

A. LONG-TERM MOVEMENT OF PRICES AND WAGES

The 'price revolution' of Tudor and early Stuart times was dramatic in proportions and violent in impact. By 1640, when our study commences, it had almost run its course. A final paroxysm at the mid century was followed by a hundred years in which prices, though volatile, exhibited no pronounced secular trend. Over the period 1640–1750 as a whole, agricultural prices in general changed by only a few percentage points, compared with the sixfold increase recorded in the preceding century and a half.[1]

General statistical averages, however, can be misleading; and in the period covered by our study not all commodity prices exhibited almost complete long-term stability, nor did they all move in the same direction. Thus, while grain prices, which had spearheaded the inflation of Tudor and early Stuart times, declined by an average of approximately 12 per cent between 1640/79 and 1710/49, livestock prices increased by almost 18 per cent during the same period (see Table 14). At the individual commodity level, a decline of 24

Table 14. *Indices of prices of agricultural commodities*[2] *(1640–1749 = 100)*[3]

	Grains	Other field crops	Livestock	Animal products	All agri-cultural products
1640–79	107	96	91	103	99
1680–1709	98	101	105	100	101
1710–49	94	104	107	98	101
% change 1640/79 to 1710/49	−12.1	+8.3	+17.6	−4.9	+2.0

I wish to acknowledge my great obligation to Mr Giles Harrison, who undertook the prodigious task of compiling from the original sources most of the raw price and wage data incorporated in Appendix 5.III. My wife, Jeanne, helped greatly with the organization, processing, and typing of the material. I am indebted also to Miss Mary Anderson, who prepared the diagrams.

[1] For the movement of agricultural prices in Tudor and early Stuart times, see above, pp. 116–72.

[2] Annual and decennial price indices will be found on pp. 319–94 below.

[3] All price indices mentioned in the text refer to this base, unless otherwise specified, and relate to harvest years (= HY) (i.e. 29 September to 28 September).

per cent in the price of rye was more than offset by an increase of over 71 per cent in the price of pigs; a drop of almost 33 per cent in the price of wool (included under "Animal products") was almost matched in proportionate terms by like increases in the prices of hops, hay, and straw (categorized under "Other field crops").

Although the magnitude of these various movements was extremely modest when contrasted with previous – or, indeed, more modern – experience, this should not necessarily be taken as precluding the presence of underlying forces making for economic growth and change. However, while long-term price stability should not thus automatically be equated with economic stagnation, from an analytical standpoint it does pose particularly difficult problems of interpretation. There are, for example, many indications that the rapid rise in agricultural prices in the sixteenth century was closely associated with the growing pressure of population upon natural resources. The subsequent levelling off of prices in the middle years of the seventeenth century supposes an easing of this pressure. Hypothetically, such a development could have been the combined result of a falling off, or even absolute decline, in the rate of population growth in conjunction with a stagnant, non-innovative agricultural sector. Alternatively, improved techniques of agricultural production, better land utilization, or reduced costs of distribution could have held prices in check in spite of expanding demand generated by population growth and/or rising levels of consumer income. It is by no means crystal clear which of these sets of circumstances most closely approximated actual developments, nor, for that matter, is it readily apparent what weight, if any, should be attached to general monetary (as opposed to real or physical) considerations. Accordingly, the best that one can hope for is to be able to determine without too large an element of conjecture the most likely causes and consequences of price changes, given the data and other available evidence.

So far as factors on the demand side are concerned, our knowledge with respect to both the size and the movement of population before 1801 is very imperfect. Towards the end of the seventeenth century, Gregory King, on the basis of the hearth-tax returns, calculated the population of England and Wales at 5.5 million, and the corresponding estimates of most modern authorities have approximated this figure fairly closely. Brownlee, for example, on the basis of the burial and baptism series published by Rickman in 1843, puts the population of England and Wales at 5.83 million in 1701.

Whether this (or some other figure) represented an increase in comparison with the population one hundred years earlier is perhaps more of an open question than is sometimes supposed. Certainly, it would seem that there was little or no population growth between 1620 and 1670: a period characterized, not only in England but also in most other parts of Europe, by exceptionally severe visitations of pestilence and chronic dearth. The effects of war and emigration further reduced a population already lowered by natural forces. By the early 1670s complaints about an overplus of people, widespread in Elizabethan and early Jacobean times, had given way to a concern that England was underpopulated. "There is nothing so much wanted in England as people", said the author of *The Grand Concern of England Explained* (1673). Although these sentiments were apparently being voiced less frequently at the end of the century, thus suggesting some recovery of population in the intervening period, Brownlee's figures for the early eighteenth century show little upward movement before the 1740s and a population of only 6.14 million in 1751.[4]

In sum, therefore, the general impression is that over the period 1640–1750 as a whole a moderate increase in population may have occurred, although this is far from certain. With somewhat more confidence, it may be asserted that such population growth as did occur was uneven and spasmodic, being interpolated by lengthy periods of stagnation, if not actual decline. These observations are not obviously contradicted by the general body of documentary evidence, while they appear to gain some support from a more detailed analysis of price and wage movements.

With respect to wage movements, our knowledge is very imperfect, as it is on the subject of the condition of labour in general. In the first place, there is an almost complete lack of information about annual earnings, payments to wage earners being recorded almost entirely on a daily basis or in terms of piece rates for specific tasks. The number of days on which wage earners worked in the course of a year is an unknown quantity, although there must have been considerable underemployment and irregularity of employment during the winter months in seasonal activities such as agriculture.

So far as wage rates are concerned, the data are largely piecemeal, although there are some fairly continuous (mainly institutional) series pertaining to the building trades. Entries relating to agricultural wages are to be found in many estate accounts but not usually over extended periods of time. Indices based upon a selection of some of the longer-term series are contained on pp. 000–0 of this volume and are presented in summary form in Table 15. As revealed in this table, between 1640/79 and 1710/49 the rate of wages paid to agricultural workers increased by 5 per cent in money terms and 12 per cent in real terms.

---

[4] E. Lipson, *The Economic History of England*, III, 4th edn, London, 1947, pp. 164–6; Phyllis Deane and W. A. Cole, *British Economic Growth, 1688–1959*, Cambridge, 1962, pp. 5–6; Karl F. Helleiner, 'The Population of Europe from the Black Death to the Eve of the Vital Revolution', in Edwin E. Rich and Charles Wilson, eds., *The Cambridge Economic History of Europe*, IV, Cambridge, 1967, pp. 42–95; D. C. Coleman, 'Labour in the English Economy of the Seventeenth Century', EcHR, 2nd ser., VIII, 1956, pp. 280–95; G. S. L. Tucker, 'Population in History', EcHR, 2nd ser., XX, 1967, pp. 131–40.

Table 15. *Indices of agricultural wage rates and their purchasing power*

	Average money wage rate	'Cost of living'	Purchasing power of wage rate
1640–79	98	103	95
1680–1709	99	100	100
1710–49	103	97	106
% change 1640/79 to 1710/49	+5.1	−5.8	+11.6

To put these figures into perspective, it should be recalled that the century and a half preceding 1640 had witnessed a prolonged decline in the purchasing power of wage rates, bringing the wage earner's standard of living by the early decades of the seventeenth century to its lowest level in three hundred years. Thus, the modest rise in real wages which apparently occurred during the course of our period seemingly did no more than restore to the farm labourer the meagre comforts enjoyed by his predecessor during the third quarter of the sixteenth century: comforts which, in turn, equated to only two-thirds of those within the competence of the agricultural worker in the second half of the fifteenth century. Put another way, the prelude to the era of the 'industrial revolution' was a century and a half in which real wage rates, at least in agriculture, stayed depressed in terms of past experience.

However, to say this is not necessarily to conclude that the common people were, on average, no better off in 1750 than they were in 1640. Indeed, this seems unlikely, given the various facts, pointers, and intuitions which we now possess with respect to the industrial distribution of the labour force and the rates of pay in different occupations.

In the first place, as is brought out in Table 16, farm labourers were poorly paid in relation to other workers (although the disparity would be reduced somewhat by customary 'fringe benefits' and seasonal bonuses), while employment in agriculture was declining in relative, if not absolute, terms. Hence, the tendency was for an increasing proportion of the labour force to enter better-paid jobs (in manufacturing, mining, and construction), with reduced dependence upon agriculture. Other things being equal, such a structural change in the composition of the work force would raise the average level of wages in the economy, irrespective of whether rates of pay increased more rapidly in the growth sectors than in agriculture. On this latter point, it will be noted from Table 16 that there was, in fact, no significant movement in wage differentials as between agriculture and building in the first half of the eighteenth century.

Secondly, as a corollary of the aforementioned structural shift in the

Table 16. *Average daily wage rates in agricultural and building trades (in pence)*

	1700–9	1740–9	Percentage change 1700/9 to 1740/9
Agricultural labourer	11.12	12.07	+8.5
Building labourer	15.75	16.72	+6.2
Building craftsman	23.69	25.44	+7.4

distribution of employment, the probability is that over the period 1640–1750 as a whole the average number of working days per member of the labour force tended to increase in consequence of the reduced emphasis upon agriculture with its marked seasonal work pattern. Even so, at the end of the eighteenth century over one-third of the country's labour force was still employed in agriculture, and before the middle of the century the proportion was possibly as high as one-half.

In the third place, given the large reservoirs of unused and under-used labour in the countryside, industrial growth, especially under the domestic system, could have been achieved primarily by means of an increase in the labour force participation rate, without entailing any, or any significant, decline in the absolute number of man hours devoted to agriculture. Growing demands for labour were reflected not only in fewer complaints respecting unemployment but also in attempts by the state to prevent skilled workers from leaving the country. The spate of innovations which characterized industrial development in the eighteenth century was doubtless in part a response to the tightening labour market situation.

It seems probable that many, if not most, of the new workers drawn into industrial production under the putting-out system, especially in textiles, were women and girls; and, just as the greater participation of females in the work force has been one of the major forces making for higher living standards in industrialized countries in the twentieth century, so the same consideration may have done much to make life more comfortable in the pre-'industrial revolution' era. Thus, even though the available data are not indicative of a significant rise in the purchasing power of the average daily wage rate, yet, for the various reasons mentioned, average family living standards could have improved substantially.

Reverting to the issue of population change, and invoking the 'iron law of wages', the price of labour in a static economy operating under conditions of decreasing returns would be directly and inversely related to the supply of labour or, more basically, to the size of population. If, in such an economy, population increased, the tendency would be for real wages to decline. Since, as we have seen, the purchasing power of wage rates apparently rose, if not very markedly, during the period 1640–1750, the presumption is either that population did not grow or, if it did, that there was an even greater increase in the total output of goods and services, part of the benefit of which was passed on to the workers in the form of higher wages. As a postscript, it is worthy of note that the tendency for the purchasing power of wages to rise in the longer term was reversed in the 1690s and again in the 1710s, suggesting the probability of fairly rapid population growth in these decades. By the same token, the improvement in real wages in the period 1720–50 is compatible with a fall in population.

All this, of course, has relevance for the longer-term movement of relative prices, some of the broader aspects of which are brought out in Table 14. With rising real wages and increasing participation by the labour force, it can be assumed that a declining proportion of family income was spent on the basic necessities of life, especially bread. Accentuating this tendency, and becoming especially noticeable towards the end of our period, new tastes were developed as fresh horticultural produce and the staples of colonial trade became more readily available. Thus, the expectation is for the prices of grains to fall relative to the prices of other commodities and for the price of rye (the inferior bread grain) to fall in relation to the price of wheat. In this connection, attention is drawn to Table 17, which depicts the longer-term price movements with respect to the main field crops.

Table 17. *Indices of prices of field crops*

	Wheat	Barley & malt	Oats	Rye	Beans	Peas	Hops	Hay	Straw
1640–79	110	101	105	115	111	107	86	86	87
1680–1709	99	97	97	98	100	98	101	108	100
1710–49	91	102	98	87	89	95	113	107	113
% change 1640/79 to 1710/49	−17.3	+1.0	−6.7	−24.3	−19.8	−11.2	+31.4	+24.4	+29.9

In the light of what has been said above it is interesting to note that two of the major grains – barley and oats – did not decline in price in the early eighteenth century. One possible explanation, of course, is that these crops were being produced in smaller quantities. However, it would seem more appropriate to associate the slight rise in the price of barley (the principal malting grain) with the more substantial rise in the price of hops and – at a further remove – with the increase in drunkenness decried by contemporary observers and later historians as constituting one of the major social evils of the age. As an aside, it may be ventured that while living conditions in the early eighteenth century were undoubtedly very hard for the majority of people, drunkenness as a mode of behaviour becomes economically feasible only at a subsistence level somewhat above the bare minimum.

So far as oats are concerned, the rise in the relative price of this crop *vis-à-vis* the main bread cereals might simply have reflected the fact that the horse population was growing more rapidly than the human population. We know that horses were replacing oxen for draught purposes in the period 1640–1750. However, the fact that hay and straw were also becoming relatively dearer at this time (see Table 17) would seem to suggest that the growth in the animal population (or the better feeding thereof) was not limited to horses; it would also appear to indicate that the demand for these traditional fodder crops remained strong in spite of the spread of the new roots, clover, and grasses.

Of course, the long-term movement of agricultural prices over the period 1640–1750 was determined not only by demand considerations such as these but also by factors on the supply side. Here, the basic question is whether the supply of agricultural produce was expanded over the longer term. So far as domestic output is concerned, there were three principal ways in which farmers could increase their production: by the use of larger quantities of the prime factors of production (land and labour); by the application of improved farming methods, capital outlays often being a necessary adjunct; and by changes involving the more effective utilization of land through a higher degree of economic specialization or a different product mix.

Respecting the first of these possibilities, the period 1640–1750 did not apparently witness a marked expansion in the area of land devoted to agriculture. There was a burst of drainage activity in the fens in the middle years of the seventeenth century and piecemeal intakes from forest and waste. But the process of land reclamation does not appear to have proceeded with the same vigour as in Tudor and early Stuart times; indeed, the documentary evidence suggests that there may well have been periods of contraction in the total amount of land used for farming purposes. In part, this surmised slowing down or retrenchment in the reclamation process may have reflected the fact that much of the land most easily accessible from the physical standpoint had already been taken in hand, while the reduced dependence upon the fallowing process must have lessened the need for new ground. Barriers of an institutional or legal nature (enshrined in prevailing systems of land tenure) may also have proved more intractable than formerly. However, even more to the point must have been the lack of incentive to break down such barriers in the absence of the powerful stimulus provided by rapidly rising agricultural prices.

It seems even less likely that larger agricultural output was achieved as a result of more labour being used (no changes in productivity taking place). In the first place, as already discussed, it is far from certain that the period under review witnessed an increase in population, while there seems no doubt that the proportion of the labour force engaged in agriculture declined as a corollary of industrial growth. Secondly, the propensity of agricultural wages to rise, if only slightly, over the longer term, at a time when the prices of most arable crops were falling, must have lent some encouragement to a more economical use of labour, at least by capitalist farming enterprises. Reinforcing such a tendency over the period as a whole was the likely shift in the balance of land use away from labour-intensive arable husbandry and towards pasture farming. It is also conceivable that the introduction of improved farming methods resulted in the displacement of labour by capital, but there seems little evidence in support of this supposition. On the other hand, increased agricultural output, achieved by whatever means, would necessitate the use of more labour to tend stock or to gather, move, store, and prepare crops for market or domestic consumption; and some of the new agricultural crops of the seventeenth century required more labour in setting, hoeing, and gathering than the old.

Whereas changes in the amounts of labour and land devoted to agriculture during the period under review must remain a matter of considerable conjecture, less uncertainty would seem to exist with respect to the application of improved farming practices. Evidence has already been adduced of the more efficient use of agricultural land consequent upon the introduction of new fallow-free crop rotations, of which the Norfolk four-course system (alternating turnips and clover with wheat or rye and spring-sown cereals) is the best known. Pre-dating these rotations, other improvements, such as the enclosure of common field land, the use of lime and marl, the floating of water meadows, and the practice of 'convertible husbandry', had begun to make an impact on agricultural productivity prior to the commencement of our period and continued to do so thereafter.

The extent to which these improvements and the new rotations had been adopted by the middle of the eighteenth century cannot be determined with any degree of precision. Hedges, fences, and irrigation systems could not be provided without the outlay of capital, while fertilizing agents, whether lime, marl, or animal manure (needed in a predominantly arable operation), also cost money to acquire, transport, and apply. It might be concluded, therefore, that lack of financial resources would tend to limit such improvements mainly to home farms and larger tenanted holdings. At the same time, it would also appear from extant documentary references that while the new grasses and turnips had gained widespread acceptance in parts of southern, eastern, and Midland England by the middle years of the eighteenth century, the custom of fallowing one-third – or even, in some instances, one-half – of the area of productive arable farmland remained a not uncommon practice in other parts of the country.

Overall, however, there can be little doubt that the period 1640–1750 witnessed substantial progress in the application of improved farming methods which, for present purposes, may be equated with increased output per acre. Such progress, one may surmise, was facilitated by changes in farming organization associated with the decline of the small landowner and the concentration of agricultural holdings in fewer hands. Coincidental with these changes, the expansion of the market for agricultural products – consequent upon the rise of classes of professional middlemen and carriers, together with developments in coastwise and internal transportation – encouraged greater regional economic specialization, with resulting improvements in farm output.

The overall effect of all these influences cannot be precisely determined. However, documentary evidence indicates that crop yields per acre on some farms in the 1730s and 1740s were already approaching and, on occasion, exceeding average British yields during the first decade of the present century. Thus, at Arreton, Isle of Wight, during the period 1732–50, average yields per acre of wheat, barley, and oats were 23.8 bushels, 32.5 bushels, and 29.3 bushels respectively. In one-third of the years in question, barley yields exceeded the aforementioned British average.[5]

Of course, crop yields varied greatly both from area to area and from year to year; and the probability is that land at Arreton was inherently more fertile than land in most other parts of the country, while the 1730s and 1740s were exceptional decades for good harvests. Hence, the figures cited may give a somewhat exaggerated impression of agricultural productivity towards the middle of the eighteenth century. Nevertheless, the wheat yield accords closely with the national estimate of 23 bushels per acre made by Arthur Young, the noted agricultural writer, in 1771. This estimate was somewhat summarily dismissed by M. K. Bennett some forty years ago, partly on account of its closeness to modern experience, but also because it suggested an improbably large increase of yield between 1650 and 1750, given Bennett's figure of 11 bushels per acre for the earlier date. In place of Young's estimate Bennett put forward a figure of 15 bushels per acre as the average British wheat yield in the middle of the eighteenth century. This figure, which Bennett derived from an analysis of agricultural statistics published by Charles Smith in 1764, still gave an implied trend increase of yield of 36 per cent between 1650 and 1750, compared with 30 per cent during the preceding two hundred years. Although these percentage changes may not have been too wide of the mark, the actual yields obtaining seem to have been consistently underestimated by Bennett. Indeed, in relation to the mid eighteenth century, an average British wheat yield in the range 18–23 bushels per acre would seem more in keeping with individual farm accounts and other

---

[5] See Table XLVIII, p. 374. For Britain as a whole during the period 1900–9, average yields per acre of wheat, barley, and oats were 31.6 bu, 33.4 bu, and 39.9 bu respectively – B. R. Mitchell and Phyllis Deane, *Abstract of British Historical Statistics*, Cambridge, 1962, p. 90.

relevant data than Bennett's somewhat arbitrarily selected figure of 15 bushels. Put into a broader context, a higher yield would appear to accord with Aldo de Maddalena's conclusion (based on crop:seed ratios) that the level of productivity in agriculture in the early eighteenth century was higher in England than in other parts of Europe with the exception of Holland. On the other hand, we are unable to find, either in Maddalena's work or elsewhere, any substantiation for his assertion that agricultural productivity in England (as elsewhere in Europe) fell between the mid sixteenth and the mid eighteenth century. Indeed, as already noted, quite the opposite appears to have been the case.[6]

With respect to livestock, information on weights is rather more plentiful than data on cereal yields. On the basis of this information it is clear that Gregory King's estimates made at the end of the seventeenth century – which put the average weight of bullocks killed at Smithfield at 370 lb (exclusive of offal) and of sheep at 28 lb – were either too low or pertained to an unrepresentative sample of stock. Respecting the latter consideration, the weights of beasts appear to have varied much more with breed than they do nowadays. Cattle from Scotland, Wales, and adjoining areas were generally very undersized, being frequently referred to as "runts" in the records of lowland English farmers. Many of these beasts ended up, in a fatted condition, at Smithfield, a factor which would seem to lend a degree of credibility to King's estimate. Among other breeds, beasts in the 500–900 lb (liveweight) range appear to have been commonplace in the early eighteenth century, and Sir John Sinclair's end-of-century estimate of 800 lb for an average-sized bullock does not seem out of line. Indeed, an ox "of the Holderness or Dutch breed" weighing 2,083 lb was slaughtered at Newby in the West Riding in 1707, while a cow weighing 1,741 lb was likewise despatched at New Market, Shropshire, in 1749, having been displayed to crowds of incredulous townsfolk beforehand. Animals of this size would have been exceptional – indeed, 1,500 lb is nowadays regarded as a respectable weight for a fatted steer. In 1683, Navy Victualling contracts required a standard ox carcase for salting to weigh 5–5½ cwt (560–616 lb); by the end of the eighteenth century the stipulated weight had risen to 6–7 cwt (672–784 lb), an increase of roughly 24 per cent. By way of comparison, oxen purchased for the household of the bishop of Winchester in 1567–8 averaged only 484 lb liveweight. Thus, casting backward and forward, the figures seem to indicate a substantial increase in the size of cattle during the period under review, although the skimpiness of the evidence makes it difficult to express this in precise quantitative terms. Similarly with sheep and pigs. Extant farm

[6] M. K. Bennett, 'British Wheat Yield per Acre for Seven Centuries', *Econ. Hist.*, III, 1935, pp. 12–29; above, pp. 71–2; Aldo de Maddelena, 'Rural Europe 1500–1750', in Carlo M. Cipolla, ed., *The Fontana Economic History of Europe: The Sixteenth and Seventeenth Centuries*, Glasgow, 1974, pp. 339–40.

accounts pertaining to the first half of the eighteenth century record sheep weights (probably liveweight) ranging between 33 lb and 88 lb and averaging somewhat over 50 lb. Most mature hogs apparently weighed 200–300 lb, approximating present-day standards for size, although probably not for leanness.[7]

The belief that there was a significant increase in the weights of livestock between the mid seventeenth and the mid eighteenth century is strengthened by a review of certain other considerations. In the first place, as is brought out in the regional chapters of Part 1 of the hardback, an expansion in the production of fodder crops was pivotal to the advances achieved on the agricultural front, making the over-wintering and fattening of stock easier. Secondly, there seems little evidence, so far as cattle are concerned, that these increased supplies of feed went to support a larger livestock population. Thus, while Gregory King put the numbers of cattle in England and Wales at the end of the seventeenth century at $4\frac{1}{2}$ million, Arthur Young in 1779 made a corresponding estimate of under $3\frac{1}{2}$ million. If a significant expansion in the production of beef is assumed, these figures can be taken to imply either that cattle were becoming heavier, or otherwise putting on flesh in place of bone and offal (in consequence of better breeding or a change· in the composition of herds), or else that the turnover of total stock was becoming more rapid (in consequence of a reduced maturative period associated with improvements in feed). The extent to which these various factors made themselves felt is unknown. However, in sum, they could have resulted in an increase in the *per capita* consumption of beef in spite of the suggested (but by no means proven) decline in the size of the cattle population. In the case of sheep a substantial increase in numbers is indicated by contemporary sources. Thus, Gregory King gave a figure of 11 million as the sheep population of England and Wales in 1688–95, while the anonymous author of *A Short Essay upon Trade* estimated that there were 16,640,000 sheep in Great Britain in 1741. Of these, it seems unlikely that Scotland would have accounted for more than, say, 3,640,000, leaving England and Wales with a round 13 million, or 2 million more than King's estimate a half-century earlier. Such an increase in numbers does not, of course, rule out the possibility that sheep were becoming heavier. Indeed, as we have seen, this possibility appears to be borne out by direct evidence. Given the further probability of low or negative population growth during the early eighteenth century, it seems reasonable to conclude that this period witnessed a marked increase in the *per capita* consumption of mutton. The same was also possibly true of pig meat and poultry.

If, as it appears, the productivity of animal husbandry was rising (in terms

[7] Table XLIX, p. 376; Deane and Cole, *op. cit.*, pp. 69–70; Bowden, *op. cit.*, pp. 23–4; W. Beveridge, L. Liepmann, F. J. Nicholas, *et al.*, *Prices and Wages in England from the Twelfth to the Nineteenth Century, I*, London, 1939, p. 548.

of greater livestock weights, heavier fleeces, or otherwise) we should expect this to be reflected in a changing relationship between the price of stock and the price of animal produce. Other things being equal, stock should have become relatively more expensive. The summary data featured in Table 18 appear to bear out this hypothesis and, in so doing, point to the continuation of tendencies which had been even more marked during Tudor and early Stuart times.[8]

Table 18. *Percentage changes in the prices of livestock and animal products, 1640/79 to 1710/49*

Sheep	+4.0	Wool	−33.0
		Mutton	−11.3
Dairy cattle	+9.4	Milk	−10.6
		Butter	−7.6
		Cheese	−22.6
Beef cattle	−6.8	Beef	+2.0
Pigs	+71.4	Pork	+4.1
Poultry	+25.0	Eggs	+27.4
Horses	+11.1		

As in these earlier times, however, it would be misleading to view the divergences between stock and produce prices as being attributable, solely – or, perhaps, even mainly – to increased yields of meat and other produce. In the first place, the demand for stock was determined not only by their direct contribution towards consumption. Stock also produced manure, without which arable land lost heart and declined in fertility. In the conditions of the early eighteenth century, more dung (resulting in higher output) must have been the course which commended itself to many individual farmers faced with falling grain prices. The demand for sheep, in particular, would have been affected by this kind of realization. Hence, it is possible to rationalize the increase in the sheep population, mentioned earlier, in spite of the apparently weak price incentive to expand the production of wool or mutton. Moreover, as already implied, substantial increases in the average yields of these products over the longer term also served to compensate for deficiencies in price.[9]

With respect to the other types of livestock featured in Table 18, dairy cattle, pigs, and poultry required comparatively large amounts of labour in relation to capital and provided regular returns to the owner in the form of produce (milk, butter, cheese, pork, bacon, and eggs). They were, therefore, especially well suited to the particular circumstances of the

[8] Above, pp. 22–3.
[9] P. J. Bowden, *The Wool Trade in Tudor and Stuart England*, London, 1962, pp. 26–7.

numerous cottars and smallholders who, possessing little or no land of their own but having traditional grazing rights on the common, had somehow or other to eke out a meagre existence. The data would seem to suggest that the number of such small farm entities, with their corresponding demands for livestock, was tending to increase, although (in line with an assumed lessening of population pressure) not as rapidly as in the sixteenth century. This view is by no means incompatible with the parallel thesis that, in general, the ownership of land was becoming concentrated in fewer hands.

Reference has already been made to the possibility of a substantial decline in the size of the cattle population in the early eighteenth century. If this possibility is accepted, the implication of an increase in the number of dairy cattle (as suggested above) would be a decline in the number of animals kept primarily for beef production in England and Wales. Conceivably one could explain such a decline in terms of a falling off in the consumption of beef; but this explanation hardly seems to accord with the evidence of our price data (which appear to indicate a comparatively strong demand for beef) or with the expectation that an increasing proportion of rising incomes would be spent on this product. Another and more likely explanation is that at the level of the farm (as opposed to that of the kitchen) there was less demand for beef-producing animals than formerly because the economics of com-parative advantage were resulting in a growing dependence upon 'external' sources of supply, notably Scotland and (prior to 1667) Ireland, especially for store cattle. On the basis of our price data it does, indeed, appear that the demand for bullocks and runts was less buoyant than that for either dairy cattle or oxen (which increased in price by approximately 7 per cent over the relevant period). The price of the latter, of course, would be influenced by the amount of land under the plough as well as by the demand for beef and hides. Similarly, horses would be required primarily for ploughing and carting, though their non-agricultural uses, notably in the field of transportation, were tending to increase. In particular, estate records point to a growing market for coach horses and geldings.

It seems clear that the supply of agricultural goods during the period encompassed by our study was very largely determined by the volume of domestic production. Limitations of transportation and marketing organiza-tion severely restricted the movement of most primary products in international trade. In spite of the corn bounties, exports of grain, when measured on a quinquennial basis, at no time exceeded 5 per cent of gross domestic output (estimated by Deane and Cole at about 16 million quarters per year in 1745–9), while imports remained negligible throughout the period (in most years amounting to well under 1 per cent of output). The general effect of such bounties on prices could not have been large.[10] For almost all other agricultural products, the indications are that domestic production

[10] For a fuller discussion of this issue see vol. 4 of the paperback series, pp. 157–253.

and domestic consumption were even more closely equated. The most notable exception to this situation was wool, the high value of which in relation to weight made it particularly well suited for longer-distance transportation. Whereas in the Middle Ages England had been a major exporter of raw wool, by the early eighteenth century she had become a substantial importer of Spanish and Irish wools, while the export of wool from England was prohibited. At the beginning of the eighteenth century it appears that perhaps one-quarter of the wool consumed by the domestic textile industry was imported. However, by the mid century, with the probable significant expansion in the English wool supply on the one hand, and the decline in the south-western textile industry (the main consumer of Irish wool) on the other, imports of raw wool had declined to about half their earlier level. Next to the traffic in wool, the trade in cattle seems to have shown least compatibility with the requirements of a closed economy for agricultural produce. Mention has already been made of the growth in the export of Scottish store cattle to England – a development evidently, if not intentionally, encouraged by the act passed in 1667 for the protection of English breeders, prohibiting the importation of cattle from Ireland "or any other place beyond the seas". While there is no firm measure of the numbers of Scottish cattle exported to England, the abundance of references to "Scots" and "Scots runts" in English farm account books of the period makes it clear that the trade was of substantial proportions. Postlethwayt, writing in the mid eighteenth century, estimated Scottish cattle exports at 80,000 head annually, which may not have been too wide of the mark, and translated into perhaps 10 per cent of English and Welsh beef requirements. Large numbers of sheep may also have entered England from Scotland, although the annual passage of 150,000, as reported by Postlethwayt, seems difficult to credit, given the paucity of references to Scottish sheep in the extant accounts of English graziers.[11]

So far our analysis has been in terms of individual commodities and groups of commodities. The analysis may now be taken further by contrasting the general price movements of agricultural goods with those of industrial products. This comparison becomes more revealing when it is pushed back in time, as in Fig. 7.[12]

During the century and a half preceding the commencement of our study period, the purchasing power of agricultural commodities over industrial goods had progressively increased as the pressure of population on the means of subsistence had mounted. By 1630–9 it needed 226 units of industrial goods

[11] See Tables L, LI, pp. 379, 380. Deane and Cole, op. cit., p. 65; Bowden, Wool Trade, pp. 61–2, 214–17; Lipson, op. cit., p. 198; G. E. Fussell and Constance Goodman, 'Eighteenth-Century Traffic in Livestock', Econ. Hist., III, 1936, pp. 218–21, 226–7; Malachy Postlethwayt, Britain's Commercial Interest Explained and Improved ... I, London, 1757, p. 57.

[12] See also Table XXVIII, p. 348; Table XIII, p. 164.

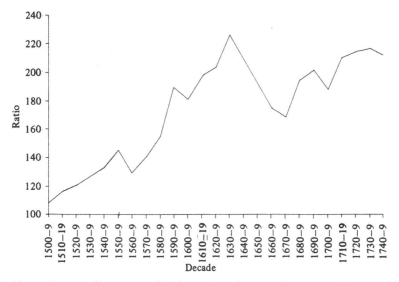

Fig. 7. Commodity terms of trade. Ratio of prices of agricultural commodities to prices of industrial products: decennial averages (1450–99 = 100).

to buy the same volume of agricultural products that 100 industrial units would have bought in the late fifteenth century. The reversals of population in the middle decades of the seventeenth century temporarily eased the pressure on resources, resulting in a relative cheapening of agricultural products *vis-à-vis* industrial goods. However, from the 1680s onwards the terms of trade again moved against industrial products – a development which, viewed from certain standpoints, might seem somewhat surprising.

Thus, given the tendency of real incomes to rise, especially in the latter part of our period, the expectation is for an increasing proportion of consumer spending to be on manufactured articles and for a decreasing proportion to be on basic foodstuffs and other essential items; as a corollary, one would look for a rise in industrial prices relative to agricultural prices. Secondly, industrial goods would normally have a larger labour component than agricultural products. If, as it appears, money wages were tending to rise in the latter part of our period, the supposition is that industrial costs would have been especially sensitive in this regard. Thirdly, the evidence reviewed in the earlier part of this chapter points to the probability of substantial real improvements in the agricultural sphere in the period 1640–1750. Given such improvements, the expectation from the supply side is for a cheapening of agricultural commodities relative to other goods *unless* the production of these other goods were subject to even greater decreases in the real costs of production. Can such an assumption be made in the present instance? There are certainly some pointers in this direction.

In the first instance (discounting the once widely held thesis originally propounded by J. U. Nef regarding the pace of technological change during the period 1540–1640) most modern scholars would now probably hold that the decades after 1660 witnessed more rapid industrial development than the period reviewed by Nef. Thus, E. L. Jones remarks that during the late seventeenth and early eighteenth centuries "domestic industries like cloth-making, hosiery, lace and leather work and nail-making thickened in the areas less favoured for farming". There was a vigorous growth in the metal trades, both in size and number, during the same period, especially from 1710 to the late 1720s. Cloth exports almost doubled in value between 1660 and 1700, while total exports trebled. Even so, according to C. H. Wilson, "it is doubtful whether even these increases in foreign trade reflect anything like the full extent of the industrial change and growth of these years".[13]

It does not necessarily follow, of course, that expanding industrial output meant decreasing real costs of production in manufacturing and allied activities, although the evidence of falling industrial prices (by 11.4 per cent between 1640/79 and 1710/49) does, indeed, indicate that this was very probably the case. Even without such statistical indicators, however, the presumption is that the supply of industrial goods could be increased more easily than that of agricultural commodities and at smaller marginal cost. More precisely, it may be hazarded that decreases in industrial costs were accomplished not as a result of any great spate of technological innovations – these belonged rather to a later age – but by virtue of the mobilization and more efficient organization of a labour force hitherto under-utilized, poorly trained, and ill disciplined. Thus, the commercial capitalism of the domestic or putting-out system paved the way for the more blatant industrial capitalism of the factory system, and the technological advances of the later era are seen to assume an evolutionary rather than a revolutionary aspect. In agriculture, with its innate conservatism, technical advance was no less a long-drawn-out evolutionary process, as other chapters in this volume show.

B. REGIONAL PRICES AND WAGES

So far our analysis of agricultural prices has been couched in terms of national secular trends, no attempt being made to point up regional or local differences in price levels or price behaviour. Yet such differences, glossed over in the

[13] J. U. Nef, 'The Progress of Technology and the Growth of Large-Scale Industry in Great Britain, 1540–1640', EcHR, v, 1934, pp. 3–24; id.,'A Comparison of Industrial Growth in France and England, 1540–1640', EcHR, vii, 1937, pp. 155–85; E. L. Jones, 'Agricultural Productivity and Economic Growth, 1700–1760', in Jones, ed., *Agriculture and Economic Growth in England, 1650–1815*, London, 1967, p. 37; W. H. B. Court, *The Rise of the Midland Industries, 1600–1838*, rev. edn, Oxford, 1953, pp. 43–4, 70, 141–2, 145; Henry Hamilton, *The English Brass and Copper Industries to 1800*, London, 1926, pp. 124–5, 138–9; C. H. Wilson, *England's Apprenticeship, 1603–1763*, London, 1965, p. 185.

process of aggregation, were in some instances quite pronounced, reflecting not only the uneven geographical distribution of factor endowments but also the imperfections of a market patchily served by a grossly inadequate, if improving, system of transportation and by an organizational structure for internal trade still largely rooted in individual regions and localities.

On the supply side, regional price disparities were influenced by a welter of factors bearing on productivity and costs. Of these, soil type, topography, and climate, being prime determinants of the inherent capabilities of land, spring most readily to mind. It requires no profound knowledge of agriculture to appreciate the physical difficulties implicit in the practice of tillage on a mountainside, the cultivation of grain on heavily stoned ground, or the ripening of wheat in wet, cold, or sunless conditions. The raising of livestock has always been somewhat less circumscribed by such considerations. Within limits, animals (like people) can survive in a variety of environments, given that the land is not overstocked or that supplies of feed are not otherwise inadequate. Thus, farmers in the wetter, bleaker, and less fertile areas, notably in Wales and northern and western England, tended to place a heavy emphasis upon livestock husbandry, with beef cattle, cows, and sheep being variously favoured according to the nature of the terrain, the scale of farm enterprise, and opportunities for marketing. In these as in other areas, pigs were often kept as an adjunct to dairying, while tillage, where practised, was directed primarily at the production of hardy grains and fodder crops.

In the more temperate and fertile lowland regions, farming options were more numerous and a greater degree of competitiveness existed in respect of agricultural land use. Even so, in most lowland districts climatic considerations and the nature of the soil served to rule out certain types of farming activity in other than highly favourable price conditions. By the same token, long before our period commenced, patterns of regional agricultural specialization, rooted in the peculiar characteristics of the physical environment, had emerged in various parts of the Midlands and southern and eastern England. Thus, in the clay vales and marshlands cattle fattening and (in some cases) dairy farming and horse rearing were favoured forms of agricultural enterprise. On the drier, lighter soils sheep tended to dominate the livestock scene. The limestone soils were also well suited to the production of barley, whereas wheat flourished best on rich, well-drained land. On thin, sandy, or gravelly soils, on the other hand, the preferred cereals were more likely to be oats or rye. Among the newer crops, both turnips and sainfoin grew better on drier, limestone soils than on heavy clayland.

However, the costs of agricultural production depended not only upon the inherent or natural capabilities of the land, as determined by soil type, topography, and climate, but also upon the man-derived inputs of labour, capital, and enterprise. Regional and local differences with respect to the usage and costs of these inputs are difficult to pin down with any degree of exactitude. Labour was a major element in the costs of commercial agriculture, especially for the larger cereal producer or market gardener. However, while extant farm accounts contain much scattered data on agricultural wage rates in different parts of the country, there is a paucity of directly corresponding information on physical output such as would permit some regional comparisons to be made of labour productivity and unit labour costs. So far as wages are concerned, several conclusions would seem possible. In the first place, reflecting the predominance of (labour-intensive) arable and mixed farming in the southern and eastern parts of England, agricultural wages in these regions were generally substantially higher than in the other, more pastoral, areas. Secondly, as might be expected, this relationship was emphasized or modified by the availability, or otherwise, of alternative employment opportunities outside agriculture. The presence of a large town, with its competing demands for labour, tended to raise the level of agricultural wages in surrounding districts. This was most manifestly the case in the vicinity of London. In this connection it would seem relevant to note that ordinary wage rates paid on estates in northern Buckinghamshire during much of the period under review were apparently only two-thirds of those paid in the southern parts of the same county adjoining the capital. Finally, with respect to changes in relative regional wage rates over time, the data are too thin to permit of any definite conclusions, although there is some suggestion that south–north differentials may have narrowed somewhat towards the end of our period, presumably on account of industrial development north of the Trent.[14]

Regional differences with respect to the application of capital and enterprise are even more difficult to establish. At the general level, it may be assumed that a considerable degree of interdependence existed between these two variables (as already noted, most estate improvements necessitated the use of capital); it also seems very probable that, in turn, there was a direct or causal relationship between each of these variables and, respectively, the scale of farm enterprise, the system of land tenure, and the pattern of landholdings. Thus, it is to be expected that the large farmer, producing for the market, would have at his command greater financial resources than the small subsistence operator, and for this reason – if for no other – would tend to be more innovative; again, knowledge of human nature suggests that a leaseholder paying a full market-value rent on a commercial property would have more inclination and a greater economic incentive to maximize his production possibilities than a customary copyhold tenant imbued with the farming traditions and attitudes of his forefathers; finally, it has long been recognized – and, indeed, has been a central theme of early-modern agrarian history – that the occupier of a compact, enclosed holding would be in a better position than the cultivator of scattered strips in the open fields to adopt new crops or improved techniques, or otherwise to rationalize his operation.

14 See Table XLIV, pp. 369–70.

However, for us to be able to express these various considerations in terms of regional cost differences, even loosely, would require much more detailed information than we now possess. The traditional view is that agriculture in the early eighteenth century was at its most progressive in the eastern and south-eastern parts of the country, Norfolk being especially cited in this regard. Here, the physical characteristics of the land, the pattern of farm holdings, the system of land tenure, and the pull of market forces were seemingly conducive to agricultural improvement. However, quite patently, not every farmer in these parts was a Walpole, Coke, or Townshend and, from a general standpoint, we should obviously not place too much weight upon the reported practices of a handful of such notables. Equally clearly, we cannot assume, as most historians did thirty years ago, that farming in the open-field districts of central England, and in the pastoral areas to the north and west, was universally weak on capital and strong on ignorance. Certainly, this often seems to have been the case, but the practice of farming in these areas could also, on occasion, be flexible and innovative, as recent research has shown.[15] Moreover, while there is a presumption that, where put into effect, technically superior farming methods and estate improvements would have resulted in increased agricultural output, it does not automatically follow that average unit costs of production were decreased thereby. Put slightly differently, we should not fall into the trap of assuming that agricultural production costs were necessarily lowest in the most 'progressive' farming districts.

Nor, to bring the discussion to bear more directly on the subject at issue, should we equate regional agricultural costs and regional agricultural prices, although a significant relationship must obviously have existed. Produce not intended for domestic consumption by the farming community had to be marketed; and here the issue of accessibility to consumers was of prime importance. Accessibility was less a matter of distance than of transport possibilities. Since roads (other than the turnpikes introduced in the latter part of our period) were generally poor and often impassable to heavy traffic, water carriage, where available, was the preferred mode of transport for extra-regional consignments of agricultural produce other than livestock and, in some cases, wool. Differences in the costs of transportation by land and by water could be very considerable. In 1686–8, Sir Daniel Fleming was paying a charge of 1s. 4d. per quarter (or about 0.80d. per quarter per mile) for the land conveyance of oats between Ulverston (Lancs.) and Rydal (Westmor.). At the other end of the country, in 1746 oats were being shipped along the coast from Plymouth to Southampton at a freight of 2s. 3d. per quarter (or the equivalent of approximately 0.18d. per quarter per land mile).[16]

---

[15] See e.g. Eric Kerridge, *The Agricultural Revolution*, London, 1967, *passim*.
[16] Westmor. RO, D/Ry, Sir Daniel Fleming's Account Book, 1656–88; Devon RO, Duke of Bedford MSS W1,258/LP1/3.

The value of produce in relation to bulk or weight was obviously a fundamental consideration in the determination of distribution costs and marketing possibilities. Thus, among the main cereals, oats, being the cheapest to buy per given measure of capacity, were also the dearest to transport. In the second example cited above, the cost of freight between Plymouth and Southampton added 34 per cent to product cost. Patently, the need for regional self-sufficiency was greater in regard to oats than in relation to the other, more highly priced, grains. Wheat, in particular, being up to three times as expensive as oats, could be transported substantially further without distribution costs becoming prohibitive. Even so, the necessity for corn bounties would seem to indicate that, in normal circumstances, these costs could serve as an effective barrier to international trade. Such restrictions applied with less severity in the case of wool, which had long been a major item of international commerce. At home, in 1732, it was possible to transport Irish wool (valued at between one-third and one-half of the equivalent weight of fine Spanish or Herefordshire wool) from Bristol to Colchester or Norwich at 15 per cent of prime cost. Even lower costs of passage applied in the case of livestock. Driving expenses incurred on behalf of Sir Henry Howard in 1748 in connection with the movement of oxen from Wales to manors in Wiltshire amounted to only 1.5 per cent of the purchase price. Other figures, reported by Chartres in vol. IV of this series, indicate driving costs in some ten instances between 1663 and 1744 averaging approximately 4.5 per cent of the final gross value of sales. These costs would normally include drovers' wages, tolls (if any), and pasturage *en route*; a further 'cost', not entered in the accounts, would be the value of flesh lost by animals while in transit.[17]

Clearly, from an extra-regional marketing standpoint, areas poorly endowed with transport possibilities were at an especial disadvantage in the disposal of low-value, bulky produce. In such areas (located primarily in the central, northern, and western parts of the country) regional economic specialization simply did not make sense except in relation to goods which were easily or cheaply transportable. Livestock husbandry and/or wool production provided the principal agricultural solution for most of these transport-deficient areas; another solution, of no small significance for the country's long-term economic future, was the development of a range of industrial activities based, in most cases, upon locally available raw materials. In this regard it may be concluded that the substantial addition to value normally resulting from manufacturing activity permitted a favourable trade-off to be achieved between the relatively low labour costs obtaining in the aforementioned areas and the relatively high distribution costs applying to commodities emanating therefrom.

Coastal areas and districts near major markets were less inhibited by

17 Bowden, *Wool Trade*, p. 75; Wilts. RO, 88/9/26.

transport considerations in the determination of the nature and range of their economic activities. In so far as there tended to be any marked degree of regional specialization with respect to the production of low-value or bulky products, it would have been in these parts. Thus, in the vicinity of London much hay was grown with a view to conversion into meat, milk, and horse power for the ultimate benefit of the metropolitan population. The capital likewise provided a ready market for Kentish hops and East Anglian malt, to mention but two commodities capable of coastwise shipment. Accessibility to a large body of consumers similarly made possible a degree of specialization upon the production of perishable produce. Liquid milk was a case in point; it had to be drunk almost on the spot, or else made into butter or cheese. It is not surprising that ale, with its superior keeping quality, should have been a more universally preferred beverage for quaffing. Market gardening, as the name implies, was another market-oriented activity, although many smallholders in the countryside grew fruits and vegetables for domestic use, just as they might also keep one or two cows for subsistence purposes.

In seeking to fit these various considerations into a more rigorous framework of regional analysis, we should be aware of the tenuity of the undertaking, given the weakness of the statistical base. The peculiarities and imperfections of the data are discussed in more detail in the Appendix,[18] which also presents regional price averages, calculated on a decennial basis, in respect of certain of the major agricultural commodities. Of particular relevance in the present context is the fact that, even within the same region, agricultural prices could sometimes vary quite markedly from one area to another – or from one estate or institution to the next – as a result of local differences in demand and supply conditions. Since only a very small scattering of these different price situations are recorded in the data which have come down to us, there is no assurance that our regional price averages, derived therefrom, are reasonably representative of the broad spectrum of regional experience. Secondly, it should be noted that the characteristics of like-named products may have varied from one part of the country to another (as well as from one statistical series to the next). The wheat grown in Hampshire, for example, may have been of a different average quality from that grown in Lancashire and, other things being equal, this should have been reflected in the relative price relationship. Our data on livestock are especially sensitive to this kind of influence, since the price of animals could vary significantly with size, age, and condition, and these latter criteria admitted of considerable regional bias. A fattened four-year-old bullock sold at 700 lb weight to a London butcher would obviously command a much higher price than a young 300 lb Scots runt purchased for rough pasturing in Westmorland. It is only occasionally, however, that the finer details pertaining to stock are entered in the records of transactions, and without these details we do not

18 Below, pp. 381–4.

have any very precise idea of the extent to which lack of product homogeneity may provide an explanation of apparent differences in regional price levels. In the case of wool, there is less of a problem in this regard, since the existence of significant regional differences in the quality and price of this commodity has long been recognized.[19]

Figures relating to the average prices of arable crops in the different regions of England in the earlier and later parts of our period are presented in Table 19. The regional breakdown adopted in this table (and subsequently) has been influenced primarily by an attempt to group together areas with broadly similar price characteristics, as revealed by the data, rather than with an eye to physical farming patterns; hence, the regions differ in some respects from those treated elsewhere in this volume. The county groupings constituting each of our regions are specified in the Appendix.[20]

Turning more specifically to Table 19, this may be read as indicating that over the period 1640–79 as a whole wheat prices were highest in the Home Counties (averaging 51.35s. per quarter) and lowest in the north Midlands and Lincolnshire (averaging 31.34s. per quarter). The price leadership of the Home Counties with respect to wheat is not unexpected in view of the fact that London's consumption of grain at this time probably accounted for about 10 per cent of total net domestic output. In volume terms the capital was consuming perhaps 1.3 million quarters of grain annually in the 1670s. Much of this came from surrounding areas by waggon; some came by barge downriver from Berkshire and Oxfordshire; while a further quantity, amounting to possibly 15 per cent of the total (judging by figures pertaining to 1680–1) was received by coastwise shipment, mainly from ports in eastern and south-eastern England. The extent to which the city's need for supplies enhanced prices in regions outside the Home Counties must be a matter for conjecture. Wheat – and possibly rye – prices in the south Midlands (encompassing much of the fertile Thames valley area) may have been significantly affected by metropolitan demand, as Gras appreciated more than half a century ago. More generally, it appears that oats were relatively expensive in every region within two or three days' journey of the capital, a finding which seems to make sense in the light of the large and rising volume of horse-drawn traffic to and from London. Houghton's price currents, compiled at the turn of the century, suggest a similar, if somewhat less widespread, influence with respect to the price of hay, without which the city's requirements for meat and milk could not be met (see Table 20). On the other hand, the strength of metropolitan demand was seemingly not able to negate the comparative cost advantages enjoyed by the eastern and southern parts of the country in relation to the production of barley. Even

[19] See, for example, T. H. Lloyd, *The Movement of Wool Prices in Medieval England*, EcHR suppl. 6, Cambridge, 1973, pp. 52–61, 70–1; Bowden, *Wool Trade*, pp. 25–37.

[20] Below, p. 382.

in the vicinity of London it was possible to purchase barley or malt more cheaply than in several of the more distant regions.[21]

These other regions included the south-west of England, where the prices of field crops in general appear to have been more or less on a par with those in the Home Counties. A degree of price leadership in this area appears to have been exerted by Bristol, the second-ranking city and port in the kingdom, described by Pepys as being "in every respect another London". However, the pressure on prices did not stem only from this town of fewer than 30,000 inhabitants (as compared with London's half a million). The south-west was also one of the country's foremost industrial areas and, after Middlesex and Yorkshire, Devonshire probably contained more people than any county in England. The population had to be fed, essentially by an agriculture operating in physical conditions which were not ideally suited to the efficient production of arable crops. Hence, while our suggestion of high prices in the south-west may be somewhat exaggerated in the case of oats (reflecting the dominance of data derived from sources in north-eastern Somerset and other places close to Bristol), the position in relation to other crops does not appear to be significantly misrepresented so far as relative regional price levels are concerned. Further north, in the region encompassing Yorkshire, Nottinghamshire, and Derbyshire, the basic structure of economic activities was reminiscent of that in the south-west of England, with the city of York providing price leadership in the same way as Bristol. Much of the land in this region was not well suited for arable husbandry; hence, the relatively high average prices of wheat and barley, as brought out in Table 19; hence, also the popularity of oatcake and porridge, as economically preferred staples of human diet. Expensive barley and cheap oats also seem to have been the general rule in the largely pastoral western region bordering upon the Marches of Wales. The contemporary appellation "Ryelands" to part of this area would seem to place a question mark against the high-price rating which we have accorded to rye. However, a review of the sources has not uncovered any statistical aberration which might account for this rating, and it would seem possible to conclude that rye was more expensive in this region simply because, in relation to other parts of the country, it was in greater demand.[22]

At the lower end of the price scale, two regions – the north Midlands and Lincolnshire, and the north and north-west of England – command particular attention. It is quite possible that the cheapness of produce in these

[21] N. S. B. Gras, *The Evolution of the English Corn Market from the Twelfth to the Eighteenth Century*, Harvard Ec. Studies, XIII, Cambridge, Mass., 1915, pp. 77, 104–9; T. S. Willan, *The English Coasting Trade 1600–1750*, Manchester, 1938, pp. 78–84; F. J. Fisher, 'The Development of the London Food Market, 1540–1640', EcHR, V, 1935, pp. 47–51 (repr. in *Essays in Economic History*, I, ed. E. M. Carus-Wilson, London, 1954).

[22] *Diary of Samuel Pepys*, ed. Lord Braybrooke, 4th edn, London, 1854, II, p. 336; Deane and Cole, *British Economic Growth*, pp. 7, 103.

Table 19. Comparisons (in rank order) of regional average price levels, 1640–79 and 1710–49: field crops

	Regions in 1640–79[a]			Regions in 1710–49		
	High price	Average price	Low price	High price	Average price	Low price
Wheat	Home Counties	South-west	West	North & north-west	West	South-west
	Yorks., Notts., & Derbs.	North & north-west	South	South Midlands	Home Counties	East
	South Midlands	East	North Midlands & Lincs.	Yorks., Notts., & Derbs.	South	North Midlands & Lincs.
		Range: 51.35s.–31.34s. per qtr			Range: 36.93s.–26.90s. per qtr	
Barley & malt	South-west	North Midlands & Lincs.	South Midlands	Yorks., Notts., & Derbs.	Home Counties	South Midlands
	Yorks., Notts., & Derbs.	Home Counties	North & north-west	South-west	South	East
	West	South	East	West	North Midlands & Lincs.	North & north-west
		Range: 26.62s.–14.30s. per qtr			Range: 24.46s.–14.06s. per qtr	
Rye	West	Yorks., Notts., & Derbs.	North Midlands & Lincs.	West	North Midlands & Lincs.	Yorks., Notts., & Derbs.
	South Midlands	East	North & north-west	South Midlands[b]	North & north-west	East
	Home Counties	South	South-west	Home Counties	South	South-west
		Range: 27.28s.–21.89s. per qtr			Range: 25.12s.–18.01s. per qtr	

The following presents rank‑orderings of regions by grain price, arranged as two sets of columns, with each grain followed by its price range.

First set

Oats	South-west / Home Counties / East	South Midlands / South / Yorks., Notts., & Derbs.	West / North & north-west / North Midlands & Lincs.	Range: 17.47s.–9.94s. per qtr
Beans	South-west / Yorks., Notts., & Derbs. / Home Counties	South Midlands / West / North & north-west	South / East / North Midlands & Lincs.	Range: 37.89s.–19.29s. per qtr
Peas	South-west / Home Counties / South	East / West / South Midlands[b]	North Midlands & Lincs. / Yorks., Notts., & Derbs. / North & north-west	Range: 33.91s.–17.45s. per qtr

Second set

Oats	South-west / Home Counties / East	South / South Midlands / Yorks., Notts., & Derbs.	West / North & north-west / North Midlands & Lincs.	Range: 14.28s.–9.82s. per qtr
Beans	West / Home Counties / South Midlands	South-west / East / North & north-west	South / North Midlands & Lincs. / Yorks., Notts., & Derbs.	Range: 28.26s.–16.17s. per qtr
Peas	South-west / Home Counties / South	West / South Midlands / East	North Midlands & Lincs. / Yorks., Notts., & Derbs. / North & north-west	Range: 29.28s.–15.74s. per qtr

[a] 1680–1709 with respect to rye.
[b] Assumed.

. Table 20. *Average price of hay, selected towns,[a] 1698–1701*
(in shillings per load)

Hereford	50.00	Andover	38.67
London	47.42	Newcastle upon Tyne	35.39
Wycombe	47.16	Norwich	31.11
Bristol	38.93	Stamford	30.06

[a] Town with highest price in each of our regions. Insufficient data with respect to towns in Yorks., Notts., and Derbs.

regions has been exaggerated by our data, since, in the one instance, we have been forced to rely heavily upon observations pertaining to Lincoln, where prices appear to have been exceptionally low, and, in the second instance, our coverage largely excludes Lancashire, where prices were probably higher than in areas further north. However, it may be hazarded that a more representative sampling of the data would still probably leave these two regions, together with eastern England, in the below-average price category for arable crops. At first sight, this may seem somewhat surprising. Neither region was evidently in the vanguard of agricultural progress. Indeed, it would not be inapt to describe northern England as a backwater in this regard, while the system of open-field farming still persisted over much of the north Midlands. However, the latter was an inherently fertile area, while the productive capability of Lincolnshire, along with that of districts to the south, was being significantly enhanced as a result of the drainage operations engineered by Vermuyden. No less significant from the standpoint of price determination must have been the fact that both regions (at least those parts covered by our data) were primarily agricultural, with low densities of population, few towns with more than eight or nine hundred inhabitants, and (except for districts adjacent to King's Lynn, Boston, and other such east-coast ports) lacking major marketing outlets for arable produce. To a considerable extent, therefore, and more especially in northern England, arable farming was for the purpose of subsistence or as an adjunct to pastoral activity. Hence, the commercial stimulus conducive to a price-setting situation was missing. In the more isolated areas of the north, following the line of argument propounded by Thorold Rogers, a shortage of coin might possibly have served to provide a further depressant influence on prices.[23]

Turning more generally to Table 19, it will be evident that the regional price relationships applying in the period 1710–49 were not, in general, very different from those just discussed. In all regions the prices of most crops were lower than in 1640–79. The Home Counties, not unexpectedly, continued to rank as a high-price region overall. However, in the light of the data

[23] J. E. T. Rogers, *A History of Agriculture and Prices in England*, 7 vols., Oxford, 1866–1902, *V*, p. 241.

pertaining to wheat, it would appear that substantial progress had been made in meeting London's requirements for bread. A different conclusion might be drawn in regard to alcoholic drink, judging by the general rise in barley and malt prices in the southern and eastern regions of England since 1640–79. As a result of the various changes affecting this part of the country, prices in the south appear, on average, to have moved rather closer to those in the Home Counties and south Midlands, while those in the east seem to have slipped somewhat, at least so far as the principal bread cereals are concerned. It may be hypothesized that this latter development had its main origins in a combination of increased agricultural production in eastern England, especially in the reclaimed fenland districts of Cambridgeshire, and lower industrial income in the region, reflecting the general *malaise* of the wool textile manufacture in East Anglia. Slow or negative industrial growth, with little or no population increase, could also account for the relative decline of wheat, barley, and bean prices in the south-west of England. On the other hand, a relatively buoyant regional economy – or an exceptionally unresponsive agricultural sector – is suggested by the comparative stickiness of cereal and pulse prices in our western area (encompassing Staffordshire, Shropshire, and neighbouring counties and comprising part of what was to become the Black Country). A similar interpretation might be applied to the situation in the northern and north-western region, where wheat and rye prices stayed firmer than elsewhere. However, for those who savoured oatcake, porridge, and pease pudding, this remained a cheap area for food, as did the north Midlands and Lincolnshire.[24]

From a more quantitative standpoint, it may be noted that the range of average prices, as between the different regions, was significantly narrower in 1710–49 than in 1640–79 with respect to all crops except rye (for which the data are very piecemeal). It may be further observed that this narrowing was brought about primarily by a reduction in prices at the top, rather than at the bottom, of the regional price scale. Thus, in relation to wheat, there was a decline of 14.42s. per quarter (from 51.35s. to 36.93s.) at the top of the regional price range, compared with a decline of 4.44s. per quarter (from 31.34s to 26.90s.) at the lower extreme. In the case of beans, there were corresponding decreases of 9.63s. and 3.12s. per quarter at the top and bottom respectively. Various hypotheses come to mind in explanation of this development. One possibility is that the real costs of arable production were most sharply reduced in the erstwhile high-price (high-demand) regions of the country, these being particularly susceptible to improved methods of farm management. Another possibility is that the demand for cereals and pulses increased proportionately more (or decreased proportionately less) in the low-price regions than elsewhere, possibly as a result of relatively high rates

[24] Bowden, *Wool Trade*, pp. 52–6; Deane and Cole, *op. cit.*, pp. 102–5; M. F. Lloyd Prichard, 'The Decline of Norwich', EcHR, 2nd ser., III, 1951, pp. 371–7.

of income growth associated with the spread of industrialization. Finally, and perhaps most pertinently, the narrowing of regional price differentials may be seen as providing confirmatory evidence of the effectiveness of improvements in transportation and marketing organization. The ultimate effect of such improvements, of course, is the creation of a national system of uniform prices.

The pattern of regional prices in relation to sheep and cattle is presented in Table 21. When compared with Table 19, this reveals a substantial measure of agreement with the regional price structure for grains and pulses. As in the case of these crops, sheep and cattle, in general, tended to be most expensive in the south Midlands, Home Counties, and south-west of England. Large concentrations of population in or near these regions resulted in a proportionately heavy emphasis being placed on the finishing end of meat production. In consequence, it would seem safe to assume that an unusually large percentage of the animals marketed in these areas were in or approaching the prime of condition – a factor tending towards the establishment of relatively high price levels. The prices of sheep, oxen, and beef cattle sold in the north Midlands and Lincolnshire were also above average, whereas, as we have seen, this was a low-price region for field crops. It has already been suggested that marketing restraints on farming activity in this area affected arable production much more severely than livestock husbandry.[25] Indeed, as early as the 1560s and 70s Northamptonshire sheep and lambs were being supplied to London butchers. However, the relatively high prices indicated in Table 21 as being generally paid for stock in the north Midlands and Lincolnshire may have owed less to metropolitan demand – or to regional differences in the industrial structure of meat production – than to the fact that the rich grasslands, marshes, and fens of central England and Lincolnshire tended to produce animals which were large in size and, therefore, relatively expensive. It was in this region (and the south Midlands) that most of the country's long-staple wool was produced, the fleeces of sheep grazed upon enclosed pastures in Lincolnshire, Leicestershire, and adjoining counties to the south being in some cases three or four times heavier than those of downland shortwool breeds.[26]

At the opposite end of the regional price scale, livestock were generally cheapest in the northern and north-western parts of the country and in eastern England, these being areas where, as we have seen, arable produce also tended to be relatively inexpensive. In the northernmost counties much of the grazing land was rough pasture, and a heavy emphasis was placed upon breeding and rearing (as opposed to finishing), while the local breeds of both cattle and sheep were usually undersized. Accordingly, since most sales

[25] Above, p. 214.

[26] Bowden, *Wool Trade*, pp. 30–7; above, p. 64; Joan Thirsk, 'Farming Techniques', in vol. 3 of the paperback series, pp. 42–5.

featured young, small, or unfattened stock, average prices were generally low. Similar considerations prevailed, somewhat less pervasively, in Yorkshire, Nottinghamshire, and Derbyshire and in the west of England. In the latter region the small size of sheep was redeemed somewhat by the high quality of their wool. How far these kinds of consideration applied to livestock in eastern England is impossible to determine. The low average price of cattle in this region could reflect a predominance of undersized stock and, while the local breeds do not appear to have been especially small, there is some evidence of runtish Scottish and northern beasts being bought and sold by Suffolk farmers in the third quarter of the seventeenth century. At the same time, in coastal and marshland districts, large numbers of old cows, young bullocks, and surplus heifers were doubtless sold off every year by dairy farmers. In the case of sheep, our data indicate that prices in the eastern region were not generally low – a fact which probably reflected both the largish size of the local breeds and the importance of sheep in the system of arable cultivation.[27]

The general regional price pattern reviewed above had not greatly changed by 1710–49. As with cereals, there was a relative strengthening in the prices of all types of cattle in the south of England and a relative (and absolute) weakening in these prices in the south-west. Demand considerations, already discussed,[28] may have been primarily responsible in each instance. However, at least part of the decline in cattle prices in the south-western region would appear to have been associated with the assumed increase in traffic in small Welsh beasts through this area – a factor which would also seem relevant to the downward movement of bullock and heifer prices in the west of England. With respect to sheep, it may be noted that while the most expensive animals continued to come from the central area of England and Lincolnshire, the price of wethers from these areas seems to have been particularly adversely affected by the fall in the price of wool which occurred during the first half of the eighteenth century. As in the case of arable crops, the range of average regional prices with respect to all types of livestock tended to narrow over time. Thus, whereas a difference of 43.97s. (i.e. 93.04s.–49.07s.) separated the highest and lowest regional price averages for cows in the period 1640–79, a corresponding margin of 38.92s. (i.e. 104.70s.–65.78s.) separated these averages in 1710–49. To some extent such narrowing seems to have resulted from a greater geographical diffusion of livestock from different areas; it must, however, be a matter of conjecture whether this factor was of more consequence than underlying changes in demand and supply conditions.[29]

[27] W. Suffolk RO, Badmondisfield estate accounts, 1,341/5/2; Lord Francis Hervey, ed., *Suffolk in the Seventeenth Century: A Breviary of Suffolk by Robert Reyce, 1618*, London, 1902, pp. 28, 38; Robert Trow-Smith, *A History of British Livestock Husbandry to 1700*, London, 1957, pp. 196–7.

[28] Above, p. 215.

[29] Fussell and Goodman, 'Eighteenth-Century Traffic in Livestock', pp. 217–18, 223–4.

Table 21. Comparisons (in rank order) of regional average price levels, 1640–79 and 1710–49: livestock

	Regions in 1640–79			Regions in 1710–49		
	High price	Average price	Low price	High price	Average price	Low price
Sheep (type unspecified)	South Midlands	North Midlands & Lincs.	South	South Midlands	Home Counties	West
	Home Counties	South-west	Yorks., Notts., & Derbs.	East	South-west	South
	East	West	North & north-west	North Midlands & Lincs.	Yorks., Notts., & Derbs.	North & north-west
		Range: 14.34s.–5.83s. each			Range: 14.43s.–6.89s. each	
Wethers	South Midlands	South-west	West	South Midlands	North Midlands & Lincs.	Yorks., Notts., & Derbs.
	South	East	North & north-west	South	Home Counties	West
	North Midlands & Lincs.	Home Counties	Yorks., Notts., & Derbs.	South-west	East	North & north-west
		Range: 19.34s.–7.25s. each			Range: 14.23s.–8.68s. each	
Oxen	South-west	South	Yorks., Notts., & Derbs.	North Midlands & Lincs.	South Midlands	Yorks., Notts., & Derbs.
	North Midlands & Lincs.	South Midlands	East[a]	South	West	East
	Home Counties	West	North & north-west	South-west	Home Counties	North & north-west
		Range: 161.09s.–72.35s. each			Range: 159.79s.–86.06s. each	

218

Bullocks

Home Counties	North & north-west	South Midlands	South Midlands	South	West
North Midlands & Lincs.	West	Yorks., Notts., & Derbs.	North Midlands & Lincs.	Yorks., Notts., & Derbs.	North & north-west
South-west	South	East	Home Counties	South-west	East

Range: 151.07s.–61.18s. each   Range: 116.28s.–58.48s. each

Cows

South Midlands	Yorks., Notts., & Derbs.	North Midlands & Lincs.	South Midlands	Home Counties	West
South-west	South	East	South	North Midlands & Lincs.	Yorks., Notts., & Derbs.
West	Home Counties	North & north-west	South-west	North & north-west	East

Range: 93.04s.–49.07s. each   Range: 104.70s.–65.78s. each

Heifers

South Midlands	Yorks., Notts., & Derbs.	South-west	Home Counties	South	North Midlands & Lincs.
South	North Midlands & Lincs.	West	Yorks., Notts., & Derbs.	South Midlands	South-west
Home Counties	North & north-west	East	East	North & north-west	West

Range: 103.56s.–46.21s. each   Range: 97.30s.–52.32s. each

[a] Assumed.

Data relating to the prices of other types of livestock are much less comprehensive than they are for cattle and sheep, and quantitative comparisons on a regional basis are not possible. It can, however, be stated that the prices of pigs and poultry, like those of other farm animals, were strongly influenced by the costs of feed. Pigs were generally cheapest in woodland and dairy farming districts, where they could be fed acorns, beechmast, and the waste products of milk processing, and dearest in unwooded areas devoted mainly to grain production. Size was also, of course, an important consideration in the determination of price. The largest pigs came reputedly from Midland counties, such as Leicestershire and Northamptonshire, where they were fattened on a diet of beans and peas produced specifically for them at comparatively low cost (see Table 19). Cheap buckwheat and barley encouraged a degree of specialization upon poultry keeping in East Anglia. Outside this area, poultry – and especially geese – tended to be cheapest in moorland and fenland districts, where extensive commons were available. Horse breeding was mainly a speciality in pastoral areas, and the expectation is that horses would be cheapest in these areas. However, in qualification, we should perhaps remind ourselves that horses were probably even less homogeneous than they are today. They ranged greatly in size, from the forest pony to the Midland shire horse and, according to their individual capabilities and the inclinations of their owners, could be called upon to serve in one or more of a number of capacities, viz. cart horse, plough horse, packhorse, saddle horse, coach horse, etc. Because they supplied a service rather than a tangible product, and because they provided a means of enhancing their owner's social standing, horses (including mares, geldings, colts, and fillies) were probably valued from a more subjective standpoint than most other commodities; in consequence, the price at which they exchanged hands varied within much wider limits than the prices of other categories of livestock. Thus, our data show horse prices ranging from £1 5s. for a "grey galloway" sold in Northumberland in 1746 to £53 15s. for a "grey stone horse" purchased in Hertfordshire in 1699. Although, by implication, the prices of horses within individual regions did not vary to this extent, yet the range of prices from transaction to transaction was often very large, making any attempt at regional comparisons extremely hazardous.[30]

In the case of farm animals other than horses, local differences in the price of stock arose partly, if not mainly, from differences in the value of their produce. As we have seen, the largest (lowland-reared and fattened) animals normally commanded the highest prices, and quite clearly this was primarily attributable to their superior weight of meat. In addition, the largest animals normally yielded the heaviest hides or pelts and the greatest quantities of tallow. Judging by the piecemeal sales of slaughtered bullocks from the duke

[30] Thirsk, op. cit., pp. 45–8; Northumb. RO, Allgood MSS ZAL box 46/1; Herts, RO, Capell MSS 10,459.

of Bedford's Devonshire estates in 1743–4, these by-products could account
for 18–29 per cent of the total value of a dead beast. All live animals, of
course, provided manure, the value of which one would expect to be highest
in arable districts, while dairy cattle, poultry, and sheep also supplied other
produce on an ongoing basis. Over the lifetime of such animals, the value
of the milk, cheese, butter, eggs, and wool which they variously produced
could substantially exceed the value of their flesh. We know very little about
regional differences in the value of dairy produce and eggs and the extent
to which the yield of these products may have varied from one part of the
country to another. Whether Cheshire cows, for example, gave more milk
or 'better' milk than cows bred in other areas is a moot question. Certainly,
the Cheshire farmers seem to have believed in the superiority of their cheese,
and St Bartholomew's Hospital, Sandwich, was willing to pay 60–70 per cent
more for it than for cheese produced in Suffolk. Of all the different livestock
products none was subject to such wide regional price variations as wool.
The quality of wool, the length of staple, and the weight of fleece varied
greatly from one part of the country to another, reflecting differences in the
nature of pasturage and climate. The criterion of high quality was fineness of
fibre and the finest wools normally commanded the highest prices. The finest
wool grown in England (which, like most fine wools, was of the short-staple
variety) came from the small Ryeland or Herefordshire breed of sheep; at
the beginning of our period this was five times as expensive as the very coarse
wools produced in the northern counties and in Suffolk. The fleece of the
Ryeland sheep, however, was very light, usually weighing no more than one
pound. As already noted, the heaviest fleeces were produced by the longwool
sheep of central and eastern England, whose principal habitats were the
enclosed pastures and rich marshland grazings. Although much of the wool
grown by these sheep was comparatively coarse in character, the rising
demands of the worsted industry (as opposed to the woollen manufacture)
helped to ensure a generally expanding market for this wool over the period
of our study.[31]

C. SEASONAL PRICE MOVEMENTS

It is a characteristic of foodstuffs in their natural state that they are perishable
and need to be consumed within a limited – sometimes very short – space
of time. Nowadays, the period of marketability of most crops may be
extended by a variety of preserving techniques and by storage under carefully
controlled conditions. In the seventeenth and eighteenth centuries, however,
preserving methods were rudimentary and storage facilities were largely
lacking. Milk could, of course, be converted into butter or cheese, but, as
a liquid product, its marketing possibilities were very limited before the

[31] Devon RO, 1,258M/F27; Cheshire RO, DAR/A65/2; Beveridge *et al.*, *Prices and Wages*,
I, pp. 239–40; Bowden, *Wool Trade*, pp. 25–37, 44–5, 72–3.

arrival of the railways and the development of refrigeration. Indeed, it is difficult to see how a dairyman could gain a livelihood from the sale of liquid milk unless his cows were actually stalled inside a town or very close thereto. Similarly with meat. The keeping – if not the eating – qualities of pork and beef could be improved by treatment with smoke or salt, but fresh meat had, of necessity, to be kept on the hoof for as long as possible prior to sale and consumption. Most institutions and large private households, in fact, did their own slaughtering for the kitchen. The rapidity of product deterioration, allied to exceptionally high costs of transport, also made horticultural produce generally unsuitable for movement over long distances. Certain horticultural crops – notably, roots, onions, and apples – could be eaten after several months in storage while, in the west country, surplus apples might be made into cider and shrivelled apples were fed to pigs. Moreover, producers and consumers took full advantage of the differing ripening dates of the many varieties of fruits and vegetables available to them, and some took considerable pains in devising ways of storage, as the books on husbandry and horticulture bear witness. However, before the advent of modern processing methods, the difficulties of disposing of large quantities of fruits and vegetables during the very short marketing seasons generally pertaining thereto must have served as a significant restraining influence upon the commercial production of such commodities.[32]

On the other hand, under suitable conditions, most grains could be stored for a number of years, although it was claimed in the early eighteenth century that "barley is worth nothing after it is a year old and by keeping it rats and mice might eat it". On reflection, however, it will be apparent that in temperate climates, where one crop per year is the norm, the discovery of a storable food staple must have been an essential prerequisite for the establishment of a settled arable agriculture. Without such a staple, capable of being stored at least from one harvest period to the next, man would have remained dependent upon livestock (wild or domestic) for his sustenance during the greater part of the year.[33]

Agricultural production before 1750, as now, was highly seasonal in character. While wheat and rye (the principal bread corns) were sown in the autumn, oats, barley, and most other field and garden crops (other than tree fruits) were planted in the spring. Depending upon the crop, time of planting, and the weather, the main harvest period for arable products fell between June and October, although there were certain commodities, among which the turnip has particular significance for our study, with an extended growing season. Livestock production was also seasonally oriented, the cattle and sheep populations reaching a peak in the springtime, when herds and flocks underwent the process of natural renewal. The increased availability of feed resulting from the growth of spring and summer pasture permitted the

[32] UCNWL, Penrhos i, 587.   [33] E. Sussex RO, FRE 6,766.

subsequent maturing and fattening of stock so that in spite of decreased numbers (attributable to planned slaughter, accident, and disease) the volume of meat on the hoof was probably at a maximum in the months of June and July, thus coinciding with the period of hay harvest. During these months milk yields would also tend to be comparatively high, while June was the usual time for the shearing of sheep.[34]

One expression of the seasonal character of agricultural operations was a shifting demand for farm labour, most especially by the larger arable undertakings. Employment in arable agriculture reached a peak during the cereal harvest, at which time many casual workers were taken on to assist with the reaping, stooking, and carting of crops in a race against the uncertain English weather. Other busy, though less hectic, phases occurred in the autumn and spring in connection with the ploughing of land and sowing of seed. Apart from these periods of brisk activity, agricultural work generally proceeded at a slow or steady pace. Most of the outdoor jobs were undertaken in the warmer seasons of the year, with threshing of corn providing the main source of employment during the winter months. This seasonal work rhythm was modified somewhat as the new rotations gained acceptance.

Similar, though less marked, seasonality permeated the labour demands of other types of farming. Among livestock enterprises, the need for extra helpers was particularly great during the haymaking season, which usually lasted for several weeks. While this was taking place many sheep farmers were hiring skilled workers and day labourers to assist with the washing and shearing of sheep and the winding of wool. Subsequently, there was little call for extra help until lambing time the following spring. Similarly, dairy farmers had to cope with a flush of milk in the early summer and with a reduced supply thereafter. In comparison with sheep farmers and dairymen, cattle graziers had less total need for labour and experienced much lighter seasonal fluctuations in activity.

Overall, however, the seasonal pattern of employment in agriculture provided considerable scope for month-to-month variations in the farm wage bill. These appear to have been due primarily to variations in the volume of employment, rather than fluctuations in the rate of wages. Indeed, an analysis of extant farm accounts reveals that similar tasks, or different tasks demanding similar levels of skill, were generally reimbursed at the same rates of wages throughout the year (as well as year after year). Thus, on the Essex estates of the Petre family at West Horndon and Thorndon Hall, 1s. per day was paid at various times in 1666–78 for haymaking, cutting corn, threshing, carting, and spreading dung. Similarly, on the Buckinghamshire estates of the Chester family at Chicheley and Lidlington, 9d. per day was the going rate in 1747–8 for weeding bean and wheat crops, raking stubble, sawing

[34] Cornwall RO, Rashleigh DDR 5,299.

wood, and stone gathering. However, irrespective of whether farm wage rates generally remained stable over the course of the year, the changing volume of agricultural earnings obviously had great significance for the whole economy. Harvest wages, and the payments which farmers themselves received from their first marketings of the recently gathered corn crops, gave the economic system its biggest injection of cash during the course of the year. Outstanding debts were paid off and a general process of stocking up for the months ahead occurred through the medium of the great fairs held in the early autumn.[35]

The spillover effects from agriculture served to reinforce or cut across the direct effects of the seasons on the economy at large. Outdoor trades, grain milling, and industrial operations powered by wind or water were particularly liable to be affected by changes in the weather. While conditions of drought could bring mills driven by water power to a halt, heavy rains or snowfalls were particularly severe in their impact on outdoor activities such as building and transport. The frosts that made the carriage of goods overland easier might snarl traffic on the rivers and canals. Severe weather conditions not only seized up the outlets for the products of mining and manufacturing industry but were also capable of causing a general scarcity of provisions. Thus, the icing over of the river Severn in the winter of 1683 prevented the transportation of supplies to Bristol from upriver.[36]

With activity so much at the mercy of the elements, the expectation is for agricultural prices to exhibit a pronounced seasonal pattern. However, so far as the major arable crops are concerned, this was not the case. Certainly, the prices of cereals sometimes fluctuated quite sharply from one month to the next but there was little consistency in the timing of such movements over the years. Consequently, long-term averages of monthly grain prices differed little from each other. Thus, over the period 1710–49 as a whole, the average monthly price of wheat at Bear Key, London, ranged between a low of 28.97s. per quarter (in January) and a high of 30.40s. per quarter (in November), the difference being a mere 4.9 per cent.[37] Likewise, there was little difference in the average monthly prices of other cereals and pulses sold at Bear Key during this period (see Table 22). Examination of a number of other sources also leads to the same conclusion: although crop prices could vary significantly over the course of a year, no regular or clear seasonal pattern can be discerned.

One may attempt to explain this apparent lack of short-term periodicity by dismissing as of small consequence the impact of seasonal influences in

[35] Essex RO, Petre MSS D/DP/A55; Bucks. RO, Chester MSS D/C/2/45; E. L. Jones, *Seasons and Prices: The Role of Weather in English Agricultural History*, London, 1964, pp. 66–7.

[36] Jones, *Seasons and Prices*, pp. 21–7; E. Suffolk RO, HA 49/A III/Gen. 5.

[37] For the sources of these and other unreferenced prices, see 'Note on Statistical Methods and Sources', pp. 381–94 below.

Table 22. Prices of cereals and pulses at Bear Key, London: lowest and highest monthly averages, harvest years 1710–49 (in shillings per quarter)

	Wheat	Rye	Barley	Oats	Beans	Peas
Lowest	28.97 (Jan.)	17.05 (Sept.)	16.35 (Apr./ Feb.)	12.21 (Feb.)	18.84 (July)	22.48 (June)
Highest	30.40 (Nov.)	18.20 (Apr.)	17.43 (Nov.)	12.91 (Dec.)	20.05 (Nov.)	24.27 (Dec.)
Highest as % of lowest	104.9	106.7	106.6	105.7	104.9	108.0

the determination of agricultural price movements, but such a viewpoint hardly seems to accord with the already noted vulnerability of the economy to changes in climatic conditions. The likeliest explanation would seem to be that the underlying tendency for prices to rise and fall with the changing seasons was frequently swamped by stronger forces attendant upon the annual harvest.

Looked at from the standpoint of supply, the presumption is that in a largely closed economy during the course of a normal year, the price of grain would be lowest in the months immediately following the harvest, subsequently rising as stocks became depleted. This seasonal tendency had apparently established itself by the end of the eighteenth century but it was not in evidence during the period covered by our study nor in the years preceding 1640. This is brought out in Table 23, which summarizes, with respect to the period under review, seasonal price movements pertaining to the major cereals and pulses, based on the Bear Key data and Houghton's nation-wide weekly price currents.[38]

As these figures indicate, there was no marked tendency for the prices of cereals and pulses to rise towards the end of the harvest year. Indeed, it seems that they were more likely to peak in November and December than in June and July, from which it might reasonably be concluded that during the course of a harvest year consumer purchasing power not uncommonly declined at a faster rate than the supply of grain. Given that the flow of cash into the pockets of consumers tended to reach a high point at harvest time or shortly thereafter, one would generally expect demand considerations to exercise their greatest upward pressure on prices at the beginning of the harvest year. At this time, increased supplies of grain would tend to be matched by greater purchasing power and willingness to spend on the part of the general body of consumers. Thus, cereal prices in the period 1640–1750 did not, as in a

[38] T. S. Ashton, Economic Fluctuations in England, 1700–1800, Oxford, 1959, p. 11; above, pp. 40–1.

Table 23. *Indices of quarterly average prices of major cereals and pulses*
(1st qtr (Oct.–Dec.) = 100)

	2nd qtr (Jan.–Mar.)	3rd qtr (Apr.–June)	4th qtr (July–Sept.)
	Houghton (HY 1693–1701)		
Wheat	101.5	100.0	94.9
Rye	100.5	99.6	97.0
Oats	101.0	101.2	97.3
Barley	99.0	101.1	101.6
Beans	100.1	99.1	98.1
Peas	100.3	100.9	100.0
Average	100.4	100.3	98.2
	Bear Key (HY 1710–49)		
Wheat	97.4	100.5	98.7
Rye	98.7	100.6	95.4
Oats	96.6	97.2	99.5
Barley	96.2	94.9	96.3
Beans	97.7	96.4	96.0
Peas	99.3	95.3	94.8
Average	97.7	97.5	96.8

later age, exhibit a general tendency to fall at the beginning of a harvest year, rising subsequently, but rather they tended to move in a contrary manner. It may be surmised that the shift to the subsequent seasonal price pattern was associated with the seasonal redeployment of economic activity coincident upon industrial growth and reduced dependence upon agriculture. It may also have been related to a greater availability of alternative foods, especially fruits and vegetables, although the increased availability of such foods would not have been limited to the autumn months. In the case of crops used partly for fodder purposes (especially oats, beans, and peas), the failure of prices in the late seventeenth and early eighteenth centuries to rise in the spring and summer months, when the animal population was at a maximum, was doubtless partly associated with the increased availability of alternative supplies of feed resulting from the growth of meadow land and pasture. However, over a period of years, the average prices of these crops did not vary greatly from one season to the next.

Of course, the seasonal averages depicted in Table 23 mask considerable fluctuations within individual years. From the standpoint of supply, prices depended not only upon what was available in the barns and granaries but also upon what the next harvest was expected to bring. Reasonably reliable estimates of the yield of the forthcoming harvest of winter-sown cereals could usually be made by early summer, and market prices were influenced accordingly. Forecasts of a bountiful harvest tended to encourage the owners of stocks of corn to sell without delay, before prices tumbled in the autumn, while anticipations of a bad crop had the opposite effect. At times, of course, forecasts went awry, and sellers and buyers of grain cursed themselves for opportunities lost or risks miscalculated. Reporting on the situation in Herefordshire at the beginning of June 1730, one correspondent noted: "The rates of corn are fallen v. much... Several granaries are full of corn expecting the markets to advance to 10s. per bus. with design to grind the face of the poor but God's Providence has ordered it otherwise." Ten years later the story would have been very different, as is brought out by the figures presented in Table 24 with reference to the prices paid for wheat by Sherborne almshouses in Dorset.[39]

Table 24. *Quarterly average price of wheat, Sherborne almshouses, Dorset, harvest years 1738–41 (in shillings per quarter)*

Harvest year	1st qtr (Oct.– Dec.)	2nd qtr (Jan.– Mar.)	3rd qtr (Apr.– June)	4th qtr (July– Sept.)	Annual average
1738	52.61	52.81	50.00	56.92	53.09
1739	60.31	60.21	80.67	90.15	72.84
1740	98.46	102.31	107.09	78.14	96.50
1741	55.41	56.83	50.57	47.38	52.55

A comparison of average seasonal prices in different parts of England (*vide* Houghton's price quotations for the period 1693–1701) reveals a certain correspondence of movement as between the various regions, especially with respect to the main bread cereals and the seasons of minimum prices. In this regard, it would perhaps be unreasonable to expect a high degree of correlation in view of regional differences in growing seasons, variations in climate, and impediments to transport. Nevertheless, of the nine major regions of England, as categorized in the Appendix,[40] only two (viz. south-western England, and Nottinghamshire, Derbyshire, and Yorkshire) did not record their lowest average wheat prices in the fourth quarter of the harvest year, while only one (viz. Nottinghamshire, Derbyshire, and Yorkshire) did not show a similar disposition with respect to rye.[41]

Among arable crops other than cereals and pulses, hops is the only one

[39] UCNWL, Penrhos i, 587.   [40] Below, p. 382.
[41] However, no rye prices were reported by Houghton for markets in the south and south-west of England.

for which seasonal price data are available in any quantity. Quarterly price indices with respect to this commodity, as illustrated in Table 25, based on London Navy Victualling transactions, reveal similar seasonal tendencies to those already noted in relation to the major arable products.

Table 25. *Indices of quarterly average prices of hops, London Navy Victualling contracts, harvest years 1686–1749*

1st qtr (Oct.–Dec.)	2nd qtr (Jan.–Mar.)	3rd qtr (Apr.–June)	4th qtr (July–Sept.)
100	99.1	95.9	94.0

By contrast, there is a strong presumption that in the case of highly perishable crops, notably fruits and vegetables, prices would tend to rise quite sharply from one harvest to the next. Indeed, the probability is that towards the end of the normal marketing season even common vegetables would be priced beyond the pockets of all but the well-to-do, while some products would be unavailable at any price during a substantial part of the year. Data from various sources seem to point to these conclusions but are too piecemeal to permit the construction of reliable price series on either a seasonal or annual basis.

In the case of meat the data are more plentiful. The principal statistics are summarized in Table 26. It will be noted that the price range of the

Table 26. *Indices of quarterly average prices of beef, pork, and mutton, 1683–1759 (1st qtr (Oct.–Dec.) = 100)*

	2nd qtr (Jan.–Mar.)	3rd qtr (Apr.–June)	4th qtr (July–Sept.)
Beef			
London Navy Victualling (1683–1759)	113.3	120.7	108.3
Portsmouth Navy Victualling (1700–59)	112.3	116.0	110.9
Plymouth Navy Victualling (1700–39)	109.3	118.5	112.0
Pork			
London Navy Victualling (1683–1743)	108.2	111.7	100.7
Mutton			
Westminster School and Abbey (1688–1749)	105.0	107.1	100.4

specified products, especially beef, is greater than that for the main arable crops, with the maximum being reached in the third quarter of the harvest year. In the case of beef, in respect of which monthly prices are available, it is possible to be somewhat more precise and to pinpoint May in each instance as marking the high point of the annual price curve. In contrasting the shape of this curve with that for arable crops it may be postulated first of all that the larger part of the population seldom ate meat and its price would therefore be influenced to a much lesser extent than that of corn by fluctuations in the level of agricultural earnings. Secondly, the amount of meat coming on the market, and hence its supply price, was influenced to a significant extent by the availability of feed in the shorter term. The decline in meat prices during the latter part of the calendar year suggests a certain pressure to dispose of stock at this time which, in turn, could be attributed to anticipatory action with respect to supplies of feed.

D. ANNUAL PRICE MOVEMENTS

Annual movements in the average prices of the major grains are presented graphically in Figs. 8 and 9. On referring to these graphs, one is immediately struck by the close comparability between the price paths

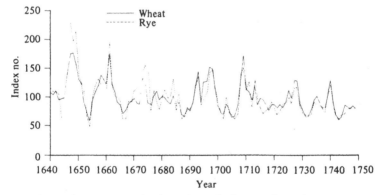

Fig. 8. Annual movements in the prices of wheat and rye (1640–1749 = 100).

charted by the different cereals. This correspondence, of course, is not unexpected in view of the possibilities for substitution in the usage of the various grains and the basic similarities in the conditions necessary for their effective production. Wheat and rye, the autumn-sown bread cereals, not surprisingly, possessed a greater degree of price affinity with each other than with either of the spring-sown cereals (barley and oats), which were used more largely to meet the needs for drink and animal fodder respectively.

The highly volatile nature of the price movements portrayed in Figs. 8 and 9 serves to underline the inelasticity in demand and supply conditions

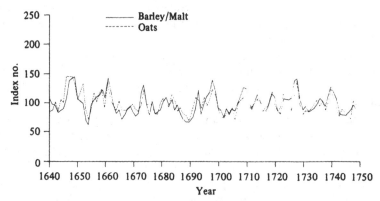

Fig. 9. Annual movements in the prices of barley/malt and oats
(1640–1749 = 100).

which has always characterized agricultural commodities in general, and cereals in particular. During our period, the only farm product to exhibit a greater degree of price volatility than cereals was hops – a crop whose production was subject to wide variations in yield and whose sales hinged upon the highly unstable output of malted grain. Because of the comparatively long-drawn-out processes of agricultural production and the difficulties inhibiting an expansion of agricultural inputs in the short run, supplies of grain, even today, cannot be rapidly increased. In the seventeenth and eighteenth centuries this inelasticity in supply – and the instability in prices associated with it – was heightened by the fact that (as in the less developed countries of the modern world) production was essentially for consumption within the current harvest year. In consequence, once allowance had been made for seed, stocks of grain were generally too small to provide much of an equilibrating influence with respect to supplies and prices. At the same time, the prospect of meeting any substantial deficiencies in home corn production through imports at moderate prices was remote: for one thing, as we have seen, costs of transport were comparatively high;[42] for another, the probability is that extreme harvest conditions in England were generally replicated to a greater or lesser extent in other grain-producing areas in northern and western Europe. Even so, it is somewhat surprising to find that in the famine year of 1728 (which accounted for almost two-thirds of total imports of wheat and wheaten flour into Great Britain during the first fifty years of the eighteenth century), imports of wheat and wheaten flour – at 74,574 quarters – amounted to a mere 2 per cent or so of gross domestic production. In 1740, when the price of wheat in England stood at about the same level as in 1728, imports amounted to only 5,469 quarters. There were, of course, other parts of the world outside Europe whence grain might be

[42] Above, pp. 207–8.

obtained, but North America – the most likely alternative source of supply
– was far away and the prairie grasslands were, as yet, undeveloped. In the
meantime, as in 1740, some relief might be obtained – at a price – through
the importation of rice from South Carolina.[43]

Most ordinary people, however, must have looked to pulses and garden
crops, rather than to rice, as a substitute for bread during periods of grain
scarcity. Since horticultural produce is generally very expensive to transport,
it seems unlikely that imports of fruits and vegetables would have increased
very substantially in years when the grain harvest failed. There are, however,
some indications that – by providence rather than by foresight – poor crops
of grain were not uncommonly accompanied by good harvests of fruits and
vegetables. Thus, as in Devonshire in 1744, a "great quantity" of apples for
cider making could compensate for a "spoiled" crop of barley for brewing.
Unfortunately for the consumer, however, horticultural products in fresh
form were not generally available at affordable prices throughout the year;
indeed, on account of their short growing season and perishable nature, most
indigenous fruits and vegetables would have ceased to be marketable well
before the end of the year. Among other types of agricultural produce, meat
was probably too expensive to be eaten daily by common folk; dairy produce
was less expensive, but lacked the bulk desirable in a food staple. Even at
famine prices, therefore, bread almost certainly remained the cheapest source
of year-round sustenance: a consideration which made it difficult to reduce
consumption substantially when times were hard. However, while we are
quite well informed about the household expenditures of many of the noble
families in the land, there is a remarkable paucity of information with respect
to the consumption patterns of ordinary people. The evidence, however (such
as it is), suggests that, on balance, the average wage-earning family may have
spent one-half of its total income on farinaceous products. In periods of famine
prices, this proportion would presumably have been higher; indeed, in many
instances, money for the purchase of bread would simply not have been
available, posing a by no means self-evident choice between starvation, theft
(with the possibility of discovery), and the rigours of the poor law.[44]

Of the four principal grain crops under review, rye exhibited the most
volatile price behaviour, especially during the earlier part of our period. This
is not surprising when it is recalled that rye was generally regarded as the
inferior bread cereal – a consideration reflected in an average price per quarter

[43] Above, pp. 37–8; M. J. Elsas, 'Price Data from Munich, 1500–1700', *Econ. Hist.*, III, 1935, p.
65; D. G. Barnes, *A History of the English Corn Laws from 1660–1846*, repr. New York, 1965, p. 299;
T. S. Ashton, *An Economic History of England: The Eighteenth Century*, London, 1955, p. 192.

[44] Devon RO, Duke of Bedford MSS W1,258/LP1/1 (16/9/1744); Lipson, *Economic History
of England*, II, London, 1931, pp. 392–3, 501; E. H. Phelps Brown and Sheila V. Hopkins,
'Builders' Wage-Rates, Prices and Population; Some Further Evidence', *Economica*, NS XXVI, 1959,
p. 29.

approximately two-thirds that of wheat. When grain prices were very low the expectation is that some people would switch their consumption from rye bread to the more expensive wheaten bread; as a result there would be a relative rise in the price of wheat (or relative fall in the price of rye). Conversely, when grain prices were high, wheaten bread would move out of the price range of some consumers, who would fall back on rye bread, resulting in a strengthening in the relative price of this grain.

With respect to the other major grains, it should be mentioned that our price indices relating to barley also incorporate data pertaining to malt, the price of which would have been affected by additional costs of labour and (in the case of some series) excise duties. Since these additional costs seem to have remained more or less constant from one year to the next, the effect of their inclusion in our calculations is to underestimate, although probably very marginally, the degree of price fluctuation in relation to barley. A real, as opposed to an apparent, influence serving to reduce the volatility of barley prices vis-à-vis those of wheat and rye was the observed tendency for people to drink more beer when bread was cheap, being better able from a financial standpoint to do so, and conversely when bread was dear. In the case of oats (the principal animal feed grain), the movement of prices must have hinged to some extent upon the supply of hay and other sources of fodder, e.g. pulses and turnips. The presumption is that, other things being equal, an abundance of these other crops would result in a reduced demand for oats, leading to a fall in the relative price of the latter, and vice versa. In fact, as we shall see subsequently,[45] there was a reasonable prospect of a plentiful harvest of hay occurring in the same year as a poor crop of oats. The effect of this, so far as the present discussion is concerned, would be to make the price of oats somewhat less volatile than the prices of the other major cereals.[46]

In regard to grains in general, reference to Figs. 8 and 9 reveals a narrowing in the amplitude of annual price fluctuations between the beginning and end of our study period. We may interpret this development as indicating that while famine still remained a real threat to life in the middle of the eighteenth century, it was less to be feared than formerly. Since, as we have seen, imports of grain were negligible throughout the period, the presumption is that internal factors were primarily responsible for this reduced susceptibility. Elaborating further, the most obvious considerations which spring to mind are improvements in transportation and in marketing organization, on the one hand, and the development of supplementary sources of food supply, on the other, horticultural produce being particularly worthy of mention in this regard. The operation of the corn laws (providing generally for bounties on the export of grain, with embargoes in times of exceptional scarcity) may also have contributed, if somewhat marginally, to the greater stability of grain prices in the early eighteenth century.[47]

[45] Below, p. 235. [46] Ashton, *Economic Fluctuations*, pp. 37–8.
[47] Embargoes were applied in 1698, 1709, and 1741 – Lipson, *op. cit. II*, p. 452.

In seeking to account for the volatility of grain and other agricultural prices during the period 1640–1750, we may recall that this was an age of political upheaval, characterized by civil unrest and military conflict, both at home and abroad. Since armies must eat as well as fight, and since wars have a habit of interfering with commercial intercourse, one might hypothesize that the price of provisions would be significantly affected by major military campaigns and associated political developments. However, while the disturbances created by the English Civil War may well have lent added emphasis to the violent disposition of agricultural prices in the middle years of the seventeenth century, civil disorders of a less revolutionary nature were much more likely to be caused by the high price of bread than the converse. With respect to events further afield, it is difficult to discern any consistent cause and effect relationship between military activities abroad and the price of necessities at home, possibly because warfare was less all-embracing than it is today, while distance greatly lessened its impact. Again, since wool was apparently the only domestically produced agricultural commodity whose sale (in the form of cloth) was substantially dependent upon export markets, this was seemingly the only farm product whose price was directly vulnerable to policies of trade protection pursued by foreign governments. Of course, a contraction in the demand for cloth (the country's largest manufacturing industry) could result in industrial unemployment and a reduction in the demand for, and price of, things in general, including grain.

At home, government initiatives with respect to the production and sale of individual commodities such as corn may be presumed to have exerted some influence on the prices of the products in question, but the effects are difficult to pin down in particular instances. On a broader front, the presumption is that government monetary and fiscal policies, by affecting the supply of money, would have implications for the general level of prices. However, seemingly perversely, the great recoinage of 1696–8, designed to restore money to its full face value after the depredations caused by clipping, was accompanied by a rise, instead of a fall, in the price of grain and other provisions. Apparently the impact of the recoinage was insufficiently strong to offset the effect of other, more powerful, influences tending to push prices upwards.

Predominant among these other influences must have been the weather, whose vagaries were clearly at the bottom of many of the annual, like the seasonal, fluctuations in agricultural prices. Extremes of temperature or rainfall, occurring at crucial times in the farming calendar, could add substantially to the costs of sowing or harvesting field crops, while the yields obtained by some farmers might be only one-half or one-third of those achieved in more favourable years. The climate, however, did not affect all agricultural areas equally nor all branches of farming in the same manner. Since the weather varied from place to place within the country, and since the characteristics of the soil, as well as the times of sowing and reaping, also varied, a very wet or exceptionally dry spell would have caused more damage in some areas than in others. Thus, for example, the expectation is that in a year of prolonged rainfall, cereal production on heavy, moisture-retaining clayland would suffer more than that on sandy, free-draining soils; conversely, one would expect the latter to be harder hit by severe drought. These expectations, discussed more fully by E. L. Jones in his historical treatise on the weather and English agriculture, are to some extent borne out by our regional price data, which point to the southern, western, and northern parts of the country as generally experiencing the smallest increase in grain prices in harvest years characterized by heavy and sustained rainfall. Having said this, however, it may need to be stressed that agricultural prices in different parts of the country normally tended to move in the same general direction from one year to the next, there being little likelihood, in the case of individual crops, of bumper harvests in some areas coinciding with seriously deficient yields in others. Indeed, as already implied earlier, in years of extreme climatic conditions, general farming experience in western and northern Europe as a whole was likely to parallel that in England.[48]

So far as the different kinds of grain are concerned, the same broad conclusions may be drawn. While optimum growing conditions – in terms of soil requirements, times of sowing, and other production variables (including the weather) – varied from one cereal to another, all would have thrived when summers were warm and mainly dry. Lack of moisture over very long periods could, of course, pose problems; but partly reflecting the preponderance of cereal production on heavy clayland, the weather could seldom have been too dry, especially for wheat. Thus, of a total of twenty-six years[49] which extant contemporary sources indicate as featuring long spells of dry weather in one or another part of the country during the period covered by our study, only five years – 1652, 1684, 1714, 1719, and 1740 – were apparently followed by deficient harvests (as measured by price indices for "all grains" in excess of 100). In the case of wheat, there were only two such years of crop deficiency (1684 and 1740). Of the major cereals, that most vulnerable to drought was oats. Describing the impact of the drought of 1719, Ashton noted that "the oats were so badly scorched that, in the south of England, the price was nearly as high as that of wheat". From the standpoint of wheat and rye production, the worst possible combination of climatic circumstances comprised a long spell of very wet or severely cold weather in the latter months of the year (whereby ploughing and sowing would be delayed), followed by severe frosts in springtime (with damaging, if not fatal, consequences for the development of the grain), succeeded by heavy and prolonged rainfall in summer (leaving crops flattened – if not waterlogged – and grain unripened). Thus, the record price attaching to the wheat harvest

---

[48] Jones, *Seasons and Prices*, pp. 58, 110–14; above p. 230.
[49] These were 1652, 1665–7, 1669–70, 1675, 1684, 1691, 1705–6, 1714, 1719–20, 1722–3, 1729, 1733–4, 1737, 1740–3, and 1746–7.

of 1648 had been preceded, in parts of Essex at least, by "terrible frosts" at the end of April and by "flouds every week" in the summer. Barley and oats, being spring-sown cereals, were scarcely affected by the weather in winter, but a cold spring made sowing more difficult, while a late frost could damage the growing grain. Although both of these cereals stood up to heavy rainfall better than wheat, a wet summer was normally a precursor of poor to middling yields and high prices. The same could be said of peas and beans, the other principal Lent crops.[50]

We may suppose that, in addition to susceptibility to unseasonable weather, all field and garden crops were liable to depredations caused by insect and animal life. In 1737, "bugs" destroyed almost the entire pea crop of one large Sussex farmer, leaving behind a meagre yield of 1.9 bushels per acre. The incidence of such occurrences is unknown, but contemporary sources appear to be remarkably free from adverse comment concerning insect infestations. It is possible, of course, that contemporaries did not always recognize such infestations for what they were, but, even so, it is perhaps surprising that, compared with our own times, which have seen the mushrooming of a gigantic pesticide industry, the threat to human food supplies by insects should not apparently have been recognized as a matter of pressing concern.[51]

Among the sources of human food supply, there were few, if any, which were not also used, on occasion, for animal feed. If grains and pulses were relatively cheap (as they were during much of our period), it might make good economic sense to use these and turnips, rather than hay, for the fattening or over-wintering of stock. Natural forces tended to conspire towards this end, since the climatic conditions favourable to bumper crops of cereals were, in general, less conducive to the plentiful production of grass (whether in the form of pasture land or hay). Heavy rainfall, providing it was interspersed with spells of warm, sunny weather, was normally beneficial to the growth of grass, while prolonged drought was detrimental. Hence, the yields of arable and grassland frequently diverged, and so, in consequence, did the prices of their products. This is brought out graphically in Fig. 10, which presents (by way of seven-year moving averages) a 'smoothed' version of the price data pertaining to wheat and hay.

In plain statistical terms, there were forty-seven years in our study period when the price of hay was above average (i.e. when the price index number was greater than 100), but in only thirteen of these years was the price of wheat also above average. One such year was 1740, when the price of hay reached record heights and (a fact glossed over by the 'smoothed' observations in Fig. 10) wheat was also very expensive. In accounting for these developments, we may note that the winter of 1739–40 was exceptionally

[50] Ashton, *Economic Fluctuations*, p. 15; A. Macfarlane, ed., *The Diary of Ralph Josselin, 1616–1683*, British Acad. Records of Social & Ec. Hist., NS III, 1976.

[51] E. Sussex RO, Add. MS 4,461.

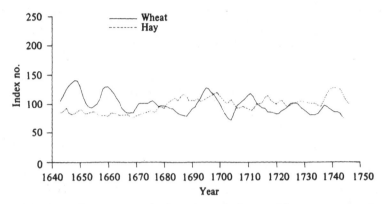

Fig. 10. Annual movements in the prices of wheat and hay: seven-year moving averages (1640–1749 = 100).

severe, the spring of 1740 was very late, and the summer of that year was cold and dry, with a notable lack of sunshine. Under such conditions, little could be expected to thrive. Writing to his sister in July 1740, Dr Edward Wynne reported that wheat and rye had failed in many of the richest grounds in the Welsh Marches, "from whence they will scarce have their seed". As if this were not misfortune enough, "as good meadows as lie in England" were "no worth mowing", while of pasture there was "none". Even in less extreme years, a backward spring could cause problems for the livestock farmer by delaying the growth of grass and making it necessary for foddering to be continued into the early summer or, because of the costs associated with this course of action, for cattle to be sold prematurely in a buyer's market. Likewise, a dry summer, such as occurred in the west of England in 1684, could make it necessary for farmers to fodder their cattle in early September, rather than late October. If the winter were hard, turnips could rot in the ground. In times such as these, farmers had to supplement the more palatable forms of fodder with whatever came to hand. Straw was one obvious possibility; another, more desperate, expedient was fern, used in the Ludlow district of Shropshire in 1740. The supply of straw, of course, depended on the bounty of the grain harvest, and this, as we have noted, tended to be most generous when the hay crop was poor. However, the general tendency was for the price of straw to reach a peak when hay was dear, in spite of the greater availability of straw at such times.[52]

As already implied, the cost of feed exercised an important influence on the short-run price of livestock. When fodder was expensive, the demand

[52] UCNWL, Penrhos i, 883; E. Suffolk RO, HA 49/A III/Gen. 5 (13/9/1684); HD 148/7; HD 148/8; Redstone S6/1/1.1, Diary of Daniel Gwilt of Icklingham, Suffolk (1693–1776); Staffs. RO, Anglesey D603/C51(55); E. Riding RO, DDWA/12/1(e); Wilts. RO, 184/1 (28/6/1743); GMR, LM 778/28/18; Herts. RO, Ashridge A.H. 997; Oxon. RO, Dil 1/K/Ly.

for leanstock for fattening tended to fall and so, too, did the price of such stock. Thus, in May 1723 it was reported that "by reason of the shortness of grass and the poor prospect of fodder" cattle in Monmouthshire yielded "no price at all". Conversely, an abundant hay harvest, or a plentiful supply of turnips or coleseed, could be calculated to encourage farmers to visit markets and fairs in search of likely runts or wethers for fattening. Reviewing the state of his charge in February 1689, the steward of a prominent Birstall (W. Riding) landowner noted: "As the winter is mild there is a surplus of hay which cannot be sold for any reasonable price"; in this situation his orders were "to feed it with cattle bought out of the rents". Similarly, in December 1693, hay again being plentiful, the steward of Sir Abstrupus Danby of Steningford Hall, near Ripon (Yorks.), wrote to his master, informing him: "I have bought in 22 steers to eat up the old hay. All manner of cattle are dear in these parts." Thus, a negative correlation is suggested between the price of feed and the price of leanstock; by inference, in the light of previous comment respecting the different climatic preferences of cereals and grass, one might also look for a positive relationship between the price of leanstock and the price of grain. The existence of such a relationship was, in fact, clearly recognized by some, at least, of the more market-conscious agriculturalists of the day. Commented one contemporary observer: "Lean cattle are indifferent plentifull but low, as is corn of all sorts, for generally both rise and sink together."[53]

The growing dependence upon roots, artificial grasses, and coleseed (as well as upon cereals and pulses) for the foddering of livestock made a failure of the conventional hay crop a less disastrous matter than in earlier times. Even so, when the hay harvest was very poor the ability of many, if not most, farmers to carry stock through the winter in good condition must have been seriously impaired. We may assume that in such situations large numbers of hapless animals were slaughtered or marketed, with a depressant short-run effect upon the prices of livestock and (dead) animal products, notably meat, hides, pelts, and tallow. Subsequently, we should expect shortages of these products, as well as of dairy produce and young stock, to develop, leading to a firming of prices, while the growth of spring grass would encourage graziers to look around for replacements for their flocks and herds. A backward spring would tend to delay this restocking process. Depending upon the extent to which animal populations had been depleted, and conditional upon the future supply of food (as determined essentially by the climate in the short to medium term), recovery might take two or three years, during which time there would be a tendency for the price of livestock and animal produce (on a seasonally adjusted basis) to remain comparatively buoyant.

[53] Gwent RO, Medlycott D760/135; Leeds AO, TN/BL/C5; He 37(e) (16/3/1729); Bradford City Library, Cunliffe Lister, box 77 (10/12/1693); Cheshire RO, DAR/C/5.

It was not only by affecting the supply of feed that the climate exerted an influence over the prices of stock and their produce; animal diseases and mortality rates – and hence, livestock numbers – were also, to some extent, functions of the weather. Severe winters, whereby animals were liable to perish from lack of food or shelter, were one aspect of this relationship, as recorded in the diary of Daniel Gwilt of Icklingham, Suffolk, in April 1740: "The hardness of the winter has damaged the growth of furze upon the heath and delayed the growth of grass which, with the loss of the turnips has occasioned the dying of vast numbers of sheep and lambs." Even when turnips were available (in the ground), snow or frost might make them inaccessible. In such circumstances it was not only domesticated farm animals which suffered. In the severe winter of 1739–40, John Wybarne of Flixton, Suffolk, "lost a great many deer"; while one hundred years earlier, in the hard winter of 1641–2, the warrener of the earl of Bridgewater's estates was fearful that many of the conies would be lost. Flooding, which could occur at almost any time of the year after excessive rain or heavy snow, presented another threat to livestock husbandry, especially sheep farming. In November 1729 Sir George Saville was informed by his steward at Thornhill (Yorks.) that following the "greatest flood in living memory" he had "no fat sheep left undrowned that were in the pastures of Calder, Aire, Wharf, Nid and Ouse by all reports". Earlier, in December 1701, "a great part" of the sheep in the Cannington district of northern Somerset suffered a similar fate when a breach in the sea wall caused extensive flooding. Such occurrences were apparently not all that uncommon, but the direct losses attributable thereto were probably small in comparison with the casualties induced by the sequential spread of animal disease, especially the liver fluke (or "rot") among sheep.[54]

References to "rotten sheep" in extant correspondence and farm records of the period are not, of course, reliable as a guide to the general severity or incidence of the condition. There were probably few years without some tainted sheep in one or another part of the country. However, so far as documentary sources are concerned, the 1670s and 1730s seemingly qualify as the decades with the most recorded references to the "rot". With respect to the period following the excessively wet winter of 1672–3, it was claimed that "never was there such a general rott of all sorts of beasts knowen in England". The initial reaction of owners of infected animals was to sell them as quickly as possible; if buyers were wary, prices tended to fall. However, for those farmers whose livestock were not tainted, there was a brighter side. Writing in October 1735 from Warter in the East Riding, the steward of Sir Joseph Pennington reported: "There seems to be a pretty good prospect for these Wold farms at present on account of a great many of ye lower ground sheep being rotten, which...very probably will in a little time advance ye price of ye Wold sheep."[55]

Whereas excessively wet weather was a cause of apprehension on the part of sheep farmers, the worst enemy of graziers was drought. In addition to causing suffering to stock through want of food and water, long spells of very dry weather were also conducive to the spread of the cattle plague or "distemper". The most severe outbreaks of cattle plague appear to have occurred towards the end of our period, starting in 1745 and continuing in various parts of the country for the next twelve years. Earlier, in 1730–2, the murrain was reported to have been "very violent" in parts of Wales. Most such visitations appear to have been followed by a tendency for the prices of calves and other young cattle to rise in the short to medium term; however, since hay was also likely to be in short supply, as a consequence of drought, the deliberate slaughter of stock, rather than attrition through disease, could have been the main causative factor in this situation. Horses, as well as "horned cattle", might suffer from "distemper", and in 1699 horse populations as far apart as Somerset and Northamptonshire were said to be affected by the disease.[56]

At this point, it may be useful to reiterate that our price data pertaining to livestock and animal produce have certain underlying weaknesses (discussed more fully in the Appendix) which make it unwise to push year-to-year comparisons too far. Reference has already been made to the lack of product homogeneity which characterizes these data;[57] when to this is added the comparative scarcity of observations for some years, the probability is that the annual price movements calculated therefrom will, in certain instances, be exaggerated. Thus, it would not be surprising if our price indices for the various individual categories of livestock and types of animal produce exhibited a greater degree of volatility than our price aggregates for field crops. However, for the principal groupings of these commodities (as well as for most of the pertinent individual products) this does not appear to be the case. On reference to Fig.- 11, it will be readily apparent that, compared with the year-to-year fluctuations in the price of grain, annual movements in the prices of livestock and animal produce were generally much less pronounced.

This is not entirely unexpected. In the first place, since most types of farm livestock would require several years to achieve prime marketability, the annual production or consumption thereof would generally account for a

---

[55] Staffs. RO, Stafford D 641/2/G/3/2; E. Riding RO, DDWA/12/1(b) (21/10/1735); E. Sussex RO, FRE 8,973; Derby Library, D231M/E4,525; Gale bdle 6 (5/12/1673); Cheshire RO, DCH/K/3/4; Hants. RO, 27 M54/3 (27/5/1740); Northants. RO, Isham IC 576; Herts. RO, DE4,123.

[56] GMR, PSH/OCK/1/1; UCNWL, Penrhos i, 376, 587; Leeds AO, Ingilby 3,591; Somerset RO, DD/BR/e.l.y. 5/6; Northants. RO, F(M)C1,080. [57] Above, pp. 209–10.

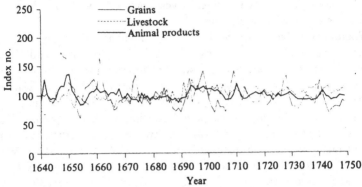

Fig. 11. Annual movements in the prices of grains, livestock, and animal products (1640–1749 = 100).

significantly smaller proportion of total supply (or inventory) than would be the case with arable produce. The impact on prices of any short-term disruptions to the normal supply process would, therefore, predictably be smaller. Secondly, in so far as bread and beer were more basic elements of consumption than animal-derived products such as meat and woollen clothing, this also would tend to make grain prices more volatile. However, cereals and edible animal products were to some extent substitutable, and in periods of extreme dearth, such as the late 1640s, the mid 1690s, and the early 1740s, consumer attempts to reduce the pressure of exceptionally high grain prices were likely to have exacerbated existing scarcities of dairy produce, meat, and eggs.

Although, as we have seen, the prices of livestock and animal produce were generally less volatile than those of cereals, the 'smoothed' curve of cattle prices over the period of our study presenting a broadly similar configuration to the corresponding curve of grain prices. This is brought out in Fig. 12 which charts seven-year moving averages of the prices of bullocks, cows, and wheat.

How far this correspondence in price movements was representative of a cause and effect relationship is difficult to say. We have already noted that the price of cattle tended to be negatively correlated with the price of hay,[58] while the latter, in turn, tended to be negatively correlated with the price of grain. Thus, an indirect relationship is indicated. However, there is the further probability that in periods of high grain prices, large farm enterprises of a mixed character would have surplus proceeds from the sale of arable produce to apply to the purchase of stock, the demand for which would thereby be stimulated.

A further feature of Fig. 12 which calls for comment is the fairly close

[58] Above, p. 237

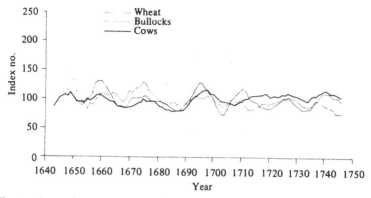

Fig. 12. Annual movements in the prices of wheat, bullocks, and cows: seven-year moving averages (1640–1749 = 100).

degree of correspondence between the short- to medium-term price movements of bullocks, on the one hand, and cows, on the other. The most apparent departure from this parallelism occurred in 1710–13, when a sharp fall in the price of bullocks was accompanied by a rise in the price of cows. It is tempting to associate the decline in the price of bullocks during these years with an envisaged increase in the influx of Scottish beef cattle consequent upon the Act of Union; this may, indeed, have been a relevant consideration. However, since the price of wheat (as well as that of dairy produce) also fell during the same period, while the price of hay increased, it would appear to have been the rise in the price of cows, rather than the fall in the price of bullocks, which represented a departure from the more usual price relationships. An apparent strengthening in the demand for calves may have been a factor in this aberration.

While, as indicated above, the prices of cows and dairy produce could sometimes move in different directions, in general a considerable degree of sympathy appears to have existed between the prices of cattle and their principal products. This is brought out in Figs. 13 and 14, which chart the 'smoothed' annual price movements of cows and dairy produce and of bullocks and beef respectively.

When we come to the prices of sheep and sheep products the position is somewhat more complex. Not uncommonly, the price of mutton moved in one direction (often the same as that taken by beef), while the price of wool took a quite different course. In consequence, it is difficult to discern any clear or consistent relationship between movements in sheep prices, on the one hand, and aggregated wool and mutton prices, on the other. The relevant indices are compared in Fig. 15, our sheep prices being those for wethers (gelded male sheep), which normally produced both the largest carcases and heaviest fleeces.

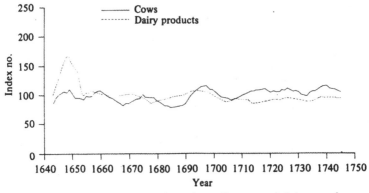

Fig. 13. Annual movements in the prices of cows and dairy products: seven-year moving averages (1640–1749 = 100).

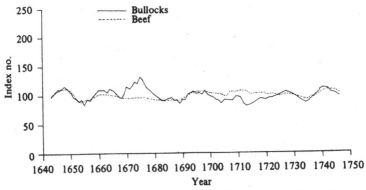

Fig. 14. Annual movements in the prices of bullocks and beef: seven-year moving averages (1640–1749 = 100).

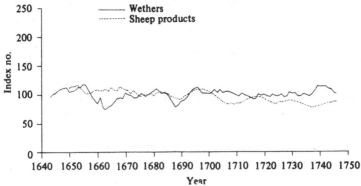

Fig. 15. Annual movements in the prices of wethers and sheep products: seven-year moving averages (1640–1749 = 100).

The price of wool reflected the demand for cloth, both at home and abroad, and this, in turn, hinged to a considerable extent upon the state of the grain harvest. A crop failure meant high bread prices, with less for consumers to spend upon other things, including clothing. Moreover, when grain was scarce, the demand for clothing was also likely to be curtailed as a result of unemployment in industries such as milling, brewing, and distilling, dependent upon agriculture for material supplies. Thus (in line with experience before 1640), one might expect to find a direct relationship between high wheat prices, on the one hand, and low wool prices, on the other. Such a relationship is, indeed, indicated by Fig. 16, especially with respect to the period after 1700, for which our wool price data are most abundant and reliable.[59]

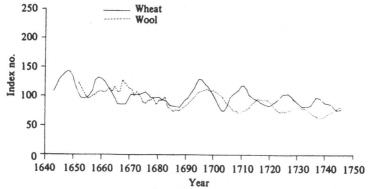

Fig. 16. Annual movements in the prices of wheat and wool: seven-year moving averages (1640–1749 = 100).

E. SOME OTHER ASPECTS OF PRICE BEHAVIOUR

Although agricultural prices, and more especially cereal prices, sometimes moved violently and seemingly unpredictably from one year to the next, their course over the longer term demonstrated a pronounced periodicity, as is evidenced by the diagrammatic representations in Figs. 8–16. In the case of wheat, this periodicity was reflected in a tendency for prices to peak every twelve or thirteen years, high points being recorded in 1648, 1661, 1673, 1684, 1697, 1709, 1727, and 1740. Troughs were similarly spaced, occurring in 1654, 1666, 1676, 1688, 1705, 1718, and 1731. It is noteworthy that the periodicity of wheat prices during the two centuries preceding 1640 was governed by a shorter time span; in the late sixteenth century, for example, ten or eleven years was the normal interval between the peaks of the price cycle for wheat. It seems not unreasonable to suppose that this change in periodicity was in some way associated with the fundamental shift in weather

[59] Above, p. 49.

conditions which climatologists claim occurred in Europe during the course of the early modern period.[60]

The cyclical disposition of grain prices to attain peaks and troughs at regular intervals was reinforced by a tendency for good harvests and bad harvests to alternate in clusters. For Europeans living in the seventeenth and eighteenth centuries there was no need to labour the Old Testament episode of Joseph and the ancient Egyptians confronted by seven "fat" years followed by seven "lean" years; [61] until the development of the complementary potentialities of the New World, alternate periods of glut and scarcity were an inescapable part of the pattern of agricultural production. Thus, equating low prices with bumper crops, uninterrupted runs of good wheat harvests were recorded in England in 1664–72, 1685–91, 1714–24, and 1741–9. In contrast, poor yields characterized the years 1645–51, 1656–63, and 1695–9.

By extending and combining certain of these runs of years it is possible to distinguish four main phases during the course of our study period (1640–63, 1664–91, 1692–1713, and 1714–49) when the price of wheat was alternately high and then low in relation to the price of agricultural commodities in general (see Table 27). The existence of similar phases in the two centuries prior to 1640 was noted by us in Volume IV of *The Agrarian History of England and Wales*, where we expressed the opinion that "the outstanding feature of those years when grain prices surged upwards, was relative economic stagnation or decline; whereas in the alternate periods when corn was cheap, the economy was buoyant and growth comparatively rapid". There would seem no good reason in the present instance to depart from the substance of this opinion nor to modify in any fundamental respect our previous explanation of these alternating price phases. In essence, this explanation was couched in terms of weather cycles, whereby different sectors of farming activity were favoured in turn. Thus, the relatively high average level of wheat prices in the periods 1640–63 and 1692–1713 may be taken as implying that weather conditions in these years were, on the whole, less conducive to the production of cereals than to other agricultural activities (especially hay production and cattle farming), while in the alternate periods 1664–91 and 1714–49 the converse was the case.[62]

Documentary support for this thesis is not lacking. Thus, the "merveylous wett", "vehement cold", and "wonderfull sad" seasons of the middle years of the seventeenth century are dismally recorded in the diary entries of the Reverend Ralph Josselin of Earls Colne (Essex), as are also the times of

---

[60] *Supra.*, p. 54; G. Utterström, 'Population Problems in Pre-Industrial Sweden', *Scand. Ec. Hist. Rev.*, II, 1954, pp. 132–4; *id.*, 'Climatic Fluctuations and Population Problems in Early Modern History', *ibid.*, III, 1955, pp. 24–5, 32–3, 42–4; C. E. P. Brooks, *Climate through the Ages*, 2nd edn, London, 1949, p. 313; G. Manley, *Climate and the British Scene*, London, 1952, pp. 239ff.

[61] Genesis 41.   [62] Above, pp. 54–6.

Table 27. *Agricultural price phases: price index number for agricultural commodities as percentage of price index number for wheat, 1640–1749*

	1640–63	1664–91	1692–1713	1714–49
Wheat	100	100	100	100
Grains	97	101	96	105
Hay	71	105	96	123
Other field crops	84	102	95	117
Wethers	81	102	98	113
Breeding sheep	87	106	86	119
Sheep	84	107	95	116
Beef cattle	84	112	98	108
Dairy & breeding cattle	82	98	97	119
Cattle	85	102	99	114
Horses	71	117	100	112
Pigs	51	98	115	134
Poultry	—	80	93	123
Livestock	76	104	100	120
Wool	96	103	88	88
Mutton, beef, & pork	86	107	97	110
Dairy products	100	106	91	104
Eggs	—	97	97	122
Animal products	89	106	96	110
Agricultural products	87	104	97	113

"great dearth and want of all things". Reflecting milder climatic circumstances, a short run of good harvests between 1652 and 1654 afforded only a limited respite from the terrible distress which appears to have afflicted the opening twenty-three years of our period. By contrast, weather conditions throughout much of the succeeding period to 1691 seem to have been almost ideal for the production of grain, though not of grass. Outside the 1670s, when the cereal harvest in several years was adversely affected by heavy rainfall and flooding, the period 1664–91 appears to have been remarkable for the number of its warm, dry summers. The high point of this climatic phase seems to have occurred in 1684 when, as already observed, even the wheat crop was adversely affected by drought, while Sir John Wittewronge of Rothamsted (Herts.) was able to record the growth of 203 bunches of ripe grapes before Bartholomewtide (24 August), noting that it had been "a hot dry summer – more like Spain than England". Conditions became distinctly less congenial in the 1690s, the unusual cold, exceptional rainfall, and consequent crop failures of 1692–9 leading contemporaries to look back on these times as "the barren years". Judging by the price statistics, the period 1708–13 was little, if at all, better, with 1709 establishing itself as possibly the worst year for the production of bread cereals in over half a century. Sandwiched between these two periods of dearth, the years 1700–7 provided some relief, being apparently blessed with a mild, dry climate and bumper crops of grain. Viewed overall, however, the years 1692–1713 clearly constituted a bad weather phase, generally unfavourable to cereal production. During the ensuing phase of low grain prices, between 1714 and 1749, the converse situation obtained. In spite of a tendency towards keen winters in the 1740s, the summers during this period as a whole seem to have been generally warm and dry, the only really disastrous years from a harvesting standpoint being 1725–8 and 1739–40. So beneficent was the climate and so generous the bounty of nature that Daniel Gwilt of Icklingham (Suffolk), writing in his diary in the spring of 1738, was moved to eloquence, reminding himself that "we are in this kingdom bless'd with healthy & fruitful seasons, our oxen are strong to labour, our sheep bring forth thousands and ten thousands and our vallies are so thick with corn that they laugh & sing". Our price data for grain suggest that the crops obtained in the years immediately preceding this diary entry were probably no more plentiful than many others produced during the good weather phase encompassing the latter decades of our study.[63]

In addition to playing a fundamental role in the determination of the supply of cereals and other farm produce, the climate, through its effects on the human population, also helped to shape the demand curve for these commodities. In the first place, of course, excessively cold or wet weather – especially when inflicted upon a population in the main wretchedly housed and inadequately clothed – must have significantly increased the incidence of respiratory disease and generally weakened resistance to other ailments. At the same time, the possibilities of starvation (most likely when seasons were inclement) must have further reduced the chances of survival for the poorer sections of society, who often went hungry, even in times of comparative abundance. In the "wonderfull hard" times of 1649 "many gentlemens houses were sett upon and pilfered", while grain shortages in 1728 necessitated the dispersal of several hundred redcoats in and about Hereford to quieten the mob which had proved "very troublesome to the corn factors and to some few that had sold corn to them".[64]

Not surprisingly, mortality rates during such periods of distress tended to rise sharply. According to the bills of mortality, burials in London (for years beginning in September) rose from 16,100 in 1707 to 22,100 in 1709 and to 24,700 in 1710. Sharp increases in mortality did not, of course, occur only in the two periods (1640–63 and 1692–1713) which we have designated as

[63] Macfarlane, *op. cit., passim*; Staffs. RO, Stafford D641/2/G/3/2 (12/2/1673); Derby Library, Gale bdle 6 (5/12/1673); Herts. RO, D/ELW/F19; Ashton, *The Eighteenth Century*, p. 4; *id.*, *Economic Fluctuations*, pp. 16–20; E. Suffolk RO, Redstone S6/1/1.1.

[64] Macfarlane, *op. cit.*, entry dated 25 Nov. 1649; UCNWL, Penrhos i, 807.

"bad weather phases", although the presumption is that they would have been more characteristic of these periods. The largest such increase, in fact, occurred in 1665, with the Great Plague of London. According to Sir John Clapham, at least 80,000 Londoners (equivalent to perhaps one-quarter of the city's population) perished as a result of the pestilence. This visitation, the last to afflict England, marked something of a departure from most previous outbreaks in that it occurred at a time when the weather was dry and the grain harvest was good. Other epidemics, such as smallpox, typhus, and influenza, could seemingly occur at almost any time, claiming a sufficiently large number of victims to cause a temporary downturn in the population. Thus, in 1740–1 typhus gained a foothold in England, where it struck at a population largely deprived of food and reeling under one of the most severe climatic spells on record. In London annual burials between 1739–40 and 1741–2 (for years beginning in September) averaged 30,320, more than twice the number of recorded births. Each such period of distress, moreover, was very probably accompanied or followed by a decrease in fertility. For not only were large numbers of potential parents swept away, but scarcity and misery, it may be supposed, led many people to postpone marriage until the arrival of better times.[65]

For the farming community, the changes of climate and population referred to above affected agricultural price relationships and enhanced or decreased the possibilities for profit from existing land use. The expectation is that when grain prices were relatively high (as in 1640–63 and 1692–1713) consumers would have less surplus income to spend on other things, the prices of which would tend to fall, while farmers would be encouraged to increase their output of wheat and other cereals, partly by diverting resources from other uses. The change in the balance of agricultural production might be expected to continue until such time as the pressure on grain supplies lessened as the combined result of a larger cereal acreage, a reduced population, and – probably most important – an improvement in medium- to longer-term weather conditions. In the ensuing good weather phase, the previous price relationships would be reversed as consumers spent proportionately more on woollen cloth, meat, dairy produce, and vegetables (among other things), encouraging farmers to expand their output of livestock, fodder crops, and horticultural products. This sequence, with respect to the Lubbenham (Leics.) estates of the Hon. Richard Hill, was described in 1726 in the following words: "The greatest part of the enclosures have been ploughed within memory. However there is very little of the enclosed land now in tillage and most that has been ploughed is pretty well recovered."[66]

[65] Ashton, *The Eighteenth Century*, p. 4; *id.*, *Economic Fluctuations*, p. 17; Sir John Clapham, *A Concise Economic History of Britain from the Earliest Times to 1750*, Cambridge, 1949, p. 189; Utterström, 'Population Problems', p. 122.

[66] Salop. RO, Attingham 112/2,850.

It should not, however, be assumed that all, or even most, farmers possessed the necessary flexibility to shift resources easily from one branch of husbandry to another in response to relative price movements. In the first place, the traditional conservatism of the farming population must have worked against this possibility. Commented Thomas March in a letter written from the West Riding to his master, Stamp Brooksbank, Esq., dated March 1729: "I tell the people at Heal and Catterton [Healaugh and Cattal?] that dairying would be much more profitable than ploughing...but like old cart horses, one can't thrust 'em out of their old beaten track." Even with a greater awareness of commercial realities, however, the freedom of manoeuvre of many farmers, especially in the more remote, hilly areas, must have been severely limited by considerations of soil, topography, and climate, as well as by marketing possibilities. Without adequate means of transportation, land which lay "very inconveniently for liming and manuring" might be condemned to continue as pasture, irrespective of the level of corn prices. Of course, the expenditure of capital could often help to overcome such physical obstacles, although not always as an economic proposition. However, for subsistence operators in particular, it may be supposed that once ongoing expenditures had been met there was usually little in reserve for capital-intensive improvements. In general, lack of capital was more likely to impede the development of livestock husbandry (especially sheep farming and beef production) than to pose problems in relation to the output of arable crops. Without capital for the purchase of stock, potentially good pasture land might stay in tillage, while, as mooted at Warter in the East Riding in 1742, sheep gates might be ploughed up. On the other hand, the freedom of many tenants to convert pasture or meadow to arable, or otherwise to extend the area of ploughland, was frequently restricted in the eighteenth century by lease covenants designed, in the landlord's interest, to prevent the soil from being worked to exhaustion.[67]

Furthermore, it should be borne in mind that the interpretation of developments which we have put forward has been postulated in terms of general tendencies or trends. Where freedom of action did exist, we may be certain that changes in agricultural land use were not always in the direction which we have indicated. Accordingly, we should allow that some farmers may have decided to expand their production of corn when grain prices were low or to add to their flocks of sheep when wool prices were depressed. If prices did not stand still, neither did costs and yields, and all three variables were relevant to the optimum deployment of land for farming purposes. Shifts at the margin of regional agricultural specialization must have continued throughout the period as technical developments and the

[67] Leeds AO, He 37(a); Bradford City Library, Cunliffe Lister, box 74 (7/5/1697), box 77 (17/2/1700); E. Riding RO, DDWA/12/1(e) (17/1/1742).

movement of market forces exposed the weaknesses and emphasized the strengths of existing farm systems and crop distributions. Thus, according to E. L. Jones, there was a longer-term propensity for the heavier claylands of central England to go down to grass (particular emphasis being given to the production of long-staple wool) and for the lighter, free-draining lands of eastern and southern England to be converted to tillage; at the same time, there is evidence that dairying districts in Suffolk were increasing their dependence upon the production of butter and cheese. In addition, we may note that in various parts of the country intakes from the forest and waste continued piecemeal, primarily, it may be assumed, for the purpose of growing cereals.[68]

While the good harvests which served to depress the price of corn were inimical to the financial interests of the larger cereal producers, they obviously benefited the general body of bread-eating and liquor-drinking consumers and provided livestock farmers with a degree of compensation for deficient crops of hay. In addition to permitting an increase in the consumption of other domestically produced agricultural commodities, the purchasing power released by low grain prices also resulted in a more buoyant demand for manufactured goods and imported foodstuffs. R. Pares has pointed out that the demand for sugar increased in each period of plenty, and the same appears to have been true of the demand for clothing, footwear, and other requirements of the poorer classes. Conversely with bad harvests. All this, however, has been argued in more detail elsewhere.[69]

In the context of the present discussion, the presumption is that the economy as a whole experienced a measure of sustained growth during the periods 1664–91 and 1714–49, when harvests were mainly good, while general economic malaise affected the periods 1640–63 and 1692–1713. This thesis is difficult to underpin statistically owing to the paucity of pertinent data, especially with respect to the years before 1700 and in relation to domestic production in the different economic sectors. We know that the fortunes of the cloth trade figured prominently in the determination of national prosperity, it having long been recognized that "when woolls were dearest then was this kingdom the richest". The price of wool fluctuated with the demand for cloth, and this, as we have seen, was sensitive to the size of the grain harvest, both at home and abroad.[70] Writing in 1662, near the end of the series of disastrous harvests which helped decimate the population of

---

[68] E. L. Jones, 'Agriculture and Economic Growth in England, 1660–1750: Agricultural Change', *J. Ec. Hist.*, XXV, 1965, pp. 11–13; A. H. John, 'Agricultural Productivity and Economic Growth in England, 1700–1760', *ibid.*, p. 21; E. Suffolk RO, HA49/IV/14 (31/1/1723); Salop. RO, 112/box (27/7/1735); Bedford RO, Russell R3/12; Dorset RO, D29/E68.

[69] Richard Pares, 'The London Sugar Market–1740–1769', *EcHR*, 2nd ser., IX, 1956, p. 259; Ashton, *Economic Fluctuations*, pp. 27–48; Jones, *Seasons and Prices, passim*; John, *op. cit.*, pp. 19–34; above, pp. 54–9.   [70] Above, p. 233.

mid-seventeenth-century Europe, Petty referred to the trade in cloth as being "almost totally lost". However, better things were on the way, the Commissioners for Trade and Plantations recording that "trade in general did considerably increase from the end of the Dutch War in 1673" to the Revolution. Child in his *Discourse about Trade*, published in 1690, reiterated this view, affirming that "in the gross we ship off now one-third part more of the manufactures, as also lead and tin, than we did twenty years past".[71]

Some of this growth we may assume was lost during the ensuing quarter of a century, with the deterioration in harvest conditions. Subsequently, the statistical indicators, such as they are, point to a degree of economic expansion. Exports of woollen and worsted goods, which accounted for approximately 70 per cent of total exports in the first decade of the eighteenth century, increased from an annual average of £2.8 million in 1697–1713 to £3.2 million in 1725–49. Since the long-term trend of wool prices was markedly downwards, the probability is that these rising values significantly underestimated the increase in volume terms. In terms of value, both exports and imports in general showed substantial growth, rising by an average of over 50 per cent between 1697–1713 and 1725–49. Our figures of home production are limited essentially to excisable commodities, notably, spirits, beer, malt, and hops. In the case of spirits, average annual production doubled between 1692–1713 and 1714–24, and doubled again between the latter period and 1725–49. By contrast (and somewhat surprisingly in view of the recorded growth in the production of hops), the output of beer and malt seemingly changed little over the longer term, the highest levels being attained in the period 1714–24. With respect to other industrial activities, Flinn has claimed that the output of pig iron increased in the century preceding 1760, especially after 1710, while Ashton and Sykes have estimated that the output of coal increased from 2½ to 4¾ million tons between 1700 and 1750.[72] In sum, these and various other pointers taken together appear to indicate a measure of growth across a broad economic front in the years 1714–49, with the fastest rate of expansion seemingly occurring in the years 1714–24, a period which, as we have already observed, was characterized by an uninterrupted run of exceptional harvests.[73]

F. FARM RENTS

Rent, in the strict economic sense, is essentially a premium payment made to a factor of production by virtue of its superior quality or advantageous

[71] *Commons Debates, 1621*, ed. W. Notestein, F. H. Relf, and H. Simpson, New Haven, 1935, V, p. 468; W. Petty, *Economic Writings*...ed. C. H. Hull, Cambridge, 1899, I, p. 30; CJ, XII, 1697, p. 432; J. Child, *Discourse about Trade*, London, 1690, Preface.

[72] Mitchell and Deane, *Abstract*, pp. 247, 250–1, 254–5, 279–80, 293–4; M. W. Flinn, 'The Growth of the English Iron Industry, 1660–1760', EcHR, 2nd ser., XI, 1958, p. 145; T. S. Ashton and J. Sykes, *The Coal Industry in the Eighteenth Century*, Manchester, 1929, p. 14.

[73] Above, p. 244.

market situation. Hence, useful, or potentially useful, farm land will attract a rent by reason of its greater utility or worth in comparison with unproductive, poorly located waste. The greater value of the former may be attributable to a more productive soil – the result of inherent characteristics or man-made improvements – or be a consequence of better marketing possibilities for agricultural produce. Patently, a piece of land which has been improved – by, for example, the clearance of scrub, the provision of drainage or irrigation, or the application of quantities of manure, lime, or marl – will be more valuable than a similarly situated tract of unimproved land and, in the absence of market rigidities, will command a higher rent. The concept of 'improvement' is important, and leads to a consideration of the compound nature of farm rent.

As has long been recognized, farm rent, in the common usage of the term, will very often include elements of interest and depreciation in respect of capital invested by the landlord in improvements. This feature is most readily apparent in relation to the provision of fixed physical assets, such as farm buildings and fences, but it is also applicable to the supply of circulating capital, such as dressings applied directly to the soil. Clearly, the eighteenth-century landlord who provided his tenants with assistance of this sort, whether in the form of fixed capital, materials, or manpower, would expect to recoup his outlays through increased rents; and, since most such expenditures would be motivated primarily by a desire to enhance the value of land by making it more productive, the probability is that, unless agricultural prices collapsed, tenants would thereby be enabled to meet higher rent demands. Of course, depending in many instances upon the terms of tenure, these various expenditures, especially those involving circulating capital, were not uncommonly undertaken by the tenant in the expectation of higher output, although the probability is that in the longer term some, at least, of the resultant benefits accrued to the landlord. However, the achievement of more efficient farming units was not always dependent upon extraordinary expenditures of capital or labour. The introduction of new crops, the elimination of the fallowing process, the practice of 'alternate husbandry', and the use of the seed drill, for example, represented technical departures which could significantly increase the value of farm output, although they probably added little to the capital intensity of farming operations and made no exceptional demands with respect to labour. Again, we may suppose that while some, if not all, of the initial benefits of such technical improvements were enjoyed by the tenant, in the longer run the likelihood is that a share of the gains would be translated into higher rent payments.

In contrast to the century and a half preceding 1640, when the long-term movement of land values and rents was dominated by the inflationary course of agricultural prices, in the subsequent period covered by our study the determination of these matters was influenced to a much greater extent by the trend towards agricultural improvement and by the more effective utilization of land in the context of production and marketing possibilities. Indeed, even though grain prices in the first half of the eighteenth century were significantly lower than in the middle decades of the seventeenth century (by almost 20 per cent, on average, in the case of wheat), it would be wrong to rule out the possibility of rising land values and enhanced rents on this account. This point may be illustrated by reference to some hypothetical situations as set out in Table 28.

In this table we assume the existence of 100 acres of arable land devoted exclusively to the production of wheat. The base situation, represented in column 1, is probably close to that obtaining on many of the larger tenanted farms in the south of England in the middle decades of the seventeenth century. Putting the price of wheat at 40s. per quarter, and assuming an average yield of 2 quarters (i.e. 16 bushels) per acre, we obtain a figure of £400 as the value of farm output. Of this amount, farm costs (excluding rent) and tenant's remuneration are assumed to account for £350, leaving £50 (or 10s. per acre) for the landlord's rent. In the other situations represented in the remaining columns of the table, with the 1730s and 1740s particularly in mind, wheat is priced at 32s. per quarter, while in those instances (columns 2 to 5) where an increase in the value of farm output is stipulated – whether as a result of capital investment, technical improvement, fair weather, or otherwise – a yield of 3 quarters per acre is assumed, giving gross farm receipts of £480. It will be evident that the landlord's ability to benefit from such increased receipts must have been limited, in the first instance, by the other (non-rent) costs of agricultural production. Obviously, no tenant who farmed for a livelihood would be willing to continue in occupation indefinitely unless he could cover his costs of operation (including depreciation and interest on any fixed capital invested) and, at the same time, obtain a reasonable reward for his labour and enterprise. If it is assumed that the tenant's remuneration was 'fair' in the initial instance, and did not change subsequently, it follows that any increase in the value of land achieved as the result of higher farm output would accrue to the landlord as rent once any additional costs of obtaining such higher output had been met. It is to be noted that in some circumstances the increase in rent could be *proportionately* much greater than the increase in the value of farm output. In our example, such a situation is represented in column 2, where it is assumed that (non-rent) farm costs and tenant's remuneration amount to £375, leaving a margin of £105 available for rent. Compared with the preceding situation, illustrated in column 1 of the table, rent has more than doubled, compared with an increase in the value of farm output of 20 per cent. In an era of stable or declining agricultural prices, rent increases of this order of magnitude – in the framework of a flexible system of land tenure – would most likely be associated with expenditure on estate improvement by the landlord and

Table 28. *Effect of changes in agricultural prices, output, and costs on value of land, landlord's rent, and tenant's remuneration*

| | Before change in value of output (1) | Increase in value of output: investment by landlord | | Increase in value of output: investment/improvement by tenant | | No change in value of output: some improvement (6) | Fall in value of output: no improvement (7) |
		Benefit to landlord (2)	Benefit shared (3)	Benefit shared (4)	Benefit to tenant (5)		
Wheat: output (qtrs)	200	300	300	300	300	250	200
price (s. per qtr)	40	32	32	32	32	32	32
Value of output (£)	400	480	480	480	480	400	320
Landlord's rent (£)	50	105	95	65	50	135	70
Tenant's remuneration (£)	100	100	110	115	130	90	46
Other farm costs (£)	250	275	275	300	300	265	250
Index numbers							
Wheat: output	100	150	150	150	150	125	100
price	100	80	80	80	80	80	80
Value of output	100	120	120	120	120	100	80
Landlord's rent	100	210	190	130	100	270	140
Tenant's remuneration	100	100	110	115	130	90	46
Other farm costs	100	110	110	120	120	106	100

would substantially comprise a return on such investment. Hence, the heading of column 2. However, given our limiting assumptions with respect to wheat prices, physical output, tenant's remuneration, and other farm costs, it is immaterial to the calculation of rent in this – or, indeed, any other – column of the table whether higher land values are engineered by the landlord or by the tenant, or whether they are the result of fortuitous circumstances (e.g. exceptional weather or external marketing considerations). Rent, it may bear repeating, is in essence a residual payment and, in a perfectly competitive market for agricultural land, represents the difference between the value of farm output, on the one hand, and farm costs (including tenant's 'fair' remuneration), on the other. Accordingly, if the value of farm output is constant, the sum potentially available for rent will vary inversely with the level of farm costs. In column 2, farm costs are assumed to be 10 per cent higher than in the initial instance, compared with the envisaged 50 per cent increase in physical output (from 200 quarters of wheat to 300 quarters). The basic premise here is that some farm costs (notably, overheads and pre-harvesting operational costs) will not rise proportionately to output; indeed, some costs will not rise at all. Moreover, so far as operational expenditures are concerned, to put the matter into a historical context, the slight upward movement of agricultural wages between the mid seventeenth and the mid eighteenth century would have been more than offset by the significant fall in the unit price of seed, the other major (non-rent) input. In this kind of situation, as already noted, it was theoretically possible for the landlord to more than double his rent receipts. In practice, allowing that the market for land is not perfectly competitive, a compromise situation, such as that indicated in column 3, might result, whereby some of the benefits of improvement would be shared with the tenant. In the situations represented in columns 4 and 5 it is assumed that the enhancement in the value of land is initiated by the tenant, and since extraordinary capital expenditures could be involved, we have indicated a somewhat higher figure for "Other farm costs" to allow for the inclusion of interest and depreciation in relation to such expenditures.

Of course, it is possible to envisage situations less favourable to both landlord and tenant than any of the foregoing. For example, we may assume, as in column 6, that the value of farm output, as compared with that represented in column 1, remains unchanged at £400, with an improvement in the yield of wheat just high enough to compensate for the reduction in its price. As a corollary of this larger output we may further assume an increase in farm costs, so that a smaller residual amount (£135) remains, out of which the claims of both tenant and landlord have to be met. If the return obtained by the tenant beforehand had been barely adequate, the presumption is that the main brunt of any downward adjustment would be borne by the landlord. In the more extreme situation represented in column 7, no increase in physical farm output is assumed, receipts from the sale or produce being reduced to £320 on account of the fall in price, leaving a mere £70 to be shared between tenant and landlord. Assuming that this situation persists and that £100 represents the minimum average level of remuneration acceptable to the tenant, three possible outcomes may be postulated: first, if the land has potential, it may be 'improved' by landlord or tenant, or both, to make it more productive in its existing use; alternatively, depending upon a reassessment of production and marketing possibilities, a more profitable agricultural use for the land may be found; or lastly, particularly in the case of very marginal land, it may be decided to abandon the practice of farming completely or, at best, to allow the land to revert to rough pasture until such time as the structure of prices once again dictates its more intensive cultivation.

Thus, to pursue the first of these possibilities a stage further, agricultural improvement, when cost-consciously undertaken, provided the farmer and landlord with an appropriate response to declining prices. At the level of the individual farm, such improvement – whether in the form of the productive utilization of additional capital, the application of more progressive farming methods, the introduction of new high-yield/low-cost crops, or the otherwise more rational organization of agricultural inputs – meant higher profits for the producer and – depending upon tenurial relationships – larger rent receipts for the landowner. At the level of the industry, as opposed to that of the farm, it may be postulated that agricultural improvement, by effecting a reduction in the costs of farm production (in economic terms, by causing a shift in the aggregate supply curve to the right), would tend towards a decline in the prices of the products affected. This, in turn, would adversely affect farm profits and rents on unimproved, less viable holdings. These different tendencies may be illustrated more explicitly by reference to artificial grasses and turnips, the most widely cultivated of the so-called new crops. Since these were essentially fodder crops which enabled stock to be fattened more cheaply and quickly than hitherto, their cultivation and use were most likely to be encountered on the farms of livestock producers, whose profits would thereby be increased; in some instances we may suppose that such enhanced profitability would be siphoned off, in whole or in part, by the landlord as rent. At the industry level, the presumption is that the growing use of clover, sainfoin, other grasses, and turnips would, by reducing the costs of feed, tend to depress the price of stock, thus, lessening the profitability of unimproved farm enterprises and their associated rents. Since artificial grasses were close substitutes for ordinary hay, it might be expected that their introduction would exercise a depressing influence upon the value of conventional meadow land. Claimed Sir Roger Twysden in the early 1660s, "Now there is a new devise of clover seed that spoyles all meadowland, so as wee are forced to abate 5 or 6s. the acre of good land in Romney Marsh." Somewhat later, in the early eighteenth century, a similar viewpoint was expressed by James Frampton with particular reference to meadow land in the vicinity of Dorchester, Dorset.[74]

Among other forms of agricultural improvement, the floating of water meadows, especially in the south of England, has been accorded greater recognition by economic historians in recent years in the light of the researches by E. Kerridge. It was not at all uncommon for water meadow to command twice the rent of conventional hay-bearing grassland. Thus, at Compton, Hampshire, in 1738 the rent per acre of fine water meadow was 40s., while that of ordinary meadow was 20s.[75] However, this should not necessarily be taken as indicating that the grass yield of water meadows was twice that of dry meadows, although the former might in some instances be mowed two or three times a year. At the same time, the increase in the value of output would need to be sufficient to permit recovery over time of the considerable costs of associated capital works.[76]

Of all forms of agricultural improvement none has been the subject of more economic eulogies (or more adverse social comment) than enclosure. Although research in recent years has demonstrated that the rigidities and other disadvantages of strip farming have generally been overstated, there seems little doubt that enclosure permitted a more flexible and, at the same time, more tightly controlled farming operation than was possible under the open-field system of arable cultivation. However, certain vital questions remain largely unresolved. In the first place, remarkably little seems to have been done to translate these differences between agricultural systems into comparative cost terms. It is generally assumed that crop yields on enclosed land were substantially higher than in the open fields, although this notion would seem to stem more from the not entirely trustworthy writings of pamphleteers and agricultural journalists than from concrete examples based on first-hand experience. It is also assumed that the transition to a more compact farming operation permitted some economies to be effected in the use of labour, although, for the small subsistence cultivator, costs of labour were scarcely a problem. Probably more to the point, the provision and upkeep of hedges and fences – the physical means of enclosure – entailed considerable capital investment and maintenance charges, and these expenditures would have to be accommodated in the landlord's rent and the farmer's cost structure. However, once these expenditures had been covered, the additional 'economic surplus' available for rent might be smaller than in the case of less capital-intensive forms of improvement. Thus, reverting to the

[74] BL, Add. MS 34,164, f. 86; Dorset RO, D29/E68.

[75] E. Kerridge, 'The Sheepfold in Wiltshire and the Floating of the Water Meadows', EcHR, 2nd ser., VI, 1954, pp. 282–9; id., Agricultural Revolution, pp. 256–67; Hants. RO, 18M54/coffer 6, box H.

[76] For more on the construction of water meadows, see pt 1 of the hardback edition, ch. 10, by R. Wordie, pp. 329–31.

situation at Compton (Hants.) in 1738, enclosed arable (with certain rights of pasture upon downs and common fields) might rent at 10s. per acre, compared with 7s. per acre for open-field land (with more generous rights of pasture). Most differences between the respective rents of arable before and after enclosure appear to have been of this order of magnitude, although in some instances enclosed land was rated much more highly. For example, Robert Vyner was informed in 1722 that the rent of field land at Withern in north-eastern Lincolnshire could be raised, by means of enclosure, from 2s. 6d. to 13s. 4d. per acre. From our present standpoint such a projected increase in rent seems improbably large unless it is assumed that the land in question was under-rented to start with, or unless some other improvement is visualized as forming part of the enclosure process. Writing from Lancashire in 1726, John Hindley informed his master, Sir Thomas Moly-neaux, that tenants at West Houghton did not expect to pay any more rent when enclosed lands were laid out than they had done previously, since "or [= our] comons are never broke up without improvement which is alwaies made by marling which with the levelling will cost ner Ten pound an acare".[77]

With the removal of the comfortable cushion provided by secularly rising agricultural prices, the period under review − perhaps more than any other before the late nineteenth century − witnessed a rationalization of farming operations and a parting of the ways between the more efficient and less efficient units of agricultural production and ownership. Agricultural improve-ment, in whatever form and whoever the instigator, when pursued in a cost-conscious manner, provided one of the main determinants of economic viability. In response to its impact, as already noted, the spread of leasehold rents tended to widen in both directions, a factor which needs to be kept in mind in any discussion of the general trend of rents during the period under review.

The most precise sources of information with respect to the level and movement of rents during our study period are provided by contemporary estate rental accounts and lease books. But while these records have survived in some quantity, the interpretation of the data which they contain is fraught with difficulty. In the first place, much of the pertinent information is piecemeal, with few uninterrupted series extending over long periods of time. The characteristics of individual holdings are generally very sketchily described, making it impossible in the great majority of instances either to follow the progress of rents on individual farms from one letting to another or to relate changes in rents to changes in the character of the land and in its capital appurtenances. Moreover, the estates featured in extant documentation are unlikely to have comprised a completely representative sample of all estates, either in respect of land characteristics or in regard to terms of tenure.

Similar problems exist with respect to the interpretation of non-statistical

[77] Hants. RO, 18M54/coffer 6, box H; Leeds AO, NH 2,368; GMR, LM778/28/28.

sources, of which particular mention should be made of correspondence on estate matters between landowners and their stewards. Not surprisingly, matters pertaining to larger leasehold properties (of, say, over one hundred acres) were the focus of much of this correspondence. However, while such properties might in many instances account for the major part of the landlord's rent receipts, they often composed well under one-half of the total area of tenant-occupied land (including copyholds and tenures-at-will, as well as leaseholds). The fortunes of the small tenant cultivators and those of the large leasehold farmers by no means followed a parallel course, and there is, therefore, the likelihood that estate correspondence – by concentrating primarily upon the affairs of the latter – will convey a somewhat unbalanced impression of the market for tenanted farm holdings as a whole. Moreover, human nature being what it is, the expectation is that landowners would be more inclined to correspond with their stewards when rents were in arrear and holdings unoccupied than when estate affairs were progressing smoothly. Consequently, the relative frequency of references to such problem areas, when viewed in isolation, may be somewhat misleading.

A further complicating consideration with respect to the appraisal of farm rents during the period 1640–1750 resides in the mixture of elements, of unknown or indeterminate value, featured in many tenancy agreements. In certain instances part of the rent received by the landlord might be in the form of corn or other produce, or the commuted money equivalent thereof. Thus, the rental accounts of the bishop of Worcester for 1689 refer to almost 1,250 bushels of rent grain (mainly wheat, but also rye and oats), 59 hens, and a cock. Produce rents had an especial appeal for institutional landowning bodies with many mouths to feed, the colleges of Oxford and Cambridge and the schools of Eton and Winchester having been empowered by act of parliament in 1576 (18 Eliz. I, c. 6) to take one-third of their leasehold rents in corn or its maximum current market value, a provision for which the price historian, in gaining access to some lengthy series of such recorded market values, has some reason to be thankful. In the sixteenth and early seventeenth centuries rents in kind had provided a practical way of maintaining the purchasing power of estate revenues in the face of rapidly rising prices. However, produce rents could be an encumbrance to landowners with small households to feed, and with the arrival of more stable monetary conditions it appears to have become increasingly unusual for the payment of large produce rents to be written into the terms of new leasehold agreements. At the same time, it was not at all uncommon for leaseholders to make token payments in the form of produce (e.g. "a fat turkey cock at Christmas") as part of their larger obligations, while many cottagers rendered part payment for their small properties in capons, hens, eggs, butter, and the like.[78]

[78] Worcs. RO, 099: B.A. 2,636/9iii; Beveridge et al., Prices and Wages, I, pp. 101–5; above, pp. 102–3; Essex RO, D/DM/F27/2; N. Riding RO, ZNK v 3/3/119; Bucks. RO, D42/c.25; Norfolk RO, Clayton 17 MS 3,226; Bedford RO, Russell R3/64.

Less common, although by no means rare at the beginning of our period, was the exaction of labour services or a money payment in lieu. In spite of their feudal origin, such boon works might occasionally be asked of leaseholders as well as customary occupiers. In themselves, obligations of this kind were usually trivial – e.g. one day's work per year with horse and cart. However, in the case of small holdings, labour services, together with produce rents and heriot payments – where these were also levied – might account for a sizeable part of the tenant's obligations. Thus, under a lease for three lives in the north-west of England in 1670 the following annual payments were due: £1 1s. 4d. in money, 2 hens, 1 load of coals, 4 loads of turf, 1 day's ploughing, 1 day's mucking, 2 day's transporting wood for the weir, and 2 day's shearing (or a total of 11s. 4d. in lieu of these various provisions and services); in addition, a heriot comprising the "best good" of the deceased tenant, or £4 in money, was exactable.[79]

Rents, in money or in kind, boon works, and heriots were rendered direct to the landlord by the tenant. Other elements entering into the determination of the landlord's net rent receipts and the tenant's gross rent outgoings were of a less direct nature and hinged essentially upon the division of responsibilities with respect to farm repairs and improvements and the payment of charges levied by external authorities. During the period under review repairs to farm buildings were most often the responsibility of the tenant, although materials such as timber might be provided by the landlord. In addition, the tenant's obligations in many instances extended to the maintenance and repair of fences, hedges, and ditches, and – less commonly – paths, gates, stiles, and ponds. In appropriate circumstances the tenant might be obliged to assume responsibility for the upkeep of ferries and jetties on or bounding the property which he occupied and for the maintenance of defences against encroachment by the sea or floodwater. Considerable expenditures – of labour or money or both – might be incurred thereby. Thus, in the East Riding manor of Patrington in the mid seventeenth century, Sir R. Hildyard, who leased seven closes of land at an annual rent of £26, was "at his own cost and charge to keep the sea walls, banks, jettyes, mounds and fences of the premises in good repair", at an estimated cost of £22 per annum. Failure to carry out such responsibilities conscientiously could saddle the landlord with a sizeable bill for repairs at the termination of a tenancy as a necessary condition for the attraction of a new tenant. Alternatively, the landlord might be obliged to accept a reduction in rent in order to persuade an incoming tenant to undertake the needed repairs.[80]

[79] Above, pp. 100, 103; Bedford RO, Russell R boxes 252, 253; Devon RO, Bedford L1,258/Casebook 1; GLCRO, E/BER/S/E/8/2/3; Univ. of Manchester, John Rylands Library, Yatton 342.

[80] Bedford RO, Russell R4/4,016, 4,021; R boxes 248–55; Lyall LL1/132, 133; LL17/3, 44; Ashburnham RO, 1/126, 127; N. Riding RO, ZAG/187; E. Riding RO, DDCC/71/5; Essex RO, D/DFa/e 44/1; Bodleian Library, MS Top. Lincs. c.3, f. 37; Northants, RO, Fitzwilliam F(M)C1,207.

Obligations with respect to the maintenance and repair of farm premises seldom fell upon tenants-at-will, who occupied holdings for uncertain terms and were liable to be dispossessed at short notice. There was even less likelihood of such tenants being required to carry out any permanent improvements to their holdings. Neither were such obligations normal in the case of leaseholders; and in those instances where they were imposed, it was primarily in connection with longer-term tenures of, say, more than ten years. Thus, in regard to one of his Hampshire farm properties in 1750, William Heathcote instructed that a twenty-one-year lease should be negotiated with the tenant "so that it will be in his interest to go to the expense of chalking". In some instances the landlord might supply the materials or make a money payment in lieu. In Sussex in 1745, the bishop of St David's agreed to provide chalk to be burnt into lime for the improvement of a tenant-occupied farm in Great Bayndene parish. At about the same time, one of the tenants on Petre's Essex lands was being allowed £10 per annum during the first three years of his term towards the cost of buying chalk. Among the improvements sometimes required of tenants, those most frequently mentioned in tenancy agreements related to the provision of fences, hedges, and ditches, the planting of trees, and the application of soil dressings (mainly chalk, lime, marl, or manure). Occasionally the obligations could assume formidable proportions, as in the case of a twenty-one-year lease granted in 1737 with respect to a farm in the Isle of Wight, whereby (in addition to the payment of a substantial money rent and the observation of certain husbandry clauses) the tenant was required to grub up, "cleanse", plough, score, and marl (with 30 waggon loads of marl per acre) "full" fifty acres of heathy land. Certain large-scale improvements, such as the enclosure of commons and the floating of water meadows, were often made the subject of collective agreements, with the mutuality of benefits clearly acknowledged. Thus, towards the beginning of our period the earl of Suffolk agreed to finance the provision of water meadows at Winfrith Newburgh in Dorset, subject to receiving from the leaseholders, freeholders, and copyholders of the manor "one moiety of the clear profits" resulting therefrom, as determined by two "indifferent" men. With respect to buildings erected upon tenanted holdings, principal dwellings and large farm outhouses, such as hay barns, were normally supplied by the landlord, while the provision of pigsties, calf houses, and suchlike premises were not uncommonly left to the tenant.[81]

The other major component entering into the calculation of net rent receipts or outgoings was that of taxes and other impositions levied by state, local authority, and church. In the latter part of our period the land tax was one of the more substantial of these charges. Levied at 4s. in the pound, it

---

[81] Hants. RO, 18M54/coffer 4, pkt E, bdle E; E. Sussex RO, Glynde MS 3,039; Essex RO, D/DP/E 182; D/DL/C9/2; D/DM/F27/2; D/DFa/e44/1; Isle of Wight RO, FLM/179; Dorset RO, D10/E 130; Somerset RO, DD/BR/e.l.y. 5/6, 9; Northants. RO, F(M)C1,122; ML1,291/2; Derbs. RO, D258/47/22; Bodleian Library, MS Top. Yorks. c.11, ff. 42–3.

raised £160 from nine tenanted holdings at Flixton, Suffolk, renting for £887 per annum in 1742. Most commonly this charge, together with the window tax, was paid by the landowner, while tithes and parochial rates – principally those imposed in connection with the support of the poor, the maintenance of order, the repair of highways, and the upkeep of sewers, sea walls, and the like – were paid by the tenant. However, this kind of arrangement was far from universal. In some instances (most generally in relation to short-term leases) the landlord assumed responsibility for payment of all taxes and assessments imposed by external authorities; in other instances this burden was not uncommonly shouldered by the occupier. In between these extreme situations, obligations with respect to state taxes and other institutional charges were split in a variety of ways. However, as with farm repairs and improvements, produce rents, and the like, it is seldom possible to quantify the value of such impositions in even approximate monetary terms.[82]

Hence, as already indicated, the task of tracing the movement of rent during the period of our study assumes formidable proportions. There would, however, appear to be enough empirical evidence and theoretical pointers for us to be able to conclude with a reasonable degree of confidence that the average level of farm rents in 1740–9 was somewhat higher than in 1640–9, in spite of the generally lower level of agricultural prices obtaining in the later years. In the first place, while the data are admittedly piecemeal and defy any attempt at precise statistical interpretation, a general review of tenurial arrangements places most of the more highly rented farm holdings in the closing decades of our study period. On reflection, this is not entirely surprising. As discussed earlier, the more effective utilization of land – whether achieved through the application of improved agricultural techniques, a better geographical deployment of crops, or otherwise – must considerably have enhanced not only the volume, but also the value, of output on many farm undertakings. In this connection, we should not forget the trend (evident to contemporaries since early Tudor times) towards the creation of larger units of agricultural production by the throwing together or consolidation of smaller farm entities. The benefits of such rationalization to the landowner were recognized by Francis Guyton, steward to Lord Fitzwilliam, in 1702, when he advised his master that the demolition of cottages on Fitzwilliam's estate at Aylesworth, Northamptonshire, would enhance the value of the land, even though the cottages in question were in good repair.[83]

[82] E. Suffolk RO, HD 148/13; Bodleian Library, MS Top. Yorks. c. 11, ff. 42–3; John Rylands Library, B 13/3/434; Oxon. RO, Dil. IV/i/12; Berks. RO, D/EPb/E3; Salop. RO, B01/2/219; Venables 484/294; Somerset RO, DD/SY/39; Lancs. RO, DD/Ke/14/37; GLCRO, E/DCA 170; E/BER/S/L/10/1; Essex RO, D/DP/E 34; D/DB/F17; E. Riding RO, DD HO/15/9; Bedford RO, Russell R4/4.016; boxes 250, 254, 255; Lyall LL1/133; Ashburnham RO, 1/126.

[83] Northants. RO, Fitzwilliam F(M)C1,207, 1,208; above, pp. 100–1, 109.

Changes in the system of land tenure, by introducing a greater degree of flexibility into tenurial relationships, undoubtedly served to reinforce these various tendencies making for higher levels of farm rent. One such change was a shortening in the average length of lease. Already, by the end of Elizabeth I's reign, the lessons of inflation had taught most landlords to avoid entering into contracts which would immobilize their rents for the next forty, fifty, sixty, or more years. With certain regional exceptions, leases for such lengthy terms were seldom granted after the beginning of our study period, and many of those then in effect were replaced during the course of the next half-century by shorter-term lettings at commercial rents. Thus, of 136 leases whose terms were recorded in a survey of the duke of Bedford's lands at Thorney (Hunts.) in 1720, 64 were for periods varying between three and twenty years, 71 (or rather over half) were from twenty-one years, and one was for thirty-one years. At the same time, the continued erosion in the once dominant position of copyhold tenure (whereby land was generally held by payment of an entry fine and a very low annual reserved rent) served to bring a larger area of agricultural land under leasehold provisions, as well as under other forms of occupancy arrangement. As part of this process, entry fines, which by the mid seventeenth century were no longer being exacted on many leasehold properties, continued to decline in relative importance as a source of rent receipts, and in the early eighteenth century were seldom imposed in connection with the grant or renewal of leasehold tenures.[84]

However, to revert to the main issue under discussion, while it seems likely that farm rents at the end of our study period were, on average, higher than at the beginning, the distinction was not so pronounced as to rule out the possibility of numerous exceptions at the level of the individual farm. Copyhold tenures continued to determine the conditions under which many small cultivators occupied their holdings, while long leases (such as that for three lives coupled with a definite term of ninety-nine years) remained commonplace in the west of England and parts of the north. Lands held by virtue of such forms of tenure were largely insensitive to happenings in the commercial market for rented farm properties. On unimproved holdings (whatever the form of tenure), especially those persisting with the production of bread cereals, the presumption is that between 1640 and 1750 the economic increment available to the landlord as income will have decreased significantly, resulting in either major rent adjustments in a downward direction or the withdrawal of land from agricultural use. Finally, in no area of the country does it seem at all probable that the perceived increase in rent occurred in evenly graduated steps over the period 1640–1750. In so far as farm rents generally tend to move in sympathy with changes in the value of farm output, we should expect the movement of rent in the late seventeenth and early eighteenth centuries to have progressed in a somewhat irregular fashion, at times reversing itself, in line with the ebb and flow of agricultural prices.

[84] Above, pp. 104–7; Bedford RO, Russell R5/4,010.

This expectation appears to gain a fair measure of support from the available documentary evidence.[85]

As we have already seen, the period 1640–63 was one in which (reflecting a combination of poor harvests, wartime conditions, and probable population pressure) agricultural prices, and especially grain prices, were generally high. The indications are that for substantial tenant farmers and their landlords this was a period of comparative prosperity, although, from time to time, extreme scarcities of food must have caused much hardship among small subsistence cultivators and agricultural labourers, as well as industrial consumers. Higher rents on renegotiated takings and a probable extension in the area of cultivated land must have considerably strengthened the financial position of many landowners. In support of this view it is noteworthy that estate records pertaining to the period 1640–63 as a whole reveal no general tendency for rent arrears to accumulate or for landlords to be otherwise hard pressed by their tenants. This global picture, however, requires qualification in several respects. In the first place, as is brought out by correspondence pertaining to Sir Edmund Bacon's estates in Essex in 1642–3, the contingencies of war could create conditions unconducive to the payment of rent. Especially was this likely to be the case when property was requisitioned, crops were damaged, and normal marketing arrangements were interrupted. Secondly, even though economic circumstances in the middle years of the seventeenth century were generally favourable to the comfort of the wealthier agricultural classes, there were some years of exceptional abundance, and some of exceptional scarcity, when distress among different sections of the farming population communicated itself to the landowning community through a weakening in the payment of rent. Thus, in December 1653, Henry Houghton, owner of farm properties in the Horsford area of Norfolk, near Norwich, was informed by his agent, Robert Carne, that "money was never so harde to gett with fearmers as now it is for nayther corn nor cattle nor butter nor cheese will give anye price". Three years later, in November 1656, the agent was again bemoaning the difficulties of obtaining money, this time laying the blame upon "the drought and the great storm of hail which beat out most of our corn and destroyed it". In such years – as in 1661–2, when there was a more widespread failure of the grain harvest – many farmers probably fell into arrears with their rent payments, but these situations do not appear to have happened with sufficient frequency as to cause a reversal in the general upward trend of farm rents over the period as a whole.[86]

This could not be said of the succeeding period, 1664–91, during which

[85] Devon RO, Bedford MSS L1,258/casebook 1; T1,258M/E48b; Lancs. RO, DDF/85; DDB1/54/8.
[86] W. Suffolk RO, "Calendar of Bacon MSS", items 4,257, 4,261; Cheshire RO, DAR/D/79/5; Essex RO, Belkus D/DL/c2/5, 8, 11; Norfolk RO, NRS 15,994; Worcs. RO, 705: 349/2x B.A. 5,117.

agricultural prices, in general, appear to have sunk to even lower levels than those subsequently obtaining during the more widely publicized 'depression' of the second quarter of the eighteenth century. The probable causes of this situation have already received attention in the earlier parts of this study. For now it may suffice to remind ourselves that the high farm commodity prices of the middle years of the seventeenth century must have called into agricultural production substantial acreages of hitherto unutilized or under-utilized land, so that when the London Plague of 1665 carried off a large body of consumers (comprising, perhaps, one-twelfth of the nation's urban population) a position of oversupply, at previously ruling levels of price, must have ensued. Compounding this situation during the following years, a number of other factors, working principally on the side of supply, served to raise levels of agricultural productivity, open up supplementary (foreign) sources of supply, and reduce the costs of getting goods to market, thus making life more comfortable for the ordinary consumer. These factors acted with varying impact upon different branches of the agrarian economy.

The improvement in the climate, which (enhanced by longer-term improvements of a technical nature) seemingly brought markedly increased yields in the arable sector, had less favourable consequences for farmers and landlords whose receipts depended more largely upon the raising of cattle. The long spells of hot, dry weather which apparently characterized much of the 1670s and 80s appear to have been particularly unwelcome in the uplands of Wales and west of England, resulting in periodic scarcities of fodder which, in turn, hindered the profitable marketing of beasts and the payment of rents. Occasionally, as in 1673, high grain prices added to the problems of small breeders. Writing in November 1673, John Wilson, steward of Sir John Wittewronge's estates in Montgomeryshire and Cardiganshire, informed his employer: "The corn prices are at a great rate and most of yr tenants at Carno buy in their rye. The markets are so slack that there are no rates for cattle unless they be very fat." On this and various other occasions during the next twenty years, Wittewronge's agent interceded with him on behalf of his Welsh tenants, urging the exercise of patience in the matter of rents.[87]

To what extent the fortunes of such tenants and their landlords were affected by imports of cattle from Ireland and Scotland is difficult to determine. Assuming that legislation was efficacious, imports of Irish cattle should have ceased after 1667,[88] while, so far as can be ascertained, the growing traffic in Scottish cattle did not prejudice the values of hill and moorland grazings in England's northern border counties. More susceptible

[87] Herts. RO, D/ELW/E60; E. Suffolk RO, HA 49/A III/Gen. 5 (13/9/1684); Nottingham Univ. Library, Middleton of Wollaton Coll. Mi/E3/1.

[88] See *Statutes of the Realm*, V, p. 597, which forbade the importation of cattle from Ireland or "any other place beyond the seas".

to external influence than cattle farming was wool production. During much of the period 1664–91 trade depression in overseas markets for English cloth adversely affected the demand for English wool. At the same time, partially as a response to this situation, English cloth manufacturers demonstrated an increasing awareness of the virtues of wools grown in Ireland and Spain. Irish wool was cheap, the 1667 prohibition of cattle imports into England encouraging Irish livestock farmers to stock "their pasture-grounde with sheep instead of great-cattel". As early as 1674 it was alleged that "the Irish wool buyers…may gainfully undersell the English wool-sellers whereby both the freeholders and tenants of England and Ireland, who are sheepmasters, visibly decay". Even more substantial during these years were imports of wool from Spain. In 1675 the import of Spanish and other foreign wools was said to have reduced the amount of English wool used in the manufacture of fine thin cloth to one-third of what it had been thirty years previously; and in 1684 it was submitted that the duty-free import of such foreign wools "is a very great prejudice to the price of English wool and so consequently contributes much to the abatements of rents and profits issuing from lands".[89]

Imports of Spanish wool posed a particular threat to the prosperity of sheep farmers and landowners in the Welsh Marches, the Midlands, and Lincolnshire, where the bulk of the country's fine wool was produced. Kent, and more especially Romney Marsh, was another area seemingly hard hit by declining wool prices. The introduction of clover seed was a further factor which served to reduce the value of meadow land, rent abatements of 5s. or 6s. per acre being cited with respect to the Kentish Weald in the 1660s. Without going into the question of the accuracy of such analytical insight, it is clear that these were difficult times for farmers in the Kentish marshland grazing districts, as is further evidenced by the accumulation of rent arrears owed by the Romney Marsh tenants of Sir John Banks in 1688. Further north, on the East Bradenham (Norfolk) estate of Mr Hungate, lettings of meadow land and pasture in 1674 were at rents 10 to 20 per cent less than they had been fifteen or twenty years previously. As a corollary of this development, some of the appurtenant farm houses had become "much decayed", while fences and ditches had fallen into a state of disrepair.[90]

[89] Bowden, *Wool Trade*, pp. 54–5, 215–17; Lipson, *Economic History of England*, 4th edn, III, pp. 198–200; *CSPD 1673–5*, pp. 168, 170–1; *1675*, p. 376; *1677–8*, p. 37; W. Carter, *The Proverb Crossed*, London, 1677 (BL, MS 712, g. 16/4), pp. 23–4; R. L'Estrange, *A Treatise of Wool and Cattel*, London, 1677 (BL, MS 712, g. 16/15), p. 7; Anon., *A Treatise of Wool and the Manufacture of It*, 1685 (NL, MS 712, g. 16/17), p. 24.

[90] Margaret Gay Davies, 'Country Gentry and Falling Rents in the 1660s and 1670s', *Midland Hist.*, IV, 2, 1977, pp. 86–96; Wilts. RO, 413/103 (12/3/1680–1); E. Sussex RO, FRE 8,973; LAO, Mon 7/12/41, 69; Bodleian Library, MS Top. Kent a.1, ff. 26–7; BL, Add. MS 34,163, f. 33; D. C. Coleman, *Sir John Banks – Baronet and Businessman*, Oxford, 1963, pp. 175–6; Norfolk RO, Clayton 17 MS 3,226; Derby Library, Gale bdle 6 (5/12/1673).

Corn-producing lands fared little, if at all, better, especially in the latter part of the 1660s and the 1680s. In November 1668 the executors of Lord Iwin were informed with respect to his estates in the West Riding that "both the manor of Hatfield and the Rectory of Birdsall consist much if not altogether of tillage and daily their rents lessen by reason of the great discouragements the tenants are under". Twenty years later, Fitzwilliam of Milton (Northants.), whose rent receipts hinged partly on the market for wool, was being urged by his steward, Francis Guybon, to exercise restraint with tenants on account of the fall in the price of corn. Referring to a property likely to fall vacant, the steward observed: "where to gitt a tenant yt will give ye rent I knowe not". Elsewhere, in relation to estates in various other parts of the country, the same message was being conveyed by stewards to their employers. Thus, to quote but one example, in March 1691, Thomas Hales, who owned land in northern Somerset, was advised by his agent: "severall of your tenants here will leave off their bargaines unlesse you please to abate them in their rents". With an apparent surfeit of farm properties at ruling levels of rent, tenants were in a strong position not only to negotiate reduced money terms but also to press for, and sometimes secure, capital improvements to holdings; how best to please "clamorous" tenants was, indeed, a worrisome problem for conscientious or financially insecure landlords, upon which the views of stewards were sometimes actively sought.[91]

By 1692–3, however, the pendulum was poised to move in the other direction, and some landlords were quick to note the change in their bargaining position. Wrote Sir Abstrabus Danby to his steward in Yorkshire in May 1693: "I shall not be satisfied to see the arrears any more postponed in your accounts, you must extremely lessen them or I shall be greatly dissatisfied." The recovery in the price of corn, which promoted Danby to write thus, and the strengthening in the prices of livestock and cattle products, which accompanied it, led Fitzwilliam the following year to take up the issue of rent increases with his steward. The latter's response was not very encouraging, but, given the continuing powerful stimulus of prices to agricultural production, it seems unlikely that the empty farms noted by the agent stayed vacant for long. During the remainder of the century landlords seemingly had little to complain about, and although there is a remarkable lack of positive evidence to show that rents were tending to rise, there is a strong presumption that this was so. One aspect of this apparent strengthening in the demand for land was the readiness of some tenants to

[91] Sheffield City Library, Wentworth Woodhouse WWM/BR75/55; Northants. RO, Fitzwilliam F(M)C496, 642, 674, 685, 703; Somerset RO, Brymore DD/BR/e.l.y. 5/6; Derbs. RO, D258/47/22; D1,101/F9; Lancs. RO, Petre DD Pt/39/9; E. Sussex RO, Danny MS 854; Staffs. RO, D593/L/1/8; Leeds AO, TN/BL/C5, 6; Suffolk RO, HA49/A III/Gen. 5 (19/8/1685); LAO, Mon 7/12/70; Leics. RO, Finch DG 7/2/32; Wilts. RO, 413/103 (22/11/1680); Oxon. RO, Dash x/xiii/5.

ask that their leases should be renewed at existing rents (without abatements) and for longer terms. Moreover, even though the upsurge in agricultural prices had run its course by 1700, increases in rent of almost 30 per cent (from 11s. to 14s. per acre) were being advised by one Norfolk agent in November 1703.[92]

However, it is clear that, with the deflation in the general level of agricultural prices, the market for farm land in the first decade of the eighteenth century was becoming less buoyant. In 1704 the owner of lands in Norfolk was told by his agent that rents could not be raised, "the prices of corn and cattle being so very low". In the same year Sir John Ingilby received word that rents due from tenants in Yorkshire were slow in coming in. Two years later Lady Anne North was informed by her agent that legal action was pending against certain of her tenants at St Briavels (Gloucs.) who had fallen behind with their rent payments. Among the different branches of farming activity, dairy farming and cattle rearing appear to have been the most adversely affected by the downturn in prices; in Cheshire, dairy farms were at a discount and some landlords found it necessary to abate rents. There is, however, nothing substantive to indicate that this was other than a transitory reversal, or that it was generally replicated in districts with lands less highly specialized upon dairying and cattle rearing. Thus, in December 1709, it was possible for the Essex steward of the earl of Nottingham to confess himself "ashamed" at having allowed tenants occupying land at Foulness to get into arrears, especially as the price of corn was "so good". In defence of the steward, however, we should note that in this year of exceptionally severe harvest failure, higher prices for grain did not necessarily mean increased receipts from sales, while sheep—corn enterprises would have been adversely affected by the depressed market for wool. Subsequently, somewhat reduced, but historically high, grain prices continued until 1713, while wool prices made a moderate recovery.[93]

Between 1713 and the end of our study period in the mid eighteenth century the trend of agricultural prices in general was slightly downward, thus pointing to a reversal, or at least a moderation, in the upward course of farm rents. As always, however, the movement of economic forces was irregular and uneven, and these broad conclusions require modification in a number of respects. On the matter of prices, our data point to the second half of the 1720s as a period of comparative prosperity so far as the wealthier agricultural classes were concerned. During this period (1725–9) the average price of wheat was 3 per cent higher than in 1692–1713, while most other

[92] Bradford City Library, Cunliffe Lister box 75; Northants. RO, F(M)C835; Bodleian Library, MS Top. Yorks. c.11, ff. 42–3; Norfolk RO, HOW 733.
[93] Norfolk RO, HOW 731/1; Leeds AO, Ingilby 1,709; E. Suffolk RO, HA 49/A iii/Gen. 3 (23/11/1706); Cheshire RO, Arderne DAR A/65/2; Leics. RO, Finch DG 7/1/58; Bradford City Library, Cunliffe Lister box 77 (5/5/1704); Wilts. RO, 184/1; GMR, LM 778/28/2.

farm prices were also buoyant. Secondly, over the period 1714–49 as a whole, the deflation in farm prices was more pronounced with respect to arable crops than in relation to the products of pastoral activity, with the major exception of wool. Indeed, in the case of dairy cattle, sheep, hay, and straw (as well as hops) average prices in the years 1714–49 were higher than in 1692–1713. On the other hand (seemingly reflecting, in part, the overlarge sheep population),[94] the average price of wool was almost one-fifth lower than in the earlier period. Among arable crops, wheat and rye registered approximately the same proportionate decrease in price as wool. Other cereal crops – notably, barley, oats, peas, and beans – fared much better. Indeed, unlike wheat and rye (whose average prices declined more between 1692/1713 and 1714/29 than between 1714/29 and 1730/49), these other cereals demonstrated considerable price resilience in the decades preceding 1730; after that date their prices dropped sharply.

It is to be expected that these and other developments in the market for agricultural commodities would be reflected by developments in the market for rented farm properties. Thus, the decade after 1713 appears to have been one in which rent arrears tended to mount in the face of the general lowering in the prices of arable produce. By 1722 at least one steward was conceding that "landlords must comply with there tennents upon terms not altogether agreeable if times hold thus bad". However, attempts by "rascally" tenants to secure abatements of rent were not always sympathetically received; and while individual cases to the contrary may be cited, the balance of evidence does not indicate a general erosion of land values and farm rents at this time. Indeed, writing from Yorkshire in June 1722, Lady Pembroke's steward reported "many offers" for farms at Grafton vacated by tenants unwilling to bid up former rents. Likewise, writing from Suffolk in 1723–4, Dudley North's agent noted that dairy farms were "enquired after" and that increased rents had been negotiated on two such properties.[95]

With respect to the subsequent years, Mingay's conclusions, based primarily upon a study of the (mainly Midland) estates of the duke of Kingston, show rents rising until 1731. Certain other pieces of evidence also point in the same direction. Thus, we are informed by Mingay that rents on the Lincolnshire lands of Richard Wynn were increased by 15 per cent between 1723 and 1727. In the area around Burton upon Trent (Staffs.), where livestock husbandry would have been an important part of the agrarian scene, there were "bidders one upon another" for any farms which fell vacant in the late 1720s. In 1728 the Thornhill (W. Riding) tenants of the earl of Cardigan were willing to pay "good rents" to continue with tillage, while

[94] See above, pp. 199–200.

[95] Notts. RO, Saville DDSR 211/2; Salop. RO, Attingham Papers of Hon. Richard Hill 112/2,424, 2,698, 2,703; Gwent RO, Medlycott D760/135; Bedford RO, Russell R5/4,010–15; E. Suffolk RO, HA 49/IV/14; Nottingham Univ. Library, Galway G12, 206/22, 23; G12, 207/1.

at Hitchin (Herts.) rents applying to hop gardens belonging to the Radcliffe family were reappraised upward. However, this period, like any other, was not entirely without problems for the farming community. Several years were characterized by deficient harvests, and these were seldom welcomed by subsistence cultivators. Following the hard winter of 1728–9 "meaner" tenants on the Saville family's Nottinghamshire estates experienced difficulties in meeting their rent obligations. Commented Sir George Saville's agent: "They complain not only about fodder for their cattle but also provisions for their families." A year previously similar difficulties had forced several of the earl of Cardigan's poorer tenants at Thornhill to give up farming, their holdings seemingly acquired (at probably enhanced rents) by more well-to-do operators.[96]

So far as the movement of rent in the 1730s and 1740s is concerned, there seems little reason to depart far from the main conclusions of Mingay's analysis, whereby the trend of rents is depicted as being slightly downward and arable farmers are perceived as being in especial need of relief. Difficulties with respect to the payment of rents on the Kingston estates were evidenced in a variety of ways: by mounting rent arrears (with peaks occurring in 1732–3 and again in 1739–40), by the granting of rent abatements in relation to large farm properties which might prove difficult to relet, by reductions in rent for the purpose of attracting new tenants, by the easing of tenants' obligations in connection with the upkeep of farm premises and the payment of external taxes, by the landlord subsidizing some of the costs of farming (e.g. by payment for, or otherwise providing, seed, stock, or materials), and by an increase in the area of unoccupied land. In referring to these developments, Mingay makes the point that the concessions were often individually of small importance, while the total of unoccupied land was never large and even at the peak of 1739 amounted to only about 1 per cent of the total rentals of the estates.[97]

Be that as it may, there is ample documentary evidence of similar developments taking place on many other estates in different parts of the country. It is also possible to find examples – much less common – of converse tendencies. On the Kingston estates in the mixed farming area of east Derbyshire rents were increased by 40 per cent between 1736 and 1743; at Tong, Shropshire, a number of seven-year leases expiring in 1746–7 were replaced by agreements for three years at enhanced rents; while in the Merthyr district of Glamorgan in 1743 at least one landlord was able to transfer responsibility for the discharge of parish rates to his tenant without any reduction in money rent. In general, such pointers as these tend to show

---

[96] G. E. Mingay, 'The Agricultural Depression, 1730–1750', EcHR, 2nd ser., VIII, 1956, pp. 324, 333; Staffs. RO, Paget D 603 C 50 XVII (26/8/1732); Northants. RO, Brudenell F iii 184, 194; Herts. RO, Delme Radcliffe DE 4,121; Notts. RO, Saville DDSR 211/58/3, 13.

[97] Mingay, op. cit., pp. 328–9.

the market for farm land at its firmest in the northern and western parts of the country, where pastoral farming, and more especially cattle husbandry, was the main form of agricultural activity. With respect to these areas it is possible to envisage a significant increase in the average level of rent in the second quarter of the eighteenth century. At the other extreme, substantial decreases in rent are likely to have occurred in areas (mainly in eastern and southern England) devoted to sheep–corn husbandry or heavily biased towards the production of arable crops. Among the districts most seriously affected by the fall in agricultural prices was the Lincolnshire Wolds, where much of the farmer's (and landlord's) income was derived from the sale of wool and grain. In June 1735, for example, Samuel Dakin, writing to Mrs Massingberd from South Ormsby in Lincolnshire, reported lands remaining unlet and farmers likely to be "broken" by low prices. On Lord Monson's farm properties in the same county rent arrears accumulated by 1741 amounted to £7,548, almost twice the annual rent roll (£4,127). Landlords owning wheat-growing and barley-producing lands in southern England seemingly fared little, if at all, better. In the late 1730s Sir William Heathcote, who had made considerable purchases of land in Hampshire, was left with much of it in hand, and spent the next few years "bitterly" regretting his investment.[98]

By the late 1740s, however, things had begun to pick up, in spite of the losses of stock and disruption to markets caused by the cattle plague. Enjoying the sun at Leghorn, Italy, in the spring of 1749 the Hon. Thomas Barrett was doubtless gratified to receive word from his Horsford (Norfolk) steward that "every tenant is paid up and there is not one peny in arrear". Three years later, the agent was expressing the certain opinion that a farm about to be vacated could be let for double the existing rent, and with the erection of a dwelling house "would admit of a further advancement".[99]

The latter point brings us back to the issue of the part played by agricultural improvement in counterbalancing any tendency for rents to decline as a consequence of falling farm produce prices. Landowners did not need to be exceptionally shrewd to recognize that outlays designed to raise agricultural productivity not only made it easier to attract and keep good tenants when times were hard, but also afforded better than average opportunities to obtain a high return on investment at comparatively small risk. Even when farm prices were depressed, a judicious investment in improvement might well increase the rent potential of land by 50 or 60 per cent – say, from 5s. to 8s. per acre. Such a financial return compared extremely favourably with the modest 3–4 per cent yield to be derived from the purchase of government stock. This point is brought out by the

[98] *Ibid.*, pp. 325, 330, 333; Glam. RO, Nicholl of Methyr Mawr D/DN 230/1; Oxon. RO, Massingberd-Mundy MMII/7; LAO, Mon 10/3/8; Hants. RO, 27 M54/3.
[99] Essex RO, D/DL/C6/13, 26.

hypothetical example contained in Table 29. Here it is assumed that the return which the improving landlord could obtain was more than four times that available to the investor in government securities. Judging by the somewhat flimsy evidence bearing on this matter, such a comparative return would not have been in any way extraordinary.[100]

Table 29. *Landlord's proceeds from agricultural improvement compared with proceeds from investment in consolidated stock, c. 1730–50*

Agricultural improvement to 200 acres of land (£)		Purchase of consolidated stock (£)	
Initial investment (depreciated over 20 years) at 10s. per acre	100	Initial investment	100
		Compound interest at	
		$3\frac{1}{2}\%$ p.a. over 20 years	99
Annual rent			
Before improvement, at 5s. per acre	50		
After improvement, at 8s. per acre	80		
Additional rental income of £30 p.a., invested at end of year for 20 years at $3\frac{1}{2}\%$ compound interest			
p.a.	848	Principal and interest over 20 years	199

G. COSTS AND PROFITABILITY

1. Introduction

Although land is seemingly the most obvious and vital element in the production of agricultural commodities, it is only one of a number of necessary inputs whose use represents a cost to the commercial farmer. Capital (in the form of fixed appurtenances, movable equipment, and materials), labour – albeit possessing comparatively low levels of skill – management, and enterprise denote other principal factor inputs. In the seventeenth and eighteenth centuries, as today, the relative importance of these different elements varied with the character, scale, and productivity of the agricultural enterprise, the latter factor (productivity), in turn, being influenced by such considerations as the nature of the terrain, the

[100] Ashton, *The Eighteenth Century*, Table XIII, p. 251; G. E. Mingay, *English Landed Society in the Eighteenth Century*, London, 1963, p. 183; J. D. Chambers and G. E. Mingay, *The Agricultural Revolution*, London, 1966, pp. 83–5.

properties of the soil, the vicissitudes of the climate, and the technical expertise and organizational ability of the farmer.

In England the typical farming entity has always comprised a diversity of activities, with the highly specialized, single-crop enterprise the exception rather than the rule. In the period 1640–1750, more so than in less distant times, the marketing limitations imposed by deficiencies in transport, and the technical interdependence of livestock and tillage, served to promote this diversification of farm operations. More explicitly, fodder crops, especially hay, were comparatively expensive to transport and thus might justify production by animal husbandmen. Arable farmers, on the other hand, needed fertile soil, and the most widely recognized fertilizing agent was animal manure produced upon the farm or neighbouring common. Location close to an urban centre or navigable waterway or (in the case of arable production) nearness to supplies of lime or marl (widely used as substitutes for animal dung) served to reduce this mutual dependence of hoof and plough. Reporting, in 1754, on a 388-acre farm constituting part of the Horsford (Norfolk) estate of the Hon. Leonard Barrett, a correspondent noted: ".'This farm is, by its situation, preferable to any other part of Mr. Barrett's lordship for getting muck from Norwich which is but 3 miles away and but little more from a navigable river." Farms thus situated clearly enjoyed a premium in the market-place, reflecting the relatively high degree of operational flexibility permitted to their occupiers. The improvement in the system of inland waterways which occurred towards the end of our period, and the development of the turnpikes, patently served to extend such flexibility, in greater or lesser degree, to areas where economic specialization had hitherto been held tightly in check. Even when transport possibilities were good, however, a mixture of agricultural activities provided an income-stabilizing influence which the farmer must have welcomed when one or another crop proved unrewarding, though, obviously, this protection was achieved at some sacrifice to economic efficiency.[101]

However, irrespective of the degree of economic specialization, there could have been few farm enterprises where the main activity did not obtain at least some of its necessary inputs from subsidiary lines of production, or vice versa. Indeed, given these interrelationships, any marked change in the price structure of agricultural commodities could result in a marked shift in the emphasis of farm operations, without radical changes to the structure of farm output. Thus, it may be hypothesized that unremunerative prices for grain, especially when accompanied by buoyant markets for animal produce, must have led some farmers with mixed arable and pastoral interests to view their cereal crops more in terms of feed for livestock than as commodities to be sold in their own right.[102]

[101] Essex RO, D/DL/C22.
[102] GMR, Howard 1/53/2; Bedford RO, R4/4,022/4; E. Suffolk RO, HA 1/GB 3/2; Devon RO, Bedford L 1,258/F26.

These kinds of changing interrelationships, and the related problem of how best to allocate overheads in a diversified enterprise, obviously serve to complicate attempts to assess farm profitability on a sectoral or individual product basis. This would be so even if comprehensive data pertaining to farm costs, crop yields, commodity prices, and related matters were available in fine detail. However, while from the long historical viewpoint the period 1640–1750 is comparatively well endowed with farm records, for the purpose of determining profitability the source documents suffer from the same basic defects as those of earlier years. In particular, even the most detailed of contemporary farm accounts are incomplete or insufficiently broken down. Normally, overheads are completely disregarded; capital and income are seldom distinguished; capital assets are not depreciated; entries relating to household expenditures are not uncommonly mixed with those of farming transactions; while the value of domestically consumed agricultural produce is not recorded. Moreover, such data as are available pertain essentially to the doings of great families, gentlemen, and substantial yeomen. Since the mass of peasant cultivators were illiterate, there is little in the way of written records to inform us of the operations of small farm entities.[103]

2. Arable farming

The imperfections of the data mean that we cannot rely upon actual case histories, as recorded in contemporary documentation, to obtain an accurate representation of the profit situation of individual agricultural producers. The development of notional farm accounts, based upon piecemeal data drawn from a variety of contemporary sources, offers one way of circumventing this difficulty. Thus, our model of an arable enterprise illustrated in Table 30 is based upon data gleaned from the records of several farm properties situated in the county of Surrey in the early eighteenth century.[104] Allowing that most farm enterprises were of a mixed character. Table 30 sets out only those costs and receipts associated with the arable part of farming activity. It should be noted that, reflecting the strength of metropolitan demand, both the costs and prices indicated in our examples are generally higher than they would have been in most other parts of the country. It should also be borne in mind that the structure of costs would not have been identical for all sizes of undertaking. For example, the typical unit of peasant agriculture would have incurred little or nothing by way of labour charges, most or all of the necessary manual work being performed by the cultivator and members of his family. The structure of costs and the level of profitability

---

[103] Above, pp. 69–70.

[104] The principal records used in this connection are those pertaining to the Ashtead and Epsom estates of the Howard family (GMR, 1/53/2–9a), the Marden estate of the Clayton family (GMR, 84/2/2), the West Horsley estate of Edward Nicholas (GMR, 22/1/1–3), and land at Streatham belonging to the Du Cane family (GLCRO, E/DCA 164, 175).

would also have been affected by the system of farming – i.e. according to whether the land was enclosed or whether it was farmed under open-field arrangements.

In our model an enclosed arable area of 100 acres is assumed. The question arises as to how this acreage might have been utilized. The percentage distribution indicated in our example approximates to that recorded with respect to land at Streatham owned by the Du Cane family and farmed by John Blumson in about 1739. Perhaps the most surprising aspect of this distribution is the relatively small area, amounting to only 5 acres, devoted to barley. This contrasts with the allocation of 30 acres for oats and 20 acres each for wheat and peas. The fact that one-quarter of the arable acreage is shown as lying fallow is a reminder of the general reliance which was still being placed up to the end of our period upon this traditional method of restoring the soil, in spite of the alternative possibilities presented by the growing, but still limited, field cultivation of artificial grasses and root crops and the assumed increasing availability of animal manure. In this regard the general practice of agricultural producers may have differed little from that reported by Sir Norton Knatchbull with respect to Kentish agriculture during the reign of Charles II: "to keep the land in good heart for 30 or 40 yeares wee must fallow it every third yeare which if we doe there need noe improvement by dung or otherwise". Of course, when land was expensive, as was generally the case in the London area, there were clearly some possible diseconomies in letting too large an acreage lie idle. The rent of 15s. 3d. per acre, assumed in connection with our notional farm, parallels the rent payable by the aforementioned John Blumson under the terms of a twenty-five-year lease negotiated in 1718. In our example it is further assumed that all external taxes (including tithes) are shouldered by the landlord, while farm maintenance and repair costs are the responsibility of the occupier. Most of the expenses incurred in the latter regard, at least on enclosed farm properties, are likely to have been labour charges in connection with hedging and ditching, the necessary materials being provided by the landlord. Our figure of £7 12s. 6d. (representing 10 per cent of the annual money rent) approximates the average recorded labour costs of maintaining the hedges, ditches, and fences on the land (of unknown acreage) farmed by the Clayton family at Marden (Surrey) during the years 1714–20.[105]

In Table 30 it will be seen that rent costs incurred in connection with the occupation of land account for almost one-third of total farming expenditures. This proportion is almost certainly greater than it would have been a century or more earlier, especially if the comparison were to be made with the cost structure of a holding lying in the open fields or governed by traditional copyhold tenure. On the other hand, partly reflecting the shift

105 GLCRO, E/DCA 164, 175; GMR, 84/2/2; R. V. Lennard, 'English Agriculture under Charles II: The Evidence of the Royal Society's "Enquiries"', EcHR, IV, 1932, p. 35.

in price levels, the cost of seed, in relative terms, would have been significantly less than formerly. We estimate it at only one-eighth of total costs, deriving our prices for seed from valuations applied to John Blumson's crops and approximating our sowing rates (of $2\frac{1}{4}$, $3\frac{1}{2}$, $3\frac{3}{4}$, and $4\frac{1}{4}$ bu per acre for wheat, peas, barley, and oats respectively) to those obtaining on Wykes farm in West Horsley (Surrey) in 1670. Whereas some farmers purchased seed in the market-place, others used seed saved from previous crops, there being little to choose either way in terms of relative costs.[106]

Outlays on soil dressings were probably of the same order of magnitude as those on seed, although information on this aspect of costs is almost nonexistent. The husbandry covenants of some leases specify the amounts of animal manure and/or lime to be applied between one rotation of crops and the next – e.g. every acre of ploughed land to be dressed with "8 hogsheads of good well burnt store lime or 160 horseloads of good rotten dung" for every three crops of corn taken from the ground. Converting the hogsheads to bushels (to be exact, 6.5625 bu per hogshead), and allowing for land lying fallow every fourth year, we may calculate that the application of lime under the terms of this covenant, when translated to our model farm, would average 1,312.5 bu per year. At a cost of 6d. per bu, we arrive at an annual charge of £32 16s. 3d. for soil dressings. Of course, animal dung, marl, or some other fertilizing agent might be used instead of, or in addition to, lime; and in our example, manure produced by the farm's draught animals is assumed to account for one-fifth of the value of soil dressings.[107]

Even on a highly specialized arable undertaking, of course, some draught animals would be necessary for ploughing and carting purposes. In the chalk districts of Wiltshire, E. Kerridge found that a plough team of three or four horses was normally employed to work an arable area of up to 60 acres. Our model farm, of 100 acres, is assumed to provide sufficient work for six horses. These horses (together with their 'gear') are further assumed to have cost the farmer a total of £60, being sold fourteen years later for £18. Hence, the depreciation in value over the fourteen-year period amounts to £42, or £3 per year, while the annual money interest forgone by the farmer by virtue of this element of capital expenditure, given a compound rate of $3\frac{1}{2}$ per cent, may be calculated at £2 13s. Thus, we arrive at a combined figure of £5 13s. in respect of the full annual cost to the farmer of his capital outlay on draught animals. A more substantial charge, even in years when grass was plentiful and cereals were cheap, was that of feed. Our figure of £31 4s. reflects the cost of agistment – amounting to 2s. per horse per week – on land owned by the Chester family at Chicheley (Bucks.) in 1743–4, and involving the supply of grass and/or hay throughout the year. Approximately

[106]Above, pp. 72–4; GLCRO, E/DCA 175; GMR, 22/3/1.
[107] Cornwall RO, Buller DDBU 531; Dorset RO, Weld of Lulworth D10/E81; Lennard, *op. cit.*, pp. 32–6.

Table 30. Expenditures and receipts of notional arable farm of 100 acres, c. 1700–50

Expenditures

	£. s. d.	Percentage distribution
Rent		
100 acres arable @ 15s. 3d.	76. 5. 0.	28.5
Farm maintenance & repairs	7. 12. 6.	2.9
Subtotal	83. 17. 6.	31.4
Seed		
45 bu wheat @ 4s. 6d.	10. 2. 6.	3.8
18¾ bu barley @ 2s. 6d.	2. 6. 11.	0.9
127½ bu oats @ 1s. 10½d.	11. 19. 1.	4.5
70 bu peas @ 2s. 6d.	8. 15. 0.	3.3
Subtotal	33. 3. 6.	12.4
Soil dressings (lime, manure)	32. 16. 3.	12.3
Draught animals		
Feed (grass, hay, oats)	31. 4. 0.	11.7
Interest & capital depreciation	5. 13. 0.	2.1
Miscellaneous (litter, shoes, medicaments)	3. 0. 0.	1.1
Subtotal	39. 17. 0.	14.9

Receipts

	£. s. d.	Percentage distribution
Fallow: 25 acres	—	—
Grain		
20 acres wheat, 400 bu @ 4s. 6d.	90. 0. 0.	29.8
5 acres barley, 120 bu @ 2s. 6d.	15. 0. 0.	5.0
30 acres oats, 1080 bu @ 1s. 10½d.	101. 5. 0.	33.5
20 acres peas, 560 bu @ 2s. 6d.	70. 0. 0.	23.1
Subtotal	276. 5. 0.	91.3
Straw		
37½ tons @ 10s. 6d.	19. 13. 9.	6.5
Manure	6. 11. 3.	2.2

	£. s. d.	%
Equipment: interest & capital depreciation	3. 11. 3.	1.3
Labour		
Ploughing, harrowing & carting – 600 man days @ 1s. 2d.	35. 0. 0.	13.1
Harvesting		
20 acres wheat @ 5s. 0d.	5. 0. 0.	1.9
5 acres barley @ 2s. 2d.	10. 10.	0.2
30 acres oats @ 2s. 2d.	3. 5. 0.	1.2
20 acres peas @ 2s. 0d.	2. 0. 0.	0.7
Threshing		
50 qtr wheat @ 2s. 0d.	5. 0. 0.	1.9
15 qtr barley @ 1s. 0d.	15. 0.	0.3
135 qtr oats @ 1s. 0d.	6. 15. 0.	2.5
70 qtr peas @ 1s. 6d.	5. 5. 0.	2.0
Miscellaneous (e.g. dunging, sowing, weeding)	7. 10. 0.	2.8
Subtotal	71. 0. 10.	26.6
Marketing and other	3. 0. 0.	1.1
Total expenditures	267. 6. 4.	100.0
Total receipts	302. 10. 0.	100.0
Net profit	35. 3. 8.	11.6

the same figure would be reached by alternatively assuming that each horse consumed 1–1¼ bu of oats per week, which appears to have been about the normal ration. In addition to feed, well-tended horses would be provided with straw or other litter (posing no problem to the arable enterprise), shoes (costing 4d. to 6d. each), and medicaments or veterinary treatment in the case of illness or injury. We have allocated an arbitrary sum of £3 per year to cover these incidental outgoings. Thus, in all, our farmer's six horses were costing him £39 17s. per year, making this one of the largest and the principal components of cost, after rent and labour. Instead of investing in draught animals, farmers could, of course, hire them; even large producers might do this on occasion when their own animals were either too few or not available for a particular job. On the Ashtead and Epsom estates of the Howard family at the beginning of the eighteenth century, plough teams (including the driver) were not uncommonly hired, the usual charge being 5s. per acre. For a single horse the cost was 1s. per day.[108]

Reflecting the low capital intensity of non-mechanized agriculture, the costs of farm appliances were much smaller than those of draught animals. On arable undertakings the major items of equipment were ploughs, harrows, and carts or waggons. Of these, ploughs and harrows usually cost only a few shillings each. The new wheel plough purchased for the Howards' farm at Ashtead in 1696 must have been rather exceptional to have cost £1 3s. Just as expensive, in a relative sense, was the new cart purchased in 1700 for £8 5s. – more than twice the usual amount. At the other end of the scale, rakes could be purchased for 3d. each and pitchforks for 1s. 1d. or 1s. 2d. apiece. In sum, it seems unlikely that the appliances employed on an arable undertaking of 100 acres would normally cost more than, say, £15, and this is the figure which we have used in our calculations. We have further assumed that equipment was replaced, on average, every five years and have calculated the loss of interest thereby at the same rate (3½ per cent) as before. On the basis of these assumptions it emerges that less than 1½ per cent of our farmer's total expenditures were attributable to the cost of equipment. Of course, most of the appliances, being mainly of wood, were comparatively simple to make and would have been produced by the farmer himself.[109]

The occupier of a holding of 100 acres or so was also likely to perform some of the manual work about the farm, with assistance from his family, but there would also be a need for hired labour. A two-plough farm, such

[108] E. Kerridge, 'The Agrarian Development of Wiltshire, 1540–1640', unpub. London Univ. Ph.D. thesis, 1951, pp. 133, 181–2; Bucks. RO, Chester of Chicheley D/C/2/43; Herts. RO, Ashridge AH 1,000; Capell 10,449; Broadfield Hall 70,474A; GMR, 1/53/2–9a.

[109] Univ. of Reading Library, Farm Rec. Coll. SALOP 5/1/1, ff. 33, 36, 39; NORF 14/1/1, f. 37; BUC 11/1/5, f. 22; Surrey Room, Minet Library, Knatchbull Rd, London SE5, Account Book of the Howard Estates at Ashtead and Epsom, 1693–1701; Hunts. RO, Manchester Coll. dd M5/bdle 4; Devon RO, Bedford 1,258 M/F27; Bedford RO, Boteler T.W. 809; Orlebar O.R. 1,352; Herts. RO, 26,294; Essex RO, Petre D/DP/A47; Cumb. RO, D/Sen. Fleming 20.

as that envisaged, would probably provide fairly regular employment for two or three labourers, plus additional workers at harvest time. The most demanding task, in terms of labour requirements, was that of ploughing. Normally, arable land (including fallow) was ploughed at least twice a year, with additional ploughings being given in the case of heavy soils. Likewise, land might, on occasion, receive four or five harrowings. At the same time, there was an ongoing requirement for carting services on and about the farm. Dung and other materials had to be conveyed to various parts of the holding, crops needed to be gathered and stored after harvest, produce had to be transported to market, and supplies needed to be fetched. In our example, it is assumed that ploughing, harrowing, and carting provide full-time employment (amounting to 600 man days) for two hired workers. At the going rate of 1s. 2d. per day, the annual earnings of these workers come to £35, i.e. approximately half the total wage bill of the enterprise (excluding the labour costs of hedging and ditching). Wage payments in connection with harvesting and threshing would ordinarily account for the bulk of the remaining expenditures on labour, although the situation would vary somewhat with the individual crop. Wheat was the most expensive cereal to harvest; at 5s. per acre (as on the Howard estates) the piece rate paid to workers for gathering this grain was rather more than twice the corresponding rates for harvesting barley, oats, and peas. Piece rates for threshing wheat, at 2s. per quarter, were also up to twice as high as those for threshing the spring-sown cereals. The task of threshing a large crop was an onerous one, requiring much time and labour. If, referring to Table 30, we assume that our farmer's total threshing costs of £17 15s. are determined on the basis of daily wage payments at the rate of 1s. 2d. per day (instead of by piece-rate wages), we may calculate that it would take 303 man days for all crops to be completely threshed. In other words, there would be sufficient work to keep two men fully occupied over a period of six months. It was doubtless partly on account of this time constraint that many substantial farmers and wealthy landowners marketed their grain in small quantities on a weekly, biweekly, or monthly basis, rather than disposing of their cereal crops in bulk.[110]

Whereas ploughing, carting, harvesting, and threshing accounted for the bulk of the labour costs of the typical arable enterprise in the early eighteenth century, there were a variety of other tasks entailing wage expenditures on the part of the farmer. Among these other tasks, "filling the dung cart" and "spreading dung" (rewarded at rates ranging between 1s. and 1s. 4d. per day) are probably mentioned the most frequently in contemporary farm accounts. Sowing was another obviously necessary task. An entry in the West Horsley (Surrey) accounts of Edward Nicholas in 1714 indicates a labour cost

[110] Lennard, op. cit., pp. 30–2; Herts. RO, 82,919; GMR, 1/53/2–9a; 84/2/2; Univ. of Reading Library, Farm Rec. Coll. KEN 13/1/1.

of 5s. 6½d. per acre for the setting of beans. However, at this time seeds were more generally sown broadcast, for which the wage rate was a mere 3d. or 4d. per acre. Also of comparatively small consequence as a cost in the cultivation of field crops (as opposed to garden crops) were expenditures on weeding, an activity infrequently undertaken, and then most usually by women at about half the normal daily wage rate for men. Juveniles were also employed on this and other suitable tasks, as, for example, on the Sackville family's Kentish lands at Knole in July and August 1750, when a boy was paid at the rate of 4d. per day for thirty-three days for "keeping rooks from barley". For all these miscellaneous wage expenditures we have allocated an arbitrary sum of £7 10s. Finally, on the side of expenditures, we have allowed a further sum of £3 to cover external marketing costs (such as tolls, accommodation, and special transport services) and any other expenses of an occasional or incidental nature. Thus, we arrive at a grand total of £267 6s. 4d. for all expenditures incurred in connection with the operation of our arable enterprise.[111]

On the revenue side of the balance sheet, the key variables are, of course, those of output and price. Our farmer's crop yields, ranging from 20 bu per acre in the case of wheat to 36 bu per acre in the case of oats, are derived from data pertaining to John Blumson's crops, and in the light of other pieces of evidence would seem to represent average experience for the type of enterprise envisaged.[112] On the basis of the sowing rates assumed in Table 30, these yields would give returns on seed ranging from 6.4 for barley to 8.9 for wheat. At the price levels already indicated in connection with the cost of seed – i.e. 36s., 20s., 20s., and 15s. per quarter for wheat, barley, peas, and oats respectively – we calculate the total value of cereal production at £276 5s. To this, an arbitrary amount of £19 13s. 9d. has been added to allow for the value of the straw resulting as a by-product of the cereal harvest, it being assumed that each of the 75 acres under cultivation yields an average of 10 cwt of straw, marketable at 10s. 6d. per ton.[113] Adding, further, the value of horse manure produced on the farm, we obtain a figure of £302 10s. as the total income of the enterprise, giving a net profit of £35 3s. 8d. This represents a ratio of net profits (before tax) to total income of 11.6 per cent, a return which most present-day farmers would be very happy to achieve.

Since even exceptional results can generally be improved upon, the question arises as to whether this return by our notional farm undertaking represents the maximum that the enterprise would be capable of achieving.

[111] GMR, 1/53/2–92; 84/2/2; 22/1/1–3; Essex RO, D/DM/A20; Kent AO, U269, A49/2; U386, A1.   [112] GLCRO, E/DCA/175.

[113] Straw was normally sold by the load, the weight of which is uncertain. We have assumed a 2-ton load, priced at 21s. This would seem to accord better with the evidence than Beveridge's assumption of a 10-cwt load. See Beveridge et al., Prices and Wages, I, p. 21; Reading Univ. Library, Farm Rec. Coll. BUC 11/1/5.

Because the production capabilities of land are not everywhere the same, sometimes differing quite markedly within the confines of a single farm entity, this is a question which cannot be answered definitively in the absence of an appreciation of the potentialities of the soil in different uses. This, of course, we do not have in the present instance. However, with or without such an appreciation, one of the necessary steps in evaluating profitability would be to disaggregate the relative contribution of each crop to the farm's finances. This is done in Table 31, in which the identifiable receipts and costs are itemized for each cereal separately, while the remaining (non-identifiable) revenues and expenditures are rated on the basis of the percentage use of the cultivated area.

The result of this financial breakdown is to reveal wheat as the most profitable of our farmer's crops (yielding a net profit of £1 2s. o½d. per acre) and to point to barley (burdened with a net loss of 2s. 4½d. per acre) as a crop to be avoided. The unsatisfactory showing of barley may well explain why the real-life farm upon which our model is based should have devoted such a relatively small acreage to the cultivation of this crop. Other things (including soil types and rotational flexibility) being equal, it would obviously pay our farmer to increase his production of wheat and decrease his production of other cereals, especially barley. For other farms, particularly those with markedly different soil characteristics, the optimum allocation of resources might well be very different. Equally, given a revised structure of cereal prices, wheat might appear lower down the scale of profitability on our model farm.

In relation to the determination of prices, as opposed to that of output, individual farmers were, of course, unable to exercise any control. To a large producer it may have mattered little whether increases in the value of produce were achieved through larger output or higher prices. In each instance some offsetting costs were entailed: a larger crop meant additional expenditures in connection with gathering and threshing, while higher prices portended increased costs for next year's seed. To a small subsistence cultivator, consuming most of his produce at home and selling little in the market-place, the issue was more critical and its resolution more self-evident. Up to the point where domestic consumption needs were fully satisfied the expectation is that the small operator would be primarily concerned with the size of his crop yield; subsequently, he would look to obtain high prices for any marketable surplus. It was, of course, rarely that bumper crops and high prices went together. Fortunate was the farmer when this occurred! More typically, high prices were the outcome of poor harvests and food scarcities; at such times many small cultivators were likely to be forced into the market-place as buyers of grain (at famine prices) rather than as sellers of surplus produce.[114]

[114] Above, pp. 77–9.

Table 31. Comparison of profitability of different arable crops

| | Income | | | Expenditure | | | | | Net profit (+) or loss (−) |
	Cereal £ s. d.	Other £ s. d.	Total £ s. d.	Seed £ s. d.	Harvesting £ s. d.	Threshing £ s. d.	Other £ s. d.	Total £ s. d.	£ s. d.
Wheat	90. 0. 0.	7. 0. 0.	97. 0. 0.	10. 2. 6.	5. 0. 0.	5. 0. 0.	54.16. 6.	74.19. 0.	+ 22. 1. 0.
Barley	15. 0. 0.	1.15. 0.	16.15. 0.	2. 6.11.	10.10.	15. 0.	13.14. 2.	17. 6.11.	— 11.11.
Oats	101. 5. 0.	10.10. 0.	111.15. 0.	11.19. 1.	3. 5. 0.	6.15. 0.	82. 4.10.	104. 3.11.	+ 7.11. 1.
Peas	70. 0. 0.	7. 0. 0.	77. 0. 0.	8.15. 0.	2. 0. 0.	5. 5. 0.	54.16. 6.	70.16. 6.	+ 6. 3. 6.
Total	276. 5. 0.	26. 5. 0.	302.10. 0.	33. 3. 6.	10.15.10.	17.15. 0.	205.12. 0.	267. 6. 4.	+ 35. 3. 8.

| | Per acre | | Net profit (+) or loss (−) |
	Income s.	Expenditure s.	s.
Wheat	97.00	74.95	+ 22.05
Barley	67.00	69.38	− 2.38
Oats	74.50	69.46	+ 5.04
Peas	77.00	70.82	+ 6.18
Total	80.66	71.28	+ 9.38

3. New arable crops

Problems encountered in connection with the determination of profitability in relation to cereal production are multiplied when the focus is switched to the more innovative horticultural products and industrial crops grown increasingly in England from the sixteenth century onwards. By 1695 it was possible for Gregory King to estimate the domestic production of these less conventional crops at £2.2 million, or 9 per cent of total farm output.[115] However, in spite of their widespread acceptance by the end of our period, for most such commodities empirical data bearing upon the economics of production are almost totally lacking, there being a great paucity of information with respect to costs (other than those of seed) and crop yields. In part, this data deficiency doubtless reflects the fact that among large farm undertakings, even in the early eighteenth century, horticultural products and industrial crops (except wool) were seldom more than very subsidiary lines of production, the foodstuffs, in particular, being often regarded primarily from the standpoint of domestic household provisioning rather than commercial sales. In so far as enterprises specialized upon the commercial production of fruits, vegetables, hemp, flax, madder, and the like, the great majority, it may be assumed, were small family entities, of which little documentary trace now remains. However, even when grown on a limited acreage, alongside more traditional forms of tillage, such crops often must have made the difference between starvation and survival in years when grain prices sagged or the cereal harvest failed.

Many of the new arable crops to appear on the scene were initially cultivated under garden, as distinct from field, conditions. This was so in the case of turnips, probably the most extensively cultivated of these new crops, although by the middle of the eighteenth century some individual farmers were devoting considerable acreages of open-field or enclosed land to turnip production. Being grown primarily for the purposes of animal fodder, turnips were normally sold and consumed *in situ*. Expenditures on harvesting and marketing were saved thereby, the costs of labour being substantially lower than those incurred in connection with the production of most other non-cereal crops. There was also a considerable cost saving with respect to soil dressings, since manure – a very necessary input in intensive horticultural operations – was generously supplied by the grazing livestock.[116]

Some useful piecemeal data pertaining to the field cultivation of turnips

[115] *Two Tracts by Gregory King*, ed. G. E. Barnett, Baltimore, 1936, p. 54 (repr. in T & C, p. 782); Joan Thirsk, *Economic Policy and Projects: The Development of a Consumer Society in Early Modern England*, Oxford, 1978, p. 177. Output of the remaining crops was estimated at £10 million in the case of grain and £12 million in the case of pastoral and woodland products.

[116] Herts. RO, Sebright 18,104; Hunts. RO, Thornhill 148/4/8; Bucks. RO, D/MH/33/8; Hants. RO, 27 M54/3; GLCRO, E/BER/S/E/7/4/6, 7; Surrey RO, Clayton 60/5/760, 764; GMR, Clayton 84/2/3; Howard 1/53/7.

are contained in extant estate accounts relating to Welbeck Park (Notts.), where thirty-five acres of enclosed land belonging to the duke of Portland were used for the production of turnips in 1731–3. Manipulating and rounding out these data, we calculate the costs and receipts of this venture in 1731 as set out in Table 32. Compared with the more traditional forms

Table 32. *Costs and receipts in connection with production of 35 acres of turnips, Welbeck Park (Notts.), 1731*

	£ s. d.	s. per acre
Costs		
Seed: 42 lb @ 5.14d. per lb	18. 0.	0.51
Ploughing, harrowing 3 times, & sowing @ 9s. 0d. per acre	15. 15. 0.	9.00
Hoeing @ 3s. 6d. per acre	6. 2. 6.	3.50
Other costs and profit (loss)	8. 9. 6.	4.84
Receipts	31. 5. 0.	17.86

of husbandry, one of the most noteworthy aspects of turnip production, as revealed by this table, is the very low expenditure on seed – a reflection of the fact that the crop:seed ratios for horticultural products were (and still are) impressively greater than those for cereals. Even so, the indicated cost of seed (in excess of 5d. per lb) is high in comparison with the 3–4d. per lb paid in the Home Counties at this time. Other expenditures at Welbeck were generally less than those incurred further south. Thus, the 9s. per acre expended on ploughing, harrowing, and sowing may be compared with a corresponding charge of 15s. per acre on a Wiltshire farm. In each instance we may assume that a hired plough team was used. While ploughing and related costs probably differed little, if at all, from those incurred in connection with the production of cereals, expenditures on hoeing and weeding were normally substantially higher for turnips and other horticultural crops than for more traditional agricultural outputs. As the Welbeck farm records contain no reference to the hoeing of turnips, a charge of 3s. 6d. per acre has been assumed for this activity on the basis of contemporary Norfolk experience.[117]

Receipts from the *in situ* sale of the Welbeck crop are recorded as £31 5s. (or 17.86s. per acre). This compares very unfavourably with the 70s. per acre received by one Surrey farmer in 1754 and the more usual payments of 20–40s. per acre obtained in southern and eastern England generally.

[117] Notts. RO, Portland DD5P1/1; Herts. RO, 48,688; Sebright 18,104; GMR, Weston 22/1/2, 3; Clayton 84/2/2; LM 1,087/2/16; Surrey RO, Clayton 60/5/506; GLCRO, E/BER/S/E/4/4, 6; Wilts. RO, 184; Norfolk RO, BAR 22; Hare 5,331.

Possibly the soil in Welbeck was not well suited for turnips or the year (1731) may have been a bad one for this crop. Whatever the cause, the result, given the outlays and receipts noted above, was to leave a margin of only £8 9s. 6d. (or 4.84s. per acre) to meet all other costs, including overheads, and provide a profit on the enterprise. Clearly, the duke's venture would hardly have been an economic proposition on leasehold land, with rent for enclosed arable in Nottingham at this time generally in the range 5–8s. per acre.[118]

Turnips apart, the only 'new' arable crop for which we possess a modicum of analytical information is hops. Seemingly grown on a very limited geographical basis before 1640, and then primarily in south-eastern localities settled by immigrants from the Low Countries, this crop spread slowly within the Home Counties and Sussex, with another significant region of production developing in the general vicinity of the Vale of Evesham. By 1736, reflecting the long-term increase in the price of this commodity, it could be reported from eastern Sussex that "everybody is now in the humor of planting hops". In spite of this growing popularity, hops remained essentially a subsidiary garden crop cultivated on plots of land of one acre or less. Some hop enterprises, however, were on a substantially larger scale. In September 1657 the Reverend Ralph Josselin, vicar of Earls Colne near Colchester (Essex) was noting in his diary that Mr Harlakenden, a neighbouring farmer, had "made" £790 from the sale of hops the previous year; in an earlier entry (dated September 1649) the vicar had recorded that the same Mr Harlakenden was devoting twenty acres of land to the cultivation of this crop. Some years later, in 1679–80, Sir John Banks had hop grounds covering twenty or thirty acres at Aylesford in Kent. Not far away, at Brasted, near Westerham, Sir John Heath was also cultivating a hop garden which, although occupying only two acres, was still larger than the average. The farm accounts pertaining to these two latter ventures are among the most complete that we possess dealing with the cultivation of hops during our study period, and, accordingly, they are reviewed in some detail by C. W. Chalklin in his study of seventeenth-century Kent. Summary versions of these data, reconstructed on a cost-per-acre basis, are presented in Table 33, together with some comparative cost figures derived by D. Baker from extant farm accounts pertaining to the production of hops by the Tylden family at Hogshaw farm in the downland parish of Milstead, Kent, during the years 1722–34 and 1744–52.[119]

Quite evidently, the production of hops required considerable amounts of capital and labour. Indeed, total expenditures per acre, as indicated in Table

[118] Notts. RO, Portland DD5P1/1; Hunts. RO, Thornhill 148/4/8; GLCRO, E/BER/S/E/7/4/6, 7; Surrey RO, Clayton 60/5/760.

[119] E. Sussex RO, SAS/RF 15/25; Macfarlane, *Diary of Ralph Josselin*; C. W. Chalklin, *Seventeenth Century Kent: A Social and Economic History*, London, 1965, pp. 92–5; D. Baker, 'Agricultural Prices, Production and Marketing, with Special Reference to the Hop Industry: North-East Kent 1680–1760', unpub. Kent Univ. Ph.D. thesis, 1976, pp. 561–9.

Table 33. *Costs per acre of hop production in Kent, 1679–80 and 1722–52*
(s. per acre)

	Aylesford (Banks)	Brasted (Heath)	Milstead (Tylden)
Poles	42.42–63.63	80.00	49.25
Hop bags, bagging, & drying	24.44–36.67	22.50	
Coal & wood	18.30–27.45	63.50	18.00
Dressing	45.64–68.46	51.75	67.00
Picking	44.28–66.42	118.54	52.17
Manure			20.50
Rent			20.00
Transport, taxes, & miscellaneous	24.31–36.47	32.08	57.83
Total	199.39–299.10	368.37	284.75

33, could be up to five times those estimated for our notional arable enterprise.[120] Moreover, not all pertinent expenditures are included in our table.[121] There is, for example, no specific reference in the earlier accounts to the annual value of land, and this could be very substantial, rents of £7 or £8 per acre allegedly being obtained in 1744 for choice hop grounds in the vicinity of Farnham (Surrey); however, in relation to less well-favoured sites, rents of about £1 per acre appear to have been the norm, with tithes rated at a further 10s. per acre. Nor is there any mention in Table 33 of annual capital charges in connection with oasthouses for the drying of hops. Most large hop-growing operations of more than a few acres probably encompassed such facilities, and their use by Banks, Heath, and Tylden may be inferred from the substantial expenditures on coal and wood indicated in Table 33. Other elements of expenditure apparently omitted from the reckoning include costs incurred in connection with the acquisition and use of farm implements, draught animals, soil dressings, and hop plants. The plants, being perennial, would not have to be purchased every year, but, in any event, at 6d.–1s. per 100 hop sets, and allowing approximately 1,200 sets per acre, the cost of plants would be negligible. A much more significant expense, especially on well-tended holdings, would be that of providing manure. With respect to Tylden's hop venture at Milstead, Baker indicates an average expenditure of 20s. 6d. per acre for this input (including costs

[120] See above, p. 282.
[121] Since Table 33 is based upon the data reproduced by Chalklin and Baker, it is not known whether any of the missing items of expenditure are mentioned in the original accounts.

of spreading), with yearly totals ranging between 16s. 8d. and 50s. per acre. Moreover, although labour charges (notably those denoted as "dressing" and "picking") comprise 40–50 per cent of all items of expenditure specified in Table 33, it would be unwise to assume the inclusion of all such charges in contemporary farm accounts. The process of growing hops included digging hills and spreading dung; setting up poles; tying and pruning the plants; hoeing between the rows; picking, drying, and bagging the hops; and taking down and stacking the poles. Dressing generally appears to have encompassed these tasks up to, but not including, that of picking. In some instances workers carrying out these jobs were paid piece-rate wages; at other times wages were calculated on a daily basis. In yet other instances special hop dressers were hired by the year. Thus, in 1652–3 and 1653–4 Thomas Kempe was paid £5 a year to look after a one-acre hop garden near Hythe (Kent) belonging to the Brockman family, doing all the manual work except picking, drying, and taking down the hop poles. Hop picking was costly for the grower because many workers, mostly women, had to be employed. Of the £299 1s. 9d. total recorded expenses on Sir John Banks's hop grounds in the year ending November 1680, £66 8s. 4d. (or between one-quarter and one-fifth) was indicated as being payments to hop pickers. At the going female wage rate of 10d. per day (as paid on the estate of the Darell family at Barksore, near Sittingbourne, in the 1720s), this represents the equivalent of approximately 1,600 'man' days of employment, or a month's work for 65–70 workers. It is not clear whether the expenditures on picking indicated in Table 33 include payments for 'pole pulling', in respect of which task the daily wage rates in early-eighteenth-century Kent ranged between 1s. 6d. and 2s. per day, making this one of the best-paid of agricultural occupations. We have, however, adjusted Sir John Heath's picking expenses to include disbursements entered in the accounts as payments "to the bin men" – bins being the receptacles used in hop picking.[122]

Among the relevant items of capital expenditure, mention has already been made of oasthouse drying facilities. The costs of providing such facilities, and the distribution of these costs between landlord and tenant, seem to have varied considerably. As in the case of one 1737 lease, there might be an arrangement whereby the landlord supplied any necessary timber, while the tenant erected the hop kiln and provided the bricks and tiles for it. In some other instance it might prove possible to convert a barn into an oasthouse, and thus effect a saving in construction costs. Hop poles were another major item of capital expenditure, two or three poles being used for the support and training of each plant. This requirement necessitated the use of 2,000–3,600 poles for each acre of hop-ground. Accordingly, with poles generally priced at between 5s. and 15s. per 100, the hop grower could look to an initial

[122] Chalklin, op. cit., pp. 93–4; Baker, thesis, pp. 562–3, 565–6; GMR, 51/5/67; LM 1,087/2/16; Kent AO, U269, A49/2; U386, A2; Hereford City Library, Scudamore 631: 16.

investment of £5–27 per acre for poles. This investment would not, of course, need to be repeated every year, and the expenditures for poles indicated in Table 33 are possibly larger than those which would normally be incurred on an average annual replacement basis; however, the average hop pole appears to have lasted about six years. A more constant, if smaller, expense was that of bagging. On the basis of Sir John Heath's accounts, six bags, costing 3s. 7½d. each, might suffice for the marketing of the yield from a one-acre plot. A more substantial charge in the latter part of our period was excise duty, first imposed in 1711 at the rate of 1d. per pound of home-grown hops.[123] Since liability to pay this tax was related directly to the level of hop output, its imposition on Tylden's Milstead hop venture, in the amount of 47s. 10d. per acre (equivalent to 16.8 per cent of total recorded costs), may be taken to imply an average hop yield by this enterprise of 574 lb (or 5⅛ cwt) per acre.[124]

Just how representative such a yield would have been is difficult to determine in view of the lack of individual farm production data and the wide variability in annual output. Assuming (on the basis of the prices paid for hops by Winchester College in 1679–80) that Heath obtained a price somewhere between 3d. and 7d. per lb for his produce, his receipts (amounting to £54 5s. 9d. for the production of two acres) would indicate a crop yield in the range 8–20 cwt per acre. This may be compared with the 40s. worth of produce obtained by one unfortunate grower from three acres in 1696, when the hop crop was "blacked and spoyled with the blaste". Prices were also subject to wide fluctuation. Thus, the average annual price of hops in Winchester between 1644 and 1702 ranged from 28s. 5d. per cwt in 1679 to 219s. 10d. in 1687. Likewise, in the years 1711 to 1750, the price obtained by Tylden for Milstead-grown hops sold at Southwark ranged from 32s. per cwt in 1729 to 210s. in 1725. Patently, this great variability in yield and price made hop growing a very risky proposition. In some years profits might be high, but for those whose first farming priority was income stability, hops were a crop to be avoided or, at best, grown on a very limited scale. This fact, allied to the substantial amounts of capital and labour needed for its production and the several years' delay between planting and any returns from sales, clearly limited its appeal for the small holder or subsistence farmer,[125] although the gross returns which could be obtained from this kind of activity, such as the £27 per acre registered by Heath in 1679–80 or the

[123] *Statutes of the Realm*, 9 Anne, c. 12. For the excise revenues collected, see Ashton, *The Eighteenth Century*, p. 240.

[124] C. W. Chalklin, 'The Rural Economy of a Kentish Wealden Parish 1650–1750', AHR, x, 1962, p. 42; E. Sussex RO, SAS/RF15/25; GMR, 51/5/67; 121/1/1,114; Kent AO, U386, A2; Eleanor C. Lodge, ed., *The Account Book of a Kentish Estate, 1616–1704*, Oxford, 1927, p. 234; E. Sussex RO, FRE 520; Notts. RO, Franklin DDF1/1; Baker, thesis, p. 565.

[125] Rogers, *History of Agriculture and Prices in England*, VI, *passim*; Chalklin, *Seventeenth Century Kent*, p. 93; Baker, thesis, p. 538.

£20 14s. per acre (net of freightage and selling commission) recorded by Tylden in 1722–52, must have seemed like riches indeed to a cereal producer grossing £3–5 per acre from traditional crops (see Table 31).[126]

Of course, an appreciation of the differing levels of associated expenditures (£10–20 per acre in the case of hops, compared with £3–4 per acre for cereals and pulses) might be calculated to temper any enthusiasm for hops. Even so, while the profitability of this crop could seldom, if ever, have measured up to the remarkable claims made for it by contemporary propagandists, there seems little reason to doubt that – on a suitable site, under proper management, and in a favourable price environment – the growing of hops could be a very rewarding activity. Such a view gains some support from the data presented in Table 34, which compares the financial results

Table 34. *Comparison of profitability: hops, wheat, and peas*

| | | Per acre | | | Net |
| | | Ex-penditure | Income/sales | Net profit | profit on sales |
Location	Crop	(s.)	(s.)	(s.)	(%)
Brasted	Hops	368.37	542.87	174.50	32.1
Milstead	Hops	284.75	414.00	129.25	31.2
Tatlingbury	Hops	374.00	424.00	50.00	11.8
Notional	Wheat	74.95	97.00	22.05	22.7
Notional	Peas	70.82	77.00	6.18	8.0

attributed to the two most profitable crop segments of our notional arable undertaking with those achieved by Heath at Brasted and Tylden at Milstead and with the financial performance of another hop-growing venture (located at Tatlingbury farm near Tonbridge in the Kentish Weald) whose extant accounts – also analysed by Baker – pertain to the years 1744–57.[127]

Allowing that, as between the real and notional enterprises represented in this table, the elements entering into the measurement of costs and profits may differ in certain significant respects, a general, if tentative, conclusion would be that, on balance, the relevant business ratios point to the production of hops as being the most attractive economic proposition. In particular, the hop-growing ventures of Heath and Tylden, whether viewed in terms of net profit per acre or net profit on sales, appear to present a very healthy business aspect.

[126] Above, p. 282; Baker, thesis, pp. 562, 567.
[127] D. Baker, 'Tatlingbury: An Eighteenth Century Wealden Hop Farm', *Cantium*, III, 1, 1971, pp. 3–14. I have used Baker's revised figure of £21 4s. for the average income per acre at Tatlingbury (see thesis, p. 567).

The superior performance of Tylden's hop enterprise in comparison with that at Tatlingbury appears to have been essentially on account of better hop prices – those paid to Tylden in 1722–34 and 1744–52 being, on average, 35 per cent higher than the prices obtained for the Tatlingbury farm produce in 1744–57.[128] As Table 34 makes apparent, the Tatlingbury enterprise was operated at a substantially higher level of costs than the hop grounds at Milstead, although (projecting an increase in the value of output to compensate for the above-mentioned differential in prices) the yield of hops per acre at Tatlingbury must have been almost 40 per cent greater than that achieved by Tylden. Accordingly, had the prices paid for Tylden's hops in 1722–34/1744–52 also applied to the output of the Tatlingbury hop farm in 1744–57, the latter venture would have yielded its owner an average gross income of 572s. per acre and a ratio of net profit to sales of 35 per cent.

Among other forms of arable cultivation, tobacco growing was affected by many of the same constraints as hop production: expenditures were heavy, output was uncertain, and prices were highly volatile; in addition, land used to grow tobacco was quickly exhausted. However, in spite of the economic risks attendant upon this activity, and in spite of government efforts to eradicate it (finally successful in the late seventeenth century), the promise of excessive profitability seemingly served to persuade cultivators in more than a score of English and Welsh counties to plant some experimental acreages with tobacco, and many small plots of land were set aside for this purpose.[129]

A much less speculative proposition, more suited to the resources and particular circumstances of the small to middling cultivator, was the production of fruits and vegetables. With the exception of tree fruits, the maturative period, between seed time and harvest, in relation to such produce, was comparatively short, and while superior results necessitated the input of substantial quantities of labour and manure, other (non-rent) elements of cost were not especially burdensome. Furthermore, although the prices of horticultural commodities exhibited a pronounced seasonal pattern, they were not, in general, subject to violent year-to-year fluctuations. Hence, as already surmised, impediments to the commercial production of horticultural produce were likely to stem more largely from lack of easy access to urban consumers than from shortages of capital or peculiarities of price behaviour.

4. Livestock husbandry

Livestock were kept by farmers for a variety of reasons and for varying lengths of time. Their place in the operation of arable enterprise – as

---

[128] Baker, thesis, pp. 532, 538; *id.*, 'Tatlingbury', p. 7.

[129] Joan Thirsk, 'New Crops and their Diffusion: Tobacco-Growing in Seventeenth Century England', in C. W. Chalklin and M. A. Havinden, eds., *Rural Change and Urban Growth, 1500–1800*, London, 1974, pp. 76–103.

producers of dung or as suppliers of muscle power – has already been noted. In a less subservient role, livestock were, of course, valued in their own right for the products which they provided and (in the case of horses) for the services which they performed. Within the system of livestock farming economic specialization occurred in various forms. For example, many farmers concerned themselves primarily with the production of wool or dairy products, breeding their own stock and selling animals which were mainly old, inferior, diseased, or surplus to requirements. Other farmers, particularly those in possession of good fattening pastures, might do little or no breeding, buying in stock for subsequent resale at higher prices. Specialization upon different types of stock might take the form of purchases of couples (of cows and calves or ewes and lambs) in the spring for resale separately in the autumn. In enterprises where the production of beef or mutton was a prime aim of livestock husbandry, mainly oxen, bullocks, or wethers would probably be kept, perhaps for a few months, possibly for a year or longer, depending upon the age and condition of the stock, the financial resources of the grazier, the availability of feed, and the movement of market prices. Animals reared for meat production, in particular, might be bought and sold a number of times before reaching peak marketable condition. In the case of cattle the normal maturation period was four or five years, though heifers made "very pretty beef" at three.[130]

The period of keep and the related appreciation in market value were, of course, fundamental considerations in the determination of profitability. Unfortunately, few contemporary farm accounts have anything to say on these matters, and for empirical detail we are essentially limited to the examples summarized in Table 35, relating to certain livestock fattening operations involving the Lowther family at Lowther in north Westmorland, Sir Daniel Fleming at Rydal, also in Westmorland, and Francis Cholmeley at Sutton upon Derwent in the East Riding of Yorkshire. These transactions were perhaps typical of many others emanating from the aforementioned estates, but other trading situations are also documented in the pertinent records, including occasional sales of "old stock" by Cholmeley and of "my own breed" of oxen by Fleming.[131]

However, referring to Table 35, it will be noted that most of the listed transactions relate to beef-producing animals (oxen being included in this category), some cows and sheep also being traded. Price levels, especially with respect to purchases for the Westmorland estates, appear to be on the low side in relation to general averages for the years in question, an outcome, it may be supposed, of the smallness of breed, the immaturity of stock, or a combination of both. A comparison of the dates of purchase and sale indicate that while some of the animals were over-wintered, the bulk were

[130] Edward Lisle, *Observations in Husbandry*, 2nd edn, 2 vols., London, 1757, *II*, pp. 5–6, 9.
[131] Cumb. RO, D/Lons/L/A1/5; D/Sen. Fleming 20; Westmor. RO, WD/Ry; N. Riding RO, ZQG/Accounts.

acquired in the spring and early summer for disposal in the autumn. All the trading situations depicted in the table, with one exception (involving sheep), reveal an enhancement in price upon resale. Moreover, in the case of sheep kept during the summer months considerable financial benefits would normally be derived from the sale of the wool clip. Likewise, cows might produce milk or even calves, and the value of these assets would need to be taken into the reckoning in any assessment of profitability. In Table 35 the average daily gain in the value of cattle during the period of keep is shown as ranging between 0.61d. and 4.88d. Doubtless some of the differences in this regard may be explained by seasonal considerations, while the generally better results achieved by Cholmeley in comparison with the other two landowners probably owed something to the richer natural pasturage available in the Vale of York.

Of course, the difference between the price paid for stock and the price received, whether calculated on an average *per diem* basis or otherwise, was not pure profit. Indeed, before any profit could be registered, this difference would have to be sufficient to cover costs of feed, overheads, and other necessary expenses. Feed costs – the largest of these elements – reflected a variety of considerations, including the type, size, and age of stock; the quality and location of grazing land; the prices of fodder crops; and the amount of forage provided. At Rydal in the 1690s, the agistment charge for keeping an ox on Fleming's demesne lands was normally 6d. per week (or 0.86d. per day). This was twice the (1s. per week) agistment charge which Cholmeley received and paid on occasion for "grass for beasts" at Sutton upon Derwent in the 1730s. Like other upland farmers, Fleming relied primarily upon comparatively cheap feed in the form of extensive natural pasturage in order to operate a low-output system of livestock farming economically. Viewed from a slightly different angle, since the price of beef during the period under review was approximately 3d. per lb, Fleming's oxen needed to put on at least 2 lb per week for him merely to meet his costs of feed, quite apart from other expenses. In Cholmeley's case, a comparable increase of 4 lb per week would have been required. Further south, especially in the vicinity of London, where one might expect forage rations to be more generous at the end of the fattening process, graziers would probably look to obtain substantially larger increases in output on account of higher feed bills. The winter stall-feeding of a bullock in order to bring it to prime condition was likely to have required a ration of at least 2 cwt of hay a week for a period of twenty weeks; even in years when hay was comparatively plentiful, the cost of this operation would have amounted to about 2s. per week for a total of £2.[132]

The relative importance of feed costs to the livestock farmer is brought

[132] Lisle, *op. cit.*, II, pp. 5–6, 9; Devon RO, 1,508M/V3; 1,258M/F27; Wilts. RO, 9; Savernake Estate Accounts.

Table 35. *Purchases and sales of livestock: some individual transactions*

No. and type of stock	Date of purchase	Average purchase price per beast (s. d.)	No. of days kept	Date of sale	Average sale price per beast (s. d.)	Gain in average price per beast (d.)	Average gain in price per day (d.)	By whom purchased and sold
2 steers	20 Oct. 1668	41. 8.	408	2 Dec. 1669	62. 3.	247	0.61	Lowther of Lowther (Westmor.)
2 steers	1 June 1669	55. 0.	184	2 Dec. 1669	68. 4.	160	0.87	
2 oxen	26 Jan. 1669	60. 0.	310	2 Dec. 1669	84. 9.	297	0.96	
2 oxen	27 May 1672	82. 6.	85	20 Aug. 1672	90. 0.	90	1.06	
6 oxen	1 June 1692	70. 0.	28	29 June 1692	76. 8.	80	2.86	Fleming of Rydal (Westmor.)
5 oxen	28 May 1692	66. 6.	102	7 Sept. 1692				
10 oxen	1 June 1692	55. 11½	98	7 Sept. 1692	59. 2.	91	1.23	
6 oxen	23 July 1692	57. 8.	46	7 Sept. 1692				
3 oxen	7 Sept. 1692	44. 5.	0	7 Sept. 1692				
11 cows	25 Mar. 1741	68. 2.	168	9 Sept. 1741	99. 10.	380	2.26	Cholmeley of Sutton upon Derwent (E. Riding of Yorks.)
2 cows	25 Mar. 1741	50. 0.	222	2 Nov. 1741	74. 6.	294	1.32	
2 oxen	25 Mar. 1741	121. 3.	222	2 Nov. 1741	189. 0.	813	3.66	
3 oxen	8 May 1741	90. 0.	173	28 Oct. 1741	132. 10	514	2.97	
2 oxen	8 May 1741	105. 0.	178	2 Nov. 1741	147. 6.	510	2.87	
2 oxen	20 May 1741	102. 6.	161	28 Oct. 1741	152. 0.	594	3.69	
2 oxen	26 June 1741	128. 0.	129	2 Nov. 1741	179. 9.	629	4.88	
56 Scots	30 Sept. 1741	47. 4.	213	1 May 1742	63. 5.	169	0.79	
20 sheep	7 Apr. 1741	8. 9.	100	16 July 1741	11. 0.	27	0.27	
8 sheep	7 Apr. 1741	8. 9.	135	20 Aug. 1741	8. 4½	−4½	−0.03	
36 sheep	29 Oct. 1741	8. 7.	184	1 May 1742	11. 0.	29	0.16	

out by a financial analysis of pastoral activity. For purposes of illustration, Table 36 envisages a mixed cattle-farming enterprise of 100 acres engaged in beef production, dairying, and rearing. Of the total farm area, 70 acres are allocated to pasture and 30 acres to meadow. In a comparatively fertile pastoral region, rents of 16s. and 24s. per acre respectively might have to be paid for the use of such lands, resulting, in the case of our model farm, in a total rent cost of almost £100, including maintenance and repair charges. In connection with this notional enterprise, bullocks are purchased in the spring at an average price of 86s. 6d. each, and, after fattening, are resold six months later at 147s. 6d. Heifers and young cows cost 61s. 6d. and after five years of bearing calves and providing milk are completely replaced, being sold at 74s. 6d. each. All calves are marketed in May or June at an average price of 15s. Bulls, which, in common with other stud animals, did not normally fetch high prices at this time, are purchased at 68s. 6d. and sold three years later at 57s. 6d. All of these prices are based upon transactions involving the south Devonshire estates of the Courtenay family in the 1730s and 40s.[133]

We have little of substance to guide us with respect to the number of stock which our 100 acres could maintain. Here, the key issue (assuming the enterprise to be self-supporting with regard to the provision of cattle fodder) is the stock-carrying capacity of the farm during the winter months. In this connection the prime determinant would be the supply of hay. If it is assumed that each of our 30 acres of meadow produces 1½ tons of hay, making a total of 900 cwt, this would permit a weekly ration of 1½ cwt to be fed to 30 beasts over a period of 20 weeks. In the context of our example, we may translate this into a dairy herd of 28 cows, plus 2 bulls. A more plentiful supply of feed during the remainder of the year, from the grazing of pasture and the aftermath of meadow, should make possible the maintenance of these beasts, their offspring, and 20 beef cattle. This would give an average stocking rate of 40–45 beasts over the year as a whole, which would be on the low side of present-day practice for a 100-acre farm in a moderately good grazing area – the modern farmer being better able to supplement the diet of his animals with concentrates and other purchased feedstuffs.[134]

If, in our example, haymaking expenditures are included, the costs of cattle forage amount to almost three-fifths of total outgoings. When allowance is also made for the purchase of feedstuffs for working animals – it being assumed that two horses are kept for general draught purposes – this proportion is exceeded. Our figures for interest and capital depreciation on

[133] Devon RO, 1,508M/V3, 7, 10, 16, 36. The Courtenay family estates were located at Powderham, Exminster, Kenton, Ford, Teignmouth, Moretonhampstead, N. Bovey, Whitchurch, S. Huish, Melborough, and Chivelstone. See also the accounts of the west-country estates of the dukes of Bedford, Devon RO, 1,258M/F26, 27.

[134] Somerset RO, Consistory Court Papers, D/D/C 1747; K. Dexter and D. Barber, *Farming for Profits*, London, 1961, pp. 74–6, 144, 170.

Table 36. Expenditures and output of notional cattle farm of 100 acres, c. 1730–50

Expenditures

	£ s. d.	Percentage distribution
Rent		
70 acres pasture @ 16s.	56. 0. 0.	32.0
30 acres meadow @ 24s.	36. 0. 0.	20.6
Farm maintenance & repairs	7.12. 6.	4.4
Subtotal	99.12. 6.	57.0
Cattle		
Interest & capital depreciation		
Cows	3. 4. 8.	1.9
Bulls	12. 4.	0.4
Bullocks	4.19. 9.	2.9
Miscellaneous (litter, medicaments)	2. 0. 0.	1.1
Subtotal	10.16. 9.	6.2
Horses		
Feed (grass, hay, oats)	10. 8. 0.	6.0
Interest & capital depreciation	1.17. 8.	1.1
Miscellaneous (litter, shoes, medicaments)	1. 0. 0.	0.6
Subtotal	13. 5. 8.	7.6
Equipment: interest & capital depreciation	3.11. 3.	2.0
Labour		
Cowherd's wages	18. 0. 0.	10.3
Haymaking 30 acres @ 4s. 6d.	6.15. 0.	3.9
Miscellaneous (e.g. carting, collecting dung, mole catching)	10. 0. 0.	5.7
Subtotal	34.15. 0.	19.9
Marketing and other	12.13. 8.	7.3
Total expenditures	174.14.10.	100.0

Output

	£ s. d.	Percentage distribution
Milk: 5,000 gal @ 6d.	125. 0. 0.	55.0
Calves: 25 @ 15s.	18.15. 0.	8.2
Gross profit on resale		
Cows, 28 @ 2s.6d.	3.10. 0.	1.5
Bullocks, 19 @ 61s.	57.19. 0.	25.5
Subtotal	61. 9. 0.	27.0
Manure	22. 5. 7.	9.8
Total output	227. 9. 7.	100.0
Net profit	52.14. 9.	23.2

horses, the cost of their feed, and other miscellaneous expenditures pertaining thereto are based on assumptions similar to those made in connection with our notional arable farm per Table 30. Likewise, in the calculation of interest foregone as a result of the investment in cattle, we have used the same compound rate ($3\frac{1}{2}$ per cent per annum) as previously. Further, our figure with respect to the cost of appliances and other farm equipment replicates that in Table 30, since there would appear to be little overall difference in this regard between a cattle undertaking and an arable enterprise. Our cattle farmer would probably have possessed one or two carts, some general agricultural implements, and various specialized utensils, notably, milking pails, sieves, butter churns, cheese tubs, and presses. Even in a large buttery the value of the latter items would not have exceeded a few pounds.

A more substantial charge, exceeded only by that of feed, was the cost of labour. Our cattle enterprise is assumed to provide full-time employment for the farmer and his family and one hired man. The latter we will suppose is paid a wage of £18 per year. In addition to the regular labour demands imposed by the routine of a dairy undertaking, there would also be a variety of occasional or seasonal tasks to be undertaken. The nature of some of these tasks is indicated in Table 36. On a pasture farm the largest requirement for casual labour during the period under review would normally be in connection with the mowing and gathering of hay. Variations in haymaking costs could result from differences in the local level of wage rates and the yield of grass. Our figure of 4s. 6d. per acre reflects average experience.[135] If the costs of haymaking are added to other labour charges we obtain a total wage bill of £34 15s., this approximating to 20 per cent of all farm expenditures.

With respect to the costs of marketing there is very little by way of hard data to guide us. Milk would be expensive to distribute in a liquid state even in a semi-urban locality, and the probability is that much of it would be converted into butter or cheese. So far as the expense of marketing livestock is concerned, drivers had to be hired, tolls paid, and feed provided *en route*. These expenses would tend to increase with the distance covered. An October 1748 entry in the Brandsby (North Riding) farming accounts of the Cholmeley family records driving expenses of £8 4s. in connection with the sale of 11 oxen at Smithfield, the price received being £63 7s. 3d. Much smaller charges would be incurred when local markets were frequented. Hence, the figure in our table assumes a maximum average marketing charge of 3 per cent on all purchases and sales.[136]

---

[135] For example, the cost of mowing and making hay on certain of the Courtenay family estates in 1744 is entered as £5 5s. 9d. for 28 acres (or 3.78s. per acre), while the "total expense" of haymaking at Beaminster (Dorset) and neighbouring parishes in 1737 is given as £24 3s. 1d. for 99 acres (or 4.88s. per acre). See Devon RO, 1,508M/V36; Dorset RO, D279.

[136] N. Riding RO, ZQG/Accounts; Cumb. RO, D/Lons/LA/2/66; Wilts. RO, 88/9/26.

Turning to the income side of the balance sheet, it emerges that milk accounts for more than one-half of the value of farm output. Our figure of £125 for the value of milk production assumes (in line with certain contemporary sources) that each fertile cow produces milk worth £5 per annum and that 3 of our dairy herd of 28 are barren. Assuming that milk is priced at 6d. per gallon (as paid by Westminster School at this time), this translates into an annual farm output of 5,000 gallons, or 200 gallons per milking cow. This, of course, compares very unfavourably with present-day milk yields of 700–1,000 gallons per year or more, and on very lush pastures, such as those of the fens, substantially better results would have been achieved. As already noted, approximately 10 per cent of our cows are (arbitrarily) assumed to be infertile; hence 25, rather than 28, calves are offered for sale. Receipts for this source (£18 15s.) are indicated as being only one-seventh of those from dairying.[137]

Of the £61 9s. added to the value of stock by fattening or otherwise, £3 10s. represents the annual capital appreciation on dairy animals since the time of purchase, while the remaining £57 19s. (amounting to approximately one-quarter of the total value of farm output) comprises the increase in the value of store cattle. Spread over a six-month period, the gain in value of 61s. per beast averages out at very slightly over 4d. per day (or 2s. 4d. per week), thus approximating some of the more profitable of Cholmeley's cattle-fattening ventures, as set out in Table 35. It will be noted that only 19 of the 20 bullocks acquired by our farmer are shown as being resold. This is because some allowance should be made for casualties resulting from accident or disease. We have assumed one casualty, in this case a bullock, although it could equally well have been a cow or calf. Casualties, however, were probably seldom a complete write-off, and we have assumed that the bullock's hide was sold for 17s., resulting in a loss of 69s. 6d. on an animal which originally cost 86s. 6d. This loss has been taken into account by including it on the expenditure side under the heading of interest and capital depreciation on cattle.[138]

The value of the manure produced by our farmer's livestock is impossible to determine with any pretence of precision. Our figure of £22 5s. 7d. assumes a 5:1 relationship between the value of feed input (appraising each acre of mown and made hay at 30s.) and the value of dung. On this basis the financial contribution of manure to the enterprise exceeds that of calves. This may seem an unlikely conclusion, but before dismissing it out of hand it is pertinent to note that the amount of manure thus estimated to be

[137] Devon RO, Consistory Court Papers, CC27/71, 104; CC44; CC50/98; Somerset RO, Consistory Court Papers, D/D/C 1739, 1747; Wilts. RO, 9: Savernake; Beveridge et al., Prices and Wages, I, pp. 168–9; Trow-Smith, History of British Livestock Husbandry, pp. 237–8; Kerridge, The Agricultural Revolution, pp. 328–9.
[138] Devon RO, 1,258 M/F27.

produced would seemingly be inadequate for the requirements of a 100-acre arable farm, such as that featured in Table 30, in which expenditures of £32 16s. 3d. on soil dressings are indicated. Put another way, the implication is that well over one-half of the acreage of the self-sufficient mixed farm enterprise would need to be devoted to the support of livestock in order to maintain the fertility of the arable land. Hence the need to supplement animal manure by other soil dressings; and hence the importance of the new grasses and root crops in permitting higher stocking rates and, in consequence, larger supplies of dung.

Turning to the overall position on our cattle farm, we find that total expenditures amount to £174 14s. 10d., while the value of output is £227 9s. 7d. The net profit of the undertaking is thus £52 14s. 9d., which averages 10.55s. per acre. This compares with the overall net profit of 9.38s. per acre which we calculated in connection with our notional arable enterprise (see Table 31). In neither case, of course, should these figures be regarded in any definitive sense.

Before leaving the subject of cattle farming, it may be instructive to make a comparative analysis of the profitability of the two main sectors of our model enterprise. The pertinent data are set out in Table 37. In this table the value of manure output has been rated in proportion to the estimated division of feed costs. The costs of forage, in turn, have been rated on the

Table 37. *Comparison of profitability of different branches of cattle farming*

	Dairying (£ s. d.)	Beef production (£ s. d.)
Output		
Milk	125. 0. 0.	
Calves	18. 15. 0.	
Capital appreciation on stock	3. 10. 0.	57. 19. 0.
Manure	17. 11. 2.	4. 14. 5.
Total	164. 16. 2.	62. 13. 5.
Costs		
Feed	72. 9. 11.	19. 10. 1.
Interest & capital depreciation on stock	3. 17. 0.	4. 19. 9.
Other	53. 0. 8.	20. 17. 5.
Total	129. 7. 7.	45. 7. 3.
Net profit		
Total	35. 8. 7.	17. 6. 2.
Per acre	9. 9½.	12. 7.
% of value of output	21. 5.	27. 6.

assumption that each cow–calf unit consumes, on average, 25 per cent more feed per day than a barren cow, bull, or bullock – the latter being counted for half a year only. All costs pertaining to bulls have been charged to the dairying side of the undertaking. "Other" (non-specific) costs have been apportioned on the basis of the relative contribution to output of the two sectors of the enterprise, and this criterion has also been used in determining the allocation of acreage. The result of this financial breakdown is to reveal beef production as the more profitable of our cattle farmer's ventures, yielding a net profit of 12s. 7d. per acre, compared with a corresponding figure of 9s. 9½d. for dairying. In this instance, therefore, there would seem to be a good *prima facie* case for a relative expansion in the fattening side of the business.[139] However, with a different set of assumptions (e.g. if one assumes a milk yield of, say, 500 gallons per cow) one might well arrive at the opposite conclusion.

Further, we have assumed in our model that the agricultural–economic environment is normal or average. But suppose that it is not. Suppose, for example, that due to abnormal weather conditions there are serious deficiencies in the supply of feed, as well as a general downturn in economic activity. Not only would this result in some shifts in the relative profitability of different sectors of livestock production, but it would also be likely to have a marked detrimental effect on the prosperity of the livestock industry as a whole. The latter point is illustrated in Table 38, in which we set out pertinent financial data with respect to a notional sheep farm of 100 acres. The data are gleaned primarily from certain Buckinghamshire and Northamptonshire estate accounts for the years 1740 and 1741,[140] which must surely rank among the most disastrous ever experienced by the British livestock industry.

The sheep-farming enterprise in our model will be seen to comprise 70 acres of pasture and 20 acres of meadow, with the remaining 10 acres used for the production of turnips. The land is envisaged as being of good quality, rents averaging out at rather more than 16s. per acre. In normal times, and with moderate inputs of purchased feed, such a farm should have been capable of maintaining a breeding flock of 300 ewes and 10 rams, plus their progeny for a six-month period, and a few draught animals. These make up the livestock population in our example. The ewes are assumed to cost an

---

[139] Such apparently was the conviction of John Wynne, one of the duke of Bedford's west-country agents, in 1744, when he notified his intention of buying more heifers and steers, "which at present are the cattle that turn out the best" – Devon RO, Bedford W1,258/LP1/1.

[140] These accounts pertain to the farming activities of the Chester family at Chicheley and Sherington, as well as at Lidlington, Beds. (Bucks. RO, D/C/2/35, 38); the Hampden family at Great Hampden, Little Hampden, Wendover, Great Kimble, and Monks Risborough (Bucks. RO, D/MH/33/1–3); Richard Temple Grenville, later Earl Temple, at Wotton (Reading Univ. Library, Farm Rec. Coll. BUC 11/1/5); and the Isham family at Lamport (Northants. RO, IL 3,945).

Table 38. *Effect of poor hay crop on profitability of notional sheep farm of 100 acres, c. 1740–1*

Expenditures

	£ s. d.	Percentage distribution
Rent		
70 acres pasture @ 14s.	49. 0. 0.	21.1
20 acres meadow @ 21s.	21. 0. 0.	9.1
10 acres arable @ 8s.	4. 0. 0.	1.7
Farm maintenance & repairs	7. 12. 6.	3.3
Subtotal	81. 12. 6.	35.2
Sheep		
Feed (purchased hay, etc.)	84. 6. 8.	36.4
Interest & capital depreciation	15. 9. 1.	6.7
Miscellaneous (pitch, ruddle, grease, veterinary)	1. 13. 1.	0.7
Subtotal	101. 8. 10.	43.8
Oxen		
Feed (purchased hay, etc.)	10. 8. 0.	4.5
Interest	19. 1.	0.4
Miscellaneous (litter, shoes, medicaments)	2. 0. 0.	0.8
Subtotal	13. 7. 1.	5.8

Output

	£ s. d.	Percentage distribution
Wool: 1,806 lb @ 5¼d.	39. 10. 2.	19.5
Lambs: 270 @ 9s.3d.	124. 17. 6.	61.5
Manure	38. 14. 11.	19.1

	£. s. d.	%
Equipment: interest & capital depreciation	3. 11. 3.	1.5
Turnip seed, 10 lb @ 4d.	3. 4. 0.	0.1
Manure	7. 15. 0.	3.3
Labour		
Shepherd's wages	5. 17. 0.	2.5
Shearing time	1. 18. 4.	0.8
Haymaking, 20 acres @ 3s. 6d.	3. 10. 0.	1.5
Turnip production (ploughing, hoeing)	4. 10. 0.	1.9
Miscellaneous (e.g. gelding lambs, carting, mole catching)	2. 0. 0.	0.9
Subtotal	17. 15. 4.	7.7
Marketing and other	6. 2. 4.	2.6
Total expenditures	231. 15. 8.	100.0
Total output	203. 2. 7.	100.0
Net loss	(28. 13. 1.)	(14.1)

average of 13s. 3d. each and to fetch 12s. apiece on resale three years later. The rams are kept for the same period of time, being bought for 15s. and resold for 12s. 6d. Ten per cent of the ewes are assumed to be infertile, while 3 per cent are designated as springtime casualties, their carcases fetching 3s. 3d. apiece. Hence, 270 lambs are produced and marketed each year, while 301 sheep (291 ewes and 10 rams) are shorn. Partly because of the ploughing requirements of arable agriculture, but also because a certain amount of carting would be needed, even on a sheep farm, our enterprise is credited with 4 oxen. These are assumed to cost an average of 127s. each, and to fetch exactly the same price when resold five years later. Interest forgone, and, where applicable, capital depreciation in relation to stock and farm equipment are calculated on the same basis as previously. The costs of equipment replicate those in Table 30, since while there are likely to be fewer aids to tillage than on a predominantly arable undertaking, various specialist items will be used in sheep farming, such as shears and – more important from a financial standpoint – hurdles for penning purposes. Isham's Lamport (Northants.) estate accounts for the 1730s and 1740s indicate the purchase of almost 1,000 hurdles "for the fold" or "to fence turnips", at prices generally ranging between 3s. 8d. and 8s. 2d. per dozen. Miscellaneous expenditures on materials for sheep were likely to include some small outlays on tar and grease for salve and ruddle for marking. We have arbitrarily estimated these costs at 0.5 per cent of the value of sheep purchases and lamb sales, obtaining thereby a figure of £1 13s. 1d. The cost of turnip seed is negligible, while labour costs (amounting in all to less than £18) constitute a much smaller proportion of total costs (7.7 per cent) than in the case of our other notional enterprises. The relatively low level of expenditure on wages primarily reflects the small regular requirement for hired labour. A sheep farm of 100 acres would be unlikely to require a full-time shepherd, and our figure of £5 17s. for a shepherd's wages is based upon the payments which Isham was making at this time for the shepherding of approximately the same acreage. At shearing time and during the lambing season additional helpers would be required, but the cost would not be great. At Lamport, labour costs incurred in connection with the washing, tagging, and shearing of sheep worked out at approximately 1½d. per head, while the piece rate for wool winding was 1d. for five fleeces. More substantial would be the payments made to labour for ploughing and hoeing the arable land, amounting in our example to £4. 10s. – i.e. more than one-quarter of the total wage bill.[141] Among other expenditures, the costs of marketing are likely to have been smaller than those incurred in connection with cattle farming, since the entire year's output of wool, unlike that of dairy products, would normally be disposed of in one transaction – often without moving from the farm – while sheep were seemingly less likely than cattle to be driven long distances to and from market. For these charges, therefore, we have

[141] Northants. RO, IL 3,945.

assumed a maximum outlay equivalent to 2 per cent of the value of all purchases and sales of sheep and wool.[142]

We have deliberately left to the end of this discussion of costs any reference to expenditures on feed (other than rent) or to manure. From the premise that the production of grass is seriously deficient, a number of things may be expected to follow. In the first place, given a low yield of grass, the costs of haymaking will predictably be less than usual. Thus, we have assumed our farmer's hay yield to drop from a norm of 30 cwt per acre to 15 cwt, and have assessed his haymaking costs on the basis of the comparatively low wage rate of 3s. 6d. per acre. Reflecting the shortage of hay, its price may be predicted to rise, possibly quite sharply. Our calculations, which will be explained shortly, assume a hay price of 2s. per cwt (approximately twice the norm), Richard Temple Grenville of Wotton (Bucks.) paying as much as 2s. 2d. per cwt in June of 1742. Agistment charges for grass and other forms of feed (e.g. oats and turnips) are also likely to rise. Hence, we value our farmer's turnip crop at 40s. per acre, whereas 30s. might represent more normal experience. Consequent upon the assumed poor condition of grazing land, the expectation is that stock will have to be foddered at an earlier date than usual. Thus, livestock farmers are likely to find themselves in the position not only of having to pay higher prices for purchased fodder, but also of having to do this over longer periods of time. In calculating the cost of purchased feed we have allowed for 26 weeks' rations at a weekly cost of 4d. per sheep (compared with the more usual 2½d. or 3d.) and 2s. per ox (compared with the more normal 1s. 4d. or 1s. 6d.). On this basis the total bill for winter feed (excluding natural pasture) amounts to £144 14s. 8d. Output of fodder crops by the farmer is valued at £50, comprising 300 cwt of hay at 2s. per cwt and 10 acres of turnips at 40s. per acre. Thus, there is a deficiency of £94 14s. 8d., which will have to be met through purchases of feed, unless – as will often be the case – a decision is made to carry less livestock. If stock numbers are, in fact, maintained, and if rent and fodder-crop production costs are included, it emerges that approximately three-quarters of the total costs in our example are concerned with the production or purchase of feed. In less difficult times, assuming an average yield of grass and hay priced at 1s. per cwt, the corresponding proportion would be approximately two-thirds.[143]

As in Table 36, we have used the cost of feed as a basis for determining the value of manure output on the farm. The value of manure production

[142] A March 1724 entry in the Chester family estate accounts indicates charges of 6s. in connection with the purchase of 61 sheep for £28 16s. at Northampton fair (Bucks. RO, D/C/2/35(ii)).

[143] Reading Univ. Library, Farm Rec. Coll. BUC 11/1/5; Bucks. RO, D/MH/33/1; Northants, RO, YZ997; Essex RO, D/DP/A57; Herts. RO, 63,795 and 18,104; Devon RO, 1,508M/V3; Somerset RO, DD/TB boxes 13, 14; Surrey Room, Minet Library, Knatchbull Rd, London SE5, Account Book of the Howard Estates at Ashstead and Epsom, 1693–1701; Surrey RO, 1/53/5.

is enhanced thereby. This would seem to be a reasonable conclusion, not only on account of the higher stipulated cost of feed input, but also because during periods of serious feed deficiency – as envisaged in our example – it is to be expected that the farm livestock population as a whole will undergo a sharp decline. As a further consequence, we should expect the presumed shortage and high price of dung to have an adverse effect on arable production during the subsequent period.

In Table 38 the value of manure produced on our model sheep farm is shown to approximate that of wool production. In more normal circumstances the value of the wool clip would be substantially greater. However, in 1740–1 demand for wool was at a very low ebb. Only 12s. per tod (of 28 lb) could be obtained for wool produced on the south-central Buckinghamshire estates of the Hampden family, while only a few pence more per tod was paid for the Grenville wool clip, grown nearby. In the early years of the seventeenth century Sir Thomas Temple of Stowe (Bucks.) had marketed several wool clips at a price of 28s. per tod (i.e. 1s. per lb), but fleeces then were considerably lighter and wool was finer. In 1740 the average weight of the fleeces produced by Grenville's sheep – being probably mainly wethers – was 7.8 lb. Our calculations assume an average fleece weight of 6 lb, since ewes were usually smaller and carried less wool than wethers. Lambs were not normally clipped, and we have, therefore, made no especial allowance for the value of their wool. Accordingly, assuming that wool is priced at 12s. 3d. per tod (or 5¼d. per lb), our farmer's wool clip should sell for £39 10s. 2d. This sum is less than one-third of that estimated to be derived from the sale of lambs (£124 17s. 6d.), thereby underlining what appears to have been a significant change in the general emphasis of sheep-farming activity, from wool growing to meat production, since earlier times.[144]

Turning to the overall financial position of our notional enterprise, we find that total expenditures amount to £231 15s. 8d., while the value of output comes to £203 2s. 7d. Hence, there is a net loss of £28 13s. 1d. This result, of course, has been predicated on the assumption of exceptionally disadvantageous circumstances – i.e. a severe shortage of feed and a depressed market for wool. With respect to the latter, the price of Buckinghamshire wool would need to reach £1 0s. 11d. per tod – a level not attained for many years – for the enterprise to break even. A more fundamental determinant of profitability, in the present instance, would be the cost of hay and other fodder crops. Thus, a plentiful supply of grass and a good harvest of hay could lower our farmer's feed bill by £70–80, leaving him with a net profit of £40–50.

In the context of our study period the contrasting situations illustrated above have very real significance. In spite of the technical and organizational

---

[144] Bucks. RO, D/MH/33/1; Reading Univ. Library, Farm Rec. Coll. BUC 11/1/5; above, p. 86; id., Wool Trade, pp. 30–3.

advances described elsewhere in this volume, the events of the early 1740s demonstrated with untoward harshness the vulnerability of agriculture to the capriciousness of nature, exposing its general inability to respond quickly or largely to contingent situations, and underlining the delicacy of the balance between comparative abundance and dearth. Among the lessons to emerge from the harrowing experiences of this period, the need for greater flexibility with respect to supplies of feed must have been one which few thinking agriculturalists could have failed to grasp. Clover, sainfoin, lucerne, trefoil, ryegrass, and turnips had been on the scene for many years, and their cultivation undoubtedly increased throughout our study period. But it is hardly fanciful to see in the mounting purchases of seed clover and grasses,[145] recorded in the extant farming account books of the 1740s, an enhanced recognition of the role which such crops might play in providing a cushion against the worst effects of climatic regression. The value of clover and the other legumes was not so much that they resulted in higher yields of hay than traditional meadow land – although there is some evidence that this was, indeed, the case[146] – as that, when worked into the arable rotation, some use could be made of otherwise bare fallow, while, since legumes fix their own nitrogen, their cultivation actually contributed to soil fertility.

H. CONCLUSIONS

In our consideration of the issue of profitability we have been able to touch upon only a limited range of farming situations. The variety of farm systems throughout the country was much greater than presented in our simplistic models, while many additional refinements could have been introduced into our examples in terms of scale of enterprise, organization of production, or market conditions. Among different types of farming activity, the rearing of pigs and poultry and the breeding of horses, for example, have received no mention, even though some of these animals would have been found on most farm undertakings. However, their presence, at least on the vast majority of holdings of more than a few acres, would seemingly have been dictated primarily by the need to provision the household, or to assist in the operation of the farm, rather than to provide a major or steady source of income. Comparatively few farming accounts of the period indicate sales of pigs, poultry, or eggs on other than a very incidental basis,[147] while prices

---

[145] See, for example, Dorset RO, D 10/E81, AE8; Devon RO, L1,258/F26; Herts. RO, 18,104; Bucks. RO, D/MH/33/8; D/W 61/64; Oxon. RO, J via 4, 5; GLCRO, E/BER/S/E/7/4/4, 6; Surrey RO, 60/5/508; 183/33/21; Cornwall RO, DDEN 1,190; DDBU 140. The price of clover seed at about this time was generally in the range 2½–5d. per lb.

[146] Cheshire RO, DAR/A/30/1; Hants. RO, 27 M54/3.

[147] A comparatively large number of references to sales of eggs and pigs occur in the Hughenden (Bucks.) estate accounts of the Way family in the mid 1740s, but even so, in the accounting year ending 17 Mar. 1747, the value of pigs and eggs sold amounted to only £16 14s. and 14s. respectively, out of total receipts of £371 3s. 7d. (Bucks. RO, D/W61/64).

received for horses suggest mainly sales of old animals rather than the fruits of breeding activity.

If the market-oriented pig breeders and poultry farmers were mostly men at the lower end of the scale of production, so also, by definition, were the subsistence cultivators, whose lack of resources, it may be supposed, led to a primary emphasis upon tillage. Specialization upon cattle or sheep required an initial outlay of £80–100 on stock and the possession of at least fifty acres of good pasture in order to provide a livelihood only moderately above the bare minimum. For the ordinary husbandman, with a more limited acreage, arable production or mixed farming was a more obvious choice. Compared with the situation on our notional arable enterprise of 100 acres, a much smaller proportion of the typical husbandman's expenditures would be on wages, since hired help would not normally be required. Proportionately less would probably be spent on soil dressings, especially in the case of open-field land trodden by the livestock of the village. A lower rent, reflecting differences in productivity, as well as tenurial rigidities, might also be exacted. Unlike the large cereal grower, the small cultivator would be adversely affected by a failure of the grain harvest; conversely, if he kept livestock he would suffer, like the substantial grazier, from any serious deficiencies in feed. In any event, whatever the catastrophe, economic survival would be rendered more difficult by meagre savings. For most of those farmers, great as well as small, who successfully weathered the economic stresses which periodically pulled at the traditional fabric of rural society, the rewards of agricultural endeavour were probably not so rich, nor so easily come by, as in the sixteenth century. But for those with an especial flair for farming, high profits were possible, given a fair share of good fortune, an enterprising disposition, and sound business acumen.

5

STATISTICAL APPENDIX, 1640–1750

AGRICULTURAL WEIGHTS AND MEASURES

The multitude of differing weights and measures used in the sale of agricultural produce in 1750 provides one of the most vivid reminders of how much more accurately England and Wales could be described as a chain of local and regional markets at this date than as one emerging national economy. Before any accurate analysis of regional price levels and trends can be undertaken, it is essential to understand the comparative value of different local measures, and to recognize the range of limitations presented by price entries in farm account books and similar documents of the period. These problems have attracted relatively little research in the past and this present essay must necessarily be of an exploratory nature.

Stated in a simplified form, price depends basically on quantity and quality. In the seventeenth and eighteenth centuries poor and costly transport meant that prices were also heavily dependent upon the local harvest: it was quite usual for two distant parts of the country producing grain of a similar quality to exhibit large differences in price levels as a result of contrasting harvest conditions. Too little is known, unfortunately, to say whether regional differences in farm labourers' wages and hence in costs of production also influenced agricultural prices to any significant extent. Insufficient attention is paid, moreover, to the fact that in any area at any given time there was not one price for a commodity but, instead, a wide range of prices according to quality. This range could be very large. In 1712 it was stated that "the price of potatoes when sold in Bristol market is from 8d. a bushel to 4s. a bushel according to their goodness".[1]

This essay will primarily be concerned with the subject of quantity, i.e. weights and measures, in agriculture, but some consideration will be given to quality. Apart from the problems of the comparative values of different local measures and the qualities of produce which different prices represent, it should be recognized that there are many other pitfalls in analysing the prices given for a stated quantity of produce in estate and farm accounts of the period. Some price entries, for example, may include a hidden charge for transport or even expenses in attending the market, whilst care must be exercised in distinguishing farm gate prices from market sales.

Measures varied extensively both between different regions of the country

[1] PRO, E 134, 11 Anne, Mich. 3.

308 APPENDIX I

and within a county. In the 1740s there were still substantial discrepancies between the measures of the adjoining counties of Devon and Dorset. An entry in an account book of the Weld estate at East Lulworth, Dorset, for 9 December 1742 records payment to " Mr Lille of Weymouth for three score quarters of oats which he bought in Devonshire", adding that "it proved only fifty quarters of our measure".[2] Perhaps the most significant point arising from this particular entry lies in its wording, since it suggests that even within the confines of the west country the local variations in measures were not widely appreciated.

A more general variance prevailed between the measures of the south-eastern counties on the one hand and those of the south-western and northern counties of England on the other. In these northern and western regions the measures were commonly two or three times larger than the Winchester bushel measure used in south-eastern counties. In Cumberland the most usual measure was equivalent to three Winchester bushels (i.e. 24 gallons); Carlisle and Cockermouth were two of the more important towns in the county employing this measure.[3] Variants of this measure, however, abounded. Even in Carlisle, rye, unlike the other grains, was sold by the different measure of 18 gallons to the bushel.[4] At Braithwaite in Cumberland oats and bigg were measured in bushels of 19 gallons in the late seventeenth century.[5] At the same date in the markets of Penrith in Cumberland and Appleby in Westmorland wheat, rye, and peas were sold in bushels of 16 gallons, and barley, bigg, malt, and oats in bushels of 20 gallons.[6] In the accounts of the Rydal estate, Westmorland, entries specify individual measures for Penrith, Kendal, and Staveley, and for Lancaster and Lancashire.[7] The differences among many of these local measures are unfortunately not known, but they were probably generally very small and in some cases possibly uncertain. The reliability of some of the local measures was definitely open to question in this period. Egremont in Cumberland was stated in 1702 to be "a great market town for corn, and that several country people reporting there are much abused in measuring their corne, there being no true measure there".[8]

In Northumberland, too, the most usual measure, especially in the seventeenth century, was three times larger than the Winchester standard, but again small local variations abounded, and different measures were distinguished for Morpeth, Hexham, Brampton, Alnwick, and Newcastle, amongst the more important markets in the county.[9] Accounts for an estate

[2] Dorset RO, D.10/AF.1.
    [3] CRO, DRC 1/4 (last page); Q.S. [box] 103: 1728 (formerly marked 102: 1727); J. Houghton, A Collection for Improvement of Husbandry and Trade, no. 47 (23 June 1693), p. 1.
    [4] CRO, DRC 1/4; DRC 2/48.   [5] PRO, E 134, 11 Wm III, Mich. 15.
    [6] Houghton, op. cit., no. 47 (23 June 1693), p. 1.
    [7] Westmor. RO, D/Ry: Account Books; CRO, D/S/20, 21.
    [8] CRO, Q.S. Q/6/1, p. 266.
    [9] Northumb. RO, ZSW 228/4; ZAL 44/11; Q.S.O.B., II, f. 135.

at Stonyhurst in Lancashire for the late seventeenth century further contain an entry which specifies "setle bushels" of oats: this measure refers to Settle in Yorkshire and presumably differed from the local bushel measure of the Stonyhurst area.[10] Any record of the precise relationship among the sizes of all these differing measures has apparently been lost.

In the west country, measures twice and three times as large as the Winchester standard were in common use. The double Winchester measure of 16 gallons was most common in Devon, and is recorded as being in use for barley both at Bridestowe in 1700 and in the Tavistock area in 1744.[11] Variations in the measure were frequent, both in different localities and for the different grains. In the Tavistock area at the same date a "Devon bushel" of oats was stated to contain $17\frac{1}{2}$ gallons, and a bag of oats 28 gallons.[12] In 1746, however, a bag of oats of Tavistock measure is specified as 31 gallons.[13] In Cornwall the bushel was most commonly measured as three Winchesters, and this particular measure was in use, for example, in the St Ive area near Liskeard in the 1740s.[14] Thorold Rogers gives the Falmouth bushel as containing 22 gallons and the Looe bushel 18 gallons in this period, but Houghton states that the Falmouth bushel for commodities other than coal measured 20 gallons or, "usually", 21 gallons.[15] At Poundstock, near the Devon border, a bushel of corn was regarded as containing 20 gallons in the 1660s.[16] Confusion with respect to measures was widely prevalent in the west country, and at the Somerset Assizes at Chard in 1656 it was recorded that "there is great complainte made unto this court of the unjustnes and inequallity of weights and of the measures both of corne and other commodities and not observinge the due assize of ale, bread and beere in the markett townes and other places in this county...whereby the poor people are much oppressed and other[wise] deceaved".[17] Houghton reported in 1692 that "all the mayors in Cornwal have been presented for permitting other bushells than by statute".[18]

Discrepancies among weights from market to market were also a constant complaint in several of the west Midlands counties. In 1656 a petition to the Worcestershire Sessions stated that the measures for corn, especially bushels and strikes, varied from one borough and market town to the next, and that they "doe differ soe farr that the husbandman knows not which measure

---

[10] Lancs. RO, DDSt: Accounts 1695–9.

[11] PRO, E 134, 12 Wm III, Trin. 8; Devon RO, L.1,258M./F.27.

[12] Devon RO, L.1,258M./F.27; W.1,258/LP1/1.

[13] Devon RO, W.1,258/LP1/3.   [14] Cornwall RO, DDR 5,299.

[15] J. E. Thorold Rogers, *A History of Agriculture and Prices in England from 1259 to 1793*, 7 vols., Oxford, 1866–1902, *VII*, pt 1, p. 3 [B2]; Houghton, *op. cit.*, no. 47 (23 June 1693), p. 1.

[16] PRO, E 134, 21 Chas II, Easter 6.

[17] J. S. Cockburn, ed., *Somerset Assize Orders, 1640–59*, Somerset Rec. Soc., LXXI, 1971, p. 46. See also p. 39 for a similar complaint placed before the Assizes at Taunton in 1651.

[18] Houghton, *op. cit.*, no. 2 (6 Apr. 1692), p. 2.

will serve".[19] In 1709 a petition of the Gloucestershire justices called for a standard measure of corn.[20] As late as the 1780s, the usual bushel measure in Shropshire contained a minimum 9 gallons or 36 quarts, and in market towns throughout the county the bushel varied from 36 to 40 quarts in measure.[21] A Warwickshire farm account records oats being sold at 9 strikes or bushels to the quarter in 1741.[22] Even within one town there were sometimes significant variations in the size of a measure. At Bridgnorth in Shropshire wool was still sold by a stone of 14 lb on the "Rye Land or Morse Side" of the town and by a stone of 12½ lb on the "Wheatland or Clee Hill Side" in the 1780s.[23]

The localized valuation of a measure used by name nationally was the paramount feature of marketing in this period. The proliferation of different measures resulted substantially from the failure of previous legislative attempts to abolish many of the old measures. Similarly, the continuing use of different multiples of sizes for one named measure is better understood if one consults early medieval descriptions of vehicles; the mode of conveyance adopted differed according to the state of a road or track, and this led inevitably to greater or lesser loads being carried in different parts of the country. This fact particularly accounts for the frequent discrepancies found in the size of the load measure across England in the seventeenth and eighteenth centuries: the load, of different sizes, was extensively used as a measure throughout the country and Rogers was incorrect in implying that its use had died out in northern England and that it remained only in southern counties.[24]

In south-east England, and particularly in Surrey, Essex, Berkshire, and Buckinghamshire, a load consisted of 5 quarters.[25] However, in the late seventeenth century at least, a load of only 5 bushels was also used in Buckinghamshire, and this smaller measure was the usual one for a load in Hertfordshire in the century before 1750.[26] Elsewhere in the country the load had other values. Farm account books record grain being measured in loads of 3 bushels in Nottinghamshire in the 1650s and in Cumbria in the 1660s.[27] According to Houghton, a load of 4 bushels was used for wheat, rye, and peas, and a load of 5 bushels for barley and bigg in both Appleby,

---

[19] Worcs. RO, Quarter Sessions 110: 1656 (2) Epiph./11 B.A.1.

[20] Glos. RO, D214/B 10/4.   [21] Salop. RO, QS F4/490–7.

[22] War. RO, CR.233.   [23] Salop. RO, QS F4/497.

[24] Rogers, op. cit., VI, p. 4; VII, 1, pp. 3–4.

[25] GMR, L.M. 1,087/2/5, 12, 13, 16; Essex RO, D/DBe A.1; D/DM A.20; Berks. RO, D/EPb/E.13; D/EWe/A.3; Bucks. RO, D/W bundle 61/vol. 64; D/MH/33/1.

[26] Bucks. RO, D/C/2/35(ii), 36(iii), Uthwatt: General Estate Account Books nos. 3–6 (uncatalogued collection in 1971); Herts. RO, 40,689; Houghton, op. cit., no. 47 (23 June 1693), p. 1.

[27] Reading Univ. Library: Farm Records Collection, NOT 5/1/1; CRO, D/Lons/L/A1/5: entries for Feb./Mar. 1667.

Westmorland, and Penrith, Cumberland, in the late seventeenth century, whereas at Wakefield in Yorkshire wheat, rye, peas, and beans were sold in loads of 3 bushels, and barley, malt, and oats in loads of 4 bushels at the same date. Houghton also mentions a load of 6 bushels being used for malt in Derbyshire at this time.[28] The 4-bushel load was widely used in county Durham in the eighteenth century.[29] A load of 7½ bushels was in use in Staffordshire in the mid eighteenth century for barley and probably for other grains too.[30] The 7½-bushel load was used for oats in the Kendal area of Westmorland in the early nineteenth century, and it seems likely therefore that this particular size of load was to be found in many other areas of the north in the eighteenth century.[31]

The bag was another measure that varied in size from one part of the country to another. In Staffordshire a bag of wheat contained 3 Winchester bushels, whilst in Shropshire it measured 3 bushels of 9 gallons.[32] The Staffordshire bag of oats, however, contained 6 standard bushels, which measure also apparently applied to malt in the county.[33] In south-west England the measure varied with respect to both grain and apples. In Devon, at Lympstone in 1689 a bag of apples contained 2 bushels of unstated size, whilst at Down St Mary in 1695 a bag of apples was stated to contain 24 gallons.[34] In Devon as a whole, the bag was most usually a measure of 3 Winchester bushels for grains and apples alike. In the St Germans area of Cornwall, though, in the early eighteenth century apples were sold by measure of a bag which contained 16 or 17 and sometimes 18 gallons, which bag measure was the equivalent of the local bushel.[35]

Apart from the large regional variations in the bushel measure already mentioned, there were several other minor discrepancies in bushel sizes among markets, particularly in central southern England, and some irregular bushel measures in a few localities. At Kingston upon Thames the bushel contained 8½ gallons, at Farnham, Reading, and High Wycombe 8¾ gallons and at Abingdon, Newbury, and Andover 9 gallons. At Dorchester a bushel of 10 gallons was used for oats and malt, whilst all other grains were measured by the standard Winchester bushel of 8 gallons. At Stamford a 16-gallon bushel was used, whilst at Chester giant bushels of 32 gallons for wheat and rye and 40 gallons for oats were employed.[36]

In some parts of the country, primarily regional terms of measure were

---

[28] Houghton, *op. cit.*, no. 39 (28 Apr. 1693), p. 1; no. 47 (23 June 1693), p. 1.
[29] Co. Durham RO, D/SA/E 167–72.
[30] Staffs. RO, D590/616: entry for 8 Oct. 1750.
[31] F. W. Garnett, *Westmorland Agriculture, 1800–1900*, London, 1912, p. 108.
[32] Staffs. RO, D590/616: entry for 4 May 1748; Salop. RO, QS F4/494.
[33] Staffs. RO, D593/F/3/2/1–25.
[34] PRO, E 134, 1 Wm & M., Mich. 8; 6 Wm & M., Trin. 5.
[35] *Ibid.*, 5 Geo. I, Hil. 1; 11 Geo. I, Hil. 4.
[36] Houghton, *op. cit.*, no. 47 (23 June 1693), p. 1.

in use. In East Anglia the coomb, equivalent to 4 Winchester bushels, was commonly used. In many other areas of England the sack was used as a measure containing 4 standard bushels; St Albans, where a sack contained 5 bushels, appears to have been one of the very few market towns in the country where the uniformity of the sack measure was not adhered to.[37] The last was also most frequently used as a measure in East Anglia: it generally contained 10 quarters, but at Norwich and King's Lynn, in the late seventeenth century at least, it apparently measured 10½ quarters.[38] The seam, equivalent to 1 quarter, was another measure that was particularly widely used in eastern England. In the west Midlands and parts of northern England the bushel was more usually referred to as a strike or, in a few instances, simply as a measure. In Northumberland and county Durham the boll or bowl, a measure of Scottish origin, was in common use in the seventeenth and eighteenth centuries: in the north of Northumberland the old, or Scottish, boll containing 6 standard bushels survived longest, but elsewhere in the county, as also in county Durham, the new boll of 2 Winchester bushels was most frequently used by 1750. In Lancashire the windle was an important measure, most commonly containing 3½ bushels, but subject to numerous local variations in size.[39]

Changes in the size and value of certain terms of measure during the period 1640–1750 add a further dimension to the confusion of measures in use. Very little is known about the circumstances of these changes, but they appear to date from the two decades after the Restoration, and to have represented an attempt to bring provincial measures into line with the Winchester standard used almost universally in south-east England at this date. The changes were only a partial success, and in many areas of England the old measure remained in use at the middle of the eighteenth century and later alongside the new measure of the same name but of different value. In certain estate accounts used in this volume it is not always clear whether transactions are recorded in units of old or new measure. In the Somerset parish of Swell in the 1670s, old and new measure bushels, more generally referred to locally as 'great' and 'small' measure respectively, were used in selling grain, and it was stated that a great measure bushel contained 5 pecks of Winchester measure.[40] In 1737 old measure bushels were still used in Glastonbury market in Somerset: in this case 3 Winchester bushels were apparently the equivalent of 2 of the old measure bushels used in the Glastonbury area.[41] In the accounts of the Willoughby family for their Payhembury estate in south-east Devon, references to both old and new measures for wheat and malt appear in entries

[37] *Ibid.*, no. 20 (15 June 1692), p. 2; no. 47 (23 June 1693), p. 1.

[38] *Ibid.*, no. 47 (23 June 1693), p. 1.

[39] Lancs. RO, DDSt: Accounts, 1703–4: entry for 24 Dec. 1703. Houghton, *op. cit.*, no. 47 (23 June 1693), p. 1, gives the windle as containing 12 gal in Manchester and 26 gal in Lancaster and markets to the north of Lancaster.

[40] PRO, E 134, 31 Chas II, Mich. 26.   [41] Somerset RO, DD/SAS, C/1,193.

covering the years 1679–82: although not specifically stated, 3 old measure bushels would appear to be the equivalent of 4 of the new bushels, but it is not clear whether the latter are Winchester measure, though they appear to be.[42]

In the north of England, several Northumberland farm accounts record entries in old and new measures between 1675 and 1750, and it is clear that in many parts of the county the use of the old measures had declined little by the mid eighteenth century. The old boll of 6 standard bushels remained in considerable use alongside the new boll of 2 bushels at this date, and in some areas old and new bushel measures were also employed.[43] In county Durham the accounts of Salvin of Croxdale include an entry specifying a "new bowl" of malt in 1711.[44] Accounts for the Temple Newsam estate in Yorkshire contain numerous entries for both old and new loads of oatmeal in the period 1694–7, and an entry for 3 "old measure" quarters of malt in 1672.[45] The accounts for the Ingilby estate at Ripley, Yorkshire, contain further entries specifying old measure bushels and quarters of malt in the years 1702, 1703, and 1710.[46] In Cumbria, the old bushel of 3 Winchesters was still widely used alongside the new measure in the first half of the eighteenth century.[47]

In those areas of the country where a conversion to Winchester measure was introduced in the seventeenth century, it was intended that the latter should replace an assortment of traditional measures of widely differing values. However, it is less clear whether the Winchester measures introduced in replacement actually signified a common standard of size throughout the country at this date. It is recorded, for example, that the Northumberland Quarter Sessions considered a request in 1684 to have the "towne" and "country" Winchester bushel made equal in the county.[48] It is not impossible that similar small discrepancies in Winchester measure existed between one part of the country and another in this period.

Wool and dairy products, too, were subject to an array of differing local measures. At St Mewan in Cornwall wool was measured at 18 ounces to the pound in the 1740s.[49] The usual weights were the stone of 14 lb and the tod of 28 lb. But wool was sold off Spindleston farm, near Bamburgh, Northumberland, at the measure of 18 lb to the stone in the 1670s, which particular measure was also used for wool in Newcastle market in the 1690s.[50]

---

[42] For a statute to enforce the use of Winchester measures for corn and salt, see 22 Chas II, c. 8, 1670, and for an amending act (because that of 1670 was being evaded), see 22 & 23 Chas II, c. 12, 1670/1 – *Statutes of the Realm*, v, pp. 662. 722. Somerset RO, DD/WO box 53.

[43] See e.g. Northumb. RO, ZSI/1–4; ZSW/240–4 and 344; ZAL/44/13; ZAL/60–2.

[44] Co. Durham RO, D/SA/E 167: entry for 6 Sept. 1711.

[45] Sheepscar Branch Library, Leeds: Archives Dept. TN/EA/12/1, 12.

[46] *Ibid.*, Ingilby 1,811, 1,814.   [47] CRO, D/Lons/A/A/2/32; D/Lec/289–90.

[48] Northumb. RO, Q.S.O.B. vol. 1, pp. 189, 203.   [49] PRO, E 134, 22 Geo. II, Hil. 1.

[50] Northumb. RO, ZSI/1; Houghton, *op. cit.*, no. 2 (6 Apr. 1692), p. 2.

Wool was sold at Pembroke at 17 lb to the stone and at King's Lynn at 14 lb
in the 1690s and in Cumbria at 16 lb per stone in the 1690s and 1740s.[51]
In Warwickshire wool was being sold at both 28 and 30 lb to the tod in the
1740s, and as late as the 1780s wool was being sold in Shropshire at 12 lb
to the stone in Bishop's Castle and at 12½ lb in Ludlow and some districts
of Bridgnorth.[52] Meat was sold in most parts of the country by the butcher's
stone of 8 lb, used to weigh meat after slaughter, and to accord with the
loss from a 14-lb stone between live and dead weight.[53] At St Ive near
Liskeard in Cornwall, a pound of 18 ounces was used locally in selling mutton
in the 1740s.[54] At Derby a pound of butter contained 18 ounces in the 1690s,
and in many Shropshire markets butter was sold at 18 ounces per lb and 12 lb
per stone as late as 1790.[55]

Various other local measuring customs and irregularities operated in
certain parts of the country. A Warwickshire farm account records oats being
sold at 22 strike to the score in 1741, and wool was sold off the Courtenay
estate at Powderham in Devon at a measure of 21 lb to the score in the
1730s.[56] On the Cholmeley estate at Brandsby in Yorkshire, labourers were
paid for peeling bark per bushel at the rate of 9 gallons to the bushel in 1750.[57]
Such a payment and those paid per hundredweight of bark "ripped" on the
Dunster Castle estate in Somerset in the 1740s are very difficult to compare
with the wages paid for peeling bark per yard on the Drake estate in the
Amersham area of Buckinghamshire in the 1690s, or per fathom of 6 feet
in east Suffolk in the eighteenth century.[58]

In some instances produce was sold by a heaped measure. More serious,
and perhaps more frequent, was the problem of short measures, particularly
in times of scarcity.[59] Moreover, a discrepancy frequently appeared between
the measures adhered to in the public markets and those given at the farm
gate. In an account of the measures still current in the Shropshire market
town of Ludlow in the 1780s it was stated that "the customary measure of
all sorts of grain is 9 gallons to the bushel" with the added note that "the

[51] Houghton, *op. cit.*, no. 2 (6 Apr. 1692), p. 2; no. 47 (23 June 1693), p. 1; CRO,
D/Lons/L/A2/66–81: entry for 20 Dec. 1740.
[52] War. RO, CR. 233: entries for 28 June 1741 and 13 Sept. 1743; Salop. RO, QS F4/490,
492, 497.
[53] See e.g. Herts. RO, 70,474 A: entry for 27 Jan. 1602.
[54] Cornwall RO, DDR 5,299.
[55] Houghton, *op. cit.*, no. 47 (23 June 1693), p. 1; Salop. RO, QS F4/492, 494–6.
[56] War. RO, CR. 233: entry for 8 July 1741; Devon RO, 1,508M/v.7: entry for 10 Nov. 1732.
[57] Yorks. N.R. RO, ZQG: Francis Cholmeley – Voucher no. 25. See also Voucher no. 8 in
this series, which records payment for "chopping" bark per ton in the 1740s.
[58] Somerset RO, DD/L 1/5/16; Bucks. RO, D/DR/2/89; E. Suffolk RO, E.1/11/2.
[59] E. Suffolk RO, 105/2/1, f. 136v, records a complaint to Quarter Sessions by the inhabitants
of Woodbridge against the bakers there making bread under weight in the high-price years of
the late 1640s.

farmers generally sell 9 gallons and a half".[60] A petition of the inhabitants of the Devon market town of Okehampton in the 1730s stated that

"for about ten years last past, there hath been a great abatement in the revenue arising from the said markets and fairs [in Okehampton], by reason of a great number of spinning-houses being set up in the neighbourhood, whereby the dealers in wool set out certain quantities thereof to the poor for spinning, at a very low price; and, instead of setting out 16 ounces, generally allot such poor people 18 or 20 ounces to the pound, which is never brought to any publick market".[61]

Hops were one commodity for which short-weight selling appears to have been a real and persistent problem in the early eighteenth century, the discrepancy usually being deliberately masked by their sale in excessively heavy bags or sacks. After two meetings at the Crown Tavern in London in March 1748, brewers and hop merchants in the City passed a resolution that the weight of a hop bag should not exceed 16 lb, and that a fine or 'allowance' would thereafter be payable for any bag exceeding that weight. This decision was reached after the meetings had been informed that "of late years" consumers had suffered "great injury" and "imposition" by the substantial increases in the weight of hop bags, these frequently having been as heavy as 32 lb.[62] The prices of hops, too, show particularly marked fluctuations from year to year, and cannot satisfactorily be analysed unless the year of growth and also the growing region of the hops are stated. To a lesser extent this qualitative information, too often lacking, is necessary for the analysis of series of malt prices: Newcastle, Yorkshire, Derby, and Nottinghamshire malt all represented different qualities, commanded different prices in any given year, and were in most cases marketed over wide areas of England.

Increasing market demand for improved quality-related pricing and the thorny problem of local customary measures combined to promote a movement towards selling by weight instead of by capacity in some areas of the country, although the evidence suggests that this had not been carried very far by 1750, in comparison with the quite substantial changes made in this direction in the succeeding seventy years. In many areas, too, such a change was of a partial nature, the practice being adopted of selling some grains by capacity and others by weight. The provision accounts for the Petre estate in Essex show that, while wheat, peas, and oatmeal were purchased by measure, barley was bought by weight in the years 1690–4.[63]

In the early eighteenth century the Navy Board, concerned to guarantee a minimum quality for the lower-priced tenders that it accepted for the provision of wheat at the ports, was stipulating a given weight per measure

[60] Salop. RO, QS F4/492.   [61] CJ, xxii, 1732–7, p. 805.
[62] Kentish Post, no. 3,170, 23 Mar. 1748; no. 3,172, 30 Mar. 1748.
[63] Essex RO, D/DP A.48.

(i.e. quarter) of grain offered. In 1717 and 1718 tenders of wheat for Dover
and London were accepted with the specification that the wheat had to weigh
either 58 or 60 lb per bushel.[64]

Where weight was used instead of measure for the sale of grain it was
not employed in isolation from measure: sale by weight actually entails sale
by measure but with a fixed weight per measure. Whereas measure alone
is little more than a crude test of quantity, weight and measure together
provide a better account of quantity combined with an indication of quality,
and hence of the real value of the corn sold.[65]

Fixed weight-per-measure sales, however, should more accurately be seen
as a step towards narrowing regional and local variations in measures in the
eighteenth century rather than eliminating them, since marketing by weight
introduced new problems which were not widely appreciated at the time.
By specifying that a quarter should weigh a certain fixed number of pounds,
it meant that the actual quantity sold would automatically vary according
to the heavier or lighter weight of the particular grain in question. Thus,
weight was not an absolute standard but was instead a function of the
goodness of the growing season and of the type and grade of grain and of
the locality in which it was grown. In his evidence before the Select
Committee on the Sale of Corn in 1834, Sir Patrick Stead, a corn merchant
and maltster of Yarmouth, illustrated this vital point when he stated that in
bad seasons wheat weighed 3 to 5 lb lighter than in good seasons, and that,
taking just one interregional comparison, Scottish wheat was not so valuable
as Norfolk wheat of the same weight.[66] Houghton, too, had recognized the
differing weights of grain from different areas: in May 1692 he had reported
in his newspaper that "a bushel of good wheat" weighed 66 to 68 lb at
Newbury and 60 to 63 lb at Dorchester.[67]

On the basis of facts such as these, the Select Committee of 1834 in its
report concluded that fixed weight-per-measure selling, whilst an improvement upon sale by measure alone, and a more accurate indicator of quantity,
was not an adequate guide to quality, and to remedy this it suggested
combined weight-and-measure selling which also embodied a description of
the actual weight of the corn per given measure in each transaction.[68] The
wisdom of such advice was clearly not being widely heeded at the time, yet
it had been recognized over a century earlier by the Navy Board. A general
tender for wheat in June 1717 had prompted the board to report that there
had appeared to be "a great difference in ye samples, Mr. Gascoigne's [who

[64] PRO, ADM 111/15.
[65] See *Select Committee on Sale of Corn, 1834*, BPP, 1834, *VII*, Q.1676–86, evidence of Mr
C. T. Dunlevie.
[66] *Ibid.*, Q.737, 742.
[67] Houghton, *op. cit.*, no. 10 (11 May 1692), p. 2. In issue no. 8 (4 May 1692), p. 2, the same
bushel is described as being of new measure.
[68] *Select Committee on Sale of Corn, 1834*, *VII*.

offered the cheapest wheat at 30s. 6d. per quarter on the second call, against the dearest tender of 34s.] being Yorkshire wheat, and much inferior to ye others", and the board concluded that it would be "for ye advantage of ye service to buy only Kentish or other wheat of equall goodness which will come up to 60 pound ye bushel".[69]

It has been the purpose of this essay to indicate some of the salient variations in measures across the country and to draw attention to some of the problems of both a quantitative and qualitative nature influencing weights and measures and hence prices in this period. No attempt has been made to provide a complete catalogue of known measures, and, doubtless, in the present state of research on this subject, much necessarily remains unsaid. Much printed information on weights and measures appears in the county agricultural surveys and amidst the Parliamentary Papers for the period 1790–1835, but it would be a gross inaccuracy to assume that a similar pattern of measures applied equally a century earlier. In those hundred years many of the old, and the smaller, local measures had died out and surviving measures had assumed a wider, more regional significance. Further research on the pre-1750 period will almost certainly unearth an even denser assortment of localized measure variations in some parts of the country than has been shown to exist in this paper, and re-emphasize the primarily local nature of agricultural marketing in this period.

[69] PRO, ADM 111/15: entry for 5 June 1717.

Land measures, like measures of agricultural produce, presented important variations across the country. In England and Wales as a whole, a wide range of local customary measures were collectively more significant than statutory measure even as late as 1750. Unfortunately, the sizes of relatively few of these historic local measures are now known with exactitude. All that can be done here is to draw attention to the scale of the differences.[1]

In parts of northern England customary measures with a country-wide validity commonly prevailed in the seventeenth and eighteenth centuries. The Cheshire acre, universally used in Cheshire in this period, represented about 2½ statute acres: 10,240 square yards represented an acre, against 4,840 square yards statute.[2] The Lancashire acre represented almost 2 statute acres, 651 Lancashire acres being the equivalent of 1,210 statute acres.[3] In south-west England, on the other hand, numerous local measures were used rather than one 'county measure'. In south-east Somerset a series of customary acre measures, approximately four-fifths to five-sixths of the statute acre, persisted into the early nineteenth century.[4] In parts of Devon a double measure, sometimes termed 'wood measure', existed, by which each (square) yard of the local acre contained eighteen feet.[5] A survey of the Milton Abbot estate in west Devon in 1726 used a measure of eighteen feet to the pole or perch instead of the statutory 16½ feet.[6] By contrast, the statute pole was the normal measure of the Moor Crichel area of east Dorset in the mid seventeenth century.[7]

---

[1] For different acres, see I. H. Adams, *Agrarian Landscape Terms: A Glossary for Historical Geography*, London, 1976, p. 2.

[2] H. Holland, *General View of the Agriculture of Cheshire*, London, 1808, p. 342; J. Holt, *General View of the Agriculture of the County of Lancaster*, London, 1795, p. 125. UCNWL, Baron Hill 335, and Cheshire RO, DDX 267, also record the use of the Cheshire acre in the county in 1648 and 1658 respectively.

[3] T. Woodcock, *Haslingden: A Topographical History*, Chetham Soc., 3rd ser., IV, 1952, p. 8. I am indebted to Dr David Hey for the references in respect of the Cheshire and Lancashire measures.

[4] M. Williams, 'The 1801 Crop Returns for Somerset', *Somerset Arch. & Nat. Hist. Soc.*, CXIII, 1968–9, p. 71.

[5] PRO, E 134, 12 Wm III, Trin. 8.

[6] Devon RO, T 1,258 M/E48 b.   [7] PRO, E 134, 1656, Mich. 5.

A. Price indices of agricultural commodities: national annual averages

1640–1749 = 100

Table XVII. Price indices of field crops

Harvest year	Grains					Other field crops						Average – all field crops
	Wheat	Barley & malt	Oats	Rye	Average – all grains	Beans	Peas	Hops	Hay	Straw	Average – all other field crops	
1640	106	109	86	115	104	122	98	79	—	—	100	102
1641	104	99	87	109	100	81	109	103	83	85	92	96
1642	111	98	103	109	105	85	103	151	104	75	104	105
1643	95	84	85	104	92	83	67	135	—	66	88	90
1644	97	88	106	62	88	107	105	70	79	93	91	90
1645	98	91	102	—	97	—	97	51	83	75	77	87
1646	140	108	147	—	132	137	95	65	—	79	94	113
1647	175	140	148	230	173	112	149	84	—	—	115	144
1648	176	144	147	196	166	98	188	89	113	—	122	144
1649	158	146	136	214	164	117	170	137	69	—	123	144
1650	132	106	108	139	121	134	118	52	75	—	95	108
1651	123	104	120	124	118	—	146	83	—	—	115	117
1652	89	101	135	109	109	—	125	68	99	—	97	102
1653	70	70	90	56	72	—	111	93	106	—	103	88
1654	57	63	71	47	60	—	79	122	69	85	89	75
1655	96	96	94	101	97	—	114	118	89	—	107	102
1656	109	106	119	121	114	141	145	174	78	—	135	125
1657	120	112	102	131	116	120	101	75	82	—	95	106
1658	138	114	118	120	123	128	124	104	90	—	112	118
1659	130	125	123	—	126	130	112	62	81	—	96	111
1660	122	108	94	115	110	91	110	69	79	86	87	99
1661	174	145	140	195	164	99	142	57	77	—	94	129
1662	123	121	107	124	119	110	97	67	81	83	88	104

Year												
1663	109	95	97	103	101	112	86	79	68	—	86	94
1664	92	82	88	99	90	64	72	81	124	81	84	87
1665	87	89	105	92	93	83	93	158	86	172	118	106
1666	72	73	88	61	74	128	83	64	72	89	87	81
1667	76	80	88	61	76	117	77	71	68	—	83	80
1668	89	91	88	91	90	71	75	62	75	—	71	81
1669	92	95	94	92	93	88	98	62	86	75	82	88
1670	97	86	99	110	98	106	106	62	68	75	83	91
1671	90	78	90	115	93	85	84	67	95	73	81	87
1672	87	83	86	—	85	78	84	114	86	108	94	90
1673	132	119	99	142	123	124	101	81	86	102	99	111
1674	129	132	124	155	135	184	137	97	84	97	120	128
1675	90	96	98	93	94	125	99	117	80	75	99	97
1676	86	80	99	75	85	99	84	72	103	86	89	87
1677	102	104	99	112	104	125	91	56	80	81	87	96
1678	110	81	82	92	91	78	88	57	102	81	81	86
1679	95	85	81	79	85	97	93	42	80	81	79	82
1680	100	87	102	98	97	97	92	74	86	86	87	92
1681	99	105	109	111	106	123	106	79	140	106	111	109
1682	92	111	102	99	101	131	97	92	86	89	99	100
1683	88	96	94	101	95	88	102	84	86	97	91	93
1684	103	107	115	131	114	160	121	108	131	154	135	125
1685	78	88	106	83	89	116	119	118	149	150	130	110
1686	92	97	86	105	95	93	92	150	88	95	104	100
1687	70	83	92	62	77	95	76	156	105	92	105	91
1688	66	73	83	70	73	90	69	76	—	77	78	76
1689	82	67	79	77	76	82	74	44	131	98	86	81
1690	76	66	72	77	73	87	73	43	112	98	83	78
1691	93	77	94	87	88	84	81	37	105	102	82	85
1692	120	94	112	121	112	97	110	89	101	103	100	106

Table XVII. (cont.)

Harvest year	Grains					Other field crops						
	Wheat	Barley & malt	Oats	Rye	Average – all grains	Beans	Peas	Hops	Hay	Straw	Average – all other field crops	Average – all field crops
1693	144	124	107	140	129	94	108	65	92	103	92	111
1694	91	83	93	86	88	89	90	112	108	79	96	92
1695	127	104	114	98	111	112	108	138	119	87	113	112
1696	128	114	98	107	112	106	114	163	113	77	115	114
1697	152	119	106	143	130	109	93	198	119	93	122	126
1698	149	142	125	147	141	122	122	198	124	118	137	139
1699	115	124	117	115	118	111	117	103	114	119	114	116
1700	85	94	97	88	91	95	95	76	114	89	94	93
1701	74	89	78	74	79	76	94	52	123	95	88	84
1702	68	75	75	62	70	70	79	90	137	95	94	82
1703	87	92	84	101	91	71	87	69	75	97	80	86
1704	77	80	83	74	79	70	78	96	75	100	84	82
1705	65	91	94	69	80	90	100	131	92	107	104	92
1706	66	87	74	62	72	92	75	94	112	94	93	83
1707	82	102	101	70	89	111	92	88	149	121	112	101
1708	134	114	108	124	120	108	106	95	82	86	95	108
1709	172	129	111	152	141	129	147	108	75	100	112	127
1710	115	127	104	113	115	117	120	143	82	102	113	114
1711	110	106	95	127	110	99	106	82	82	97	93	102
1712	94	90	92	83	90	81	94	90	82	97	89	90
1713	122	105	104	130	115	100	101	128	101	129	112	114
1714	86	117	109	96	102	115	110	187	131	91	127	115
1715	98	102	93	82	94	115	98	129	103	91	107	101
1716	?6	??	??	??	??	??	?-	???	--	--	--	??

Year												
1717	88	88	95	76	87	82	89	110	84	91	91	89
1718	78	97	97	80	88	80	97	165	93	108	109	99
1719	87	118	121	92	105	118	118	116	149	134	127	116
1720	87	114	100	82	96	84	92	87	120	129	102	99
1721	82	87	88	70	82	76	79	68	78	86	77	80
1722	87	82	94	76	85	79	96	82	78	86	84	85
1723	82	109	119	88	100	99	123	96	112	113	109	105
1724	91	107	101	89	97	98	98	109	112	113	106	102
1725	113	107	95	100	104	96	109	184	106	99	119	112
1726	99	109	89	90	97	82	100	78	106	148	103	100
1727	129	140	116	115	125	97	116	71	94	116	99	112
1728	129	144	141	118	133	109	125	71	95	116	103	118
1729	87	110	97	86	95	111	96	63	95	108	96	96
1730	77	89	83	74	81	84	82	87	111	134	94	88
1731	67	95	88	69	80	87	87	158	136	97	120	100
1732	67	85	85	68	76	74	79	184	111	97	109	93
1733	79	87	91	72	82	75	86	132	90	97	96	89
1734	95	91	98	93	94	77	82	125	90	97	94	94
1735	101	99	107	87	99	84	87	118	90	97	95	97
1736	93	109	95	87	96	89	107	154	94	97	108	102
1737	82	105	104	83	94	100	114	112	110	129	113	104
1738	81	94	89	72	84	74	83	73	110	113	91	88
1739	109	114	102	106	108	78	100	81	101	129	98	103
1740	132	129	125	123	127	119	126	87	157	151	128	128
1741	90	118	107	84	100	109	110	68	157	113	111	106
1742	68	105	93	70	84	93	89	74	157	113	105	95
1743	60	79	78	62	70	67	66	84	112	102	86	78
1744	66	79	90	70	76	72	71	132	118	118	102	89
1745	86	78	85	72	80	71	73	173	98	129	109	95
1746	84	81	79	78	81	69	78	110	89	140	97	89
1747	80	86	74	81	80	78	72	112	90	129	96	88
1748	85	97	104	81	92	80	80	108	86	129	97	95
1749	81	89	98	81	87	83	80	136	131	129	112	100

Table XVIII. Prices indices of sheep

Harvest year	Breeding sheep					Other sheep			Average – all sheep
	Type unspecified	Wethers	Ewes	Ewes & lambs	Average – all breeding sheep	Tups	Lambs	Average – all other sheep	
1640	85	72	116	62	89	—	106	106	88
1641	87	86	67	—	67	—	—	—	80
1642	71	59	113	—	113	—	66	66	77
1643	85	97	97	—	97	—	50	50	82
1644	88	95	133	—	133	—	—	—	105
1645	120	114	—	—	—	—	117	117	117
1646	110	151	49	149	99	—	112	112	119
1647	—	105	101	—	101	—	129	129	106
1648	104	99	79	103	91	73	118	96	106
1649	—	96	119	—	119	—	124	124	104
1650	—	100	—	—	—	—	—	—	124
1651	106	—	—	—	—	—	—	—	103
1652	94	123	—	—	—	—	55	55	91
1653	136	—	—	—	—	—	—	—	136
1654	131	113	—	—	—	—	—	—	122
1655	98	—	79	—	79	—	81	81	86
1656	119	117	105	—	105	88	86	87	104
1657	91	—	—	—	—	—	75	75	94
1658	70	—	—	—	—	—	81	81	76
1659	—	—	—	—	—	—	114	114	114
1660	84	89	151	146	149	—	—	—	107
1661	93	85	105	—	105	105	96	101	96
1662	98	67	—	—	—	—	97	97	87

Year									
1663	80	—	—	—	—	—	—	69	91
1664	115	132	—	132	178	—	178	71	78
1665	116	111	53	168	178	—	178	89	87
1666	69	66	—	66	50	—	50	56	102
1667	115	124	124	—	140	—	140	117	78
1668	119	153	153	—	112	—	112	95	116
1669	109	103	103	—	72	—	72	122	138
1670	93	113	113	—	74	—	74	100	84
1671	122	101	101	—	218	—	218	87	80
1672	84	79	79	—	83	72	94	79	94
1673	107	88	88	77	117	102	131	124	97
1674	82	75	73	—	—	—	—	83	88
1675	88	74	74	—	—	—	—	96	94
1676	90	88	88	—	70	42	70	91	110
1677	82	66	66	—	62	—	81	108	90
1678	86	48	48	—	—	45	—	109	100
1679	87	119	119	126	45	—	—	101	84
1680	101	105	84	142	96	—	96	90	111
1681	113	124	106	107	133	—	133	89	107
1682	116	99	91	—	—	82	—	125	124
1683	105	99	99	115	84	—	86	110	127
1684	127	119	123	174	—	—	—	138	124
1685	96	112	49	119	87	—	87	84	102
1686	88	119	—	134	53	69	53	79	99
1687	92	106	78	92	57	—	57	93	110
1688	92	92	91	88	107	—	107	74	96
1689	74	80	71	159	57	—	45	78	79
1690	76	114	69	98	67	—	67	60	61
1691	88	98	—	137	96	—	96	77	81
1692	104	137	—	66	84	—	84	111	82
1693	100	72	78	—	83	75	90	113	130

Table XVIII. (cont.)

Harvest year	Type unspecified	Breeding sheep				Other sheep			Average – all sheep
		Wethers	Ewes	Ewes & lambs	Average – all breeding sheep	Tups	Lambs	Average – all other sheep	
1694	113	119	109	—	109	123	119	121	116
1695	100	101	88	—	88	82	—	82	93
1696	85	128	87	83	85	93	131	112	103
1697	131	105	129	87	108	116	104	110	114
1698	106	98	111	105	108	—	135	135	112
1699	109	123	123	104	114	102	93	98	111
1700	104	63	99	—	99	61	65	63	82
1701	103	104	86	—	86	—	142	142	109
1702	92	102	97	—	97	—	119	119	103
1703	129	119	96	99	98	98	68	83	107
1704	88	111	89	108	99	—	93	93	98
1705	90	131	81	110	96	86	104	95	103
1706	102	101	96	113	105	66	100	83	98
1707	98	94	100	60	80	107	118	113	96
1708	111	67	79	66	73	120	93	107	90
1709	87	115	89	89	89	—	125	125	104
1710	92	115	87	66	77	—	111	111	99
1711	99	108	85	83	84	119	94	107	100
1712	117	105	94	92	93	85	115	100	104
1713	104	92	99	93	96	206	118	162	114
1714	106	78	86	—	86	85	95	90	90
1715	102	95	98	119	109	—	109	109	104
1716	104	97	104	118	111	87	113	100	103
1717	121	107	102	106	104	—	106	106	110

Year									
1718	99	93	101	111	106	93	104	99	99
1719	85	80	103	108	106	73	106	90	90
1720	97	104	95	82	89	126	115	121	103
1721	111	121	125	87	106	57	107	82	105
1722	78	82	100	124	112	—	103	103	94
1723	93	113	77	103	90	135	85	110	102
1724	99	95	111	115	113	61	93	77	96
1725	91	78	86	106	96	—	113	113	95
1726	100	103	101	111	106	91	—	91	100
1727	91	96	92	127	110	87	136	112	102
1728	84	109	95	133	114	87	123	105	103
1729	102	108	96	113	105	—	86	86	100
1730	120	79	102	—	102	—	88	88	97
1731	167	98	109	104	107	46	102	74	112
1732	117	132	108	64	86	40	100	70	101
1733	94	91	92	114	103	78	90	84	93
1734	86	96	116	110	113	241	141	191	122
1735	94	75	98	108	103	—	109	109	95
1736	98	109	94	110	102	—	149	149	115
1737	97	99	104	112	108	—	94	94	100
1738	98	89	88	117	103	132	97	115	101
1739	96	123	76	116	96	138	80	109	106
1740	94	116	112	110	111	—	101	101	106
1741	105	143	129	118	129	124	106	115	123
1742	110	123	108	135	113	88	—	88	109
1743	114	88	119	104	127	114	73	94	106
1744	112	99	120	103	112	125	112	119	111
1745	102	95	106	116	105	—	117	117	105
1746	81	96	121	114	119	84	126	105	100
1747	94	102	96	85	105	135	116	126	107
1748	89	107	99	109	92	112	115	114	101
1749	99	112	100	109	105	120	121	121	109

Table XIX. *Price indices of cattle*

Harvest year	Beef cattle				Dairy & breeding cattle				Other cattle			Average – all cattle
	Oxen	Bullocks	Runts	Average – all beef cattle	Cows	Heifers	Cows/heifers & calves	Average – all dairy & breeding cattle	Bulls	Calves	Average – all other cattle	
1640	80	88	—	88	71	86	78	78	111	—	111	89
1641	85	81	—	81	72	82	84	79	108	53	81	82
1642	128	131	115	123	86	105	86	92	58	—	58	100
1643	80	77	84	81	—	108	—	108	—	—	—	90
1644	160	—	—	—	96	103	—	100	—	—	—	130
1645	135	93	95	94	80	90	111	94	183	—	183	127
1646	101	117	124	121	108	90	118	105	103	65	84	103
1647	95	112	101	107	130	106	94	110	132	—	132	111
1648	98	118	—	118	103	106	95	101	141	158	150	117
1649	109	139	—	139	107	106	—	107	144	—	144	125
1650	118	96	156	126	127	112	110	116	77	—	77	109
1651	83	138	—	138	80	133	83	99	95	81	88	102
1652	78	49	—	49	120	72	—	96	100	—	100	81
1653	79	93	76	93	65	46	—	56	73	124	99	82
1654	76	56	82	66	76	89	—	83	108	—	108	83
1655	80	92	76	87	94	59	—	77	93	77	85	82
1656	88	108	76	92	101	36	—	69	99	—	99	87
1657	92	115	81	98	124	94	119	112	92	—	92	99
1658	110	73	71	72	118	178	—	148	—	—	—	110
1659	107	113	—	113	110	111	93	105	—	—	—	108
1660	140	81	80	81	78	115	—	97	62	—	62	95
1661	125	112	83	98	113	117	94	108	62	85	74	101
1662	100	118	—	118	107	92	103	101	107	85	96	104
1663	106	152	74	113	105	—	91	98	67	160	114	108

1664	107	127	127	—	96	123	62	102	111	—	111	92
1665	88	83	83	—	78	—	65	91	85	—	85	104
1666	70	73	53	92	79	92	58	87	64	52	75	64
1667	80	92	76	107	69	—	72	65	95	65	125	64
1668	111	—	—	—	94	102	88	91	120	133	107	120
1669	88	88	93	83	84	95	79	79	84	90	77	94
1670	88	68	51	85	102	88	121	96	97	78	116	86
1671	88	95	115	75	82	93	82	71	86	85	86	88
1672	100	94	58	129	106	—	97	115	124	—	124	74
1673	106	81	66	96	96	107	100	82	168	—	168	77
1674	107	118	132	103	108	127	106	92	108	116	99	93
1675	111	100	104	95	118	120	134	99	142	151	132	84
1676	101	84	73	94	103	105	103	102	110	87	133	105
1677	106	83	65	100	105	114	97	103	128	141	115	107
1678	108	104	61	146	106	99	—	112	122	92	151	99
1679	87	84	81	86	98	99	99	96	89	—	89	78
1680	96	87	—	87	96	74	130	85	100	111	89	102
1681	100	88	81	95	90	92	92	85	83	95	70	138
1682	94	82	74	90	103	94	121	95	86	—	86	80
1683	96	106	94	118	87	104	87	71	110	102	117	82
1684	87	93	82	103	88	94	—	81	84	—	84	83
1685	93	87	—	87	88	103	69	92	112	104	120	84
1686	80	92	—	92	81	116	52	74	78	77	79	67
1687	85	92	—	92	73	90	54	74	96	96	96	79
1688	75	81	—	81	74	80	—	67	91	97	84	53
1689	86	94	114	73	79	65	73	98	89	—	89	83
1690	79	93	107	78	66	—	56	76	84	—	84	71
1691	91	94	—	94	73	86	50	83	119	136	102	77
1692	95	102	94	110	101	—	98	103	83	90	76	94
1693	116	104	100	108	112	121	123	92	119	—	119	127
1694	113	139	175	102	94	83	96	104	119	139	98	101
1695	133	154	139	168	134	—	132	135	124	104	144	121
1696	128	114	102	126	120	120	111	128	124	141	106	154

Table XIX. (*cont.*)

Harvest year	Beef cattle				Dairy & breeding cattle				Other cattle			Average – all cattle
	Oxen	Bullocks	Runts	Average – all beef cattle	Cows	Heifers	Cows/heifers & calves	Average – all dairy & breeding cattle	Bulls	Calves	Average – all other cattle	
1697	114	102	90	96	112	104	81	99	114	96	105	104
1698	104	78	92	85	106	116	103	108	100	162	131	107
1699	97	84	97	91	128	102	121	117	90	115	103	102
1700	105	—	55	55	98	100	105	101	99	167	133	99
1701	121	125	—	125	104	139	95	113	90	155	123	121
1702	96	107	130	119	103	120	125	116	115	98	107	110
1703	104	89	166	128	119	126	94	113	160	97	129	119
1704	91	97	120	109	87	—	—	87	92	63	78	91
1705	115	56	130	93	82	116	—	99	86	114	100	102
1706	138	64	150	154	92	86	131	103	130	118	124	130
1707	75	63	89	76	86	61	—	74	—	97	97	81
1708	88	173	115	144	96	112	—	104	100	89	95	108
1709	121	112	108	110	99	144	98	114	88	122	105	113
1710	115	77	130	104	93	93	85	90	102	95	99	102
1711	107	96	92	94	104	94	77	92	112	85	99	98
1712	77	—	100	100	103	100	93	99	90	135	113	97
1713	92	67	111	89	106	109	116	110	66	119	93	96
1714	99	52	—	52	107	81	103	97	95	133	114	91
1715	103	104	64	84	102	120	108	110	125	160	143	110
1716	117	91	—	91	119	94	99	104	117	116	117	107
1717	144	88	—	88	116	128	93	112	111	121	116	115
1718	105	104	—	104	106	86	119	104	96	134	115	107
1719	104	106	89	98	107	90	74	90	99	111	105	99

1720	106	101	90	112	98	78	109	107	106	121	91	119
1721	89	90	121	58	103	103	94	112	75	—	75	—
1722	108	98	100	96	104	94	107	111	95	—	95	133
1723	100	108	110	105	93	81	99	99	100	107	92	99
1724	98	97	107	86	101	100	107	96	94	82	105	99
1725	109	97	87	107	121	113	135	115	103	104	102	116
1726	119	123	141	105	114	118	123	100	120	121	119	119
1727	97	90	85	95	109	96	120	111	104	110	98	86
1728	113	92	114	69	136	118	154	135	96	86	105	126
1729	102	105	109	100	110	108	111	110	89	79	98	104
1730	106	104	127	81	108	111	94	119	110	105	114	100
1731	106	91	100	81	110	113	135	82	115	135	94	108
1732	93	93	91	94	97	98	103	91	94	97	91	89
1733	102	96	106	85	127	154	116	111	83	81	84	101
1734	81	78	71	85	88	81	90	94	79	68	89	78
1735	85	78	71	84	98	98	89	106	68	70	66	94
1736	82	80	91	69	88	81	87	97	79	70	87	80
1737	98	103	91	114	107	94	114	112	86	80	91	96
1738	104	87	72	102	117	130	101	120	98	87	108	114
1739	104	91	93	88	93	65	100	113	120	105	134	111
1740	116	120	118	121	120	—	129	111	104	108	99	120
1741	109	104	94	113	119	138	100	118	106	81	131	108
1742	104	92	94	90	110	107	94	129	116	112	120	98
1743	108	105	105	—	115	110	124	112	93	89	96	120
1744	89	91	92	89	95	85	94	106	85	82	87	84
1745	100	115	86	144	93	76	110	93	102	100	104	91
1746	97	94	86	102	97	88	95	107	94	95	92	102
1747	101	106	90	121	112	101	130	104	98	96	99	87
1748	100	110	102	117	94	90	87	105	101	89	113	95
1749	109	109	109	108	102	80	116	110	124	153	95	100

Table XX. *Price indices of livestock*

Harvest year	Sheep	Cattle	Horses	Pigs	Poultry	Average – all livestock
1640	88	89	58	48	—	71
1641	80	82	59	48	—	67
1642	77	100	53	48	—	70
1643	82	90	80	48	—	75
1644	105	130	75	48	—	90
1645	117	127	83	48	—	94
1646	119	103	85	48	—	89
1647	106	111	78	—	—	98
1648	106	117	81	—	—	101
1649	104	125	103	64	—	99
1650	124	109	100	—	—	111
1651	103	102	90	56	—	88
1652	91	81	90	48	—	78
1653	136	82	83	—	—	100
1654	122	83	90	—	—	98
1655	86	82	101	—	—	90
1656	104	87	69	—	—	87
1657	94	99	64	81	—	85
1658	76	110	127	58	—	93
1659	114	108	68	—	—	97
1660	107	95	100	—	—	101
1661	96	101	88	81	—	92
1662	87	104	100	99	—	98
1663	80	108	99	80	—	92
1664	115	107	109	67	—	100
1665	116	88	82	84	—	93
1666	69	70	101	63	—	76
1667	115	80	71	103	—	92
1668	119	111	102	66	—	100
1669	109	88	76	73	88	87
1670	93	88	94	80	88	89
1671	122	88	104	83	87	97
1672	84	100	75	86	87	86
1673	107	106	109	85	88	99
1674	82	107	103	88	87	93
1675	88	111	127	90	87	101
1676	90	101	103	87	87	94
1677	82	106	117	90	87	96
1678	86	108	117	88	87	97
1679	87	87	91	93	87	89
1680	101	96	81	95	87	92
1681	113	100	115	79	87	99
1682	116	94	64	101	87	92

Table XX. (*cont.*)

Harvest year	Sheep	Cattle	Horses	Pigs	Poultry	Average – all livestock
1683	105	96	147	98	87	107
1684	127	87	92	100	96	100
1685	96	93	153	108	96	109
1686	88	80	80	91	93	86
1687	92	85	173	98	93	108
1688	92	75	87	105	93	90
1689	74	86	121	101	94	95
1690	76	79	79	112	94	88
1691	88	91	224	110	94	121
1692	104	95	71	94	101	93
1693	100	116	101	108	101	105
1694	116	113	172	129	101	126
1695	93	133	94	126	101	109
1696	103	128	129	117	101	116
1697	114	104	104	105	101	106
1698	112	107	109	96	101	105
1699	111	102	134	135	101	117
1700	82	99	73	138	101	99
1701	109	121	114	124	101	114
1702	103	110	143	119	83	112
1703	107	119	112	154	93	117
1704	98	91	126	—	95	103
1705	103	102	171	124	95	119
1706	98	130	83	120	96	105
1707	96	81	89	134	96	99
1708	90	108	62	164	100	105
1709	104	113	104	107	110	108
1710	99	102	91	150	110	110
1711	100	98	124	98	110	106
1712	104	97	85	98	110	99
1713	114	96	97	175	95	115
1714	90	91	92	124	106	101
1715	104	110	95	118	107	107
1716	103	107	120	111	107	110
1717	110	115	130	107	107	114
1718	99	107	103	123	105	107
1719	90	99	101	120	107	103
1720	103	106	117	111	107	109
1721	105	89	98	100	107	100
1722	94	108	80	153	107	108
1723	102	100	90	102	107	100
1724	96	98	83	119	107	101
1725	95	109	101	92	107	101

Table XX. (*cont.*)

Harvest year	Sheep	Cattle	Horses	Pigs	Poultry	Average – all livestock
1726	100	119	98	98	114	106
1727	102	97	108	111	110	106
1728	103	113	122	113	110	112
1729	100	102	109	124	110	109
1730	97	106	102	111	110	105
1731	112	106	64	106	110	100
1732	101	93	67	132	110	101
1733	93	102	105	89	110	100
1734	122	81	116	107	111	107
1735	95	85	122	100	104	101
1736	115	82	107	145	106	111
1737	100	98	90	161	106	111
1738	101	104	116	143	106	114
1739	106	104	133	148	106	119
1740	106	116	92	68	115	99
1741	123	109	86	128	115	112
1742	109	104	89	148	115	113
1743	106	108	110	134	115	115
1744	111	89	90	101	115	101
1745	105	100	95	112	115	105
1746	100	97	84	139	115	107
1747	107	101	78	129	115	106
1748	101	100	107	131	115	111
1749	109	109	93	124	115	110

	Sheep products			Cattle products								
Harvest year	Wool	Mutton	Average – all sheep products	Milk	Butter	Cheese	Average – all dairy products	Beef	Average – all cattle products	Pork	Eggs	Average – all animal products
1640	—	92	92	—	98	—	98	97	98	—	—	95
1641	156	—	156	—	96	109	103	98	101	—	—	129
1642	—	—	—	—	99	113	106	103	105	97	—	101
1643	—	—	—	—	103	101	102	96	99	88	—	94
1644	—	—	—	—	106	95	101	88	95	—	—	95
1645	—	—	—	—	106	82	94	99	97	93	—	95
1646	—	92	92	—	—	—	—	110	110	134	—	112
1647	—	92	92	—	145	239	192	127	160	100	—	117
1648	—	92	92	—	145	209	177	138	158	100	—	117
1649	—	128	128	—	175	239	207	135	171	107	—	135
1650	144	138	141	—	145	209	177	87	132	—	—	137
1651	132	130	131	—	—	—	—	88	88	—	—	110
1652	94	115	105	—	97	89	93	97	95	—	—	100
1653	—	107	107	—	92	88	90	88	89	—	—	98
1654	—	100	100	—	—	—	—	85	85	66	—	84
1655	99	100	100	—	—	—	—	85	85	66	—	84
1656	101	100	101	—	110	110	110	94	102	67	—	90
1657	102	112	107	—	—	105	105	89	97	100	—	102
1658	95	108	102	—	123	117	120	103	112	—	—	107
1659	84	110	98	90	99	100	96	108	102	123	—	108
1660	119	110	115	123	97	104	108	97	102	118	—	112
1661	111	104	108	90	97	100	94	103	103	111	—	106
1662	134	104	119	112	92	105	103	103	103	97	—	106
1663	112	109	111	90	90	105	95	105	103	117	—	109
1664	89	115	102	112	100	90	101	100	101	93	—	99

Table XXI. (cont.)

Harvest year	Sheep products				Cattle products								Average – all animal products
	Wool	Mutton	Average – all sheep products	Milk	Butter	Cheese	Average – all dairy products	Beef	Average – all cattle products	Pork	Eggs		
1665	—	106	106	112	97	98	102	104	103	105	—		105
1666	—	111	111	112	83	—	98	101	100	105	—		105
1667	89	112	101	—	100	104	102	98	100	—	—		101
1668	155	106	131	—	97	83	90	92	91	94	84		111
1669	93	109	101	122	91	—	107	97	102	94	84		95
1670	—	103	103	117	96	93	102	93	98	94	84		95
1671	167	103	135	112	104	97	104	97	101	94	84		104
1672	96	98	97	112	96	98	102	92	97	94	84		93
1673	82	108	95	112	103	121	112	96	104	94	84		94
1674	86	103	95	112	99	109	107	99	103	94	84		94
1675	73	105	89	—	83	—	83	96	90	84	—		88
1676	144	105	125	—	94	83	89	94	92	94	—		104
1677	59	105	82	—	91	86	89	96	93	98	—		91
1678	—	103	103	—	99	91	95	97	96	94	—		98
1679	78	103	91	—	94	81	88	96	92	96	—		93
1680	112	103	108	—	91	81	86	91	89	94	—		97
1681	92	103	98	—	91	86	89	89	89	93	—		93
1682	—	105	105	—	91	87	89	93	91	94	—		97
1683	—	109	109	—	87	94	91	88	90	93	—		97
1684	90	115	103	—	105	106	106	100	103	102	84		98
1685	—	110	110	112	86	96	98	89	94	103	98		101
1686	—	101	101	112	92	89	98	90	94	93	98		97
1687	67	100	84	112	93	77	94	89	92	88	98		91
1688	—	100	100	112	98	95	102	91	97	86	98		95

Year												
1690	87	73	97	97	97	97	100	95	112	88	96	80
1691	95	98	94	99	92	105	109	95	112	90	97	82
1692	95	98	95	95	88	101	94	97	112	100	106	94
1693	99	94	99	102	98	106	105	101	112	102	107	97
1694	111	110	122	108	107	109	111	106	112	109	115	103
1695	116	124	122	109	108	109	110	104	112	114	113	115
1696	112	104	120	111	113	109	109	105	—	105	100	110
1697	100	82	106	107	106	107	109	104	—	114	106	121
1698	113	—	116	110	106	113	116	110	112	110	106	114
1699	116	126	120	108	106	110	115	104	112	104	102	105
1700	113	126	120	100	98	101	94	98	112	106	103	108
1701	110	110	121	103	106	99	86	100	112	107	104	109
1702	110	107	120	106	108	104	98	103	90	95	94	95
1703	98	97	102	99	105	93	91	98	93	101	93	109
1704	98	102	96	94	97	91	90	90	90	89	89	—
1705	94	99	94	92	98	85	79	85	90	93	88	98
1706	100	105	99	101	107	94	89	102	90	82	84	79
1707	93	105	95	91	96	86	75	92	90	82	89	74
1708	93	105	96	90	95	84	77	86	90	76	89	63
1709	95	102	108	94	98	90	87	94	90	82	93	71
1710	103	102	127	100	105	95	97	97	90	81	99	62
1711	120	105	166	128	138	117	128	133	90	98	98	—
1712	104	105	113	98	103	93	93	96	90	86	92	79
1713	97	102	103	96	101	90	87	93	90	87	86	88
1714	94	92	101	94	102	85	83	83	86	88	94	81
1715	96	106	99	92	102	81	79	75	90	87	94	80
1716	99	114	99	94	100	88	87	87	92	94	101	87
1717	101	111	106	94	103	85	84	86	98	103	99	106
1718	105	115	108	95	102	87	83	87	98	107	95	119
1719	102	111	97	94	100	88	85	87	98	96	95	97
1720	102	113	99	99	107	90	87	86	98	94	94	93
1721	106	109	119	100	106	94	93	90	98	83	93	73
1722	99	109	106	98	103	92	89	89	98	87	91	83
1723	97	109	96	94	97	90	85	87	100	84	93	75

337

Table XXI. (cont.)

Harvest year	Sheep products			Cattle products								Average – all animal products
	Wool	Mutton	Average – all sheep products	Milk	Butter	Cheese	Average – all dairy products	Beef	Average – all cattle products	Pork	Eggs	
1724	64	94	79	98	89	89	92	98	95	99	106	95
1725	74	98	86	98	95	89	94	102	98	117	106	102
1726	71	96	84	98	97	91	95	102	99	104	106	98
1727	71	102	87	97	94	89	93	98	96	106	106	99
1728	82	102	92	98	101	97	99	103	101	106	106	101
1729	72	103	88	97	102	95	98	106	102	118	109	104
1730	88	101	95	91	101	88	93	100	97	104	109	101
1731	81	94	88	91	97	88	92	99	96	91	109	96
1732	85	89	87	91	93	82	89	94	92	85	109	93
1733	83	85	84	91	93	83	89	93	91	84	109	92
1734	80	84	82	91	94	77	87	90	89	86	109	92
1735	65	90	78	91	94	78	88	90	89	87	109	91
1736	68	89	79	91	98	84	91	93	92	89	111	93
1737	62	90	76	91	96	83	90	88	89	89	106	90
1738	60	89	75	91	95	87	91	93	92	93	102	91
1739	60	94	77	91	104	89	95	103	99	92	102	93
1740	59	100	80	91	115	104	103	117	110	111	104	101
1741	62	97	80	96	118	107	107	115	111	122	118	108
1742	75	96	86	91	106	89	95	113	104	106	100	99
1743	80	92	86	88	100	82	90	106	98	97	104	96
1744	86	91	89	86	100	77	88	99	94	83	104	93
1745	82	92	87	88	106	85	93	102	98	89	104	95
1746	78	90	84	91	112	88	97	104	101	88	104	94
1747	78	93	86	97	109	95	100	108	104	96	114	100
1748	85	92	89	88	111	91	97	102	100	98	114	100
1749	84	85	85	91	112	89	97	99	98	94	114	98

Table XXII. *Price indices of all agricultural products*

Harvest year	Grains	Other field crops	Livestock	Animal products	Average – all agricultural products
1640	104	100	71	95	93
1641	100	92	67	129	97
1642	105	104	70	101	95
1643	92	88	75	94	87
1644	88	91	90	95	91
1645	97	77	94	95	91
1646	132	94	89	112	107
1647	173	115	98	117	126
1648	166	122	101	117	127
1649	164	123	99	135	130
1650	121	95	111	137	116
1651	118	115	88	110	108
1652	109	97	78	100	96
1653	72	103	100	98	93
1654	60	89	98	84	83
1655	97	107	90	84	95
1656	114	135	87	90	107
1657	116	95	85	102	100
1658	123	112	93	107	109
1659	126	96	97	108	107
1660	110	87	101	112	103
1661	164	94	92	106	114
1662	119	88	98	106	103
1663	101	86	92	109	97
1664	90	84	100	99	93
1665	93	118	93	105	102
1666	74	87	76	105	86
1667	76	83	92	101	88
1668	90	71	100	111	93
1669	93	82	87	95	89
1670	98	83	89	95	91
1671	93	81	97	104	94
1672	85	94	86	93	90
1673	123	99	99	94	104
1674	135	120	93	94	111
1675	94	99	101	88	96
1676	85	89	94	104	93
1677	104	87	96	91	95
1678	91	81	97	98	92
1679	85	79	89	93	87
1680	97	87	92	97	93

Table XXII. (*cont.*)

Harvest year	Grains	Other field crops	Livestock	Animal products	Average – all agri-cultural products
1681	106	111	99	93	102
1682	101	99	92	97	97
1683	95	91	107	97	98
1684	114	135	100	98	112
1685	89	130	109	101	107
1686	95	104	86	97	96
1687	77	105	108	91	95
1688	73	78	90	95	84
1689	76	86	95	87	86
1690	73	83	88	95	85
1691	88	82	121	95	97
1692	112	100	93	99	101
1693	129	92	105	111	109
1694	88	96	126	116	107
1695	111	113	109	112	111
1696	112	115	116	100	111
1697	130	122	106	113	118
1698	141	137	105	116	125
1699	118	114	117	113	116
1700	91	94	99	110	99
1701	79	88	114	110	98
1702	70	94	112	98	94
1703	91	80	117	98	97
1704	79	84	103	94	90
1705	80	104	119	100	101
1706	72	93	105	93	91
1707	89	112	99	93	98
1708	120	95	105	95	104
1709	141	112	108	103	116
1710	115	113	110	120	115
1711	110	93	106	104	103
1712	90	89	99	97	94
1713	115	112	115	94	109
1714	102	127	101	96	107
1715	94	107	107	99	102
1716	87	111	110	101	102
1717	87	91	114	105	99
1718	88	109	107	102	102
1719	105	127	103	102	109
1720	96	102	109	106	103
1721	82	77	100	99	90

Table XXII. (cont.)

Harvest year	Grains	Other field crops	Livestock	Animal products	Average — all agricultural products
1722	85	84	108	97	94
1723	100	109	100	93	101
1724	97	106	101	95	100
1725	104	119	101	102	107
1726	97	103	106	98	101
1727	125	99	106	99	107
1728	133	103	112	101	112
1729	95	96	109	104	101
1730	81	94	105	101	95
1731	80	120	100	96	99
1732	76	109	101	93	95
1733	82	96	100	92	93
1734	94	94	107	92	97
1735	99	95	101	91	97
1736	96	108	111	93	102
1737	94	113	111	90	102
1738	84	91	114	91	95
1739	108	98	119	93	105
1740	127	128	99	101	114
1741	100	111	112	108	108
1742	84	105	113	99	100
1743	70	86	115	96	92
1744	76	102	101	93	93
1745	80	109	105	95	97
1746	81	97	107	94	95
1747	80	96	106	100	96
1748	92	97	111	100	100
1749	87	112	110	98	102

B. PRICE INDICES OF AGRICULTURAL COMMODITIES: NATIONAL
DECENNIAL AVERAGES

1640–1749 = 100

Table XXIII. *Price indices of field crops*

	Grains					Other field crops						
Decade	Wheat	Barley & malt	Oats	Rye	Average – all grains	Beans	Peas	Hops	Hay	Straw	Average – all other field crops	Average – all field crops
1640–9	126	111	115	142	122	105	118	96	88	79	101	112
1650–9	106	100	108	105	106	131	118	95	85	85	104	105
1660–9	104	98	99	103	101	96	93	77	82	98	88	95
1670–9	102	94	96	108	99	110	97	77	87	86	91	96
1680–9	87	91	97	94	92	107	95	98	111	104	103	98
1690–9	120	105	104	112	110	101	104	115	111	98	105	108
1700–9	91	95	90	88	91	91	95	90	103	98	96	94
1710–19	97	104	100	95	99	98	102	131	104	105	108	104
1720–9	99	111	104	91	101	93	103	91	100	112	100	101
1730–9	85	97	94	81	89	82	91	122	104	110	102	96
1740–9	83	94	93	80	88	84	84	108	119	125	104	96

Table XXIV. *Price indices of sheep*

Decade	Type unspecified	Wethers	Breeding sheep			Other sheep			Average – all sheep
			Ewes	Ewes & lambs	Average – all breeding sheep	Tups	Lambs	All other sheep	
1640–9	94	98	97	105	101	73	100	97	98
1650–9	106	113	92	—	92	88	88	88	105
1660–9	96	86	123	146	123	118	104	111	101
1670–9	92	98	111	65	96	77	85	85	92
1680–9	108	96	83	76	84	122	88	106	100
1690–9	100	103	98	91	94	108	104	108	102
1700–9	100	101	91	92	92	90	103	102	99
1710–19	103	97	96	99	97	107	107	107	101
1720–9	94	101	98	110	104	92	107	100	100
1730–9	107	99	99	106	102	112	105	108	104
1740–9	100	108	111	110	112	113	110	110	108

Table XXV. *Price indices of cattle*

	Beef cattle				Dairy & breeding cattle				Other cattle			
Decade	Oxen	Bullocks	Runts	Average – all beef cattle	Cows	Heifers	Cows/ heifers & calves	Average – all dairy & breeding cattle	Bulls	Calves	Average – all other cattle	Average – all cattle
1640–9	107	106	104	106	95	98	95	97	122	92	118	107
1650–9	91	94	91	93	102	93	101	96	92	94	94	94
1660–9	101	104	83	97	92	83	100	90	83	95	90	95
1670–9	89	122	107	117	97	104	105	102	101	81	91	100
1680–9	85	91	97	93	82	85	91	86	92	89	90	89
1690–9	106	99	111	104	107	99	102	102	109	121	114	107
1700–9	105	98	118	111	97	112	108	102	107	112	109	107
1710–19	106	87	98	90	106	100	96	101	101	121	111	102
1720–9	111	98	101	98	110	116	101	109	93	107	100	104
1730–9	97	96	90	93	104	103	102	103	88	91	90	96
1740–9	101	104	100	102	109	108	97	106	112	98	105	103

Table **XXVI.** *Price indices of livestock*

Decade	Sheep	Cattle	Horses	Pigs	Poultry	Average – all livestock
1640–9	98	107	76	50	—	85
1650–9	105	94	88	61	—	93
1660–9	101	95	93	80	88	93
1670–9	92	100	104	87	87	94
1680–9	100	89	111	98	91	98
1690–9	102	107	122	113	100	109
1700–9	99	107	108	132	97	108
1710–19	101	102	104	123	106	107
1720–9	100	104	101	112	109	105
1730–9	104	96	102	124	108	107
1740–9	108	103	92	121	115	108

Table XXVII. Price indices of animal products

Decade	Sheep products			Cattle products								Average – all animal products
	Wool	Mutton	Average – all sheep products	Milk	Butter	Cheese	Average – all dairy products	Beef	Average – all cattle products	Pork	Eggs	
1640–9	156	99	109	—	119	148	131	109	119	103	—	109
1650–9	106	112	109	90	111	117	113	93	99	84	—	102
1660–9	113	108	111	109	94	99	100	100	100	105	84	105
1670–9	98	104	102	113	96	96	97	96	97	94	84	95
1680–9	86	104	100	112	93	91	95	92	94	94	92	95
1690–9	102	105	104	112	102	107	107	102	105	111	107	107
1700–9	90	93	91	95	95	87	92	102	97	106	103	99
1710–19	89	95	93	91	91	89	90	106	98	109	107	102
1720–9	76	97	86	98	93	90	94	101	98	106	107	99
1730–9	73	91	82	91	96	84	91	94	93	90	107	93
1740–9	77	93	85	91	109	91	97	106	102	98	108	98

Table XXVIII. Price indices of all agricultural products and industrial products

Decade	Grains	Other field crops	Livestock	Animal products	Average – all agricultural products	Industrial products[a]	$\dfrac{\text{Agricultural}}{\text{Industrial}} \times 100$
1640–9	122	101	85	109	104	97	107
1650–9	106	104	93	102	101	103	98
1660–9	101	88	93	105	97	109	89
1670–9	99	91	94	95	95	111	86
1680–9	92	103	98	95	97	98	99
1690–9	110	105	109	107	108	105	103
1700–9	91	96	108	99	99	103	96
1710–19	99	108	107	102	104	97	107
1720–9	101	100	105	99	101	93	109
1730–9	89	102	107	93	98	89	110
1740–9	88	104	108	98	100	93	108

[a] Based on figures contained in E. H. Phelps Brown and Sheila V. Hopkins, 'Wage Rates and Prices: Evidence for Population Pressure in the Sixteenth Century', *Economica*, ns XXIV, 1957, p. 306; Elizabeth B. Schumpeter, 'English Prices and Public Finance, 1660–1822', *Rev. Ec. Stat.*, XX, I, Cambridge, Mass., 1938.

C. PRICE INDICES OF AGRICULTURAL COMMODITIES: REGIONAL
AVERAGES

'ENGLAND' 1640–1749 = 100

Table XXIX.   Field crops
Table XXX.   Sheep and cattle
Table XXXI.   All agricultural products

Table XXIX. *Price indices of field crops*

Period	Wheat	Barley & malt	Rye	Oats	Beans	Peas	Average – all field crops
(a) South							
1640–79	101	93	—	98	100	104	99
1680–1709	102	102	99	102	103	99	101
1710–49	94	103	85	99	91	98	95
Average s.	34.40	17.76	20.87	13.26	20.86	25.08	—
(b) South Midlands							
1640–79	131	91	—	106	125	—	113
1680–1709	117	89	118	91	116	90	104
1710–49	104	99	—	95	103	81	96
Average s.	40.74	16.72	27.12	13.06	24.56	21.38	—
(c) Home Counties							
1640–79	148	100	112	127	128	113	121
1680–1709	114	116	115	108	151	112	119
1710–49	98	111	100	105	129	107	108
Average s.	41.82	19.44	24.62	15.03	29.17	27.59	—
(d) South-west							
1640–79	120	149	—	131	177	136	143
1680–1709	102	119	—	101	145	120	117
1710–49	93	115	79	107	97	117	101
Average s.	36.71	22.97	18.01	15.02	29.87	31.21	—
(e) West							
1640–79	101	122	—	83	124	85	103
1680–1709	99	111	119	80	114	102	104
1710–49	98	114	110	80	132	85	103
Average s.	34.64	20.32	26.05	10.81	26.66	22.67	—
(f) North Midlands and Lincs.							
1640–79	90	104	102	74	90	73	89
1680–1709	84	95	98	71	94	69	85
1710–49	77	103	99	74	81	67	84
Average s.	29.19	18.04	22.29	9.77	18.78	17.34	—
(g) North and north-west							
1640–79	112	88	112	76	108	70	94
1680–1709	113	82	96	75	96	67	88
1710–49	106	78	88	74	92	63	84
Average s.	38.23	14.84	22.58	10.01	21.01	16.61	—
(h) Yorks., Notts., and Derbs.							
1640–79	139	136	110	93	130	70	113
1680–1709	107	117	107	87	82	66	94
1710–49	100	137	85	91	76	65	92
Average s.	40.33	23.45	22.93	12.10	20.37	16.65	—

Table XXIX. (*cont.*)

Period	Wheat	Barley & malt	Rye	Oats	Beans	Peas	Average – all field crops
(*i*) *East*							
1640–79	110	80	117	112	99	89	101
1680–1709	101	69	106	97	88	85	91
1710–49	91	80	85	101	93	74	87
Average s.	34.99	13.76	23.05	13.91	20.09	20.67	—
(*j*) *'England'*							
1640–79	110	101	115	105	111	107	108
1680–1709	99	97	98	97	100	98	98
1710–49	91	102	87	98	89	95	94
Average s.	34.80	17.90	22.92	13.36	21.43	25.02	—

Table XXX. Price indices of sheep and cattle

Period	Sheep			Cattle				
	Type unspecified	Wethers	Average	Oxen	Bullocks	Cows	Heifers	Average
(a) South								
1640–79	91	105	98	98	96	94	87	94
1680–1709	97	89	93	97	90	97	86	93
1710–49	100	104	102	108	112	108	124	113
Average s.	10.28	12.45	—	145.10	90.92	82.94	77.01	—
(b) South Midlands								
1640–79	134	156	145	93	91	112	134	108
1680–1709	155	110	133	68	103	104	151	107
1710–49	135	115	125	93	128	126	91	110
Average s.	15.25	15.18	—	127.01	103.43	98.71	87.92	—
(c) Home Counties								
1640–79	123	78	101	107	166	93	75	110
1680–1709	129	103	116	110	131	90	105	109
1710–49	114	91	103	89	118	124	126	114
Average s.	12.99	11.43	—	139.56	125.78	87.79	83.11	—
(d) South-west								
1640–79	102	89	96	113	115	107	87	106
1680–1709	99	110	105	103	82	102	85	93
1710–49	107	103	105	100	90	96	88	94
Average s.	11.00	12.38	—	150.29	86.29	83.97	66.71	—

(e) West

1640–79	92	76	84	86	105	105	75	93
1680–1709	88	73	81	85	119	101	78	96
1710–49	101	83	92	92	85	109	68	89
Average s.	10.22	9.69	—	126.01	92.36	87.42	56.11	—

(f) North Midlands and Lincs.

1640–79	117	105	111	112	165	90	86	113
1680–1709	118	126	122	103	126	84	75	97
1710–49	115	93	104	112	118	99	112	110
Average s.	12.43	13.09	—	155.95	115.41	77.22	73.03	—

(g) North and north-west

1640–79	54	63	59	51	105	59	64	70
1680–1709	48	61	55	53	74	78	72	69
1710–49	65	70	68	60	80	90	79	77
Average s.	6.02	8.00	—	78.37	79.41	62.70	54.86	—

(h) Yorks, Notts., and Derbs.

1640–79	91	60	76	71	90	98	102	90
1680–1709	110	89	100	86	83	81	112	91
1710–49	107	87	97	86	93	98	105	96
Average s.	11.13	10.55	—	117.66	81.12	77.09	81.59	—

(i) East

1640–79	122	78	100	—	67	89	60	72
1680–1709	106	76	91	—	43	96	57	65
1710–49	122	88	105	73	64	79	79	74
Average s.	12.56	10.07	—	104.05	54.65	72.41	51.04	—

(j) 'England'

1640–79	97	99	98	97	107	97	95	99
1680–1709	103	100	102	99	96	95	99	97
1710–49	101	101	101	104	96	107	107	104
Average s.	10.70	12.41	—	142.92	90.92	82.94	77.01	—

Table XXXI. *Price indices of all agricultural products*

Period	Wheat, barley, & rye	Oats, beans, & peas	Sheep	Cattle	Average – all agricul tural products
(a) *South*					
1640–79	97	101	98	94	98
1680–1709	101	101	93	93	97
1710–49	94	96	102	113	101
(b) *South Midlands*					
1640–79	111	116	145	108	120
1680–1709	108	99	133	107	112
1710–49	102	93	125	110	108
(c) *Home Counties*					
1640–79	120	123	101	110	114
1680–1709	115	124	116	109	116
1710–49	103	114	103	114	109
(d) *South-west*					
1640–79	135	148	96	106	121
1680–1709	111	122	105	93	108
1710–49	96	107	105	94	101
(e) *West*					
1640–79	112	97	84	93	97
1680–1709	110	99	81	96	97
1710–49	107	99	92	89	97
(f) *North Midlands and Lincs.*					
1640–79	99	79	111	113	101
1680–1709	92	78	122	97	97
1710–49	93	74	104	110	95
(g) *North and north-west*					
1640–79	104	85	59	70	80
1680–1709	97	79	55	69	75
1710–49	91	76	68	77	78
(h) *Yorks., Notts., and Derbs.*					
1640–79	128	98	76	90	98
1680–1709	110	78	100	91	95
1710–49	107	77	97	96	94
(i) *East*					
1640–79	102	100	100	72	94
1680–1709	92	90	91	65	85
1710–49	85	89	105	74	88
(j) *'England'*					
1640–79	109	108	98	99	104
1680–1709	98	98	102	97	99
1710–49	93	94	101	104	98

D. PRICES OF AGRICULTURAL COMMODITIES: REGIONAL DECENNIAL AVERAGES

Table XXXII. *Price of wheat (in s. per quarter)*

Decade	South	South Midlands	Home Counties	South-west	West	North Midlands & Lincs.	North & north-west	Yorks., Notts., & Derbs.	East	'England'
1640-9	38.15	50.76	60.34	44.95	44.40	—	56.56	58.57	40.82	43.88
1650-9	33.68	43.25	45.18	43.01	33.06	35.39	32.60	47.47	36.09	37.02
1660-9	33.17	44.77	45.38	40.82	30.24	30.44	31.97	44.76	39.20	36.11
1670-9	35.26	43.17	54.51	38.40	32.60	28.19	34.10	42.19	36.96	35.43
1680-9	29.96	34.73	31.86	31.16	31.10	27.37	33.32	36.50	30.56	30.31
1690-9	44.00	50.12	49.63	40.61	41.80	34.11	46.98	43.36	43.26	41.60
1700-9	32.97	36.74	37.07	34.63	31.01	26.47	37.27	31.80	31.36	31.63
1710-19	36.49	41.90	37.81	34.84	34.68	32.10	36.74	33.67	34.95	33.92
1720-9	33.99	38.38	35.36	35.30	39.01	—	41.35	38.29	33.86	34.33
1730-9	31.48	32.31	31.79	30.39	31.01	25.47	33.98	34.02	29.66	29.60
1740-9	29.25	31.96	31.11	29.70	32.14	23.14	35.65	32.98	28.16	28.98
Average	34.40	40.74	41.82	36.71	34.64	29.19	38.23	40.33	34.99	34.80

Table XXXIII. *Price of barley and malt (in s. per quarter)*

Decade	South	South Midlands	Home Counties	South-west	West	North Midlands & Lincs.	North & north-west	Yorks., Notts., & Derbs.	East	'England'
1640–9	17.04	17.57	20.13	28.34	—	—	21.26	30.36	15.51	19.82
1650–9	16.42	15.49	14.98	26.54	21.79	21.34	14.07	23.52	14.19	17.85
1660–9	16.46	16.33	16.01	25.44	—	17.56	14.41	22.25	14.97	17.50
1670–9	16.82	15.95	20.50	26.16	22.66	17.17	13.30	21.15	12.54	16.91
1680–9	16.00	14.80	19.09	17.28	21.96	16.77	14.16	20.74	11.97	16.36
1690–9	19.86	17.26	22.78	23.47	14.61	18.11	16.11	20.61	13.40	18.73
1700–9	18.93	15.87	20.63	23.30	21.78	15.88	13.68	21.47	11.64	17.06
1710–19	19.77	18.37	21.46	20.02	21.78	18.33	13.87	25.01	14.50	18.66
1720–9	19.65	19.60	21.72	23.14	23.15	18.80	15.65	26.13	15.64	19.84
1730–9	17.69	16.60	18.57	18.64	18.68	19.61	13.59	22.62	13.81	17.30
1740–9	16.68	16.06	17.98	20.36	17.90	16.80	13.14	24.09	13.23	16.84
Average	17.76	16.72	19.44	22.97	20.32	18.04	14.84	23.45	13.76	17.90

Table XXXIV. Price of rye (in s. per quarter)

Decade	South	South Midlands	Home Counties	South-west	West	North Midlands & Lincs.	North & north-west	Yorks., Notts., & Derbs.	East	'England'
1640–9	—	—	—	—	—	—	31.98	—	33.39	32.64
1650–9	—	—	—	—	—	24.34	23.88	25.02	19.34	24.10
1660–9	—	—	20.75	—	—	24.88	21.98	24.54	27.45	23.64
1670–9	—	—	30.25	—	—	24.94	24.22	26.38	—	24.76
1680–9	20.25	—	23.51	—	33.10	21.90	20.40	—	23.24	21.48
1690–9	25.17	31.16	33.18	—	27.97	24.13	25.60	25.65	28.34	25.69
1700–9	22.71	23.08	22.38	—	20.77	19.68	19.68	23.45	21.36	20.07
1710–19	22.82	—	25.03	—	25.89	22.03	19.67	—	21.27	21.82
1720–9	19.65	—	24.98	—	27.52	20.85	21.72	21.30	20.53	20.94
1730–9	17.79	—	20.16	18.48	23.22	17.88	20.42	19.72	17.48	18.60
1740–9	17.67	—	21.37	17.53	23.86	—	18.81	17.40	18.10	18.37
Average	20.87	27.12	24.62	18.01	26.05	22.29	22.58	22.93	23.05	22.92

Table XXXV. Price of oats (in s. per quarter)

Decade	South	South Midlands	Home Counties	South-west	West	North Midlands & Lincs.	North & north-west	Yorks., Notts., & Derbs.	East	'England'
1640–9	13.97	15.03	—	—	12.54	—	12.21	14.64	16.77	15.32
1650–9	13.30	14.48	20.61	19.65	9.81	11.68	9.88	12.25	15.15	14.40
1660–9	12.84	13.40	15.36	18.76	9.76	9.58	9.27	10.72	14.53	13.22
1670–9	12.10	13.86	14.87	14.00	12.19	8.57	9.14	11.86	13.38	12.78
1680–9	13.57	14.37	15.26	9.35	—	9.13	9.54	12.00	12.49	12.93
1690–9	13.94	13.04	14.67	16.19	11.76	9.78	12.23	11.96	12.89	13.86
1700–9	13.22	8.95	13.50	15.09	9.57	9.69	8.33	10.88	13.77	12.08
1710–19	13.56	12.87	13.81	15.25	9.77	11.15	9.67	13.00	13.26	13.35
1720–9	13.84	13.12	14.29	14.80	12.04	10.42	10.94	12.89	14.60	13.92
1730–9	13.13	12.12	13.92	13.66	10.37	9.19	9.40	11.30	13.08	12.59
1740–9	12.37	12.39	14.00	13.40	10.29	8.53	9.53	11.61	13.14	12.47
Average	13.26	13.06	15.03	15.02	10.81	9.77	10.01	12.10	13.91	13.36

Table XXXVI. Price of beans (in s. per quarter)

Decade	South	South Midlands	Home Counties	South-west	West	North Midlands & Lincs.	North & north-west	Yorks., Notts., & Derbs.	East	'England'
1640–9	19.94	27.25	—	29.47	—	—	23.17	29.19	22.76	22.44
1650–9	23.60	29.19	—	40.96	—	21.81	—	31.57	—	28.03
1660–9	17.51	22.88	26.05	44.53	—	17.32	18.10	23.10	20.04	20.67
1670–9	24.61	28.02	28.98	36.58	26.50	18.73	28.42	—	20.71	23.60
1680–9	24.76	28.91	36.70	37.03	26.85	19.07	18.60	—	—	23.03
1690–9	22.08	22.49	31.92	32.58	22.82	20.14	24.79	20.12	20.86	21.67
1700–9	19.22	23.16	28.73	23.89	24.05	21.10	18.45	14.72	17.03	19.59
1710–19	21.05	23.24	28.99	25.57	25.85	21.38	20.99	20.54	24.14	21.04
1720–9	20.90	24.39	28.50	18.83	29.04	18.49	22.33	11.56	19.70	19.99
1730–9	17.60	20.87	25.89	19.36	26.61	14.64	17.99	15.92	18.23	17.64
1740–9	18.17	19.80	26.73	19.76	31.53	15.15	17.27	16.64	17.34	18.07
Average	20.86	24.56	29.17	29.87	26.66	18.78	21.01	20.37	20.09	21.43

Table XXXVII. *Price of peas (in s. per quarter)*

Decade	South	South Midlands	Home Counties	South-west	West	North Midlands & Lincs.	North & north-west	Yorks., Notts., & Derbs.	East	'England'
1640–9	30.98	—	—	35.10	—	—	24.92	—	23.57	29.53
1650–9	26.15	—	27.75	36.19	—	20.69	18.56	20.79	24.51	29.41
1660–9	21.47	—	28.12	34.40	26.33	16.35	11.38	15.60	21.02	23.32
1670–9	25.26	—	28.67	29.94	15.94	17.73	14.92	16.11	20.37	24.22
1680–9	24.21	23.28	26.58	27.25	22.89	16.42	14.82	18.24	21.73	23.70
1690–9	25.46	22.76	31.07	29.88	24.91	18.81	19.21	16.06	20.96	26.05
1700–9	24.78	21.60	26.57	33.40	28.62	16.32	15.94	14.91	20.72	23.83
1710–19	27.33	—	30.70	28.67	23.11	20.43	16.71	16.11	17.86	25.50
1720–9	25.76	22.54	28.55	32.00	24.88	19.48	17.62	17.04	19.64	25.87
1730–9	22.53	17.59	24.28	29.03	18.94	15.41	15.12	16.36	19.91	22.70
1740–9	21.90	20.53	23.61	27.41	18.41	11.72	13.52	15.32	17.08	21.11
Average	25.08	21.38	27.59	31.21	22.67	17.34	16.61	16.65	20.67	25.02

Table XXXVIII. Price of sheep (type unspecified) (in s. each)

Decade	South	South Midlands	Home Counties	South-west	West	North Midlands & Lincs.	North & north-west	Yorks., Notts., & Derbs.	East	'England'
1640–9	11.46	—	—	9.49	—	8.10	5.93	—	13.49	10.03
1650–9	8.14	—	16.93	12.62	10.45	13.46	6.20	—	—	11.30
1660–9	11.62	14.34	12.03	11.98	—	—	6.13	8.84	11.18	10.31
1670–9	7.83	—	10.60	9.43	9.21	15.81	5.06	10.61	14.65	9.86
1680–9	7.38	14.47	16.04	10.91	—	16.25	5.67	8.19	14.49	11.54
1690–9	11.57	15.12	13.43	10.42	9.55	9.28	4.53	15.38	6.12	10.67
1700–9	12.21	20.36	12.03	10.47	9.32	12.24	5.13	11.57	13.48	10.75
1710–19	10.78	17.20	12.42	11.36	12.37	10.64	4.62	16.03	13.21	11.01
1720–9	9.62	11.24	10.43	9.96	9.55	14.47	7.05	8.87	12.28	10.11
1730–9	12.07	14.62	15.32	12.54	10.60	11.76	8.09	9.51	13.29	11.43
1740–9	10.42	14.67	10.64	11.82	10.69	12.31	7.80	11.16	13.37	10.69
Average	10.28	15.25	12.99	11.00	10.22	12.43	6.02	11.13	12.56	10.70

Table XXXIX. Price of wethers (in s. each)

Decade	South	South Midlands	Home Counties	South-west	West	North Midlands & Lincs.	North & north-west	Yorks., Notts., & Derbs.	East	'England'
1640-9	13.70	—	—	11.46	11.06	10.16	7.74	—	9.36	12.10
1650-9	14.06	20.75	—	—	9.89	—	8.34	—	—	14.06
1660-9	12.19	—	9.10	10.42	8.96	—	7.27	7.25	9.55	10.68
1670-9	12.18	17.93	10.19	11.20	7.70	15.72	8.11	8.33	10.10	12.12
1680-9	10.38	12.80	10.69	—	8.02	14.87	9.15	12.17	10.02	11.91
1690-9	10.97	15.33	16.83	11.39	9.88	—	7.27	12.93	11.02	12.84
1700-9	11.63	12.91	10.81	15.85	—	16.32	6.11	9.79	7.17	12.50
1710-19	12.86	16.69	12.66	9.45	11.21	12.52	—	9.92	9.63	12.03
1720-9	13.06	13.61	12.47	12.91	11.56	9.81	7.36	11.59	10.88	12.52
1730-9	12.47	13.52	10.11	15.78	9.26	—	7.21	12.41	10.59	12.31
1740-9	13.44	13.08	10.00	12.99	9.36	12.25	11.48	12.41	12.35	13.42
Average	12.45	15.18	11.43	12.38	9.69	13.09	8.00	10.55	10.07	12.41

Table XL. Price of oxen (in s. each)

Decade	South	South Midlands	Home Counties	South-west	West	North Midlands & Lincs.	North & north-west	Yorks., Notts., & Derbs.	East	'England'
1640–9	166.51	—	—	185.00	140.73	160.26	75.94	—	—	153.08
1650–9	135.22	98.07	153.50	157.41	107.16	—	77.86	78.55	—	130.37
1660–9	141.88	167.04	—	168.40	120.57	—	69.46	—	—	144.32
1670–9	117.19	—	—	133.55	124.77	—	66.15	123.69	—	127.48
1680–9	101.84	97.10	—	109.79	120.26	147.80	65.68	119.30	—	121.62
1690–9	169.15	—	133.11	142.43	137.59	—	72.14	136.57	—	151.43
1700–9	147.36	—	182.07	186.66	107.77	—	90.57	111.80	—	150.57
1710–19	182.04	118.52	82.35	134.55	134.73	—	85.08	121.76	—	151.87
1720–9	135.57	—	220.87	166.72	129.21	—	92.69	132.90	—	158.99
1730–9	146.19	173.35	88.63	129.24	123.87	159.79	75.88	123.89	104.05	138.62
1740–9	153.14	107.99	116.38	139.47	139.42	—	90.60	110.46	—	143.81
Average	145.10	127.01	139.56	150.29	126.01	155.95	78.37	117.66	104.05	142.92

Table XLI. *Price of bullocks (in s. each)*

Decade	South	South Midlands	Home Counties	South-west	West	North Midlands & Lincs.	North & north-west	Yorks., Notts., & Derbs.	East	'England'
1640–9	98.68	—	—	83.58	101.09	—	107.65	—	58.69	96.72
1650–9	87.23	—	106.09	—	89.76	—	85.60	51.17	—	85.08
1660–9	64.36	127.47	140.30	99.13	102.33	—	84.73	112.43	51.04	95.00
1670–9	97.64	37.52	206.83	129.61	89.36	149.59	104.90	—	73.80	110.53
1680–9	84.66	93.95	126.16	70.47	105.90	91.75	71.47	54.59	44.97	83.12
1690–9	79.82	—	135.39	75.21	108.91	120.92	62.96	80.34	—	90.41
1700–9	79.83	—	94.84	78.48	109.21	130.63	66.11	93.15	33.28	89.45
1710–19	110.37	107.61	95.95	74.71	50.46	78.64	53.54	110.75	44.56	79.50
1720–9	71.39	120.58	—	95.55	92.51	115.12	74.25	64.67	—	89.11
1730–9	120.38	112.21	132.53	63.78	97.40	142.90	77.51	68.27	62.21	87.02
1740–9	105.76	124.70	93.90	92.34	69.07	93.70	84.82	94.71	68.67	94.24
Average	90.92	103.43	125.78	86.29	92.36	115.41	79.41	81.12	54.65	90.92

Table XLII. *Price of cows (in s. each)*

Decade	South	South Midlands	Home Counties	South-west	West	North Midlands & Lincs.	North & north-west	Yorks., Notts., & Derbs.	East	'England'
1640–9	74.43	—	75.02	73.44	94.09	—	47.98	—	70.67	78.51
1650–9	79.32	—	79.32	114.33	95.62	—	58.01	84.07	66.67	84.22
1660–9	76.52	105.48	—	79.00	74.12	82.10	42.53	81.51	76.93	76.13
1670–9	81.34	80.60	—	87.59	84.55	67.43	47.77	79.94	80.16	80.33
1680–9	70.72	—	47.48	84.68	78.09	62.39	53.85	60.74	61.53	68.14
1690–9	88.14	—	90.77	77.44	91.17	—	78.00	74.37	104.14	88.54
1700–9	84.06	86.10	85.90	90.92	81.37	77.38	62.04	65.72	73.29	80.13
1710–19	92.78	111.76	89.90	76.88	96.17	80.67	76.56	78.84	59.71	88.14
1720–9	85.43	85.45	125.81	79.22	85.27	81.46	75.62	74.40	77.13	90.85
1730–9	75.44	119.00	93.84	76.00	92.32	92.95	66.89	84.09	72.51	86.59
1740–9	104.14	102.57	102.04	84.12	88.85	73.36	80.45	87.21	53.76	90.72
Average	82.94	98.71	87.79	83.97	87.42	77.22	62.70	77.09	72.41	82.94

Table XLIII. *Price of heifers (in s. each)*

Decade	South	South Midlands	Home Counties	South-west	West	North Midlands & Lincs.	North & north-west	Yorks., Notts., & Derbs.	East	'England'
1640–9	67.50	—	—	64.82	62.56	69.11	42.45	—	46.72	75.58
1650–9	86.89	103.56	54.45	67.30	49.84	61.17	49.60	73.34	—	71.75
1660–9	48.72	—	61.21	62.65	54.24	—	42.60	—	39.43	63.98
1670–9	64.53	—	—	73.15	65.30	68.81	61.23	84.14	52.47	80.35
1680–9	51.37	—	70.17	60.97	—	56.28	49.10	—	44.71	65.17
1690–9	70.64	108.44	66.51	69.04	64.23	—	62.21	62.13	—	75.98
1700–9	77.38	124.36	106.47	—	55.61	58.28	54.40	110.20	43.09	85.87
1710–19	82.96	44.93	95.65	63.65	41.37	73.33	58.88	66.38	—	76.63
1720–9	91.59	63.81	100.85	78.03	61.26	73.17	67.91	77.32	79.84	89.26
1730–9	100.89	79.24	100.26	58.37	55.16	109.89	56.87	85.31	47.64	79.37
1740–9	104.64	91.13	92.42	69.14	51.48	87.24	58.16	93.90	54.40	83.15
Average	77.01	87.92	83.11	66.71	56.11	73.03	54.86	81.59	51.04	77.01

E. WAGES AND COST OF LIVING

Table XLIV. Daily wage rates in certain areas of England (in d.)

(a) Agricultural labourers[a]

Decade	Essex	Sussex	Suffolk	Hunts.	South Bucks.	North Bucks.	W. Riding	Average[b]
1640–9	—	—	—	—	—	8	—	11.00
1650–9	12–16	—	—	—	—	8	—	11.00
1660–9	12–16	—	—	—	—	8	—	11.00
1670–9	12–16	—	8–12	—	—	8	—	11.00
1680–9	12–16	—	10–12	—	—	8	—	11.14
1690–9	—	12–14	—	12	12	—	8	11.28
1700–9	—	12	—	10	12–14	—	8	11.12
1710–19	—	12–14	12	10	—	8	—	11.29
1720–9	—	12	12	8–10	—	—	—	11.13
1730–9	16–18	—	—	12	—	—	8	11.64
1740–9	18	—	—	12	10–12	9–10	8–12	12.07

(b) Building labourers[c]

Decade	Westminster Abbey	Southwark	Greenwich Hospital	Maidstone	Guildford	Exeter	Oxford	W. Riding	Lancs.	Average[b]
1700–9	20–24	22	20	—	—	14–15	14	8–12	8–9½	15.75
1710–19	22–22½	22	20	16	14½	14	14	10–12	8–10	15.86
1720–9	21–22½	24	20	16	15–18	14–16	14	8–12	10–12	16.47
1730–9	22–24	24	20	16	15–16	14–16	14	8–12	11–12	16.56
1740–9	23½–24	22–24	20	16	—	14–16	13–14	12	11½–12	16.72

Table XLIV. *(cont.)*

(c) *Building craftsmen*[c]

Decade	West-minster Abbey	South-wark	Green-wich Hospital	Maid-stone	Exeter	Oxford	W. Riding	Lancs.	Average[b]
1700–9	30–34	32	30	—	20–24	20	12–17	12–18	23.69
1710–19	32–36	30–36	30–31	—	20–21	20	16–18	12–16	24.13
1720–9	36	30–36	31–33½	24	19½–22	20–24	12–18	18	25.13
1730–9	36	32–36	30–31	24	20–22	24	18	16–18	25.56
1740–9	36	34–36	30	24	20–24	22½–24	16–18	14½–18	25.44

[a] The wage rates are those commonly paid for ordinary day-to-day agricultural operations performed by male workers – e.g. hedging, ditching, spreading dung. Seasonal tasks, such as mowing and haymaking, normally paid at higher rates, are not included. Also excluded are rates supplemented by payments in kind.
[b] For method of calculation, see Sect. H below.
[c] Data from Elizabeth W. Gilboy, *Wages in Eighteenth-Century England*, Cambridge, Mass., 1934. App. II. *Sources*: Essex RO, Petre MSS (West Horndon, Thorndon Hall), D/DP/A47, A54–7; Tylers Hall farm (Upminster), D/DM/A20; Lennard estate (Aveley), D/DL/E1, E81; Gidea Hall (Gidea Park), D/DBe/A1–2; J. E. T. Rogers, *A History of Agriculture and Prices in England*, *VI*, Oxford, 1887 (Harting, Sussex); GMR, Wyatt MSS (Horsted Keynes), LM1,087/2/8; W. Suffolk RO, Warner MSS (Badmondisfield), 1,341/5/2; Stanton accounts, E1/11/2; E. Suffolk RO, Parson accounts (Onehouse), N9/1/1.2; Hunts. RO, Bernard MSS (Grafham, etc.), Manchester Coll. ddM5/4, 5; Trevor accounts (Houghton, etc.), Manchester Coll. ddM44B/2; Bucks. RO, Drake MSS (Amersham, etc.), D/DR/2/48, 51, 89; Earl of Buckinghamshire MSS (Great Hampden, etc.), D/MH/33/1–8; Way MSS (Hughenden), D/W60/1–5, D/W61/64; Uthwatt MSS (Great Linford, etc.), Account Nos. 1–6, 11; Chester MSS (Chicheley, etc.), D/C/2/33–45, AR18/69 box 1; Bedford RO, ref. CH938; Reading Univ. Library, Farm Rec. Coll., Grenville estate (Wotton), BUC 11/1/5; Sheepscar Pub. Library, Leeds, Temple Newsam farm, TN/EA/12/11; Gilboy, *op. cit.*

Table XLV. *Indices of wage rates of agricultural labourers in England and their purchasing power (1640–1749 = 100)*

Decade	Average money wage rate[a]	'Cost of living'[b]	Purchasing power of wage rate
1640–9	98	108	91
1650–9	98	104	94
1660–9	98	101	97
1670–9	98	99	99
1680–9	99	97	102
1690–9	100	107	94
1700–9	99	96	103
1710–19	100	102	98
1720–9	99	99	100
1730–9	104	93	112
1740–9	107	95	113

[a] Calculated on the basis of data in Table XLIV(a)
[b] Based on the preceding price tables using the following weights: field crops, excluding hay (5), animal products (3), industrial products (2).

Table XLVI. *Sowing rates of seed: bushels per acre*

Crop year	Wheat	Barley	Rye	Oats	Beans	Peas	Location
1649	—	2.00	—	—	6.00	4.00	Barnes, Surrey
1655	—	4.67[a]	—	—	—	—	Puttenham, Surrey
1670	2.25[b]	3.82[c]	—	4.19[d]	2.00	3.54	W. Horsley, Surrey
1680	3.20	4.49	3.31	4.54	—	5.07	Hatfield, Herts.
1681	3.37	4.92	3.25	4.99	—	4.81	Hatfield, Herts.
1687	3.33	—	—	—	—	2.67[e]	"Winterborne", Wilts.
1738	—	—	—	—	3.80	—	Stoke Bruerne, Northants.
1745	2.00	—	—	—	—	—	Bridgnorth, Salop.

[a] Plus 15.33 lb per acre of clover.
[b] 2.21–2.40.
[c] 3.40–3.89.
[d] 3.50–4.67.
[e] Vetches.
Sources: Sheffield Univ. Library, Hartlib MS 62/6/3; GMR, 51/5/67; Misc. bdle 22/3/1; Herts. RO, Hatfield est. acc., ref. 152; Wilts. RO, Acc. 1,164, Myers c.17; Northants. RO, G3,884, ML1,291; Univ. of Reading Library, Farm Rec. Coll., SALOP 5/1/1.

Table XLVII. *Crop–seed ratios: bushels of output per bushel of seed*

Crop year	Wheat	Barley	Oats	Beans	Peas	Location
1670–1[a]	14.2[b]	12.0[c]	8.2[d]	15.0	12.2[e]	W. Horsley, Surrey
1682–3	14.8	17.9	—	—	10.4	Fowlmere, Cambs.
1684	—	—	11.6	—	—	Fowlmere, Cambs.
1737–8	6.1	4.1	—	3.5	—	Stoke Bruerne, Northants.
1738	—	9.0	—	—	—	"Tern", Salop.

[a] Yields calculated on the assumed basis of 40 bu (5 qtr) to the load.
[b] 10.5–20.0.
[c] 8.4–14.1.
[d] 7.6–13.3.
[e] Peas and tares.
Sources: GMR, Misc. bdle 22/3/1; Cambs. RO, P72/3/1; Northants. RO, G3,884, ML1,291; Salop. RO, Letters of Thos. Bell 112, box 20, 19/8/1738.

Table XLVIII. Crop yields in bushels per acre

Harvest year	Wheat	Barley	Rye	Oats	Beans	Peas	Buckwheat	Location
1671[a]	32.0[b]	45.9[c]	—	34.4[d]	30.0	43.3[e]	—	W. Horsley, Surrey
1682	10.0[f]	16.0	10.0	20.0	—	—	—	Horsham St Faith, Norfolk
1732	17.4	32.2	—	—	—	17.6	—	Arreton I.O.W.
1733	20.2	29.6	—	26.2	—	24.5	—	Arreton, I.O.W.
1734	20.4	34.2	—	35.7	—	21.0	—	Arreton, I.O.W.
1735	—	—	—	50.5	—	7.5	—	Arreton, I.O.W.
1736	—	26.0	—	—	—	—	—	Arreton, I.O.W.
1737	26.5	39.7	—	30.4	—	—	—	Arreton, I.O.W.
1738	22.1	32.2	—	—	—	—	—	Arreton, I.O.W.
1739	26.3	32.3	—	30.6	—	—	—	Arreton, I.O.W.
1740	18.1	35.4	—	—	—	—	—	Arreton, I.O.W.
1741	17.3	25.6	—	10.9	—	—	—	Arreton, I.O.W.
1742	26.2	18.7	—	—	—	—	—	Arreton, I.O.W.
1743	23.4	43.2	—	21.1	—	—	—	Arreton, I.O.W.
1744	26.4	32.9	—	—	—	—	—	Arreton, I.O.W.
1745	—	29.8	—	—	—	—	—	Arreton, I.O.W.
1746	—	33.1	—	—	—	20.8	—	Arreton, I.O.W.
1747	29.3	39.3	—	37.2	—	—	—	Arreton, I.O.W.
1748	27.4	31.1	—	25.9	—	22.8	—	Arreton, I.O.W.

1749	30.0	36.4	—	—	—	—	Arreton, I.O.W.
1750	26.5	32.8	24.9	—	—	—	Arreton, I.O.W.
1737	—	14.8	—	—	13.4	—	Stoke Bruerne, Northants.
1738	22.4	39.2	—	—	15.0	—	Stoke Bruerne, Northants.
1737	—	—	16.8	1.9[g]	—	12.5	Lewes (?), Sussex
1747	16.1	31.5	19.1	12.9	—	—	Lewes (?), Sussex
1748	—	25.8	24.6	21.0[h]	—	18.7	Lewes (?), Sussex
1749	—	—	—	—	—	—	Lewes (?), Sussex
1752	22.6[i]	21.9	18.9[j]	25.3	—	—	Pirton, Herts.
1754	19.9[i]	27.5	28.0[j]	21.8[i]	—	—	"Wellbury Farm", Herts.

[a] "Yields calculated on the assumed basis of 40 bu (5 qtr) to the load.

[b] 23.2–45.7.

[c] 32.0–52.9.

[d] 26.7–60.6.

[e] 40.0–43.8 (peas and tares).

[f] 10.0–12.0.

[g] "Peas almost all destroyed by bugs."

[h] Tares.

[i] Assuming 1 load = 1 qtr.

[j] Oats and "bullimon".

Sources: GMR, Misc. bdle 22/3/1; Norfolk RO, NRS16,023; Isle of Wight RO, Blake Coll. BRS/J/1; Northants. RO, G3,884; ML1,291; E. Sussex RO, Add. MS 4,461; Herts. RO, 48,685, 48,688.

Table XLIX. *Weights of livestock*

Type of livestock	Harvest year	No. of stock/ sales	Weight (lb)[a]			Family and/or estate	County	Reference[b]
			Average	Highest	Lowest			
Sheep	1694–5	6	43	45	40	Ticehurst	Sussex	1
Sheep	1732–7	32	55	70	44	Tyrell, Benhall	Suffolk	2
Sheep	1737–9	5	40	50	36	Frampton, Moreton	Dorset	3
Sheep	1740–1	18	55	—	47	Phillipps, Garenton	Derbs.	4
Sheep	1742–3	8	53	59	47	Grenville, Wotton	Bucks.	5
Sheep	1744–5	7	63	88	51	Hervey, Ickworth	Suffolk	6
Wethers	1740–3	20	48	53	40	G. Capell (Clerk), Stanton	Suffolk	7
Ewes	1740–3	11	44	58	33	G. Capell (Clerk), Stanton	Suffolk	7
Lambs	1737–8	1	18	—	—	Frampton, Moreton	Dorset	3
Lambs	1740–1	1	26	—	—	G. Capell (Clerk), Stanton	Suffolk	7
Oxen	1692–3	1	2037	—	—	Newby area (W. Riding)	Yorks.	8
Oxen	1707–8	1	2083	—	—	Newby area (W. Riding)	Yorks.	8
Oxen	1728–9	1	1262	—	—	More-Molyneaux, Loseley, etc.	Surrey	9
Steers	1691–2	5	467	496	450	Broadfield Hall	Herts.	10
Bullocks	1740–1	2	381	—	—	Phillipps, Garenton	Derbs.	4
Bullocks	1745–7	12	513	700	378	Kimbolton Castle	Hunts.	11
"Welch beasts"	1743–4	1	531	—	—	Duke of Bedford, Tavistock	Devon	12
"Scotts"	1740–3	18	394	452	324	G. Capell (Clerk), Stanton	Suffolk	7
Cows	1726–42	10	622	764	494	More-Molyneux, Loseley, etc.	Surrey	9
Cows	1729–30	1	813	—	—	Frewen, Northiam	Sussex	13
Cows	1745–7	17	300	384	234	Coton Hall, Bridgnorth	Salop.	14
Cows	1748–9	1	1741	—	—	New Market area	Salop.	15
Heifers	1737–41	2	788	808	768	More-Molyneaux, Loseley, etc.	Surrey	9
Calves	1740–2	4	65	75	56	G. Capell (Clerk), Stanton	Suffolk	7
Pigs	1702–7	4	206	272	100	West Chelborough	Dorset	16
Pigs	1707–19	5	271	310	221	Howe, Greatworth	Northants.	17
Pigs	1711–18	3	193	208	174	Carew, Camerton	Somerset	18
Pigs	1720–1	1	98	—	—	G. Capell (Clerk), Stanton	Suffolk	7
Pigs	1732–3	1	248	—	—	Popham, Hunstrete, & Nyland	Somerset	19
Pigs	1740–1	1	44	—	—	G. Capell (Clerk), Stanton	Suffolk	7
Pigs	1748–9	2	127	149	105	Earl of Ailesbury, Savernake	Wilts.	20

Type	Years	No.				Place	County	Source
						retd, West Horndon, etc.	Essex	21
Hogs	1707–19	6	235	284	196	Glynde Place, nr Lewes	Sussex	22
Hogs	1715–25	9	238	295	202	Howe, Greatworth	Northants.	17
Hogs	1720–4	4	175	203	147	Duke of Grafton, Thetford	Norfolk	23
Hogs	1731–2	11	232	236	228	Wyatt, Horsted Keynes	Sussex	24
Hogs	1736–7	2	217	—	—	Weald Hall, South Weald	Essex	25
Hogs	1743–6	1	154	178	132	Shieffner	Sussex	26
Hogs	1746–7	1	112	—	—	Hickstead Place	Sussex	27
Hogs	1746–7	1	264	—	—	Tithe accounts, Abinger	Surrey	28
Hogs	1747–8	2	227	250	240	Clayton, Marden	Surrey	29
Hogs	1747–9	1	245	—	—	Earl of Ailesbury, Savernake	Wilts.	20
Porkers	1704–5	4	88	160	—	Glynde Place, nr Lewes	Sussex	22
Porkers	1745–7	1	94	—	60	Coton Hall, Bridgnorth	Salop.	14
Porkers	1749–50	1	146	—	—	Isham, Lamport	Northants.	30
Boars	1748–9	1	230	249	163	Clayton, Marden	Surrey	29
Sows	1748–9	4	200	—	—	Clayton, Marden	Surrey	29
Geese	1748–9	2	9	10	9	Barker, Coleshill	War.	31

a Most weights are documented in lb. Where weights are given in stones, conversion has been on the basis of either 8 or 14 lb to the stone, according to the indications and balance of probabilities in individual cases.

b See the sources listed below.

Sources:

1 E. Sussex RO, Tichurst MS A6, A11–13, A16.
2 E. Suffolk RO, S1/5/3–4.
3 Dorset RO, D29/E1.
4 Derby Central Library, MS 10,627.
5 Reading Univ. Library, Farm Rec. Coll. BUC 11/1/5.
6 W. Suffolk RO, 941/46/14.
7 W. Suffolk RO, E1/11/2.
8 Leeds Archives Dept., Ingilby 3,591.
9 GMR, LM1,087.
10 Herts. RO, 70,474 A–N.
11 Hunts. RO, Manchester Coll. dd1,722/13.
12 Devon RO, W1,258/LP1/1.
13 E. Sussex RO, FRE7,331.
14 Reading Univ. Library, SALOP 5/1/1.
15 Salop. RO, Letters of Thos. Bell 112/box 20, 15/1/1749.
16 Dorset RO, P16/M11.
17 Northants. RO, YZ997.
18 Somerset RO, DD/TB, boxes 13, 14.
19 Somerset RO, DD/PO32.
20 Wilts. RO, Savernake estate accounts, ref. 9.
21 Essex RO, D/DP/A47.
22 E. Sussex RO, Glynde Place MSS 2,931–5.
23 Norfolk RO, MS11,355.
24 GMR, LM1,087/2/8/1–8.
25 Essex RO, D/DTW/A2.
26 E. Sussex RO, Shiffner MS1,999.
27 E. Sussex RO, Hickstead Place MSS 457–74.
28 Surrey RO, P1/7/1.
29 GMR, 84/2/3.
30 Northants. RO, H3,945.
31 War. RO, CR233.

G. OVERSEAS TRADE IN AGRICULTURAL COMMODITIES

Table L. *Net exports of wheat and wheat flour (Great Britain) and imports of raw wool (England and Wales), 1697–1749 (annual)*

Year	Net exports[a] Wheat & wheat flour (000 qtr)	Imports Irish wool (000 great stones)[b]	Imports Spanish wool (bags)[b]	Year	Net exports[a] Wheat & wheat flour (000 qtr)	Imports Irish wool (000 great stones)[b]	Imports Spanish wool (bags)[b]
1697	14.3	—	—	1724	247.0	113.3	4,220
1698	5.2	—	—	1725	211.2	75.6	5,961
1699	0.1	—	—	1726	143.6	51.4	6,395
1700	49.1	304.2	5,778	1727	31.0	58.2	2,624
1701	98.3	290.0	8,740	1728	−70.6	49.8	3,700
1702	90.2	303.9	4,605	1729	−21.3	38.7	3,755
1703	106.6	352.3	34	1730	94.5	19.8	6,859
1704	90.3	333.8	356	1731	130.6	13.0	4,455
1705	96.2	—	—	1732	202.6	9.7	5,594
1706	188.3	278.6	4,037	1733	427.4	64.7	4,996
1707	174.2	247.8	2,970	1734	498.7	88.2	3,815
1708	83.9	217.4	404	1735	155.3	96.7	4,777
1709	70.1	224.3	3,626	1736	118.2	68.0	4.680
1710	16.2	269.8	2,522	1737	466.0	61.4	4,986
1711	80.9	268.2	7,695	1738	588.3	55.1	5,356
1712	148.5	—	—	1739	285.5	45.1	2,157
1713	180.0	157.4	5,712	1740	48.9	31.3	2,828
1714	180.6	210.6	4,076	1741	37.9	39.6	49
1715	173.2	145.5	3,771	1742	295.7	35.6	7,148
1716	75.9	207.8	5,984	1743	376.0	20.8	7,630
1717	25.6	144.4	4,749	1744	234.3	13.5	1,184
1718	74.4	144.2	3,606	1745	325.3	21.6	4,769
1719	130.5	75.4	1,588	1746	131.1	71.4	4,395
1720	84.3	79.1	4,701	1747	270.5	187.7	2,387
1721	82.7	139.4	2,766	1748	545.2	42.8	6,675
1722	178.9	129.6	3,266	1749	630.6	43.2	3,312
1723	158.1	98.5	4,188				

[a] Imports were generally very small or nil, exceeding 1,000 quarters in only six of the years covered, viz. 1698, 1709, 1728, 1729, 1740, and 1741.
[b] The equivalent modern weights of a great stone and a bag are uncertain.
Sources: D. G. Barnes, *A History of the English Corn Laws from 1660–1846*, repr. New York, 1965, p. 299; Elizabeth B. Schumpeter, *English Overseas Trade Statistics, 1697–1808*, Oxford, 1960, Table xvi. See also B. R. Mitchell and P. Deane, *Abstract of British Historical Statistics*, Cambridge, 1962, pp. 94–6, 190 − 1.

Table LI. *Average annual net exports of grains (Great Britain) and imports of raw wool (England and Wales), 1697–1749 (quinquennial averages)*

	Net exports[a] (000 qtr)				Imports	
Period	Wheat & wheat flour	Barley	Malt	Oats	Irish wool (000 great stones)[b]	Spanish wool (bags)[b]
1697–9	6.5	21[c]	37[c]	− 1[c]	—	—
1700–4	86.9	33	77	—	316.8	3,903
1705–9	122.5	21	125	—	242.0	2,759
1710–14	121.2	22	170	—	226.5	5,001
1715–19	95.9	24	248	—	143.5	3,940
1720–4	150.2	22	301	− 12	112.0	3,828
1725–9	58.8	4	239	− 51	54.7	4,487
1730–4	270.8	29	191	− 25	39.1	5,144
1735–9	322.7	43	180	− 1	65.3	4,391
1740–4	198.6	17	180	− 17	28.2	3,768
1745–9	380.5	97	315	—	73.3	4,308

[a] See Table L, note *a*. Most of the wheat imports and over half of the barley imports occurred during the period 1725–9. The figures for malt are of exports only, while those for oats are of imports only.

[b] See Table L, note *b*.

[c] The period Michaelmas 1696 to 25 Dec. 1698 has been counted as two years in computing the averages for 1697–9. All other figures are for years ended 25 Dec.

Sources: See Table L.

H. NOTE ON STATISTICAL METHODS AND SOURCES

Although seventeenth- and eighteenth-century agricultural price data are somewhat more plentiful than for earlier periods, there are comparatively few farm products for which we possess continuous time series extending over all, or the larger part, of the period covered by our study. Most series, especially those derived from farm accounts, are either discontinuous or cover only short runs of years. Almost without exception, the longer series are of Assize prices or pertain to institutional purchases.

Additional, but related, problems arise in connection with the comparability of the data. Thus, goods were marketed under a variety of conditions of sale, with uneven or distorting effects upon prices. Apart from underlying dissimilarities in demand and supply situations – which are, of course, of legitimate concern in the present instance – there may have been differences in, for example, the level of trade, the scale of transaction, or the method of payment (whether cash or credit) – all of which could have affected the price paid, or received, for goods. Likewise, there may have been significant differences with respect to product characteristics, such as quality, type, condition, age, or weight. The prices of livestock and of certain animal products, such as wool and cheese, were especially sensitive to such considerations, although there appear to have been clearly recognized, and separately priced, grades of grain.[1] Unfortunately, these distinctions are seldom spelled out in the accounts of the period, and, other than being able to differentiate between goods on the basis of broad categories or types, it has not generally been possible to acknowledge these differences in the treatment of the data. As highlighted by G. Harrison in Appendix I, lack of standardization in the use of weights and measures introduces the possibility of further distortion into our analysis of prices. Occasionally, information has been available which has provided a reasonably sure basis for adjustment in this regard, but in most instances it has been necessary to accept commonly used units of measurement, such as quarters and bushels, at their normal present-day values. There has been even less to guide us with respect to indeterminate units of weight or capacity, such as the load.

In developing our indices of prices, the first step was to recast all transactions on a unit-price basis (e.g. shillings per quarter, shillings per cow).

---

[1] See above, pp. 209–21.

For each source, or series of related sources, these unit prices were then grouped on a commodity basis by harvest years (29 September to 28 September). The number of annual observations thus grouped ranged from one or two to forty or fifty per source. Subsequently, simple arithmetical averages were calculated on a yearly basis for each commodity–source combination. The volume of data thus assembled varied considerably as between commodities, with grains being best served in this respect.

Both in order to assist in the process of regional historical analysis and to provide geographical balance to our country-wide price indices, the possibility of developing regional price averages was examined. In the case of certain commodities such an undertaking seemed feasible, although the uneven geographical coverage of the data posed problems for the determination of appropriate price regions. After considerable experimentation, the country was divided into nine county groupings, using one or more of the following criteria in addition to geographical proximity: approximate equivalence in regard to the prices of agricultural products generally; broadly similar patterns of agricultural land use; and/or a sufficiency of price data (i.e. observations for over half of the years in question) with respect to most of the major commodities treated. The nine county groupings, or regions, finally decided upon were as follows:

1   Home Counties and London: Surrey, Middx, Essex, Herts.
2   South Midlands: Berks., Bucks., Oxon.
3   South: Kent, Sussex, Hants., Dorset, Wilts.
4   South-west: Somerset, Glos., Devon, Cornwall
5   West: Worcs., Staffs., Herefords.
6   North and north-west: Cheshire, Lancs., Westmor., Cumb., Northumb., Durham
7   Yorks., Notts., and Derbs.
8   North Midlands and Lincolnshire: War., Northants., Leics., Rutland, Lincs.
9   East: Norfolk, Suffolk, Cambs., Hunts., Beds.

It will be noted that these regions are not identical with those featured elsewhere in this volume

For those commodities in respect of which it proved possible to construct regional price averages, the statistical procedure used may be illustrated using wheat as an example. First, short or very broken price series were discarded unless examination showed them to encompass years for which regional data would otherwise be lacking. The next step was to select for each region a series of wheat prices against which other wheat price series could be measured. In most instances the longest series was chosen as the standard. In the case of the south of England the selected series was that of Winchester College; in the south-west it was that of the Exeter Assize. Subsequently, using the south of England as an illustration, an average price differential coefficient was established between the prices in each non-Winchester series and the Winchester prices in corresponding years. For example, the average price of wheat in Maidstone was found to be 0.982 times that of wheat in Winchester for the same years. Each Maidstone wheat price was, therefore, multiplied by a factor of 1.018, or $\frac{1}{0.982}$. After each south series of wheat prices had been treated in this way, simple arithmetical averages were obtained of the adjusted prices. This process was repeated for every region. Where, as was sometimes the case, it was not possible to establish a direct relationship between a series and the series selected as the standard, an indirect relationship was established through some third overlapping series the ratio of whose average price to the average price of the basic series was known. Then, using the statistical procedure described above, the resulting regional averages were combined into a wheat price series for 'England', with the south price averages as the standard series.

As a further step in this statistical exercise, decennial price averages were calculated for 'England' and for the individual regions. In the calculation of these averages, a problem was posed by gaps in some of the regional series. In instances where such gaps affected short runs of years, rather than whole decades, the regional decennial average was estimated by inflating or deflating the relevant decennial average for 'England' by an average price differential coefficient reflecting the relationship between regional annual prices in the decade and corresponding national prices. Consequent upon the use of this procedure, some slight discrepancies may be found in particular instances between the average decennial price for all regions and the 'England' decennial price. Finally, the annual and decennial price averages for 'England', and the decennial averages for the various regions, were converted into indices, with the average price ruling in 'England' over the period as a whole as the base (= 100).

Essentially the same procedure was followed with respect to all cereals. In the case of other products various shortcomings in the data necessitated some modifications in approach. In regard to most types of livestock the main problem was less one of lack of data than their diffusion over many comparatively short series. The principal solution adopted was to group the different series on a county basis, using the average prices for one county as the standard series for the purpose of calculating regional averages. Thus, in the case of bullocks, taking the south-west of England as an example, the price averages for Devonshire incorporated prices derived from six different sources or sets of sources, and these averages became the standard against which the average prices pertaining to other counties in this region were measured. In turn, the south-west price series for bullocks was used as the standard series in the calculation of 'England' bullock prices. In the case of six livestock categories – sheep, wethers, oxen, bullocks, cows, and heifers

– sufficient data were obtained on a countrywide basis to permit the construction of decennial price averages for all regions. In the case of three other livestock groups – ewes, lambs, and bulls – this exercise was precluded by gaps in the data for several regions. At a still lower level of data availability – in connection with the price of ewes, ewes and lambs, tups, runts, cows and calves, calves, horses, and wool – lack of observations precluded any attempt at statistical manipulation on a regional basis, and the 'England' price averages were, therefore, constructed using the averages of a particular county as a reference point. Finally, there were a number of other agricultural commodities – including hops, hay, straw, meat, and dairy products – pertaining to which only a few (primarily institutional, although generally long) price series could be found. In the case of these commodities, the predominant individual series was used as the standard in the calculation of the 'England' averages.

The standard series and base price for each commodity covered by these various operations are listed in the accompanying table (p. 385).

In the calculation of average price indices for each major group of commodities (e.g. grains, cattle) no attempt has been made to weight products according to their relative importance, since the necessary information respecting production or consumption patterns is not available. In years for which there are no data for some products in a group, simple arithmetical averages have been calculated in respect of those commodities for which data exist. Similarly, the indices for 'All agricultural commodities' are simple unweighted averages of indices of major groups of products.

As already noted elsewhere,[2] the statistical procedures which we have adopted are open to criticism on theoretical grounds. In particular, there is the possibility that the long-term trend of prices for individual commodities will be misrepresented if the trend of the standard series is markedly different from that of other series, especially if the total number of observations is small. Further, the extent, although probably not the direction, of year-to-year variations may also be misrepresented. It may hardly be necessary to note that national price averages will fluctuate to a lesser extent than the individual price series from which they are ultimately derived. As for our regional price averages, these should not be pushed too hard in view of the thinness of the data with respect to certain commodities and regions.

Because of their piecemeal nature, seventeenth- and eighteenth-century wage data are, if anything, more difficult than price data to assemble and integrate into an analytically useful form. None of the many sources investigated was found to yield enough data to permit the construction of a lengthy time series of wage rates for any one agricultural occupation in any one locality. Accordingly, the data presented in Table XLIV draw upon a sampling of sources in a cross-section of counties for wage rates for ordinary

[2] *Supra*, p. 172.

Standard series and base prices for all commodities

Commodity	'England' base price (average 1640–1749)	Region	County	Individual series
Wheat	34.80s. per qtr	South		Winchester College
Barley & malt	17.90s. per qtr	South		Maidstone Qtr Sess.
Oats	13.36s. per qtr	South		Winchester College
Rye	23.03s. per qtr	N. & N.W.		Northumb. Qtr Sess.
Beans	21.45s. per qtr	South		Maidstone Qtr Sess.
Peas	25.02s. per qtr	South		Maidstone Qtr Sess.
Hops	106.62s. per cwt			Eton College
Hay	53.55s. per load			Lord Steward's
Straw	18.60s. per load			Lord Steward's
Sheep (unspecified)	10.70s. each	South	Sussex	
Wethers	12.41s. each	South	Sussex	
Ewes	8.57s. each	South	Hants.	
Ewes & lambs	21.86s. per couple		Surrey	
Tups	9.11s. each		Westmor.	
Lambs	9.08s. each	South	Sussex	
Oxen	142.92s. each	South	Sussex	
Bullocks	85.27s. each	S.W.	Devon	
Runts	84.57s. each		Sussex	
Cows	84.96s. each	West	Staffs.	
Heifers	65.45s. each	S.W.	Devon	
Cows/heifers & calves	96.01s. per couple		Surrey	
Bulls	41.78s. each	S.W.	Devon	
Calves	13.51s. each		Surrey	
Horses (unspecified)	147.39s. each		Surrey	
Pigs (boars)	83.15s. each			Oxford, All Souls'
Hens (chickens)	1.67s. each			Lord Steward's
Ducks	1.79s. each			Lord Steward's
Geese (green)	3.47s. each			Lord Steward's
Turkeys (poults)	2.56s. each			Lord Steward's
Wool	22.24s. per tod		Lincs.	
Mutton	2.17s. per (8 lb) stone			Eton College 'A'
Milk	2.23s. per doz. qt			Lord Steward's
Butter	5.68s. per doz. lb			Sandwich (St Bart's)
Cheese (Cheshire)	3.80s. per doz. lb			Sandwich (St Bart's)
Beef	2.31s. per (8 lb) stone			Charterhouse
Pork	1.98s. per (8 lb) stone			Navy Vict., London (1st qtr)
Eggs	7.13s. per 120			Lord Steward's

day-to-day agricultural operations. In order to arrive at the decennial average wage rates presented in Table XLIV a number of arbitrary steps were necessary. First, in instances where a range of wage rates was found to apply, the median rate was taken for the purpose of calculation. Secondly, the wage rate applicable to the nearest point of reference was used to fill gaps in the data at the beginning or end of a county series. Other gaps were filled by a process of extrapolation assuming a constant rate of change. Subsequently, simple arithmetical averages were calculated to give the figures indicated in the last column of Table XLIV.

The sources of price and wage data which have been utilized in connection with this study extend over a wide range of printed and manuscript material. For purpose of identification they are listed alphabetically below under three main heads: (a) Publications, (b) County Record Offices, and (c) Other record repositories.

Individual series are identified either by the name of the pertinent institution, municipality, or other organ of government, or, in the case of private sources, by the name of the family or record collection, followed by a listing of the pertinent estate or estates. Dates have been attached to most series. In the case of the institutional series these generally refer to the periods over which substantially continuous tabulation of data is possible. In the case of other records there is likely to be much more discontinuity, at least over long periods.

For ease of reference, documentary sources have been identified by their collection and/or manuscript classification or number.

Publications

Beveridge, W. H. (Lord). 'A Statistical Crime of the Seventeenth Century', *J. Ec. Bus. Hist.*, 1929.

Beveridge, W. H. (Lord), *et al. Prices and Wages in England from the Twelfth to the Nineteenth Century*. London, 1939. Vol. *I*.

    Charterhouse, 1644–1830.
    Chelsea Hospital, 1702–1810.
    Eton College, 1444–1831.
    Greenwich Hospital, 1695–1828.
    Lord Steward's Department, 1659–1830.
    Navy Victualling: London, Plymouth, and Portsmouth, 1683–1826.
    Westminster (School and Abbey), 1564–1830.
    Winchester College, 1393–1817.

Brown, E. H. Phelps, and Hopkins, Sheila V. 'Wage-Rates and Prices: Evidence for Population Pressure in the Sixteenth Century', *Economica*, NS XXIV, 1957.

    Indices of prices of industrial products, England, 1401–1700.

Gilboy, Elizabeth W. 'The Cost of Living and Real Wages in Eighteenth Century England', *Rev. Ec. Stat.*, XVIII, 3, 1936.

    Wages in Eighteenth Century England. Cambridge, Mass., 1934.

Hill, J. W. F. *Tudor and Stuart Lincoln*. Cambridge, 1956.

    Corn prices returned by leet juries, 1513–1712.

Lodge, E. C., ed. *The Account Book of a Kentish Estate, 1616–1704*. Records of the Social and Economic History of England and Wales, VI. London, 1927.

Macfarlane, A., ed. *The Diary of Ralph Josselin, 1616–1683*, British Acad. Rec. of Soc. and Ec. Hist., NS III, 1976.

Mitchell, B. R., and Deane, Phyllis. *Abstract of British Historical Statistics*. Cambridge, 1962.

    Indices of wages of labourers in London and Lancashire, 1700–96.

    Price of Lincoln long wool, 1706–81.

    Prices of wheat at Exeter, 1316–1820; Eton, 1594–1820; and Winchester, 1630–1817.

    Schumpeter–Gilboy price indices, 1661–1823.

Rogers, J. E. T. *A History of Agriculture and Prices in England from 1259 to 1793*. Oxford, 1866–1902. Vols. *VI* and *VII*.

    Basingstoke, Hants., 1722–30.

    Biggin, Cambs., 1640–1750.

    Brandsby, Yorks., 1735–50.

    Bristol, Glos., 1727–37.

    Cambridge colleges & market, 1640–1750.

    Castle Howard, Yorks., 1716–29.

    Coxwold, Yorks., 1740–8.

    Essex, 1640–52.

    Foxcombe, Hants., 1699–1703.

    Gloucester, Glos., 1728–50.

    Hardwick, Bucks., 1649–1750.

    Harting, Sussex, 1696–1750.

    London (Bear Key), 1697–1750.

    Oxford colleges & market, 1640–1750.

    Portsmouth, Hants., 1662–1750.

    Reading, Berks., 1710–50.

    Weedon, Bucks., 1649–1750.

    Winchester, Hants., 1644–1702.

    John Houghton's price currents, 1691–1703.

Schumpeter, Elizabeth B. 'English Prices and Public Finance, 1660–1822', *Rev. Ec. Stat.*, XX, 1, 1938.

Thirsk, Joan, ed. *The Agrarian History of England and Wales, IV: 1500–1640*. Cambridge, 1967.

    Statistical appendix: Prices of agricultural commodities, 1450–1649.

Yorkshire Diaries and Autobiographies in the 17th and 18th Centuries. Surtees Soc., LXV, 1875.

    Journal of John Holson of Dodsworth, 1726–34.

County Record Offices

Bedford

Ashburnham: Ampthill, 1737–8. R.O.1/128.

Becher: Howbury, Salphoberry, Favills, 1663–89. P.O.3.

Boteler: Biddenham, 1634–63. T.W.800–9.

Chester: Chicheley (Bucks.), Lidlington, 1658–1708. CH938; BC482.

Francklin: 1668–9. F.N.994.

Hanscombe: Shillington, 1693–1727. H.E.259–64.

Orlebar: Hinwick, Podington, 1732–50. O.R.1,352, 1,355.

Russell (duke of Bedford): Thorney (Hunts.), 1734–47. R4/4,011, 4,022; R5/4,311–14.

Berkshire
Allen: Streatley, 1675–6. D/EBp/E24.
Burdett: Horemarke (Derbs.), 1738–50. D/EBu/A1/1.
Clarke: Ardington, Isbury, 1656–1732. D/ECw/M2.
Craven: N. & W. Berks., 1725–46. D/EC/A3.
Pleydell-Bouverie: Coleshill, N. Wilts., 1725–50. D/EPb/E5–14.
Stonehouse: Radley, Abingdon, 1712–18. D/EP1/E1.
Throckmorton: Buckland, Weston Underwood (Bucks.), Derbs. estates, 1695–1750. D/EWe/A1–3; D/EBu/A4/1.

Buckingham
Chester: Chicheley, Sherington, Lidlington (Beds.), 1645–1750. D/C/2/33–45; AR18/69 box 1.
Drake: Shardeloes, Amersham & area, 1692–1707. D/DR/2/48, 51, 89.
Hampden: Great Hampden, Little Hampden, Wendover, Great Kimble, Monks Risborough, 1740–9. D/MH/33/1–8.
Uthwatt: Great Linford & area, 1678–1750. Account nos. 1–13.
Way: Hughenden, 1738–50. D/W bdles 60, 61, 64.

Cambridge
North (Lord): Kirtling, 1639–62. L95/12.

Cheshire
Rode: Rode, 1669. DBW/M/A39.

Cornwall
Buller: Sherford (Devon), 1692–6. DDBU145.
Erys: Lambridgan, 1722–9. DDEN 1,357.
Rashleigh: St Minver, 1647–1741. DDR3,858, 4,461, 4,543, 5,399.

Cumberland
Curwen: Workington, 1625–46. D/Lons.
Fleming: Rydal (Westmor.), 1688–1737. D/Sen. Fleming 20, 21.
Leconfield: Cockermouth, 1665–1735. D/Lec/289, 290.
Lowther/Lonsdale: Lowther (Westmor.), Whitehaven, 1639–1742. D/Lons/L/A1/5; D/Lons/LA/2/32, 66–81; D/Lons/W lists 1, 2.
Pennington: Muncaster, 1695–1708. D/Pen/203.
Quarter Sessions: Carlisle, Penrith, Cockermouth, 1694–1750. Q.S.Q/1–8; Q.S.124, 125.

Devon
Courtenay: Powderham & other estates, 1688–1750. 1,508M/V2–38; 19M/E2.
Crosse: Bampton, Morebath, 1688–1750. 1,160M/Accounts A9.

Drake: Sherford & other estates, 1734–50. 346M/E1.
Ilbert: W. Alvington, S. Milton, 1738–46. 316M/EA13–14.
Quarter Sessions: Exeter, 1733–50. III 3A 5C.
Russell (duke of Bedford): Tavistock & other estates, 1743–50. 1,258M/F26, 27.

Dorset
Almshouses: Sherborne, 1642–1750. D204/217–668, 1,108.
Bragge: Sadborrow for Thorncombe, 1726–50. D83/1.
Larder: W. Chelborough, 1700–50. P16/M11.
Strode: Parnham, Mosterton, Chantmarle, Bilsay, 1730–50. D279/E4.
Tilly: Thornford, 1746–8. D188A/E22.
Weld: E. Lulworth & other estates, 1643–1750. D10/AE1–8, AF1.

Durham
Salvin: Croxdale, 1709–49. D/Sa/E167–195.

Essex
Gidea Hall: Gidea Park, 1746–50. D/DBe/A1–2.
Howard: Conyers nr Epping, 1741–8. D/DW A1, 3.
Lennard (or Barrett): Aveley, 1724–39. D/DL/E1, E81.
Petre: W. Horndon, Ingatestone, 1656–1702. D/DP/A47–57.
Savill, Joseph, of Bocking: Stourbridge Fair, 1743–50. D/DCd/A1.
Tylers Hall: Upminster, 1732–5. D/DM/A20.
Weald Hall: S. Weald, 1733–47. D/DTW/A2.

Greater London County
Russell (duke of Bedford): Streatham, Cheam, 1747–50. E/BER/S/E/7/4/4, 6.
—: Ruislip, 1723. Middx Div., Acc 249/3,010.

Hampshire
—: Millcourt, Binstead, 1678–1738. 3M51/605.
Overseers accounts: Appleshaw, 1707–21. 2M37/21, 25(332).

Hereford
Foley: Almeley, 1742–4. E12/F/A III/40.
Guy's Hospital: Llangarron, 1741–4. C99/III/305.
Noble: Hellens, Much Marcle, 1740–1. F35/RC/M III/279.
Partridge: Llangarron, 1747–8. K2/III/9.

Hertford
Aldenham Parish: Markets at Watford, Hemel Hempstead, St Albans, 1661–5.
    D/P3.1/2.
Brand: Kimpton, Barnet, 1728–50. 40,688; 40,690.
Broadfield Hall: Cottered, 1690–6. 70,474A, B.
Capell: Watford, Cassio & other estates in Herts. & Norfolk, 1678–1702. 10,447–69.
Hatfield (earl of Salisbury): Bygrave, 1677–1716. 26,294.

Parish Register: Little Hormead, 1690–1715. D/P 56.1/2.
Radcliffe: Hitchin, 1730–8. DE4,209–634.
Rolt: Sacombe Park, 1699–1700. D/EAS 2,171C.
Sebright: Beechwood, Flamstead, 1702–48. 63,795; 18,104.
Wilshere: Wymondley, 1745–7. 61,589; 61,590.

Huntingdon
Bernard: Grafham & other estates, 1679–1750. Manchester Coll. ddM5/4, 5;
     ddM16/39; ddM29/6; ddM44B/1, 2.
Cromwell: Dalby, 1658–80. Cromwell 25.
—: Kimbolton Castle, 1746. Manchester Coll. ddM22/13.
St John: Longthorpe (Northants.), Doddington (Cambs.), and the Fens, 1702–14.
     Manchester Coll. ddM16/59.
Thornhill: Great Dingle (Suffolk), 1735–45. 148/4/8.

Kent
Darell: Barksore nr Sittingbourne, 1726–9. U386/A1–2.
Rockingham, earl of: Waldershare Park nr Dover, 1740–50. U471 A18–19.
Sackville: Knole, 1646–1739. U269/A41–9.

Lancashire
Cavendish: Dalton in Furness, 1682–1708. DDCa 12/5–10.
Clifton: Lytham, Layton, Lathom, Westby, 1696–1706. DDCl 386, 399.
Farington: Worden, Leyland, Ulnes Walton, Penwortham, Whittle-le-Woods,
     1695–1750. DDF27–33.
Hawkshead-Talbot: Chorley, Euxton, 1676–1746. DDHk.
Lathom: Scarisbrick, 1723–50. DP/385.
Molyneaux (earl of Sefton): Sefton, 1712–46. DDM140–2.
Pedder: Finsthwaite, 1712–50. DDPd26/337.
Stanley (earl of Derby): Bickerstaffe, Knowsley, & other estates, 1714–50.
     DDK2,012/1, 2,021/1–6.
Weld (Shireburne): Stonyhurst, Chaigley, Dalton, Clitheroe, & areas, 1690–1714.
     DDSt.

Leicester
Heyrick, Beaumanor, 1688–1703. No ref.
Nottingham and Winchelsea, earl of: Burley & other estates in Rutland, Norfolk,
     & Essex, 1667–1727. DG7/1, 2.

Norfolk
—: Horsham St Faith, 1686. NRS16,023.

Northampton
Brudenell (earl of Cardigan): estates in Leicester & Yorkshire, 1713–29. Bru
     A.S.R.116, 117.
Dryden: Chesterton, Canons Ashby, Weekley, Blakesley, 1655–1737. D(CA)305–8,
     312, 789.

Fitzwilliam: Castor-cum-Milton, Aylesworth, Helpston, 1685–1710. Fitzwilliam Misc. Vols. 714, 790.
Howe: Greatworth, 1707–24. YZ997.
Isham: Lamport, 1717–50. IL3,945, 5,278.
Langham: Walgrave, 1710–15. ML783.

Northumberland
Allgood. Nunwick, 1709–50. Allgood ZAL boxes 44, 46, 60–2.
Atkinson: Longbenton, 1728–40. Griffiths ZGR.
Blackett: Newby (Yorks.), 1690–8. ZBL 273/2–4.
—: Haggeston, 1675–80. ZHG IV/3.
Radcliffe: Spindleston farm nr Bamburgh, 1676–95. Simpson ZS1/1–4.
Swinburne: Capheaton, 1667–1750. Swinburne ZSW 228–46, 344–6.
Quarter Sessions: Newcastle, Alnwick, Morpeth, 1693–1742. Q.S.O. vols. I–IV; Q.S.B. vols. 8–86.

Nottingham
Monoux: Gonalston, 1739–40. Franklin DDF1/1.

Shropshire
Charlton: Apley, 1677–8. 625/box 19.
Corbet: Adderley, Drayton, 1667–74. Corbet Family Archives.
Hill: London & other places, 1735–6. Attingham Coll. boxes of vouchers.
Parish Overseers accounts: Childs Ereall, 1715–50. 2,182/3/1–3.
Parish Overseers accounts: Ightfield, 1738–50. 975/9.

Somerset
Carew: Camerton, Clatworthy, Crowcombe, 1694–1750. DD/TB boxes 13, 14.
—: Hestercombe, nr Taunton, 1696–1723. DD/SAS, C/795, P.R.70.
Hylton: Holcombe, Kilmersdon, Writhlington, 1679–95. DD/HY box 12.
Luttrell: Dunster, Minehead, Carhampton, Withycombe, 1747–50. DD/L1/5/16.
Popham: Hunstrete, Nyland, 1649–1750. DD/PO32.
Parsonage accounts: Weston Zoyland, 1689–97. DD/X/REE C/1,308.
Willoughby: Payhembury, 1650–1714. DD/WO boxes 49, 53.

Stafford
Chetwynd: Ingestre, Wood Eaton, Church Eaton, Brereton, 1622–1750. D240/E/219–22.
Gifford: Chillington, Brewood, Marston, Walton-in-Eccleshall, 1662–1750. D590/613–17, 663.
—: Horninglow, 1715–50. DD512(30).
Leveson-Gower: Trentham, 1678–1750. D593/F/2–3; D593/N/2.

Suffolk (East)
—: Blythburgh, Walberswick, 1647. HA30:50/22/27.3(7).
Crowley: Barking-cum-Needham, 1728–36. HA1/GB3/2/1.
Tyrell (duke): Benhall, 1732–7. S1/5/3.1–4.

Suffolk (West)
Clerk: Rectory of Stanton, 1713–49. E1/11/2.
Gwilt: Icklingham, 1730–1. E3/10/9.20.
Hanmer: Mildenhall, 1700–20. E18/660/1–2.
Hervey (earl of Bristol): Ixworth, 1688–1750. 941/46/13, 13A, 14.
Warner: Badmondisfield, 1659–1750. 1,341/5/1–3.

Surrey
Effingham, earl of: Lingfield, 1745–50. 63/1/97–102.
Frederick: Burwood, Walton, 1743–8. 183/33/18, 21a.
Tithe accounts: Abinger, Oxted, Woking, 1664–1744. P1/7/1; P3/5/3; P22/5/66; P52/7/1–174.

Sussex (East)
Ashburnham: Ashburnham & area, 1678–80. Ashburnham 1,630.
Frewen (Evenden): Sedlescombe & other estates, 1642–76. FRE520, 1,729, 7,331, 8,974.
—: Glynde Place nr Lewes, 1675–1721. Glynde 2,931–5.
—: Hickstead, Twineham, 1662–1747. Hickstead 457–74.
Parson: Onehouse, 1708–20. N9/1/1.2.
Shiffner: 1731–50. Shiffner 1,999, 3,609.
—: Ticehurst, 1661–1728. Ticehurst A6, 11–14, 16.
—: Wivelsfield, 1749. Add. 1,778.

Sussex (West)
Derby, dowager countess of: Halnaker, 1740–8. Goodwood E5,530–2.
Somerset, duke of: Petworth & other estates, 1700–48. Petworth 493–7, 2,782–94.

Warwick
Barker: Coleshill, 1715–52. CR233.
Chesterfield: Bretby (Derbs.), 1746–50. CR229/110.
Conway, Lord: Whittington (Glos.), 1739–41. CR114A/250.
Newdigate: Ashtead (Surrey), Arbury nr Coventry, 1644–52. CR136/box 14/B1,104, 1,106, 1,110.
Northampton, earl of: Compton Wynyates & other estates, 1671–6. CR556/275–6.
Taylor: South Littleton (Worcs.), 1709–22. L3/675.
Warwick Priory: Warwick, 1727–9. CR26/2/1.

Westmorland
Browne: Troutbeck, 1715–46. Accounts of Ben Browne, Troutbeck.
Fleming: Rydal, 1656–1750. WD/Ry.

Wiltshire
Ailesbury, earl of: Savernake Forest & area, 1698–1750. 192/41, A, B, G; 9.
Ashe: Wingfield, Stoford, Langley Burrell, 1709–50. 118/140(b), 145.
—: Enford, 1726–37. 415/86, 89.

Howard (earl of Suffolk & Berkshire); Charlton, Hankerton, Brinkworth, Broken-borough, 1748–50. 88/9/26.
Osgood: Normanton in Wilsford, 1676–81. 91/1, 1–22.

Worcester
Berington: Castlemorton, Coddington (Herefords.), 1711–34. 705: 24/355, 381, 1,360, 1,361.

Yorkshire (*N. Riding*)
Cholmeley/Fairfax: Brandsby, Stevesby, Gilling, Sutton upon Derwent, 1650–1750. ZQG; ZDV(F).

Other record repositories
Bodleian Library, Oxford
Hussey: Keal (Lincs.), 1689–90. MS Top. Lincs. B.4, ff. 225–6.

Dudley Central Library
—: Dudley (Worcs.) Horse Fair, 1702–9. Box 24/5.

Guildford Museum and Muniment Room
Clayton: Marden (Surrey), 1707–50. 84/2/2, 3.
—: Conny farm at Addlestone (Surrey), 1724–44. 22/1/4.
Hedley: Bentley in Street hundred (Sussex), 1656–61. LM1,087/1/10. (The generosity of Mr J. More-Molyneux of Loseley Park in permitting use of data from this document and the other Loseley MSS listed below is gratefully acknowledged.)
Howard: Ashtead, Epsom (Surrey), 1693–1722, 1/53/1–9a.
More-Molyneux: Loseley Park, Artington, Compton (Surrey), 1689–1750. LM1,087/1/7, 8, 10; LM1,087/2/5, 16.
Nicholas: W. Horsley (Surrey), 1701–22. 22/1/1–3.
Orslow: Guildford area (Surrey), 1691–1718. 97/11/6.
Shallett: Exton, Eyles Watton, Meonstoke (Hants.), 1750. 121/1/11/3–5.
Wyatt: Horsted Keynes (Sussex), 1718–19. LM1,087/2/8/1–8.

Hereford City Library
—: Holme Lacy farm (Herefords.), 1667–1709. Scudamore 631: 16.

Leicester Museum and City of Leicester Record Office
Cave: Stanford, Swinford, Theddingworth, S. Kilworth (Leics.), 1670–1744. 23D57/1,456, 1,479.
Ferrers: Staunton Harold & other estates in Leics., Chartley (Staffs.), 1703–50. 26D53/2,335, 2,408–10, 2,485.
—: Rothley (Leics.), 1674–1707. 2D31/187, 241.

London School of Economics, British Library of Political and Economic Science: Beveridge Collection of Price Material
Assize Prices of Grain: Canterbury & Maidstone, 1687–1750; Kingston upon Hull, 1708–50; Nottingham, 1640–1750; Shrewsbury, 1640–1737; York, 1671–1750. Misc. Coll. boxes D6, I14, I15/1, 2, 4.

—: sales of horses & cattle, Shrewsbury market, 1646–74. Misc. Coll. box I15/3.
—: Bushey (Herts.), Horton (Bucks.), 1729–39. Misc. Coll. box H12/3.
—: Cambridge colleges (King's, St John's, Trinity), 1640–1750. Boxes G2, G3.

Minet Library, Knatchbull Rd, London SE5: Surrey Room
Howard: Ashtead, Epsom, 1693–1701. "Account Book of the Howard Estates at Ashstead and Epsom, 1693–1701".

Odiham (Hants.) Parish
Lady Gurney's gift: beef prices at Odiham, 1658–1750. Churchwarden's accounts. (The assistance of Mr Barry Stapleton in extracting these data is gratefully acknowledged.)

Reading University Library
Baxendon: Collingham (Notts.), 1748–50. NOT 4/1/1.
—: Coton Hall farm, Bridgnorth (Salop.), 1744–50. SALOP 5/1/1.
Creswick: Bristol (Glos.), 1738–50. GLOU 6/1.
Dixwell: Broome (Kent), 1662–5. KEN 17/1/1.
Grenville: Wotton (Bucks.), 1741–3. BUC 11/1/5.
Halfehide: Babworth (Notts.), 1650–89. NOT 5/1/1.
Luscombe: South Milton (Devon), 1739–50. DEVON 3/2/9.
—: Tatlingbury farm, Tudeley (Kent), 1744–50. KEN 13/1/1.
Temple: Stowe (Bucks.), 1677–80. BUC 11/1/1.
—: Thame (Oxon.), 1742–50. OXF 11/1/1.
Wych: Hockwold (Norfolk), 1681–1723. NOR 14/1/1, 15/1/1, 17/1/1.

Sheepscar Branch Public Library, Leeds
Gascoigne: Aberford, Garforth, Fenton & area (Yorks.), 1724–35. GC/EG/32, 33B, 35.
Ingilby: Ripley, Harrogate & area (Yorks.), 1701–47. Ingilby 1,811–41.
Ingram/Irwin (Lord): Temple Newsam, nr Leeds (Yorks.), 1619–1750. TN/EA/ 12/1, 11(a)–(c), 12.
Lascelles: Harewood (Yorks.), 1749–50. Harewood estate accounts 225, 269.
Robinson/Weddell: Newby Hall, Dishforth, Worden (Yorks.), 1656–1732. NH 2,175, 2,175B, 2,187, 2,194B.

6

SELECT BIBLIOGRAPHY

Addison, W. *English Fairs and Markets*. London, 1953.

Airs, M. *The Making of the English Country House, 1500–1640*. London, 1975.

Albert, W. A. *The Turnpike Road System in England and Wales, 1663–1840*. Cambridge, 1972.

Alcock, N. W. *Stoneleigh Houses*. Birmingham, 1973.

Allison, K. J. *The East Riding of Yorkshire Landscape*. London, 1976.

'Flock Management in the Sixteenth and Seventeenth Centuries', EcHR, 2nd ser., XI, 1958.

'The Norfolk Worsted Industry in the Sixteenth and Seventeenth Centuries', *Yorks. Bull. Ec. & Soc. Research*, XII–XIII, 1960–1.

'The Sheep–Corn Husbandry of Norfolk in the Sixteenth and Seventeenth Centuries', AHR, v, 1, 1957.

Ambler, L. *Old Halls and Manor Houses of Yorkshire*. London, 1913.

Amery, C. *Period Houses and their Details*. London, 1974.

Andrews, J. H. 'The Port of Chichester and the Grain Trade, 1650–1750', *Sussex Arch. Coll.*, XCII, 1954.

Andrews, L. S. 'Vaynor Lands during the Eighteenth Century', *Mont. Coll.*, XLVI, 1940.

Appleby, A. B. 'Disease or Famine? Mortality in Cumberland and Westmorland, 1580–1640', EcHR, 2nd ser., XXVI, 1973.

Ashton, T. S. *Economic Fluctuations in England, 1700–1800*. Oxford, 1959.

An Economic History of England: The Eighteenth Century. London, 1955.

Ashworth, G. J. 'A Note on the Decline of the Wealden Iron Industry', *Surrey Arch. Coll.*, LXVII, 1970.

Astbury, A. K. *The Black Fens*. Cambridge, 1957.

Atwell, G. *The Faithfull Surveyor*. Cambridge, 1662.

Aubrey, J. *The Natural History of Wiltshire*, ed. J. Britton. London, 1847.

Austen, R. *The Spiritual Use of an Orchard; or Garden of Fruit Trees*. Oxford, 1653.

Bailey, J. *A General View of the Agriculture of Durham*. London, 1810.

Bailey, J. and Culley, G. *General View of the Agriculture of Cumberland*. London, 1794.

General View of the Agriculture of the County of Northumberland. 3rd edn. London, 1805.

Baker, A. H. R. and Butlin, R. A. (eds.). *Studies of Field Systems in the British Isles*. Cambridge, 1973.

Banister, J. *A Synopsis of Husbandry*. London, 1799.

Bankes, J. and Kerridge, E. *The Early Records of the Bankes Family at Winstanley*. Manchester, 1973.

Barley, M. W. 'The Double-Pile House', *Arch. J.*, CXXXVI, 1979.

The English Farmhouse and Cottage. London, 1961.

'A Glossary of Names for Rooms in Houses of the Sixteenth and Seventeenth Centuries', in *Culture and Environment*, ed. I. Ll. Foster and L. Alcock. London, 1963.

The House and Home. London, 1963.

Barley, M. W. and Summers, N. 'Averham Park Lodge and its Paintings', *Thoroton Soc.*, LXV, 1961.

Barnes, D. G. *A History of the English Corn Laws from 1660–1846*. London, 1930. Repr. New York, 1965.

Barratt, D. M. (ed.). *Ecclesiastical Terriers of Warwickshire Parishes, II*. Dugdale Soc., 1971.

Batchelor, T. *General View of the Agriculture of the County of Bedford*. London, 1808.

Batey, Mavis. 'Oliver Goldsmith: An Indictment of Landscape Gardening', in P. Willis (ed.), *Furor Hortensis*. Edinburgh, 1974.

Baxter, R. *The Reverend Richard Baxter's Last Treatise*, ed. F. J. Powicke. Manchester, 1926.

Beale, J. *Herefordshire Orchards*. London, 1657.

Beale, J. and Lawrence, A. *Nurseries, Orchards, Profitable Gardens and Vineyards Encouraged*...London, 1677.

Beastall, T. W. *A North Country Estate*. London and Chichester, 1975.

Beavington, F. 'Early Market Gardening in Bedfordshire', *Inst. Brit. Geographers*, XXXVII, 1965.

Beckett, J. V. *Coal and Tobacco: The Lowthers and the Economic Development of West Cumberland, 1660–1760*. Cambridge, 1981.

'English Landownership in the Later Seventeenth and Eighteenth Centuries: The Debate and the Problems', EcHR, 2nd ser., XXX, 4, 1977.

'Regional Variation and the Agricultural Depression, 1730–50', EcHR, 2nd ser., XXXV, 1982.

Bell, V. *To Meet Mr. Ellis: Little Gaddesden in the Eighteenth Century*. London, 1956.

Bennett, M. K. 'British Wheat Yield per Acre for Seven Centuries', *Ec. Hist.*, III, 1935.

Beresford, M. W. 'The Common Informer, the Penal Statutes, and Economic Regulation', EcHR, 2nd ser., X, 1957.

'Glebe Terriers and Open Field Leicestershire', in *Studies in Leicestershire Agrarian History*, ed. W. G. Hoskins. Leicester, 1949.

'Glebe Terriers and Open-Field Yorkshire', *Yorks. Arch. J.*, XXXVII, 1951.

'Habitation versus Improvement', in *Essays in the Economic and Social History of Tudor and Stuart England*, ed. F. J. Fisher. Cambridge, 1961.

Best, Henry. *Rural Economy in Yorkshire in 1641, being the Farming and Account Books of Henry Best of Elmswell, East Riding of Yorkshire*. Surtees Soc., XXXIII. 1851.

Bettey, J. 'The Cultivation of Woad in the Salisbury Area during the Late Sixteenth and Early Seventeenth Centuries', *Textile Hist.*, IX, 1978.

Bigmore, P. *The Bedfordshire and Huntingdonshire Landscape*. London, 1979.

Billing, R. *An Account of the Culture of Carrots*. London, 1765.

Blake, S. *The Compleat Gardener's Practice*. London, 1664.

Blith, W. *The English Improver*. London, 1649. 2nd edn. 1649.

The English Improver Improved. 3rd edn. London, 1652. 4th edn. 1653.

Blome, R. *Britannia*. London, 1673.

Blomefield, F. *An Essay towards a Topographical History of Norfolk.* 5 vols. Norwich and King's Lynn, 1739–75. 2nd edn. 11 vols. 1805–20.

Blundell, N. *The Great Diurnall of Nicholas Blundell of Little Crosby*, ed. J. S. Bagley. 3 vols. Lancs. & Cheshire Rec. Soc. Manchester, 1968–72.

Bonfield, L. 'Marriage Settlements and the "Rise of Great Estates"': The Demographic Aspect', EcHR, 2nd ser., XXXII, 1979.

Bonser, K. J. *The Drovers.* London, 1970.

Bouch, C. M. L. and Jones, G. P. *The Lake Counties, 1500–1830.* Manchester, 1961.

Bowden, P. J. *The Wool Trade in Tudor and Stuart England.* London, 1962.

Boys, J. *General View of the Agriculture of the County of Kent.* London, 1813.

Brace, H. W. *A History of Seed Crushing in Great Britain.* London, 1960.

[Braddon, L.]. *To Pay Old Debts without New Taxes by Charitably Relieving, Politically Reforming, and Judiciously Employing the Poor.* London, 1723.

Bradley, R. *A General Treatise of Husbandry and Gardening, II.* London, 1726.

Brigg, M. 'The Forest of Pendle in the Seventeenth Century', *Hist. Soc. Lancs. & Cheshire*, CXIII, 1961.

Broad, J. 'Alternative Husbandry and Permanent Pasture in the Midlands, 1650–1800', AHR, XXVIII, 2, 1980.

Brodrick, G. C. *English Land and English Landlords.* London, 1881.

Brooks, C. E. P. *Climate through the Ages.* 2nd edn. London, 1949.

Brown, E. H. Phelps and Hopkins, S. V. 'Builders' Wage-Rates, Prices and Population: Some Further Evidence', *Economica*, NS, XXVI, 1959.

'Seven Centuries of the Prices of Consumables, compared with Builders' Wage-Rates', *Economica*, NS, XXIII, 1956.

Brown, J. *General View of the Agriculture of the County of Derby.* London, 1794.

Brunskill, R. W. *Illustrated Handbook of Vernacular Architecture.* London, 1970.

Buchanan, K. M. 'Studies in the Localisation of Seventeenth-Century Worcestershire Industries, 1600–1650', *Worcs. Arch. Soc.*, XVII, 1940; XIX, 1943.

Bulkeley, W. 'The Diary of William Bulkeley of Brynddu, Anglesey', ed. H. Owen, *Anglesey Antiq. Soc.*, 1931.

Campbell, Colin. *Vitruvius Britannicus, or the British Architect.* 3 vols. London, 1715–25.

Campbell, M. *The English Yeoman.* New Haven, 1942.

Carter, E. *A History of Cambridgeshire.* London, 1819.

Carter, W. *The Proverb Crossed.* London, 1677.

Cartwright, J. J. (ed.). *The Travels through England of Dr. Richard Pococke.* 2 vols. Camden Soc., NS, XLII, XLIV, 1888–9.

Cathcart, Earl. 'Jethro Tull, his Life, Times and Teaching', *J. RASE*, 3rd ser., II, I, 1891.

Chalklin, C. W. 'The Rural Economy of a Kentish Wealden Parish, 1650–1750', AHR, X, 1962.

Seventeenth Century Kent: A Social and Economic History. London, 1965.

Chalklin, C. W. and Havinden, M. A. (eds.). *Rural Change and Urban Growth, 1500–1800: Essays in English Regional History in Honour of W. G. Hoskins.* London, 1974.

Chambers, J. D. *Nottinghamshire in the Eighteenth Century.* London, 1932.

Chambers, J. D. and Mingay, G. E. *The Agricultural Revolution, 1750–1880.* London, 1966.

Chapman, S. D. 'The Genesis of the British Hosiery Industry, 1600–1750', *Textile Hist.*, III, 1972.

Chartres, J. A. *Internal Trade in England, 1500–1700*. London, 1977.
'Road Carrying in England in the Seventeenth Century: Myths and Reality', EcHR, 2nd ser., xxx, 1977.
Chauncy, H. *Historical Antiquities of Hertfordshire* (1700). Bishop's Stortford, 1826.
Chesney, H. E. 'The Transference of Lands in England, 1640–60', *Trans. RHS*, 4th ser., xv, 1932.
Chibnall, A. C. *Sherington: The Fiefs and Fields of a Buckinghamshire Village*. Cambridge, 1965.
Child, Sir J. *Discourse about Trade*. London, 1690.
New Discourse of Trade. London, 1694.
Clapham, Sir John. *A Concise Economic History of Britain from the Earliest Times to 1750*. Cambridge, 1949.
Clarke, P. and Slack, P. (eds.). *Crisis and Order in English Towns, 1500–1700*. London, 1972.
Clarkson, L. A. 'The Leather Crafts in Tudor and Stuart England', AHR, xiv, 1, 1966.
The Pre-Industrial Economy in England, 1500–1750. London, 1971.
Clay, C. '"The Greed of Whig Bishops"? Church Landlords and their Lessees, 1660–1760', PP, no. 87. 1980.
'Marriage, Inheritance, and the Rise of Large Estates in England, 1660–1815', EcHR, 2nd ser., xxi, 3, 1968.
'The Misfortunes of William, Fourth Lord Petre', *Recusant Hist.*, xi, 2, 1971.
'The Price of Freehold Land in the Later Seventeenth and Eighteenth Centuries', EcHR, 2nd ser., xxvii, 2, 1974.
Public Finance and Private Wealth. Oxford, 1978.
Cliffe, J. T. *The Yorkshire Gentry from the Reformation to the Civil War*. London, 1969.
Clifton-Taylor, A. *The Pattern of English Building*. London, 1972.
Coate, M. *Cornwall in the Great Civil War and Interregnum*. 2nd edn. Truro, 1963.
Coleman, D. C. *The Economy of England, 1450–1750*. Oxford, 1977.
'Growth and Decay during the Industrial Revolution: The Case of East Anglia', *Scand. Ec. Hist. Rev.*, x, 1962.
'An Innovation and its Diffusion: The "New Draperies"', EcHR, 2nd ser., xxii, 1969.
'Labour in the English Economy of the Seventeenth Century', EcHR, 2nd ser., viii, 1956.
'Naval Dockyards under the Later Stuarts', EcHR, 2nd ser., vi, 1953.
Sir John Banks – Baronet and Businessman. Oxford, 1963.
Coleman, D. C. and John, A. H. (eds.). *Trade, Government and Economy in Pre-Industrial England*. London, 1976.
Colville, James (ed.). *Letters of John Cockburn of Ormistoun to his Gardener, 1727–1744*. Scottish Hist. Soc., xlv. 1904.
Colvin, H. M. *Biographical Dictionary of British Architects*. London, 1978.
History of the King's Works, V. London, 1976.
Colvin, H. M. and Harris, J. (eds.). *The Country Seat*. London, 1970.
Colvin, H. M. and Newman, J. (eds.). *Of Building – Roger North's Writings on Architecture*. Oxford, 1981.

Colyer, R. J. 'Cattle Drovers in the Nineteenth Century', *Nat. Lib. Wales J.*, xviii, 1973–4.

The Welsh Cattle Drovers. Cardiff, 1976.

Cooper, J. P. 'Patterns of Inheritance and Settlement by Great Landowners', in J. Goody *et al.* (eds.), *Family and Inheritance*. Cambridge, 1976.

'The Social Distribution of Land and Men in England, 1436–1700', EcHR, 2nd ser., xx, 1967.

Cordingley, R. A. 'British Historical Roof-Types and their Members', *Ancient Monuments Soc.*, ns, ix, 1961.

Cornwall, J. C. K. 'Agricultural Improvement, 1560–1640', *Sussex Arch. Coll.*, xcviii, 1960.

Court, W. H. B. *The Rise of the Midland Industries, 1600–1838*. Rev. edn. Oxford, 1953.

Cox, T. *Magna Britannia*. London, 1720.

Cracknell, B. E. *Canvey Island*. Leicester, 1959.

Cranfield, G. A. *The Development of the Provincial Newspaper, 1700–1760*. Oxford, 1962.

Crosweller, W. T. *The Gardeners' Company: A Short Chronological History, 1605–1907*. London, 1908.

Darby, H. C. *The Draining of the Fens*. Cambridge, 1940. 2nd edn. 1956.

Davies, Margaret G. 'Country Gentry and Falling Rents in the 1660s and 1670s', *Midland Hist.*, iv, 2, 1977.

Davies, Walter. *A General View of the Agriculture and Domestic Economy of South Wales*. 2 vols. London, 1815.

Davis, O. R. F. 'The Wealth and Influence of John Holles, Duke of Newcastle, 1694–1711', *Renaissance & Mod. Stud.*, ix, 1965.

Davis, R. *General View of the Agriculture of the County of Oxford*. London, 1794.

Davis, T. *General View of the Agriculture of the County of Wiltshire*. London, 1794.

Deane, P. and Cole, W. A. *British Economic Growth, 1688–1959*. Cambridge, 1962. 2nd edn. 1969.

Defoe, Daniel. *The Complete English Tradesman*. 2 vols. London, 1745.

A Tour through the Whole Island of Great Britain, ed. G. D. H. Cole and D. C. Browning. 2 vols. London, 1962.

Dell, R. F. 'The Decline of the Clothing Industry in Berkshire', *Newbury & Dist. Field Club*, x, 1954.

Dexter, K. and Barber, D. *Farming for Profits*. London, 1961.

Dodd, A. H. 'Caernarvonshire in the Civil War', *Caerns. Hist. Soc.*, xiv, 1953.

'The Civil War in East Denbighshire', *Denbs. Hist. Soc.*, iii, 1954.

'Flintshire Politics in the Seventeenth Century', *Flints. Hist. Soc.*, 1953–4.

The Industrial Revolution in North Wales. Cardiff, 1933.

Life in Wales. London, 1972.

'The North Wales Coal Industry during the Industrial Revolution', *Arch. Cambrensis*, lxxxiv, 1929.

'The Pattern of Politics in Stuart Wales', *Hon. Soc. Cymmrodorion*, 1948.

Studies in Stuart Wales. 2nd edn. Cardiff, 1971.

Doddington, George Bubb. *The Political Journal of George Bubb Doddington*, ed. J. Carswell and L. A. Dralle. London, 1965.

Donnelly, T. 'Arthur Clephane, Edinburgh Merchant and Seedsman', AHR, xviii, 2, 1970.

Dony, J. G. *A History of the Straw Hat Industry*. Luton, 1942.

Doughty, H. M. *Chronicles of Theberton*. London, 1910.

Douglas, J. 'The Culture of Saffron', *Philos. Trans. Roy. Soc.*, xxxv, 1728.

Downes, K. *English Baroque Architecture*. London, 1966.

Driver, A. and Driver, W. *General View of the Agriculture of the County of Hampshire*. London, 1794.

Drummond, J. C. and Wilbraham, A. *The Englishman's Food*, rev. D. Hollingsworth. London, 1957.

Dugdale, W. *The History of Imbanking and Drayning*. London, 1662.

Dyer, Alan. 'Growth and Decay in English Towns, 1500–1700', *Urban Hist. Yearbook*, 1979.

Eaton, Daniel. *The Letters of Daniel Eaton to the Third Earl of Cardigan, 1725–32*, ed. Joan Wake and Deborah Champion Webster. Northants. Rec. Soc., xxiv. 1971.

Edie, C. A. *The Irish Cattle Bills: A Study in Restoration Politics*. Amer. Philos. Soc., ns lx. 1970.

Edmunds, Henry. 'History of the Brecknockshire Agricultural Society, 1755–1955', *Brycheiniog*, iii, 1957.

Edwards, J. K. 'The Gurneys and the Norwich Clothing Trade in the Eighteenth Century', *JFHS*, l, 1962–4.

Edwards, P. R. 'The Cattle Trade of Shropshire in the Late Sixteenth and Seventeenth Centuries', *Midland Hist.*, vi, 1981.

'The Development of Dairy Farming on the North Shropshire Plain in the Seventeenth Century', *Midland Hist.*, iv, 3–4, 1978.

'The Horse Trade of the Midlands in the Seventeenth Century', AHR, xxvii, 2, 1979.

Ellis, W. *Chiltern and Vale Farming Explained*. London, 1733.

A Compleat System of Experienced Improvements. London, 1749.

The Compleat Planter and Cyderist. London, 1756.

The Practical Farmer, or The Hertfordshire Husbandman. London, 1732. 2nd edn., 2 pts. 1732.

The Modern Husbandman. 8 vols. London, 1750.

Emery, Frank V. 'Early Cultivation of Clover in Gower', *J. Gower Soc.*, xxvi, 1975.

'The Mechanics of Innovation: Clover Cultivation in Wales before 1750', *J. Hist. Geog.*, ii, 1, 1976.

'A New Account of Snowdonia, 1693, Written for Edward Lhuyd', *Nat. Lib. Wales J.*, xviii, 1974.

Emery, Frank V. and Smith, C. G. 'A Weather Record from Snowdonia, 1697–98', *Weather*, xxxi, 1976.

Evans, E. J. *The Contentious Tithe*. London, 1976.

'Tithing Customs and Disputes: The Evidence of Glebe Terriers, 1698–1850', AHR, xviii, 1, 1970.

Evans, G. N. 'The Artisan and Small Farmer in Mid-Eighteenth Century Anglesey', *Anglesey Antiq. Soc.*, 1933.

Evelyn, John. *Acetaria: A Discourse of Sallets*. London, 1699.

Diary, ed. E. S. de Beer. 6 vols. Oxford, 1955.

Sylva...to which is annexed Pomona. London, 1664.

Everitt, Alan M. 'The English Urban Inn, 1560–1760', in *Perspectives in English Urban History*, ed. Alan Everitt. London, 1973.

'Social Mobility in Early Modern England', *PP*, no. 33, 1966.

Eversley, D. E. C. 'A Survey of Population in an Area of Worcestershire from 1660 to 1850 on the Basis of Parish Registers', in *Population in History*, ed. D. V. Glass and D. E. C. Eversley. London, 1965.

Ferris, J. P. and Oliver, R. C. B. 'An Agricultural Improvement of 1674 at Trewern, Llanfihangel-Nant-Melan', *Radnors. Soc.*, XLII, 1972.

Fieldhouse, R. T. 'Agriculture in Wensleydale from 1600 to the Present Day', *Northern Hist.*, XVI, 1980.

Fieldhouse, R. T. and Jennings, B. *A History of Richmond and Swaledale*. Chichester, 1978.

Fiennes, Celia. *The Journeys of Celia Fiennes*, ed. C. Morris. London, 1947.

Firth, C. H. and Rait, R. S. (eds.). *Acts and Ordinances of the Interregnum, 1642–60*. 3 vols. London, 1911.

Fisher, F. J. 'The Development of London as a Centre of Conspicuous Consumption in the Sixteenth and Seventeenth Centuries', in *Essays in Economic History, II*, ed. E. M.Carus-Wilson. London, 1962. (Repr. from RHS, 4th ser., XXX, 1948.)

'The Development of the London Food Market, 1540–1640', in *Essays in Economic History, I*, ed. E. M. Carus-Wilson. London, 1954. (Repr. from EcHR, V, 1935.)

Fisher, F. J. (ed.). *Essays in the Economic and Social History of Tudor and Stuart England.* Cambridge, 1961.

Fisher, H. E. S. 'Anglo-Portuguese Trade, 1700–1770', EcHR, 2nd ser., XVI, 1963.

Fletcher, A. J. *A County Community in Peace and War: Sussex, 1600–1660*. London, 1975.

Flinn, M. W. 'The Growth of the English Iron Industry, 1660–1760', EcHR, 2nd ser., XI, 1958.

Fowler, J. and Cornforth, J. *English Decoration in the Eighteenth Century*. London, 1974.

Fox, Sir Cyril and Raglan, Lord. *Monmouthshire Houses*. 3 vols. Nat. Museum of Wales, 1953–4.

Fox, H. S. A. and Butlin, R. A. (eds.). *Change in the Countryside: Essays on Rural England, 1500–1900*. Inst. Brit. Geographers, Special Publ., no. 10. London, 1979.

Freeman, C. *Pillow Lace in the East Midlands*. Luton, 1958.

Fuller, T. *The Worthies of England*, ed. J. Freeman. London, 1952.

Fussell, G. E. *The English Dairy Farmer, 1500–1900*. London, 1966.

'Four Centuries of Farming Systems in Hampshire, 1500–1900', *Hants. Field Club & Arch. Soc.*, XVII, 3, 1949.

'Four Centuries of Leicestershire Farming', in *Studies in Leicestershire Agrarian History*, ed. W. G. Hoskins. Leicester, 1949.

'History of Cole (*Brassica* sp.)', *Nature, London*, 9 July 1955.

The Old English Farming Books from Fitzherbert to Tull, 1523 to 1730. London, 1947.

Fussell, G. E. and Goodman, Constance. 'Eighteenth-Century Traffic in Livestock', *Ec. Hist.*, III, 1936.

Garret[t], Daniel. *Designs and Estimates for Farm Houses...* 3rd edn. London, 1772.

Gazley, J. G. *The Life of Arthur Young, 1741–1820*. Philadelphia, 1973.

Gentles, I. 'The Sales of Bishops' Lands in the English Revolution, 1646–1660', EHR, xcv, 1980.

'The Sales of Crown Lands during the English Revolution', EcHR, 2nd ser., xxvi, 4, 1973.

Gerarde, John. *The Herbal, or General Historie of Plantes.* London, 1636.

Gill, H. and Guilford, E. L. (eds.). *The Rector's Book of Clayworth, Notts.* Nottingham, 1910.

Girouard, M. *Robert Smythson.* London, 1966.

Girouard, Mark. *Life in the English Country House: A Social and Architectural History.* New Haven and London, 1978.

Godber, Joyce. *History of Bedfordshire, 1066–1888.* Bedford, 1969.

Godfrey, W. H. *The English Almshouse.* London, 1955.

Gooder, A. *Plague and Enclosure: A Warwickshire Village in the Seventeenth Century.* Coventry & N. War., Hist. Pamphlets, no. 2. 1965.

'The Population Crisis of 1727–30 in Warwickshire', *Midland Hist.*, 1, 4, 1972.

Gough, R. *Antiquityes and Memoyres of the Parish of Myddle.* London, 1875.

Grainger, J. *General View of the Agriculture of Co. Durham.* London, 1794.

Granger, C. W. J. and Elliott, C. M. 'A Fresh Look at Wheat Prices and Markets in the Eighteenth Century', EcHR, 2nd ser., xx, 1967.

Gras, N. S. B. *The Evolution of the English Corn Market from the Twelfth to the Eighteenth Century.* Harvard Ec. Stud., xiii. Cambridge, Mass., 1915.

Gray, H. L. *English Field Systems.* Cambridge, Mass., 1915.

'Yeoman Farming in Oxfordshire from the Sixteenth Century to the Nineteenth Century', *Qtly J. Ec.*, xxiv, 1910.

Green, D. *Gardener to Queen Anne: Henry Wise and the Formal Garden.* Oxford, 1956.

Green, F. 'The Stepneys of Prendergast', *W. Wales Hist. Rec.*, vii, 1917–18.

Green, I. M. 'The Persecution of Parish Clergy during the English Civil War', EHR, xciv, 1979.

Gunther, R. T. *The Architecture of Sir Roger Pratt.* Oxford, 1928.

Habakkuk, H. J. 'Daniel Finch, 2nd Earl of Nottingham: His House and Estate', in *Studies in Social History*, ed. J. H. Plumb. London, 1955.

'The English Land Market in the Eighteenth Century', in *Britain and the Netherlands*, ed. J. S. Bromley and E. H. Kossmann. London, 1960.

'English Landownership, 1680–1740', EcHR, x, 1940.

'The Land Settlement and the Restoration of Charles II', RHS, 5th ser., xxviii, 1978.

'Landowners and the Civil War', EcHR, 2nd ser., xviii, 1965.

'Marriage Settlements in the Eighteenth Century', RHS, 4th ser., xxxii, 1950.

'Public Finance and the Sale of Confiscated Property during the Interregnum', EcHR, 2nd ser., xv, 1962–3.

'The Rise and Fall of English Landed Families, 1600–1800', RHS, 5th ser., xxix–xxx, 1979–80.

Hadfield, Miles. *A History of British Gardening.* London, 1969.

Halfpenny, William. *Twelve Beautiful Designs for Farmhouses.* London, 1750.

Hammersley, G. 'The Charcoal Iron Industry and its Fuel, 1540–1750', EcHR, 2nd ser., xxvi, 1973.

'The Crown Woods and their Exploitation in the Sixteenth and Seventeenth Centuries', *Bull. IHR*, xxx, 1957.

Harris, A. 'The Agriculture of the East Riding before the Parliamentary Enclosures', *Yorks. Arch. J.*, XL, 1962.

The Open Fields of East Yorkshire. York, 1959.

Hartley, M. and Ingilby, J. *The Old Hand-Knitters of the Dales*. Clapham, 1951.

Hartlib, S. *His Legacie, or An Enlargement of the Discours of Husbandrie Used in Brabant and Flanders*. London, 1651. 2nd edn. 1652.

[C. Dymock]. *A Discovery for Division or Setting Out of Land*. London, 1653.

Harvey, John H. *Early Gardening Catalogues*. London, 1972.

Early Nurserymen. London, 1974.

'The Family of Telford, Nurserymen of York', *Yorks. Arch. J.*, XLII, 167, 1969.

'Leonard Gurle's Nurseries and Some Others', *Garden Hist.*, III, 3, 1975.

'The Nurseries on Milne's Land-Use Map', *London & Middx Arch. Soc.*, XXIV, 1973.

'The Stocks Held by Early Nurseries', *AHR*, XXII, 1, 1974.

Havinden, M. A. 'Agricultural Progress in Open Field Oxfordshire', *AHR*, IX, 2, 1961.

Henrey, Blanche. *British Botanical and Horticultural Literature before 1800*. 3 vols. Oxford, 1975.

Henstock, A. 'Cheese Manufacture and Marketing in Derbyshire and North Staffordshire, 1670–1870', *Derbs. Arch. J.*, LXXXIX, 1969.

Hervey, Lord Francis (ed.). *Suffolk in the Seventeenth Century: A Breviary of Suffolk by Robert Reyce, 1618*. London, 1902.

Hey, D. *An English Rural Community: Myddle under the Tudors and Stuarts*. Leicester, 1974.

Packmen, Carriers and Packhorse Roads. Leicester, 1980.

The Rural Metalworkers of the Sheffield Region. Leicester, 1972.

Hill, M. C. 'The Wealdmoors, 1560–1660', *Shrops. Arch. J.*, LIV, 1951–3.

Hill, O. and Cornforth, J. *English Country Houses: Caroline*. London, 1966.

Holderness, B. A. 'The Agricultural Activities of the Massingberds of South Ormsby, Lincolnshire, 1638 – c. 1750', *Midland Hist.*, I, 3, 1972.

'Capital Formation in Agriculture', in *Aspects of Capital Investment in Great Britain, 1750–1850*, ed. J. P. P. Higgins and S. Pollard. London, 1971.

'Credit in English Rural Society before the Nineteenth Century', *AHR*, XXIV, 1976.

'The English Land Market in the Eighteenth Century: The Case of Lincolnshire', *EcHR*, 2nd ser., XXVII, 4, 1974.

Holiday, P. G. 'Land Sales and Repurchases in Yorkshire after the Civil Wars, 1650–1670', *Northern Hist.*, V, 1970.

Holland, H. *General View of the Agriculture of Cheshire*. London, 1808.

Hollingsworth, T. H. 'The Demography of the British Peerage', suppl. to *Pop. Stud.*, XVIII, 1964.

Holmes, G. S. 'Gregory King and the Social Structure of Pre-Industrial England', *RHS*, 5th ser., XXVII, 1977.

Holt, J. *General View of the Agriculture of the County of Lancaster*. London, 1795.

Hopkins, E. 'The Bridgewater Estates in North Shropshire during the Civil War', *Shrops. Arch. Soc.*, LVI, 2, 1960.

'The Re-Leasing of the Ellesmere Estates, 1637–42', *AHR*, X, 1, 1962.

Hoskins, W. G. 'Harvest Fluctuations and English Economic History, 1620–1759', AHR, XVI, 1, 1968.

Houghton, John. *A Collection for Improvement of Husbandry and Trade*. 9 vols. London, 1692–1703. Ed. R. Bradley. 4 vols. London, 1727–8.

A Collection of Letters for the Improvement of Husbandry and Trade. 2 vols. London, 1681–3.

Howard, C. 'The Culture of Saffron', *Philos. Trans. Roy. Soc.*, XII, 1678.

Howells, B. E. (ed.). *A Calendar of Letters relating to North Wales*. Cardiff, 1967.

Hughes, E. *North Country Life in the Eighteenth Century: The North-East, 1700–1750*. Oxford, 1952.

North Country Life in the Eighteenth Century, II, Cumberland & Westmorland, 1700–1830. Oxford, 1965.

Hull, F. 'The Tufton Sequestration Papers', *Kent Rec.*, XVII, 1960.

Hussey, C. *English Country Houses: Early Georgian*. London, 1965.

Innocent, C. F. *The Development of English Building Construction*. Cambridge, 1916. Newton Abbot, 1971.

Jacob, G. *The Country Gentleman's Vade Mecum*. London, 1717.

James, M. 'The Political Importance of the Tithes Controversy in the English Revolution, 1640–60', *Hist.*, XXVI, 1941.

James, W. and Malcolm, J. *General View of the Agriculture of the County of Buckingham*. London, 1794.

General View of the Agriculture of the County of Surrey. London, 1793.

Jancey, E. M. 'An Eighteenth-Century Steward and his Work', *Shrops. Arch. Soc.*, LVI, 1, 1957–8.

'The Hon. and Rev. Richard Hill of Hawkstone, 1655–1727', *ibid.*, LV, 1954–6.

Jenkins, J. G. *The Welsh Woollen Industry*. Cardiff, 1969.

The English Farm Waggon: Origins and Structure. Newton Abbot, 1972.

Jenkins, R. 'Suffolk Industries: An Historical Survey', *Newcomen Soc.*, XIX, 1940.

Jennings, B. (ed.). *A History of Harrogate and Knaresborough*. Huddersfield, 1970.

A History of Nidderdale. Huddersfield, 1976.

John, A. H. 'Agricultural Productivity and Economic Growth in England, 1700–1760', *J. Ec. Hist.*, XXV, 1965.

'The Course of Agricultural Change, 1660–1760', in *Studies in the Industrial Revolution*, ed. L. S. Pressnell. London, 1960. Repr. in W. E. Minchinton (ed.), *Essays in Agrarian History, I*. Newton Abbot, 1968.

'English Agricultural Improvement and Grain Exports, 1660–1765', in D. C. Coleman and A. H. John (eds.), *Trade, Government and Economy in Pre-Industrial England*. London, 1976.

The Industrial Development of South Wales, 1750–1850. Cardiff, 1950.

'Iron and Coal on a Glamorgan Estate, 1700–40', *EcHR*, XIII, 1943.

Johnson, George W. *A History of English Gardening*. London, 1829.

Jones, E. L. 'Agricultural Conditions and Changes in Herefordshire, 1600–1815', *Woolhope Naturalists' Field Club*, XXXVII, 1962.

'Agricultural Origins of Industry', *PP*, no. 40, 1968.

'Agricultural Productivity and Economic Growth, 1700–1760', in E. L. Jones (ed.), *Agriculture and Economic Growth in England, 1650–1815*. London, 1967.

'Agriculture and Economic Growth in England, 1660–1750: Agricultural Change', *J. Ec. Hist.*, XXV, 1965.

'Eighteenth-Century Changes in Hampshire Chalkland Farming', AHR, VIII, I, 1960.

Seasons and Prices: The Role of Weather in English Agricultural History. London, 1964.

Jones, F. 'The Old Families of Wales', in Wales in the Eighteenth Century, ed. D. Moore. Swansea, 1976.

'A Squire of Anglesey', Anglesey Antiq. Soc., 1940.

'The Vaughans of Golden Grove. I, The Earls of Carbery', Hon. Soc. Cymmrodorion, 1963, pt 1.

'The Vaughans of Golden Grove. II, Anne, Duchess of Bolton, 1690–1715', ibid., 1963, pt 2.

'The Vaughans of Golden Grove. III, Torycoed, Shenfield, Golden Grove', ibid., 1964, pt 2.

Jones, G. P. 'Sources of Loans and Credits in Cumbria before the Rise of Banks', CW2, LXXV, 1975.

Jones, Stanley and Smith, J. T. 'Breconshire Houses', Brycheiniog, IX, 1963.

Kalm, Pehr. Kalm's Account of his Visit to England on his Way to America in 1748, ed. J. Lucas. London, 1892.

Kelch, R. A. Newcastle: A Duke without Money: Thomas Pelham-Holles 1693–1768. London, 1974.

Kent, N. General View of the Agriculture of Norfolk. London, 1796.

Hints to Gentlemen of Landed Property. London, 1775.

Kenyon, G. H. 'Kirdford Inventories, 1611 to 1776, with Particular Reference to the Weald Clay Farming', Sussex Arch. Coll., XCIII, 1955.

'Petworth Town and Trades, 1610–1760', ibid., XCVI, 1958.

Kerridge, E. The Agricultural Revolution. London, 1967.

Agrarian Problems in the Sixteenth Century and After. London, 1969.

'The Sheepfold in Wiltshire and the Floating of the Water Meadows', EcHR, 2nd ser., VI, 1954.

'Turnip Husbandry in High Suffolk', EcHR, 2nd ser., VII, 1956.

Lambton, L. Temples of Convenience. London, 1978.

Lane, Carolina. 'The Development of Pastures and Meadows during the Sixteenth and Seventeenth Centuries', AHR, XXVIII, 1980.

Langley, Batty. The City and Country Builder's and Workman's Treasury of Designs. London, 1745. Repr. 1969.

La Quintinye, M. de. The Complete Gard'ner, tr. G. London and H. Wise. London, 1701.

Laurence, Edward. The Duty of a Steward to his Lord. London, 1727.

Laurence, John. A New System of Agriculture. London, 1726.

Law, C. M. and Hooson, D. J. M. 'The Straw Plait and Straw Hat Industries of the South Midlands', E. Midlands Geographer, IV, 6, 1968.

[Lee, J.]. Considerations concerning Common Fields. London, 1654.

Lees–Milne, J. English Country Houses: Baroque, 1685–1715. London, 1970.

Leigh, C. The Natural History of Lancashire, Cheshire and the Peak of Derbyshire. Oxford, 1700.

Lennard, R. V. 'English Agriculture under Charles II: The Evidence of the Royal Society's "Enquiries"', EcHR, IV, 1932.

L'Estrange, R. A Treatise of Wool and Cattel. London, 1677.

Lewis, W. J. 'The Cwmsymlog Lead Mine', *Ceredigion*, II, 1, 1952.

Lightoler, Thomas. *Gentleman and Farmer's Architect*. London, 1762.

Linnard, W. 'A Glimpse of Gwydyr Forest and the Timber Trade in North Wales in the Late 17th Century', *Nat. Lib. Wales J.*, XVIII, 1974.

Linnell, C. D. 'The Matmakers of Pavenham', *Beds. Mag.*, I, 1947.

Lisle, Edward. *Observations in Husbandry*. London, 1757. 2nd edn. 2 vols. London, 1757.

Lloyd, T. H. *The Movement of Wool Prices in Medieval England*. EcHR suppl., no. 6. Cambridge, 1973.

Lodge, E. C. (ed.). *The Account Book of a Kentish Estate, 1616–1704*. Oxford, 1927.

Long, W. H. 'Regional Farming in Seventeenth-Century Yorkshire', AHR, VIII, 2, 1960.

Loudon, J. C. *An Encyclopaedia of Gardening*. London, 1822.

Lowe, N. *The Lancashire Textile Industry in the Sixteenth Century*. Manchester, 1972.

Lowe, R. *General View of the Agriculture of Nottinghamshire*. London, 1798.

McCutcheon, K. L. *Yorkshire Fairs and Markets*, Thoresby Soc., XXXIX. 1940.

Machin, R. 'The Great Rebuilding: A Reassessment', *PP*, no. 77, 1977.

Machin, R. (ed.). *Probate Inventories and Memorial Excepts of Chetnole, Leigh and Yetminster*. Bristol, 1976.

Madge, S. J. *The Domesday of Crown Lands*. London, 1938.

Manley, G. *Climate and the British Scene*. London, 1952.

Manning, B. *The English People and the English Revolution*. London, 1976.

Markham, G. *The Inrichment of the Weald of Kent*. London, 1625.

Marshall, G. 'The "Rotherham" Plough', *Tools & Tillage*, III, 3, 1978.

Marshall, J. D. *Furness and the Industrial Revolution*. Barrow in Furness, 1958.

Kendal, 1661–1801: The Growth of a Modern Town. Kendal, 1975.

Old Lakeland. Newton Abbot, 1971.

Marshall, W. *Review and Abstract of the County Reports to the Board of Agriculture*. 5 vols. London and York, 1808–17. 5 vols. in 1. 1818.

The Rural Economy of Gloucestershire. 2 vols. Gloucester, 1789.

The Rural Economy of the Midland Counties. 2 vols. London, 1790. 2nd edn. 1796.

The Rural Economy of Norfolk. 2 vols. London, 1787.

Rural Economy of the Southern Counties. 2 vols. London, 1798.

The Rural Economy of Yorkshire. 2 vols. London, 1788.

Mathias, P. *The Brewing Industry in England, 1700–1830*. Cambridge, 1959.

Mavor, W. *General View of the Agriculture of Berkshire*. London, 1809.

Meager, Leonard. *The English Gardener*. London, 1670.

Meek, M. 'Hempen Cloth Industry in Suffolk', *Suffolk Rev.*, II, 1961.

Mercer, Eric. *English Vernacular Houses: A Study of Traditional Farmhouses and Cottages*. RCHM (England). London, 1975.

Meredith, R. 'A Derbyshire Family in the Seventeenth Century: The Eyres of Hassop and their Forfeited Estates', *Recusant Hist.*, VIII, 1965.

Michell, A. R. 'Sir Richard Weston and the Spread of Clover Cultivation', AHR, XXII, 2, 1974.

Middleton, J. *General View of the Agriculture of Middlesex*. 2nd edn. London, 1807.

Millward, R. 'The Cumbrian Town between 1600 and 1800', in *Rural Change and Urban Growth, 1500–1800*, ed. C. W. Chalklin and M. A. Havinden. London, 1974.

Mingay, G. E. 'The Agricultural Depression, 1730–1750', EcHR, 2nd ser., VIII, 1956.
'The Eighteenth Century Land Steward', in Land, Labour and Population in the Industrial Revolution, ed. E. L. Jones and G. E. Mingay. London, 1967.
English Landed Society in the Eighteenth Century. London, 1963.
'Estate Management in Eighteenth-Century Kent', AHR, IV, 1, 1956.
'The Size of Farms in the Eighteenth Century', EcHR, 2nd ser., XIV, 3, 1962.
Mitchell, B. R. with Deane, P. Abstract of British Historical Statistics. Cambridge, 1962.
Moore, B. J. S. Goods and Chattels of our Forefathers: Frampton Cotterell and District Probate Inventories, 1539–1790. Chichester, 1976.
Morant, P. A History of Essex. London, 1768.
Mordant, J. The Complete Steward. 2 vols. London, 1761.
Mortimer, J. The Whole Art of Husbandry. London, 1707.
Mullett, C. F. 'The Cattle Distemper in Mid-Eighteenth Century England', Agric. Hist., XX, 3, 1946.
Munby, L. N. (ed.). East Anglian Studies. Cambridge, 1968.
Myddelton, W. M. (ed.). Chirk Castle Accounts, 1666–1753. Manchester, 1931.
Neve, Richard. City and Country Purchaser and Builder's Dictionary. 3rd edn. London, 1736. Repr. Newton Abbot, 1969.
Nichols, J. The History and Antiquities of the County of Leicester...4 vols. London, 1795–1811.
Norden, J. The Surveyor's Dialogue. London, 1607.
North, Roger. The Lives of the Norths, ed. A. Jessopp. 3 vols. London, 1890.
Oliver, J. 'The Weather and Farming in the Mid-Eighteenth Century in Anglesey', Nat. Lib. Wales J., X, 1958.
Ormrod, D. J. 'Dutch Commercial and Industrial Decline and British Growth in the Late Seventeenth and Early Eighteenth Centuries', in Failed Transitions to Modern Industrial Society: Renaissance Italy and Seventeenth-Century Holland, ed. F. Krantz and P. M. Hohenberg. Montreal, 1975.
Osborne, B. S. 'Glamorgan Agriculture in the Seventeenth and Eighteenth Centuries', Nat. Lib. Wales J., XX, 1979.
Outhwaite, R. B. 'Dearth and Government Intervention in English Grain Markets, 1590–1700', EcHR, 2nd ser., XXXIII, 3, 1981.
Overton, M. 'Computer Analysis of an Inconsistent Data Source: The Case of Probate Inventories', J. Hist. Geog., III, 4, 1977.
Owen, L. 'Letters of an Anglesey Parson', Hon. Soc. Cymmrodorion, 1961, pt 1.
Owen, W. Owen's Book of Fairs. London, 1756.
Parker, R. A. C. Coke of Norfolk: A Financial and Agricultural Study 1707–1842. Oxford, 1975.
Parkinson, John. Paradisi in Sole. London, 1629.
Parkinson, R. General View of the Agriculture of Huntingdonshire. London, 1813.
Patten, J. 'Patterns of Migration and Movement of Labour to Three Pre-Industrial East Anglian Towns', J. Hist. Geog., II, 1976.
'Population Distribution in Norfolk and Suffolk during the Sixteenth and Seventeenth Centuries', Inst. Brit. Geographers, LXV, 1975.
'Village and Town: An Occupational Study', AHR, XX, 1972.
Peate, I. C. 'A Flintshire Barn at St. Fagan's', Country Life, July–Dec. 1952.
The Welsh House. Liverpool, 1944.

Pelham, R. A. 'The Agricultural Revolution in Hampshire, with Special Reference to the Acreage Returns of 1801', *Hants. Field Club & Arch. Soc.*, XVIII, 1953.

Penney, N. (ed.). *The Household Account Book of Sarah Fell*. Cambridge, 1920.

Perkins, J. A. *Sheep Farming in Eighteenth- and Nineteenth-Century Lincolnshire*. Occ. Papers in Lincs. Hist. & Arch., no. 4, Soc. Lincs. Hist. & Arch. Sleaford, 1977.

Peters, J. E. C. *The Development of Farm Buildings in...Staffordshire*. Manchester, 1969.

Pettit, P. A. J. *The Royal Forests of Northamptonshire: A Study in their Economy, 1558–1714*. Northants. Rec. Soc., XXIII. 1968.

Petty, W. *Economic Writings...ed.* C. H. Hull, Vol. I. Cambridge, 1899.

Pilkington, J. *A View of the Present State of Derbyshire*. Derby, 1789.

Plot, Robert. *The Natural History of Oxfordshire*. Oxford, 1676/7. 2nd edn. 1705.
The Natural History of Staffordshire. Oxford, 1686.

Plumb, J. H. *Sir Robert Walpole.* 3 vols. London, 1956.
'Sir Robert Walpole and Norfolk Husbandry', *EcHR*, 2nd ser., v, 1952.

Plumb, J. H. (ed.). *Studies in Social History*. London, 1955.

Plymley, J. *General View of the Agriculture of Shropshire*. London, 1803.

Postgate, M. R. 'The Field Systems of Breckland', *AHR*, x, 1961.

Postlethwayt, Malachy. *Britain's Commercial Interest Explained and Improved...I.* London, 1757.

Poynter, F. N. L. *A Bibliography of Gervase Markham, 1568?–1637.* Oxford, 1962.

Prichard, M. F. Lloyd. 'The Decline of Norwich', *EcHR*, 2nd ser., III, 1951.

Priest, St John. *General View of the Agriculture of Buckinghamshire*. London, 1813.

Prince, H. *Parks in England*. Shalfleet Manor, I.O.W. 1967.

Pringle, A. *General View of the Agriculture of Westmorland*. Edinburgh, 1794.

Radley, J. 'Holly as a Winter Feed', *AHR*, IX, 2, 1961.

Raistrick, A. and Jennings, B. *A History of Lead Mining in the Pennines*. London, 1965.

Ramsay, G. D. *The Wiltshire Woollen Industry in the Sixteenth and Seventeenth Centuries*. Oxford, 1943.

Ravensdale, J. R. *Liable to Floods*. Cambridge, 1974.

Rawson, H. Rees. 'The Coal Mining Industry of the Hawarden District on the Eve of the Industrial Revolution', *Arch. Cambrensis*, XCVI, 1941.

Rees, Alwyn. *Life in a Welsh Countryside*. Cardiff, 1950.

Rennie, G. B., Brown, R., and Shirreff, S. *General View of the Agriculture of the West Riding*. London, 1794.

Reyce, R. *See* Hervey (ed.).

Riches, N. *The Agricultural Revolution in Norfolk*. Chapel Hill, 1937.

Roberts, P. 'The Decline of the Welsh Squires in the Eighteenth Century', *Nat. Lib. Wales J.*, XIII, 1963–4.

Roebuck, P. 'Absentee Landownership in the Late Seventeenth and Early Eighteenth Centuries: A Neglected Factor in English Agrarian History', *AHR*, XXI, 1, 1973.
'The Constables of Everingham: The Fortunes of a Catholic Royalist Family during the Civil War and Interregnum', *Recusant Hist.*, IX, 1967.

Roebuck, P. (ed.). *Constables of Everingham Estate Correspondence, 1726–43.* Yorks. Arch. Soc. Rec. Ser., CXXXVI. 1974.

Rogers, Benjamin. *The Diary of Benjamin Rogers, Rector of Carlton*, ed. C. D. Linnell. Beds. Rec. Soc., XXX. 1950.

Rogers, J. E. T. *A History of Agriculture and Prices in England from 1259 to 1793*. 7 vols. Oxford, 1866–1902.

Rogers, Nathan. *Memoirs of Monmouthshire*. London, 1708.

Rowlands, Henry. *Idea Agriculturae*. Dublin, 1764.

Rowlands, M. B. *Masters and Men in the. West Midland Metalware Trades before the Industrial Revolution*. Manchester, 1975.

Salaman, R. N. *The History and Social Influence of the Potato*. Cambridge, 1949.

Salmon, N. *The History of Hertfordshire*. London, 1728.

Scarfe, N. *The Suffolk Landscape*. London, 1972.

Schumpeter, E. B. *English Overseas Trade Statistics, 1697–1808*. Oxford, 1960.

Seaborne, M. *The English School*. London, 1971.

Sharp, Lindsay. 'Timber, Science and Economic Reform in the Seventeenth Century', *Forestry*, XLVIII, 1, 1975.

Sharrock, Robert. *The History of the Propagation and Improvement of Vegetables*. Oxford, 1660.

An Improvement to the Art of Gardening. London, 1694.

Sheail, J. 'Rabbits and Agriculture in Post-Medieval England', *J. Hist. Geog.*, IV, 4, 1978.

Sheppard, J. A. *The Draining of the Hull Valley*. York, 1958.

Sidwell, R. W. 'A Short History of Commercial Horticulture in the Vale of Evesham', *Vale of Evesham Hist. Soc., Research Papers*, II, 1969.

Simpson, A. 'The East Anglian Fold-Course: Some Queries', AHR, VI, 1958.

Skipp, V. *Crisis and Development: An Ecological Case Study of the Forest of Arden, 1570–1674*. Cambridge, 1978.

'Economic and Social Change in the Forest of Arden, 1530–1649', in *Land, Church and People: Essays Presented to Professor H. P. R. Finberg*, ed. Joan Thirsk. Suppl. to AHR, XVIII, 1970.

Slicher van Bath, B. H. 'Yield Ratios, 810–1820', *A.A.G. Bijdragen*, X, 1963.

Smith, J. T. 'The Evolution of the English Peasant House in the Late Seventeenth Century: The Evidence of Buildings', *J. Brit. Arch. Assoc.*, XXXIII, 1970.

'The Long-House in Monmouthshire, a Reappraisal', in *Culture and Environment*, ed. I. Ll. Foster and L. Alcock. London, 1963.

'Medieval Roofs: A Classification', *Arch. J.*, CXII, 1958.

Smith, Peter. *Houses of the Welsh Countryside*. London, 1975.

Smith, W. J. (ed.). *Calendar of Salusbury Correspondence*. Cardiff, 1954.

Herbert Correspondence. Cardiff, 1963.

Smout, T. C. *Scottish Trade on the Eve of Union, 1660–1707*. Edinburgh, 1963.

Speed, Adolphus [Adam]. *Adam Out of Eden*. London, 1659.

Spenceley, G. F. R. 'The Origins of the English Pillow Lace Industry', AHR, XXI, 1973.

Spufford, Margaret. *A Cambridgeshire Community: Chippenham*. Leicester, 1965.

Contrasting Communities: English Villagers in the Sixteenth and Seventeenth Centuries. Cambridge, 1974.

Stanes, R. G. F. (ed.). 'A Georgicall Account of Devonshire and Cornwalle in Answer to Some Queries concerning Agriculture, by Samuel Colepresse, 1667', *Devonshire Assoc.*, XCVI, 1964.

Steer, F. W. (ed.). *Farm and Cottage Inventories of Mid-Essex, 1635–1749*. Chelmsford, 1950.

Steers, J. A. *The Coastline of England and Wales.* Cambridge, 1946.
Steers, J. A. (ed.). *Cambridge and its Region.* Cambridge, 1965.
Stern, W. M. 'Cheese Shipped Coastwise to London towards the Middle of the Eighteenth Century', *Guildhall Misc.,* IV, 1973.
Stone, L. *Crisis of the Aristocracy, 1538–1641.* Oxford, 1965.
    Family and Fortune: Studies in Aristocratic Finance in the Sixteenth and Seventeenth Centuries. Oxford, 1973.
    The Family, Sex and Marriage in England, 1500–1800. London, 1977.
Stone, Lawrence and Stone, Jeanne C. F. 'Country Houses and their Owners in Hertfordshire, 1540–1879', in *The Dimensions of Quantitative Research in History,* ed. W. O. Aydelotte *et al.* Princeton and Oxford, 1972.
Stout, William. *The Autobiography of William Stout of Lancaster, 1665–1752,* ed. J. D. Marshall. Manchester, 1967.
Straker, E. *Wealden Iron.* London, 1931.
Strickland, H. E. *General View of the Agriculture of the East Riding of Yorkshire.* London, 1812.
Summerson, J. *Architecture in Britain 1530 to 1830.* London, 1953.
    'The Classical Country House in 18th-Century England', *J. Roy. Soc. Arts,* CVII, 1959.
Switzer, Stephen. *A Compendious Method for the Raising of Italian Brocoli.* London, 1729.
Tate, W. E. 'Cambridgeshire Field Systems', *Proc. Cambridge Arch. Soc.,* XL, 1939–42.
    A Domesday of English Enclosure Acts and Awards, ed. M. Turner. Reading, 1978.
    'Inclosure Movements in Northamptonshire', *Northants. Past & Present,* I, 2, 1949.
Taylor, C. C. *The Cambridgeshire Landscape.* London, 1973.
Thirsk, Joan, 'Agrarian History, 1540–1950', in *VCH Leics.,* II. London, 1954.
    Economic Policy and Projects: The Development of a Consumer Society in Early Modern England. Oxford, 1978.
    English Peasant Farming: The Agrarian History of Lincolnshire from Tudor to Recent Times. London, 1957. Repr. London, 1981.
    'The Fantastical Folly of Fashion: The English Stocking Knitting Industry, 1500–1700', in *Textile History and Economic History,* ed. N. B. Harte and K. G. Ponting. Manchester, 1973.
    'Horn and Thorn in Staffordshire: The Economy of a Pastoral County', *N. Staffs. J. Field Stud.,* IX, 1969.
    Horses in Early Modern England: For Service, for Pleasure, for Power. Stenton Lecture, 1977. Reading, 1978.
    'Industries in the Countryside', in *Essays in the Economic and Social History of Tudor and Stuart England,* ed. F. J. Fisher. Cambridge, 1961.
    'New Crops and their Diffusion: Tobacco-Growing in Seventeenth Century England', in *Rural Change and Urban Growth, 1500–1800,* ed. C. W. Chalklin and M. A. Havinden. London, 1974.
    'Plough and Pen: Agricultural Writers in the Seventeenth Century', in T. H. Aston *et al.*, *Social Relations and Ideas.* Cambridge, 1983.
    'Projects for Gentlemen, Jobs for the Poor: Mutual Aid in the Vale of Tewkesbury, 1600–1630', in *Essays in Bristol and Gloucestershire History,* ed. P. McGrath and J. Cannon. Bristol. 1976.

'The Restoration Land Settlement', *JMH*, xxvi, 4, 1954.

'The Sales of Royalist Land during the Interregnum', EcHR, 2nd ser., v, 1952–3.

'Seventeenth-Century Agriculture and Social Change', in *Land, Church and People: Essays Presented to Professor H. P. R. Finberg*, ed. Joan Thirsk. Suppl. to AHR, xviii, 1970.

Thirsk, Joan (ed.). *The Agrarian History of England and Wales, IV, 1500–1640.* Cambridge, 1967.

Thirsk, Joan and Cooper, J. P. (eds.). *Seventeenth-Century Economic Documents.* Oxford, 1972.

Thomas, D. 'The Social Origins of the Marriage Partners of the British Peerage', *Pop. Stud.*, xxvi, 1972.

Thomas, H. *A History of Wales, 1485–1660.* Cardiff, 1972.

Thomas, K. R. 'The Enclosure of Open Fields and Commons in Staffordshire', *Staffs. Hist. Coll.*, 1931.

Thompson, E. P. 'The Moral Economy of the English Crowd in the Eighteenth Century', *PP*, no. 50, 1971.

Whigs and Hunters: The Origins of the Black Act. London, 1975.

Thompson, F. M. L. 'The Social Distribution of Landed Property in England since the Sixteenth Century', EcHR, 2nd ser., xix, 1966.

'Landownership and Economic Growth in England in the Eighteenth Century', in *Agrarian Change and Economic Development*, ed. E. L. Jones and S. J. Woolf. London, 1969.

Thomson, G. Scott. *Family Background.* London, 1949.

Life in a Noble Household, 1641–1700. London, 1937.

Tibbutt, H. G. *Bedfordshire and the First Civil War.* 2nd edn. Elstow, 1973.

Torrington Diaries, ed. C. Brayn Andrews. London, 1954.

Trinder, B. S. *The Industrial Revolution in Shropshire.* Chichester, 1973.

Trinder, B. S. and Cox, J. *Yeomen and Colliers in Telford.* Chichester, 1980.

Trow-Smith, R. *A History of British Livestock Husbandry to 1700.* London, 1957.

A History of British Livestock Husbandry, 1700–1900. London, 1959.

Tubbs, C. R. 'The Development of the Smallholding and Cottage Stock-Keeping Economy of the New Forest', AHR, xiii, 1965.

Tucker, G. S. L. 'Population in History', EcHR, 2nd ser., xx, 1967.

Tuke, J. *General View of the Agriculture of the North Riding of Yorkshire.* London, 1800.

Tull, J. *A Supplement to the Essay on Horse-hoing Husbandry...* London, 1736.

Tupling, G. H. 'The Early Metal Trades and the Beginnings of Engineering in Lancashire', *Lancs. & Cheshire Arch. Soc.*, lxi, 1951.

Turner, J. 'Ralph Austen, an Oxford Horticulturist of the Seventeenth Century', *Garden Hist.*, vi, 2, 1978.

Turner, M. *English Parliamentary Enclosure: Its Historical Geography and Economic History.* Folkestone, 1980.

Underdown, D. 'A Case concerning Bishops' Lands', EHR, lxxviii, 1963.

Unwin, R. W. 'The Aire and Calder Navigation, Part II: The Navigation in the Pre-Canal Age', *Bradford Antiq.*, ns xliii, 1967.

Utterström, G. 'Climatic Fluctuations and Population Problems in Early Modern History', *Scand. Ec. Hist. Rev.*, iii, 1955.

Vanbrugh, Sir John. *The Complete Works, IV, Letters.* London, 1928.

Vancouver, C. *General View of the Agriculture in the County of Cambridge.* London, 1794.

General View of the Agriculture of Essex. London, 1795.

General View of the Agriculture of Hampshire. London, 1813.

Verney, F. P. *Memoirs of the Verney Family during the Civil War.* 2 vols. London, 1892.

Verney, F. P. and Verney, M. M. *Memoirs of the Verney Family during the Seventeenth Century.* 2nd edn. 2 vols. London, 1904.

Veysey, A. G. 'Col. Philip Jones, 1618–74', *Hon. Soc. Cymmrodorion.* 1966, pt 2.

Warner, J. 'General View of the Agriculture of the Isle of Wight', in A. and W. Driver, *General View of the Agriculture of the County of Hampshire.* London, 1794.

Watts, S. J. 'Tenant-Right in Early Seventeenth-Century Northumberland', *Northern Hist.,* VI, 1971.

Weatherill, L. *The Pottery Trade and North Staffordshire, 1660–1760.* Manchester, 1971.

Webber, Ronald. *Covent Garden, Mud-Salad Market.* London, 1969.

Market Gardening. Newton Abbot, 1972.

Webster, C. *The Great Instauration.* London, 1975.

Westerfield, R. B. *Middlemen in English Business, Particularly between 1660 and 1760.* Conn. Acad. Arts & Sci., XIX. New Haven, 1915. Repr. Newton Abbot, 1968.

Weston, R. *A Discours of Husbandrie Used in Brabant and Flanders.* London, 1605 [*recte* 1650].

Weston, Richard. *Tracts on Practical Agriculture and Gardening.* London, 1773.

Whetter, J. *Cornwall in the Seventeenth Century: An Economic Survey of Kernow.* Padstow, 1974.

Whistler, L. *The Imagination of Vanbrugh.* London, 1954.

White, Gilbert. *The Natural History of Selborne,* ed. G. Allen, London, 1908.

Wiliam, Eurwyn. 'Adeiladau Fferm Traddodiadol yng Nghymru' (with English summary), *Amgueddfa,* XV, 1973.

Willan, T. S. *The English Coasting Trade 1600–1750.* Manchester, 1938.

The Inland Trade. Manchester, 1976.

'The River Navigation and Trade of the Severn Valley, 1600–1750', EcHR, VIII, 1937–8.

River Navigation in England, 1600–1760. Oxford, 1936. New impr. London, 1964.

[William, Richard]. *Wallography, or the Britton Described.* London, 1673.

Williams, Glanmor (ed.). *The Glamorgan County History, IV.* Cardiff, 1976.

Williams, J. E. 'Whitehaven in the Eighteenth Century', EcHR, 2nd ser., VIII, 1956.

Williams, L. A. *Road Transport in Cumbria in the Nineteenth Century.* London, 1975.

Williams, Michael. *The Draining of the Somerset Levels.* Cambridge, 1970.

Wilson, C. H. *England's Apprenticeship, 1603–1763.* London, 1965.

Wood-Jones, R. B. *Traditional Domestic Architecture of the Banbury Region.* Manchester, 1963.

Woodward, D. M. 'The Anglo-Irish Livestock Trade in the Seventeenth Century', *Irish Hist. Stud.,* XVIII, 72, 1973.

'Cattle Droving in the Seventeenth Century: A Yorkshire Example', in *Trade and Transport: Essays in Economic History in Honour of T. S. Willan,* ed. W. H. Chaloner and B. M. Ratcliffe. Manchester, 1977.

'A Comparative Study of the Irish and Scottish Livestock Trades in the Seventeenth Century', in *Comparative Aspects of Scottish and Irish Economic and Social History, 1600–1900*, ed. L. M. Cullen and T. C. Smout. Edinburgh, 1977.

Wordie, J. R. 'Social Change on the Leveson-Gower Estates, 1714–1832', EcHR, 2nd ser., XXVII, 4, 1974.

Worlidge, J. *Systema Agriculturae.* London, 1669.

Systema Horti-Culturae, or the Art of Gardening. London, 1677.

Wrigley, E. A. 'A Simple Model of London's Importance in Changing English Society and Economy, 1650–1750', *PP*, no. 37, 1967.

Yarranton, Andrew. *England's Improvement by Sea and Land.* London, 1677.

The Improvement Improved, by a Second Edition of the Great Improvement of Lands by Clover. London, 1663.

Yates, E. M. 'Aspects of Staffordshire Farming in the Seventeenth and Eighteenth Centuries', *N. Staffs. J. Field Stud.*, XV, 1975.

'Enclosure and the Rise of Grassland Farming in Staffordshire', *ibid.*, XIV, 1974.

Yelling, J. A. 'Changes in Crop Production in East Worcestershire, 1540–1867', AHR, XXI, 1, 1973.

'The Combination and Rotation of Crops in East Worcestershire, 1540–1660', AHR, XVII, 1, 1969.

Common Field and Enclosure in England, 1450–1850. London, 1977.

Youd, G. 'The Common Fields of Lancashire', *Hist. Soc. Lancs. & Cheshire*, CXIII, 1961.

Young, A. *The Farmer's Tour in the East of England.* 4 vols. London, 1771.

General View of the Agriculture of Hertfordshire. London, 1804.

General View of the Agriculture of the County of Lincoln. London, 1799.

General View of the Agriculture of the County of Norfolk. London, 1804.

General View of the Agriculture of Oxfordshire. London, 1809.

A Six Months Tour through the North of England. 4 vols. London, 1770.

A Six Weeks' Tour through the Southern Counties. 3rd edn. London, 1772.

Tours in England and Wales (Selected from 'The Annals of Agriculture'). London, 1932.

Young, A. (ed.). *The Annals of Agriculture.* 46 vols. London, 1784–1815.

Young, the Rev. A. *General View of the Agriculture of the County of Sussex.* London, 1813.

INDEX

Printed in the United States
By Bookmasters